Engineering Investment Process

Quantitative Finance Set

coordinated by
Patrick Duvaut and Emmanuelle Jay

Engineering Investment Process

Making Value Creation Repeatable

Florian Ielpo
Chafic Merhy
Guillaume Simon

ISTE PRESS
ELSEVIER

First published 2017 in Great Britain and the United States by ISTE Press Ltd and Elsevier Ltd

ISTE Press Ltd
27-37 St George's Road
London SW19 4EU
UK

www.iste.co.uk

Elsevier Ltd
The Boulevard, Langford Lane
Kidlington, Oxford, OX5 1GB
UK

www.elsevier.com

British Library Cataloguing-in-Publication Data
A CIP record for this book is available from the British Library
Library of Congress Cataloging in Publication Data
A catalog record for this book is available from the Library of Congress
ISBN 978-1-78548-162-8

Contents

Foreword

Jean-Philippe BOUCHAUD - Chairman & Chief Scientist, CFM, PARIS.

"The time is gone when asset managers could deal from the seat of their pants with portfolio construction, risk constraints and transaction costs. These issues deserve to be treated with scientific tools and watch-maker precision, whether or not trading decisions themselves come from quantitative models. This book provides a comprehensive and insightful account of the recent breakthroughs in the world of quantitative asset management."

Albert DESCLÉE - Managing Director, Quantitative Portfolio Strategy, BARCLAYS, LONDON.

"The authors are market practitioners who provide realistic, implementable approaches to portfolio construction. This is an excellent book that should appeal to all professional investors."

Fiona FRICK - Chief Executive Officer, UNIGESTION, GENEVA.

"Models in finance are not grounded on "laws of nature" but are built through a process of statistical learning guided by economic and market intuition. This book creates a bridge between the academic financial theory and the practicality of managing money on a day by day basis. It articulates one by one all the steps that need to be engineered in order to build a sound investment process from market analysis, allocation process or risk management. The book also illustrates that risk belongs at the centre stage of asset allocation and shows the value of an holistic approach to risk management embracing its different aspects from statistical measures to market valuation , macro-economic assessment or liquidity criteria.

I would have loved to have such a book when I started working in asset management."

Ibrahima KOBAR - CIO Fixed Income, NATIXIS AM, PARIS.

"I've always been a huge fan and advocate of investment processes based on the combination of a skilled portfolio manager supported by strong quantitative and qualitative analysis. This approach is key for a value creation for the investors. No other book serves the need of a reader who seeks a fuller understanding of the quantitative analysis of an investment process. This is a must read for any practitioner: portfolio manager, investor, consultant..."

Charles-Albert LEHALLE - Senior Research Advisor, CFM - Visting Researcher, IMPERIAL COLLEGE, LONDON - Member of the Scientific Committee of the French regulator, AMF - Chair of Euronext Index Advisory Group.

"Ielpo, Merhy and Simon's book is unique in the way it combines theory and practice, with no concession on the statistical science. Far from a boring list of well known formulas, each chapter covers an important building block of quantitative portfolio management. Examples are carefully chosen not only to explain how to use theory, but each of them sheds an interesting light on important features of returns dynamics. Authors cover reliable beta estimation, alpha identification, inter-temporal portfolio construction, back testing and performance analysis. It gives crucial clues to combine in practice these essential steps of the lifecycle of a portfolio. The two last chapters focus on very important topics that are often addressed in a few paragraphs and deserve more. I strongly recommend this book to young practitioners and young researchers who want to invest themselves in quantitative asset allocation. Bibliographical references will allow readers to go further on their own, and an appendix covers necessary mathematics. Therefore more experienced practitioners would read it with interest too."

Thierry RONCALLI - UNIVERSITY OF EVRY.

"This book covers everything from asset universe and risk factors to portfolio construction and backtesting in order to understand and build investment processes. Besides theoretical aspects of quantitative strategies, the authors also provide an extensive treatment of practical aspects of these topics. This book is highly recommended for students and investment professionals, who want to benefit from the long experience of the authors in quantitative asset management."

Preface

Quantitative finance literature has made countless contributions in various fields, from very general topics to very specific ones. To our surprise, we rarely found books dealing with the *complete* investment process. With more and more sophisticated products, an increasing number of participants, increasing complexity and continuously increasing assets, it is becoming necessary to handle an investment process with an engineering approach. We wanted to write the book we would have wanted to read as young practitioners. Therefore, our goal is to make it as useful a tool for readers, from students to experienced professionals, by presenting the concepts of financial markets as much as possible through a pedagogical prism.

Daily work on the financial markets is often a production concern and a quest for performance that makes it very difficult to step back and have a critical viewpoint of one's own process. It makes it difficult to have the clarity of mind to discard the use in production of a seemingly profitable strategy. When performing some research, it is not so easy to assess the quality of a given research paper that is found randomly. And most of the time (fortunately not always), books focus on very specific issues and theoretical aspects, which may be far from practical considerations and applicability. Conversely, students have time to study but it is difficult for them to have a neat idea of what the daily life of a financial practitioner is. Learning sophisticated techniques is a necessity to survive in today's quantitative financial world; however, it may sometimes be difficult to get a clear picture of the pertinence of each technique on real data. Moreover, some aspects of the "practical survival kit" of a quantitative analyst are not taught and have to be discovered "live" when working with empirical data.

What is this book about? When building or analyzing an investment process, there are a couple of essential steps to be followed: we particularly want to highlight and explain throughout the following chapters the articulation of all these steps. Despite the large literature dedicated to selected pieces of this sequence of steps, few people have taken on the difficult task of articulating each of these elements together. This book aims at providing a stylized view on the key elements on which any investment process should be built by bringing consistency to the engineering of this process.

We want to bring a unified and scientific view of what an investment process should be, in order to allow investors to generate performance recurrently. The principles and features of a fund's investment process are unique to each fund and reflect its managers' experience and beliefs. They nonetheless drive the resilience of the fund's performance. We also conceive this book as a sanity checklist for any manager to assess the quality of her or his process. It may also be viewed as a road map for quants, whatever their asset class and whatever their experience. However, this is not a financial econometrics textbook *per se,* and for lack of space, we cannot deal with every subject or every detail of the points we tackle. In this respect, we have made a particular effort to indicate the major references in each field, also considering our work as a "scientific hub" to guide our readers towards the most useful and qualitative contributions in specific fields. We will not provide a guide to so-called winning strategies either. Strategies illustrate the idiosyncrasies of fund managers, therefore strategy construction is out of the scope of this book. This book will be neither a handbook of techniques nor a collection of recipes. We do not aim to provide a heavy encyclopedia of unreadable equations and will carefully select the theoretical aspects that are relevant in the daily life of fund management in order to wrap up concepts, make links and explain theory when needed. We do not disregard theory as we truly believe in the power of a quantitative approach. We simply want to put financial mathematics and econometrics in their rightful place: an incredibly useful set of tools to increase our understanding of markets.

We see this book as the blending of our academic research with our practical daily experience as quantitative analysts, fund managers and economists. We believe that this balance, between academic and practical experience as investment management professionals, will give this book a specific identity for readers interested in finance, whatever their degree of experience. And if it turns to be a useful tool for our readers, our wish will have been fulfilled!

Acknowledgments

The present work owes a lot to enlightening discussions with a lot of people. We would like to thank people who had, directly or indirectly, a concrete influence on the writing and content of this book. First, we would like to thank Patrick Duvaut and Emmanuelle Jay for their support, help and advice in the development of this project. We also want to thank (in alphabetical order) Philippe Bernard, Guillaume Bernis, Ling-ni Boon, Axel Botte, Jean-Philippe Bouchaud, Joël Bun, Mabrouk Chetouane, Rémy Chicheportiche, Stefano Ciliberti, Albert Desclée, Grégoire Docq, Fiona Frick, Matthieu Garcin, Ibrahima Kobar, Laurent Laloux, Charles-Albert Lehalle, Yves Lempérière, Angelo Pessaris, Nathalie Pistre, Marc Potters, Sara Razmpa, Thierry

Roncalli, Mathieu Rosenbaum, Emmanuel Sérié, Benoît Sévi, Anna Simoni and Jérôme Teiletche for indirect or direct discussions, encouragements, remarks, comments or ideas.

F.I. will never be able to thank enough Patrick Zweifel for having inspired once again the elements of macroeconomics in this book. He also wishes to thank Dominique Guégan for not having let go of the preposterous student he was in 2004.

C.M. would like to thank Jacques Aben, Dominique Guégan and Jean-Marie Rousseau for their support and enlightenment.

G.S. would also like to thank Serge Darolles and Jean-Pierre Florens for their help, support, influence and scientific inspiration through years.

We moreover bear alone the responsibility of the views and thoughts exposed in the present book. And obviously, all the errors remain ours.

Florian IELPO
Chafic MERHY
Guillaume SIMON
December 2016

Introduction

"It takes 20 years to build a reputation and five minutes to ruin it. If you think about that, you'll do things differently."

Warren Buffet[1]

I.1. Making value creation repeatable

Since the financial crisis of 2008, financial markets have been under pressure and heavily criticized. Their role and nature are challenged, heated public debates on their claimed usefulness for the real economy have taken place. In this context, bad performance could wreck a fund manager's reputation and perspectives. Performance can be disappointing because of bad strategies and a low ability to forecast markets moves. Outstanding prediction skills can also be spoiled by a poor risk management, an inaccurate allocation scheme, or a lazy study of the overall process.

Such systematic weaknesses of the industry appear in the data. Studying hedge funds' databases, academics have observed that the reason for a fund to exit from a database may be explained by a voluntary exit (funds locking up after reaching a sufficient capacity and in no need of more clients) or more simply by the death of the fund. Hedge funds show in general a high degree of attrition within each year, even in favorable periods[2] which is much higher than for mutual funds. Statistical counting for attrition and the instantaneous probability of failure are two different concepts, yet provide the same message: funds are more fragile in their early years. Young funds have a greater probability of dying and disappearing from databases [BRO 01], [AMI 03]. The most fragile funds do not even have the opportunity to survive long enough to enter databases: they die before having time to display figures and collect

1 Source: http://business.time.com/2010/03/01/warren-buffetts-boring-brilliant-wisdom/.

2 Around 15 or 20% in the 1987–2001 period ([FUN 97], [BRO 99], [AMI 03]).

assets. The estimation of the instantaneous probability of dying is still a debate [GRE 02], [GRE 07] but it asks fundamental questions. Do fund managers benefit from their experience, does this explain why aged funds are less likely to die? Do young managers have the time to show their skills? Does it depend on market conditions? It all boils down to a simple yet striking fact: typically, all things being equal, after three years of activity, half of the funds may have shut down or have gone bankrupt. This proves that a robust investment process is necessary to survive sufficiently longer in the financial universe. This may not be sufficient but having a world class and organized process should help in making value creation repeatable.

I.2. Why do we allocate?

I.2.1. *From passive to active management : the rise of indices*

The historical context of indices and risk-based investment throughout the 20th Century and the beginning of the 21st helps a lot to understand how people conceive the evolutionary links between performance and portfolio allocation. In the 1950s, Harry Markowitz, through his contributions in [MAR 52], [MAR 59], laid the foundations of Modern Portfolio Theory: his work helped to improve the understanding of diversification as a way to increase risk-adjusted returns. He also settled the use of (co)variance to model risk and gave birth to the concept of efficient frontier. In an illuminating review of the historical aspects of Markowitz allocation, Mark Rubinstein recalls that initially, the link between the variance of assets and the variance of the portfolio was also identified at the same period by [ROY 52] who also developed an equivalent concept of efficiency. Markowitz's theory allows the investor to shift himself along the efficient frontier (Markowitz however recognizing the novelty of the approach of Roy at the same time, see [RUB 02]).

Beyond the mean-variance optimization framework, the Capital Asset Pricing Model (henceforth CAPM) states that when markets are at equilibrium, any efficient portfolio should be a combination of a risk-free asset with an optimal-tangency portfolio whose weights are only determined by market capitalization of the stocks. The messages of the CAPM must not been assimilated to those of mean-variance allocation. However, they share an important influence on modern finance. CAPM has been independently developed by [TRE 07], [TRE 61], [LIN 65], [SHA 64], and [MOS 66] (see also e.g. [KOR 99] or a the recent review by [PER 04]). CAPM builds on the work initiated on mean-variance by Markowitz in the 1950s with his seminal paper [MAR 52]. The optimal portfolio is made of all available assets whose weights are all relatively proportional to their market capitalization. This portfolio helps the theory of efficient markets to be self-fulfilling since tracking this portfolio will naturally reinforce the relative market-capitalization structure at equilibrium.

However, if investors seek to replicate this target, their resulting portfolios are bound to be sub-optimal with respect to this benchmark once costs are taken into account. Any investor deviating from this target should end within the efficient set, due to fees and transaction costs. And this is even if the turnover of the portfolio is the lowest possible since the natural evolution of prices univocally affects the market capitalization and therefore determines the weights of the portfolio. Consequently, it was easier for investors to buy ready-made market-capitalization indices. Those indices have naturally gained the name "*passive*" investing because of this mechanism and the self-realizing way of computing weights. This explains, for years, the success of market capitalization indices since they offer the most straightforward and direct access for investors seeking exposure to equity markets, added to the fact that they have deep roots in academic literature and the theory of efficient markets.

Does this leave some space for generating extra performance? If not, close this book and contact any market participant able to sell you some market-capitalization weighted index. End of the story? Of course not. The CAPM bridged a gap at a time where empirical evidence between risk and return were not heavily investigated and rather helped to formalize the theory of decision in the presence of uncertainty. Naturally, not all market participants abide by this approach, and this creates distortions that prevent markets from being at equilibrium, generating trading.

Are market-cap indices problematic? Obviously not since they are still the object of a large amount of money invested and bear an economic representiveness. Yet, it is difficult to conceive nowadays market-cap indices as the one and only holy grail for every investor. Why? First, their optimality is questioned. Empirically, it has been reported that market-cap indices are in fact not optimal according to real data (see e.g. [THO 06], [CLA 13b] and also our discussion below on the low-volatility anomaly). And there are also theoretical arguments that disqualify passive indices as optimal investments. Those arguments, that we relay here, have been addressed in the work of [HAU 91] which is one of the first contributions to consider market-capitalization weighted indices as "*inefficient investments*". They underline that as soon as the usual fundamental assumptions behind the theory do not hold, the capitalization-weighted portfolios are no longer efficient.

Second, investors may be constrained in practice: this invalidates the full application of the theoretical CAPM setting. Examples of such constraints are those related to short-selling. Since they appear to be constraints that are (excluding frictions due to broker and exchange fees) the more binding ones, and the first departure from theory one investor may face when trading in practice (see for instance [JAC 05] and references therein). In addition to the constraints they may face, and independently of their own appreciation of future market evolution, investors may differ on numerous aspects: regulation; geographical parameters and exposition to taxes; operational constraints: infrastructures, execution abilities, latency; access to data; disagreement on return and risk estimation; etc. There consequently remains an *uncompensated risk* meaning that for the given level of return of market-cap indices, there are still portfolios with lower risk. Let us highlight that those conclusions are valid even in an informationally efficient world, this not being a case against market efficiency in itself [HAU 91].

Elaborating on this, a (bad) argument to convince yourself that all hope is not gone would be that trading still occurs every day on the markets! Investors and market participants still try to reap each day some benefit from the financial markets with a variety of views and bets, in a context close to that of [HAU 91]. What would be the motivation for hundred of thousands of practitioners to fight for portfolios that would be doomed to be sub-optimal and inefficient? Of course, this cannot be considered as a grounded argument. Yet, it illustrates that even with the same constraints and mandates, investors differ in their views and habits and have heterogeneous expectations and behaviors. There are also biases and preferences for domestic assets; divergence on macro and economic forecasts; different risk estimation methods and measures; wide scope of risk aversion; overconfidence; appetite for lottery-like assets or alternatively seeking defensive bets; etc.

I.2.2. *Beating the benchmark*

But is everyone able to *beat* (or at least consistently positively deviate from) the market-capitalization benchmark? This is a more subtle question. In order to outperform, you must have a strategy, and also some *skills* to follow and implement this strategy. Not every investor is qualified or able to do it (see again e.g. [PER 07]). The fact that managers *effectively* add value is still part of a live debate. Therefore, any investor willingly and dynamically managing his or her portfolio with an aim to produce a better performance than the passive indices has naturally been called an *active manager*. *Managing actively* is a notion that is relative in time and style (see below) and therefore quite diffuse, but the first meaning is that an active manager is believed to add value by deploying skills to deviate from passive benchmarks represented by market-cap indices.

I.2.3. *Deviating from a benchmark*

A major contribution to understanding the debate between passive and active management is the paper of [CAR 97] that dismisses the general existence of added skills in mutual performance, in contradiction to the first results of [HEN 93]. *Deviating from a benchmark* may be understood under a quite general meaning: all fund managers do not compare, of course, to a benchmark, equity or no equity. We want to dissect and illustrate here the historical mechanisms that help to understand how performance generation is considered nowadays. Of course, managers seeking total returns, managing absolute return processes, Hold to Maturity, etc. qualify for the definition of *active managers* in such a discussion, and the notion is, in a way, related to the message conveyed by [GRI 00] who consider that active management is intrinsically linked to *forecasting*.

In the following, we will use the term *alpha* as a proxy for extra-performance with respect to "a" benchmark. The true econometric definition of the alpha, as originally introduced by [JEN 68], is linked by essence to the beta, i.e. the sensitivity to the benchmark, the two quantities having to be determined jointly. However, in this qualitative introduction, we instead speak about a general and fuzzy view of *alpha*, which has to be understood under a lazy proxy of the extra-performance generated when compared loosely to benchmarks including performance of competitors. Under this very crude view of alpha, we may also understand this term as the attractiveness that a fund manager may have in the eyes of potential investors. The more precise the definition of the benchmark, the more relevant the alpha. In this context, the *active shares* are the measure of the proportion of a portfolio that differs from a market-cap weighted benchmark (based on the individual deviations of the weights at the asset level). Whereas the tracking error measures how much the portfolio differs from the benchmark at the aggregated risk level. Technically, is market-capitalization the only prism through which we must see passive investment?

The notion of an index was not new in the middle of the 20th Century when the Modern Portfolio Theory arose[3]. The DJIA (Dow Jones Industrial Average) equity index was created in 1896, whereas the first index, the DJTA (Dow Jones Transportation Average, still defined today) was created in 1884. Standard & Poor's developed its first index around 1923, and built the current S&P500 equity index as we know it now in 1957. At this time, an index was most of all designed to tell an economic story and to aggregate in one single number the state and economic perspectives of an equity market, of one sector or of one geographical area. Dow indices began to show a non-trivial weighting in 1928 where some price-weighting was introduced, whereas S&P indices were already market-cap weighted, following Irving Fisher's intuition. However, things really began to change in the 1970s. In 1971, Wells Fargo launched the first indexed *account* for the Samsonite company; the people behind this product were John McQuown, James Vertin and William Fouse, elaborating on the previous works of [SHA 64], [FAM 65] or [JEN 68]. Wells Fargo continued an indexed investing activity in the following years, while in 1975 Vanguard and John Bogle launched the Vanguard First Index Trust, one of the first index *mutual funds*. What really changed is that such an index became *investable* i.e. buying one single product allows you to track the desired index. In the stream of the disaster of October 1987, the first ETF (Exchange Traded Fund), the SPY, was created in January 1993 to replicate the S&P500 index. John Bogle even assisted Nathan Most and Steven Bloom as the Vanguard fund could be considered as an inspiration for ETF creation. SPY is the security that is now the most traded in the world, ETFs representing a worldwide asset of $3 trillion and may now be the easiest way to gain exposure to nearly any given index. For more figures and an inside story on ETFs see the fascinating story related in [BAL 16]. Before that, the first bond

3 [LO 16] provides an interesting review of the history of indices from which some of the events described here are taken.

index fund appeared in 1986, and the first international share index fund was created in 1990 (see [LO 16]). This is the history of descriptive, investable or non-investable indices.

In fact, other indexing strategies may integrate the category of passive investing. Key elements for an index definition are for example defined and highlighted in [GAN 12]: a great capacity and a sufficient liquidity; it can be replicated in a systematic and objective way; finally, the index that is built must have a representativeness. [LO 16] proposes a definition that is quite similar, that is to say "*a portfolio strategy that satisfies three properties*": a strategy that is transparent, investable, and systematic in the sense that it is completely rule-based and without any discretionary intervention. Lo asks as Merton the fundamental question of "*what function does an index serve*" and identifies two different aspects of modern indices: informational purpose to wrap up economic insights; and benchmarking purpose to serve as a reference for active managers.

Rather than separating active and passive indices through a proximity with market-cap weighting, [LO 16] makes a distinction in the sense that traditional indices are called "static" and sophisticated ones "dynamic". [GAN 12] identifies for instance 5 indexation schemes: their categorization (that we restate here) is not an official representation but it enlightens the debate. The first set of indices covers *price-focused* indexing (which is clearly related to market-capitalization indices). The second kind is *price-agnostic* indexing, quite well illustrated by equally-weighting the assets within the index (see section 3.6.1.1). Third, *fundamental* indexation (see also [ARN 05] or [CLA 13a] as a reference) uses variables such as dividends and fundamentals (income, book equity, sales, employment, etc.) to propose new, transparent weights as an alternative to generate mean-variance efficient portfolios. We may also speak about *return-focused* indexing (quite close to the Markowitz framework) and about *risk-focused* indexing (risk-parity, minimum variance: we will handle this approach in detail throughout section 3.6.1). All these approaches are only ways to propose alternatives to market-capitalization indices while sharing the fact that they are clearly defined, transparent and explicit. Recently, [CLA 13b] finds that in recent years, a rather large number of alternative indexing methods would have given more profitable risk-adjusted performance than the traditional market-capitalization index. And even that many random choices could have led to more satisfying *a posteriori* results than the market-cap index! Their point is that since the end of the 1990s and the beginning of the 2000s, the market-cap indices have provided disappointing results in the absolute. See also [CHO 11] for an in-depth study, comparison and factor analysis. Those alternatives are still trying to redefine not the notion but the definition of a benchmark, several of them are trying to be more mean-variance efficient (fundamental indexation for instance) whereas for others (minimum variance e.g.) mean-variance efficiency should (optionally) arise empirically as a by-product.

I.2.4. *Active management and the financial industry*

It is interesting to discover how the industry, seen as a whole, has positioned itself with respect to the *active management* question. We want to make it clear that we are not expressing a personal view on the topic detailed below: by restating the figures and findings drawn from the academic literature, we instead want to illustrate the difficulty of reaching a clear consensus on the sources and drivers of alpha generation.

Alternative indexation methods remain transparent benchmarks and we will extend below the discussion on extra-performance and indices built on systematic strategies. But generating performance remains hard work for institutional investors like mutual and pension funds, as well as for other participants from traditional asset managers to hedge funds. For instance, the evidence that mutual funds managers are able to generate a significantly superior performance is, if not unclear, at least not so frequent or not so persistent (see for instance [FAM 10] or [WIM 13]). [JOH 15] finds for instance that even recently in the US, actively managed funds are not able to over-perform their passive counterparts (when profit is computed net of fees).

Moreover, this incapacity is more pronounced for funds that ask for large fees, and those funds survive even on a shorter period. In a recent piece of literature, [KOS 06], [JIA 07] or [CRE 09] among others give insights to show that in some situations managers may have some added value in their investments. [KOS 06] shows that the distribution of the cross-section of mutual fund estimated *alphas* is non-normal and rather complex. They conclude that funds or managers heavily diverge in their attitude towards risk, and in their idiosyncratic *alpha*: this may be explained by the diversity of approaches, cultures, constraints and mandates. Only a fraction of managers end-up with a profitable stock-selection after costs, but hopefully this superior *alpha* seems to be persistent. [CRE 09] finds that funds that allow us to deviate in a large proportion from the benchmark tend to outperform the benchmark after costs, in contrary to less actively managed funds (with the smallest deviation relative to the benchmark). This is consistent with the findings of [KAC 05] whose results are in favor of active management delivering performance in the stream of effective bets on industry.

The contradictions of the academic literature also appear in the contrasted results on factor timing. An early work of [DAN 97] finds that mutual funds managers may add some alpha with a pertinent stock picking rather than with an effective factor timing, whereas some years later, [JIA 07] finds some evidence to the fact that mutual funds do gain performance due to their timing ability. In fact, using a superior framework for information processing, they may appear more concentrated and playing some industrial bets. This is quite in-line with the arguments of [WIM 13] who finds that performing, actively managed funds may experience alternated and long periods of poor performance with no effective *alpha*, after several consecutive years of successful investments. This may be the sign that performance may also come from an ability to *time* or take benefit from an identified economic cycle or regime.

Moreover, it is not clear that every fund manager is shifting toward an active management. [CRE 09] monitored through time the evolution of active shares of funds from 1980 to 2003. Surprisingly, the proportion of active share shows a clear decrease towards a lower active share. Among many figures, [CRE 09] identified in 2003 a percentage of assets under management with active share greater than 80% was around only 23% in 2003. In 2016, the lack of active management is still identified by the suite of proprietary SPIVA Scorecard reports delivered along the years by S&P Dow Jones. The proportion of active funds is revealed to be very tiny, less than 5% of funds in some countries. For instance, [UNG 15] identifies an inverse link between the holding period of the fund and the ability of the best funds to remain performing ones. A vast majority of funds (including in Europe or US) cannot over-perform their benchmarks over the mid or long periods (typically 3, 5, or 10 years). In the 1980s, most of mutual funds were genuinely active: with more and more available data, increased automated trading, more anomalies discovered, it may seem paradoxical to observe that the proportion of indexed fund with passive management has in fact increased since then. But it is quite natural to think that with a low active management, there is little room for pure alpha generation. However as [CRE 09] notes, the active bets of the mutual funds as a whole remains significant when aggregated.

I.2.4.1. *On the importance of factors*

A sector index remains useful since it bears a true economic justification and afterwards provides a coherent risk description. Sector investing may be therefore conceived as a true investment possibility or mandate. Yet, the work of [BRI 15] highlights the fact that factor investing is preferable to sector investing as long as shorting is allowed and, in this context, it performs better than sector and industry-based allocation both in bear and bull markets. However, with a no-short-selling constraint, sector-based allocation gives better risk-return profiles in both bear and bull periods (at least for US equities). Such a finding was already underlined in [IDZ 13] whose work put some emphasis on the importance of the short-selling possibility for factors to work well.

One cannot disentangle the profusion of (academic and empirical) work on factors from the theoretical developments that started at the end of the 20th Century. The original work of [FAM 92] was as the driver of a huge academic work in the following two decades and indirectly irrigated a complete stream of business. The core of their work was that they identified systematic, persistent and interpretable sources of risk which could be qualified as persistent drivers of returns. The first two explanatory *factors* they found were relative market-capitalization ("SMB" : Small stocks Minus Big stocks). The second one was the book-to-market or *value* component of stocks i.e. the comparison between the market value of the stock with the accounting value of the company ("HML" : High book-to-market stocks Minus Low book-to-market stocks). Some years later, a third factor was identified, namely the *momentum* factor (see [JEG 93] and [CAR 97]). Value links future asset returns with the long-term value of the company, proxied by the book (i.e. balance-sheet) value of the company. Momentum links future asset returns with its recent relative performance, often a one-year return, and emulates the *trend* propensity of the asset. Others factors have been identified as in [PÁS 03] (the liquidity factor) or in [FAM 15] which later extends the list of their identified factors.

All the aforementioned works aimed at identifying "*anomalies*" that are persistent in the long-run and are a source of risk that is consistent and somewhat interpretable: uncovering factors is satisfying when they bear a semantic interpretation that allows us to tell a story to identify investment patterns and interpret performance realization. Factors are for sure drivers of risk and...when they perform, drivers of returns. Factor identification should originally be based to their risk explanation power, but the success they encounter in practice or in the literature is paradoxically also linked to their link with performance and their potential interpretability. It is clear that the factors mentioned in the paragraph above have been present for a long time and that their discovery did not affect their pertinence in risk decomposition.

Factors are generally understood within the same asset class. But even if those factors were identified originally in the equity sphere, they may have a good generalization as explained in [ASN 13]. The authors find that those factors are quite universal across asset classes. They identify a common link through the channel of liquidity risk that explain their correlation across markets and across asset classes. They differ in the fact that value has a positive link, and momentum a negative link with liquidity risk, explaining why those two factors are negatively correlated *within* one asset class and one geographical market. The result holds for equities but also, for instance, for government bonds, indices, commodities or currencies. Generally, they are however expected to be mildly correlated within one asset class, but empirically correlations rise during market downturns, becoming closer and closer to one in the case of crisis. In conclusion, in addition to major macro risk factors like inflation or economic conditions, those style factors are an overlay to understand better the premium[4] associated with long-run returns.

The factor representation allows us to identify bets of an active investor since any performance track may be decomposed on those style factors. It became a clear manner both to identify or classify active managers to understand to which category

4 There is still an ongoing discussion on the nature of potential anomalies, their remuneration, their link with the potential risk they represent and the difference between risk premia with behavioral anomalies. This is a deep question that we will not solve, yet we will give in section 4.4.5 some insights to at least shed some light on this fascinating yet difficult debate.

they are belonging. It was then possible to *explain* (at least a part of) the extra-performance generated by active managers in a systematic manner. And if active management is not able to generate in all occasions a consistent and robust performance, it became at least possible for clients to understand which kind of risk they were facing. It was then possible for them to explicitly target, choose and focus on specific investments, depending on the risk sources they wanted to be exposed to. Then, factors evolve in a world somewhere between alpha and beta. This is also linked to the message behind the CAPM, that is to say that investing in high beta assets is easy, by simply seeking exposure to the market portfolio; while creating performance by investment in low-beta assets is much more difficult and requires some skill and experience.

I.2.4.2. *From factors to smart beta*

After years of academic work, this research led inevitably to the appearance of investable products. A plausible "kick-off" for this may have been the work of [ANG 09a] highlighting the practice of some nordic pension funds that, rather than accepting a passive management, took the initiative of active bets incorporating simple yet systematic strategies to enhance their traditional portfolios. Those products are now generally known under the term *smart beta* products, indices and ETFs. For instance, smart beta ETFs were representing a total amount of $544 billion invested as of February 2015 (see [EVA 15]). Specifically, [CHO 16] indicates that *strategic beta* Exchange Traded Products (growth, value, low-volatility, etc.) represent in June 2016 a global amount of assets under management of $550 billion. The terminology remains rather vague in the sense that those funds and products are thriving and are the subject of heavy marketing and a battle for increasing seeding. In particular, [CHO 16] attributes 80% of the growth in asset since 2000 to new inflows compared to 20% for endogenous asset performance. Their next frontier is therefore the crowding of the strategies on use, with a potential heavy in-sample bias in that case (see the detailed arguments for such a discussion as developed in [LO 16] on this precise aspect). But the interest for us here is the general pattern underlying their development. We will instead speak of *alternative risk premia* in the following: the term "alternative risk premia" may therefore encompasses all the notions like *style factors*, *factor investing*, *systematic risk premia*, *strategy beta*, *factor beta*, etc.

Some are quite universal among asset classes (carry, momentum), others more specific (quality, value, size for equities ; convexity, curve for fixed income). See for instance [ILM 12] who explores the generalization of anomalies through different asset classes. Historically, the factor that is the most trivial to undercover remains the market factor! The departure that is identified from the CAPM in this context is that the market risk premium is not the only source of systematic risk that investors may be exposed to. We are interested in them since they tell a lot about the history of passive and active management. At the time they were discovered, investing in factors was no longer *passive* management since factors were largely deviating from market-capitalization indices and needed an active management. Factors have therefore a striking universal behavior and may constitute a systematic source of performance. The extensive work of [ANG 14a] on factor investing is particularly interesting since it puts the stress on the fact that factors remain risky. It particularly put them in perspective with the fact that risky periods and different horizons have to be distinguished. Factors may perform worse in bad times (economic and financial crises for instance) but may over-perform the market on longer horizons: factors have to be qualified as such on the long-term.

We will comment on the graph we display in Figure I.1. In a way, this graph is not[5] ours. This graph may be under very similar alternatives in numerous papers, theoretical or professional presentations, with an interesting variation on words, terms and labels. What interests us for the sake of clarity is this shared consensus on the evolution of the way people are talking about risk premia. The main message of this evolution is that a large portion of what was traditionally considered as alpha has turned into a *mainstream alpha* that is now considered as being *beta*. Alpha or performance generation is therefore a matter of times and risk analysis. This trend is also confirmed by [LO 16] that underlines that the notion of indexing has evolved with years, and now encompasses a large stream of strategies that all try to gain some beta exposure with different approaches.

Following the CAPM inspiration of this decomposition, the beta or market return, was the part of performance that may be explained by market moves through the sensibility/exposition to those moves. Beta was merely conceived as the part of the returns coming from passive exposure to market-capitalization indices. Alpha, the residual part, was extra performance due to active management. Formerly, alpha was mainly asset selection with good performance believed to be only due to a manager's skill and abilities. This alpha plus beta decomposition however entailed a true quest for alpha for managers, as expressed for instance in [MON 07b]. Market returns may be described through their explicit expositions to regional, sectorial and economic risks (exposition to inflation, to some geographical zones, etc.). All of this is more description than explanation. We are here at the heart of performance generation. Extra-performance (or *alpha*) created by skilful managers has always been a relative concept across time. The more it is possible to identify the sources of risk (or bets) a manager is playing, the less freedom it leaves him to appear as a performing one. Managers playing (only) value or growth styles were no longer identified as adding value as soon as value or growth factors were identified, and momentum or growth index investable.

But with the democratization of style indices, and their diffusion as financial products, they appeared quickly themselves as common or plain vanilla. It however

5 Our sources are therefore numerous, see for instance [BEN 14] among others for a close inspiration.

left some space for talented managers to generate performance through an even more active management. The performance that is created is always function of what is easy to identify or to generate "at a cheap cost" (that is to say, with simple, audited data, using vanilla procedures and techniques). Alternative risk premia includes therefore alternative indexation (fundamental indexation, see e.g. [CLA 13a]) but also all the more or less sophisticated but systematically, reproducible, and identified strategies. This builds a space for a whole stream of strategies and potential indices whose risk is compensated for by expected returns. Let us underline that those alternative risk premia are not compulsory a hedge against market downturns and are commonly exposed to global economic and market fluctuations and, potentially, to unforeseen slow-downs at some periods. Products flagged as *alternative risk premia* obviously aim at improving returns and increasing diversification. But two things are really modified in the financial landscape. First, the notion of passivity itself, since passive investing is gradually shifting from a market-capitalization weighting notion to a broader extension encompassing factors in a rule-based, transparent way and with low implementation costs. Second, the traditional alpha component of portfolio returns are now understood as compensation for identified risk exposures and non-diversified risk. We sometimes find them under the term "units of risk".

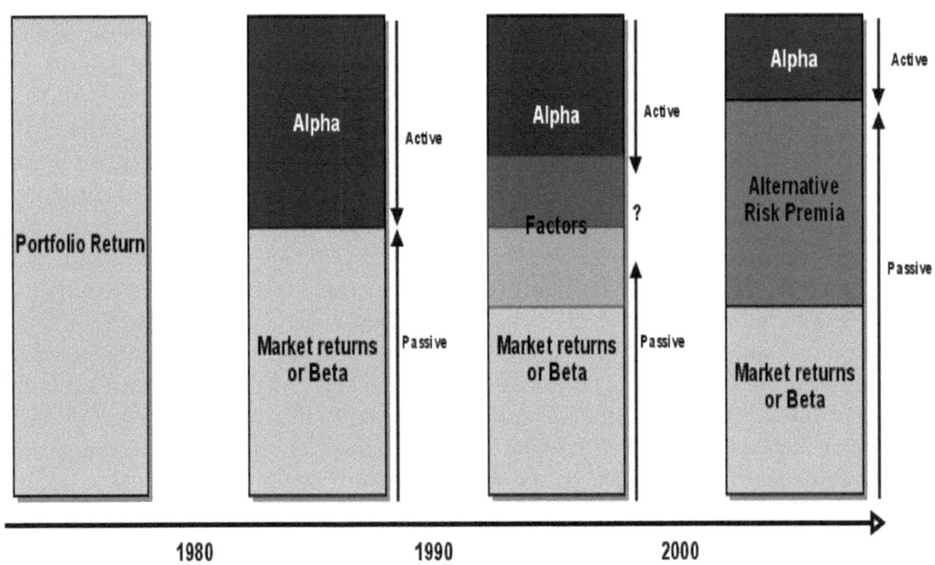

Figure I.1. *Historic evolution of the semantic vision of performance decomposition through alpha and beta*

I.2.4.3. *Alpha is not dead*

Paradoxically, we believe that all this story is in favor of the use of proprietary strategies since they are many ways to access to performance and that things are not static, a dynamic management may be the key to future profits. The role of an asset manager today is still to generate performance, with a smart security selection, coherent bets, a precise market timing and of course, a robust and repeatable investment process. The beta exposures to all kind of strategies and risks have to be carefully monitored. This means also that the fees that are paid by investors have to be justified and associated with a real, persistent and convincing alpha creation. [WER 12] has shown that an analysis of individual securities could generate profits that cannot be obtained only by industrial, sectorial or factorial exposition. However, investors have to be aware that the use of new styles or new strategies comes almost always at the cost of capacity (proxied, say, by the maximal amount of dollar-risk you may take for a given acceptable level of dollar-gain). Capacity may be limited depending on the strategy that is used. Departing from the wide capacity market-capitalization indices comes at a cost. To underline the increasing pressure of competition on alpha generation, [LO 16] identifies that "*competition suggests that alpha should be capacity-constrained, hard to come by and expensive*". Generating new sources of alpha is more and more difficult, needs a cautious process, skills and this should have a price for the investor wanting to access superior levels of performance.

On the other side, [SIE 14] pushes the argument that diversification should be the investor's concern, not necessarily the manager's one! Manager should expect and seek a high alpha to translate strong conviction, even if they end up with a concentrated portfolio[6]. The final investment decision of the final investor would simply be to blend its investment among several managers and use more simple techniques of allocation to diversify across managers. But this should also be a positive argument for managers to seek to apply strong convictions, strategies or views to step out of the crowd. We could take the example of the so-called low-volatility (or low-beta) strategy. This particular anomaly is in strong disagreement with the most fundamental CAPM lessons since it identifies that the risky stocks (with a high volatility) deliver poor returns when compared to defensive stocks (with a lower volatility). This fact has been highlighted by [HAU 91] and confirmed later by [CLA 06], [ANG 06a], [BLI 07], [ANG 09b], [BAK 11a], [HAU 12], [ASN 12], [LI 14] and [BOU 16] among others. Even if the ubiquity of the anomaly is still discussed (see [NG 15] in the case of corporate bond markets), the anomaly was barely noticed ten years ago (or was at least more an academical concern that had not percolated as an investor topic) whereas it constitutes nowadays in itself a common and recognized factor. Section 3.6 will indirectly deal with this

6 "*Diversification is protection against ignorance. It makes little sense if you know what you are doing.* Warren Buffet (again), see [BUF 06] for more words of wisdom.

issue since we will tackle the topic of minimum variance portfolios, but a huge amount of work has to be done to fully understand the finest mechanisms of the anomaly.

The proprietary use of a strategy and the details of its implementation are often of the utmost importance. For instance, it is generally well known that hedge funds are particularly focused on the confidentiality of their strategies. The study [MCL 16] confirms this rationale: studying 97 published anomalies, they identify a clear post-publication attrition of performance, caused both by statistical bias and pressure from investors probably informed of this anomaly (the anomaly is more closely followed rather than losing in trend). The performance decay is up to 30% which is statistically significant. Research publication raises the attention of investors and traders, and entails an increase in activity through volumes and short interest, along with a higher correlation with other anomalies that have been published, as stated in this paper. This finding is confirmed by [CAL 16]. Examining several well-known anomalies after their publication, they identify a rise in anomaly-based trading by institutional investors and an *a posteriori* decrease in the anomaly returns. They particularly stress the role of institutional investors such as hedge funds for this decay of anomalies' performance and therefore an improvement of the overall efficiency.

I.3. Building a process

I.3.1. *Forecasting is not a science*

We want to stress an important message. We believe that quantitative analysis may remain close to a hard science as long as it deals with risk management. It is a crucial thing to understand that the quantitative analysis involved in the study of the risk aspects of a financial process have to be ambitious. Sophistication cannot be a drawback in this precise context. Such aspects are for example related to risk decomposition, identification of risk drivers, factor model analysis, analysis of past performance, statistical analysis of a returns time series, etc.

However, as a whole, asset management can hardly be conceived as a *true* science because *repeatability* in the experiments cannot be enforced. What prevents finance from being a science is mainly the fact that investors will never be able to repeat the same experience in a fixed context to proceed to "*what-if*" scenarios[7]. And this is because forecasting is dealing with the future: not about pure randomness that can be nicely modeled with appropriate models, but with uncertainty. Yet any investor should be concerned with repeatability *of performance* since ensuring the robustness

7 We indicate at this stage a fascinating read which is the book of [MOR 15]. Even if it deals with social science concepts and not with financial ones, this work clarifies greatly the notion of counterfactual inference and analysis.

of a process by quantitatively monitoring all its aspects it the best way to circumscribe the uncertainty lying in the forecasting part of the process.

In other words, we want to clearly draw a separation between risk and performance drivers from the practitioner's point of view. It is important to distinguish the two concepts, as active risk management is a need, whatever the sophistication of the underlying strategy. Factors, that should be genuinely risk drivers and elect naturally for an essential stepping stone of the risk management part. But this qualification should be theoretically made independently of their potential remuneration: a factor may be used as as winning strategy, but such a use is not straightforward, not automatic and not a promise of profitability. Future returns forecasting is therefore not a natural counterpart of ex-post risk analysis[8].

In the more specific context of equity indices, Andrew Lo clearly restates in [LO 16] his views on the distinction that has to be made between passive and active equity indices. According to him, passivity is of course not a synonym for absence of monitoring and action. Passivity should be linked with transparency, automation and reproducibility at low cost:

> "*The functional definition of the index (...) decouples risk management from alpha generation. Passive strategies can and should be actively risk managed.*" —
> [LO 16].

This is also our opinion: whatever the sophistication of a given strategy, its risk management must be made carefully. But risk management of a *whole process* includes operational risk, which encompasses the use of bad data, the implicit biases that the investor forgets about, the poor statistical significance of the performance track, etc. This also explains why we will not tackle in this current book the forecasting part of the process related to prediction and signal construction: we have left it to the professional investor or to the motivated reader since forecasting is mainly related to beliefs, bets, and forecasts, which cannot be *objectively*[9] mastered, estimated and evaluated. Some of the aspects we deal with in the book *may* be used in a forecasting perspective, or within a signal building procedure: state-space models in section 2.3.1; risk-based allocation in section 3.6 are such examples. We do use some strategies (synthetic ones in Chapter 4, real ones in Chapter 5 for instance) but all of this is done for the purpose of illustration. We insist on the fact that our true aim is to cover all other aspects of the "life" of a strategy (data, allocation, backtesting, etc.) and we do not promote those strategies for what they are, but use them as raw material to illustrate how to dissect them, both from the statistical and the economic point of view.

8 We do not resume factors to be only an ex-post help in analyzing risk however!

9 We do use the word *objectively* and not the word *easily* on purpose.

I.3.2. *A four-step process*

In a recent contribution, Harry Markowitz described his thoughts and feelings about how academics and practitioners have used and talked about his work through the 20th Century. He particularly recalls his intuitions, assumptions and theoretical developments, how they have been used, and potentially misunderstood. He explains how in a conference, a speaker helped him to put in perspective both the theoretical importance of his work, but also how it became the stepping stone on which practitioners elaborated fifty years ago to make a whole industry grow: "*Now I understand what I have started*" [MAR 10]. He particularly underlines how this work must be understood as a building block of a "*whole process*" including potentially macro forecasts, factor models, and trading signals.

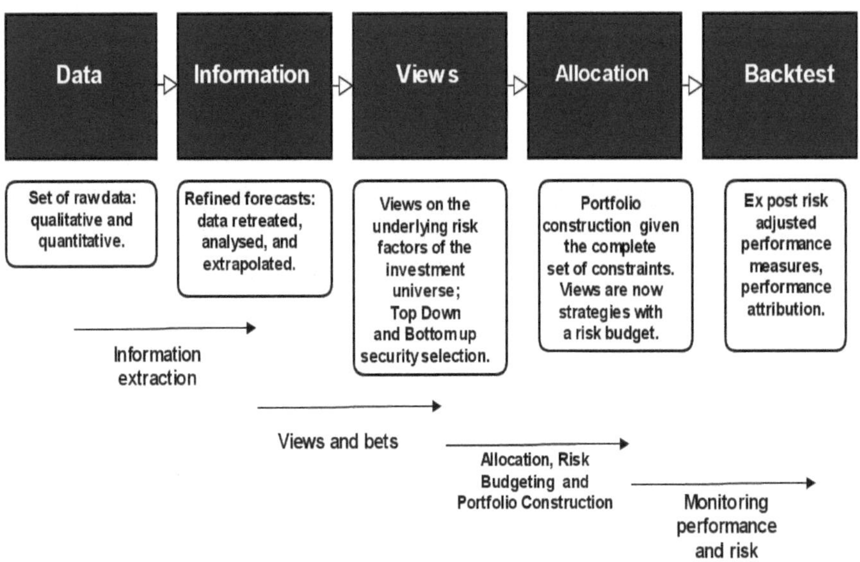

Figure I.2. *Four steps for an investment process*

So, repeatability is at the heart of financial stability as any money seeder seeking a potential investment will look for successful managers that are able to consistently deliver positive performance. A successful investment process can be viewed as a sequence of intermediate transformations contributing to the overall value which is added when compared to his competitors: the alpha of the process. We identify four critical steps that are illustrated in Figure I.2: 1) information extraction, 2) conversion of information into views and bets, 3) allocation and 4) ex post performance analysis. Although strategies are often proprietary or specific to each investor, our aim is to stress, describe and study how those steps are articulated to form a robust process in order to make any value creation consistent and robust. Therefore this book does *not* aim at providing any magic formula, or any secret strategy. We instead want this book to help to extract all the statistical and economic value of any kind of views on expected returns. This book intends in particular to accompany investors who already have an expected returns estimation methodology, and willing to transform those views into an actual investment process. The transformation of the asset management industry through the years makes it so that regulators, investors, managers, or clients are expecting more than crude performance figures: this constitutes the core motivation of the current book.

It is moreover crucial to understand that costs are present at each step and behind each action. They appear under various forms, directly and indirectly. Yet it must be stressed that repeatability is also driven by effective costs since hidden (or lightly estimated) costs may dramatically affect the *effective* value creation. Gathering data is costly: it may represent hundreds of thousands of dollars a year. Extracting information and building views has a price: hiring quantitative analysts, researchers or fund managers also constitutes a cost. Execution and implementation costs are explicitly tackled within Chapter 3 in the section dedicated to the modeling of impact. We will see that introducing costs in the allocation process does not boil down to the introduction of a simple overlay on the no-costs problem, but implies drastically changing the overall approach. Finally, overestimating the significance of a strategy, or dismissing its links with the real economy, weakens the potential added value of an investment process, if its sensitivity to extreme and/or exogenous events is not monitored: and this may be the worst cost of all. Consequently, it is recommended to read the present book having in mind that identifying costs and controlling them shapes the investment process backbone.

The first step consists of extracting information from data. Data is, in our opinion, the cornerstone of each investment process. Nowadays, finance cannot be conceived as an ethereal concept or science. Investing may in fact only be driven by data under various forms: prices, volumes, tick-by-tick data, fundamental statements; but also macroeconomic information, inflation and production figures, etc. Diving into raw data is a real challenge and before doing so each investor should carefully define, build and understand quantitative tools to understand her or his asset universes. Understanding the statistical context and the consequences of quantitative choices to model an investment universe is the first driver of repeatability of performance and the avoidance of operational risk: this will be the goal of Chapter 1. The first step of the process is related to information extraction: this will be possible thanks to a clear definition of statistical objects and concepts at hand. As often in statistics and econometrics, choosing the right tool depending on the processes we want to study is the first step of pertinent modeling. Notions dealing either with the biases due to the nature and quality of the data, or with the way the investor react to those biases (data-snooping, overfitting) will be addressed later in the book. Yet, the pedagogical role of Chapter 1 is to show that statistical models on financial data have appeared as an answer to the existence of the observed patterns in data. In order to understand the information conveyed by financial time series, data comes first, theory next.

The second step an investor should naturally turn to is the conversion of information into views and bets on his investment universe. We believe that bets, signal construction, and views on the market are not an end in itself but only a transition from the interpretation of cleaned data to an allocation process. The aim of Chapter 2 is to disentangle the sources of information one may be tempted to filter out, in order to understand which value the investor wants to add, depending on the goal She or He wants to pursue. Once again, a clear definition of aims and targets is a prerequisite. Projecting the P&L distribution of the portfolio at the investor horizon is the relevant task to conduct prior to any portfolio selection decision. One has to identify the risk factors, to model their joint distribution and to project them at the appropriate horizon before recovering the corresponding P&L distribution. Allocation decision and portfolio optimization allows to shape the *ex ante* P&L distribution according to the investor preferences. Besides standard market risk factors, we focus on liquidity risk that is incurred when trading assets and rebalancing the portfolio. All of that is analyzed under current market conditions characterized by negative rates environment.

The temptation is great to be mentally satisfied at having some forecasting abilities on the evolution of markets. But even if a good forecast is based on clean inputs, and even if the bets are in the good direction, a strategy based on a forecast may be qualified as successful only if it is converted into effective profit. Understanding what happens when converting bets into portfolios is the goal of Chapter 3. The portfolio construction step addresses the implementation of these views in the portfolio by allocating to the corresponding strategies while controlling for risk. Allocation is perturbed by estimation error, whose effects are tremendous for out-of-sample risk of the resulting portfolios. This trade-off between views' implementation and estimation error makes it so that, as developed later in the book, allocating may in fact only be an *estimation challenge*. Consequently, practitioners have developed solutions ranging from empirical to more sophisticated ones to address this problem in practice. Many contributions in the literature only compare those solutions along performance metrics, in particular contexts. We believe that such an approach is deceptive and somehow limited. We adopt in this part of the book a point of view which is, if not original, at least quite unusual since we will try to exhaust the underlying *regularization* mechanisms driving each allocation technique. We will in particular develop the mean-variance allocation procedure in specific details. Studied for decades now, the mean-variance framework still remains useful since it allows us to easily explain concepts such as covariance estimation, covariance cleaning, or out-of-sample risk; and to introduce later the notion of market impact and dynamic trading.

Finally, ex-post performance analysis identifies winning strategies and gauges their risk consumption. This part of the process is of utmost importance and we will split this task into two steps: a statistical and an economic one. On the contrary to observational sciences, it is not possible for financial actors to assess the performance of their strategies by means other than "replaying" those strategies on already-observed data. As explained before, it is difficult (impossible?) to build a whole framework that generates counterfactual scenarios of data that allow us to measure the true profitability of a strategy. In this respect, post-analysis is, in our mind, a step that is at least as important as the conception of the signal and its risk management. Why? Because it is more important not to implement a fake strategy rather than trading a strategy that is in fact pure noise (with unwanted features, disappointing performance, and a behavior unrelated to initial backtests). This will be the aim of Chapter 4: we would like to present how it is possible to criticize *statistically* any backtest in order to lift any possible doubt before implementing and trading any strategy. This chapter will be a profoundly statistical one since we will be more interested in this chapter by time series of returns rather than underlying drivers of strategies.

But in real life, any investment remains intrinsically a motivated decision. In this respect, understanding the economic drivers of a strategy with its features and peculiarities is difficult but necessary. The connections between active strategies and macroeconomic cycles is rarely done in the literature: we will however try to draw those links throughout Chapter 5, where we will take the example of an equity, a commodity and a currency strategy. We want to explore practically those links and to provide an overview of methods that may be used to connect strategy returns with economic conditions, including inflation and recession for instance.

We conceive the whole book as being equivalent to a "pipe" through which an investment idea has to transit. Chapters 1 and 2 deal with the identification, the joint modeling and the projection of risk factors. This is a prerequisite for estimating the yet to come P&L distribution of the portfolio upon which risk calculation, portfolio section, and optimization are conducted. A special focus is brought to actual market conditions regarding liquidity and negative rates within Chapter 2. With a cleaned view or bet, Chapter 3 should allow you to build a portfolio whose returns are analyzed later with the help of Chapters 4 and 5. Any investment idea should pass successfully through all those steps to be considered as being profitable and well understood.

I.4. Further reading

The core of this book is to dissect the articulation of the different steps[10] of an investment process, but having the ability to explain every detail of such a process on any asset class could not even be the objective of a lifetime! We have already made it clear that we will not elaborate much on strategy construction and we do not want either to build a cookbook of strategies. Yet we will need to use at some points some additional material and potentially advanced concepts. Obviously, we do not aim to deal with every theoretical or practical aspect of any quantitative tool we use. Unfortunately, we will not have space to recall basic notions of probabilities, econometrics or time series. And even if we did, other contributions did probably already done it before, with greater talent.

We identify some necessary fields for which extra references have to be given, in addition to the literature that we refer to all throughout the book: probabilities, time series, multivariate analysis, statistics and asymptotic statistics, econometrics and stochastic calculus. In this respect, for an introduction to probabilities, we encourage interested readers to refer to the book of [FEL 68]. The reading of that book can be completed by the reading of [BOU 09] for an alternative, data-driven approach, with an econophysics flavor. For an exhaustive review on time series analysis, we indicate the book of [HAM 94], [KIM 99] and also, as a complement, the remarkable course made by [VAN 10]. [KEN 77] is a cornerstone reading in statistics while the book of [VAN 00] will provide the necessary background to master asymptotic aspects of statistics. In the meantime, [AND 03b] and [HÄR 15] provide a nice introduction to multivariate statistical analysis. To get insights on advanced, theoretical econometric modeling we refer to [FLO 07] which is quite turned toward theory and fundamental modeling rather than empirical recipes. We make it clear by the way that the present book does not deal with stochastic calculus. Yet, readers interested in this topic may find a classic reference in stochastic calculus applied to finance with the book of [KAR 98]. Even more advanced concepts in fundamental stochastic modeling are available in the set of books of [DEL 71] which remain a major reference. Finally, some general finance books introduce and summarize with talent important concepts: we think in this respect that the reading of [GRI 00], [MEU 05], [ANG 14a] and [RON 14] (cited however later in the book) would be fruitful for interested readers.

10 We highlight here the contribution of [DID 09] whose objectives are quite close to ours: it could constitute an interesting alternative reading since this book also decomposes the investment process as a sum of elementary steps. Our contribution is however different as we put a large emphasis on the backtesting phase, on the economical dimension of the investment process, on the modeling of the market, and we seek to find theoretical frameworks to unify the concepts that are exposed.

List of Acronyms

Notations

$a, b, ...$	scalars
$\mathbf{a}, \mathbf{b}, ...$	column vectors
$\mathbf{A}, \mathbf{B}, ...$	matrices
$\mathbf{A}'$ or $\mathbf{A}^T$	transpose of a matrix $\mathbf{A}$
$\text{tr}(\mathbf{A})$	trace of a matrix $\mathbf{A}$
$det(A)$	determinant of a matrix A
$sign(x)$	vector of signs of components of x
$\|\phi\|$	modulus of a vector ϕ associated with an AR process
I_N	$N \times N$ identity matrix
$\mathbf{I}_N$	$N \times N$ matrix of ones
e_N	N-dimensional vector of ones
1	vector of ones, without precision on the dimension
t	time
T	total number of time observations
$p_{i,t}$	price of asset i at time t
$diag(x_1, ..., x_N)$	denotes the $N \times N$ diagonal matrix of statistical objects $(x_1, \ldots, x_N)$ on the diagonal, 0 elsewhere
$R_{i,t}$	random variable of the return of asset i at time t
$R_{M,t}$	random variable of the return of the market at time t
R_t	N-dimensional random vector of returns at time t
$r_{i,t}$	observed return of asset i at time t
R_t^P	random variable of return of a portfolio p at time t
r_t^P	observed return of a portfolio p at time t
$r_{M,t}$	observed return of the market M at time t
$r_{f,t}$	return of the risk-free asset at time t
$\mathbf{r}_t$	N-dimensional vector of returns at time t
$\mathbf{r}_k$	T-dimensional vector of returns for asset k

$\mathbf{R} = \{\mathbf{r}_k\}_{k=1}^N$	$T \times N$ matrix of returns for the N observed assets
σ_{ij}	covariance of two assets i and j
σ_{ii}	variance of asset i
σ_i	volatility of asset i, equal to $\sqrt{\sigma_{ii}}$
δ_{ij} or δ_i^j	Kronecker delta, equal to 1 iff $i = j$, 0 otherwise
$\mathbf{F} = \{\mathbf{f}_k\}_{k=1}^K$	matrix of the K factor returns included in factor models
$\mathbf{f}_k$	k^{th} column of $\mathbf{F}$
$\mathbf{f}_t$	t^{th} row of $\mathbf{F}$ and K-dimensional vector of the factor values at t
$1(.)$	indicator function
$\hat{\mathbf{x}}$	estimated value of an object $\mathbf{x}$
$\sim$	distributed according to
$\perp\!\!\!\perp$	statistically independent
$\mathbb{E}(.)$	statistical expectation
$\mathbb{V}(.)$	variance
$Cov(.)$	covariance
$\mathbb{V}_{as}(.)$	asymptotic variance
$Cov_{as}(.)$	asymptotic covariance
$corr(.,.)$	correlation between two variables
$\mathcal{N}(m, \sigma^2)$	Gaussian distribution with a mean m and variance σ^2
$\mathcal{N}(\mu, \Omega)$	multivariate Gaussian distribution with a mean vector μ and covariance Ω
$\mathcal{R}(T)$	range of an operator T
Dom(f)	domain (or support) of a function f
$\mathbb{R}$	real numbers
$\mathbb{R}^N$	N-dimensional space based on $\mathbb{R}$
$\mathbb{R}^+$	real positive numbers, including zero
$\mathbb{R}^-$	real negative numbers, including zero
$\mathbb{R}^*$	real, non-zero numbers
$\mathcal{M}_{k,n}$	set of $k \times n$ real-valued matrices
$\mathcal{M}_{n,n}^+$	set of $n \times n$ real-valued, symmetric, positive, semi-definite matrices

Acronyms

AIC	Akaike Information Criterion
APT	Arbitrage Pricing Theory
BIC	Bayes Information Criterion
BL	BlackLitterman
CAPM	Capital Asset Pricing Model
dof	degrees of freedom
ERC	Equal Risk Contribution
EW	Equally Weighting
FLAM	Fundamental Law of Active Management

FLS	Flexible Least Squares
GDP	Gross Domestic Product
GMV	Gross Market Value
IC	Information Coefficient
ICA	Independent Component Analysis
i.i.d.	independent and identically distributed
IR	Information Ratio
IV	Instrumental Variables
KF	Kalman Filter
LKF	Linear Kalman Filter
LSE	Least Squares Estimate
MaxDD	Maximum Drawdown
MDP	Maximum Diversification Portfolio
ML	Maximum Likelihood
MMSE	Minimum Mean Square Error
MPT	Modern Portfolio Theory
MS	Markov Switching
MSE	Mean Square Error
MV	Minimum Variance
NA	Non-Arbitrage
NMV	Net Market Value
OLS	Ordinary Least Squares
PCA	Principal Component Analysis
P&L	Profits and Losses of a portfolio
QE	Quantitative Easing
RMT	Random Matrix Theory
RP	Risk Parity
SSM	State Space Model
SVD	Singular Value Decomposition
VaR	Value at Risk

1

Understanding the Investment Universe

1.1. Introduction

With a variety of asset classes with different liquidities, constraints and characteristics, and a large number of investors with different investment horizons, speaking in general of financial returns is rather difficult. Finance is not a hard science and no statistical pattern appears with certainty and perfect regularity in the data. However, it has been known for a long time that financial returns show some *stylized facts*. Stylized facts are statistical patterns that tend to repeat in the data, for different financial instruments (stocks, indices, etc.) and markets, frequently but without certainty as they may be unobserved in some periods or under some extreme market conditions. [MAN 63] and [FAM 65] were the first to empirically question the Gaussian random walk hypothesis for prices, bringing to light various statistical properties of asset returns. Their studies paved the way to intensive empirical works trying to exhibit statistical regularities common across a wide range of financial data sets, as presented in [CON 01] and [TER 11] ([CON 01] clearly stating that there is a trade-off between the potential universality of the qualitative qualification and the quantitative precision when characterizing stylized facts).

1.1.1. *On the importance of stylized facts*

A first stylized fact is that financial returns are known to be non-Gaussian. The main drawback of the Gaussian assumption for returns is that it does not, in general, give a precise description of the tails of the return distribution. The non-Gaussianity of returns is a widely and deeply studied topic, in various aspects and details, for several asset classes. For instance, it is the main object of the book of [JON 07a], but other stylized facts are particularly striking. We recall here some of the facts already listed in [CON 01].

A very well known stylized fact is that financial returns show a low degree of linear correlation when computed on the raw returns (on a non-intra-day time scale). The picture changes if autocorrelation is computed on a nonlinear transformation of returns. The same returns, when squared or taken as their absolute value, present an autocorrelation that is, on the contrary, slowly decaying with time. Of course, empirical properties of returns distribution change dramatically with the time scale definition (for more details see Chapter 2 of [BOU 09]). For stocks, for instance, a Gaussian assumption appears less and less inaccurate as the time scale increases: for monthly returns, the Gaussian modeling may be acceptable, whereas delving into intra-day data, 5-minute returns show empirical distributions that have nothing to do with the Gaussian distribution. Conversely, some linear correlation in raw return series tends to appear as the time scale increases up to monthly scales (again, see [CON 01]).

1.1.2. *The particular role of volatility*

Two other stylized facts are particularly interesting. *Volatility clustering* translates the fact that volatility, whatever its measure, is generally positively auto-correlated. This means that volatility comes by "*clusters*", with periods of high volatility alternating with less volatile ones. See [LO 91], [DIN 93] or [GIA 03], or [CON 07] for insights and models of volatility clustering. Also linked with volatility, the *leverage effect* is the term used to qualify the fact that returns and volatility are generally negatively correlated, as reported in works by [SCH 89], [NEL 91], [GLO 92] or [BRA 95].

The time-varying dimension of univariate returns is usually described using their moments: the empirical finance literature has long been diagnosing the fact that the conditional distribution of returns is time varying. Clearly, returns are not stationary, as their historical volatility exhibits time variation. This lack of stationarity can in part explain some known stylized facts about returns: as described later, the "fat tails" of financial returns' distributions can be reproduced using conditional distributions with thinner tails combined with a stochastic volatility model. Given the difficulties of explicitly modeling time-varying distributions, the "modern" approach relies instead on time-varying moments. In a perfect world of perfectly observable returns at any point in time, the observer would be able to estimate one distribution per day – this distribution being able to change: one day a Gaussian distribution, and the next day a skewed Student distribution, for example. This is however impossible: even intra-day data are imperfect observations of our mental representation of the law of motion of financial assets and tricks need to be found in order to partially reproduce the time-varying nature of returns' distributions. One way to do so is to utilize the fact that selected moments of distribution of returns are showing signs of persistence. A very common example of that is how financial econometrics has been exploiting the persistence of the square root of the second-order moment of the returns' distributions: volatility. As will be explained later, the GARCH literature that emerged from the 1980s has been very successful at exploiting the persistence of volatility to generate time series models that generate more realistic distributions than [BLA 73]'s model (the Gaussian model). This has been one of the most significant breakthroughs of research in financial econometrics over the past 50 years or so.

Unfortunately, volatility is the only moment-related characteristic of financial returns which exhibits a measurable persistence: currently, the most realistic modeling approaches combine a time-varying volatility component with a conditional distribution with asymmetric fat tails[1]. Expected returns – the first moment of returns' distribution – cannot display persistence by essence: should there be persistence, then returns should show predictability based on their past. If a strong absolute correlation should appear in returns, it would be easy to forecast future returns with a simple contrarian strategy in case of negative autocorrelation (selling past winners and buying past losers) or a trend following strategy in case of positive autocorrelation (selling past losers and buying past winners). If such an arbitrage may exist in specific circumstances, it is natural that such a pattern is not systematically present: market participants would use this anomaly until it disappears.

The case for persistent skewness and kurtosis is difficult to make: the consensus is that they are time varying in some respect, also showing signs of a limited persistence. Regarding this point, see [JON 03] and the references within. For example, during crisis periods, returns seem to show a different kurtosis level from periods of rising equity markets. However, measuring such stylized facts is a difficult exercise, and the only thing that we really know is that volatility *is* time varying and that the conditional distribution of returns combines asymmetry *and* fat tails.

1.1.3. *Scope of this chapter*

The observation made by practitioners and academics that some statistical patterns frequently repeat in financial time series created a need for a modeling of prices and returns that would be able to reflect those statistical features. This effort is natural and necessary in order to model, analyze and forecast financial time series. Even with a lot of efforts, however, and even with a high degree of complexity, the models involved are still missing some specific features of the stylized facts. This is

1 This is at least the most common way of modeling returns in the most consensual academic literature (the top three finance journals include: *Journal of Finance, Review of Financial Studies* and *Journal of Financial Economics*). There are other approaches essentially exploiting methods coming from other fields than finance and economics and applying them to financial markets. This is not the view that intellectually dominates so far: this book focuses mainly on the current thought consensus, but an interested reader should not bind herself to what is presented here. Journals such as *Quantitative Finance* and *International Journal of Theoretical and Applied Finance* regularly provide their readers with heterodox contributions.

one of the main goals of the present chapter: we want to underline how and why the modeling of financial returns interacts with the observation of data. The qualification of the non-Gaussian nature of financial returns is not to be discussed here, and an alternative modeling for return distribution is out of our scope. It has been widely done previously with a high level of precision in the literature (see, among others, [MAN 63], [BAR 97], and [CON 97]). Financial returns are not always raw returns of single stocks, which are often the focus of return distribution studies in the literature: we may also study returns of strategies, backtests, single funds, funds of funds, portfolios, etc. In this respect, the variety of return distributions to be fitted may be large. In the case of hedge funds strategies' returns, for instance, the departure from Gaussianity is also validated, but the return distributions displayed have their own specificities (see, for example, [DAR 09] and references therein).

The question we deal with here is consequently rather different. While the forthcoming chapters will focus on the joint behavior of returns, the focus of Chapter 1 will remain on the univariate properties of financial returns. The Gaussian assumption, even if unverified in practice for single assets, may be particularly useful to draw heuristics for inferring laws of aggregated returns, both in the asset dimension and in the time dimension. Mastering at least the results for the Gaussian assumption is both necessary and insightful. In addition, the Gaussian assumption for returns helps to recover not only simple estimators, but also the asymptotic laws of those estimators, whose asymptotic properties are sometimes needed, for allocation for instance. In addition, even if returns are not strictly Gaussian, some major stylized facts on returns can be reproduced with simple statistical tools, thanks to the specification of their dynamics with the introduction of serial dependence as modeling their time series patterns in a realistic way matters both to risk management and to portfolio construction. Finally, understanding the risk factors that are priced in the cross-section of the assets' returns that make the portfolio will help to have having a better control over them.

1.2. Computing returns

As mentioned previously, the modeling of the distribution and the stylized facts supported by financial returns is the subject of a wide stream of literature. We could also call for stochastic and sophisticated mathematical tools to model the price process of a financial asset (e.g. in [KAR 98]). Nonetheless, without further sophistication, we simply need to compute returns on a given, observed time series. In addition, even with this simple goal in mind, the choices we could make can have different consequences. The aim of this section is to handle the various ways to compute returns and understand the features of one choice or another.

We will assume in section 1.2 that we follow on a liquid market a given financial asset i. We want to define a random variable, the return $R_{i,t+1}$ at date $t+1$ that quantifies the increments of the price process $(P_{i,t})$ of the asset. The return should depend not only on the value of the asset in the period, but also on the potential payoffs linked to the holding of the asset in the given period. The definition of return is not unique, and returns are always defined relatively to a time scale: fixing the length of the period determines the time scale and the "dimension" of the computed returns. We assume moreover for the moment that the process $(P_{i,t})$ is observed on a discrete-time grid $(..., t-1, t, t+1, t+2, ...)$, where the time step of the grid is fixed (day, week, month, etc.). The price of asset i at date t is denoted $P_{i,t}$, potentially delivering a dividend equal to $D_{i,t}$ in the period $[t-1; t]$. Issues related to sub-sampling or asynchronicity are not tackled yet, but the discrete sampling of the process will not prevent us from continuous-time modeling of the price process.

1.2.1. *Discrete-time modeling*

In a discrete-time view of the price process, the random value $R_{i,t+1}$ of a return at date $t+1$ is defined as:

$$R_{i,t+1} = \frac{P_{i,t+1} - P_{i,t}}{P_{i,t}} + \frac{D_{i,t+1}}{P_{i,t}}.$$

The first term is the relative gain or loss in capital. The second is the dividend rate. For a bond, $D_{i,t+1}$ is known in advance and is even null for zero-coupon bonds. For a stock, $D^i_{i,t+1}$ is positive, not stochastic but not known in advance, set by the company, either positive or equal to zero and may lead to the payment of taxes. Whatever the asset, $P_{i,t}$ is random and is known for bonds for only the maturity date. The discrete-time modeling leads to returns that are often called *arithmetic* or *simple returns*.

Now, let us consider that we want to compute the same kind of return but on H consecutive periods. We will note this return:

$$R^{(H)}_{i,t+H} = \frac{P_{i,t+H} - P_{i,t}}{P_{i,t}} + \frac{D_{i,t+H}}{P_{i,t}}.$$

Of course, both processes $(R^{(H)}_{i,t})_t$ and $(R^{(H=1)}_{i,t})_t = (R_{i,t})_t$ do not have the same dimension, but they are however related through a nonlinear relation, since we have clearly:

$$R^{(H)}_{i,t+H} = \Big(\prod_{k=1}^{k=H} (1 + R_{i,t+k})\Big) - 1.$$

We have here a first message that the most natural way of defining returns, the simple return definition, is not linearly summable in the time dimension, since:

$$R_{i,t+H}^{(H)} \neq \sum_{k=1}^{k=H} R_{i,t+k}.$$

However, it is clear that a first-order development when the realizations of $(R_{i,t})$ are close to zero, and when H is low, influences the error made in the previous inequality to be empirically weak.

1.2.2. *Continuous-time modeling*

We could also try to use a continuous-time modeling for the price process. In this case, we state that at each moment $u \in [t-1; t]$, the performance is assumed to be constant equal to $r_{i,t}$. In an elementary period $[u; u+du]$, if $dP_{i,u}$ is an elementary increase in price in u, we have:

$$r_{i,t}du = \frac{dP_{i,u}}{P_{i,u}}.$$

Integrating between $t-1$ and t, this gives:

$$r_{i,t+1} = \log\left(\frac{P_{i,t+1}}{P_{i,t}}\right).$$

This defines *geometric* or *log-returns*. A first-order development of the function $x \mapsto \log(1+x)$ gives that $\log(1+x) \sim x$ for x close to 0. For usual returns, $(P_{i,t+1} - P_{i,t})/P_{i,t}$ has no dimension and is close to 0, therefore giving:

$$\log\left(\frac{P_{i,t+1}}{P_{i,t}}\right) = \log\left(1 + \frac{P_{i,t+1} - P_{i,t}}{P_{i,t}}\right) \simeq \frac{P_{i,t+1} - P_{i,t}}{P_{i,t}}.$$

We also see that $r_{i,t+1} = p_{i,t+1} - p_{i,t}$ if $p_{i,t} = \log(P_{i,t})$. This definition of the return is exactly linear in the price increments as soon as we use log-prices rather than raw prices[2]. Here again, a strong message appears as the key property of geometric returns is that they are linear in the time dimension, contrary to simple returns. Indeed, if $(r_{i,t}(H))_t$ is the H-periods geometric return process, then:

$$r_{i,t+H}^{(H)} = \log(1 + R_{i,t+H}^{(H)}) = \sum_{k=1}^{k=H} r_{i,t+k}.$$

2 It is usual to see in the literature implicit consensus on notations that use lowercase letters for log-returns or log-prices. We keep those notations for this section only, since, everywhere else in the book, we prefer to use the widespread convention of statistical literature of uppercase letters for random variables and lowercase letters for observations.

1.2.3. *Return moments*

Mastering and understanding the computation of moments of the returns' distribution is crucial. We understand the moment of order m of a distribution here as being the probabilistic expectation of the random variable up to a power m. From a theoretical point of view, having at hand all the moments of a given distribution should help to characterize the distribution (even if, theoretically, it may not always uniquely *determine* the distribution). From a practical point of view, estimating moments may be a useful guideline to understand the specificities of the distribution: in particular, it allows us to know whether or not the return distribution matches the observations made usually through stylized facts. On the statistical side, it allows us to test for the stationarity of the return distribution, or, for example, its Gaussianity. On the financial side, return moments are extensively used in risk management, forecasting and allocation.

1.2.3.1. *Existence*

With a finite sample of observations, computing the sample mean of the series up to a given power seems to be easy. Things are in fact a bit more complicated, since if we want to estimate moments, we have at least to assume that they exist! As discussed previously, financial returns are in general non-Gaussian, and this is materialized in the fact that tails of financial returns' distributions are in general heavier than the tails of a Gaussian law, and in the existence of an asymmetry in extreme returns, with negative extreme returns being relatively more frequent than positive extreme ones. However, the fatter the tails, the less likely the possibility of computing higher moments. In some cases, distributions with extremely fat tails may not have an existing skewness or variance. Classes of distributions that are suited to model financial returns are therefore power-law or stable Pareto distributions that can be parametrized by a tuning parameter (and the Gaussian distribution is a particular case of stable Pareto distribution): see [BOU 09] or [BON 11] on this topic. More precisely, the contribution of [MAN 63] remains especially important, since it maintains the assumption of independent returns but shows that if price increments follow a stable distribution, then the central limit theorem does not help to recover Gaussian returns after aggregation. If this assumption is particularly interesting in order to model non-Gaussian returns at various scales, there is a price to pay: stable distributions do not have finite second moments, which makes in particular the use of mean-variance allocation difficult to justify.

1.2.3.2. *Interpretation*

The interpretation of the first two moments of the distribution is generally easy in the financial context. The first moment of the return distribution, expected return, is understood as a proxy of performance, since, if returns are stationary, the mean expected return is linked to the drift of the price process. The second moment, variance, has historically always been understood as a proxy of the risk of the detention of an asset. There are of course a lot of drawbacks of using only variance and correlation to model risk and dependence structure (e.g. as discussed later in Chapter 2 and section 4.3.4.1). However, under a Gaussian assumption, the first two moments are sufficient to provide a full characterization of the law of returns. The historical success of mean–variance (due to the clarity of the approach and its simplicity) therefore drove the interest for mean and covariance to model performance and risk.

There is a subtlety concerning the third and fourth moments. They are rarely estimated under their raw value; practitioners rather prefer to use *skewness* and *kurtosis* which are respectively the third and fourth moments not of the raw distribution itself but of the centered and normalized distribution. There are tight links between moments and *cumulants* as detailed in Chapter 1 of [BOU 09], and in both cases, skewness and kurtosis may be expressed as the ratio of centered, normalized moments (see below). Both are known as being the *form factors* of the distribution. In a financial context, it has been known for years that they are the easiest argument to dismiss the Gaussian[3] nature of returns: financial returns have in general a negative *skewness* and a pronounced excess *kurtosis* (see, for example [JOR 88], [BAT 96], [HAR 99], [HWA 99], [HAR 00]).

Skewness, which we will denote by s, measures the degree of asymmetry of the return distribution relative to its mean. It is a signed variable that may be even undefined for some distributions, and its interpretation depends also on the nature of the distribution. As financial return distributions are mostly unimodal, the sign of skewness in fact reveals interesting things on the distribution. A negative skewness is a sign that the left tail of the distribution has more weight than the right tail, and vice versa. However, in pathological situations, for fat-tailed distributions, the use of skewness for a diagnosis of symmetry is not convincing (see [BON 11]). This may be due to either the amplitude of the support or the form or the thickness of the tail, with no general rule: a cautious look at the empirical distribution will be the better way to truly understand skewness, since even asymmetric distributions may have a zero-skewness, as for symmetric distributions. Kurtosis, which we will denote by k, measures the thickness of the tails of the return distribution, and therefore complements skewness as it describes also the shape of the distribution. For both moments, estimation is sensible and the best estimators to choose are subject to debate, sometimes depending on the context. A high kurtosis means that volatility is driven by less frequent but extreme moves rather than mild but frequent moves.

3 For a Gaussian distribution, k is equal to 3. Then we will often find corrected values implicitly shifted towards 0, to materialize the potential deviation from the Gaussian case. "Excess kurtosis" is equal to the $k - 3$ quantity.

1.2.4. *Usual statistical assumptions on return distributions*

Until now, we only considered the *computation* of returns that can be made for any asset, without additional hypothesis: only the observation of the price process is required. We will now try to see which kind of assumption we can formulate on the *dynamic* nature of the returns, to qualify the distribution of returns at sequential dates. A crucial remark is that those assumptions will be made on returns. Indeed, it is nearly *impossible* to state an independence or a stationarity assumption (a notion to be refined later) directly on prices. Indeed, from one period to another, and even more at a high frequency, prices are often at a similar level, and if we conceive price trajectories as nearly continuous, it would be unrealistic to think the elements of this trajectory as being independent of time. In this respect, statistical assumptions are made on the price increments, or on the returns, rather on the price process in itself. As is often the case in any topic in statistics, the stronger the assumptions, the finer the results. We could set the complexity of the hypothesis at an arbitrary level but will however focus on a set of three assumptions with a decreasing level of universality.

The three assumptions (Assumptions 1.1, 1.2 and 1.3) are fairly standard in financial econometrics. Depending on their strength, those assumptions will help to:

– postulate distributions to propose estimators and models for analysis and prevision (see section 1.3);

– obtain an asymptotic diagnosis on the return moment estimators, in terms of independence, asymptotic distribution and asymptotic moments (see sections 1.3.2.2 and 1.3.3.3);

– obtain a diagnosis on estimators at finite distance (see sections 1.3.2.2 and 1.3.3.3);

– help to recover the return distributions of returns when they are aggregated along the time or the asset dimension (see sections 1.2.5 and 1.4).

We are interested here in the distribution at date t of a N-assets return vector, which we denote by R_t (recovering here its general meaning as described in the general notations of the present book).

ASSUMPTION 1.1.– (R_t) is said to be stationary at the second order (or of order 2) if the probability law of (R_t, R_{t+H}) depends on H but not on t. In particular, the moments of the marginal law of (R_t) at date t do not depend on t. Expectation and (co)variance of (R_t) are independent of time, the autocovariance of (R_t), $Cov(R_t, R_{t+H})$ is a function Γ of H only:

$$\begin{aligned}\mathbb{E}[R_t] &= \mu\\ \mathbb{V}[R_t] &= \Omega\\ Cov(R_t, R_{t+H}) &= \Gamma(H)\end{aligned}$$

with $\mu = (\mu_1, ..., \mu_N)'$ and $\Omega = (\sigma^2_{i,j})_{i,j \in [1;N]^2}$.

Even if Assumption 1.1, appears quite mild when compared with the following ones, it is still likely to fail in general for financial returns due to the existence of the volatility clustering effect. Volatility clustering stipulates that volatility switches from low to high regimes, meaning that the second moment of the return distribution changes with time, which is in opposition to Assumption 1.1. Moreover, the existence of different trends in any market is another counter-example that the first moment of the return distribution is constant in time. Assumption 1.1 is the definition of *stationarity of order 2* which is the most common and the weakest form of stationarity used in practice. This assumption remains an important statistical tool for estimation and analysis.

We will understand in the following, by autocorrelation, the function $\gamma(H)$ of order H where H is a natural integer as is defined as follows:

$$\gamma(h) = \frac{Cov(R_t, R_{t+H})}{\mathbb{V}[R_t]}. \quad [1.1]$$

For a given time series, the autocorrelogram will designate the mapping of the order $H \geq 0$ versus the empirical value of $\gamma(H) \in [-1;+1]$ for the series, for a reasonable support of H.

ASSUMPTION 1.2.– In addition to Assumption 1.1, returns $(R_t)_t$ are assumed to be independent of time. A consequence is that $\Gamma(H)$ is in particular zero-valued as soon as $H \neq 0$.

Assumption 1.2 is already very strong. It corresponds to the definition of *strict stationarity*: the joint statistical distribution of any collection of the time series variates never depends on time. For such a case, R_t follows a distribution that does not depend on time. This definition being very strict and difficult to test, most experiments would rely in practice on the milder definition of stationarity defined thanks to Assumption 1.1.

ASSUMPTION 1.3.– In addition to Assumption 1.2, the law of returns (R_t) at date t is assumed to be Gaussian, following at each date t a Gaussian distribution $\mathcal{N}(\mu, \Omega)$.

The assumption of Gaussian returns will not be compulsorily stated in the following. However, the previous discussion on arithmetic and geometric returns is in this case of interest. In the case of a single asset i, if we formulate a Gaussian assumption on $R_{i,t}$, we see that having observed $p_{i,t-1}$, the price $P_{i,t}$ of asset i follows in this case a Gaussian distribution with mean $p_{i,t-1}(1 + \mu_i)$: the support of the resulting distribution may have a negative support which means that random future prices, under this assumption, may be negative! Of course, this holds not only in the case of the Gaussian distribution, and results in fact from the choice of arithmetic returns. It shows, however, that if such an assumption has to be made on the distribution of returns, the geometric definition of returns is more adapted, since it allows us to recover a log-normal distribution for prices that are, in this case, always positive.

1.2.5. *Aggregating returns*

What are the aggregation properties of returns? We briefly explore here the way they aggregate (linearly or not) both in the time and in the asset dimension, depending on the return definition (arithmetic or geometric returns) and on the statistical assumption that is made. Let us assume that we work with a portfolio of N assets, with weights in the portfolio being represented by a vector $w \in \mathbb{R}^N$ with components w_i not necessarily positive that may be either quantities or relative proportions (i.e. summing to one $\sum_{i=1}^{N} w_i = 1$). We note, respectively, $P_{i,t}$, $R_{i,t}$ and $r_{i,t}$ as the price, the one-period arithmetic return and the one-period geometric return of assets $i = 1, ..., N$ at date t.

1.2.5.1. *Aggregation in the asset dimension in one period*

Things are pretty clear when we work with arithmetic returns. In this case, the one-period geometric return $R_{t+1}^P(w)$ of the portfolio at date t is simply:

$$R_{t+1}^P(w) = \sum_{i=1}^{N} w_i R_{i,t+1}.$$

Unfortunately, geometric returns do not have this property, since in the most general case:

$$\log\left(\sum_{i=1}^{N} w_i \frac{P_{i,t+1}}{P_{i,t}}\right) \neq \sum_{i=1}^{N} w_i \log\left(\frac{P_{i,t}}{P_{i,t-1}}\right).$$

Consequently, in general we have:

$$r_{i,t}^P(w) \neq \sum_{i=1}^{N} w_i r_{i,t},$$

even if this inequality may approximately hold, in practice, typical situations where returns have a low amplitude.

1.2.5.2. *Aggregation in the time dimension on a single asset*

This aspect has already been handled in section 1.2, where we have seen that, with a single asset, geometric returns were linear with respect to time aggregation, which was not the case for simple returns. The linearity mainly comes from the choice of the return and not from an independence assumption. In addition, if we formulate a strong assumption of independence and Gaussianity as Assumption 1.3, working with w as quantities, on a H-periods horizon, with geometric returns (for the aforementioned reasons), [GOU 97] explicitly computes the law of evolution of log-prices: we are therefore in a framework that is similar to the one of Black and Scholes. The main inference is that, in this case, we obtain the normality of log-prices both with moments depending linearly on H. In particular, under the no-rebalancing assumption (quantities fixed), the return by unit of time of asset i has a decreasing variance by unit of time.

1.2.5.3. *General case*

We will retain here the general result that arithmetic returns are not linear in the time dimension but sum linearly in the asset dimension, whereas it is the opposite for geometric returns that sum linearly in time, but not in the asset dimension. The general case is much more sophisticated. Chapter 1 of [GOU 97] explores in detail the statistical behavior of portfolios (laws, moments and expressions) in various situations (quantities/proportions), potentially also with a Gaussianity assumption. It is underlined, in particular, that the arithmetic definition of returns is much more useful in the general case, since computations in the multi-asset case become much more difficult with several assets, and this explains why arithmetic returns are often chosen in practice for statistical inference.

1.3. Moment estimation

Having defined how to compute returns, one of the key statistical challenges is to estimate the moments of the return distribution. Implicitly, we place ourselves within a context where we are interested, for now, by an unconditional distribution of returns.

1.3.1. *Sample counterparts*

As detailed in section 1.2.3.1, it is always possible to compute weighted averages of a finite time series to obtain a given quantity that we hope to represent a decent estimator of the moment of the theoretical distribution. The pertinence of this choice is more questionable and depends mainly on the thickness of the tail of the true distribution. Yet, sample counterparts are the empirical equivalent of theoretical moments. For a given asset i one-dimensional real-valued series of returns $(R_{i,t})$

with T observations $(r_{i,1},...r_{i,T})$, the sample counterpart $\hat{m}_{i,T}^{(1)}$ of the expected return (first moment) is simply given by:

$$\hat{m}_{i,T}^{(1)} = \frac{1}{T}\sum_{t=1}^{T} r_{i,t}.$$

The sample counterpart of the second moment is equivalently given by:

$$\hat{m}_{i,T}^{(2)} = \frac{1}{T}\sum_{t=1}^{T}(r_{i,t} - \hat{m}_{i,T}^{(1)})^2.$$

The sample counterpart for skewness, $\hat{m}_{i,T}^{(3)}$ and for kurtosis, $\hat{m}_{i,T}^{(4)}$ will therefore be simply obtained through:

$$\hat{m}_{i,T}^{(3)} = \frac{1}{N}\frac{\sum_{t=1}^{N}(r_{i,t} - \hat{m}_{i,T}^{(1)})^3}{\left(\hat{m}_{i,T}^{(2)}\right)^{3/2}} \quad \text{and} \quad \hat{m}_{i,T}^{(4)} = \frac{1}{N}\frac{\sum_{t=1}^{N}(r_{i,t} - \hat{m}_{i,T}^{(1)})^4}{\left(\hat{m}_{i,T}^{(2)}\right)^{2}}.$$

Those sample counterparts are obviously natural estimators for expected return, variance/volatility, skewness and kurtosis. They do present at finite distance (fixed T) a bias that is generally forgotten in practice, since it vanishes quickly with T. Now, the question is to see whether there are other estimators, whether they coincide with the previous expressions and whether the statistical theory can help us to infer on their properties.

1.3.2. *Expected return and covariance*

In the present section, we will both extend to the multi-asset case and show that the sample expressions presented before are natural estimators for expected return and variance, as they are similar to the expressions we obtain for maximum likelihood estimation (henceforth MLE) under a multivariate Gaussian assumption for returns. We assume in section 1.3.2 that returns $(R_t)_t$ are N-dimensional real-valued vectors that follow an i.i.d. Gaussian $\mathcal{N}(\mu, \Omega)$ with $\mu \in \mathbb{R}^N$, Ω a $N \times N$ real-valued square matrix, and observations $(\mathbf{r}_1, ..., \mathbf{r}_T)$. We are consequently under Assumption 1.3.

Again, the Gaussianity assumption that is made here not only serves a purely computational purpose (even if it is interesting to see that sample counterparts coincide with MLE estimators), but will also help us to understand the statistical properties of the estimators used afterwards, in particular in section 3.3.3.1. Should this assumption be relaxed, estimation and the obtainment of asymptotics would still be possible but potentially with greater difficulties or less clarity.

1.3.2.1. *Estimation*

It is possible to estimate the moments (μ, Ω) thanks to MLE. MLE is fairly standard in many statistical textbooks (see, for example [KEN 77] or [FLO 07]) especially for multivariate Gaussian law. The computation we re-do here is quite classical and is nicely exposed also in a financial context in [RON 14]. The likelihood $\mathcal{L}$ for a Gaussian distribution, as a function of the parameters, conditionally on the observations can be written as:

$$\begin{aligned}\mathcal{L}(\mu, \Omega) &= \prod_{t=1}^{T} \frac{1}{\sqrt{(2\pi)^N det(\Omega)}} e^{-\frac{1}{2}(\mathbf{r}_t-\mu)'\Omega^{-1}(\mathbf{r}_t-\mu)} \\ &= \frac{1}{((2\pi)^N det(\Omega))^{\frac{T}{2}}} e^{-\frac{1}{2}\sum_{t=1}^{T}(\mathbf{r}_t-\mu)'\Omega^{-1}(\mathbf{r}_t-\mu)}.\end{aligned}$$

Therefore, the log-likelihood l_0 is:

$$l_0(\mu, \Omega) = -\frac{NT}{2}\log(2\pi) - \frac{T}{2}\log(det(\Omega)) - \frac{1}{2}\sum_{t=1}^{T}(\mathbf{r}_t - \mu)'\Omega^{-1}(\mathbf{r}_t - \mu). \quad [1.2]$$

The couple of estimators $(\hat{\mu}_T, \hat{\Omega}_T)$ is given by the parameters obtained as an expression of the set of observations, which maximizes equation [1.2]. At the optimum, the two derivatives of the log-likelihood with respect to the parameters have to vanish. For this, differentiating $l_0(\mu, \Omega)$ with respect to parameter μ and equalizing to 0 gives:

$$\hat{\mu}_T = \frac{1}{T}\sum_{i=1}^{T}\mathbf{r}_{t-i}.$$

In the same way, plugging $\mu = \hat{\mu}_T$ into $l_0(\hat{\mu}_T, \Omega)$ gives a function of Ω only which, as we have mentioned before, is scalar-valued. We can therefore replace any term $(\mathbf{r}_t - \mu)'\Omega^{-1}(\mathbf{r}_t - \mu)$ by its trace, omit the constant term (which will disappear when differentiating), and use the commutation properties of the trace function. We finally find that:

$$l(\Omega) = -\frac{T}{2}\log(det(\Omega)) - \frac{1}{2}tr(\Omega^{-1}\sum_{t=1}^{T}(\mathbf{r}_t - \hat{\mu}_T)'(\mathbf{r}_t - \hat{\mu}_T).$$

If we differentiate with respect to Ω and equalize to zero, we finally get the expression of the estimator for Ω:

$$\hat{\Omega}_T = \frac{1}{T}\sum_{i=1}^{T}(\mathbf{r}_{t-i} - \hat{\mu}_T)'(\mathbf{r}_{t-i} - \hat{\mu}_T).$$

There is no surprise to observe that, under a Gaussian assumption, maximum likelihood estimators and sample counterparts do coincide in fact for the first (expected return) and the second moments (variance).

1.3.2.2. *Statistical properties*

We are interested here in the statistical properties of the estimators stated above. Any estimator is a random variable, and consequently has statistical properties: law, moments, etc. These properties can be studied either at finite distance (T fixed) or in the asymptotic framework (T growing to infinity). These properties may depend on the initial assumptions we made on the return distribution. The following results have to be found in contributions of [KEN 77] or [AND 03b], and are also explicitly given under the same set of assumptions in [GOU 97]. We therefore simply restate here the conclusions and properties we find under the same form in those references.

Let us take the least sophisticated assumption, Assumption 1.1, where only the stationarity of the return process is assumed. We consider the estimators $\hat{\mu}$ and $\hat{\Omega}$ of μ and Ω as described in the previous section. In this case, we find that [GOU 97]:

– $\hat{\mu}$ and $\hat{\Omega}$ converge towards μ and Ω;

– $\hat{\mu}$ and $\hat{\Omega}$ are asymptotically Gaussian;

– the asymptotic variance of $\sqrt{(\hat{\mu} - \mu)}$ can be obtained only and is equal to: $\sum_{h=-\infty}^{h=+\infty} \Gamma(h)$.

We see in particular that we are not guaranteed that the estimators are independent and the asymptotic variance of the covariance estimator is not obtained. If we are more demanding, we can assume that we shift from Assumption 1.1 to Assumption 1.2: we now assume in addition that, at two different dates, the returns are independent but follow the same law. We obtain new properties in addition to the previous ones [AND 03b]:

– the asymptotic variance of $\sqrt{(\hat{\mu} - \mu)}$ is now equal to Ω;

– $\hat{\mu}$ and $\hat{\Omega}$ are asymptotically independent as soon as the original law of returns is symmetric;

– the asymptotic variance of $\sqrt{(\hat{\Omega} - \Omega)}$ is a function of Ω, decreasing as tails of the original distribution thicken.

Assumption 1.2 is already a satisfying one, as independence and homogeneity of returns allow us to find many desirable properties for estimators at mild cost, without assuming Gaussian returns in the meantime. Stating Assumption 1.3 will finally bring us two more results: finite distance moments for $\hat{\mu}$ and a simple closed-form expression for the asymptotic variance of $\hat{\Omega}$. We have in this case ([AND 03b] again):

– $\hat{\mu}$ and $\hat{\Omega}$ are asymptotically Gaussian (still convergent with no bias);

– the asymptotic variance of $\sqrt{(\hat{\mu} - \mu)}$ is still equal to Ω, but we know now that the asymptotic covariance expression for the estimator of Ω is such that, for any vectors, v_1 and $v_2 \in \mathbb{R}^N$, we have that:

$$Cov_{as}[\sqrt{T}(\hat{\Omega}_T - \Omega)v_1, \sqrt{T}(\hat{\Omega}_T - \Omega)v_2] = v_1'\Omega v_2 \Omega + \Omega v_2 . v_1' \Omega.$$

Two remarks are that $\hat{\mu}$ and $\hat{\Omega}$ are automatically independent by a symmetry argument, and that the finite distance law of $\hat{\mu}$ is moreover Gaussian. Those expressions become simpler in the case of one single asset, in particular for the asymptotic variance, since, under Assumption 1.3, we have for a given asset i at fixed T:

$$\mathbb{E}[\hat{\mu}_T^i] = \mu_i \quad \text{and} \quad \mathbb{V}[\hat{\mu}_T^i] = \frac{\sigma_i^2}{T},$$

and asymptotically[4]:

$$\mathbb{V}_{as}[\sqrt{T}(\hat{\sigma}_i^2 - \sigma_i^2)] = 2\sigma_i^4.$$

We must add finally that, in any case, the asymptotic or finite distance moments depend on the true value of the parameter. Then, to estimate the moment of the estimator, it is common to plug the estimator in the theoretical expression to have an estimation of the moment of the estimator.

1.3.2.3. *Alternative volatility estimators*

Volatility being the square-root of variance, there are however other ways to estimate volatility. We will explore in detail in Chapter 3 alternative covariance estimators thanks to the spectral inspection of the correlation structure between assets (see sections 3.2 and 3.5). However, as detailed in section 3.4.1, it is possible to estimate separately correlation and volatility to estimate covariance. Volatility estimation may in itself be the subject of not only one more book, but of many. We expose in this section some useful contributions for alternative paths leading to alternative estimators of individual volatilities, different from the simple, usual standard deviation. We do not aim to be exhaustive due to the large amount of literature on the topic. As we will explore dynamic models for volatility in section 1.5.2, we briefly focus in this section on historical volatility estimators. Volatility annualization will be addressed later in section 4.4.1.

Working with, say, daily data, the first possibility is to compute volatility assuming either that the drift (computed as the mean return on the sample) is positive or not. The

4 This last expression will be explicitly useful later in section 3.3.3.1.

computation of volatility with zero drift is fairly standard and widely spread. Another possibility is to compute volatility as an exponential moving average of the time series of returns: this choice is quite frequent among practitioners, and a review is available in [ALE 08].

If available, another possibility is to use intra-day data. The theoretical advantage is that having access to more data is a way to increase the number of observations and then to obtain more precise estimators. Some estimators are now quite famous: [PAR 80] was one of the first contributions to use high and low prices rather than daily, close-to-close prices. The estimator is the square-root of the sum of squared logarithms of the ratio of the highest prices to the lowest prices. Elaborating on this idea, [GAR 80] corrected the squared log ratios of high to low prices, with another log term of the ratio of close to open. Another proposition for a historical volatility estimator using open, high, low and close prices is available in [ROG 91]. The Garman–Klass and Rogers–Satchell estimators are now widespread in the literature but are quite inappropriate to handle volatility on price processes with jump components. [YAN 00] provided a correction relative to those estimators that may account for both non-zero drift and jumps. In particular, this estimator allows us to obtain an overnight/intra-day decomposition of the volatility. Interested readers can also find further contributions in the papers of [BAL 84], [BAR 02], [AND 03a], [ZHA 05] or [AND 12a].

1.3.3. *Skewness and kurtosis*

The computation of empirical skewness and kurtosis on a finite sample thanks to sample moments is not a challenge *per se*. However, some estimators or the definition itself of those moments may be critical in the case of distributions with fat tails (for this, we refer to the detailed discussion of the first chapter of [BOU 09]): we may end up with huge empirical figures meaning nothing. In general, the literature on the subject is not very developed when compared with other financial fields but one reference that is often quoted is [KIM 04], which compiles robust versions of skewness and kurtosis estimators and that we will partly relay here. We will go back on the use and measure of skewness and kurtosis in the context of strategies later in section 4.3.3. As we will not explore measures of co-skewness and co-kurtosis, we will consider for the sake of clarity and ease of explanation, in section 1.3.3, a scalar, univariate return series (R_t) with sample observations $(r_t)_{t=1,\dots,N}$. On this sample, we assume that the unconditional distribution of returns R has an empirical mean μ, an empirical median $med(R)$, an empirical mode $mode(R)$ and a volatility σ. Of course, all these quantities are estimated but we skip the estimator notations for the sake of simplicity in this section. In the same way, quantiles and distributions have to be understood, for a practical estimation, as the empirical quantiles and distributions equivalents. Moreover, the series may represent the returns of any given financial asset (stocks, funds, etc.), not necessarily a component of a portfolio, which means that we also skip the asset subscript.

1.3.3.1. *Skewness estimation*

Of course, a Gaussian assumption for returns in order to derive a skewness or a kurtosis estimator would be pointless here. As the values are known and fixed, there would be nothing to estimate. On the contrary, departure from those fixed values will produce tests for the normality of a distribution. As discussed previously, the natural estimators for skewness and kurtosis are:

$$\hat{s} = \frac{1}{N}\frac{\sum_{t=1}^{N}(r_t - \mu)^3}{\sigma^3} \quad \text{and} \quad \hat{k} = \frac{1}{N}\frac{\sum_{t=1}^{N}(r_t - \mu)^4}{\sigma^4}.$$

A potential correction for the finite distance bias of the skewness estimator is given by the *adjusted Fisher–Pearson* skewness:

$$s_a = \frac{N}{(N-1)(N-2)}\frac{\sum_{t=1}^{N}(r_t - \mu)^3}{\sigma^3}.$$

As they are computed as averages of powers of observations, the sensitivity to potential outliers is huge. In this respect, estimation is in practice quite challenging, since many alternative measures have been tested, implemented and proposed, both in the theoretical statistical and in the financial literature. Explicitly removing outliers is rather subjective and empirically difficult. It is then better to seek robust measures rather than manipulate data.

In the case of unimodal, symmetric distributions, the mean, median and mode should coincide. If the distribution is not unimodal but still symmetric, the equality between the mean and the median should hold, and skewness is equal to zero: as said before, zero skewness does not however imply symmetry, and in general anything goes (skewness different from zero and mean above or below median), meaning that a cautious use and comparison of estimators for a sanity check is always preferable. Some measures may however exploit the distance between moments and quantiles to measure skewness. We will recall, for instance, the Bowley[5] formula (see [BOW 20]):

$$s_B = \frac{Q1 - 2med(R) + Q_3}{Q_3 - Q_1},$$

with Q_1 and Q_3, respectively, the 0.25 and 0.75 quantiles of the distribution. This quantity is naturally comprised between -1 and 1, leading to a "normalized" value of skewness, -1 indicating an extreme-left skewness and $+1$ an extreme-right skewness.

5 We also find the terms "Galton formula" and "Yule–Kendall index".

In the same way, *Pearson's first* and *second* skewness coefficients are written as:

$$s_{P1} = \frac{\mu - mode(R)}{\sigma} \quad \text{and} \quad s_{P2} = 3\frac{\mu - med(R)}{\sigma}.$$

For additional reading, see the works of [HOT 32] and [ARN 95] that provide a critical review of skewness measures using the distribution mode or the median.

REMARK 1.1.– The expression of s_{P2} does not come from nowhere. In fact, s_B is a particular case of the formula popularized by [HIN 75], which is a parametrized expression for the skewness estimator $s_H(\alpha)$ for α lying in $[0; 0.5]$:

$$s_H(\alpha) = \frac{F^{-1}(1-\alpha) + F^{-1}(\alpha) - 2med(R)}{F^{-1}(1-\alpha) - F^{-1}(\alpha)},$$

with F^{-1} being the inverse cumulative function of the distribution of Y. $F^{-1}(\alpha)$ is the α-quantile of the empirical distribution of R and $s_H(0.25) = s_B$ for any sample. The particular choice of α is quite uneasy that explains why this formula has not much echo in practice. However, [GRO 84] integrates the $s_H(\alpha)$ formula along α to recover a different estimator s_{GM} whose expression reads:

$$s_{GM} = \frac{\mu - med(R)}{\frac{1}{N}\sum_{t=1}^{N} |r_t - med(R)|}.$$

As $\frac{1}{N}\sum_{t=1}^{N} |r_t - med(R)|$ is a dispersion measure, it can be replaced [KEN 77] by σ and, in this case, s_{GM} coincides with s_{P2} thanks to this change of normalization.

1.3.3.2. *Kurtosis estimation*

Alternative measures for kurtosis are rather scarce. A contribution by [MOO 88] shows that sample kurtosis may be interpreted as a dispersion measure of the distribution relative to the two points $\mu - \sigma$ and $\mu + \sigma$. Then, if the distribution is concentrated around μ or far in the tails, the value of kurtosis can be huge. [MOO 88] presents a kurtosis-equivalent formula close to the idea used for defining the Bowley formula of kurtosis but using octiles rather than quartiles:

$$k_M = \frac{((O_7 - O_5) + (O_3 - O_1))}{O_6 - O_2},$$

where $O_i = F^{-1}(i/8)$ with the previous notations. For a standard Gaussian distribution, $k_M = 1.23$.

REMARK 1.2.– [BON 11] recalls the approaches of [HOG 72] and [CRO 67] who both define alternatives for kurtosis measurement by using ratio of differences of upper and lower quantiles of the distribution, each parametrized by parameters to tune. The work of [HOG 72] leads in particular to potential tests for the presence of light or heavy tails (see also [KIM 04]).

1.3.3.3. *Statistical properties*

As skewness and kurtosis are perfectly known for a Gaussian distribution, as expectation and variance fully determine the law, the asymptotical law of estimators is then a bit particular. Under Assumption 1.3, [KEN 77] provide the distribution of the sample estimators $\hat{s}$ and $\hat{k}$:

– $\sqrt{T}\hat{s}$ follows asymptotically a $\mathcal{N}(0, 6)$;

– $\sqrt{T}(\hat{k} - 3)$ follows asymptotically a $\mathcal{N}(0, 24)$.

The asymptotic variance of kurtosis is huge. This means that, in a finite sample, it is important to have large values of T, since there is a hazard of having large estimators, with a high sensitivity to outliers, that boost the final estimator value when computed at power 4. This explains why empirical values for kurtosis are often very difficult to rely on.

REMARK 1.3.– The values of skewness and kurtosis (respectively 0 and 3) for a Gaussian distribution make it easy to build normality tests relying on the departure of skewness and kurtosis from those values. Those tests are in general easy to implement in practice, even if they should rely on robust empirical measures. Such tests are, for instance, the [JAR 80] and the [D'AG 73] tests that compute a distance between empirical and theoretical moments. See [DOO 08], [RIC 93], [THO 02] and Chapter 2 of [JON 07a] for a review and developments on normality tests.

1.4. The time series properties of returns

Building[6] on the notations and concepts detailed above, we now turn our attention to the time series properties of returns. Thus far, our focus has been on how to compute returns, how to estimate their moments, and we were mainly interested in an unconditional (under the statistical meaning) view of returns. Through the notion of stylized facts, we have already seen that there are actually significant pieces of evidence that their longer run properties are time varying. However, that is not the only key dimension of the time series behavior of return. This section should help the

6 The intra-day realized variance data used in this section owes a lot to the work of Benoît Sévi. The authors wish to thank him.

reader understand where this consensus is coming from and how it matters when building an investment strategy, both from a risk and a portfolio construction perspective.

A large part of investment-related literature builds portfolios from a refined version of the original formula presented in [MAR 52] stating that the weight of a given asset in a given portfolio should be proportional to its expected return and inversely proportional to its returns' volatility. We will heavily discuss allocation (and more specifically the mean-variance setting) in Chapter 3, yet need to stress an important message: the two quantities that matter to investing in a Gaussian world are expected returns and volatility. Mean-variance solves nothing of investors' issues but helps quantifying them: it points towards a more systematic way to state how assets should be combined into a portfolio. Now, if volatility can be measured because of its persistence, creating expected returns is the basic bread and butter of the industry and the very heart of any investment process.

1.4.1. *Expected returns and how they are linked with strategies*

Every investment process is based on embedded hypotheses regarding the expected returns of its underlying markets and the ability of an investment process to predict either the sign or the magnitude of returns is precisely what makes the strategy successful in the first place. Here are a couple of examples of expected returns embedded in an investment process:

– *Trend following strategies*: in a trend following strategy, the investment process aims at exploiting a market anomaly known as "time series momentum". The sign of upcoming returns of a given asset empirically appears to be related to its past performances. This phenomenon has been more specifically isolated in [MOS 12] and seems to be robust across asset types and time periods. The reasons for this anomaly are both to be found in the behavioral patterns of financial markets such as herding and in the fact that returns respond to persistent economic conditions – not to mention liquidity issues that also play a role in this equation. For such strategies, the scale of expected returns is not specified, only their sign is.

– *Statistical arbitrage*: statistical arbitragers exploit another type of anomaly. By looking for groups of assets with long-term relationships, they seek to exploit departures from them. When the assets show a significant deviation from their relative long-term behavior, the strategy assumes some form of a mean reversion to it, forming an expected return forecast on the performance of the pair of assets. In a way, this type of strategy assumes that when two assets usually price the same information set, they will keep on doing so and any departure from it is only temporary – a short-term failure of the efficient market hypothesis. Here, expected returns are formulated for pairs or two groups of assets and their long-term relationship is used to explicitly compute an expected return of the relative value trade: the normalization of the anomaly.

– *Carry strategies*: carry strategies assume that in the long run, the spread of interest rates is a decent predictor of the performance of currencies. Such strategies buy currencies with high rates and sell the ones with lower rates. Here again, expected returns are usually not directly predicted, but their sign is modeled as a function of interest rates spread between currency zones.

– *Fundamental strategies*: fundamental strategies rely on fundamental data – like book-level information for companies, macro-economic data or information news flow coming from big data – and assume that markets fail at correctly pricing this information. The comparison between how markets should theoretically factor in these pieces of information and how they actually do it gives rise to a forecast for the sign of returns. Depending on the underlying model used to measure the fundamental inefficiency, expected returns can also be explicitly formulated.

Across each of these examples, we simply want to help the reader understand how expected returns are at the root of any investment process. This book does not aim to provide its readers with a list of expected returns formulas "that work"[7], but to help the reader optimizing the economic value of his or her expected return formulas. This book is intended for investors who already have ideas of an expected return methodology and who are interested in turning these expected returns into an actual investment process. The asset management industry has been through a certain modernization in recent decades and clients are now expecting more than just opaque past performances. They wish to invest into an investment process as much as in performance – the very reason for this book to exist. Accurate expected returns formulations can be improved in several ways. Here is a non-exhaustive list of them:

1) they can be improved by dealing explicitly with the risk management associated with each of the individual assets in the overall final portfolio. For example, in the trend-following strategy, should the exposure to each asset be constant in capital or constant in terms of risk? Volatility being time varying, a model for its measure will be necessary in this second case;

2) should the reader wish to control the losses in a better way, expected shortfall measures are then necessary, which involves working with the tails of returns, requiring an advance modeling strategy of the returns' higher order moments;

7 There are several good reasons for that but they all revolve around the same idea. If there was a method to generate accurate expected returns, and should the authors of this book know of this method, it would be foolish to write a book about it. Instead, we would be sipping mojitos on a Copacabana beach, as we would be selfish and lazy billionaires. However, writing financial books in Chexbres is, in our opinion, a decent trade-off.

3) when asset-by-asset expected returns models are aggregated in an overall portfolio, a certain market factor exposure can arise from this combination (see below). An uncontrolled exposure to global factors can undermine the quality of the expected returns formulated. This is particularly the case for bottom-up equity strategies: even though the model works well on individual stocks, once that several stocks are aggregated, the exposure to the market factor, that is an uncontrolled beta of the portfolio, can lead to mixed results. The final part of this chapter will deal with individual assets' factor exposures.

An expected return formula "that works" is not enough to create an investment process. We need to understand how the volatility and tail behaviors of returns should be integrated in any investment process. This subsection will now focus on the law of motion of financial returns, putting an emphasis on the dynamic properties of volatility, skewness and kurtosis. Since 1980, a consensus progressively appeared regarding how to model the returns on financial assets. Again, the expected return part has received much less attention than higher order moments. A consensus emerged from two different streams of the literature: the continuous-time literature and the discrete-time one. The continuous-time literature expanded from the early contribution of [BLA 73], up to [HES 93]'s stochastic volatility model, and finally, its extension with jumps as in [BAT 96]. The discrete-time literature took down a very similar route, starting with [ENG 82], [ENG 86] to be extended to include an asymmetric connection between past returns and volatility in [NEL 91] and to include jumps in [DUA 06]. The consensus is described in the following sections.

1.4.2. *The particular case of volatility*

The only investigation of rolling estimates of volatility clearly shows that volatility is time dependent and that returns are therefore non-stationary. An example of such a pattern is shown in Figure 1.1. Episodes such as the 1987 stock market crash and the 2008 financial crisis typically display heightened levels of volatility, which contrast with long-lasting periods of calmer markets. Similar patterns can be found across various types of risky assets.

Volatility is time-varying but exhibits persistence: when volatility is high or low, it remains so for a sustained period as it is now obvious from Figure 1.1. Already introduced earlier in this chapter, this phenomenon known as *volatility clustering* is usually isolated by charting the autocorrelation function of squared returns. Figure 1.2 displays the autocorrelogram – that is the structure of $\gamma(h)$ (as described in section 1.2.4) as a function of h ranging from 0 to 40 days – for the returns on the S&P500 over the 1987–2016 period. The chart shows a pattern that is now widely acknowledged across various empirical experiments: returns show an absence of autocorrelation, consistent with the efficient market hypothesis. Absolute returns being a proxy for volatility and square returns being a proxy for variance have a very different autocorrelation structure: it is more obvious in the case of absolute returns, as the autocorrelation function decays very slowly towards zero. Most volatility models describe the upcoming volatility level as a function of the past volatility level for this reason. This fact holds for the various time series volatility models, from [ENG 86]'s most ancient GARCH model to the most recent heterogeneous autoregressive volatility model presented in [COR 09]. The continuous-time literature relies on the same pattern to describe the dynamics of variance, as in the widely used [HES 93] model.

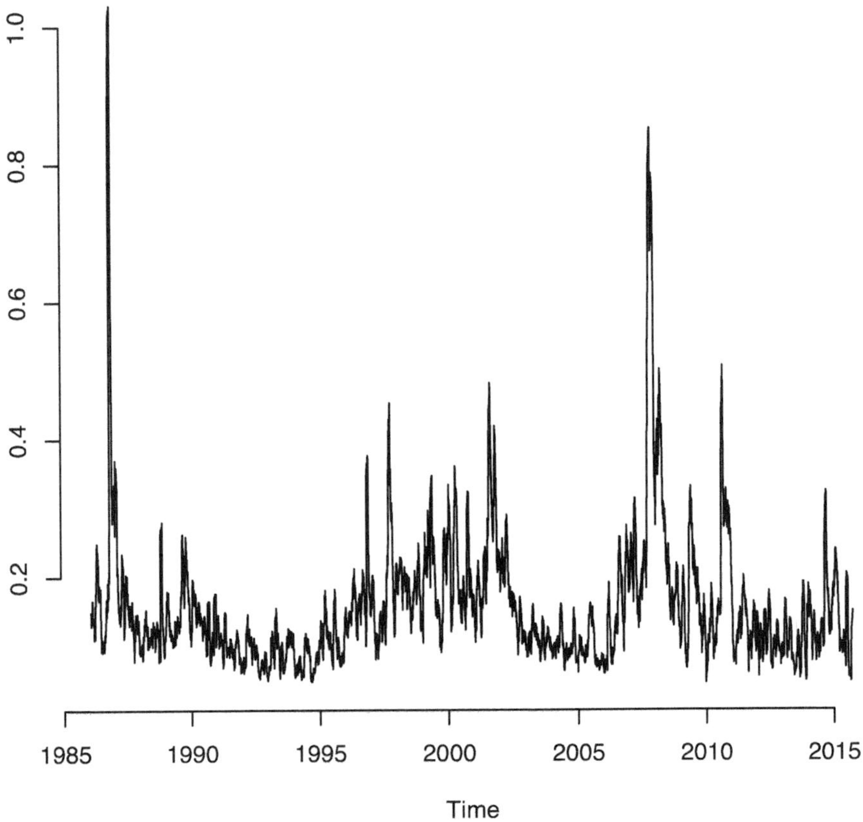

Figure 1.1. *Rolling 20-day estimates of the annualized volatility of the S&P500 using daily data over the 1987–2015 period*

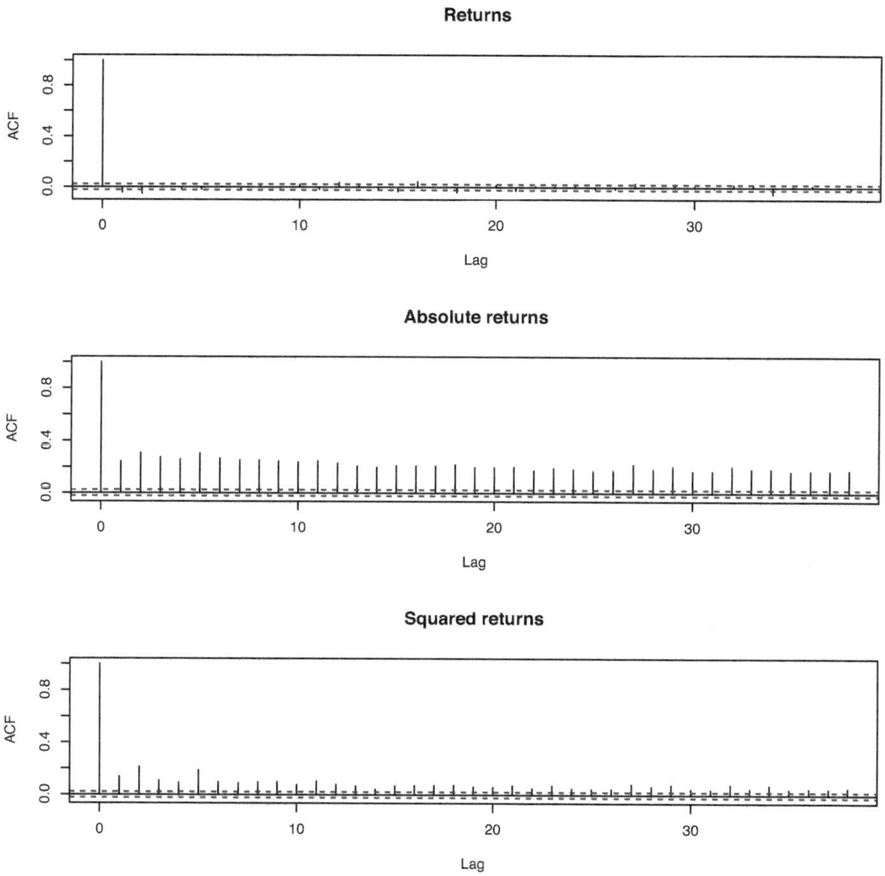

Figure 1.2. *Autocorrelogram for daily S&P500 returns over the 1987–2016 period. Top to bottom, the chart shows the autocorrelogram for returns, absolute returns and squared returns. Dotted lines show the 95% interval confidence for each estimates of autocorrelation*

There is a negative relation between past returns and the subsequent returns' volatility, at a daily frequency. In the case of equity markets, there is empirical evidence that negative returns lead to a stronger surge in volatility than positive ones. This phenomenon receives different designations in the financial economics literature: contributions call it "leverage effect", echoing the corporate finance literature[8]; others call it the returns-to-volatility feedback effect, as the explanation of the phenomenon can also come for market participants' risk aversion. Market

8 In the corporate finance literature, when the price of equities goes down, the ratio between debt and equity increases mechanically, increasing the risk of the company. This increase in risk should then show in the stock's volatility.

participants being on average long equities, their risk lies on the downside of the market. A drop in equities' prices can lead to a panic move, creating a burst in volatility. A symmetrical effect can usually be found in bonds, as waves of "flight-to-quality" imply both large negative returns on equities and large positive returns on government bonds. The case of commodities is much more asset specific: [CHE 14b] reviews the existing literature and provides empirical results as well, showing how commodities display leverage effects of various signs. Figure 1.3 shows the model-implied leverage effect obtained when estimating the parameters of [NEL 91]'s EGARCH model across different assets. The model will be introduced later, in equation [1.5]. The model's parameters have been obtained by maximizing the log-likelihood of the model using different types of returns samples. The graph[9] shows the estimated leverage parameter in the model δ. Indicative of a negative leverage effect, negative returns contribute more to the changes in volatility than the positive ones. Negative leverage effects have been estimated in the case of equities, industrial metals and energy commodities. Positive leverage effects have been found in the case of precious metals, US 10-year bonds and agriculture products. In the case of the US Dollar, a near zero parameter's value has been obtained. Here again, most assets display an asymmetric relationship between returns and variance, but of various signs, depending on the nature of the asset.

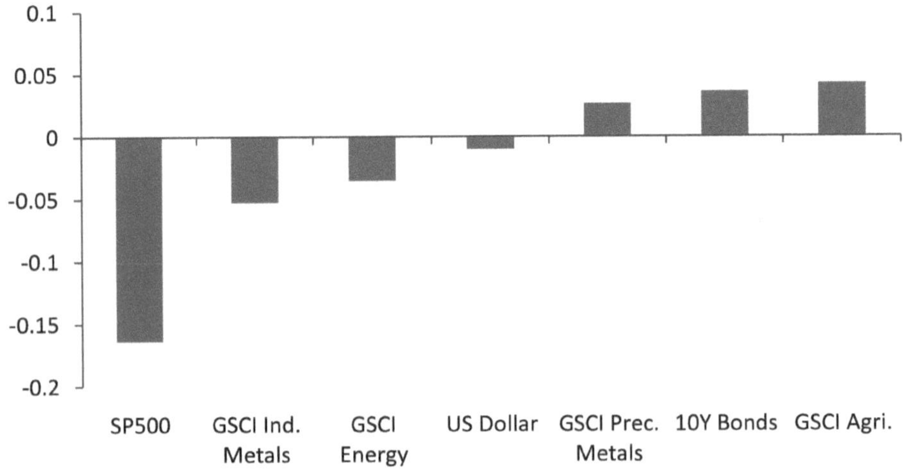

Figure 1.3. *EGARCH model-implied leverage effects across different assets: commodities, bonds and equities over the 1995–2015 period. The EGARCH model's variance dynamics is presented later in equation [1.5]. The graph shows estimated δ as obtained when maximizing the log-likelihood of the model*

9 We anticipate a bit since the meaning of the parameter δ will be elaborated later through the study of the model given in equation [1.8].

Another way to look at it is to compute the correlation between returns and a volatility index. The VIX index is an excellent candidate to perform such an estimation. The VIX index is a model-free estimate for risk-neutral volatility, and its methodology has been inspired by [JIA 05]'s article: it combines option prices of call and put options whose underlying asset is the S&P500 into a volatility index. The VDAX is another potential candidate, exploiting the same methodology as in the VIX case, but using options whose underlying asset is the DAX index. Table 1.1 shows the correlation between financial assets' returns and the changes in the VDAX and the VIX: here again, various types of stocks and credit bonds show measurable signs of negative leverage effects when government bonds show a positive correlation. These results remain naturally period specific in terms of their magnitude, but globally speaking the sign of the relationship for each asset is relatively stable across the literature on time series analysis of financial returns.

	VIX	VDAX
S&P500	–76%	–39%
NASDAQ	–64%	–31%
DAX	–42%	–67%
CAC	–41%	–66%
US Small caps	–68%	–38%
European Small caps	–42%	–68%
European High yield index	–1%	–2%
European Investment Grade index	6%	12%
Chinese equities	–11%	–20%
Emerging equities	–99%	–47%
European government bonds	8%	14%
Commodity index	–14%	–15%
Oil prices	–9%	–8%
Gold	–2%	–3%
World government bonds index	18%	25%

Table 1.1. *Correlation between various assets' returns and changes in the VIX and VDAX over the 1999–2015 period*

1.4.3. *Stylized facts for skewness*

Financial returns display a non-zero skewness: depending on the type of assets, the skewness can either be positive or negative, as a reflection of which of the returns' distribution's tail is the thickest. A common understanding of a thicker tail is that it shows the usual sign of jumps: when an asset has a tendency to be impacted by negative jumps – that is large negative returns that happen rarely – then its distribution should show a negative skewness. That is especially the case for equities and duration-hedged credit bonds. As in the case of leverage effect, the case of government bonds is usually the opposite, as their most extreme variations usually mirror the equities' during "flight-to-quality" episodes.

At this point of this chapter an important remark needs to be made: the apparent skewness found in financial returns is not always the reflection of a left-tail asymmetry. Leverage effects also have the property of creating an asymmetry in the distribution of returns as negative returns have a tendency to be larger in absolute terms than positive ones. It is therefore complex to disentangle the asymmetry coming from leverage effects – the existence of which being obvious from the previous tables and figures – and the asymmetry coming from negative or positive jumps. Skewness being influenced by both phenomena, a model incorporating both a leverage effect component and jumps stands a good chance to be non-identifiable: several parameters shape the very same part of the distribution, making their numerical estimation rather complex if not infeasible.

As a crude illustration of this phenomenon, Table 1.2 displays the skewness estimated[10] across different types of financial assets before and after their standardization – that is using returns to volatility ratios instead of using returns to compute skewness figures. Several conclusions can be made. First, the table shows that, for most standard assets but government bonds, the skewness of returns is negative. At the bottom of the table, an average is displayed and is about -0.3. A symmetric Gaussian distribution would have a 0 skewness: the non-zero skewness disqualifies the Gaussian distribution as a potential candidate to model financial returns. Second, when looking at standardized returns, the global picture remains unchanged as a negative average skewness is still obtained. Still, this average figure is lower and this finding holds across all asset categories: by eliminating the contribution of volatility[11] from assets' returns, we stand a greater chance to be accurately looking at the contribution of jumps to the shape of returns' distribution. The asymmetry remains, but on average it has been divided by two. From those very crude estimates, it seems that, on average, leverage effects explain half of returns' skewness, the remaining part being intuitively attributed to jumps.

These estimates are crude ones indeed, as it is unsure if jumps cannot have an influence on the evolution of volatility. A large return is not necessarily a jump, as long as it comes in a period of volatility. A jump is a significant change in assets' prices that is unusual, given the current level of volatility: say that a given asset's volatility is 1% per day; a one-day change of 2% in this asset's price being a two-standard deviation change, it is unusual. If the asset's returns were to be Gaussian, the chances to observe such a change would be of about 5%: very low indeed. Now, should these extreme events take place right before an increase in volatility, then there is a possibility that they can "explain" part of the increase in volatility, by using the leverage effect channel. Such a phenomenon of a negative jump triggering a significant increase in volatility is usually referred to as "jump-to-volatility" channel. An early

10 The estimators used in the remaining sections of this chapter are the sample counterparts for skewness and kurtosis, see section 1.3.

11 Note that if the distribution of returns is stationary, skewness computed on the raw series and on the centered, normalized series with unconditional moments has to be unmodified. The same conclusion should hold for kurtosis.

literature has already formed around it, and an interested reader would take interest in reading [FUL 11], [CAR 11a], [CHE 12] and [AÏT 15].

		Returns	Standardized returns
Standard assets	Govt. Debt US	0.41	0.25
	S&P500	–0.52	–0.35
	Russell 2000	–0.38	–0.34
	Investment Grade US	–0.87	–0.35
	High Yield US	–2.25	–0.64
	Govt. Debt EMU	–0.13	–0.06
	Eurostoxx	–0.50	–0.31
	MSCI Small Cap	–1.08	–0.50
	Investment Grade EMU	–1.01	–0.24
	High Yield EMU	–1.43	–0.54
	DJ Commodity	–0.74	–0.25
	MSCI EM Asia	–0.33	–0.36
	MSCI EM Latam	–0.32	–0.39
	MSCI EM Europe	0.58	–0.40
Currencies	USDCHF	0.61	–0.06
	EURUSD	–0.15	–0.20
	USDJPY	–0.25	–0.01
	GBPUSD	–0.48	–0.15
	USDNOK	0.45	0.34
	USDSEK	0.23	0.23
	AUDUSD	–1.25	–0.42
	NZDUSD	–0.63	–0.39
	USDCAD	0.86	0.18
	USDPLN	0.86	0.35
	USDMXN	1.95	0.41
	USDBRL	0.95	0.47
	USDCZK	0.34	0.18
	USDHKD	–2.01	–0.05
	USDSGD	0.42	0.25
Commodities	Gold	0.14	–0.18
	Silver	–0.79	–0.27
	Platinum	–0.42	–0.03
	Palladium	–0.04	0.08
	Aluminum	–0.29	0.02
	Copper	–0.53	–0.24
	WTI	–0.46	–0.37
	Brent	–0.47	–0.37
	Natural Gas	0.33	0.18
	Corn	0.18	0.20
	Wheat	0.34	0.37
	Rice	–0.05	0.10
	DJUBS Agri.	–0.17	0.13
	DJUBS Energy	–0.32	–0.24
	DJUBS Ind. Metals	–0.42	–0.16
	DJUBS Prec. Metals	–0.40	–0.28
Average		–0.27	–0.11

Table 1.2. *Estimated skewness across different types of assets estimated using (1) their returns and (2) their standardized returns over the 1999–2015 period. The returns have been standardized using their 20-day rolling volatility estimates. The estimation period covers from 1999 to 2016*

Intra-day datasets helped a lot when dealing with such a question: *realized variance* measures of different kinds have been introduced such as in [AND 03a] and [AND 12a], making it possible to compute model-free volatility measures and even jump estimates. The idea is always the same: when relying on a model-free volatility measure, it becomes easier to disentangle which say 30 minutes return is "normal" or not. Using estimates of this kind makes it possible to obtain charts such as Figure 1.4. The figure relates estimated jumps in the S&P500 with the next day change in daily variance: should jump have no influence on variance – and therefore on volatility – the graph should be a flat line. The U-shaped curve is consistent with the intuition that jumps contaminate volatility, contributing as well to the overall leverage effect found in returns. Again, the distinction between the contribution of jumps and leverage effects to skewness is difficult and much of the modeling choices between the two of them is usually done for convenience reasons.

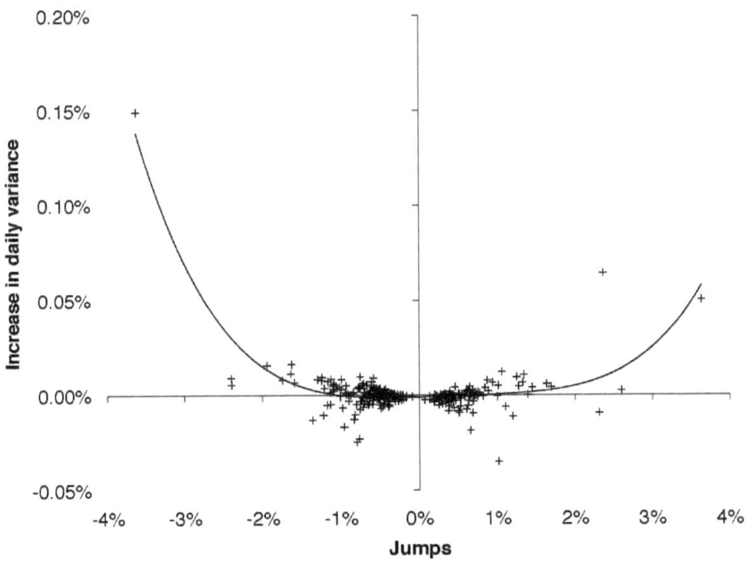

Figure 1.4. *Scatterplot between daily jumps estimated using non-parametric intra-day estimates and the next day increase in daily variance over the 1982–2013 period*

NUMERICAL EXAMPLE 1.1.– Using a dataset of intra-day returns sampled at 30 minutes intervals, daily median realized variance as presented in [AND 12a] are computed and represented in Figure 1.4. Jumps are obtained by testing for them (see [AND 12a]). The figure matches jumps with the next day increase in daily median realized variance. The line is a polynomial approximation of order 4 of the relationship estimated by ordinary least squares.

		Returns	Standardized returns
Standard assets	Govt. Debt US	1.03	–0.20
	S&P500	5.39	0.42
	Russell 2000	3.55	0.12
	Investment Grade US	5.35	–0.03
	High Yield US	25.21	1.20
	Govt. Debt EMU	0.87	–0.13
	Eurostoxx	4.28	0.01
	MSCI Small Cap	4.83	0.64
	Investment Grade EMU	5.07	0.04
	High Yield EMU	15.01	1.09
	DJ Commodity	2.96	0.15
	MSCI EM Asia	2.68	0.28
	MSCI EM Latam	5.10	0.37
	MSCI EM Europe	15.51	0.44
Currencies	USDCHF	13.05	–0.07
	EURUSD	0.91	–0.30
	USDJPY	0.98	0.18
	GBPUSD	3.41	0.01
	USDNOK	1.02	0.11
	USDSEK	1.02	–0.11
	AUDUSD	10.90	0.49
	NZDUSD	2.42	0.27
	USDCAD	5.80	0.08
	USDPLN	4.87	0.17
	USDMXN	22.77	0.48
	USDBRL	5.49	0.49
	USDCZK	1.04	–0.06
	USDHKD	20.14	2.12
	USDSGD	3.06	0.24
Commodities	Gold	3.04	0.38
	Silver	4.23	0.53
	Platinum	2.62	0.43
	Palladium	1.81	0.55
	Aluminum	1.87	–0.07
	Copper	4.03	0.24
	WTI	2.10	0.10
	Brent	2.54	0.30
	Natural Gas	1.15	0.12
	Corn	1.95	0.24
	Wheat	1.24	0.07
	Rice	1.53	0.13
	DJUBS Agri.	2.17	0.07
	DJUBS Energy	1.21	–0.02
	DJUBS Ind. Metals	1.99	–0.15
	DJUBS Prec. Metals	2.33	0.48
Average		5.10	0.26

Table 1.3. *Estimated kurtosis across different types of assets estimated using (1) their returns and (2) their standardized returns over the 1999–2015 period. The returns have been standardized using their 20-day rolling volatility estimates*

1.4.4. *Stylized facts for kurtosis*

Finally, the last key element of financial returns is their kurtosis. It is usually presented in excess of 3, the kurtosis of a Gaussian distribution, that is, a thin tail distribution. The higher the kurtosis, the thicker *both* the tails will be. Table 1.3 shows excess kurtosis figures for various assets, computed out of their returns as well as their standardized returns, similarly to what has been presented earlier in the case of skewness. All returns show excess kurtosis, with various magnitudes: currencies have the highest kurtosis, when bonds and commodities have among the weakest ones. Equities and credit bonds are lying in the middle, showing some heterogeneity.

Again, the question is now to understand the origin of kurtosis, as in the case of skewness: is it the reflection of volatility or of the jump activity beyond volatility? The second column of figures of Table 1.3 answers this question with little ambiguity: when computing the excess kurtosis across assets based on their standardized returns, there is very little remaining kurtosis. Most of the kurtosis attached to returns are actually the reflection of the time-varying property of volatility: mixing returns with different levels of volatility yields distributions with fatter tails than the Gaussian one. The larger these changes in volatility, the higher the kurtosis: the average excess kurtosis of the returns in Table 1.3 is about 5, when that of the standardized returns is about 0. This implies that in terms of modeling approach, once a time-varying component is included in the model, not much attention is required for the kurtosis of returns. An interested reader could also refer to [POO 05], [TAY 07] or [CHO 15] for more details on this topics.

1.5. Modeling financial returns and why it matters to an investment process

Once these previously stylized facts have been listed, it turns out to be much easier to understand the current modeling consensus when it comes to putting the behavior of financial returns into a few equations. As mentioned earlier, there are two different ways of thinking of modeling returns, in a continuous or in a discrete-time fashion. Historically, continuous time is used whenever closed-form expressions are required for asset price computations, such as for option pricing. Rapid and effective pricing of derivatives is a major concern of the investment banking industry. This book is intended more for an asset management-oriented audience and this audience is usually more educated in time series analysis than in stochastic calculus[12]. Time is indeed continuous – at least our perception of it – but the data that we use to create

12 The quant people in the investment banking sector are sometimes referred to as "Q-guys", "Q" being the usual way to refer to the risk neutral distribution, when asset management people are more often referred to as "P-people", "P" being the usual notation for the historical distribution of returns.

investment signals are discrete, even for high-frequency traders. The time series approach therefore makes a lot more sense: why approximate something – continuous-time processes – instead of modeling directly the data we rely on? In what follows, we will take down this discrete-time path but what is going to be presented now could also be presented with continuous-time notations with a very consistent message.

1.5.1. *Modeling returns dynamically*

Building on the previous notations, a now very standard way of modeling a series of univariate random returns R_t is as follows:

$$R_t = \mu_t + \sigma_t \underbrace{\left(\epsilon_t + \sum_{i=0}^{N_t} x_{it} \right)}_{\eta_t}, \quad [1.3]$$

$$\sigma_t^2 = f(\sigma_{t-1}^2, \eta_{t-1}), \quad [1.4]$$

where $\epsilon_t \sim \mathcal{N}(0,1)$, N_t is the number of jumps at time t, x_{it} is the size of the ith jump at time t, μ_t is the expected return at time t as discussed earlier and σ_t is the volatility of returns at time t. In addition, η_t is the combination of a Gaussian random component and a jump component: basically it is what remains of returns once the expected return and the volatility components have been stripped out of it. Then, η_t should be a random variable with expectation 0 and variance 1, so that μ_t remains the conditional expected return and σ_t^2 the conditional variance of R_t. This formulation calls for several remarks.

First, with this modeling approach, R_t is not a stationary process, both in its strict and second-order definitions (as defined in Assumption 1.1), as volatility and expected returns are both time-varying. Now, $R_t|\sigma_t, \mu_t$ has a stationary distribution: conditionally upon volatility and the expected return, returns are modeled as a stationary process, in both senses. The return process is said to be conditionally stationary. One exception to that is when N_t has time-dependent parameters as for some of the contributions that belong to the "jump to volatility" channel literature. For such a case, jumps are "self-exciting": jumps are more likely when a jump has just occurred. When $N_t \sim \mathcal{P}(\lambda_t)$, the number of jumps at time t follows a Poisson distribution with a parameter λ_t. This unique parameter controls both the expectation and the variance of the distribution. Therefore, λ_t can be a function of its own past $(\lambda_{t-1}, \lambda_{t-2}, ...)$: by doing so, η_t is no longer stationary, and the model's estimation becomes much more complex as jumps are not observable most of the time[13].

---

13 A novel literature stream emerged over the past decade using intra-day data sets to compute model-free jump estimates. [LAH 11] provides an example of such a literature and reviews the existing one.

Second, in η_t, the combination of the two random variables does not always need to be disentangled: there are various distributions that can be used to mimic a combination between a Gaussian random variable and a jump process and we will later list some of these possibilities. For such a case, a proxy distribution for η_t will be chosen. The mixture of Gaussian distribution and the generalized hyperbolic one are two decent examples of such distributions being able to generate asymmetric and fat-tailed probability densities.

Third, an extension of the model can be easily imagined to incorporate a dependence between σ_t and longer periods of its past history, or of that of η_t. In the version presented in equations [1.3] and [1.4], the model sees σ_t as a function of σ_{t-1} and η_{t-1}: it is therefore a form of autoregressive model of order 1. The usual way to run a sanity check of such an hypothesis – being that σ_t relies only on its very recent past as well as that of η_t – is to compute the *partial* autocorrelation function (PACF) of the modeled variable. The PACF[14] is very similar to the autocorrelation function presented earlier, but when correlating, say, a variable at time t with its past value at time $t - 2$, for example, it does so by removing the influence of the lag in-between: here the value at time $t - 1$. An autoregressive model typically displays one single non-zero value on its PACF for a lag of 1, and zero elsewhere.

NUMERICAL EXAMPLE 1.2.– Figure 1.5 shows such estimates in the case of the realized variance estimates[15] for four very diverse assets: the S&P500, US T-notes, the USDCAD foreign exchange rate and the WTI. All these graphs show the same image: overall, longer lags should be included in [1.4]. Still, given the increased numerical complexity and the limited improvement in terms of goodness-of-fit, this option is rarely chosen. An autoregressive structure of order 1 is the usual modeling choice commonly observed in the literature.

Fourth, most of the models created so far have a tendency to model variance rather than volatility. It is a common pattern for both continuous- and discrete-time models: variance seems to be more easily related to its past history linearly, even though models such as [DIN 96] question this usual hypothesis.

Finally, the variance dynamics should be chosen to be consistent with leverage effects. This point will be discussed later, when detailing the construction of several GARCH-type models. By doing so, when σ_t^2 depends on past values for η_t, then not

---

14 A formal presentation of PACF is actually quite complex, and this complexity is not useful here. Any reader interested in a formal presentation of the PACF should find all his or her needs in any good time series book, such as [BOX 15].

15 Realized variance estimates can be estimated as follows once the reader has at his or her disposal an intra-day data set of returns. If the trading day is cut into M parts of size δ, then $\sum_{j=2}^{M} \left(p_{j\Delta} - p_{(j-1)\Delta}\right)^2$ yields, where p_i is the log of the asset's price at time t_i, realized variance of day t. Here, the days are cut into periods of 30 minutes.

only will the model display a leverage effect but also a "jump-to-volatility" pattern as past jumps will have an asymmetric influence over the next day's volatility. It remains now to review the most common possibilities for the dynamics of σ_t^2 and the distribution of η_t that are consistent with what has been listed previously.

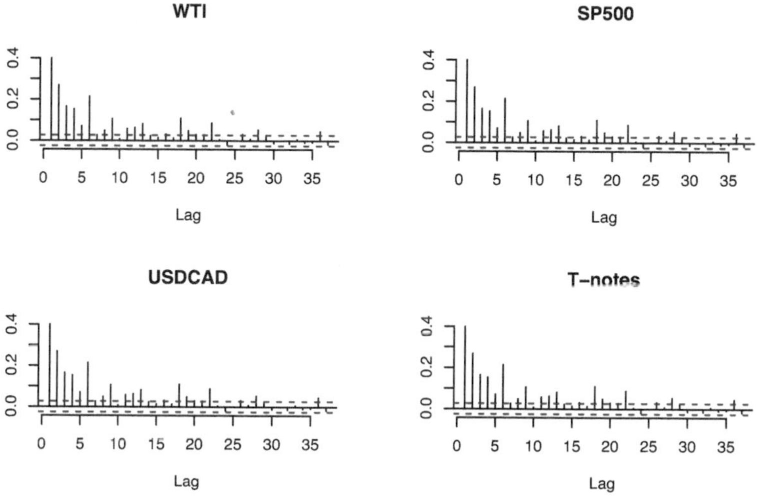

Figure 1.5. *Partial autocorrelation function for realized variance estimates of four assets. Dotted lines represent the interval confidence around the estimates at a 5% risk level. The periods cover from 1989 to 2013*

1.5.2. *Volatility models*

There are many types of models that may potentially be used for the purpose of modeling volatility, but most of them share the very same origin: GARCH models. [ENG 86] proposes the following dynamics for variance:

$$\sigma_t^2 = \omega + \alpha\sigma_{t-1}^2\eta_{t-1}^2 + \beta\sigma_{t-1}^2, \qquad [1.5]$$

where ω, α and β are usually assumed to be real-valued parameters[16], so that the variance dynamics remains positive through any time series. The variance dynamics is stationary if these three parameters fulfill the following constraint:

$$|\alpha + \beta| < 1. \qquad [1.6]$$

16 α and β have nothing in common with the usual notions of alpha and beta coming from the CAPM and exposed otherwise in the book. We keep those notations as they are very common also for GARCH-like models.

The unconditional variance of the process is therefore

$$\mathbb{E}\left[\sigma_t^2\right] = \frac{\omega}{1-\alpha-\beta}. \qquad [1.7]$$

Given that the model presented here only includes one lag for both σ_t and η_t, the model is usually referred to as a GARCH(1,1) model. The lag specification used to be a significant empirical question, but the decent performances of the GARCH(1,1) to model financial returns' volatility let many to adopt a (1,1) structure. One of the main advantage of such a choice is that the estimation is considerably eased: replacing $\mathbb{E}\left[\sigma_t^2\right]$ by an empirical estimate of the quantity creates a constraint on one of the parameters (usually ω), letting the user with only two parameters (usually α and β). These two parameters can easily be estimated using a two-dimensional grid search. The numerical cost is actually not much higher than that of a 20-day rolling estimate as long as it is done in an Matlab/R type of software. Figure 1.6 shows a typical GARCH's volatility's path.

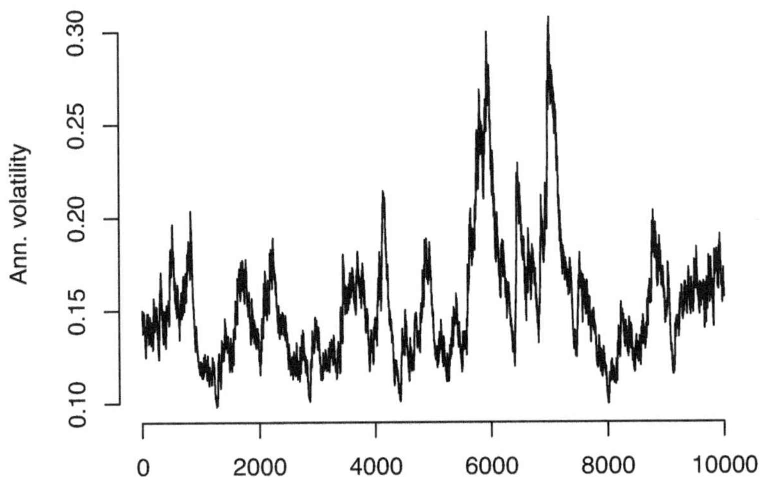

Figure 1.6. *Simulated annualized volatility from a GARCH model. The simulated GARCH model uses the following parameters: $\alpha = 0.025$ and $\beta = 0.97$. The sample size is 10 000 days. Here, η_t is assumed to be following a $\mathcal{N}(0,1)$ distribution*

One key element to be discussed here is the level of the returns' kurtosis generated by the volatility's dynamics. As detailed earlier, volatility plays a central role there and GARCH models should be able to replicate this stylized fact to be qualified as a useful volatility model. Figure 1.7 shows empirical estimates for the kurtosis implied by a GARCH model, given the realistic values for its parameters: the kurtosis's values obtained are actually similar to the values presented in Table 1.3. The higher the α (and consequently the lower the β given the constraint stated in equation [1.7]), the higher the kurtosis of the sampled returns: in a GARCH model, a higher kurtosis implies a less persistent volatility dynamics.

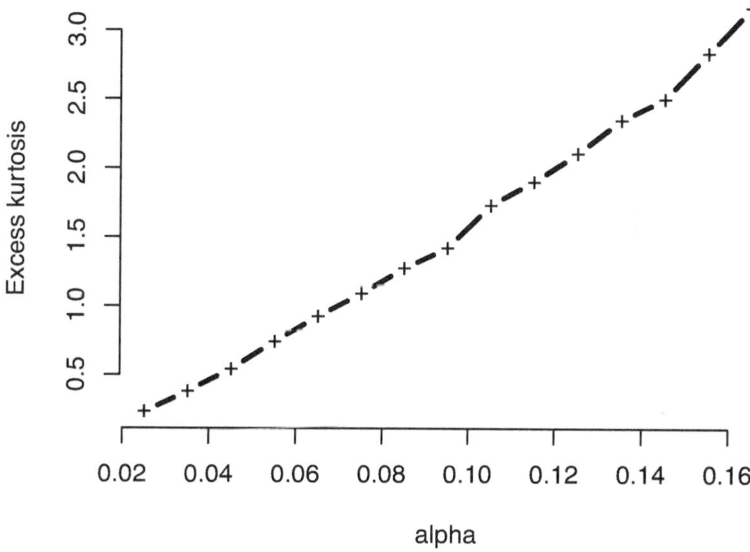

Figure 1.7. *Kurtosis as a function of the α parameter in a GARCH(1,1) model. η_t is assumed to be following a $\mathcal{N}(0,1)$ distribution. The simulated GARCH model uses the following parameters: $\alpha = 0.025$ and $\beta = 0.97$. On the chart, α is increased by steps of 0.01, when β is decreased by steps of the same size. For each value of α and β, 10 000 samples of 10 000 days have been sampled*

One of the issues now is that GARCH models fail at mimicking leverage effects: from the formulation of equation [1.5], the modeled connection between the past return's innovation and the current volatility is linear and that is at odds with the empirical evidence mentioned previously. There have been mainly two different answers to this problem. The first is that of [GLO 92], where the authors introduced a leverage effect component in the dynamics of volatility as follows:

$$\sigma_t^2 = \omega + \alpha\sigma_{t-1}^2\eta_{t-1}^2 + \beta\sigma_{t-1}^2 + \delta\max(0, -\eta_{t-1})^2, \qquad [1.8]$$

where δ is the parameter controlling the leverage effect. When the parameter is positive, a negative η_{t-1} will increase the contribution of η_{t-1} to σ_t^2: volatility will therefore increase during periods of negative innovations than during those of positive ones, that is, the typical type of values expected when dealing risky assets, as presented in Table 1.2. Figure 1.8 illustrates the model's influence over the connection between past innovations and the changes in the volatility: a positive δ parameter is able to create an asymmetry in this function, which should be a symmetric concave function under the simpler GARCH model. This is however not the only way of introducing an asymmetric component in a GARCH-like model. The aim here is not to create an extensive list of possibilities, but to emphasize one alternative, that is the Exponential GARCH model of [NEL 91].

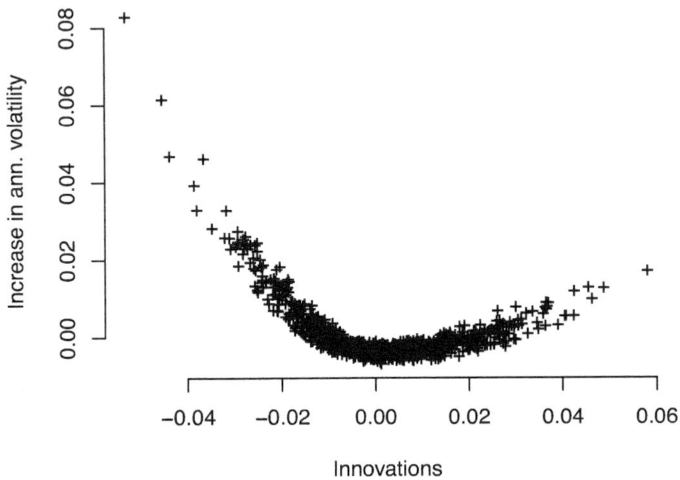

Figure 1.8. *Scatterplot between returns and changes in annualized volatilities using a GARCH-GJR model. The simulated GARCH-GJR model uses the following parameters:* $\alpha = 0.015$, $\beta = 0.95$ *and* $\delta = 0.05$. *To obtain the parameters of the model, 10,000 simulations have been used. The scatterplot compares* η_{t-1} *and* $\sqrt{252}\left(\sqrt{\sigma_t^2} - \sqrt{\sigma_{t-1}^2}\right)$. *Here,* η_t *is assumed to be following a* $\mathcal{N}(0,1)$ *distribution*

One of the pitfalls of GARCH and GARCH-GJR models is related to their estimation. The only efficient estimation method to estimate their parameters is to maximize numerically their log-likelihood. In order to do so, the numerical scheme needs to be constrained to maintain the sign of the α and the β parameters in a way that preserves the positivity of the variance's path. This can turn the estimation of the models' parameters extremely tricky, especially in the GARCH-GJR case. The originality of the EGARCH model is that it models the log of the variance instead of the variance itself. The variance dynamics becomes[17]:

$$\log \sigma_t^2 = \omega + \alpha|\eta_{t-1}| + \beta \log \sigma_{t-1}^2 + \delta\eta_{t-1}. \qquad [1.9]$$

17 The presentation here does not follow the original [NEL 91]'s notations and specification, but keeps the essence of it while making it comparable to the previous GARCH specifications.

The parameters have been kept intentionally similar to those used in the GARCH and GARCH-GJR cases, as they have the very same interpretation: β controls the persistence of the volatility process, α creates a linear connection between innovations and log-variances, ω contributes to controlling the long-term variance and, finally, δ is the leverage effect parameter. The difference is that the only constraint on the parameters is the one making sure that the log variance process does not become explosive, which is a constraint similar to that specified in equation [1.6]. The estimation of such a model is eased as none of the parameters need to have a sign constraint.

Other modeling approaches have then been proposed, but they all aim at providing a modeling of a similar understanding of the law of returns. [DIN 96] present an asymmetric power ARCH model, in which an exponent of σ_t is modeled instead of the variance itself. It also incorporates a leverage component. For such a case, the volatility dynamics is written as follows:

$$\sigma_t^\gamma = \omega + \alpha\left(|\eta_{t-1}| - \delta\eta_{t-1}\right)^\gamma + \beta\sigma_{t-1}^\gamma, \qquad [1.10]$$

with the parameters' interpretation being exactly the same as in the EGARCH and the GARCH-GJR cases. Numerically maximizing the likelihood of a model that incorporates an exponent as a parameter proves quite complex, but decent routines have been created to deal with the estimation of this model.

Another example is [CHR 06] who proposed a GARCH-type model in which the skewness is time-varying. This latter article is a very good example of what will be discussed in the next couple of sections: it is actually one of the earliest time series models, which tries to find as much value in the dynamics of volatility as in the distribution of the innovations. The distribution of the innovations is actually a key part to successfully reproduce the changes in financial assets' returns. Our aim here is to cast some light on the law of motion of assets' returns, and not to measure volatility using these models. A reader interested in measuring volatility should definitely dive into the intra-day volatility measure literature (see section 1.3.2.3 for references). Yet, an interesting remark is that [FAN 12b] find that, across different types of assets, intra-day-based volatility measures have a significant tendency to be biased measures of volatility, which GARCH models are not by construction.

1.5.3. *Conditional distributions*

The volatility structure determines the time-varying property of volatility, the kurtosis of returns and partly the skewness they will eventually display. The conditional distribution, which is the distribution of returns conditionally upon σ_t and μ_t, controls the rest of the skewness and of the kurtosis of returns. The basic formulation for η_t presented in equation [1.3] specifies its distribution as a mixture between a normal component and a jump component. By doing so, it aims at mimicking the behavior of returns: extended periods of "normal" returns and rare extreme events, of the type the industry went through in 2008. Even though a simple jump structure would reproduce these features, it is actually rare to be able to estimate the models of the jump component from a genuine sample of jumps: instead, most of the time, the only sample at hand will be normalized returns. Such standardized returns will incorporate both components. That is why it is more common to try to fit a unique distribution with fatter tails than the normal distribution directly to samples of η_t, once the volatility and expected return path have been estimated. We will review here two types of distributions that emerged from the literature in recent years: the mixture of two Gaussian distributions and the generalized hyperbolic distribution.

1.5.3.1. *Mixture of Gaussian distributions*

The mixture of two Gaussian distributions (MN) is a potentially asymmetric and fat-tailed distribution matching financial stylized facts. For $(\phi, \mu_1, \mu_2, \sigma_1, \sigma_2) \in [0,1] \times \mathbb{R}^2 \times (\mathbb{R}^*)^2$, X follows a $\mathcal{MN}(\phi, \mu_1, \mu_2, \sigma_1, \sigma_2)$ distribution if its density function is a convex combination of two Gaussian density functions, such that for all $x \in \mathbb{R}$:

$$d_{\mathcal{MN}}(x) = \frac{\phi}{\sqrt{2\pi\sigma_1^2}} e^{-\frac{(x-\mu_1)^2}{2\sigma_1^2}} + \frac{1-\phi}{\sqrt{2\pi\sigma_2^2}} e^{-\frac{(x-\mu_2)^2}{2\sigma_2^2}}. \qquad [1.11]$$

The distribution's moments are the following:

$$\mathbb{E}[X] = \phi\mu_1 + (1-\phi)\mu_2,$$

$$\mathbb{V}[X] = \phi\mu_1^2 + (1-\phi)\mu_2^2 + \phi\sigma_1^2 + (1-\phi)\sigma_2^2 - \mathbb{E}[X]^2,$$

$$s[X] = \frac{1}{\mathbb{V}[X]^{\frac{3}{2}}} \sum_{i=1}^{2} \phi_i(\mu_i - \mathbb{E}[X])(3\sigma_i^2 + (\mu_i - \mathbb{E}[X])^2,$$

$$k[X] = \frac{1}{\mathbb{V}[X]^2} \sum_{i=1}^{2} \phi_i(3\sigma_i^4 + 6(\mu_i - \mathbb{E}[X])^2\sigma_i^2 + (\mu_i - \mathbb{E}[X])^4),$$

where $\phi_1 = \phi$ and $\phi_2 = 1 - \phi$. Clearly, the skewness and the kurtosis can be, respectively, different from 0 and 3. [BER 07] showed that any possible pair of skewness–kurtosis can be reached by a mixture of only two Gaussian distributions. This distribution also allows for bimodal densities and has an intuitive economic interpretation in the sense that the components represent different states of the market (e.g. market periods with different levels of volatility). It particularly matches the needs here, as it can reproduce a mixture of a next to (0,1) Gaussian distribution with a high frequency with another Gaussian distribution with a strongly negative expectation and a very low frequency (that would be the jump component). Its estimation is also easier than for most of the asymmetric and leptokurtic distributions, as a grid search can be used for the ϕ parameter while the rest of the parameters are estimated from a Gradient-type method.

1.5.3.2. *Generalized hyperbolic and hyperbolic distributions*

The generalized hyperbolic (GH) distribution introduced in a seminal paper by [BAR 77] is a normal variance-mean mixture where the mixing distribution is the generalized inverse Gaussian distribution. Equivalently, for $(\lambda, \alpha, \beta, \delta, \mu) \in \mathbb{R}^5$ with $\delta > 0$ and $\alpha >| \beta |> 0$, the one-dimensional $GH(\lambda, \alpha, \beta, \delta, \mu)$ distribution is defined by the following density functions, such that for all $x \in \mathbb{R}$:

$$d_{GH}(x, \lambda, \alpha, \beta, \delta, \mu) = \frac{(\sqrt{\alpha^2 - \beta^2}/\delta)^\lambda}{\sqrt{2\pi} K_\lambda(\delta\sqrt{\alpha^2 - \beta^2})} e^{\beta(x-\mu)} \frac{K_{\lambda-1/2}\left(\alpha\sqrt{\delta^2 + (x-\mu)^2}\right)}{\left(\sqrt{\delta^2 + (x-\mu)^2}/\alpha\right)^{1/2-\lambda}}, \quad [1.12]$$

where K_λ is the modified Bessel function of the third kind:

$$K_\lambda(x) = \frac{1}{2}\int_0^{+\infty} y^{\lambda-1} e^{-\frac{x}{2}(y+\frac{1}{y})} dy, \ x > 0. \quad [1.13]$$

The greatest advantage of this distribution is that it nests a large spectrum of other distributions. For $\lambda = 1$, we get the hyperbolic distribution (HYP) whose log-density is a hyperbola:

$$d_{HYP}(x, \alpha, \beta, \delta, \mu) = \frac{\sqrt{\alpha^2 - \beta^2}}{2\delta\alpha K_1(\delta\sqrt{\alpha^2 - \beta^2})} e^{\beta(x-\mu)-\alpha\sqrt{\delta^2+(x-\mu)^2}}, \quad [1.14]$$

and for $\lambda = -\frac{1}{2}$, we obtain the normal inverse Gaussian distribution (NIG), the density of which is

$$d_{NIG}(x, \alpha, \beta, \delta, \mu) = \frac{\alpha\delta}{\pi} \frac{K_1(\alpha\sqrt{\delta^2 + (x-\mu)^2})}{\sqrt{\delta^2 + (x-\mu)^2}} e^{\beta(x-\mu)+\delta\sqrt{\alpha^2-\beta^2}}. \quad [1.15]$$

The GH distribution contains other distributions, among which are the Gaussian one and the Student one. The parameters μ and δ, respectively, describe the location and the scale of the distribution. The other parameters are interpreted as follows: β describes the skewness (when $\beta = 0$ the distribution is symmetric), while α drives the kurtosis.

Both distributions have three advantages: first of all, they incorporate a limited number of parameters (5 of them for each). Second, both of these distributions are able to reproduce fat and asymmetric tails. Third, they can be constrained into a pure Gaussian distribution: when scaled returns would be Gaussian, their estimation would say so. Still, their estimation remains relatively involved and usually requires the use of a statistical package: such packages are usually available for R and Matlab. Examples of use of both distributions for financial assets can be found in [EBE 02], [BER 07], [CHO 12] or [GUÉ 13].

1.5.4. *Numerical model comparison*

Now, we propose a short empirical application to help the reader understand that once each key component of the returns' distribution has been accurately modeled, all models will offer a similar goodness-of-fit. To do so, we propose to estimate the various models proposed earlier using a data set of 1509 returns on the S&P500, the American equity index, using different combinations of volatility structure and conditional distributions. The dataset starts on January 2nd 1998 and ends on December 31st 2003. It includes different market phases, both bull and bear, as it includes the 1998 market rally and the explosion of the technology bubble in 2001.

Descriptive statistics are provided by Table 1.4. The S&P500 returns are characterized by fat tails, as the excess kurtosis is positive. The skewness of the sample is close to 0: this is explained by the balance between the positive and negative momentum periods over the sample. In the sample, 49.83% of the returns are negative. This remains however compatible with leverage effects.

	Average	Standard Dev.	Skewness	Excess Kurtosis	Length
S&P500	0.02	0.21	0.01	1.68	1507

Table 1.4. *Descriptive statistics for the S&P500 returns. The data set starts on January, 2nd 1998 and ends on December, 31st 2003. It includes 1506 data points. The returns computed are logarithmic returns. The average and standard error statistics are annualized*

We estimated the parameters of the models combining two volatility structures: the EGARCH and APARCH ones. The distributions used are the MN and GH ones. The estimated parameters for the EGARCH-GH, the EGARCH-MN, the APARCH-GH and the APARCH-MN models are, respectively, provided in Tables 1.5 and 1.6. These tables are also presented for the reader to see typical values for the parameters of each model: they can be used as starting values when maximizing the log-likelihood function for estimation purposes.

Now, we are interested in comparing these models, given the sample at hand: is one model dominating the rest of them? To answer such a question, it is usual to use the joint density of the sample as a score to differentiate the estimation strategies. The test we use can be seen as an in-sample version of the test proposed for density forecast in [AMI 07]. Say we deal with a time series model for the log-returns whose conditional density at time t is $f_1(R_t|\underline{R_{t-1}}, \theta_1)$, where $\underline{R_{t-1}} = (R_0, ..., R_{t-1})$ and θ_1 is the vector of parameters describing the shape of this conditional distribution and the volatility structure. We compare this model to another one defined by the conditional density $f_2(R_t|\underline{R_{t-1}}, \theta_2)$, with θ_2 being the parameters associated with this second model. The null hypothesis of the test is "models 1 and 2 provide a similar fit of the log-return's conditional distribution". The corresponding test statistic used for a series of observed returns $(r_t)_{t\in[1;N]}$ is:

$$t_{1,2} = \frac{1}{N}\sum_{t=1}^{N}\left(\log f_1(r_t|\underline{r_{t-1}}, \theta_1) - \log f_2(r_t|\underline{r_{t-1}}, \theta_2)\right). \quad [1.16]$$

EGARCH-GH									
	α	β	δ	μ	λ	ω	α	δ	β
Estimates	1.47	–0.74	1.84	0.16	–8.55	–0.33	–0.19	0.17	0.96
EGARCH GH									
	ϕ	μ_1	σ_1	μ_2	σ_2	ω	α	δ	β
REC	0.003	–1.97	0.09	0.003	0.46	–0.33	–0.17	0.18	0.96

Table 1.5. *Estimated parameters for the EGARCH-based model using the S&P500 data set*

APARCH-GH										
	α	β	$\delta_{\text{distrib.}}$	μ	λ	ω	α	β	δ	γ
Estimates	1.27	–0.635	1.77	0.14	–7.99	0.0006	0.11	0.909	0.98	1.24
APARCH-GH										
	ϕ	μ_1	σ_1	μ_2	σ_2	ω	α	β	δ	γ
Estimates	0.9964	0.005	0.46	–1.859	0.199	0.00067	0.12	0.913	0.6549	1.16

Table 1.6. *Estimated parameters for the APARCH-based models using the S&P500 data set*

Under the null hypothesis:

$$\frac{t_{1,2}}{\hat{\sigma}_N}\sqrt{N} \underset{N\to+\infty}{\rightsquigarrow} \mathcal{N}(0,1), \quad [1.17]$$

where $\hat{\sigma}_N$ is a properly selected estimator for the statistic volatility. Here, as proposed in [AMI 07], we use a Newey–West estimator, with a lag empirically retained to be large (around 25). The test results are presented in Table 1.7. Given the transitivity of this test statistics, it is possible to rank the different models and thus decide on the model(s) that should be favored. Now, here is the key result from the table: at a 5% risk level, most models provide an equivalent fit. Overall, all models deliver a similar fit of the returns distribution: the reader should understand at this stage that given the way empirical finance research has evolved, any combination from an asymmetric and fat-tailed distribution with a realistic volatility structure will provide a good enough fit once its parameters have been properly estimated.

	EGARCH GH	APARCH GH	EGARCH MN	APARCH MN
EGARCH GH	–	–0.09	–0.88	–0.08
APARCH GH	–	–	–0.81	0.03
EGARCH MN	–	–	–	0.95
APARCH MN	–	–	–	–

Table 1.7. *Density testing model domination*

NUMERICAL EXAMPLE 1.3.– The data set starts on January 2nd 1998 and ends on December 31st 2003. It includes 1506 data points. The returns computed are logarithmic returns. When comparing the accuracy of model 1 (with parameters θ_1) vs. model 2 (with parameters θ_2) to fit the joint distribution of a given sample, the test statistic is computed as follows:

$$t_{1,2} = \frac{1}{N}\sum_{t=1}^{N}\left(\log f_1(r_t|\underline{r_{t-1}}, \theta_1) - \log f_2(r_t|\underline{r_{t-1}}, \theta_2)\right), \qquad [1.18]$$

with $f_.(.)$ the selected conditional density. The test reads as follows: when the EGARCH-GH is model 1 and the EGARCH-MN is model 2, the test statistics value is -0.88: this value being outside the $[-1.96 : 1.96]$ 5% interval confidence, the null hypothesis that both models are equivalent is accepted.

1.5.5. *What to do with it*

The key point to take from this modeling endeavor should be clear now: mastering the stylized facts of financial returns that the investment process relies on is crucial. It makes it possible to build time series models that can be used to generate reliable returns paths that can be used for two essential uses.

First, such models should be used for risk control: being able to generate sampled returns paths makes it possible to generate risk metrics for various horizons. Regulators are increasingly asking investment managers to have a better control on their volatility if not on their potential losses. Clients are now also very keen on evaluating the riskiness of a strategy from its risk metrics, such as the value-at-risk or its expected shortfall. Being able to monitor a value-at-risk for various horizons helps controlling a strategy's risk: the previously presented time series models can be used not only for individual assets' returns but also to directly model a portfolio's returns in order to compute *ex ante* metrics.

Second, "risk-based" investing has become a significant trend in the industry: this investment approach combines assets in a portfolio, so that they all contribute to the portfolio's risk the same way. Risk-based investing heavily relies on risk estimates. Again, thanks to the combination of volatility models and distributions mentioned previously, computing such measures is easy once the models' parameters have been estimated. They can also be modified in order to incorporate premiums for a phenomenon, which are difficult to capture such as liquidity risk. On such an issue, see [GUÉ 10] and [JUR 15a]. When combining strategies, an equal risk contribution also makes sense, and here again, time series modeling is required to compute the necessary risk metrics. We will come back on this point in the following chapters.

1.6. Living in a world of factors

This final section will focus on the influence of factors on portfolio returns. Aggregating the returns on different assets into a portfolio gives rise to the influence of *factors*. Factor models will be discussed in greater detail in Chapter 2, but for this section, we mean here by "factors" the latent risk factors that affect various assets in the meantime. Most of the time, those factors are unobserved, given their latent nature, and require a model to estimate them or an *ex ante* formulation of their composition. As mentioned in introduction, the very concept of factor has more or less emerged from the equity literature, as in [FAM 92]. It follows [ROS 76]'s asset pricing model, connecting the returns on individual stocks to a set of risk factors explaining a significant portion of their variability. In this section, we will rapidly discuss the existing *ex ante* factors commonly used to analyze the performance of individual stocks before turning to an overview of the latent risk factors as measured through data analysis methods, such as PCA.

1.6.1. *Why risk factors matter*

1.6.1.1. *A CAPM inspiration*

Before stating the formulation of the asset pricing theory of [ROS 76], we believe that it is essential to understand the importance of the influence of factors on the returns of assets, here on individual stocks. One of the most commonly known lessons from the literature is the seminal message behind diversification. Most portfolio managers around the world would know the famous law that states that, by increasing the number of stocks in a portfolio, its volatility is lowered: by doing so, the idiosyncratic risk attached to individual stocks is diversified away, as the risk on one stock is mitigated by the risk on another stock. Such a message will be quantitatively and cautiously discussed through Chapter 3, but this is however not the key conclusion from this experiment; volatility is indeed lowered, but at the expense of something else: as individual stocks' influences over the returns on the portfolio are lowered, another influence grows up, that of the market portfolio.

Let $R_{i,t}$ be the return of stock i at time t. A portfolio mixing different stocks together will have returns R_t^p, which is written as:

$$R_t^p = \sum_{i=1}^{N} \omega_{i,t} R_{i,t}, \qquad [1.19]$$

where $\omega_{i,t}$ is the weight (assumed to be positive) of asset i at time t and N is the total number of assets in the portfolio. The capital asset pricing model (CAPM) as presented in [MER 73] relates the returns on individual assets to the returns on the market portfolio, a portfolio that best represents the evolution of markets. Usually (see the discussion in introduction), this portfolio is chosen to be the market-capitalization benchmark attached to the individual stocks. Let $R_{M,t}$ be the returns on such a portfolio and let $R_{f,t}$ be the risk-free rate, and the yield attached to a short-term bond with the lowest achievable credit risk. The CAPM states the following relationship:

$$R_{i,t} = R_{f,t} + \beta \left(R_{M,t} - R_{f,t} \right) + \epsilon_t,$$

where β is the stock's sensitivity to the market portfolio and ϵ_t is a centered disturbance usually assumed to be Gaussian for estimation consistency reasons. In this form, a natural estimator for β is the following one:

$$\hat{\beta} = \frac{\hat{Cov}(R_{i,t}, R_{M,t})}{\hat{\mathbb{V}}[R_{M,t}]},$$

where $\hat{Cov}(.,.)$ is an estimate of the covariance operator and $\hat{\mathbb{V}}[.]$ an estimate of the variance one. This estimator does not hold any more in the presence of α attached to individual stocks (i.e. the portion of returns not coming from the market's performance). A proper econometric way of stating this relationship is as follows:

$$R_{i,t} = \alpha + R_{f,t} + \beta \left(R_{M,t} - R_{f,t} \right) + \epsilon_t, \qquad [1.20]$$

Here α is not time dependent, and neither is β. Empirical estimates for both of them suggest that they can be: we will assume for the moment they are not for the sake of simplicity. Chapter 2 will cast some light on the state-space models that can be used to turn both of them into time-varying parameters. Equation [1.20] can now be estimated using ordinary least squares estimators for α and β. On top of the usual β formula in its earliest formulation, equation [1.20] also makes it possible to measure the explanatory power of the model using the R^2 attached to the regression, which is the part of the variability of the returns that are actually explained by the model. The market portfolio is by essence a *factor*: it is a risk that is consistently priced in the cross-section of returns. The introduction of the present book provided a list of various known factors: the market factor is one of them and is the earliest factor ever mentioned in the literature.

The financial investment industry has long been aware that factors have an influence over individual assets' returns. What is important to understand for now is that, as the number of assets in a portfolio grows, the return on R_t^P will be more and more explained by factors, and that the influence of factors will become rapidly more important than that of individual assets. [MAL 04] shows that the existence and the appearance of factors in fact "*result from a collective effect of the assets*": according to this view, factors are then both a "cause" and a "consequence" of asset correlation. The essential lesson from diversification is that investors will not be rewarded for their idiosyncratic risk taking, but only for their systematic risk exposure. It simply means that when the number of assets in a portfolio grows, the regression's R^2 obtained with equation [1.20] when replacing $R_{i,t}$ by R_t^P should be increasing, and it should be above 50% as systematic risk should explain more of the cross-section of returns that individual stocks' idiosyncrasies.

1.6.1.2. *Empirical intuition*

Let us take a look at the data to see how both these statements actually hold. We now use a dataset of individual stocks contained in the S&P500. The dataset is daily. It starts in January 1999 and ends in March 2016. The experiments presented here are based on geometric returns. A standard way to assess the impact of a growing N on the characteristics of an equity portfolio is to randomly pick N stocks in the investment universe, combine them into a portfolio and then run the regression presented in equation [1.20]. In the experiments we are about to comment, we have drawn 10,000 randomly selected portfolios of size N. The regression will be the following one:

$$R_t^P = \alpha + R_{f,t} + \beta \left(R_{M,t} - R_{f,t}\right) + \epsilon_t. \qquad [1.21]$$

Each time, the R^2 of the regression, the α and β estimates and the volatility of the portfolio are collected. N goes from 2 to 50 stocks. Figure 1.9 shows the average values for each of the quantities of interest. The figure therefore shows estimates for the following values:

$$\tilde{\alpha}_N = \frac{1}{10000} \sum_{i=1}^{10000} \hat{\alpha}_{i,N} \quad \text{and} \quad \tilde{\beta}_N = \frac{1}{10000} \sum_{i=1}^{10000} \hat{\beta}_{i,N},$$

$$\tilde{R}_N^2 = \frac{1}{10000} \sum_{i=1}^{10000} \hat{R}_{i,N}^2 \quad \text{and} \quad \tilde{\sigma}_N = \frac{1}{10000} \sum_{i=1}^{10000} \hat{\sigma}_{i,N},$$

where, for instance, $\hat{\alpha}_{i,N}$ is the alpha obtained from i^{th} randomly drawn portfolio of size N. Figure 1.9 charts each of these four quantities as a function of N. Here are the conclusions the reader should reach when looking at this figure:

1) consistently with the literature, the portfolio's volatility is a decreasing function of N, the number of stocks. It seems to be reaching a floor around 16%, which happens to be the market portfolio's volatility. As idiosyncratic risk gets diversified,

the volatility of the portfolio goes down until its exposure to the market portfolio takes over the bulk of the portfolio's volatility. This explains this asymptotic result;

2) the R^2 is clearly an increasing function of N: with 2 stocks, the average R^2 is in the neighborhood of 40%, but then quickly rises above 50%. For 50 stocks, the average R^2 is around 90%, validating what has been stated earlier: as the number of assets in the portfolio grows, the exposure to market factors explains most of the performance;

3) neither α nor β show much variability depending on N: the increase in the R^2 is not explained by any pattern in these parameters.

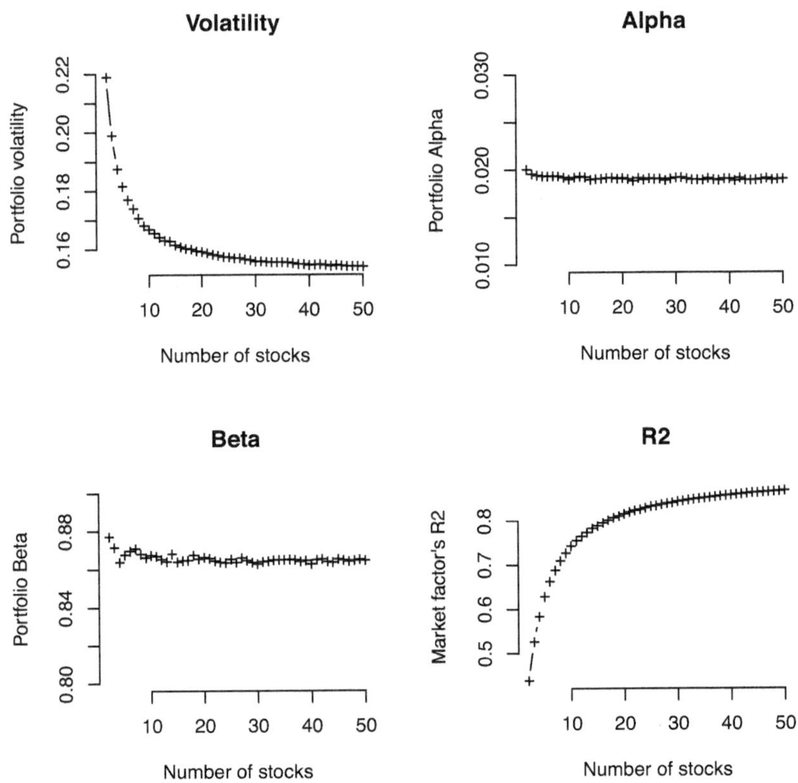

Figure 1.9. *R^2, α, β and volatility of a portfolio made of stocks belonging to the S&P500 index, as a function of the number of stocks in the portfolio. The period covers from 1999 to 2015*

Such conclusions will also be reached through another prism later in example 3.9. This pattern is usually well known when it comes to the behavior of volatility, but the R^2 pattern is usually overlooked. From the perspective of this book, and that of an investment process building, the R^2 conclusion is much more important than the volatility one: not actively dealing with risk factors amounts to giving up understanding what makes most of a portfolio's returns behavior.

1.6.1.3. *Factors and asset classes*

If these stylized facts are actually well known in the case of equity portfolios, not much attention has been dedicated to other types of assets, such as bonds, foreign exchange rates, or even portfolios of indices. In this latter case, the risk that is getting diversified by aggregating indices gives rise to more global risk factors that can be estimated via dimension reduction techniques such as a PCA.

For the time being, let us focus on the fixed income investment universe. For such a case, indices are on average much broader than their equity counterparts: in the investment grade universe – that is for bonds issued by corporates with a rating ranging from AAA to BBB – there can be several bonds issued by the very same issuer. For one company, instead of having one stock, the index can contain a higher number of bonds. Given the depth of the market-capitalization indices such as Bloomberg Barclays' indices or Bank of America Merril Lynch's indices, the reader could suspect that it will take a higher number of assets to reach an R^2 greater than 50%. In the case of high-yield bonds, the situation could even be worse than that: high-yield bonds are often seen as very illiquid assets, with a stronger influence of idiosyncrasies than elsewhere. Figure 1.10 shows similar graphs to Figure 1.9, focusing only on R^2 and using Bloomberg Barclays' fixed income indices over the 2013–2015 period for the dollar- and euro-denominated bonds belonging to the investment grade and high-yield spaces. It leads to the very same computations as presented in the S&P500 case, but for one noticeable difference. In the case of credit bonds, the factor allocation of bonds as well as their allocation by time to maturity buckets matters not to end up with a portfolio that would be very concentrated in short-term financial bonds, for example. Here, we use three sectors – financials, utilities and industrials – and two time-to-maturity buckets – 1 to 7 years and above 7 years.

This will turn our experiment into something a bit more realistic from a portfolio construction perspective, while casting light on a key element that is usually overlooked by credit portfolio managers: their β to their market portfolio matters more than their bottom-up allocation, as long as they do not display strong departures from the index's sector and time-to-maturity allocation. Figure 1.10 shows patterns comparable to the equity ones: *both* in the US and European cases, with 60 bonds in the portfolio, more than 50% of the returns on this portfolio are explained by the market portfolio. As stated earlier, the bottom-up allocation of a credit portfolio matters less than its exposure to the market portfolio, and a lot of "high conviction" credit portfolios are actually made of approximately 50 bonds. The graph also shows a comparison to the equivalent equity universes, highlighting the similarity of the pattern: R^2 is a rising function of the number of assets in the portfolio both in the equity and in the bond cases. One striking difference though is the fact in the equity case, an asymptote is found quite rapidly, around 30 assets in the portfolio. In the credit case, this pattern is much more difficult to find: for both the US and European high-yield bonds, increasing the number bonds beyond the maximum 60 bonds presented here seems to offer an increased exposure to the market factor, as, from 6 to 60 bonds, the R^2 is steadily rising. Still, the key conclusion from Figures 1.9 and 1.10 is that, when building an investment process, not taking into account the global risk factors attached to the investment universe leads to a poor control over the performance of the strategy: risk factors need to be systematically assessed and monitored. As listed in the introduction and especially in the equity case, some of these factors are built from an ex-ante formulation, such as the celebrated Fama–French factors. In the fixed income space, three factors are usually identified: a level, a slope and a curvature factor. The level factor would shift the term structure of interest rates upward or downward as a whole. The slope factor changes the slope of the term structure of rates and, finally, the curvature one changes the convexity of the curve. On this point, see [LIT 91]. When the reader has no intuition regarding the nature of the risk factors in an investment universe, then he or she could be using what will be presented in the next section.

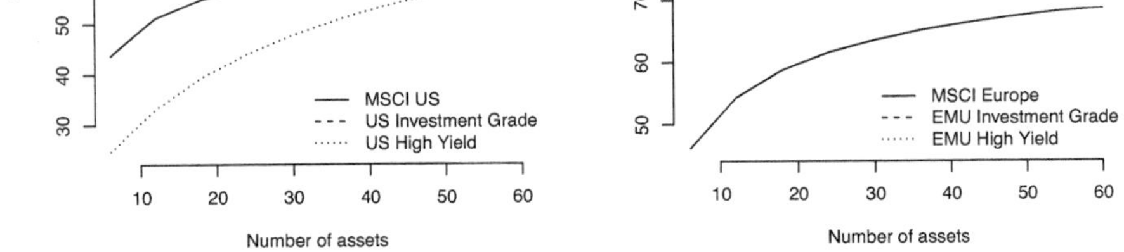

Figure 1.10. R^2 *obtained when running the regression stated in equation [1.21] in the case portfolios composed of (1) investment grade bonds, (2) high-yield bonds and (3) stocks. The period covers 2013–2015 and the data come from MSCI indices and Bloomberg Barclays indices. The graph on the left is for US dollar-denominated assets, and the one on the right is made of euro-denominated ones*

1.6.2. *Measuring risk factors*

There are two ways of measuring risk factors in financial markets, as mentioned already. The first and the most common way is to look for proxies of our theoretical representation of risk factors. The difference between the 10-year and the 2-year yield is a proxy for the slope factor to interest rates curves. The relative performance between the best and the worst performing companies within an equity index is a proxy for momentum factors. For each of these examples, the person building the factor can have a rather large influence on the composition of the factor. The slope factor could be proxied as well by the difference between the 10-year and the 1-month yield. The momentum factor could focus on the best and worst performers in terms of deciles instead of dividing companies into only two groups. Another feature of this type of risk factors is that a set of factors built that way usually remains correlated: the idea of such factors is not to span a set of non-redundant risk factors, but to look for patterns in the cross-section of returns. Among the Fama–French equity factors, a significant correlation is usually found. A similar finding arises from the usual three factors of yield curves. Overall, these *ex ante* formulations of risk factors require the user to have a knowledge of some sort about them: they cannot be unveiled and measured unless the user knows what these risk factors are made of.

Another way of looking for factors is to rely on the statistical analysis of returns: by building uncorrelated factors that span as much information embedded in the cross-section of returns as possible, a method such as the PCA makes it possible to estimate such risk factors. The issue with this approach is that the factors must be interpreted after they are estimated and no clear-cut methodology exists to do so. In the forthcoming sections, we present how a factor model of returns works, before showing how to use this methodology to analyze the factors embedded in different types of investment universes.

1.6.2.1. *Analyzing the joint behavior of returns*

The joint behavior of returns is commonly analyzed through a factor model specification, making it possible for a group of variables to either rely on components that are common or specific to each of them. An n-factor *approximate factor model* is represented by:

$$R_{i,t} = \psi_i' F_t + e_{i,t},$$

for $i \in [1; N]$ and $t \in [1; T]$, where $R_{i,t}$ is the return of the ith asset at time t, F_t is the $n \times 1$ vector of unobservable common factors, $F_t = (F_{1,t}, F_{2,t}, \ldots, F_{n,t})'$, ψ_i is the $n \times 1$ vector of factor loadings and $e_{i,t}$ is the idiosyncratic component. The following assumptions are imposed:

1) F_t and e_t are uncorrelated, so that a common factor cannot be reflected in the specificities of a given variable.

2) The matrix $\Omega = (Cov(e_{i,t}, e_{j,t}))_{i,j}$ is not necessarily diagonal, allowing for serial correlation and heteroskedasticity, but the degree of correlation between the idiosyncratic components is limited, that is, the largest eigenvalue of Ω, the $N \times N$ covariance matrix of the idiosyncratic component, is assumed to be bounded[18]. The common factors are assumed to be unobservable and must thus be measured from the cross-section of the variables $R_{i,t}$, and only a subset of them are expected to be statistically significant. The estimation of the number of factors is performed using the criterion provided in [ALE 10]. The factors are estimated using a PCA. We now briefly review the key steps of the methodology.

The first n principal components are obtained by solving a minimization problem, set up to yield the sum of squared residuals:

$$V(n) = \min_{\Psi, F^n} \quad \frac{1}{NT} \sum_{i=1}^{N} \sum_{t=1}^{T} (R_{i,t} - \psi_i^n F_t^n)^2 ,$$

with $\Psi = (\psi_1, \psi_2, \ldots \psi_N)'$ and $F = \left(F_1^k, F_2^k, \cdots, F_T^k\right)'$ with F_t^k a vector containing for date t the first k factors, subject to either $\frac{F'F}{T} = I_n$ and $\Psi'\Psi$ is diagonal, or $\frac{\Psi'\Psi}{N} = I_n$ and $F'F$ is diagonal. Linear algebraic manipulations demonstrate that the result of this minimization problem is essentially the ordered eigenvectors corresponding to the assets returns' covariance matrix.

The first step is to determine the number of factors to include. Numerous criteria have been developed but arguably the most popular technique involves using an information criterion. This approach is based on the idea that an $(n+1)$-factor model can fit no worse than an n-factor model, but is less efficient. The balance between parsimony and explanatory power is evaluated via a loss function, defined as

$$V(n, F^n) + n \times g(N, T),$$

or:

$$\log(V(n, \hat{F^n})) + n \times \bar{\sigma}^2 g(N, T),$$

18 Following [BAI 02], a strict factor model is based on the assumption that the matrix Ω is a diagonal matrix, therefore not allowing for correlation between two different idiosyncratic components. For a rigorous and detail statement of the hypothesis underlying factor models, see [BAI 02] (assumptions A-D, p. 196). Such hypothesis are beyond the scope of this empirical research piece, but any interested reader will find a finer level of details in the aforementioned article. [BAI 03] shows that the factor and loadings estimate are asymptotically normally distributed.

whereby:

$$V(n, F^n) = \min_{\Psi} \frac{1}{NT} \sum_{i=1}^{N} \sum_{t=1}^{T} (r_{t,i} - \psi_i^{n'} F_t^n)^2,$$

is the value function, $g(N,T)$ is the penalty for over-fitting, n is a constant and $\bar{\sigma}^2$ is a consistent estimate of $\frac{1}{NT} \sum_{i=1}^{N} \sum_{t=1}^{T} \mathbb{E}[e_{t,i}]^2$, which in practice can be replaced by $V(n_{max}, \hat{F}^{n_{max}})$[19]. N is the cross-section dimension while T is the time dimension. The estimated number of factors is then the n corresponding to the lowest value of the loss function among those considered.

One of the most commonly used criteria has been proposed by [ALE 10], which is a refinement of the one by [BAI 02]. [ALE 10] defines a refined loss function and evaluate it over a range of the constants and over random subsamples of the data. The estimated number of factors is then the number that is insensitive to neighboring values of the constant, and has no dependence on the sub-samples. The purpose of the constant is to tune the penalizing power of $g(N,T)$, resulting in an estimate that is empirically more robust than when this constant c is fixed. The number of factors is estimated using the following formula, which is a modified version of [BAI 02]'s original criterion:

$$n^{\text{opt}} = \underset{0 \le n \le n_{\max}}{\text{argmin}} \quad V(n, F^n) + cn \times g(N,T).$$

Commonly used loss functions are:

$$g_1(N,T) = \frac{N+T}{NT} \log(\min(\sqrt{N}, \sqrt{T})^2),$$

$$g_2(N,T) = (N+T-k) \frac{\log(NT)}{NT}.$$

g_1 is frequently used in empirical works due to its stability. Here, g_2 has been shown to have good properties when errors are cross-correlated. [BOO 14] provide a Monte Carlo-based assessment of [ALE 10]'s criteria as opposed to other methods, e.g. [BAI 02], [CON 93] or [ONA 09]. The results demonstrate that [ALE 10]'s criterion is superior in accuracy (overall best in the Monte Carlo study, even when cross-section and serial correlation exist in the data), and precision (less sensitive to whether linear dependencies exist in the financial data, yielding the same estimation regardless of whether the criterion is applied to the data, or the vector autoregressive residuals).

---

19 There is no general guide in selecting n_{max} in panel data analysis. In time series analysis, Schwert's rule (1989) of $n_{max} = 8 \times int[(\frac{T}{100})^{\frac{1}{4}}]$ is occasionally used.

1.6.2.2. *Empirical illustration*

This methodology can be applied to almost any long enough set of financial returns. Let us present two illustrations of it, one applied to a set of global indices and another applied to returns on commodities. The first case will cast some light on a rather unknown problem: how many factors are there to multi-asset investing – and what these risk factors are made of. The second will show how an asset class with cross-sectional correlations as low as the commodity complex can still be partially driven by selected factor exposures.

1.6.2.2.1. The risk factors of multi-asset investing

For this first application, we use weekly returns of global equities, U.S. and European government and corporate debt, and commodities from January 15th 1999 to January 30th 2015. These assets compose a typical pension fund portfolio. The timespan includes two full market cycles of approximately equal lengths (i.e. 1999–2007 and 2008–2015). Furthermore, the time period begins only after the European Monetary Union is adopted, excluding the period when market integration is on-going and when determinants of expected returns shift from local risk to the monetary-union-wide risk. We opt for weekly frequency as it circumvents the difficulty of reconciling the different trading hours around the world that a daily data set would entail, yet preserves more variability in returns relative to data at a lower frequency (e.g. monthly). Table 1.8 summarizes the composition of the data set.

Asset Class	Composing Assets
Equity (7 assets)	S&P 500, Russell 2000, Eurostoxx MSCI Small Cap Europe, MSCI Emerging Markets: Asia, Emerging Europe and Latin America
Debt (6 assets)	US and Europe: Government Debt, Investment Grade, High Yield
Commodities (1 asset)	Bloomberg Commodity Index

Table 1.8. *Composition of the data set of empirical experiment detailed in section 1.6.2.2.1. This table lists the assets included in the analysis, categorized by asset classes. The time period is from January* 15th *1999 to January* 30th *2015*

We perform a PCA decomposition on the covariance matrix of the excess returns. The [ALE 10] criterion points to a two factor model for our data set. Both principal components cumulatively explain 73.7% of the variation in returns, with the first principal component explaining up to 64.2% of the variation in excess returns[20]. This proportion decreases markedly for the second principal component, which explains only 9.5% of the variation.

20 Assuming that the eigenvalues are ordered by magnitude, $\lambda_1 > \lambda_2 > \ldots > \lambda_N$. For $i = 1 \ldots N$, $\frac{\lambda_i}{\sum_{k=1}^{N} \lambda_k}$ is the amount of variation explained by the ith PC.

For each of the principal components, we construct portfolios with the factor loadings (i.e. eigenvectors of the covariance matrix), ϕ_i for $i = 1, 2$. Each ϕ_i is of length N, the number of assets, and represent the weight of each asset within the portfolio. The loadings constitute portfolio weights as they express the time series evolution of the realized risk premiums. Moreover, the principal components are ordered by the amount of data variation explained, thus reinforcing the interpretation of the holding of factor portfolios as harvesting risk premiums. We thus adopt the point of view of the buyer of a risky portfolio, whose high-risk positions are potentially funded by lower risk ones. We scale the loadings by a constant, so that the annualized volatility on each factor portfolio's excess returns, over the entire data period, do not exceed 10%. Apart from allowing a better comparison of the portfolios, this volatility re-scaling also takes into consideration that pension funds are particularly concerned about the volatility of their funding ratio, by extension also the funds' asset value.

One way to interpret the factors is to compute their correlation with the underlying assets, as presented in Figure 1.11. We observe that Factor 1 is highly positively correlated with the excess returns of all assets except government bonds. Therefore, Factor 1 is a risk-on factor: it delivers positive returns when all assets deliver a performance greater than that of bonds. Factor 2 encompasses the emerging markets/energy as it is long on emerging equity indices, especially for emerging Europe and energy commodities, and short on equity indices in developed markets, being therefore a long EM versus DM type of factor. The reader should be aware that those results are dependent on the time period considered, and a longer or a shorter time frame could lead to very different results.

1.6.2.2.2. Risk factors across commodity returns

We now turn to a data set of returns on commodities, aiming at answering the question: what are the risk factors hidden behind their returns? The data come from Bloomberg from 1995 to 2012 with a daily frequency, totaling 2,757 observations. The characteristics of the time series are given in Table 1.9. Note that GSCI stands for the Goldman Sachs Commodity Index (with specific sub-indices for agricultural products, metals and energy commodities).

Prior to determining the number of factors using [ALE 10]'s criteria, the explanatory power of the first factor obtained from a PCA in this data set is analyzed. By doing so, we aim at analyzing the concentration of correlations in commodity markets. The decomposition of the amount of the variance explained by each factor is obtained by taking the ratio of the eigenvalue associated with each factor, and the sum of all eigenvalues of the entire return covariance matrix. A very concentrated market – that is a market for which correlations across assets' variations are very high – should deliver a ratio that is very close to 100%. On the contrary, when a market exhibits a low cross-asset correlation – as we suspect in the case of commodities since [GOR 06] – this ratio should be closer to 0%.

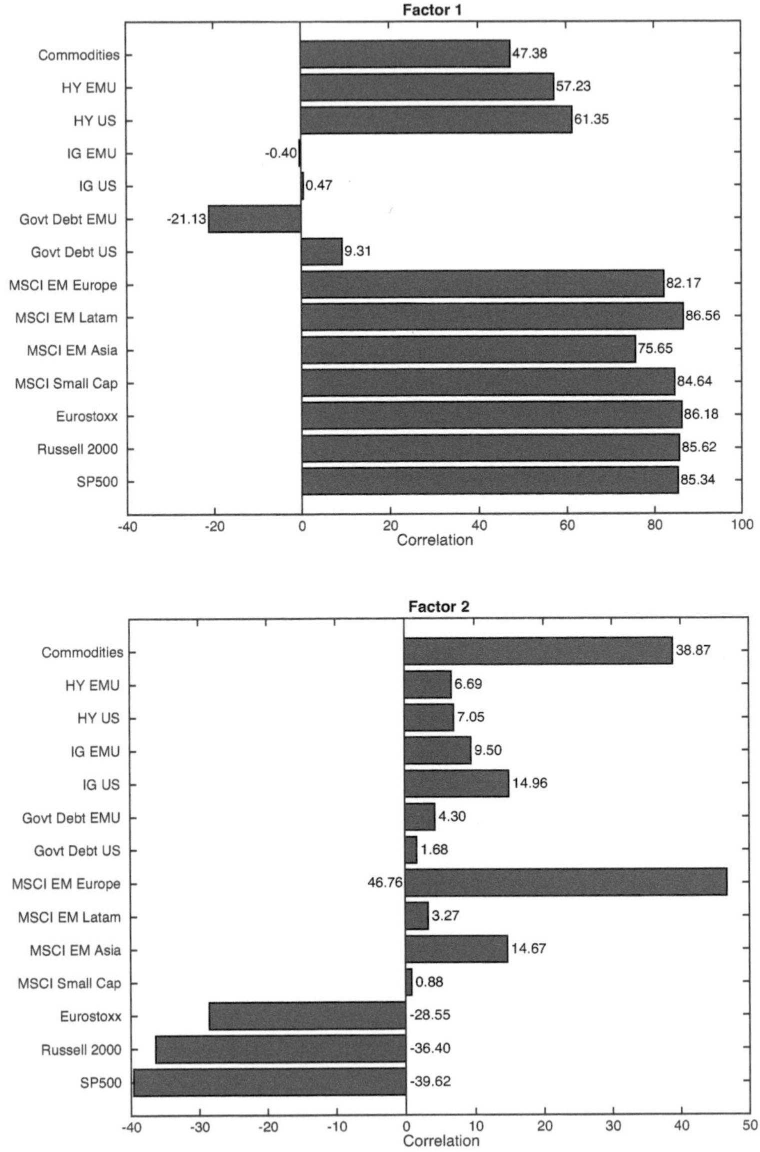

Figure 1.11. *Correlation of the factors with the underlying asset's excess return. The bars represent the Pearson correlation coefficient of either factor with the excess returns of all assets constituting the portfolio. The factors are the first two principal components obtained from PCA on the covariance matrix of the excess returns*

Data Composition	
Commodities (25 assets)	Metals: Gold, silver, platinum, aluminum, copper, nickel, zinc, lead. Fuel: WTI, Brent, Gasoil, Natural Gas, Heating Oil. Softs: Coffee, Sugar, Cocoa, Cotton. Grains: Corn, Wheat, Soybean, Rice. Financials: GSCI Agriculture, Energy, Industrial Metals, Precious Metals.

Table 1.9. *Composition of the data set and summary statistics. The data set is made of weekly data and covers a period starting on the* 19th *of January 1994 and ending on the* 24th *of August 2012*

Such results are presented in Table 1.10. As expected, this concentration is quite low in the case of commodities. In order to help the reader understand what is meant here by high and low, the table provides a comparison of the commodity results with other asset classes. In the case of interest rates' variations, the first factor obtained from the PCA explains 69% of the data set. Equities are not far behind, as their first factor explains 49% of equities' variations. Next is the currency asset class, for which the first PCA factor explains 45% of the data set. Finally, the first factor of commodities explains 28% of the returns on commodities. Thus, commodities obtain the weakest value in this first investigation of risk concentration. This finding underlines the diversification effects obtained when investing into commodities: returns on commodities are weakly related to each other, while still remaining connected as this ratio is not equal to 0.

Data set	Equities	Interest rates	FX	Commodities
Estimated number of factors by ABC	3	2	1	1
Proportion of variance explained	75%	88%	45%	28%

Table 1.10. *Estimated number of factors and proportion of variance explained by data set*

Then, we estimate the number of factors that explain the cross-section of returns on commodities and compare it with what is obtained in the case of other asset classes using [ALE 10]'s rule. These results are also presented in Table 1.10. Equities are estimated to have three factors. These three factors explain up to 75% of equities fluctuations. Interest rates are found to be driven by two factors that explain 88% of their variations, consistent with the findings by [LIT 91][21]. Hence, these two investment universes exhibit a strong concentration of risk around common risk factors. Only a weak part of their variations is explained by asset-specific factors. When it comes to currencies or commodities, we obtain a different picture: the estimation scheme only diagnoses a single common factor in these respective data

21 They actually found three factors, but the last factor explains between 1 and 2% of interest rate variations by using a data set covering a different period from ours.

sets, which explains less than half of the variance. Asset-specific risk factors dominate the evolution of these markets. Indeed, it appears that commodities and currencies have a strong bottom-up side, and a more limited top-down one.

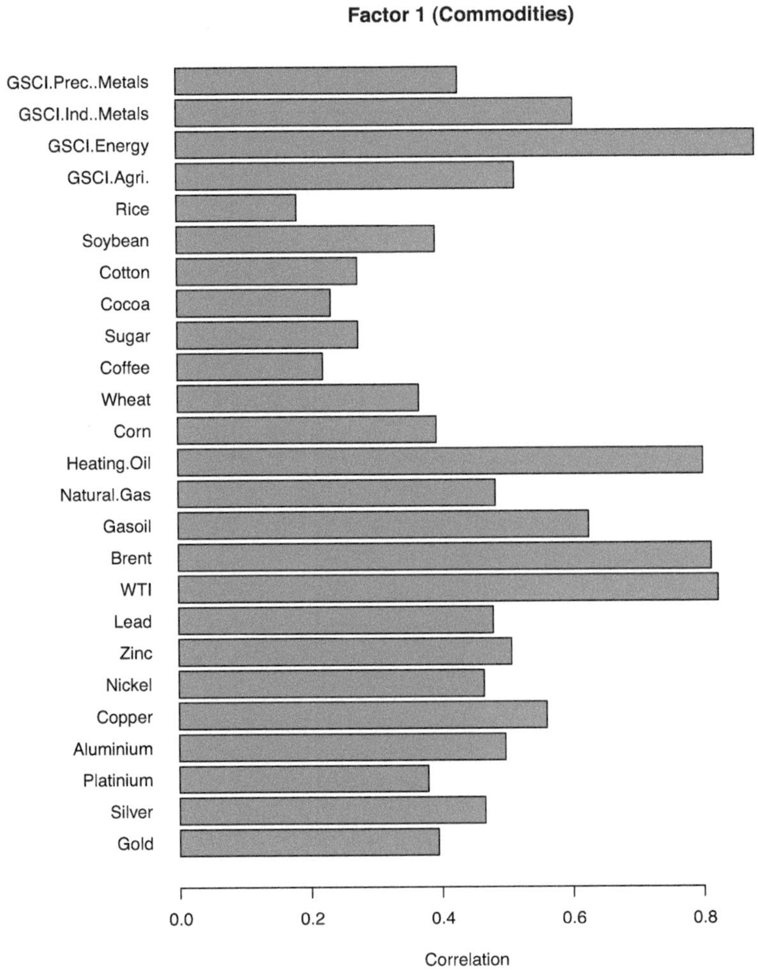

Figure 1.12. *Factor loadings bar plots for the first factor of returns on commodities*

Now, focusing on this dataset and as we did previously, we perform an identification of the first factor driving commodities. To identify this factor, the correlation between the estimated factors and the assets whose variances the factors are trying to explain is investigated. Figure 1.12 presents the correlations between commodity returns and the returns over the first factor obtained from the PCA analysis. The correlation bar plots indicate that factor 1 is a global commodity factor, with a stronger exposure to energy commodities. From this empirical analysis and despite the fact that commodities from a given sector are used for various purposes, they still share common risk factors.

2

Dealing with Risk Factors

The *ex ante* future distribution of the portfolio's P&L is the relevant objective function that a portfolio manager looks at before making an investment decision. Tracking Error Volatility (TEV) or Value at Risk (VaR) are synthetic risk statistics commonly used to measure the risk of the P&L distribution yet to come. Portfolio optimization, including mean-variance portfolios, heavily relies on the relevance of the *ex ante* P&L distribution. This chapter introduces key concepts regarding a sound projection of the *ex ante* P&L distribution and discusses the relevant modeling approaches. It brings forward the building blocks of a comprehensive framework while pointing out the pitfalls of each step.

The shape of the projected P&L distribution depends on the joint dynamics of the underlying assets. Given a joint scenario of the underlying risk factors at the projection horizon, asset prices can be recovered by a full repricing approach or by applying a linearization scheme, i.e. multiplying the scenario factors and the corresponding sensitivities. The estimation of these risk factors multivariate distribution can be made easier by separating the estimation of the univariates from their dependence structure. This can be achieved using copulas, whether they are parametric or non-parametric. Elliptical copulas have the benefit of being symmetric and tractable, which is convenient for modeling stationary symmetric market invariants. They are also stable by spatial aggregation and flexible when composing simulations in time. Another tractable class of parametric copulas is given by the family of Archimedean copula, which tolerate asymmetric risks. The parameters of both copula families can often be linked to standard measures of association such as Kendall's tau. Therefore, summarizing the dependence structure into a single figure can be tempting. Such a measure has to abide by a list of desired properties in order to be appropriate. These topics are tackled in the first section.

Moreover, when the number of assets is high, dimension issues hinder the estimation procedure of the joint distribution. Reduction techniques can be useful to address this point. Linear factor models (henceforth LFM) play a prominent role in gaining statistical efficiency. This is one of the many applications of the various types of LFM which shares the idea that a limited number of factors is able to explain a large part of the investment universe (or any vector of interest) ups and downs. We distinguish between four types of LFM depending on whether factors and loadings are observed or not. Adding financial constraints to LFM, for example, non-arbitrage, or statistical constraints such as the non-correlation of the residuals, allows them to gain economic sense and statistical efficiency on both theoretical and applied ground. Confusion arises when some implications brought under specific constraints are used in circumstances other than those under which it has been derived. Typically the systematic-idiosyncratic decomposition brings forward robustness and a lighter computational burden in portfolio optimization at the expense of some bias in risk calculations. LFM theory and applications are addressed in the second section of this chapter.

The projection of risk factors is addressed afterward. State space models (henceforth SSM) offer the benefit of a unique comprehensive framework for modeling time series. Many standard models such as auto-regressive or moving-average models under their univariate or their vector representations admit an SSM expression. Moreover, models with hidden factors can also be tackled by SSM framework, which widens their scope of application to include, among others, stochastic volatility models, with unobserved components or time-varying sensitivities. SSM can be inferred efficiently using the Kalman filter. Projection, filtering and smoothing are all made possible using the Kalman recursive algorithm. Non-stationarity stemming from structural breaks can be addressed by regime-switching models. Depending on the complexity of their expression, Hamilton's or Kim's filters can be used in order to infer the hidden process and to estimate the model parameters. The third section of the current chapter will shed light on SSM with or without regime switching.

The portfolio's future P&L is affected not only by traditional market risks but also another source of uncertainty called: liquidity risk. However, while market risks alter price fluctuations, liquidity risk is incurred when trading assets. Under the market completeness and perfection assumptions, the financial theory does not explicitly account for liquidity risk, and rather assumes that investors could buy and sell significant position sizes without affecting market prices. As a consequence, securities are priced, and their risk measured, at the mid price irrespective of any friction stemming from liquidity. However, in nervous markets, liquidity recedes and the bid price prevails. The way in which liquidity influences the P&L distribution is addressed in the last section. The roots of illiquidity as well as liquidity measures are presented. The existence of risk premia is analyzed and portfolio construction in the presence of liquidity risk is discussed.

Traditional modeling techniques are challenged by the current market environment, characterized by low yields and negative rates. For instance, in a classical log-normal framework, rates are not allowed to go into negative territories, which raises some mathematical issues, such as the logarithm of a negative number, as well as statistical issues, for example, the volatility of rates being negative, and financial ones, for example, the risk being proportional to rates; the fact that the latter decays to zero would imply that we would be living in a risk-free world! Modeling fixed-income risk in a low or negative yield environment is addressed in the last section.

2.1. Dependence among markets

The use of copula helps to alleviate the implementation of multivariate models as it separates the modeling of univariate risks from their dependence structure. It encompasses a large variety of dependence patterns. Parametric copulas, mainly elliptical, Archimedean, and non-parametric ones are presented and their statistical inference discussed. Copulas being multi-dimensional distributions, one could be tempted to collapse the global or local dependence function into one single digit. This is the object of dependence measures, whose applications and pitfalls are also discussed.

2.1.1. *Copulas*

A Copula can be thought of as a uniform multi-dimensional distribution. This statistical tool was first introduced by [SKL 59] and revisited later by [GEN 86]. It alleviates the implementation and the estimation of multi-dimensional distribution as it splits it into univariate probability laws and a dependence structure.

DEFINITION 2.1 (Bidimensional copula).– A bidimensional copula is a function C satisfying:

1) $\mathrm{Dom}(C) = [0,1] \times [0,1]$;

2) $C(0,u) = C(u,0) = 0$ and $C(1,u) = C(u,1) = u \ \forall u \in [0,1]$;

3) C is *2-increasing*: $C(v_1,v_2) - C(v_1,u_2) - C(u_1,v_2) + C(u_1,u_2) \geq 0$ $\forall (u_1,u_2) \in [0,1]^2$, $(v_1,v_2) \in [0,1]^2$ such that $0 \leq u_1 \leq v_1 \leq 1$ and $0 \leq u_2 \leq v_2 \leq 1$.

Consider the random vector $U = (U_X, U_Y)$ with U_X and U_Y, two uniformly distributed random variables. We have:

$$C(u_X, u_Y) = \Pr(U_X \leq u_X, U_Y \leq u_Y).$$

The following theorem is given with its proof in [SKL 59]:

THEOREM 2.1 ([SKL 59] - Sklar's theorem).– Let F be a bidimensional distribution function with marginals $\mathrm{F_X}$ and $\mathrm{F_Y}$. F admits a copula representation:

$$\mathrm{F}(x,y) = C\left(\mathrm{F_X}(x), \mathrm{F_Y}(y)\right).$$

The copula C is unique if the marginals are continuous.

Equivalently, we have:

$$C(u_X, u_Y) = \mathrm{F}\left(\mathrm{F_X^{-1}}(u_X), \mathrm{F_Y^{-1}}(u_Y)\right).$$

Theorem 2.1 allows us to associate a copula, which may be unique, for each bidimensional distribution law. If the bivariate distribution is absolutely continuous, then we have:

$$\mathrm{f}(x,y) = c(\mathrm{F_X}(x), \mathrm{F_Y}(y)) \times \mathrm{f_X}(x) \times \mathrm{f_Y}(y), \qquad [2.1]$$

with $c(.,.)$ denoting the density function of the copula C. It is important to note that the condition that C is 2-*increasing* is equivalent to the positivity of the density $c(u_X, u_Y) = \partial^2 C(u_X, u_Y) \geq 0$, when it exists.

One of the most remarkable features of copula is the property of *invariance* that states the following:

PROPOSITION 2.1 (Invariance).– Let X and Y be two continuous random variables whose respective probability laws F_X and F_Y are bound by a copula C. Let h_X and h_Y be two strictly increasing functions, then:

$$C\left(F_X(h_X(x)), F_Y(h_Y(y))\right) = C\left(F_X(x), F_Y(y)\right).$$

The invariance property is particularly useful for empirical modeling as the dependence structure remains unchanged when risk factors are composed by any strictly increasing function. For instance, the copula binding the log-returns is the same as that which binds the returns. This feature is not verified by the correlation measure presented in section 2.1.2.1 p. 85. Moreover, any convex linear combination of copulas is a copula. Such a mixture of copulas is useful as it can nest different patterns of dependency structures.

REMARK 2.1 ([GEN 95] - Impossibility theorem).– Some caution is required when working with higher-dimensional copulas as constructing them using lower-dimensional copulas does not always yield a copula.

Standard multivariate copulas lack flexibility in high dimension. They do not allow for different dependency structures between pairs of variables. Vine pair copulas rely on bivariate copulas as building blocks for higher-dimensional distribution. The dependency structure is determined by the bivariate copulas and a nested set of trees. The multi-dimensional density can thus be expressed as the product of the marginal densities' times and conditional pair copula densities. This approach is known as "Pair Copula Construction" (henceforth PPC). However, the decomposition is not unique because if we permute the order of variables, the conditional copulas would also change. See [JOE 96], [BED 01], [BED 02] and [AAS 09].

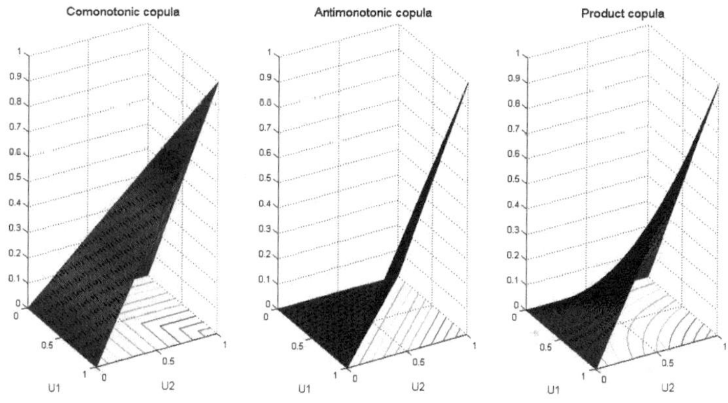

Figure 2.1. Fréchet-Hoeffding *bounds and the product copula. For a color version of the figure, see www.iste.co.uk/ielpo/investment.zip*

Any copula C is bound by the *Fréchet-Hoeffding* bounds C^- and C^+. While the latter is always a copula, the former is a copula in the bivariate case. C^-, C^+ and the *product copula* are represented in Figure 2.1[1]. They are defined as follows:

– the *upper Fréchet bound* $C^+(U_X, U_Y) = min\{U_X; U_Y\}$: two random variables are *comonotonic* if $C(F_X(X), F_Y(Y)) = C^+(U_X, U_Y)$;

– the *lower Fréchet bound* $C^-(U_X, U_Y) = max\{U_X + U_Y - 1; 0\}$: two random variables are *antimonotonic* if $C(F_X(X), F_Y(Y)) = C^-(U_X, U_Y)$;

– the *product copula* $C^\perp(U_X, U_Y) = U_X \times U_Y$: two random variables are independent[2] if their dependence structure is $C^\perp$.

1 [CHI 12] put forward the normalized difference between the selected copula and the Gaussian one, along the diagonal and the anti-diagonal, as an efficient tool of methodological interest for visualizing and comparing copulas.

2 Independence is characterized by the fact that the joint probability is given by the product of the marginals. From equation [2.1] we deduce that the density of the product copula is thus equal to 1.

The following inequality holds:

$$C^{-}(U_X, U_Y) \leq C(U_X, U_Y), C^{\perp}(U_X, U_Y) \leq C^{+}(U_X, U_Y). \qquad [2.2]$$

Equation [2.2] defines a lower and an upper boundary for any copula. Those bounds are useful for delimiting the portfolio risk measures such as *Value at Risk* irrespective of the dependence structure among the underlying assets: see section 2.1 p. 70 for a precise illustration.

The notions of *antimonotonicity* (or perfect negative dependence) and *comonotonicity* (perfect positive dependence) both generalize the notion of correlation when the latter is equal to -1 and $+1$. The closer the copula to the upper (resp. lower) Fréchet bound, the more comonotonic (resp. antimonotonic) the dependence is. [PAT 06] showed that Sklar theorem remains valid if we condition both the marginal and joint distributions by the same filtration $\mathcal{J}_t$, which proves to be useful for modeling time-varying joint distributions and copulas. Applications to risk management can be found in [FAN 08b], and copula-based risk-neutral pricing in [CHE 02] and [COU 01].

2.1.1.1. *Parametric copulas*

A small set of parameters controls the strength and structure of dependence for parametric copulas. They offer the advantage of capturing large patterns of dependence whether symmetric or not, with or without heavy tails, while remaining tractable. Among parametric copulas, we distinguish the following two popular families:

– *elliptical copulas,* which are copulas corresponding to the multivariate elliptical distributions;

– *Archimedean copulas* that allow for various dependence structures while remaining tractable and keeping a closed form (at least for the most popular choices).

2.1.1.1.1. Elliptical copulas

Elliptical copulas are copulas associated to elliptical distributions introduced by [KEL 70]. The class of multivariate elliptical distributions allows for the presence of heavy tails though it remains as a simple linear dependence structure. Their denomination stems from the shape of their density function whose isocurves form ellipsoids in $\mathbb{R}^n$. They are thus useful for modeling symmetric risks such as market invariants, i.e. stationary risk factors or its functions.

An elliptical distribution $\varepsilon(\mu, \Sigma, g_n)$ in $\mathbb{R}^n$ is characterized[3] by a set of three parameters:

– the localization vector $\mu \in \mathbb{R}^n$;

– the scatter matrix $\Sigma \in \mathbb{M}^+_{n,n}$, which is positive and symmetric;

– the characteristic generator or the tail function $g_n : \mathbb{R}^+ \mapsto \mathbb{R}$.

Its density is written as:

$$f(x) = det(\Sigma)^{\frac{-1}{2}} g_n\left((x-\mu)'\Sigma^{-1}(x-\mu)\right),$$

where g_n is a non-negative univariate function satisfying:

$$\int_0^{\infty} v^{\frac{n}{2}-1} g_n(x) dx < \infty.$$

Elliptical distributions can be classified according to their characteristic generator g_n. Distributions sharing the same generator belong to the same elliptical family. The Gaussian and the Student multivariate distributions are among popular elliptical distributions. Their elliptical representation is given in Table 2.1 and the shape of their isocurves in Figure 2.2. Elliptical distributions are stable by aggregation, which makes them a suitable candidate for modeling the portfolio P&L distribution as a linear combination of that of the underlying assets as stated in Proposition 2.2.

PROPOSITION 2.2.– Let A be a vector of $\mathbb{R}^k$ and B a matrix of $\mathcal{M}_{k,n}$. If $X \rightsquigarrow \varepsilon(\mu, \Sigma, g_n)$, then $A + BX \rightsquigarrow \varepsilon(A + B\mu, B\Sigma B', g_k)$.

Distribution	Elliptical representation
Gaussian	$\varepsilon\left(\mu, \Sigma, \frac{e^{-\frac{(x-\mu)'\Sigma^{-1}(x-\mu)}{2}}}{(2\pi)^{\frac{n}{2}}}\right)$
Student	$\varepsilon\left(\mu, \Sigma, \frac{\Gamma(\frac{\nu+n}{2})}{\Gamma(\frac{\nu}{2})(\nu\pi)^{\frac{n}{2}}}\left(1 + \frac{(x-\mu)'\Sigma^{-1}(x-\mu)}{\nu}\right)^{-\frac{\nu+n}{2}}\right)$

Table 2.1. *Elliptical representation of the Gaussian and Student distributions*

Elliptical multivariate distributions do not tolerate non-elliptical margins, which may constitute a drawback for multivariate risk modeling, where it can be realistic to consider non-elliptical margins with elliptical distributions. For a detailed presentation of elliptical distributions, we refer to the work of [FAN 90]. If

3 Existing literature offers alternative characterizations based on the characteristic function or the rotational properties [CAM 81] or also [EMB 99].

$\Sigma = c \times I_n$, with c a positive scalar and I_n the identity matrix, the distribution is spherical. In their standard formulation, elliptical distributions have a null location vector and an identity dispersion matrix $\Sigma = I_n$. An elliptical copula is invariant under any strictly increasing transformation, in particular in cases of standardization of the marginal distributions. This means that the copula of $\varepsilon(\mu, \Sigma, g_n)$ is identical to that of $\varepsilon(0_n, R_n, g_n)$ distribution, where R_n is the correlation matrix implied from Σ. The covariance matrix of an elliptical distribution is not necessarily equal to the scatter matrix, as is the case for the Gaussian distribution. For instance, the covariance of $Student(\nu)$ random vector X is given by:

$$Cov(X) = \frac{\nu}{\nu - 2}\Sigma.$$

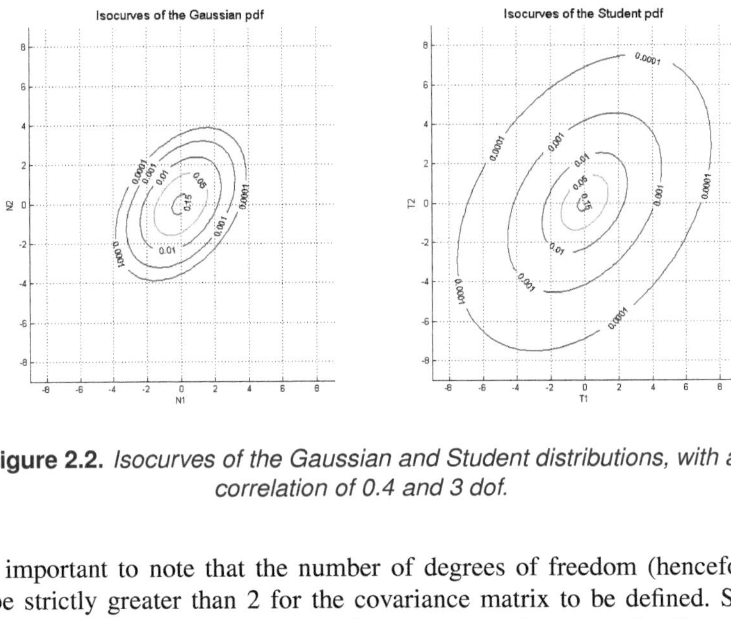

Figure 2.2. *Isocurves of the Gaussian and Student distributions, with a correlation of 0.4 and 3 dof.*

It is important to note that the number of degrees of freedom (henceforth dof) has to be strictly greater than 2 for the covariance matrix to be defined. Similarly, the Cauchy copula has a scatter matrix but not a covariance matrix. Generally, the relationship between the scatter and the covariance matrix is given by Proposition 2.3 (See [MEU 05]):

PROPOSITION 2.3.– If $X \rightsquigarrow \varepsilon(\mu, \Sigma, g_n)$, then:

$$\mathbb{E}[X] = \mu \quad \text{and} \quad Cov[X] = \frac{\mathbb{E}\left[\left\|\Sigma^{-\frac{1}{2}}(X - \mu)\right\|^2\right]}{n}\Sigma.$$

Among popular elliptical copulas, we distinguish the Gaussian copula and the Student copula.

2.1.1.1.2. Gaussian copula

The Gaussian copula is, by definition, the copula corresponding to the Gaussian distribution:

$$C(u_1,\ldots,u_n) = \Phi_{R_n}\left(\Phi^{-1}(u_1),\ldots,\Phi^{-1}(u_n)\right),$$

where Φ is the cumulative distribution function of a standard univariate Gaussian variable and Φ_{R_n} is the density given by $\phi_{R_n} = \frac{1}{(2\pi)^{\frac{n}{2}}|R_n|^{\frac{1}{2}}}e^{-\frac{1}{2}(x'R_n^{-1}x)}$. Thus, by deriving Φ_{R_n}, we obtain the density of the Gaussian copula. The scatterplot of a Gaussian vector and its corresponding copula are given in Figures 2.3 and 2.4.

DEFINITION 2.2 (density of a Gaussian copula).– The density of the normal copula is:

$$c(u_1,...,u_n) = \frac{\frac{1}{(2\pi)^{\frac{n}{2}}|R_n|^{\frac{1}{2}}}\exp(-\frac{1}{2}\zeta' R_n^{-1}\zeta)}{\frac{1}{(2\pi)^{\frac{n}{2}}},\exp(-\frac{1}{2}\zeta'\zeta)} = \frac{1}{|R_n|^{\frac{1}{2}}}\exp\left(-\frac{1}{2}\zeta'(R_n - I_n)\zeta\right)$$

where $\zeta' = \left(\Phi^{-1}(u_1)\ldots\Phi^{-1}(u_n)\right)$ and Φ is the Gaussian cumulative probability function.

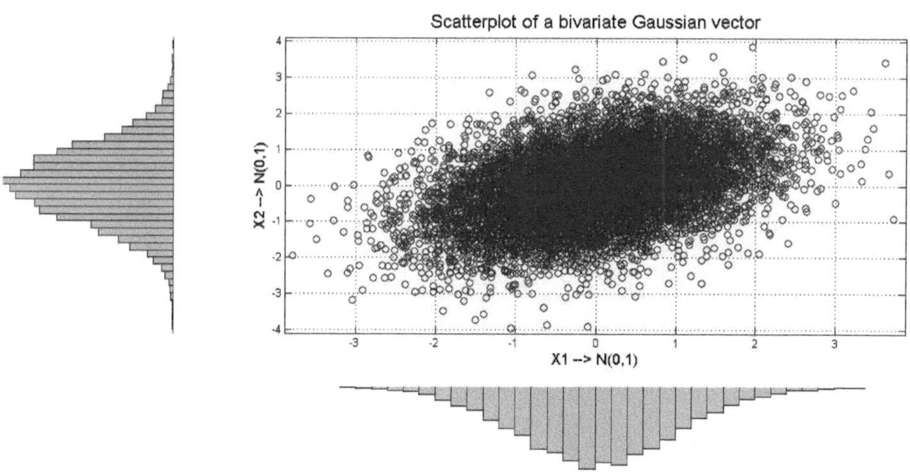

Figure 2.3. *Scatterplot of a centered Gaussian vector with correlation* 0.4 *for* $10,000$ *scenarios.*

2.1.1.1.3. Student copula

The Student copula is defined as the copula corresponding to the Student multivariate distribution.

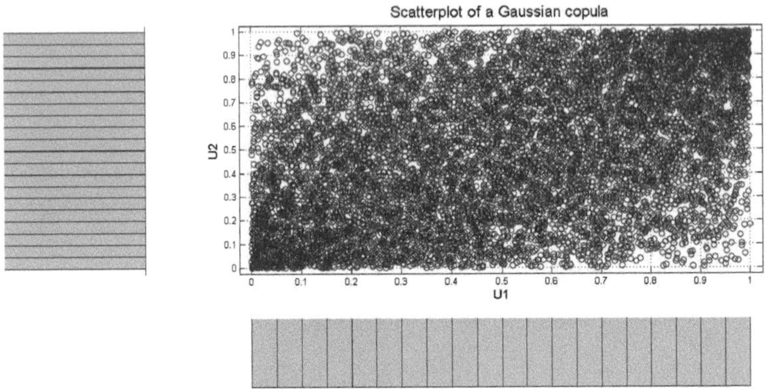

Figure 2.4. *Scatterplot of the bivariate Gaussian copula with correlation 0.4 for $10,000$ scenarios.*

DEFINITION 2.3 (t copula).– Let t_ν be a standard univariate Student distribution and $t_{R_n,\nu}$ the multivariate Student distribution with $\nu > 2$ dof and correlation matrix R_n. The Student copula is defined as follows:

$$C^t(u_1, ..., u_n; R_n, \nu) = t_{R_n,\nu}\left(t_\nu^{-1}(u_1), ..., t_\nu^{-1}(u_n)\right).$$

The density of the Student copula is given by the following equation:

$$c^t(u_1, ..., u_n; R_n, \nu) = \frac{f_{R_n,\nu}\left(t_\nu^{-1}(u_1), \ldots, t_\nu^{-1}(u_n)\right)}{\prod_{i=1}^n f_\nu(t_\nu^{-1}(u_i))},$$

where t_ν denotes the cumulative probability function of a standard Student variable, f_ν is the corresponding density function and $f_{R_n,\nu}$ is the joint density of t centered vector with correlation R_n and ν dof:

$$f^t_{R_n,\nu} = \frac{1}{(\nu\pi)^{\frac{n}{2}}|R_n|^{\frac{1}{2}}} \frac{\Gamma(\frac{\nu+n}{2})}{\Gamma(\frac{n}{2})}\left(1 + \frac{1}{\nu}x' R_n^{-1} x\right)^{-\frac{\nu+n}{2}}$$

Unlike the Gaussian copula, the t copula exhibits symmetric fat tails (see section 2.1.2.4 p. 93). This choice of copula makes it useful for modeling dependence in stressed markets with spillover effects. It converges toward the Gaussian copula as the dof grows toward infinity as highlighted in Figure 2.6. For a review of the Student copula and its related properties, see the contribution of [DEM 05].

NUMERICAL EXAMPLE 2.1.– Stress-testing the dependence among portfolios of assets

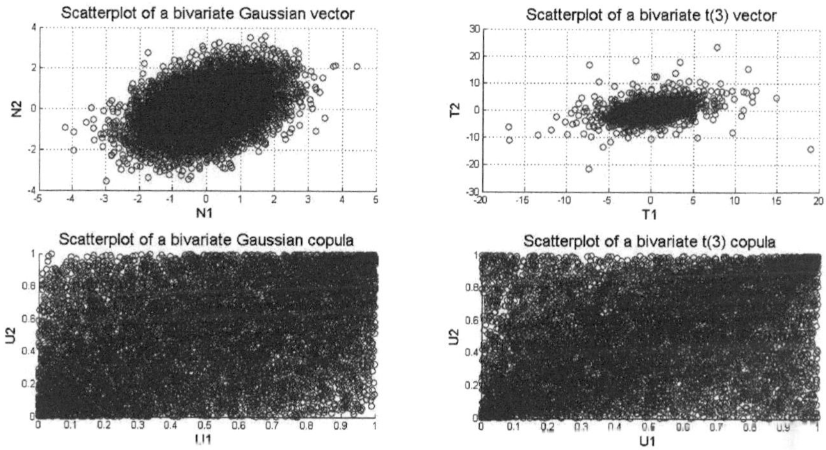

Figure 2.5. *Gaussian copula versus t copula with correlation* 0.4 *and* 3 *dof,* $10,000$ *scenarios*

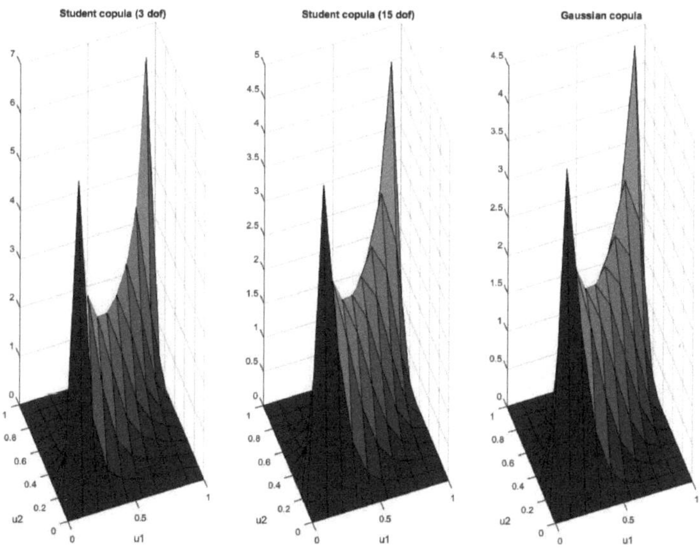

Figure 2.6. *Convergence of the Gaussian copula toward the t copula with correlation* 0.4 *and* 3 *dof,* $10,000$ *scenarios. For a color version of the figure, see www.iste.co.uk/ielpo/investment.zip*

Consider a portfolio P equally weighted in $N = 10$ assets whose returns' joint distribution R is assumed to be Gaussian with a constant correlation. We are therefore in the framework of the constant correlation model (or Single Index Model), further developed in section 3.5.1.3.2 p. 211.

$$R \equiv \begin{pmatrix} R_1 \\ R_2 \\ \vdots \\ R_N \end{pmatrix} \rightsquigarrow \mathcal{N}\left(\begin{pmatrix} 0 \\ 0 \\ \vdots \\ 0 \end{pmatrix}, \begin{pmatrix} 1 & \rho & \dots & \rho \\ \rho & 1 & \ddots & \vdots \\ \vdots & \ddots & \ddots & \rho \\ \rho & \dots & \rho & 1 \end{pmatrix}\right)$$

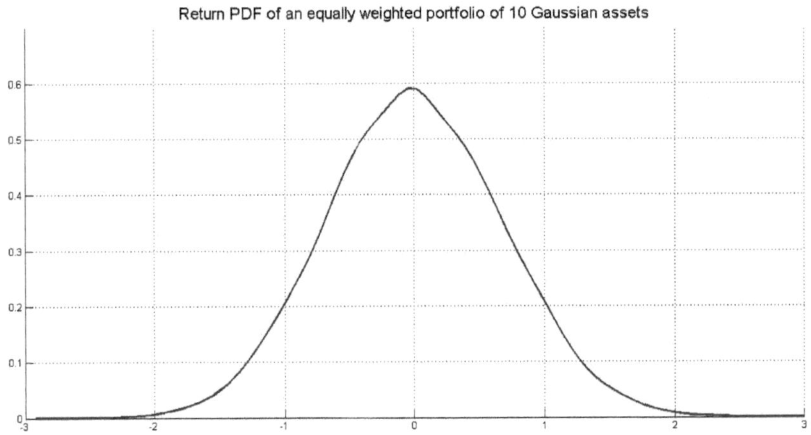

Figure 2.7. *Probability density function of returns for the equally weighted portfolio P in Gaussian assets with* $\rho = 0.4$

We simulate $10,000$ joint scenarios of R with $\rho = 0.4$. The return distribution of the portfolio plotted in Figure 2.7 is hence Gaussian, given that a linear combination of a Gaussian vector remains Gaussian. In order to stress-test the dependence among the assets, one may increase the correlation coefficient ρ, by keeping the dependence structure Gaussian, and check the impact on the VaR of the portfolio. Under such assumptions, the portfolio returns remain Gaussian irrespective of the intensity of the correlation. Spillovers, or the probability of an extreme event for an asset following the occurrence of an extreme event for another asset, are however prohibited because the Gaussian copula does not exhibit tail dependence. In order to address such extreme events, the Gaussian copula can be substituted by a t copula all others being equal. Figures 2.3 and 2.9 show how copulas permit the separation of marginals from the structure binding them.

Although each separate asset is Gaussian, the joint distribution of the assets as well as the portfolio distribution are no longer Gaussian as shown in Figure 2.9. The effect of the intensity and the structure of dependency on the risk measures of the portfolio, such as the VaR, is depicted in Figure 2.10. The VaR increases with the correlation between assets and the copula binding them. This simple approach allows us to conduct symmetric dependency stress tests. However, it is well known that markets' spillovers are not symmetric; bear markets seem to be more "correlated" (see, e.g., [PAT 06]) than bull ones. The corollary of such an asymmetric dependence is a higher downside risk. Such shocks can be addressed by asymmetric copulas such as some Archimedean copulas.

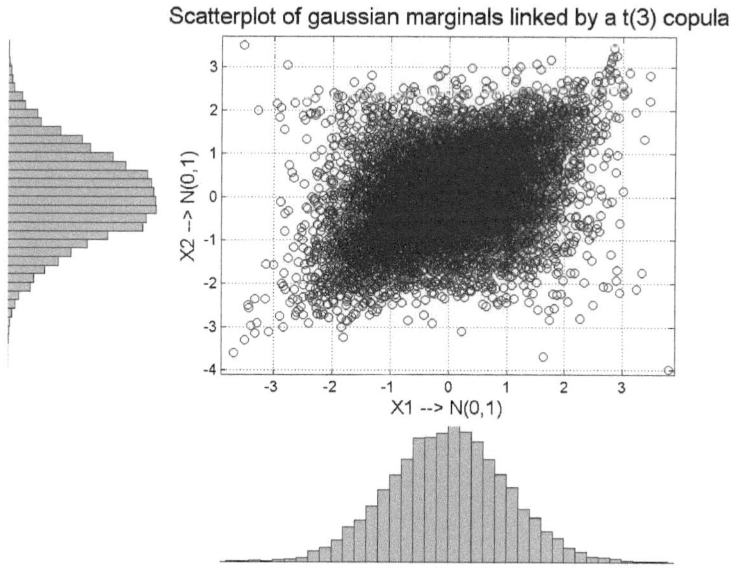

Figure 2.8. *Scatterplot of 2 Gaussian margins linked by a t copula*

2.1.1.1.4. Archimedean copulas

There are two advantages of using Archimedean copulas: unlike elliptical copulas, they have a closed form, and they allow for a large variety of dependence structures. However, they are not derived from multivariate distributions using Sklar's theorem. As a consequence, additional conditions and constraints are required to ensure that extensions to higher-dimension copulas yield proper copulas.

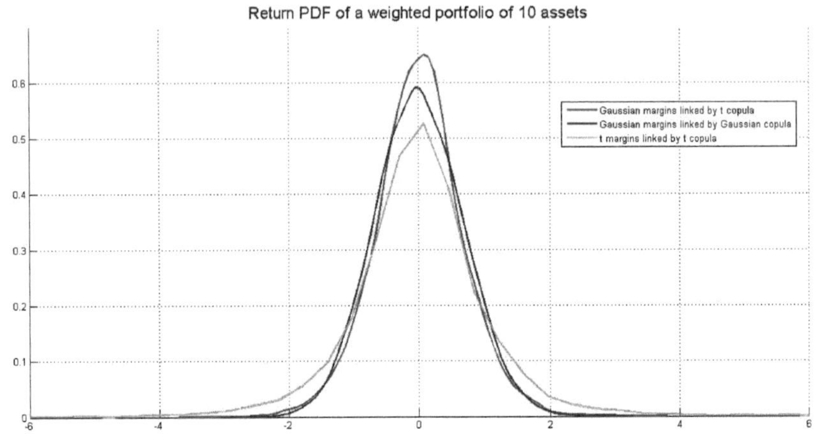

Figure 2.9. *Probability density function of an equally weighted portfolio in Gaussian assets linked by various types of copulas*

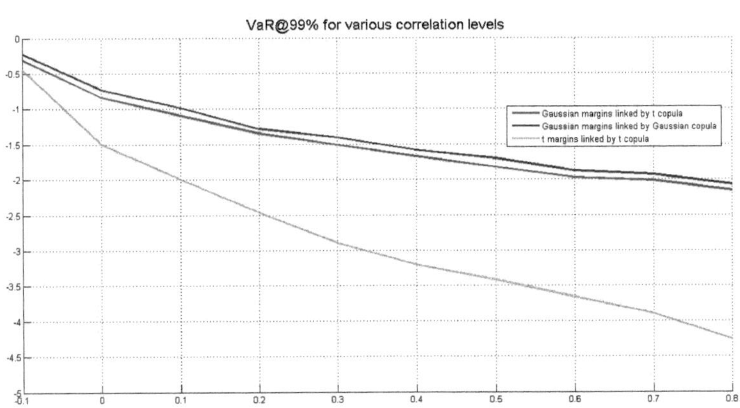

Figure 2.10. *VaR@99% for various levels of correlation. For a color version of the figure, see www.iste.co.uk/ielpo/investment.zip*

DEFINITION 2.4 (Archimedean copula).– [GEN 86] defined bivariate Archimedean copulas as:

$$C(u_1, u_2) = \begin{cases} \varphi^{-1}(\varphi(u_1) + \varphi(u_2)) & \text{if} \quad \varphi(u_1) + \varphi(u_2) \leq 0 \\ 0 \text{ otherwise} \end{cases}$$

with φ a C^2 function such that $\varphi(1) = 0$, $\varphi'(u) < 0$ and $\varphi''(u) > 0$ $\forall u \in [0,1]$. φ is the generator of the copula and φ^{-1} the pseudo-inverse of φ.

Among famous Archimedean copulas, we briefly present the Gumbel copula, the Clayton copula, the Frank copula and even the product copula whose Archimedean representations are shown in Table 2.2. Their densities are plotted in Figure 2.11. While the Gumbel copula allows for upper tail dependence, the Clayton copula is suitable for lower tail dependence. The Frank copula is the only symmetric Archimedean copula. Moreover, it converges toward Fréchet upper (resp. lower) bound as $\theta \to \infty$ (resp. $\theta \to -\infty$) and toward the product copula as $\theta \to 0$.

Copula	$\varphi(u)$	$C(u_1, u_2)$
$C^{\perp}$	$-\log u$	$u_1 u_2$
Gumbel	$(-\log u)^{\theta}$	$\exp -[(-\log u_1)^{\theta} + (-\log u_2)^{\theta}]^{\frac{1}{\theta}}$
Frank	$-\log \frac{\exp(-\theta u)-1}{\exp(-\theta)-1}$	$-\frac{1}{\theta}\log\left(1 + \frac{(\exp(-\theta u_1)-1)(\exp(-\theta u_2)-1)}{\exp(-\theta)-1}\right)$
Clayton	$u^{-\theta} - 1$	$\left(u_1^{-\theta} + u_2^{-\theta}\right)^{-\frac{1}{\theta}}$

Table 2.2. *Some Archimedean copulas*

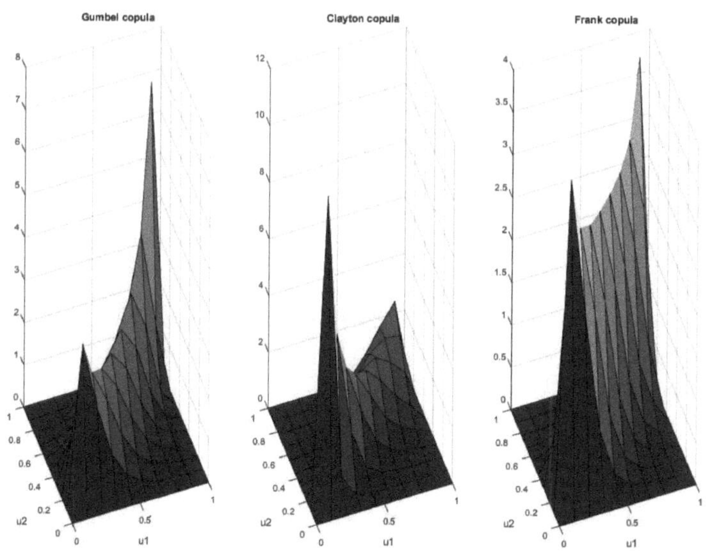

Figure 2.11. *Some Archimedean copulas with Kendall tau of* 0.7. *For a color version of the figure, see www.iste.co.uk/ielpo/investment.zip*

2.1.1.2. *Non-parametric copulas*

[DEH 79] introduced the empirical copula. Let $X_m = (X_{m,1}, \ldots, X_{m,n}) \in \mathbb{R}^n$ be a sequence of random vectors i.i.d. following the distribution F with margins $\mathrm{F}_1, \ldots, \mathrm{F}_\mathrm{n}$. We assume that F is continuous to ensure the uniqueness of the copula $C(\mathrm{F})$. Let δ_k be the Dirac measure with $k \in \mathbb{R}^n$. The empirical measure of the sample X is given by:

$$\hat{\mu} = \frac{1}{m} \sum_{j=1}^{m} \delta_{X_j},$$

and the empirical distribution is written as:

$$\hat{\mathrm{F}}(x_1, \ldots, x_n) = \hat{\mu}\left(\prod_{i=1}^{n}]-\infty, x_i]\right).$$

Denoting by $x_{j:m,1}, \ldots, x_{j:m,n}$ the order statistic, i.e. the jth–smallest value of the sample $(x_{t,1}, \ldots, x_{t,n})_{1 \leq t \leq m}$ and by $r_{j,1}, \ldots, r_{j,n}$ the rank statistic such that: $x_{r_{j,i}:m,i} = x_{j,i}$, we define the empirical copula as follows:

DEFINITION 2.5 (Empirical copula).– Any copula $\hat{C} \in \mathcal{C}$ defined on the lattice $\mathcal{J}$:

$$\mathcal{J} = \left\{\left(\frac{j_1}{m}, \ldots, \frac{j_n}{m}\right) : 1 \leq i \leq n, j_i = 0, \ldots, m\right\}$$

by the function:

$$\hat{C}\left(\frac{j_1}{m}, \ldots, \frac{j_n}{m}\right) = \frac{1}{m} \sum_{j=1}^{m} \prod_{i=1}^{n} 1\{r_{j,i} \leq j_i\}$$

is called an empirical copula.

NUMERICAL EXAMPLE 2.2.– *Empirical copula and Value at Risk trade-off.*

Consider the empirical copula binding the yields to maturity (henceforth YTM) daily movements of sovereign debt issued by Brazil and Colombia in US dollar. The empirical copula, estimated over 3,700 joint YTM observed between May 2002 and May 2016, is depicted in Figure 2.12. The copula lies between Fréchet bounds (see equation [2.2]). The closer the empirical copula is to the upper (resp. lower) bound, the more comonotonic (resp. antimonotonic) the dependence is.

Figures 2.13 and 2.14 give, respectively, the 5% and 95% bivariate isocurves (or BiVaR) for the empirical copula. The isocurves of the empirical copula lie between the product and maximal copula isocurves in both cases. This denotes a positive dependence between the Brazilian and Colombian YTM daily movements. However, the empirical isocurves are closer to the maximal copula isocurves at the 95% level than they are to the 5% level.

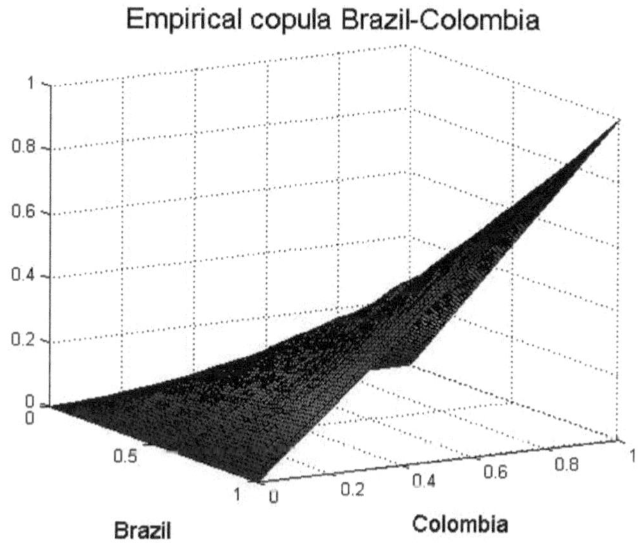

Figure 2.12. *Empirical copula of Brazil and Colombia YTM daily movements. For a color version of the figure, see www.iste.co.uk/ielpo/investment.zip*

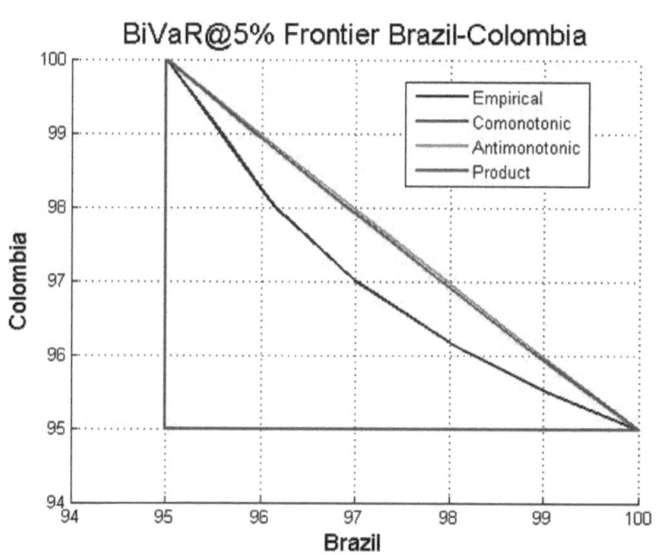

Figure 2.13. *The BiVaR@5% trade-off for Brazil and Colombia. For a color version of the figure, see www.iste.co.uk/ielpo/investment.zip*

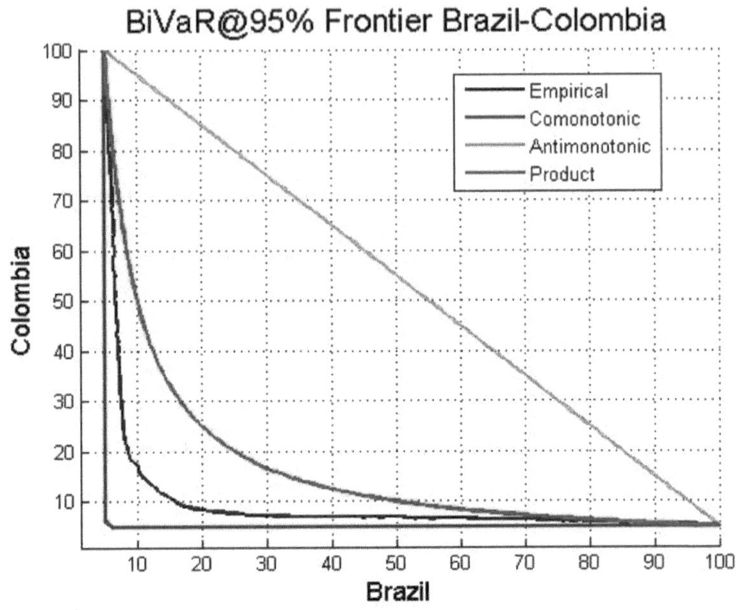

Figure 2.14. *The BiVaR@95% trade-off for Brazil and Colombia. For a color version of the figure, see www.iste.co.uk/ielpo/investment.zip*

This emphasizes the fact that an important widening on the YTM of one country is more likely to spillover to another country than a tightening. Moreover, the isocurves of the estimated copula indicate the trade-off between the risks of the countries at the corresponding level.

2.1.1.3. *Statistical inference*

In what follows, we consider a sample of N random variables $(X_1, ..., X_N)$ with T observations $\left(x_1^t, ..., x_N^t\right)_{t=1}^T$. Inferring the parameters of the copula can be done using one of the three parametric approaches which follow (see [CHE 04]). Alternatively, an efficient non-parametric algorithm is also presented.

2.1.1.3.1. Parametric approaches

Exact Maximum Likelihood Method (EML)

The EML method simultaneously estimates the parameters of the copula and those of the margins by maximizing the likelihood of the sample. Let Θ be the space of parameters and θ the k-dimensional vector of parameters to estimate. The log-likelihood $l(\theta)$ is given by:

$$\sum_{t=1}^{T} \log\Big(c\big(F_1(x_1^t), ..., F_N(x_N^t)\big)\Big) + \sum_{t=1}^{T}\sum_{n=1}^{N} \log\Big(f_n(x_n^t)\Big),$$

with F_i the cumulative probability function of x_i^t and f_i the corresponding probability density function. c denotes the density of the copula. The ML estimator is written as:

$$\widehat{\theta} := (\widehat{\theta}_1, ...\widehat{\theta}_k) = argmax\{l(\theta) : \theta \in \Theta\}$$

REMARK 2.2.– Under some regularity assumptions, the ML estimator exists, is consistent, and asymptotically efficient. Moreover, it satisfies:

$$\sqrt{T}\left(\widehat{\theta}_{EML} - \theta_0\right) \to N\left(0, I^{-1}(\theta_0)\right)$$

where $I(\theta_0)$ is the Fisher information matrix (see, e.g., [VAN 00]) and θ_0 is the true value of the parameter.

When estimating the t copula, for instance, using the EML method can be quite complex because it requires the simultaneous estimation of R, the correlation matrix, ν the dof in addition to the margins parameters. Alternative approaches are presented hereafter.

Inference for Margins Method (IFM)

IFM makes it possible to separate the estimation procedure into two steps: the estimation of the margin parameters and the estimation of the copula itself. The log-likelihood can be written as:

$$\sum_{t=1}^{T} \log\Big(c\big(F_1(x_1^t;\theta_1), ..., F_N(x_N^t;\theta_N);\alpha\big)\Big) + \sum_{t=1}^{T}\sum_{n=1}^{N} \log\Big(f_n(x_n^t;\theta_n)\Big).$$

The IFM estimator is given by the vector:

$$\theta_{IFM} = (\widehat{\theta}, \widehat{\alpha}_{IFM})$$

REMARK 2.3.– [JOE 97] shows that under some regularity conditions, the IFM estimator is asymptotically normal:

$$\sqrt{T}\left(\widehat{\theta}_{IFM} - \theta_0\right) \to N\left(0, G^{-1}(\theta_0)\right)$$

where $G(\theta_0)$ is the Godambe information matrix and θ_0 is the true value of the parameters.

Canonical Maximum Likelihood Method (CML)

EML and IFM approaches require us to parametrically estimate the margins. CML allows a non-parametric estimation of the margins to be carried out through their empirical cumulative density function:

$$\widehat{F}_n(u) = \frac{1}{T}\sum_{t=1}^{T} \mathbb{1}(\{X_{nt} \leq u\}), \text{ for } n = 1, ..., N$$

CML is therefore a two-step procedure, which:

1) transforms margins into uniform variables through their empirical cumulative density function;

2) estimates the parameters of the copula, the CML estimator being given by the vector $\widehat{\alpha}_{CML}$:

$$\widehat{\alpha}_{CML} = argmax \sum_{t=1}^{T} \log\left(c(\widehat{u}_1^t, ..., \widehat{u}_N^t; \alpha)\right).$$

Non-parametric approaches: the Copula Marginal Algorithm (CMA)

Introduced by [MEU 11], the CMA presents many advantages compared to previous estimation methods: it does not require the computation of margins and their inverse; it allows for large-scale sampling by arbitrarily weighting the joint scenarios of the sample; it applies to copulas other than elliptical or Archimedean ones. CMA is here again a two-step procedure:

– separation, to decompose joint distributions into their copula and marginals;

– combination, to bind marginals by a copula and recover the corresponding joint distribution.

For the separation step, the CMA builds on the idea that the joint distribution F_X of the n–dimensional vector $X = (X_1, \ldots, X_n)$ can be represented by a scenario probability representation:

$$\{x_{1j}, \ldots, x_{nj}; p_j\}_{j=1,\ldots,J}.$$

In practice, each scenario corresponds to a joint realization of the n variables observed at $t = j$. The joint observation of $\{x_{1j}, \ldots, x_{nj}; p_j\}_{j=\mathbb{1},\ldots,J}$ is transformed into joint realization of grades $\{u_{1j}, \ldots, u_{nj}; p_j\}$. For each variable X_l, the grade is calculated as $u_{lj} = \sum_{i=1}^{J} p_i \mathbb{1}_{\{x_{li} \leq x_{lj}\}}$. For intermediate values, the CMA interpolates/extrapolates pairs (x_{lj}, u_{lj}) with a suitable function $\delta\{x_{lj}, u_{lj}\}$ such that

$F_{X_l}(x) = \delta\{x_{lj}, u_{lj}\}(x)$. For the combination step, a set of n marginals and a copula are required. The copula is represented as a set of probability scenario $\{u_{1j}, \ldots, u_{nj}; p_j\}_{j=1,\ldots,J}$. For each marginal, we use a function δ in order to recover x_{lj} corresponding to u_{lj}: $x_{lj} = \delta\{u_{lj}, x_{lj}\}(u_{lj})$.

NUMERICAL EXAMPLE 2.3 (Historical dependence stress applied to emerging fixed-income markets).– The use of copula allows us to separate the margins from the dependence structure. Stress tests can thus be applied separately to margins, to the copula or to the joint distribution. The last two stress tests have been highlighted in a previous example on p. 70. In this example, we shock the margins while keeping the copula unchanged. More precisely, what would be the VaR of an emerging portfolio if the volatility of oil (CL1 Cmdty) were to jump to an historical level?

Consider an equally weighted portfolio in some emerging markets' fixed-income securities. We assume that the portfolio is invested in mid-term securities with maturity around 4 years. We observe daily YTM of these nine emerging countries[4] over the last 14 years, between May 2002 and May 2016. For instance, the YTM joint movements for Brazil and Colombia are given in Figure 2.15 and their copula in Figure 2.16.

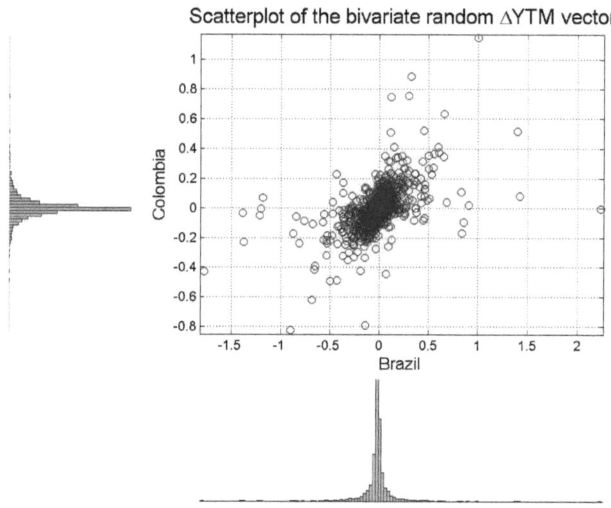

Figure 2.15. *Scatterplot of the daily movements of the YTM of Brazil and Colombia and their univariate histograms*

4 Selected countries with sound historical observations are: Brazil, Colombia, Lebanon, Mexico, Philippines, Romania, Turkey, Ukraine and Venezuela.

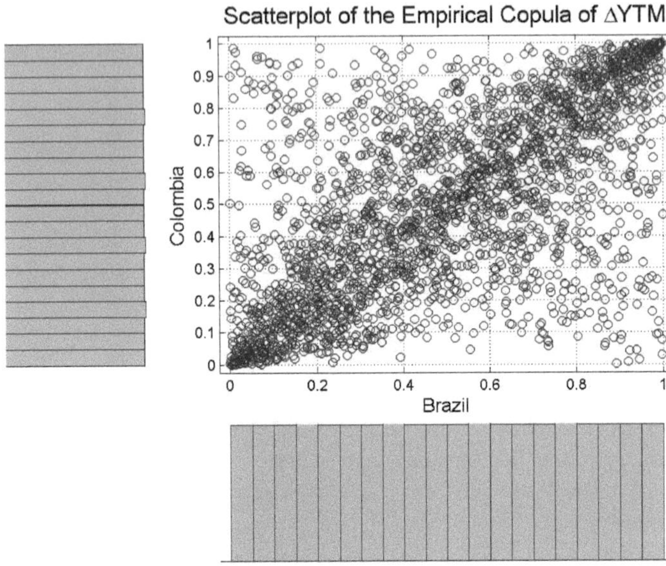

Figure 2.16. *Scatterplot of the empirical copula binding the daily movements of the YTM of Brazil and Colombia and the histograms of their uniformly distributed grades.*

For each country n, the total return over time horizon H can be approximated by the product of the modified duration times, the variation of YTM at horizon H, denoted by $\Delta_H(YTM_n)$, plus the carry:

$$R_{n,H} \approx -ModDur_n \times \Delta_H(YTM_n) + YTM_n \times \frac{H}{260}.$$

The return of the portfolio at horizon H is approximated by:

$$R_H = \frac{1}{N}\sum_{n=1}^{N} R_{n,H} \approx -\frac{1}{N}\sum_{n=1}^{N} ModDur_n \times \Delta_H(YTM_n) + \frac{H}{260}\frac{1}{N}\sum_{n=1}^{N} YTM_n.$$

The portfolio return distribution at horizon H depends thus on the joint distribution of:

$$(\Delta_H(YTM_1), \ldots, \Delta_H(YTM_n))'.$$

The accuracy of the return projections at H and that of the derived risk measures depend on the stationarity of the process steering the market invariant $\Delta_H(YTM_n)$. The joint dynamics of the N-dimensional vector of YTM are given by the following:

$$YTM_{t+1} = YTM_t + \epsilon_{t+1},$$

where $\epsilon \rightsquigarrow F_{\Delta(YTM)}$. Over horizon H, we have:

$$YTM_{t+H} = YTM_t + \sum_{h=1}^{H} \epsilon_{t+h},$$

$$\Delta_H(YTM_t) = \sum_{h=1}^{H} \epsilon_{t+h}.$$

A practical solution to stress the VaR consists of focusing on a specific stress period and calibrating the joint distribution of $\Delta(YTM)$ accordingly. However, such a solution implies a drastic shrink in the estimation sample. An alternative solution consists of keeping the original sample but weighting joint observations differently. Using CMA, it is easy to weight data according to the volatility of oil, whose evolution is shown in Figure 2.17. Thus, turmoil periods, as measured by the volatility of oil, are overweighted with respect to the traditional equally weighted scheme. Estimated marginals present higher volatility and kurtosis. We bind them using genuine original copula in order to isolate shocks on margins from those on their dependence. We project the return distribution, under standard and stressed assumptions, over horizons up to 5 days and calculate the corresponding VaR at each horizon. Results are presented in Figure 2.18.

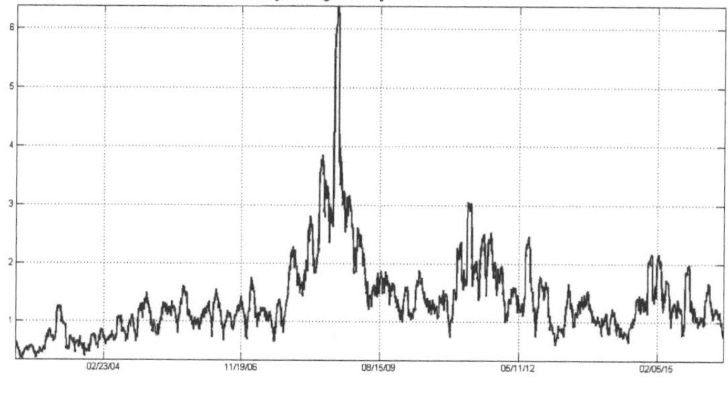

Figure 2.17. *22-Day rolling volatility of oil.*

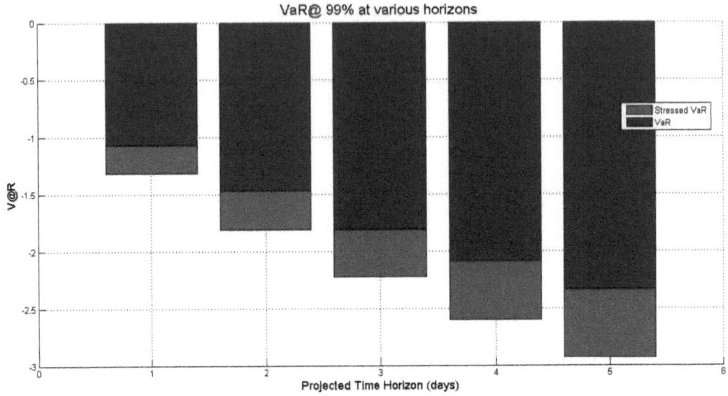

Figure 2.18. *VaR@99% at different horizons obtained under original and stressed margins.*

2.1.2. *Measures of dependence*

Let X and Y be two real continuous random variables with distributions F_X and F_Y bound by copula C and with joint distribution F. A measure of dependence between X and Y is a scalar summarizing the dependence structure in a single figure. Additional constraints are required to make this measure comprehensive, meeting a list of desired properties.

DEFINITION 2.6 (Measure of dependence).– A measure of dependence[5] is a function $\delta(X,Y)$ verifying the following properties:

1) symmetry: $\delta(X,Y) = \delta(Y,X)$;

2) normalization: $-1 \leq \delta(X,Y) \leq 1$;

3) monotonicity:
$\delta(X,Y) = 1 \Leftrightarrow X,Y$ are comonotonic;
$\delta(X,Y) = -1 \Leftrightarrow X,Y$ are anti-monotonic.

4) invariance: let $T : \mathbb{R} \rightarrow \mathbb{R}$ be a strictly monotonic function of X, then:
$\delta(T(X),Y) = \delta(X,Y)$ for T increasing;

5 Existing literature distinguishes between measures of concordance and measures of dependence (see [FUS 08]). For instance, the normalization property is limited to the unit interval according to standard definitions of dependence measures whereas measures of concordance take their values between -1 and 1 and thus account for the sign of the association between random variables. Moreover, the requirements for independence property are looser for standard definitions of concordance measures.

$\delta(T(X),Y) = -\delta(X,Y)$ for T decreasing.

5) independence: $\delta(T(X),Y) = 0 \Leftrightarrow$ X and Y are independent.

Unfortunately, [EMB 99] proved that no measure of dependence simultaneously satisfies the fourth and fifth properties, so we will settle for the following measures: the linear correlation; the rank correlation; the alternative dependence measures and the tail dependence. These measures can be grouped according to various criteria such as global or local measures, linear and nonlinear, non-parametric or not.

2.1.2.1. *Linear correlation or Pearson's coefficient*

Linear correlation is one of the most ubiquitous concepts in finance, popularized by Markowitz's seminal work on portfolio construction and diversification (see Chapter 3). We also find it in the CAPM behind the notion of beta. However, some caution is required with this often misunderstood concept, since correlation and dependence are not interchangeable concepts: correlation does not necessarily imply causality. As highlighted hereafter, small correlation does not imply a small degree of dependency and high correlation does not guarantee identical patterns.

The Pearson coefficient corresponds to the classical view of linear correlation. It measures the linear proximity between two variables and is written:

$$\rho(X,Y) = \frac{Cov(X,Y)}{\sigma_X \sigma_Y}.$$

The Pearson coefficient has advantages in terms of computation and manipulation as it is easy to estimate and can be (almost) linearly handled:

$$\rho(aX + b, cY + d) = sign(ac)\rho(X,Y),$$

where a, b, c and d are real numbers.

It can be expressed as a function of the copula and the marginals (see [DRO 14]):

$$\rho(X,Y) = \frac{1}{\sigma_X \sigma_Y} \int_0^1 \int_0^1 [C(u_X,u_Y) - u_X u_Y]\, dF_X^{-1}(u_X) dF_Y^{-1}(u_Y).$$

It respects the aforementioned symmetry and normalization properties as $\rho(X,Y) = \rho(Y,X)$ and $-1 \le \rho \le +1$. However, it does not satisfy the monotonicity, the invariance and the independence properties. In fact, if X and Y are independent, then $\rho = 0$. The reverse is not true unless the vector $(X,Y)'$ is Gaussian, in which case we have: X and Y are independent $\Leftrightarrow$ $\rho(X,Y) = 0$. Moreover, let $X \rightsquigarrow \mathcal{N}(0,1)$ and $Y = X^2$. Although X and Y are functionally related, their correlation coefficient is null as $Cov(X,Y) = E(XY) - E(X)E(Y) = E(X^3) = 0$. If we recall the definition of independence between two random variables X and Y, one should have for any choice of common and smooth functions f and g the equality $\mathbb{E}[f(X)g(Y)] = \mathbb{E}[f(X)]\mathbb{E}[g(Y)]$ for independence to hold. As the linear correlation is quite similar to the computation of $\mathbb{E}[XY] - \mathbb{E}[X]\mathbb{E}[Y]$, then confounding correlation and independence is equivalent to checking independence only with linear functions in the original definition.

The Pearson coefficient requires finite second-order moments, otherwise the correlation is not defined. It has no intrinsic interpretation; however, it can be regarded as the cosine of the angle between X and Y and its square defines the determination coefficient, i.e. the percentage of variance that can be explained by the other variable. It measures thus the intensity of the linear relationship between X and Y. It is adapted for the linear monotonic relationship between variables elliptically distributed. Besides, two perfectly positively correlated variables, i.e. $\rho = +1$, do not necessary co-move in the same direction. In fact, the correlation applies to deviations from the mean of a series and not from the series itself:

> "*Strong positive correlation indicates that upward deviations from the mean on one return time series tend to be accompanied by upward deviations from the mean in the other, and similarly downward deviations from the respective mean of the two series tend to go together.*" —— [LHA 12]

NUMERICAL EXAMPLE 2.4.– We can check in Figure 2.19 the extent to which a misinterpretation of correlation can lead to critical situations. Consider three geometric Brownian assets X, Y and Z whose dynamics are given by the following stochastic differential equations:

$$\begin{aligned} dX_t &= \mu dt + \sigma dW_t \\ dY_t &= \mu dt - \sigma dW_t \\ dZ_t &= -\mu dt + \sigma dW_t, \end{aligned}$$

where $dW_t \rightsquigarrow \mathcal{N}(0,1)$ and μ and σ are two positive scalars defining the magnitude of the process' trend and volatility. Our three assets share thus the same trend and volatility magnitude, and their movements are perfectly correlated:

$$corr\left(dX_t, dY_t\right) = -1 \text{ and } corr\left(dX_t, dZ_t\right) = +1.$$

Despite the perfect positive correlation between movements of X and Z, they follow opposite patterns as highlighted in Figure 2.19: X increases while Z decreases. In fact, when the trend is important, it steers the process irrespective of the stochastic part.

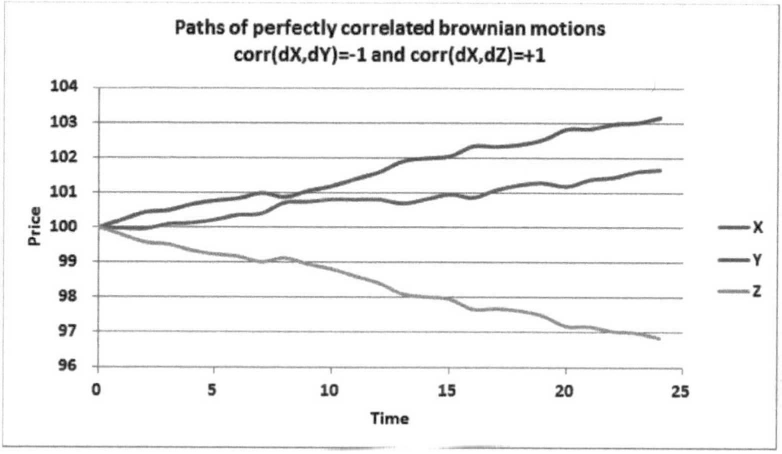

Figure 2.19. *Paths of perfectly correlated Brownian motions. For a color version of the figure, see www.iste.co.uk/ielpo/investment.zip*

If we have two sets of observations of X and Y with respective samples $(x_i)_{i\in[1;T]}$ and $(y_i)_{i\in[1;T]}$, the empirical linear correlation between the two variables is written as:

$$\hat{\rho} = \frac{\sum_i (x_i - \bar{x})(y_i - \bar{y})}{\sqrt{\sum_i (x_i - \bar{x})^2}\sqrt{\sum_i (y_i - \bar{y})^2}}$$

where $\bar{x}, \bar{y}$ are the empirical means of the two variables over their respective samples. $\hat{\rho}$ is a biased, yet convergent, estimator for ρ. In fact:

$$\mathbb{E}[\hat{\rho}] = \rho - \frac{\rho(1-\rho^2)}{2T} \longrightarrow_{T\to\infty} \rho.$$

Testing the significance[6] of linear correlation:

$$H_0 : \rho = 0 \quad \text{vs. alternative assumption } H_a : \rho \neq 0$$

can be conducted using the asymptotic distribution of the statistic:

$$t = \frac{\hat{\rho}}{\sqrt{\frac{1-\hat{\rho}^2}{T-2}}} \rightsquigarrow Student(T-2).$$

For larger T, the Student distribution converges toward the Gaussian one and the significance test can rely on the following asymptotic distribution $\hat{\rho} \rightsquigarrow \mathcal{N}(0, \frac{1}{\sqrt{T-1}})$.

6 Unilateral test is also possible, i.e. $H_a : \rho > 0$ or $H_a : \rho < 0$.

NUMERICAL EXAMPLE 2.5 (The elusive notion of beta: global average sensitivity vs. local quantile sensitivity).– Consider the spreads (s) of the Bloomberg-Barclays Euro Credit Corporates and the German rates (r) of maturity between 3 and 5 years over the same period. The choice of the 3- to 5-year bucket ensures comparable durations for both indices whose evolution is represented in Figure 2.20. We have 750 weekly observations between January 2002 and May 2016. The sensitivity of spreads relative to rates is given by the coefficient of a suitable regression, often called beta, of the relative variation of spreads to the absolute movements of the German rates. This choice is guided by empirical research (see [MEU 05] in the case of rates and [BEN 07] for the case of spreads) suggesting that rates' movement and relative spread variations are deemed to be stationary risk factors or market invariants. The traditional OLS beta can be expressed as the ratio of the covariance to variance or alternatively as the correlation scaled by the ratio of volatilities of covariates, i.e.:

$$\beta^{OLS} = \frac{Cov\left(\frac{\Delta s}{s}, \Delta r\right)}{\mathbb{V}(\Delta r)} = corr\left(\frac{\Delta s}{s}, \Delta r\right)\frac{\sigma_{\frac{\Delta s}{s}}}{\sigma_{\Delta r}}.$$

β^{OLS} can be interpreted as the average sensitivity of the relative variation of spreads to a unit shock in the rates' movements, i.e.:

$$d\left(\frac{\Delta s}{s}\right) \approx \beta^{OLS}.d(\Delta r).$$

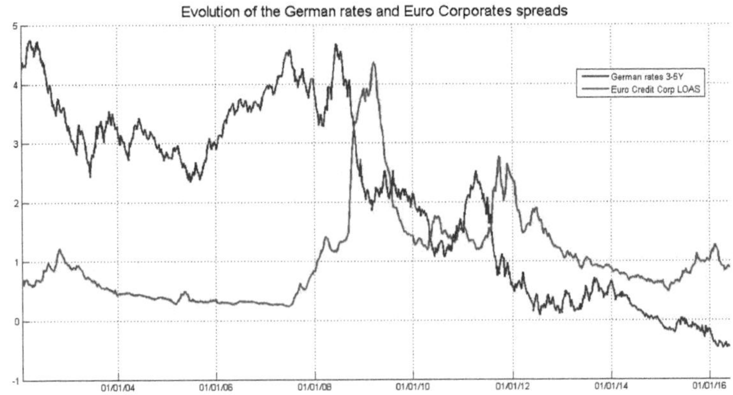

Figure 2.20. *Evolution of rates and spreads*

Quantile regression (see [KOE 05], [GIV 13]) allows for a richer analysis as it takes into account the whole conditional distribution of spreads and is not limited to the average. Quantile regression gives the sensitivity of each quantile of the spreads' relative variations to a standardized shock in rates' movements. The quantile betas are plotted in Figure 2.21. The negative sensitivity of spreads to rates seems to be more pronounced for higher quantiles suggesting an over-reaction of spreads to rates when the former exhibits important widening[7].

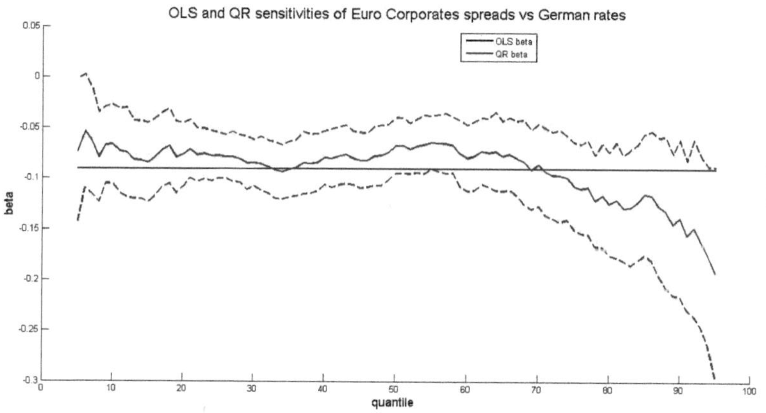

Figure 2.21. *Sensitivity of spreads' relative variations to rates' movements.*

2.1.2.2. *Rank correlation*

To avoid significance interpretation, we may seek a non-parametric version of dependence measures, i.e. a measure that does not require the knowledge of the distribution of X and Y. While the Pearson coefficient captures monotonic linear relationships, rank correlations are more suitable for monotonic nonlinear dependencies. The main advantage of the rank correlation over the Pearson coefficient is its invariance under monotonic transformations and robustness with respect to outliers. Its main disadvantage is its lack of flexibility and the ease of manipulation. It is a suitable measure of association for non-elliptical distributions. In what follows, we present the Spearman correlation, the Kendall's τ and Blomqvist's beta. These measures satisfy the aforementioned desired properties of measure of dependence except for that of independence. In fact, if variables X and Y are independent, then $\delta(X,Y) = 0$, the opposite is not always true.

7 Some caution is required for such an assertion since the impact of rates on spreads' distribution might depend on other covariates not taken into consideration by the regression.

2.1.2.2.1. Spearman's rank correlation

The Spearman correlation is defined as the Pearson coefficient computed on the ranks of X and Y. It inherits all of Pearson's properties. Estimation and significance tests are also conducted similarly. More formally, Spearman's rho is written:

$$\rho_S(X,Y) = \rho(F_X(X), F_Y(Y)).$$

Replacing the variables by their grades enhances robustness because no assumption is required for the distribution of the marginals. The distribution of the grades is well known and corresponds to the uniform distribution, i.e. $F_X \rightsquigarrow U_X$ and $F_Y \rightsquigarrow U_Y$.

Given that $\mathbb{E}[U_X] = \mathbb{E}[U_Y] = \frac{1}{2}$ and $\mathbb{V}[U_X] = \mathbb{V}[U_Y] = \frac{1}{12}$, Spearman's rho can be expressed as a function of only the underlying copula (see [EMB 99]):

$$\begin{aligned}\rho_S(X,Y) &= \rho(U_X, U_Y) \\ &= 12\mathbb{E}[U_X U_Y] - 3 \\ &= 12 \int_0^1 \int_0^1 C(u_X, u_Y) du_X du_Y - 3.\end{aligned}$$

Alternatively, following [NEL 06]:

$$\rho_S(X,Y) = 3\left\{\mathbb{P}\left[(X - \tilde{X})(Y - \tilde{Y}) > 0\right] - \mathbb{P}\left[(X - \tilde{X})(Y - \breve{Y}) < 0\right]\right\},$$

where $(X,Y)'$, $(\tilde{X},\tilde{Y})'$ and $(\breve{X},\breve{Y})'$ are independent copies.

The empirical Spearman correlation can be estimated through:

$$\hat{\rho_S}(x,y) = \frac{\sum_{i=1}^T (Rk(x_i) - \bar{Rk}(x))(Rk(y_i) - \bar{Rk}(y))}{\sqrt{\sum_{i=1}^T (Rk(x_i) - \bar{Rk}(x))^2}\sqrt{\sum_{i=1}^T (Rk(y_i) - \bar{Rk}(y))^2}}$$

where $\bar{Rk}(x) = \bar{Rk}(y) = \frac{T+1}{2}$ or alternatively

$$\hat{\rho_S}(x,y) = 12\frac{\sum_{i=1}^T Rk(x_i)Rk(y_i)}{T(T^2-1)} - 3\frac{T+1}{T-1} = 1 - \frac{6\sum_i d_i^2}{T(T^2-1)}$$

where $d_i = Rk(x_i) - Rk(y_i)$.

It is important to note that the expression of $\hat{\rho_S}$ only holds if there are no equalities in the sample, the resulting expression being far more complicated in the opposite case. In fact, in the presence of *ex aequo* observations, the variance of ranks is no longer equal to $\frac{T(T^2-1)}{6}$. In this case, it is possible to replace *ex aequo* ranks by the corresponding average and to apply the proper adjustment factor. As a function of X and Y, $t_S = \hat{\rho_S}\sqrt{\frac{T-2}{1-\hat{\rho_S}^2}}$ approximately follows a Student's distribution with $T - 2$ degrees of freedom.

2.1.2.2.2. Kendall's τ

Let $(X, \tilde{X})$ and $(Y, \tilde{Y})$ be two independent pairs of random variables drawn from the same joint distribution. Kendall's rank correlation is given by:

$$\tau(X,Y) = \mathbb{P}\left[(X-\tilde{X})(Y-\tilde{Y})>0\right] - \mathbb{P}\left[(X-\tilde{X})(Y-\tilde{Y})<0\right].$$

Kendall's τ can also be expressed as a function of only the underlying copula (see [EMB 99]):

$$\tau(X,Y) = 4\int_0^1\int_0^1 C(u,v)dC(u,v) - 1.$$

Estimating Kendall's τ between a couple of variables is based on the compared sorting of both series (see [KEN 90]). Assuming a sample of size T, we get:

$$\hat{\tau}(X,Y) = \frac{2\times\left(\sum_i\sum_j(\mathbb{1}[Y_j > X_i] - \mathbb{1}[Y_j \le X_i])\right)}{T(T-1)}.$$

$\tau = 1$ when the two series are perfectly ordered, and $\tau = -1$ in the opposite case. Independence between X and Y implies that $\tau = 0$. Therefore, the interpretation is similar to the Pearson correlation coefficient even if Kendall's τ is more robust. In fact, it only tests the presence of monotonic relations between the two variables.

At finite distance for samples of size N, the standard deviation of $\hat{\tau}(X,Y)$ is given by:

$$\sigma_\tau = \sqrt{\frac{4N+10}{9N^2-9N}}.$$

Asymptotically, $\hat{\tau}(X,Y)$ converges quickly toward a standard Gaussian. Therefore, the test statistic is simply:

$$\hat{\tau}\sqrt{\frac{9N^2-9N}{4N+10}} \rightsquigarrow \mathcal{N}(0,1).$$

Again in case of *ex aequo* observations, an adjustment has to be made. The difference between Kendall and Spearman is bounded (see [SIE 88]):

$$-1 \le 3\hat{\tau} - 2\hat{\rho_S} \le +1.$$

2.1.2.2.3. Blomqvist's beta

The medial point of a bivariate copula, $C\left(\frac{1}{2},\frac{1}{2}\right)$ gives the probability that both variables have their values below their medians simultaneously. For elliptically distributed variables, the linear correlation ρ and the medial point are related by the following equation:

$$C\left(\frac{1}{2},\frac{1}{2}\right)=\frac{1}{4}+\frac{1}{2\pi}\arcsin\rho.$$

[CHI 12] build on this relation among others to develop a visual test for the departure from elliptical models.

Introduced by [BLO 50], Blomqvist's beta or medial correlation coefficient is defined as:

$$\begin{aligned}\beta(X,Y) &= \mathbb{P}\left[\left(X-F_X^{-1}(\tfrac{1}{2})\right)\left(Y-F_Y^{-1}(\tfrac{1}{2})\right)>0\right]\\ &-\mathbb{P}\left[\left(X-F_X^{-1}(\tfrac{1}{2})\right)\left(Y-F_Y^{-1}(\tfrac{1}{2})\right)<0\right]\\ &= 2\mathbb{P}\left[\left(U_X-\frac{1}{2}\right)\left(U_Y-\frac{1}{2}\right)>0\right]-1.\end{aligned}$$

It can be also written using the following expression:

$$\beta=4C\left(\frac{1}{2},\frac{1}{2}\right)-1.$$

It evaluates the dependence at the center of the distribution and presents the advantage of low computational complexity.

The empirical $\hat{\beta}$ can be simply computed:

$$\hat{\beta}(X,Y)=\frac{2\sum_{i=1}^{N}\mathbb{1}_{\left[(Rk(X_i)-\frac{N}{2}-\frac{1}{2})(Rk(Y_i)-\frac{N}{2}-\frac{1}{2})\geq 0\right]}}{N}.$$

The asymptotic distribution of $\hat{\beta}$ can be found in [JOE 14]:

$$\frac{\sqrt{N}(\hat{\beta}-\beta)}{\sqrt{1-\beta^2}}\rightsquigarrow N(0,1).$$

2.1.2.3. *Alternative dependence measures*

Previous measures do not satisfy all the five desired requirements for a measure of dependence, mainly that of independence. However, it is possible to meet this last property by relaxing the normalization constraint and allowing the measure to take its values between 0 and 1. The degree at which two variables are mutually related is thus assessed by the distance between their copula and the product (or the maximal) copula. Examples of such measures are: Schweizer-Wolff sigma and Hoeffding's phi.

– Schweizer-Wolff sigma: two random variables are independent if and only if they are linked by the product copula, in which case the probability of any joint event is given by the product of the marginal probabilities. The closer their copula is to the product copula, the less related they are. [SCH 76] build on this idea by defining their symmetric and non-parametric dependence measure as the L_p distance between the copula and the product copula. More formally:

$$\sigma_p(X,Y) = k_p\left(\int_0^1\int_0^1 \mid C(u_X,u_Y) - u_X u_Y \mid^p du_X du_Y\right)^{\frac{1}{p}}$$

with $p \geq 1$ and k_p a normalized constant so that $0 \leq \sigma_p(X,Y) \leq 1$ (see also [SCH 81]). For $p = 1$, we have:

$$\sigma(X,Y) = 12\int_0^1\int_0^1 \mid C(u_X,u_Y) - u_X u_Y \mid du_X du_Y.$$

– Hoeffding's phi (see [FUS 08]):

$$\phi(X,Y) = 3\sqrt{10\int_0^1\int_0^1 (C(u_X,u_Y) - u_X u_Y)^2\, du_X du_Y}.$$

2.1.2.4. *Tail dependence*

While linear correlation and rank correlation are global dependency measures averaging the intensity of the association over the whole domain of definition, it can be useful to focus on the dependence of extreme events where spillover and overshooting induce a local dependency structure different from the average global one. This notion is known as the tail dependence. Introduced by [JOE 90], it measures the strength of dependence in the upper joint multivariate distribution and the lower joint multivariate distribution.

DEFINITION 2.7 (Tail dependence).– Upper and lower tail dependences are defined, respectively, as:

$$\lambda_U = \lim_{u \longrightarrow 1^-} Pr[U_Y > u \mid U_X > u],$$

$$\lambda_L = \lim_{u \longrightarrow 0^+} Pr[U_Y < u \mid U_X < u].$$

λ_U and $\lambda_L \in [0,1]$. If $\lambda_U = 0$ (resp. $\lambda_L = 0$) then X and Y are said to be independent in the upper (resp. lower) tail. Thus, these asymptotic coefficients are limit probabilities conditional on both margins exceeding a certain quantile level given that one margin does. We may note that:

$$\mathbb{P}[U_Y > u \mid U_X > u] = \mathbb{P}[Y > F_Y^{-1}(u) \mid X > F_X^{-1}(u)]$$
$$= \frac{1 - \mathbb{P}[X \le F_X^{-1}(u)] - \mathbb{P}[Y \le F_Y^{-1}(u)] + \mathbb{P}[X \le F_X^{-1}(u), Y \le F_Y^{-1}(u)]}{1 - \mathbb{P}[X \le F_X^{-1}(u)]}.$$

Consequently, the upper tail dependence can be written as a function of the copula:

$$\lambda_U = \lim_{u \longrightarrow 1^-} \mathbb{P}[U_Y > u \mid U_X > u] = \lim_{u \longrightarrow 1^-} \frac{(1 - 2u + C(u,u))}{(1-u)}.$$

Similarly, the lower tail dependence can be defined as a function of copula:

$$\lambda_L = \lim_{u \longrightarrow 0^+} \frac{C(u,u)}{u}.$$

Coefficients strictly greater than zero indicate a tendency for the copula to generate joint extreme events. In the case of elliptical distributions, the upper and lower tails are similar as the distribution is symmetric: $\lambda_U = \lambda_L = \lambda$. The value of λ is zero for the Gaussian copula and positive for the t copula. Its value in this latter case was analytically calculated[8] by [EMB 01]:

$$\lambda = 2\bar{t}_{\nu+1}\left(-\sqrt{\nu+1}\frac{\sqrt{1-\rho}}{\sqrt{1+\rho}}\right)$$

where $\bar{t}_{\nu+1}$ denotes the tail of a univariate t-distribution and ρ the correlation coefficient. The tail dependence coefficient of a convex linear combination of copulas is equal to the convex linear combination of the tails of these copulas (see, e.g., [SAL 07]). The estimation of tails is addressed by [CAI 05].

2.2. Linear factor models

A factor decomposition maps the randomness of the variables of interest into a set of other variables called factors[9], plus residuals. Although the appropriate decomposition may not be linear, a lot can be achieved with LFM. Behind the simple specification of an LFM lies a set of assumptions often neglected by practitioners and

8 [CHI 12] show that it suffers from large pre-asymptotic corrections.

9 We do not call them *explicative* variables on purpose.

which may lead to spurious conclusions. For example, the LFM representation of the CAPM and the APT are often interchangeably used although their underlying assumptions are quite different. Various LFM specifications can be found in the literature. They differ in their purposes, assumptions and constraints. They nonetheless share the idea that a small number of variables, called factors, can explain much of the market ups and downs.

More formally, an LFM decomposition of the N–dimensional market X into a set of K pervasive parts that are common to all market components, called factor F, plus a residual u for each market component, can be written as:

$$X_{(N,1)} = a_{(N,1)} + B_{(N,K)}F_{(K,1)} + u_{(N,1)}. \quad [2.3]$$

Typically, X is the variable of interest and represents the return vector of a cross-section of N assets, F is the return vector of some K risk factors and B is the sensitivity of asset returns to the risk factors. When not exogenously specified, the coefficient $a_{(N,1)}$ can be identified by setting $\mathbb{E}[u]$ to null. Factor models are widely used in the financial industry in various fields such as asset pricing, portfolio optimization, alpha extraction, risk assessment and performance attribution. LFM are not just about historical regressions run over time series data, but they are forward-looking probabilistic models imposing a dependence structure on variables describing the way randomness flows among variables X, F, B, u. For a review of LFM models see, for instance, [KNI 05], [DAR 13] or [MEU 14].

2.2.1. *Why multifactor models?*

Factor models are everywhere in the literature, but their motivation or original interest is often ignored, skipped or left aside. The following paragraph restates the economic rationale that leads to the use of factor models. Simple regressions using factor models are too often used empirically only as a blind and systematic procedure, whereas their use and understanding need a cautious modeling. Quite universally, it is admitted in economics that the price of an asset is given by the expectation of its discounted payoff. Formally, this idea can be summarized by equations [2.4] and [2.5]:

$$P_t = \mathbb{E}_t[M_{t+1}Y_{t+1}] \quad [2.4]$$

$$M_{t+1} = f(data, parameters), \quad [2.5]$$

where P_t stands for the current price, Y_{t+1} denotes the asset payoff at $t+1$, f is a function and M_{t+1} is the stochastic discount factor (henceforth SDF)[10], i.e. a random variable used for discounting the future payoff in each state of the world.

10 For the SDF approach, see [SHI 82], [HAN 91], [COC 01].

Applying equation [2.4] to the risk-free asset normalized for a current value of 1 and paying r_f in the future gives the following identity, linking the risk-free payoff to the SDF:

$$r_f = \frac{1}{\mathbb{E}_t[M_{t+1}]}.$$

Inserting r_f into equation [2.4] gives the price of the asset :

$$P_t = \frac{\mathbb{E}_t[Y_{t+1}]}{r_f} + Cov(M_{t+1}, Y_{t+1}).$$

The SDF theory states that the price of any asset is equal to the sum of two terms. The first term corresponds to the standard discounted present value or the asset price in a risk-neutral world. The second term is a risk adjustment equal to the covariance of the payoff with a single variable: the SDF. If the asset payoff co-varies positively with the SDF, then it exhibits a higher price. The SDF framework unifies different pricing approaches for various types of securities whether bonds, stocks or derivatives. The SDF can be linked to the investor preferences for consumption over time. Formally, the investor chooses its consumption and saving levels by maximizing its intertemporal utility function (U), which depends on its current (c_t) and future (c_{t+1}) consumptions. If u is an increasing and concave function denoting the period utility function and ξ the investor preference for the present, the two-period consumption model is written as:

$$\begin{aligned} \max_{\kappa} U(C_t, C_{t+1}) &= u(C_t) + \xi \mathbb{E}_t\left[u(C_{t+1})\right] \\ \text{such that:} \quad C_t &= D_t - P_t \kappa \\ C_{t+1} &= D_{t+1} + Y_{t+1}\kappa, \end{aligned}$$

where D_t denotes the original consumption level if the investor had no possibility to buy or sell the asset. Solving this problem for κ gives the price of the asset as a function of the marginal utility function (u') and the preference for the present parameter ξ:

$$P_t = \mathbb{E}_t\left[\xi \frac{u'(C_{t+1})}{u'(C_t)} Y_{t+1}\right],$$

where $M_{t+1} = \xi \frac{u'(C_{t+1})}{u'(C_t)}$ denotes the SDF. The poor empirical performance of the consumption-based model motivates a search for alternative functions $M = f(data)$. One sensible solution is to directly model marginal utility in terms of other variables:

$$M_{t+1} = a + b_1 F^1_{t+1} + b_2 F^2_{t+1} + \ldots,$$

where, a is a constant, $F^1, F^2, \ldots$ are random variables called factors and b_k is the sensitivity of the SDF to the factor k. It is important to note that those factors are proxies for the marginal utility related SDF. They constitute the market portfolio proxy in the CAPM, some broad portfolios inferred from the covariance matrix of returns in the APT, the short-rate level plus the slope of the curve in [COX 85] model, macroeconomic variables, ...

2.2.2. *Types of linear factor models*

Depending on whether F and B are observable or not, four types of LFM can be distinguished. We list the four types of LFM we have identified in Table 2.3. This table summarizes our understanding of LFM classification, with the hope that it would help practitioners to better understand the rich variety of LFM and to avoid their related pitfalls.

For each of the models in Table 2.3, the estimation technique is conducted by maximizing the R^2 measure of fitness (see [MEU 14]) or equally by minimizing the sum of squares of errors. More general objective functions such as *VaR* are also possible. Alternative estimation techniques are based on GMM (see [COC 01]) or on likelihood maximization (see [CON 10a] and [KNI 05]).

		Loadings B	
		Observable	Unobservable
Factors F	Observable	LFM1	LFM2
	Unobservable	LFM3	LFM4

Table 2.3. *Various families of LFM*

Although easy to implement, the least-squares (henceforth LS) estimation is nonetheless subject to various potential biases. Omitting a risk factor leads to a mispricing, whose magnitude is linked to the covariance matrix of the residuals. [MAC 00] suggest to use this link for estimating expected returns. [ANG 07a] highlighted the inconsistency of LS estimation in the presence of time-varying loadings. Over the period 1926-2001, the authors found little evidence that conditional alpha is statistically significant. Voluminous literature documents an impressive number of "factors". [COC 11] refers to it as the "*zoo of new factors*" explaining the cross-section of expected returns. However, [HAR 16] argued that many of the 316 documented factors since 1967 are likely to be false as they were deemed to be significant by chance.

> "*... Professionals often complain that betas and factor loadings need to be "recalibrated" all the time. Cointegration relations are notoriously unstable (i.e. useless). Millions of regressions can be performed per minute, with automated*

"factor selection" routines that lead to discoveries such as GDP being predicted by the size of the male organ ([WES 11]). A researcher dared theorize that "heightened self-esteem" may justify this finding... good grief! Beware of economists bearing "factors." . — [LOP 16]

2.2.2.1. *LFM1: the no model*

[CHI 15] developed a "nested factor model" in which standard LFM framework is extended to include an additional factor structure on the log-volatility of the factors and of the residuals. The authors suggest that their approach accounts for stylized facts such as fat tails and non-linear dependences in stock returns.

When both loadings and factors are observable, there is little room left for estimation. As such, a "no model" specification is used for *ex post* performance attribution[11] purposes. The observable return X is decomposed over various exogenous performance drivers in order to explain as much information as possible. The residual will typically converge to null as the number of factors grows. [MEU 14] notes that such "pure exogenous" LFMs:

"... *are used in practice, often as the first of a two-step approach to market analysis. First, a pure exogenous LFM is used to extract the residuals. Then a different LFM is used to analyze and impose structure on the distribution of the residuals.*" — [MEU 14]

As B and F are exogenous, the randomness of X is directly transferred to the residual $u = X - a - BF$, which is simply recovered and modeled using another type of LFM in order to achieve risk attribution, for instance.

NUMERICAL EXAMPLE 2.6.– In fixed-income markets, LFM1 are used to decompose the return of a bond into carry and price components, in which case X denotes the total return, a represents the carry, B represents the key rates' durations and F denotes key rates' movements.

Applying this to the Bloomberg Barclays Euro Treasury index weekly returns between 15 July 2011 and 15 July 2016, we obtain in Figure 2.22 the scatterplot of the estimated versus the observed weekly returns and the histogram of the corresponding residuals. The cumulative returns are plotted in Figure 2.23.

11 In performance attribution models, the number of factors used to explain the performance may be higher than that of the portfolio constituents, i.e. $K \geq N$.

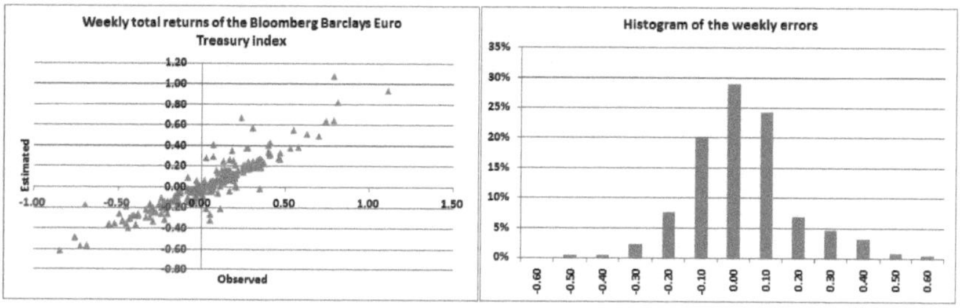

Figure 2.22. *The Bloomberg Barclays Euro Treasury index weekly return and its approximation by the product of duration time and the variation of the yield to maturity plus carry.*

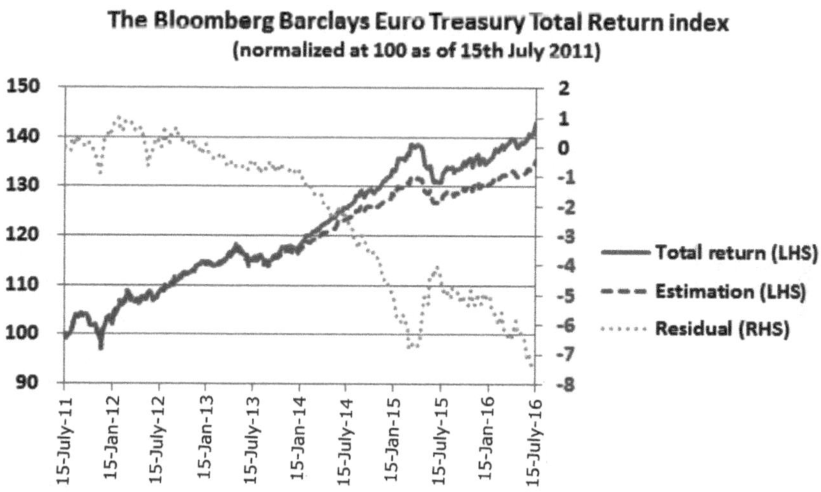

Figure 2.23. *The Bloomberg Barclays Euro Treasury index cumulative return and its approximation by the product of duration time and the variation of the yield to maturity plus carry.*

2.2.2.2. *LFM2: the classical time series model*

In an LFM2-like model, the N−dimensional market X and the factors F are observable. The coefficient a is identified by imposing the constraint $\mathbb{E}[u] = 0$. B is estimated by least-squares routines:

$$\widehat{B} = Cov(x, f)\mathbb{V}(f)^{-1}.$$

The existence and uniqueness of $\widehat{B}$ requires a minimal set of assumptions, namely that factors are not linearly correlated, so that $\mathbb{V}(f)^{-1}$ exists as well as

$Cov(x, f)$. The entries of $B = (\beta_{n,k})$ are called *betas,* which measure the sensitivity of asset n to factor k. This collapses with the general appreciation under which financial practitioners speak about the "beta", as described, for instance, in the Introduction of this book. These betas can be easily constrained while keeping a closed-form expression. Let $M_{(p,K)}$ be a matrix of rank $p < K$ and $m_{(p,1)}$ a vector defining the set of p linear constraints on vector $\beta_n = (\beta_{n,1}, \beta_{n,2}, \ldots, \beta_{n,K})'$:

$$M\beta_n = m.$$

The analytical expression and the properties of the constraint least-squares estimator (β_n^{CLS}) can be found in [CRÉ 10]:

$$\widehat{\beta}_n^{CLS} = \widehat{\beta}_n - \mathbb{V}(f)^{-1}M'\left[M\mathbb{V}(f)^{-1}M'\right]^{-1}\left[M\widehat{\beta}_n - m\right].$$

When $M\widehat{\beta}_n = m$, both estimators are identical. Divergence appears when $M\widehat{\beta}_n \neq m$.

NUMERICAL EXAMPLE 2.7 (Betas computed on S&P500 stocks).– In chapter 3, we will follow a numerical example based on stocks from the S&P500 index. This simulation exercise is described in example 3.1 p. 180. We anticipate a bit and use the same data set of daily returns from 01/01/2002 to 01/01/2015 for S&P500 components whose composition is fixed at the date of 01/01/2015. Again, this choice is made for illustrative purposes, and would not reflect a true strategy because following a fixed set of stocks in the past would induce survivorship bias. Anyway, this data set is made up of 502 stocks and 3,273 daily returns.

We can compute the betas of the stocks with respect to the index of the whole period. The histogram and the density of the 502 obtained OLS betas are shown in Figure 2.24. We observe that the betas are not so homogeneous, even for S&P500 necessarily (even if present constituents are not necessarily past constituents). The mode of the distribution is around 1.0 even if some stocks are clearly out of the bulk.

2.2.2.3. *LFM3: the cross-sectional model*

In a cross-sectional model, loadings B are specified exogenously while factors are hidden and need to be extracted from the market by means of a linear transformation $F = LX$, where $L_{(K,N)}$ is a rotational matrix to optimize. Here again, the vector a is set to $\mathbb{E}[X] - B\mathbb{E}[F]$ so that the expectation of the error is null. Similar to a cross-sectional regression, we recover factors F:

$$\widehat{F} = \left(B'\mathbb{V}(x)^{-1}B\right)^{-1} B'\mathbb{V}(x)^{-1}x,$$

which can be simplified to $\widehat{F} = (B'B)^{-1} B'x$ when data are normalized.

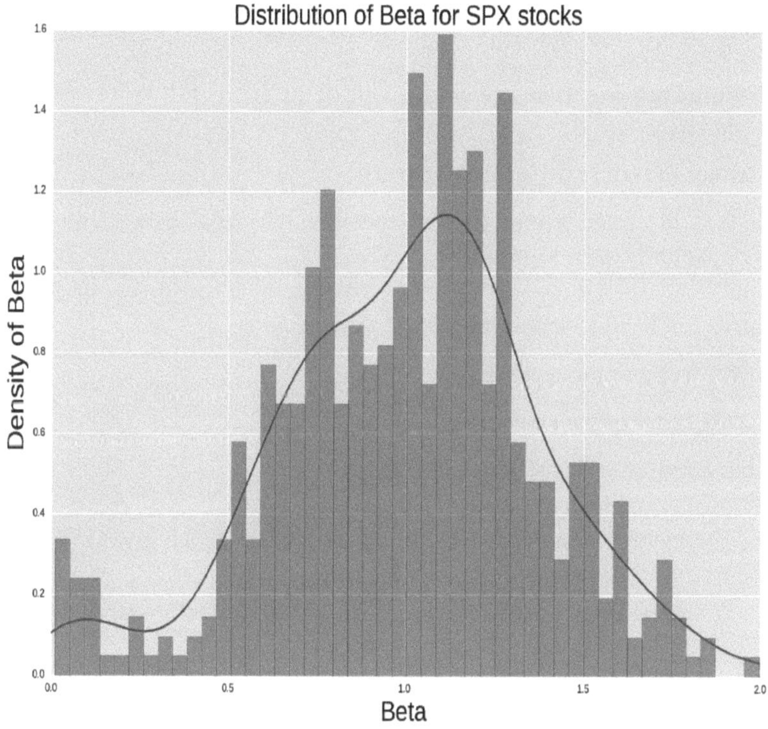

Figure 2.24. *Distribution of daily betas of S&P500 components versus the S&P500 index.*

NUMERICAL EXAMPLE 2.8 (Nelson-Siegel term structure model).– [NEL 87] developed a parametric approach to model the term structure of rates. It states that a continuously compounded zero coupon rate of maturity θ observed at time 0 can be written as follows[12]:

$$\begin{aligned} R_{0,\theta} &= \beta_0 \\ &+ \beta_1 \left[\frac{1 - \exp(-\frac{\theta}{\tau})}{\frac{\theta}{\tau}} \right] \\ &+ \beta_2 \left[\frac{1 - \exp(-\frac{\theta}{\tau})}{\frac{\theta}{\tau}}) - \exp(-\frac{\theta}{\tau}) \right] \end{aligned}$$

12 In its original specification, the Nelson-Siegel model applies to forward rates.

with:

– $\beta_0 = \lim_{\theta \to \infty} R_{0,\theta}$ compounded to the continuously compounded long-term rate level;

– $\beta_1 = \lim_{\theta \to 0} R_{0,\theta} - \beta_0$ describes the slope of the curve. It follows that $\beta_0 + \beta_1$ is the *overnight* rate;

– β_2 defines the convexity of the curve;

– $\tau > 0$ is the scale parameter that specifies the decay rate of the short and intermediate maturity rates toward 0[13].

The curve can be modeled as the sum of three factors:

– the shift factor or the level: β_0;

– the twist factor or the slope: β_1;

– the butterfly factor or the convexity of the curve: β_2.

The sensitivity of the curve to the Nelson-Siegel parameters is given in Figure 2.25.

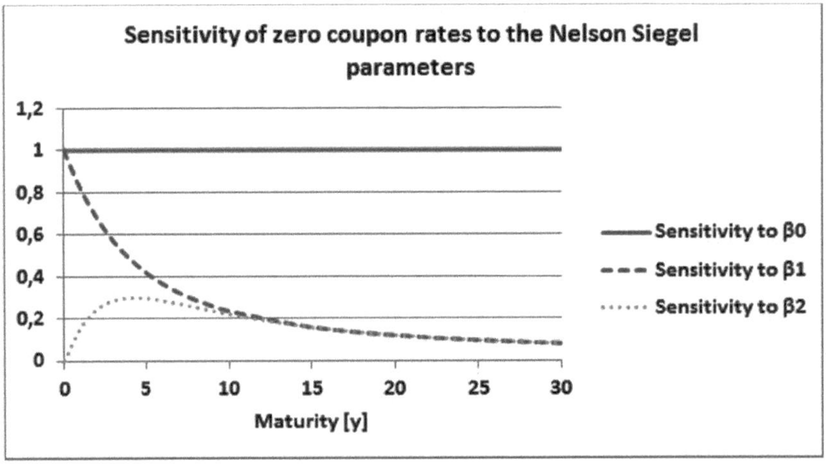

Figure 2.25. *The sensitivity of the curve to the Nelson-Siegel parameters obtained for parameter values* $\beta_0 = 3\%, \beta_1 = -2.44\%, \beta_2 = -3.34\%$ *and* $\tau = -2.38$

13 It is assigned to a fixed value in order to avoid costly nonlinear optimization. The estimation of the model is thus conditional to the value of τ. After a first estimation of parameters β_0, β_1 and β_2, we can improve the adequacy of the model by optimizing recursively the value of τ and the β parameters.

Assuming N rates with different maturities, we can write the factor decomposition as follows:

$$X = BF + u \quad [2.6]$$

where:

- X denotes the vector of N empirical rates each of maturity θ_i, i.e. $X_i = R_{0,\theta_i}$;
- F represents the vector of factors: $F = (\beta_0, \beta_1, \beta_2)'$;
- B is the pre-specified matrix of loadings of dimension $(N, 3)$:

$$B = \begin{pmatrix} 1 & \left[\frac{1-\exp(-\frac{\theta_1}{\tau})}{\frac{\theta_1}{\tau}}\right] & \left[\frac{1-\exp(-\frac{\theta_1}{\tau})}{\frac{\theta_1}{\tau}} - \exp(-\frac{\theta_1}{\tau})\right] \\ \vdots & \vdots & \vdots \\ 1 & \left[\frac{1-\exp(-\frac{\theta_i}{\tau})}{\frac{\theta_i}{\tau}}\right] & \left[\frac{1-\exp(-\frac{\theta_i}{\tau})}{\frac{\theta_i}{\tau}} - \exp(-\frac{\theta_i}{\tau})\right] \\ \vdots & \vdots & \vdots \\ 1 & \left[\frac{1-\exp(-\frac{\theta_N}{\tau})}{\frac{\theta_N}{\tau}}\right] & \left[\frac{1-\exp(-\frac{\theta_N}{\tau})}{\frac{\theta_N}{\tau}} - \exp(-\frac{\theta_N}{\tau})\right] \end{pmatrix}.$$

It is important to note that the loadings are known and the factors are estimated by $\widehat{F} = (B'B)^{-1}B'x$. Applying the model to the British sovereign curve, we get the following outputs represented in Figure 2.26.

2.2.2.4. *LFM4: the statistical model*

In an LFM4 specification, both the loadings and factors are unobservable and have to be inferred from the market by means of a rotation. We assume that factors are linear combinations of the market components: $F = LX$. The spectral decomposition of the market covariance matrix gives:

$$Cov(X) = E\Lambda E',$$

where $\Lambda_{(N,N)}$ is the diagonal matrix of the positive eigenvalues ordered according to their decreasing values $\lambda_1^2 > \lambda_2^2 > \ldots > \lambda_N^2$ and $E_{(N,N)}$ denotes the symmetric normalized matrix of the corresponding eigenvectors whose columns $(e_1, e_2, \ldots, e_N)$ are orthogonal, i.e. $e_n' e_m = 0$ and such that $EE' = I_N$. Choosing the adequate number of factors K and denoting by the matrix $E_K = (e_1, \ldots, e_K)$, we obtain $B = E_K$ and $F = E_K' X$.

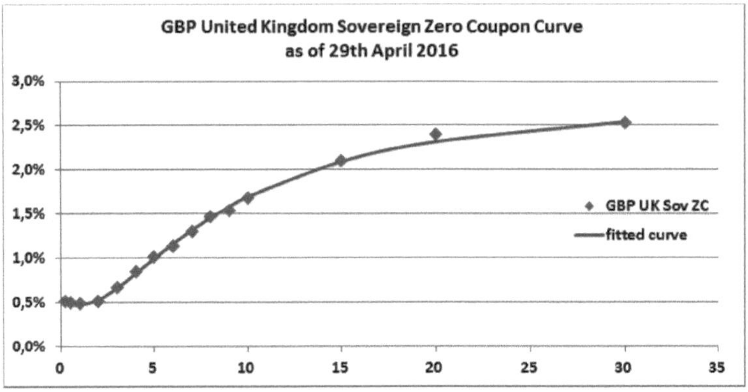

Figure 2.26. *The Nelson-Siegel fit of the GBP United Kingdom Sovereign Zero Coupon curve as of 29 April 2016. The estimated parameters are:* $\beta_0 = 3\%, \beta_1 = -2.44\%, \beta_2 = -3.34\%$ *and* $\tau = -2.38$.

NUMERICAL EXAMPLE 2.9 (PCA on the British curve).– Modeling the British curve using a PCA approach on 15 GBP UK zero coupon rates with different maturities, we find that the first three components explain more than 95% of the curve total variance. The percentage of variance explained by each of the 15 components is given in Figure 2.27.

The first component loads positively on all of the empirical rates: it is thus a market factor that affects the level of the curve. The second component loads positively on the short-term maturity rates and negatively on longer maturity ones: it is interpreted as the slope of the curve. The third component represents the convexity.

REMARK 2.4 (Identification issues).– Part of the negative side of LFM is their rotational indeterminacy, i.e. F and B are defined up to a linear transformation. Let G be a non-singular matrix. Consider $F^* = GF$ and $B^* = G^{-1}B$. B and F can be substituted by F^* and B^* without affecting the market X. Therefore, it would be convenient to impose (see [CON 10b]) the following identifying constraint:

$$Cov(F) = I_K. \qquad [2.7]$$

2.2.3. *Adding empirical restrictions, gaining economic sense*

Equation [2.3] does not add any specific restriction on the market X. Additional assumptions and constraints are required to glean some interesting insights from the original general formulation. Two restrictions are commonly added: the systematic-idiosyncratic constraint and the non-arbitrage assumption (henceforth NA).

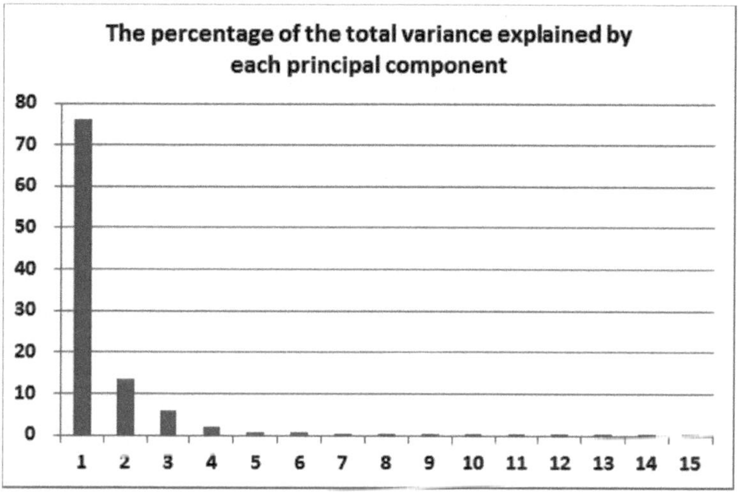

Figure 2.27. *Percentage of the total variance explained by each principal component. The first three components explain more than 95% of the total variation of the curve*

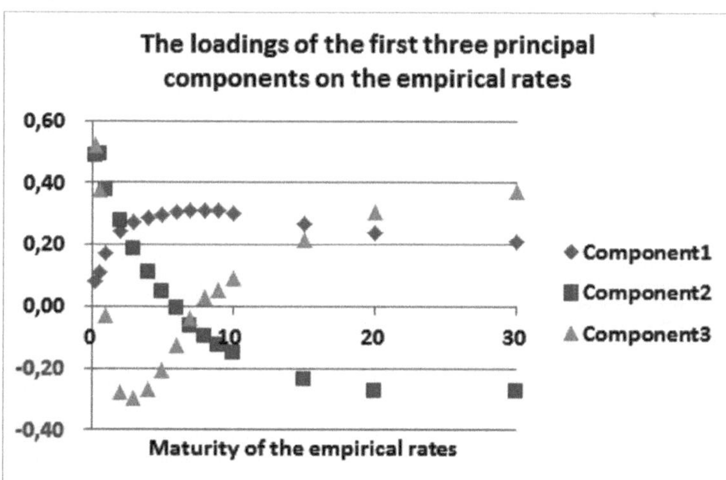

Figure 2.28. *PCA decomposition of the GBP UK curve conducted on 1,126 weekly movements between 31 December 1994 and 29 July 2016*

2.2.3.1. *The systematic-idiosyncratic constraint*

Systematic-idiosyncratic LFMs are often used for alpha generation, risk modeling purposes or portfolio optimization. For instance, the Markovian problem requires the estimation of the unknown covariance matrix of assets $\mathbb{V}(X)$ whose dimension may be high. Some entries may be insignificant and the optimal portfolio spurious. In fact, optimal portfolios are proportional to the Sharpe ratio of the underlying assets, which require computing the inverse of the variance estimate $\widehat{\mathbb{V}}(x)^{-1}$. The problem of covariance matrix estimation, inversion and cleaning will be fully handled throughout Chapter 3. Problems linked to the inversion of the covariance matrix are tackled in section 3.3.3. Giving some structure to the shape of $\mathbb{V}(X)$ helps to alleviate the computational burden of covariance matrix inversion. See again the discussion in Chapter 3. Moreover, when the number of assets grows in the investment universe, it is unlikely to observe decorrelated assets. The dependence structure is thus driven by a limited number of factors in such a way that much of the variability of the universe returns can be explained by these few factors. Assuming systematic factors implies an additive split of the total variance between factors and residuals, while idiosyncratic residuals imply that the covariance matrix of errors is diagonal. It follows that the covariance matrix of the market can be decomposed into a systematic and an idiosyncratic part:

$$\underbrace{\mathbb{V}(X)}_{total} = \underbrace{B\mathbb{V}(F)B'}_{systematic} + \underbrace{\mathbb{V}(u)}_{idiosyncratic} .$$

This is useful to invert $\mathbb{V}(X)$ in mean-variance optimizations. Using the Woodbury formula (used later in the book, and explained in Appendix A.1.2 p. 329), we get:

$$\underbrace{\mathbb{V}(X)^{-1}}_{N\times N} = \underbrace{\mathbb{V}(u)^{-1}}_{N\times N diagonal}$$

$$- \mathbb{V}(u)^{-1}B\mathbb{V}(F)\underbrace{\left[\mathbb{V}(F) + \mathbb{V}(F)B'\mathbb{V}(u)^{-1}B\mathbb{V}(F)\right]^{-1}}_{K\times K}\mathbb{V}(F)B'\mathbb{V}(u)^{-1}.$$

The computational burden of inverting $\mathbb{V}(x)$ is alleviated and the estimation errors in $\widehat{\mathbb{V}}(x)$ are mitigated by adding structure on $\mathbb{V}(x)$, when assuming that the return generating process follows a systematic-idiosyncratic factor model. Formally, an LFM model is said to be systematic-idiosyncratic if:

– residuals are uncorrelated with factors, i.e. factors are systematic:

$$\forall n \in \{1,\ldots N\}, k \in \{1,\ldots,K\}, Cov(u_n, F_k) = 0; \qquad [2.8]$$

– residuals are cross-sectionally uncorrelated, i.e. residuals are idiosyncratic:

$$\forall n \neq m \in \{1,\ldots N\}, Cov(u_n, u_m) = 0. \qquad [2.9]$$

In LFM2 models, the LS estimator performs well as it guarantees that factors and residuals are uncorrelated, i.e. $Cov(F_k, u_n) = 0$ for all $k \in [1, K]$ and $n \in [1, N]$, which defines a system of NK equations. It is easy to check that:

$$Cov(F, u) = Cov(F, X - a - BF) = Cov(F, X) - BCov(F, F) = 0.$$

Factors are thus said to be *systematic*. However, residuals are not necessarily uncorrelated among each other and thus are not idiosyncratic. In fact, the variance of residuals is not a diagonal one:

$$\begin{aligned} \mathbb{V}(u) &= Cov(X - a - BF, X - a - BF) \\ &= \mathbb{V}(X) - Cov(X, F)B' - BCov(F, X) + B\mathbb{V}(F)B' \\ &= \mathbb{V}(X) + Cov(X, F)\left(-\mathbb{V}(F)^{-1} - \mathbb{V}(F)^{-1} + \mathbb{V}(F)^{-1}\right)Cov(F, X) \\ &= \mathbb{V}(X) - BCov(F, X), \end{aligned}$$

with $\mathbb{V}(X) - BCov(F, X)$ not being diagonal in the general case. Furthermore, for the residuals to be idiosyncratic, we need to have $Cov(u_i, u_j) = 0$ for all $(i, j) \in [1; N]^2$ such that $j < i$, which defines a system of $\frac{N(N-1)}{2}$ equations.

While the *systematic-idiosyncratic* model requires $NK + \frac{N(N-1)}{2}$ constraints to be satisfied, B has only NK entries. The system is overdetermined and the solution does not exist. Moreover, when the betas are tied, the constrained least-square estimator does not guarantee obtaining systematic factors.

The systematic-idiosyncratic framework seems difficult to achieve. Identification reasons preclude such an eventuality. Therefore, in order to achieve the systematic-idiosyncratic decomposition in an LFM2 model, the off-diagonal elements of the covariance matrix of the residuals are set to zero. Such a distortion of the original market leads to erroneous risk figures. Systematic-idiosyncratic LFM2 time series models are also known as macroeconomic models because factors are typically macroeconomic variables such as inflation, growth and surveys presumed to explain securities' returns. [CHA 83] developed an approximated factor model, in which off-diagonal elements of the residuals covariance matrix are close to but not strictly equal to zero. In their asymptotic framework, the specific risk of a portfolio composed of a large number of assets will be close to zero.

In an LFM3 model, neither factors are systematic nor residuals idiosyncratic. In fact:

$$\begin{aligned} Cov(F,u) &= Cov\left((B'B)^{-1}B'X, X - a - B(B'B)^{-1}B'X\right) \\ &= (B'B)^{-1}B'\mathbb{V}(X)\left(I_N - B(B'B)^{-1}B'\right) \\ &\neq 0_{K,N}. \end{aligned}$$

Again, imposing systematic-idiosyncratic conditions for convenience implies exogenously setting the correlation between factors and residuals as well as correlation among residuals to zero. The recovered model is an approximation of the true market distribution. It achieves a lower-rank covariance matrix at the cost of an inaccurate risk estimation. Systematic-idiosyncratic LFM3 cross-sectional models are also known as fundamental or characteristic models as they rely on security characteristics such as the industry or other fundamental figures (see [FAM 92], [FAM 93] or [FAM 96]) and help recover fundamental factors.

LFM4 statistical models are typically fed by security returns and output both security betas and statistical factors. Factors recovered by PCA are uncorrelated by construction. It follows that factors are systematic in an LFM4 model. However, residuals are not uncorrelated. Any attempt to make the LFM4 systematic-idiosyncratic has to pass by an exogenous distortion of the model by setting the dependence among residuals to null. Asymptotic systematic-idiosyncratic LFM4 models were derived by [CON 86a], [CON 88] and [CON 93] who studied the case of an unknown covariance matrix and suggested that when N is much larger than T, the factor model can be estimated by applying the principal components method to the $T \times T$ covariance matrix. [BAI 03] derived the limiting distributions for factors, loadings in an asymptotic PCA approach when both N and $T \longrightarrow \infty$, under general assumptions which allow for serial and cross-section dependence for the idiosyncratic errors.

[VES 00] used ICA[14] as an alternative for PCA for estimating an LFM4 model when idiosyncratic risk is high, which hinders the classical estimation procedure. The advantage of ICA over PCA lies in its ability to take into account higher moments and to ensure independence among variables. However, there is no ordering of the independent components. Transposing the notion of dominant principal component into ICA is not henceforth, although it is possible to order the independent components along their contributions to the variances of the original variables.

The explanatory power of these models is addressed in [CON 95] who finds that fundamental and statistical models outperform macroeconomic LFMs. Indeed, in

14 For a review of ICA, see [HÉR 87], [JUT 91] and [COM 94].

highly correlated markets, statistical models are likely to achieve higher explanatory power with fewer factors. The comparison of these three types of models cannot rely exclusively on R^2 but rather should take theoretical consistency into consideration and practical considerations such as rebalancing costs and the economic sense of the factors. [PUK 15] defined a seven empirical stage protocol for sorting factors as main drivers for returns and determining the identities of these factors as well as what they represent: anomalies, risks or others. They argue that pervasive factors with risk premium should be related to the covariance of returns of real assets rather than that of the returns of bonds and derivatives.

2.2.3.2. *The non-arbitrage condition*

Arbitrage opportunities can be easily identified using LFMs. The cornerstone of this approach is that, under the NA condition, two risk-free assets must offer the same return, otherwise there is an arbitrage. Since systematic-idiosyncratic LFMs are difficult to achieve empirically, we assume in what follows that the idiosyncratic part can be completely diversified, i.e. $\mathbb{V}(u) = 0$.

Let us consider a portfolio characterized by its exposure vector to each asset in the market $w = (w_1, \ldots, w_N)'$ such that $\sum_{n=1}^{N} w_n = 1$. The return of the portfolio over period $[t-1, t]$ is:

$$w'X_t = w'a + w'BF_t.$$

In LFM1 and LFM2, factors are observable. The conditional expected return and variance are given by:

$$\mathbb{E}[w'X_t \mid f_t] = w'a + w'Bf_t,$$
$$\mathbb{V}[w'X_t \mid f_t] = 0.$$

Under the NA condition, riskless portfolios must have the same return as the risk-free asset r_f, that is, for each $w \in \mathbb{R}^N$:

$$w'a + w'Bf_t = r_f.$$

It appears that, under the above mentioned restrictions, LFM1 and LFM2 do not preclude arbitrage opportunities. Nonetheless, assumptions required for obtaining such a result, i.e. $\mathbb{V}(u) = 0$, are at best constraining if not unrealistic.

In LFM3 model, factors are unobservable. The expected return and variance are given by:

$$\mathbb{E}[w'X_t] = w'a + w'B\mathbb{E}[F_t],$$
$$\mathbb{V}[w'X_t] = w'B\mathbb{V}[F_t]B'w.$$

Riskless portfolios are those exhibiting a null variance such that:

$$w'B\mathbb{V}[f_t]B'w = 0 \Longleftrightarrow B'w = 0,$$

and their expected return simplifies to $w'a = r_f$. The NA condition implies that:

$$B'w = 0 \Longrightarrow w'(a - r_f e) = 0.$$

Under such specifications, the expected returns are linear combinations of the betas (see [GOU 97]).

2.3. Risk factor dynamics: the state-space modeling framework

Models with unobserved state variables nest a large class of stochastic models widely used in economics and finance (see, e.g., [HAR 12], [KOO 15] or [PEL 15]). Unlike standard models such as ARMA or VAR, hidden factor models have their model coefficients contingent to an unobserved latent process called the *state vector*. The latter is linked to other observable variables conditional to which it is inferred. Regime-switching models, stochastic volatility models and models with threshold effects are examples of models with unobserved state variables. *State-Space Models* (henceforth SSM) provide a unique framework for projecting loadings and factors, whether they are observable or unobserved. Contributions of [HAR 90b], [HAM 94], [COM 07], [DUR 12] or [ZEN 13] are examples of surveys of SSM with applications in economics and finance. SSM makes a simple representation of a wide range of dynamic models possible, whether standard (e.g. AR process, see example 2.1) or with a latent component, with the use of two equations:

– the *transition equation*, which describes the dynamics of the unobserved variables;

– and the *measurement equation*, which describes the relationship between the observable variables and the hidden ones.

In the case of a linear representation of an SSM, these two equations would be written in the following form at date t:

$$X_t = M_t X_{t-1} + C_t + v_t \quad \text{: transition equation;}$$
$$Y_t = O_t X_t + D_t + w_t \quad \text{: measurement equation;}$$

where:

– $Y_t \in \mathbb{R}^N$ is the observed vector;

– $X_t \in \mathbb{R}^K$ is the state vector;

– $(v_t) \in \mathbb{R}^K$ and $(w_t) \in \mathbb{R}^N$ are independent series of centered, random variables with respective variances Q_t and H_t;

– $M_t \in \mathcal{M}_K$ and $O_t \in \mathcal{M}_{N\times K}$ are two deterministic matrices;

– $C_t \in \mathbb{R}^K$ and $D_t \in \mathbb{R}^N$ are deterministic vectors.

Vector (Y_t) being the only observable process, information grows along the pace of arrival of observations $y_t, y_{t+1}, \ldots$. The hidden process (X_t) is inferred conditionally by information generated by successive realizations of (Y_t), given some initial conditions.

EXAMPLE 2.1 (SSM representation of an AR(p) process).– Consider an autoregressive process Y whose order is a strictly positive integer p. $\phi = (\phi_1, \ldots, \phi_p)$ is the vector of model coefficients such that $|\phi| < 1$, where $|\phi|$ is the modulus of ϕ[15], δ is a constant and ϵ is a white noise.

The dynamics of process Y are given by the following equation:

$$Y_t = \delta + \phi_1 Y_{t-1} + \phi_2 Y_{t-2} + \ldots + \phi_p Y_{t-p} + \epsilon_t.$$

Then, $Y \rightsquigarrow AR(p)$ and admits the following SSM representation, with a degenerated measurement equation:

$$X_t = MX_{t-1} + C + v_t,$$
$$Y_t = (1, 0, \ldots, 0)\, X_t,$$

where

$$\underbrace{\begin{pmatrix} y_t \\ y_{t-1} \\ y_{t-2} \\ \vdots \\ y_{t-p+1} \end{pmatrix}}_{X_t} = \underbrace{\begin{pmatrix} \phi_1 & \phi_2 & \ldots & \phi_{p-1} & \phi_p \\ 1 & 0 & \ldots & 0 & 0 \\ 0 & 1 & \ldots & 0 & 0 \\ \vdots & \vdots & \ddots & \vdots & \vdots \\ 0 & 0 & \ldots & 1 & 0 \end{pmatrix}}_{M} \underbrace{\begin{pmatrix} y_{t-1} \\ y_{t-2} \\ y_{t-3} \\ \vdots \\ y_{t-p} \end{pmatrix}}_{X_{t-1}} + \underbrace{\begin{pmatrix} \delta \\ 0 \\ 0 \\ \vdots \\ 0 \end{pmatrix}}_{C} + \underbrace{\begin{pmatrix} \epsilon_t \\ 0 \\ 0 \\ \vdots \\ 0 \end{pmatrix}}_{v_t}.$$

2.3.1. *Kalman filter*

The canonical statistical inference technique based on maximizing the likelihood is not adapted for models with an unobserved component whose likelihood does not have an explicit expression (see [KIM 99]). To solve this problem, we may rely on an

15 For insights on modulus of parameters of an AR process, see [HAM 94].

SSM representation and a recursive technique known as the *Kalman Filter* (henceforth KF), which was introduced by [KAL 60] for estimating the unobserved component and enabling the likelihood to be calculated.

2.3.1.1. *The underlying intuition*

How do we estimate a variable Z given a couple of its measures Z_1 and Z_2? A natural answer would be to calculate a weighted average of both measures with weights related to their reliability as captured by their respective variances $\sigma^2_{Z_1}$ and $\sigma^2_{Z_2}$. Hence, we would get with such an approach an alternative weighted measure for Z:

$$Z \sim \frac{\sigma^2_{Z_2}}{\sigma^2_{Z_1} + \sigma^2_{Z_2}} Z_1 + \frac{\sigma^2_{Z_1}}{\sigma^2_{Z_1} + \sigma^2_{Z_2}} Z_2.$$

The weight assigned to each measure decreases when the magnitude of its variance increases.

In SSM framework, these two measures are given by the transition and measurement equations that have to be weighted in order to forecast the value of the state vector X_t. Under mild assumptions, the KF gives the optimal weighting scheme. Conditional to information available up to time $t-1$, the transition and measurement equations give, respectively, the predictions of X and Y as well as their corresponding variances. Observing y_t at time t allows us to update the prediction of the state variable with mixing it with a portion of the innovation on y_t. This portion, $\mathcal{K}_t$, is called the *Kalman gain matrix*. Denoting by $y_{1:t}$ the series of observations up to time t, i.e. $y_{1:t} = (y_1, y_2, \ldots, y_t)$, we have:

$$\begin{aligned}\text{Prediction}(X_t \mid y_{1:t}) &= \text{Prediction}(X_t \mid y_{1:t-1}) + \mathcal{K}_t \left[y_t - \text{Prediction}(Y_t \mid y_{1:t-1})\right], \\ \text{Variance}(X_t \mid y_{1:t}) &= \text{Variance}(X_t \mid y_{1:t-1}) - \mathcal{K}_t \text{Variance}(Y_t \mid y_{1:t-1}) \mathcal{K}'_t.\end{aligned}$$

It is important to note that the larger the *Kalman gain* is, the smaller the *ex post* variance will be with respect to the *ex ante* one. The KF is a recursive procedure for computing optimal estimates of the state vector. It makes it possible to:

– forecast, i.e. estimate the state vector X at time t given values of y up to $t-1$;

– filter, i.e. estimate the state vector X at time t given values of y until t;

– smooth, i.e. estimate the state vector X at time t given values of y until $T > t$.

In the following section we present the Linear Kalman Filter (LKF) as well as two extensions related to the relaxation of the normality and the linearity assumptions.

2.3.1.2. *Linear Kalman filter*

Let us consider a linear SSM characterized by the following equations:

$$X_t = M_t X_{t-1} + C_t + v_t \quad \text{(transition equation)}, \qquad [2.10]$$

$$Y_t = O_t X_t + D_t + w_t \quad \text{(measurement equation)}. \qquad [2.11]$$

Moreover let us assume let that:

– Assumption $(A1)$: $(v_t, w_t)'$ are i.i.d. white noises;

– Assumption $(A2)$: X_0, the initial state vector, is independent from noises (v_t) and (w_t).

These two assumptions ensure the independence of v_t and w_t with observations $(y_1, y_2, \ldots, y_{t-1})$. The LKF still consists of the following two steps: prediction and updating.

2.3.1.2.1. Prediction

From the transition equation [2.10], we calculate the prediction and covariance matrix of X_t given information up to $t-1$:

$$x_{t|t-1} = \mathbb{E}[X_t \mid y_{1:t-1}] = M_t X_{t-1|t-1} + C_t,$$

$$P_{t|t-1} = \mathbb{V}[X_t \mid y_{1:t-1}] = M_t P_{t-1|t-1} M_t' + Q_t.$$

Similarly, using the measurement equation [2.11], we calculate the prediction and the covariance of Y_t conditional to information available up to $t-1$:

$$y_{t|t-1} = \mathbb{E}[Y_t \mid y_{1:t-1}] = O_t X_{t|t-1} + D_t,$$

$$V_{t|t-1} = \mathbb{V}[Y_t \mid y_{1:t-1}] = O_t P_{t|t-1} O_t' + H_t.$$

Moreover, we can calculate the conditional covariance between X_t and Y_t :

$$Cov[X_t, Y_t \mid y_{1:t-1}] = P_{t|t-1} O_t'.$$

2.3.1.2.2. Updating

Once y_t is realized and observable at time t, the prediction error, $\eta_t = y_t - y_{t|t-1}$, can be calculated. It brings new information that has to be exploited to update the prediction of the unobserved state vector X_t. At this stage, it is convenient to add Assumption $(A3)$, the joint normality of variables (v_t) and (w_t):

$$(A3) : \begin{pmatrix} v_t \\ w_t \end{pmatrix} \rightsquigarrow \mathcal{N}\left(\begin{pmatrix} 0 \\ 0 \end{pmatrix}, \begin{pmatrix} Q_t & 0 \\ 0 & H_t \end{pmatrix} \right),$$

from which stems the normality of X_t and Y_t :

$$\begin{pmatrix} X_t \\ Y_t \end{pmatrix} \mid y_{1:t-1} \rightsquigarrow \mathcal{N}\left(\begin{pmatrix} x_{t|t-1} \\ y_{t|t-1} \end{pmatrix}, \begin{pmatrix} P_{t|t-1} & P_{t|t-1}O_t' \\ O_tP_{t|t-1} & V_{t|t-1} \end{pmatrix}\right).$$

We now need to look for the determination of the distribution of $X_t \mid y_{1:t}$.

PROPOSITION 2.4 (Conditional law of a Gaussian variable).– Let $(X,Y)'$ be a Gaussian vector such that:

$$\begin{pmatrix} X \\ Y \end{pmatrix} \rightsquigarrow \mathcal{N}\left(\begin{pmatrix} \mu_X \\ \mu_Y \end{pmatrix}, \begin{pmatrix} \Sigma_{XX} & \Sigma_{XY} \\ \Sigma_{YX} & \Sigma_{YY} \end{pmatrix}\right).$$

The distribution of X conditional to Y, denoted by $X \mid Y$, is also Gaussian:

$$X \mid Y \rightsquigarrow \mathcal{N}\left(\mu_X + \Sigma_{XY}\Sigma_{YY}^{-1}(Y - \mu_Y), \Sigma_{XX} - \Sigma_{XY}\Sigma_{YY}^{-1}\Sigma_{YX}\right).$$

With this proposal, we are able to update the distribution law of X_t after observing y_t:

$$X_t \mid y_{1:t} \rightsquigarrow \mathcal{N}\left(\underbrace{x_{t|t-1} + P_{t|t-1}O_t'V_{t|t-1}^{-1}(y_t - y_{t|t-1})}_{x_{t|t}}, \underbrace{P_{t|t-1} - P_{t|t-1}O_t'V_{t|t-1}^{-1}O_tP_{t|t-1}}_{P_{t|t}}\right). \quad [2.12]$$

Denoting by $\mathcal{K}_t = P_{t|t-1}O_t'V_{t|t-1}^{-1}$ the *Kalman gain matrix,* we get updates for the prediction of X_t and its variance:

$$\begin{aligned} x_{t|t} &= \mathbb{E}[X_t \mid y_{1:t}] = x_{t|t-1} + \mathcal{K}_t\eta_t, \\ P_{t|t} &= \mathbb{V}[X_t \mid y_{1:t}] = P_{t|t-1} - \mathcal{K}_tV_{t|t-1}\mathcal{K}_t'. \end{aligned}$$

The gain matrix can be expressed as:

$$\mathcal{K}_t = P_{t|t-1}O_t'V_{t|t-1}^{-1} = (M_tP_{t-1|t-1}M_t' + Q_t)O_t'(O_tP_{t|t-1} + H_t)^{-1}.$$

It depends on the matrix of observation error H_t. The "smaller" the H_t, the greater the weight assigned to innovations.

REMARK 2.5 (Correlation of noises).– The assumption of uncorrelated errors v_t and w_t can be relaxed without altering the filter. Let A_t be the $K \times N$ covariance matrix of errors v_t and w_t whose joint distribution is now given by the following:

$$\begin{pmatrix} v_t \\ w_t \end{pmatrix} \rightsquigarrow \mathcal{N}\left(\begin{pmatrix} 0 \\ 0 \end{pmatrix}, \begin{pmatrix} Q_t & A_t \\ A_t' & H_t \end{pmatrix}\right).$$

The predictions $x_{t|t-1}$ and $y_{t|t-1}$ remain unchanged as well as the conditional variance of the state vector $P_{t|t-1}$. However, the conditional variance of the observed vector y_t now includes a covariance term:

$$V^a_{t|t-1} = \mathbb{V}[Y_t \mid y_{1:t-1}] = O_t P_{t|t-1} O'_t + H_t + O_t A_t + A'_t O'_t.$$

Similarly, the conditional covariance contains an additional term due to the correlation of errors:

$$Cov[X_t, Y_t \mid y_{1:t-1}] = P_{t|t-1} O'_t + A_t.$$

The Kalman gain matrix has a new expression:

$$\mathcal{K}^a_t = \left(P_{t|t-1} O'_t + A_t\right)\left(V^a_{t|t-1}\right)^{-1}.$$

The updates of the state vector are:

$$\begin{aligned} x_{t|t} &= x_{t|t-1} + \mathcal{K}^a_t \eta_t, \\ P_{t|t} &= P_{t|t-1} - (\mathcal{K}^a_t) V^a_{t|t-1} (\mathcal{K}^a_t)'. \end{aligned}$$

2.3.1.2.3. Initialization and iterations

The KF allows for recursive calculation of $x_{t|t-1}$ and $P_{t|t-1}$ as well as $x_{t|t}$ and $P_{t|t}$. It requires starting parameters $x_0^{initial}$ and $P_0^{initial}$ to initialize the algorithm.

Assuming we are given initial conditions:

$$X_0 \rightsquigarrow \mathcal{N}\left(x_0^{initial}, P_0^{initial}\right) \perp\!\!\!\perp \begin{pmatrix} v_t \\ w_t \end{pmatrix}.$$

For a stationary process x, the unconditional mean and variance can be used as proxies for $x_0^{initial}$ and $P_0^{initial}$, where:

$$\begin{aligned} x_0^{initial} &= M x_0^{initial} + C, \\ P_0^{initial} &= M P_0^{initial} M' + Q. \end{aligned}$$

For non-stationary processes, means and variances do not exist, so any guess for $x_0^{initial}$ is a valid one provided that $P_0^{initial}$ is large enough to account for uncertainty affecting the choice of $x_0^{initial}$. It is important to note that at initial time 0, conditional and unconditional moments are the same.

The KF filter can now be run following the standard two-step iteration:

1) Prediction step:

- $x_{1|0} = M_1 x_0^{initial} + C_1$
- $P_{1|0} = M_1 P_0^{initial} M_1' + Q_1$
- $y_{1|0} = O_1 x_{1|0} + D_1$
- $V_{1|0} = O_1 P_{1|0} O_1' + H_1$.

2) Updating step:

- $\eta_1 = y_1 - y_{1|0}$
- $\mathcal{K}_1 = P_{1|0} O_1' V_{1|0}^{-1}$
- $x_{1|1} = x_{1|0} + \mathcal{K}_1 \eta_1$
- $P_{1|1} = P_{1|0} - \mathcal{K}_1 V_{1|0} \mathcal{K}_1'$.

For any time $t \leq T$:

1) Prediction step:

- $x_{t|t-1} = \mathbb{E}[X_t \mid y_{1:t-1}] = M_t x_{t-1|t-1} + C_t$
- $P_{t|t-1} = \mathbb{V}[X_t \mid y_{1:t-1}] = M_t P_{t-1|t-1} M_t' + Q_t$
- $y_{t|t-1} = \mathbb{E}[Y_t \mid y_{1:t-1}] = O_t x_{t|t-1} + D_t$
- $V_{t|t-1} = \mathbb{V}[Y_t \mid y_{1:t-1}] = O_t P_{t|t-1} O_t' + H_t$.

2) Updating step:

- $\eta_t = (y_t - y_{t|t-1})$
- $\mathcal{K}_t = P_{t|t-1} O_t' V_{t|t-1}^{-1}$
- $x_{t|t} = x_{t|t-1} + \mathcal{K}_t \eta_t$
- $P_{t|t} = P_{t|t-1} - \mathcal{K}_t V_{t|t-1} \mathcal{K}_t'$.

Consequently we obtain the sequences $(x_{t|t-1})$, $(P_{t|t-1})$, $(x_{t|t})$ and $(P_{t|t})$ for $t \in \{1, \ldots, T\}$.

2.3.1.2.4. Prediction with the KF

For each integer $h \geq 0$, we can write the transition equation at each time step up to h:

$$\begin{aligned} X_{t+1} &= M_{t+1}X_t + C_{t+1} + v_{t+1}, \\ X_{t+2} &= M_{t+2}X_{t+1} + C_{t+2} + v_{t+2}, \\ &\vdots \\ X_{t+h} &= M_{t+h}X_{t+h-1} + C_{t+h} + v_{t+h}. \end{aligned}$$

Combining these equations and injecting them into the last one gives the expression of X_{t+h}:

$$X_{t+h} = \left[\prod_{j=1}^{h} M_{t+j}\right] X_t + \sum_{j=1}^{h}\left[\prod_{l=j+1}^{h} M_{t+l}\right] C_{t+j} + \sum_{j=1}^{h}\left[\prod_{l=j+1}^{h} M_{t+l}\right] v_{t+j}.$$

The predictor $x_{t+h|t}$ conditional to information up to time t is given by the conditional expectation:

$$x_{t+h|t} = \mathbb{E}\left(X_{t+h} \mid y_{1:t}\right) = \left[\prod_{j=1}^{h} M_{t+j}\right] x_{t|t} + \sum_{j=1}^{h}\left[\prod_{l=j+1}^{h} M_{t+l}\right] C_{t+j},$$

and the conditional variance is written as:

$$\begin{aligned} P_{t+h|t} &= \mathbb{V}\left(X_{t+h} \mid y_{1:t}\right) \\ &= \left[\prod_{j=1}^{h} M_{t+j}\right] P_{t|t} \left[\prod_{j=1}^{h} M_{t+j}\right]' + \sum_{j=1}^{h}\left[\prod_{l=j+1}^{h} M_{t+l}\right] Q_{t+j} \left[\prod_{l=j+1}^{h} M_{t+l}\right]'. \end{aligned}$$

Similarly, on the basis of the measurement equation, the observed process expression at time $t+h$ is written as:

$$Y_{t+h} = O_{t+h}X_{t+h} + D_{t+h} + w_{t+h}.$$

Its prediction and variance are given by:

$$y_{t+h|t} = O_{t+h}x_{t+h|t} + D_{t+h} = O_{t+h}\left(\left[\prod_{j=1}^{h} M_{t+j}\right] x_{t|t} + \sum_{j=1}^{h}\left[\prod_{l=j+1}^{h} M_{t+l}\right] C_{t+j}\right) + D_{t+h},$$

$$V_{t+h|t} = O_{t+h}P_{t+h|t}O_{t+h}' + H_{t+h}.$$

REMARK 2.6.– When the transition and observation matrices are independent of time, i.e. when we assume that $M_t = M$, $O_t = O$ and $C_t = D_t = 0$, the expression of X_{t+h} simplifies to:

$$X_{t+h} = M^h X_t + \sum_{j=1}^{h} M^{h-j} v_{t+j}.$$

Conditional predictions and variances over horizon $t + h$ can be expressed as follows:

$$\begin{aligned}
x_{t+h|t} &= M^h x_{t|t}, \\
P_{t+h|t} &= M^h P_{t|t}(M^h)' + \sum_{j=1}^{h} M^{h-j} Q_{t+j} (M^{h-j})', \\
y_{t+h|t} &= O M^h x_{t|t}, \\
V_{t+h|t} &= O \left[M^h P_{t|t}(M^h)' + \sum_{j=1}^{h} M^{h-j} Q_{t+j} (M^{h-j})' \right] O' + H_{t+h}.
\end{aligned}$$

2.3.1.2.5. Statistical inference

In the previous sections, the matrices and vectors of the SSM were assumed to be known in order to implement the algorithm. In this paragraph, they are assumed to be *unknown* and do not depend on time but on a vector of parameters $\theta \in \Theta \subset \mathbb{R}^d$ that needs to be estimated. Under this assumption, the SSM is:

$$\begin{aligned}
X_t &= M(\theta) X_{t-1} + C(\theta) + v_t, \\
Y_t &= O(\theta) X_t + D(\theta) + w_t,
\end{aligned}$$

and the joint normality of noises is expressed through:

$$\begin{pmatrix} v_t \\ w_t \end{pmatrix} \rightsquigarrow \mathcal{N}\left(\begin{pmatrix} 0 \\ 0 \end{pmatrix}, \begin{pmatrix} Q(\theta) & 0 \\ 0 & H(\theta) \end{pmatrix} \right).$$

Given a sample of observations $(y_1, y_2, \ldots, y_T)$ and initial values $x_0^{initial}$ and $P_0^{initial}$, the likelihood $L_T(\theta) := L_T(\theta; x_0^{initial}, P_0^{initial}, y_1, \ldots, y_T)$ is written as a function of observations[16]:

$$L_T(\theta) = \prod_{t=1}^{T} \frac{1}{\sqrt{(2\pi)^N det\left(V_{t|t-1}(\theta)\right)}}$$
$$\exp\left(-\frac{1}{2}[y_t - \mathbb{E}_\theta(Y_t \mid y_{1:t-1})]' V_{t|t-1}(\theta)^{-1}[y_t - \mathbb{E}_\theta(Y_t \mid y_{1:t-1})]\right).$$

The maximum likelihood estimator $\hat{\theta}_T$ is obtained by maximizing:

$$\hat{\theta}_T = \arg\max_{\theta\in\Theta} L_T(\theta),$$

or equivalently after composing the opposite of the logarithm:

$$\hat{\theta}_T = \arg\min_{\theta\in\Theta} \sum_{t=1}^{T} \eta_t(\theta)' V_{t|t-1}(\theta)^{-1}\eta_t(\theta) + \log\left(det\left(V_{t|t-1}(\theta)\right)\right).$$

NUMERICAL EXAMPLE 2.10 (Dynamic Nelson-Siegel term structure model).– Following [DIE 06b], we build on example 2.8 presented on p. 101 consisting of modeling the United Kingdom Sovereign Zero Coupon curve by allowing for the estimated factors F on [2.6] on page 103 to have some dynamics. The model admits the following SSM expression:

$$F_t = MF_{t-1} + \bar{F} + v_t,$$
$$X_t = BF_t + w_t,$$

where M denotes the (3×3) transition matrix and $\bar{F}$ represents the (3×1) vector defining the long-term level for each of the three factors: level, slope and convexity. X_t is a vector of 15 observable zero coupon rates of different maturities. Noises (v_t, w_t) are assumed to be Gaussian:

$$\begin{pmatrix} v_t \\ w_t \end{pmatrix} \rightsquigarrow \mathcal{N}\left(\begin{pmatrix} 0 \\ 0 \end{pmatrix}, \begin{pmatrix} Q & 0 \\ 0 & H \end{pmatrix}\right).$$

Applying the two-step LKF at each month t between January 1995 and July 2016, we get:

16 At initialisation time 0, conditional and unconditional moments match. The notation $y_{1:t-1}$ at time $t = 0$ reads $y_{1:0} \equiv y_0$.

1) Prediction step:

$$
\begin{aligned}
f_{t|t-1} &= M f_{t-1|t-1} + \bar{F} \\
P_{t|t-1} &= M P_{t-1|t-1} M' + Q \\
x_{t|t-1} &= B f_{t|t-1} \\
V_{t|t-1} &= B P_{t|t-1} B' + H.
\end{aligned}
$$

2) Updating step:

$$
\begin{aligned}
\eta_t &= x_t - x_{t|t-1} \\
\mathcal{K}_t &= P_{t|t-1} B' V_{t|t-1}^{-1} \\
f_{t|t} &= f_{t|t-1} + \mathcal{K}_t \eta_t \\
P_{t|t} &= P_{t|t-1} - \mathcal{K}_t V_{t|t-1} \mathcal{K}_t'.
\end{aligned}
$$

Given some initial values, the model parameters $\theta = \left(M, \bar{F}, H, Q\right)$ are estimated by maximizing the likelihood:

$$
L(\theta) = \prod_{t=1}^{T} \frac{1}{(2\pi)^{15/2} det\left(V_t(\theta)\right)^{1/2}} \exp\left(-\frac{1}{2}\eta_t' V_t(\theta)^{-1} \eta_t\right).
$$

Factor f dynamics are shown in Figure 2.29. The dynamics of the entire curve is captured by the evolution of three factors, which helps alleviate the forecasting of the curve as well as other risk calculations.

The Kalman filter allows us to recursively recover the distribution of $X_t \mid y_{1:t}$. Under Assumption $(A3)$, this distribution is likewise Gaussian, whose expectation $x_{t|t}$ provides an optimal estimator of X_t in the sense of L^2. In cases of failure of the Gaussian assumption, the filter yields optimal estimates among linear ones only. In cases of failure of linearity, nonlinear filtering has to be privileged. The Flexible Least Squares approach, detailed later in section 2.3.1.4, can help to relax the Gaussian assumption.

2.3.1.3. *Extended Kalman filter*

Let m and o be two nonlinear functions. A nonlinear SSM representation with additive noises can be expressed as follows:

$$
\begin{aligned}
X_m &= m(X_{m-1}) + v_m, \\
Y_m &= o(X_m) + w_m.
\end{aligned}
$$

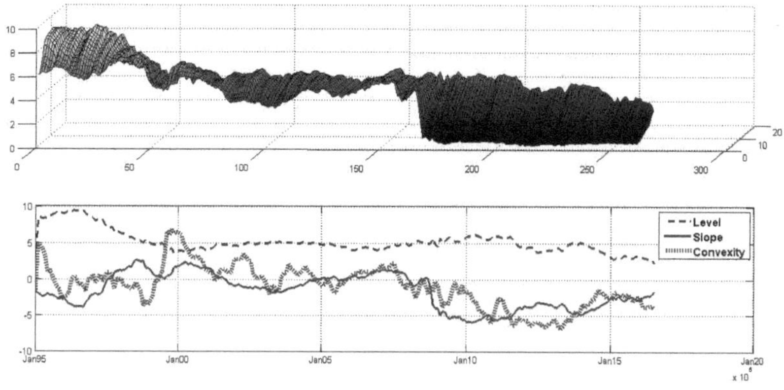

Figure 2.29. *On the first graph, we represent the term structure of the GBP zero coupon curve between January 1995 and July 2016. The Nelson-Siegel monthly factors dynamics are plotted on the second graph*

If these two equations can be applied for predicting the state vector and the vector of the observed variables, calculating their variances is much more problematic. One possible solution consists of linearizing functions m and o so that covariances can be recovered. This technique is known as *Extended Kalman filter* (see, e.g., [SOR 68]). It consists of linearizing the transition and measurement equations for each time step. Therefore, functions o and m have to be differentiable. When computing the covariances, functions o and m are substituted by their Jacobian matrix[17] so that the two-step standard LKF algorithm can be implemented for each time $t \leq T$.

1) Prediction step:

$$
\begin{aligned}
x_{m|m-1} &= m(x_{t-1|t-1}),\\
P_{t|t-1} &= \nabla m_{x_{t-1|t-1}} P_{t-1|t-1} \nabla m'_{x_{t-1|t-1}} + Q_t,\\
y_{t|t-1} &= o(x_{t|t-1}),\\
V_{t|t-1} &= \nabla o_{x_{t|t-1}} P_{t|t-1} \nabla o'_{x_{t|t-1}} + H_t.
\end{aligned}
$$

2) Updating step:

$$
\begin{aligned}
x_{t|t} &= x_{t|t-1} + P_{t|t-1} \nabla o'_{x_{t|t-1}} V_{t|t-1}^{-1} (y_t - y_{t|t-1}),\\
P_{t|t} &= P_{t|t-1} - P_{t|t-1} \nabla o'_{x_{t|t-1}} V_{t|t-1}^{-1} \nabla o_{x_{t|t-1}} P_{t|t-1}.
\end{aligned}
$$

17 The Jacobian matrix is the partial derivative matrix of a vector-valued function. For further discussion, the reader may refer to any course or textbook on differential calculus.

For highly nonlinear processes, the *Unscented Kalman Filter* can be used, see [JUL 97] for an application. The theory and application of nonlinear filtering are unfortunately beyond the scope of this book, yet interested readers can refer to [TAN 10].

2.3.1.4. *Flexible Least Squares*

In case of failure of the noises' joint normality assumption, Flexible Least Squares (henceforth FLS) provide an elegant alternative to LKF. FLS generalizes the standard least-square approach by incorporating a dynamic component in the cost function to minimize. This results in a recursive multicriteria optimization. The standard linear regression model usually assumes that the dependent variable Y_t can be explained by a set of K explanatory variables $X_t = (X_t^1, \dots, X_t^K)'$. The coefficients vector of the regression $\beta = (\beta_1, \dots, \beta_K)'$ is estimated thanks to least-squares routines through the minimization of the following objective cost function:

$$\mathcal{C}(\beta) = \sum_{t=1}^{T} (y_t - x_t'\beta)^2.$$

The resulting vector $\hat{\beta} = \hat{\beta}^{LS}$ therefore obtained is the one that minimizes the sum of square of errors over the whole estimation period $[1, T]$. For this fixed set of observations, the $\hat{\beta}$ vector is estimated for the whole set and is not intended to vary in time within the $[1, T]$ time-period. The sensitivity of the dependent variable Y_t to any explanatory variable X_t^k is the same, regardless of time t. [KAL 88] and [KAL 89] generalized the standard linear model in order to allow for time-varying coefficients:

$$\beta_{t+1} = \beta_t + v_t, \qquad [2.13]$$

$$Y_t = X_t'\beta_t + w_t, \qquad [2.14]$$

without adding any assumption regarding the distribution of residuals, presumed to be mutually and serially independent. The cost function to minimize, as described in [KAL 88], is:

$$\mathcal{C}(\beta, \mu) = \sum_{t=1}^{T} (y_t - x_t'\beta_t)^2 + \mu \sum_{t=1}^{T-1} (\beta_{t+1} - \beta_t)'(\beta_{t+1} - \beta_t), \qquad [2.15]$$

with $\mu \geq 0$. $\mathcal{C}(\beta, \mu)$ being the sum of the measurement error r_M^2 and the dynamic error r_D^2 with:

$$r_M^2 = \sum_{t=1}^{T} (y_t - x_t'\beta_t)^2,$$

$$r_D^2 = \sum_{t=1}^{T-1} (\beta_{t+1} - \beta_t)'(\beta_{t+1} - \beta_t).$$

The parameter μ defines the relative importance assigned to the dynamic error in the minimization program. The higher the value of μ, the higher the weight assigned to r_D^2 and the more stable the estimated β are. At the limit, the FLS converges toward the OLS beta when $\mu \longrightarrow \infty$. [KAL 88] proposed a recursive backward algorithm for solving 2.13. The β achieving the smallest cost at time t is given by:

$$c(\beta_{t+1}, \mu) = \inf_{\beta_t}\{(y_t - x_t'\beta_t)^2 + \mu(\beta_{t+1} - \beta_t)'(\beta_{t+1} - \beta_t) + c(\beta_t, \mu)\}.$$

Assuming a quadratic cost:

$$c(\beta_t, \mu) = \beta_t' Q_{t-1}\beta_t - 2\beta_t' p_{t-1} + r_{t-1},$$

where Q_{t-1} and p_{t-1} have respective dimensions of $K \times K$ and $K \times 1$ and r_{t-1} a scalar. Injecting $c(\beta_t, \mu)$ into $c(\beta_{t+1}, \mu)$ and deriving the latter with respect to β_t and conditioning on β_{t+1}, we obtain a recursive equation:

$$\widehat{\beta}_t = E_t + L_t\beta_{t+1},$$

where:

$$E_t = \mu^{-1} L_t(p_{t-1} + x_t y_t),$$
$$L_t = \mu(Q_{t-1} + \mu I + x_t x_t')^{-1}.$$

Given initial parameters p_0 and Q_0, [KAL 88] showed that the estimate of β_T can be obtained as:

$$\widehat{\beta}_T = (Q_{T-1} + x_T x_T')^{-1}(p_{T-1} + x_T y_T).$$

β_{T-1}, β_1 are then calculated recursively using:

$$\widehat{\beta}_t = E_t + L_t\beta_{t+1}.$$

[MON 09] proved that the LKF is equivalent to FLS with $\mu = \mathbb{V}[v]^{-1}$ when the mean and the variance of the innovations are specified, without assuming these errors to be normally distributed. For a comparison between KF and FLS, we refer to [DAR 12] and [KLA 05]. See also [MAR 04] for a constrained version of *FLS*.

NUMERICAL EXAMPLE 2.11 (FLS time-varying sensitivities).– We have estimated previously the sensitivity of the Euro Corporates spreads' relative variations to the German rates' movements of similar duration, in Figure 2.21, p. 89. This average sensitivity was spanned over the whole spectrum of spreads' quantiles using quantile regression. However, sensitivity can also vary in time. We display in Figure 2.30 the output of different $FLS(\mu)$ filters ranging from a reactive and highly volatile sensitivity pattern (μ = 1) to a more stable sensitivity path (μ = 100). In the former case, the sensitivity features some abrupt changes and moves from negative to positive territories before reverting back. It captures local dynamics that least-square estimator or smoother FLS fail to detect.

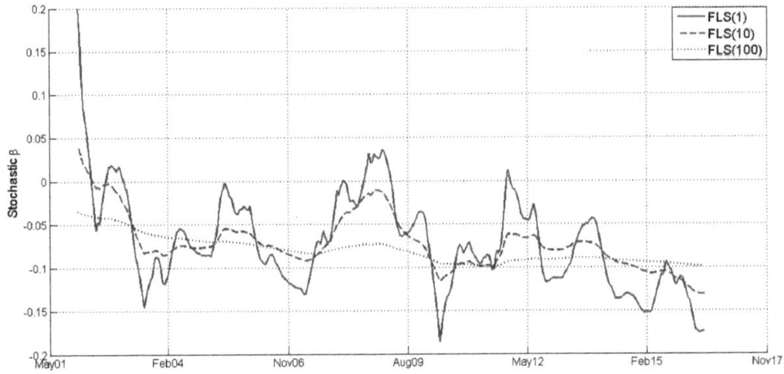

Figure 2.30. *Time-varying sensitivity of relative spreads' variation of the Bloomberg Barclays Euro Credit Corporates index to German 3-5 Yr rates' movements as recovered using different FLS filters with different μ parameters*

2.3.2. *State-space models with regime switching*

SSMs with regime switching were introduced by [HAM 89] in order to account for some types of non-stationarity in linear models due to structural breaks (see section 5.3.1, p. 312 for an illustration. Hamilton expands the KF by incorporating regime switching for serially dependent data. The Markovian switching mechanism was first considered by [GOL 73]. [HAM 94] presented a thorough analysis of the Markov switching model and its estimation method. [KIM 99] provided an in-depth analysis for MS-SSM and their related estimation methods.

In what follows, we investigate regime switching means and variance models for serially uncorrelated data. Using a two-step prediction-updating filter, the likelihood can be expressed and parameters can be estimated. The case of serially correlated data is examined a second time. They can be inferred using the Hamilton filter. Finally, we present the general case of MS-SSM where regime switching affects all of the SSM parameters including the transition and observation matrices. This results in an increased mathematical and computational complexity. The likelihood can be approximated using [KIM 94] filter. [KIM 08] developed a parsimonious model of endogenous Markov regime switching. Their model nests the exogenous switching models presented hereafter.

2.3.2.1. *Regime switching for uncorrelated data*

Consider the following regime-switching model:

$$Y_t = \mu_{S_t} + \epsilon_t \qquad [2.16]$$

where $\epsilon_t \rightsquigarrow \mathcal{N}(0, \sigma^2_{S_t})$ and $\mu_{S_t} \in \mathbb{R}$ is a parameter. Structural breaks in parameters occur when $S_t \in \{1, \dots, j, \dots, J\}$ switches from one regime into another. Conditional to the current regime $S_t = j$, we have:

$$\mathbb{E}[Y_t \mid S_t = j] = \mu_j,$$
$$\mathbb{V}[Y_t \mid S_t = j] = \sigma_j^2.$$

The conditional density of y_t, given $S_t = j$ denoted by $f(y_t \mid S_t = j)$ is then equal to $\mathcal{N}(\mu_j, \sigma_j^2)$. If S_t is perfectly observable, then the model parameters $\theta = (\mu_1, \sigma_1^2, \dots, \mu_J, \sigma_J^2,)$ can be easily estimated by maximizing the likelihood of the observed sample $y_{1:T} = (y_1, \dots, y_T)$:

$$L_T(\theta) = \prod_{t=1}^{T} f(y_t \mid S_t).$$

The estimation problem is less trivial when S_t is not observed. Following [KIM 99], the rule of thumb for determining the likelihood expression, consists of computing the conditional density of Y_t given S_t and then to integrate S_t out of it:

$$\begin{aligned} f(y_t \mid y_{1:t-1}) &= \sum_{j=1}^{J} f(y_t, S_t = j \mid y_{1:t-1}) \\ &= \sum_{j=1}^{J} f(y_t \mid S_t = j, y_{1:t-1}) \mathbb{P}(S_t = j \mid y_{1:t-1}) \\ &= \sum_{j=1}^{J} \frac{1}{\sqrt{2\pi\sigma_j^2}} \exp\left(-\frac{(y_t - \mu_j)^2}{2\sigma_j^2}\right) \mathbb{P}(S_t = j \mid y_{1:t-1}). \end{aligned}$$

This marginal density corresponds to the weighted average of the conditional densities, with weighting factors given by the probabilities of regimes. The recovered likelihood depends on the set of parameters θ^* corresponding to θ and parameters steering the probabilities of regimes:

$$L_T(\theta^*) = \prod_{t=1}^{T} \left[\sum_{j=1}^{J} f(y_t \mid S_t = j, y_{1:t-1}) \mathbb{P}(S_t = j \mid y_{1:t-1}) \right]. \qquad [2.17]$$

In order to determine this likelihood, the probabilities of the regimes $\mathbb{P}(S_t = j \mid y_{1:t-1})$ need to be assessed. At this stage, it would be useful to assume that the discrete random variable S_t follows a Markov Switching (henceforth MS) process. For convenience, a first-order MS process is presumed with transition matrix $p = (p_{ij})$, where $p_{ij} = \mathbb{P}(S_t = j \mid S_{t-1} = i)$. S_t being unobserved, the weighting factors $\mathbb{P}(S_t = j \mid y_{1:t-1})$ can be filtered following a two-step prediction-updating procedure:

1) Prediction step: the prediction of S_t given available information at $t-1$ is computed as follows:

$$\begin{aligned} \mathbb{P}(S_t = j \mid y_{1:t-1}) &= \sum_{i=1}^{J} \mathbb{P}(S_t = j, S_{t-1} = i \mid y_{1:t-1}) \\ &= \sum_{i=1}^{J} \mathbb{P}(S_t = j \mid S_{t-1} = i, y_{1:t-1}) \mathbb{P}(S_{t-1} = i \mid y_{1:t-1}) \\ &= \sum_{i=1}^{J} p_{ij} \mathbb{P}(S_{t-1} = i \mid y_{1:t-1}). \end{aligned}$$

2) Updating step: the updating of the probability following the observation of y_t is:

$$\begin{aligned} \mathbb{P}(S_t = j \mid y_{1:t}) &= \mathbb{P}(S_t = j \mid y_t, y_{1:t-1}) \\ &= \frac{f(y_t, S_t = j \mid y_{1:t-1})}{f(y_t \mid y_{1:t-1})} \\ &= \frac{f(y_t \mid S_t = j, y_{1:t-1}) \mathbb{P}(S_t = j \mid y_{1:t-1})}{\sum_{j=1}^{J} f(y_t \mid S_t = j, y_{1:t-1}) \mathbb{P}(S_t = j \mid y_{1:t-1})}. \end{aligned}$$

Recursively applying this procedure, given some initial conditions for the probabilities of S_0, allows us to express the likelihood 2.17 as a function of the set of parameters θ^*. Initial probabilities $\mathbb{P}(S_0 = j)$ can be defined as the unconditional probabilities or the steady-state ones given by:

$$\mathbb{P}(S_0 = j) = \sum_{i=1}^{J} p_{ij} \mathbb{P}(S_0 = i).$$

NUMERICAL EXAMPLE 2.12 (Gaussian Mixture).– Let (Y_t) be a real process whose value at time t depends on the regime $j \in \{1,2,3\}$ of a hidden first-order Markov process S_t whose transition probabilities $\mathbb{P}(S_t = j \mid S_{t-1} = i) = p_{ij}$ for all $i, j \in \{1,2,3\}$, are given by:

$$p = \begin{pmatrix} p_{11} & p_{12} & 1 - p_{33} - p_{23} \\ p_{21} & p_{22} & p_{23} \\ 1 - p_{11} - p_{21} & 1 - p_{12} - p_{22} & p_{33} \end{pmatrix}.$$

We assume that the process (Y_t) is a mixture of Gaussian variables whose means and variances are regime-dependent: $\epsilon_{S_t=j} \rightsquigarrow \mathcal{N}(\mu_j, \sigma_j^2)$. The process (Y_t) can thus be expressed as follows:

$$Y_t = \sum_{j=1}^{3} \mathbb{1}_{[S_t=j]} \epsilon_{S_t}.$$

The model parameters are:

$$\theta = \left(\mu_1, \sigma_1^2, \mu_2, \sigma_2^2, \mu_3, \sigma_3^2, p_{11}, p_{21}, p_{22}, p_{12}, p_{33}, p_{23}\right).$$

Given initial values, the likelihood is written:

$$L_T(\theta) = \prod_{t=1}^{T} \left(\sum_{j=1}^{3} \frac{1}{\sqrt{2\Pi\sigma_j^2}} \exp\left(-\frac{1}{2} \frac{(y_t - \mu_j)^2}{\sigma_j^2} \right) \times \pi_{t|t-1}^{j} \right)$$

where $\pi_{t|t-1}^{j} = \mathbb{P}(S_t = j \mid y_{1:t-1})$ is the projected conditional probability of $S_t = j$ given information up to $t-1$. Denoting by $\pi_{t|t-1} = \left(\pi_{t|t-1}^{1}, \pi_{t|t-1}^{2}, \pi_{t|t-1}^{3}\right)'$ the vector of regime probabilities, we have:

$$\pi_{t|t-1} = p'.\pi_{t-1|t-1}$$

Once y_t is observed, the regime probability can be updated using the following equation:

$$\pi_{t|t} = \frac{\pi_{t|t-1} \odot D_t}{\sum_{j=1}^{3} \pi_{t|t-1}^{j} \odot D_t^{j}}, \qquad [2.18]$$

with $D_t = \left(D_t^1, D_t^2, D_t^3\right)'$ denoting the vector of the densities of y_t for each regime j:

$$D_t = \left(\frac{1}{\sqrt{2\Pi\sigma_i^2}} e^{-\frac{1}{2}\frac{(y_t-\mu_i)^2}{\sigma_i^2}} \right)_{i\in[1;3]}.$$

And ⊙ the element by element product. The denominator of equation [2.18] is the likelihood to maximize. We simulate (Y_t) conditional to a given path of (S_t) with the following set of parameters:

$$\left(\mu_1 = 0, \sigma_1^2 = 1, \mu_2 = 5, \sigma_2^2 = 1.5^2, \mu_3 = 10, \sigma_3^2 = 2^2\right).$$

Maximizing the log-likelihood provides the following estimates for the Gaussian densities and the transition probabilities:

$$\left(\hat{\mu}_1 = -0.03, \hat{\sigma}_1^2 = 0.98^2, \hat{\mu}_2 = 4.85, \hat{\sigma}_2^2 = 1.38^2, \hat{\mu}_3 = 10.11, \hat{\sigma}_3^2 = 2.18^2\right),$$

$$\hat{p} = \begin{pmatrix} 0.95 & 0.02 & 0.02 \\ 0.02 & 0.93 & 0.03 \\ 0.03 & 0.03 & 0.94 \end{pmatrix}.$$

Simulated process (Y_t) and the estimated probabilities for regime 3 are shown in Figure 2.31.

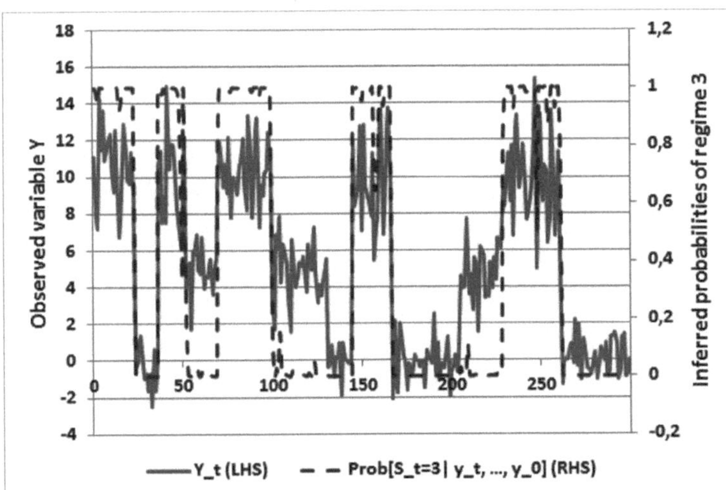

Figure 2.31. *Simulated process (Y_t) and inferred probabilities for regime 3*

2.3.2.2. *Regime switching for serially correlated data: the Hamilton filter*

In the previous section, the conditional likelihood of observation y_t given information up to $t-1$ depended on an unobserved variable S_t. In the current section, we examine the case of a likelihood depending not only on the current state but also on previous ones. For this, consider a Markov switching mean and variance autoregressive process of order 1. The model is written:

$$(Y_t - \mu_{S_t}) = \phi(Y_{t-1} - \mu_{S_{t-1}}) + \epsilon_{S_t},$$

with the autoregression coefficient such that $|\ \phi\ | < 1$, $\epsilon_t \rightsquigarrow \mathcal{N}(0, \sigma^2_{S_t})$ and $(\mu_{S_t}, \mu_{S_{t-1}}) \in \mathbb{R}^2$ are two parameters. S_t is a $J-$state Markov process of order one, with J a non-negative integer and $p_{(J\times J)}$ the corresponding transition matrix. Conditional on observations up to time $t-1$ and given the current and previous regimes, $S_t = j$ and $S_{t-1} = i$, we have:

$$\mathbb{E}[Y_t \mid y_{1:t-1}, S_t = j, S_{t-1} = i] = \mu_j + \phi(y_{t-1} - \mu_i),$$
$$\mathbb{V}[Y_t \mid y_{1:t-1}, S_t = j, S_{t-1} = i] = \sigma^2_j.$$

The conditional density of y_t, given $S_t = j$ and $S_{t-1} = i$, denoted by $f(y_t \mid S_t = j, S_{t-1} = i)$, is thus equal to $\mathcal{N}(\mu_j + \phi(y_{t-1} - \mu_i), \sigma^2_j)$.

Similar to the rule of thumb used in the previous section for deriving the likelihood expression, we compute the joint density of the observed variable and the unobserved one and then integrate the latter out of it. However, in our example Y_t depends not only on the current value of S_t but also on the previous one S_{t-1}. Therefore, we need to compute the joint density of Y_t, S_t, S_{t-1} and integrate (S_t, S_{t-1}) out of it.

The density of y_t conditional to information up to $t-1$ is written:

$$\begin{aligned} f(y_t \mid y_{1:t-1}) &= \sum_{j=1}^{J}\sum_{i=1}^{J} f(y_t, S_t = j, S_{t-1} = i \mid y_{1:t-1}) \\ &= \sum_{j=1}^{J}\sum_{i=1}^{J} f(y_t \mid S_t = j, S_{t-1} = i, y_{1:t-1})\mathbb{P}(S_t = j, S_{t-1} = i \mid y_{1:t-1}) \\ &= \sum_{j=1}^{J}\sum_{i=1}^{J} \frac{1}{\sqrt{2\pi\sigma^2_j}} \exp\left(-\frac{[y_t - \mu_j - \phi(y_{t-1} - \mu_i)]^2}{2\sigma^2_j}\right) \\ &\quad \mathbb{P}(S_t = j, S_{t-1} = i \mid y_{1:t-1}). \end{aligned}$$

The marginal density $f(y_t \mid y_{1:t-1})$ is a weighted average of J^2 conditional densities. The likelihood is therefore written as:

$$L_T(\theta^*) = \prod_{t=1}^{T}\left[\sum_{j=1}^{J}\sum_{i=1}^{J} f(y_t \mid S_t = j, S_{t-1} = i, y_{1:t-1})\mathbb{P}(S_t = j, S_{t-1} = i \mid y_{1:t-1})\right]. \quad [2.19]$$

Therefore, we need to calculate $\mathbb{P}(S_t = j, S_{t-1} = i \mid y_{1:t-1})$ in order to recover the likelihood $L_T(\theta^*)$. This can be done by applying the following two-step prediction-updating algorithm:

1) Prediction step: predicting the probability of $(S_t = j, S_{t-1} = i)$ given information up to time $t-1$:

$$\begin{aligned}\mathbb{P}(S_t = j, S_{t-1} = i \mid y_{1:t-1}) &= \mathbb{P}(S_t = j \mid S_{t-1} = i, y_{1:t-1})\mathbb{P}(S_{t-1} = i \mid y_{1:t-1}) \\ &= p_{ij}\mathbb{P}(S_{t-1} = i \mid y_{1:t-1}).\end{aligned}$$

2) Updating step: updating the probability of $(S_t = j, S_{t-1} = i)$ following the occurrence of y_t at time t:

$$\begin{aligned}&\mathbb{P}(S_t = j, S_{t-1} = i \mid y_{1:t}) = \mathbb{P}(S_t = j, S_{t-1} = i \mid y_t, y_{1:t-1}) \\ &= \frac{f(y_t, S_t = j, S_{t-1} = i \mid y_{1:t-1})}{f(y_t \mid y_{1:t-1})} \\ &= \frac{f(y_t \mid S_t = j, S_{t-1} = i, y_{1:t-1})\mathbb{P}(S_t = j, S_{t-1} = i \mid y_{1:t-1})}{\sum_{j=1}^{J}\sum_{i=1}^{J} f(y_t \mid S_t = j, S_{t-1} = i, y_{1:t-1})\mathbb{P}(S_t = j, S_{t-1} = i \mid y_{1:t-1})},\end{aligned}$$

with:

$$\mathbb{P}(S_t = j \mid y_{1:t}) = \sum_{i=1}^{J} \mathbb{P}(S_t = j, S_{t-1} = i \mid y_{1:t}).$$

Iterating these two steps for $t \in \{1, \ldots, T\}$ provides us with required weights for the likelihood expression 2.19. Initial probabilities are derived as steady-state ones.

2.3.2.3. *State-space models with Markov switching: the Kim filter*

Regime switching can affect not only means and variances of serially dependent data but also the autoregressive coefficients. Transposing this into the SSM framework implies that transition and observation matrices can also be subject to structural breaks in addition to those hitting the errors and vectors C and D. The MS-SSM expression is written:

$$\begin{aligned}X_t &= M_{S_t} X_{t-1} + C_{S_t} + v_t, \\ Y_t &= O_{S_t} X_t + D_{S_t} + w_t,\end{aligned}$$

where $S_t \in \{1, 2, \ldots, j, \ldots, J\}$ is a $J-$state MS variable with transition probabilities $p_{ij} = \mathbb{P}(S_t = j \mid S_{t-1} = i)$. Errors are assumed to be Gaussian:

$$\begin{pmatrix} v_t \\ w_t \end{pmatrix} \rightsquigarrow \mathcal{N}\left(\begin{pmatrix} 0 \\ 0 \end{pmatrix}, \begin{pmatrix} Q_{S_t} & 0 \\ 0 & H_{S_t} \end{pmatrix}\right).$$

For the estimation of this model, we use the Kim filter (see [KIM 94]). It combines the Kalman filter with the Hamilton filter and a collapsing procedure. The Kim filter is an optimal estimator in the sense that no other estimator based on a linear function of the information set yields a smaller mean square error. A detailed discussion of the Kim filter can be found in [KIM 94] and [KIM 99].

In MS-SSM framework, the prediction of the state vector x_t is done conditionally not only on $y_{1:t-1}$ but also on $S_t = j$ and $S_{t-1} = i$:

$$x^{ij}_{t|t-1} = \mathbb{E}[X_t \mid y_{1:t-1}, S_t = j, S_{t-1} = i].$$

At each time t, $J \times J$ different forecasts and $J \times J$ different variances $P^{ij}_{t|t-1} = \mathbb{V}[X_t \mid y_{1:t-1}, S_t = j, S_{t-1} = i]$ are produced, one for each regime pair (i, j). Applying the KF for pair (i, j) gives:

1) Prediction step at time $t - 1$:

– $x^{ij}_{t|t-1} = \mathbb{E}[X_t \mid y_{1:t-1}, S_t = j, S_{t-1} = i] = M_j x^{i}_{t-1|t-1} + C_j$,

– $P^{ij}_{t|t-1} = \mathbb{V}[X_t \mid y_{1:t-1}, S_t = j, S_{t-1} = i] = M_j P^{i}_{t-1|t-1} M_j' + Q_j$,

– $y^{ij}_{t|t-1} = \mathbb{E}[Y_t \mid y_{1:t-1}, S_t = j, S_{t-1} = i] = O_j x^{ij}_{t|t-1} + D_j$,

– $V^{ij}_{t|t-1} = \mathbb{V}[Y_t \mid y_{1:t-1}, S_t = j, S_{t-1} = i] = O_j P^{ij}_{t|t-1} O_j' + H_j$.

2) Updating step at time t:

– $\eta^{ij}_t = (y_t - y^{ij}_{t|t-1})$,

– $\mathcal{K}^{ij}_t = P^{ij}_{t|t-1} O_j' (V^{ij}_{t|t-1})^{-1}$,

– $x^{ij}_{t|t} = x^{ij}_{t|t-1} + \mathcal{K}^{ij}_t \eta^{ij}_t$,

– $P^{ij}_{t|t} = P^{ij}_{t|t-1} - \mathcal{K}^{ij}_t V^{ij}_{t|t-1} (\mathcal{K}^{ij}_t)'$.

The expression of the *Kalman Gain Matrix*, as well as the updated state vector and variance, also becomes dependent on pair (i, j). This leads to a drastic increase in the number of cases to consider as we move in time while iterating the prediction-updating algorithm over all possible pairs (i, j). One possible solution consists of reducing the number of cases by collapsing the $(J \times J)$ updates $x^{ij}_{t|t}$ and $P^{ij}_{t|t}$ into J posteriors $x^{j}_{t|t}$ and $P^{j}_{t|t}$ at the end of each iteration, so that the KF computations become feasible. The obtained posteriors in this way are given by:

$$x^{j}_{t|t} = \mathbb{E}[X_t \mid y_{1:t-1}, S_t = j] = \frac{\sum_{i=1}^{J} \mathbb{P}\left(S_{t-1} = i, S_t = j \mid y_{1:t}\right) x^{ij}_{t|t}}{\mathbb{P}\left(S_t = j \mid y_{1:t}\right)},$$

$$P^j_{t|t} = \mathbb{V}[X_t \mid y_t, S_t = j]$$
$$= \frac{\sum_{i=1}^{J} \mathbb{P}\left(S_{t-1} = i, S_t = j \mid y_{1:t}\right)\left[P^{ij}_{t|t} + (x^{ij}_{t|t} - x^j_{t|t})(x^{ij}_{t|t} - x^j_{t|t})'\right]}{\mathbb{P}\left(S_t = j \mid y_{1:t}\right)}.$$

Completing the filter and recovering $x^j_{t|t}$ and $P^j_{t|t}$ series requires computing the probabilities appearing in their respective expressions. This can be achieved by applying the following two-step procedure:

1) At time $t-1$, given $\mathbb{P}(S_{t-1} = i \mid y_{1:t-1})$, write the joint density of $(y_t, S_t = j, S_{t-1} = i)$:

$$f(y_t, S_t = j, S_{t-1} = i \mid y_{1:t-1})$$
$$= f(y_t \mid S_t = j, S_{t-1} = i, y_{1:t-1})\mathbb{P}(S_t = j, S_{t-1} = i \mid y_{1:t-1})$$
$$= f(y_t \mid S_t = j, S_{t-1} = i, y_{1:t-1})\mathbb{P}(S_{t-1} = i \mid y_{1:t-1})p_{ij}.$$

The marginal density $f(y_t \mid y_{1:t-1})$ can thus be obtained by summing S_t and S_{t-1} out of the joint density $f(y_t, S_t = j, S_{t-1} = i \mid y_{1:t-1})$:

$$f(y_t \mid y_{1:t-1}) = \sum_{i=1}^{J}\sum_{j=1}^{J} f(y_t \mid S_t = j, S_{t-1} = i, y_{1:t-1})\mathbb{P}(S_t = j, S_{t-1} = i \mid y_{1:t-1})$$
$$= \sum_{i=1}^{J}\sum_{j=1}^{J}\left(\frac{1}{\sqrt{(2\pi)^N \det(V^{ij}_{t|t-1})}} \exp\left(-\frac{1}{2}\eta^{ij}_t (V^{ij}_{t|t-1})^{-1}\eta^{ij}_t\right)\right)$$
$$\mathbb{P}(S_{t-1} = i \mid y_{1:t-1})p_{ij}.$$

2) Updating regime probabilities after observing y_t:

$$\mathbb{P}(S_t = j, S_{t-1} = i \mid y_{1:t}) = f(S_t = j, S_{t-1} = i \mid y_t, y_{1:t-1})$$
$$= \frac{f(y_t, S_t = j, S_{t-1} = i \mid y_{1:t-1})}{f(y_t \mid y_{1:t-1})}$$
$$= \frac{f(y_t \mid S_t = j, S_{t-1} = i, y_{1:t-1})\mathbb{P}(S_t = j, S_{t-1} = i \mid y_{1:t-1})}{f(y_t \mid y_{1:t-1})}$$
$$= \frac{f(y_t \mid S_t = j, S_{t-1} = i, y_{1:t-1})\mathbb{P}(S_{t-1} = i \mid y_{1:t-1})p_{ij}}{f(y_t \mid y_{1:t-1})}.$$

and $\mathbb{P}(S_t = j \mid y_{1:t}) = \sum_{i=1}^{J} \mathbb{P}(S_t = j, S_{t-1} = i \mid y_{1:t})$

The initial parameters for Kalman and Hamilton filters are derived as previously shown. As explained in [KIM 99], one should bear in mind that this filter relies on approximations in posteriors $x_j^{t|t}$ and $P_{t|t}^j$.

NUMERICAL EXAMPLE 2.13 (Dynamic Nelson-Siegel term structure model with regime switching).– Many argue that the dynamics of the rate curve is subject to structural breaks that can be captured by regime-switching models, with or without arbitrage constraints or macroeconomic variables, see [HEV 14], [ZHU 15], [XIA 13], [MON 07a]. Following [BER 05a] and [NYH 07], we extend the example 2.10 on p. 119 by allowing the slope mean to switch values. Three regimes are identified for the UK sovereign curve (see Figure 2.32): normal, steep, inverse. The SSM expression of the regime-switching model is:

$$\begin{aligned} F_t &= MF_{t-1} + \bar{F}^{S_t} + v_t, \\ X_t &= BF_t + w_t, \end{aligned}$$

under the usual Gaussian noises assumption:

$$\begin{pmatrix} v_t \\ w_t \end{pmatrix} \rightsquigarrow \mathcal{N}\left(\begin{pmatrix} 0 \\ 0 \end{pmatrix}, \begin{pmatrix} Q & 0 \\ 0 & H \end{pmatrix}\right).$$

$\bar{F}^{S_t}$ is a (3×1) vector of the factors' mean. In the current specification, only the slope mean changes in cases of regime switching in the first-order Markovian process (S_t) with transition matrix $p_{(3\times3)}$. Given regime j, the factors' mean vector is:

$$\bar{F}^j = \begin{pmatrix} \bar{F}_1 \\ \bar{F}_2^j \\ \bar{F}_3 \end{pmatrix}$$

At each time t, we run the two-step Kalman filter for each regime $j \in \{1, 2, 3\}$, after which we reduce the outcomes of each regime into a weighted average, with the probabilities of the regimes as weighting components:

Predicting given information available at time $t - 1$:

$$\begin{aligned} f_{t|t-1}^j &= Mf_{t-1|t-1} + \bar{F}^j, \\ P_{t|t-1} &= MP_{t-1|t-1}M' + Q, \\ x_{t|t-1}^j &= Bf_{t|t-1}^j, \\ V_{t|t-1} &= BP_{t|t-1}B' + H. \end{aligned}$$

Updating after observing the rates x_t:

$$\eta_t^j = x_t - x_{t|t-1}^j,$$
$$\mathcal{K}_t = P_{t|t-1} B' V_{t|t-1},$$
$$f_{t|t}^j = f_{t|t-1}^j + \mathcal{K}_t \eta_t^j,$$
$$P_{t|t} = P_{t|t-1} - \mathcal{K}_t B P_{t|t-1}.$$

The updated factors $f_{t|t}$ are computed as weighted averages of the regime-dependent ones $(f_{t|t}^j)$:

$$f_{t|t} = \sum_{j=1}^{3} \pi_{t|t}^j \times f_{t|t}^j,$$

with weights given by the following equation:

$$\pi_{t|t} = \frac{\pi_{t|t-1} \odot D_t}{\mathbb{1}'(\pi_{t|t-1} \odot D_t)}.$$

$\pi_{t|t-1}$ denotes the probability of regimes conditional to information up to $t - 1$. As (S_t) is a first-order Markov process, it can be projected one step ahead by multiplying the updated probabilities by the transition matrix:

$$\pi_{t+1|t} = p\pi_{t|t}.$$

Again, the likelihood corresponds to the denominator of the regime probabilities updating equation:

$$\mathbb{1}'(\pi_{t|t-1} \odot D_t).$$

Parameters are estimated by maximizing the log-likelihood. The Nelson-Siegel slope factor (F_2) as well as the inferred probabilities of regimes are plotted in Figure 2.32.

The SSM framework encompasses a large variety of models, from the standard time series models such as AR, MA or $ARCH$ to more elaborated approaches with hidden components and structural breaks. It makes it possible to forecast both observable and unobserved components. When choosing the suitable model, specification should balance the in-sample explanatory power with the out of sample prediction performance. While some tests provide guidance for practitioners, we believe that forecasting is much more of an art than it is a science.

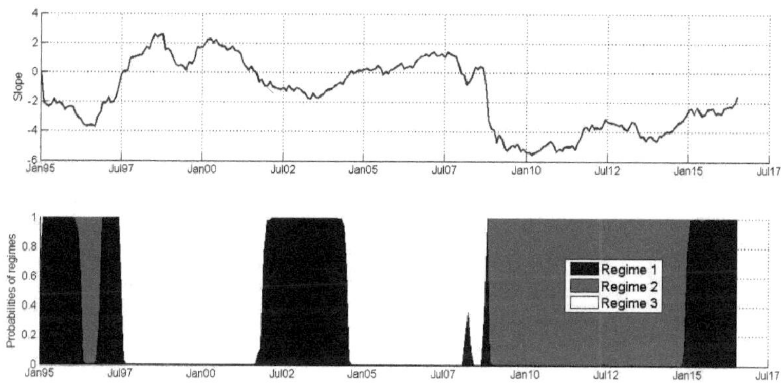

Figure 2.32. *The Nelson-Siegel slope factor F_2 for the GBP zero coupon curve between January 1995 and July 2016 and its probability of the three regimes.*

2.4. The liquidity risk factor

Market risk and liquidity risk are by far the main sources of uncertainty affecting a portfolio's future P&L. While the former can be explained by uncertainty regarding price fluctuations, the latter is incurred when trading assets. Under the market completeness and perfection assumptions, the financial theory does not explicitly account for liquidity risk, and rather assumes that investors could buy and sell significant position sizes without affecting market prices. As a consequence, securities are priced and their risk is measured at the mid-price irrespective of any friction stemming from liquidity. However, in nervous markets, liquidity recedes and the bid price prevails. Such circumstances call into question the notion of mark to market, as it no longer reflects a "fair" price[18].

Financial history is filled with liquidity crises. During the 1998 LTCM crisis, hedge fund positions had grown so large that it was impossible to liquidate them without significant price impact. More recently, in the 2007-2008 financial crisis, widespread liquidity shortage forced banks to reduce exposures by liquidating assets. Many asset managers became forced sellers to meet outflows and margin calls. Prices dropped as liquidity melted. [AMI 91a] posited that a change in investor perception of liquidity risk would push them to price securities at lower levels, which could result in a crash akin to October 1987. The root of liquidity risk lies in information asymmetries and the existence of incomplete markets, which lead to adverse selection and moral hazard situations. It follows that in order to reduce systematic liquidity risk, transparency and

18 The valuation of illiquid instruments is, for instance, addressed by [GUÉ 10].

information flow should be enhanced. Nonetheless, this could be a very expensive strategy that requires a long time before being fully operational.

2.4.1. *Liquidity: a multiform and heterogeneous concept*

When talking about liquidity, some caution is required as the nature of risk is not the same when analyzed on a global macro economic level, on a corporate level or on a specific asset level. From a broad economic perspective, liquidity risk is the ability of economic agents to exchange their wealth into goods (see [WIL 08] cited in [NIK 09] p.10). Liquidity is thus a flow notion (in contrast to the notion of stock). Illiquidity arises in the case of inability of exchanging. When money lacks in the overall economy, transactions and thus activity slow down.

Banks finance the economy through lending operations. By doing so, they boost the economic activity by supporting investment and consumption. However, banks have to meet some legal obligations in terms of reserve requirements, which create a global deficit in liquidity. Banks rely on central banks to offset this liquidity deficit and to get refinanced. Central banks can improve (or sterilize) global liquidity of the economy by acting on the monetary base through open market operations in a way to keep the interbank lending rates close to its target rate. The latter is a tool used to monitor the overall liquidity with respect to certain objectives, for example, inflation and/or growth. From a theoretical perspective, asymmetrical information hinders exchanges leading to illiquidity and market incompleteness. Central banks play an important role in managing liquidity crises. According to [NIK 09]:

> "*The central bank can act as an immediate but temporary buffer to liquidity shocks, thereby allowing time for supervision and regulation to confront the causes of liquidity risk.*" — [NIK 09]

From a corporate perspective, liquidity denotes the solvability of the firm, for example, the net liquidity of assets and liabilities. When assets' cash flows are no longer sufficient to cover liabilities, the firm faces a credit event that may lead to bankruptcy. Default risk varies from one country to another according to the economic cycle. It depends also on the sector and other factors. From a market perspective, investors are concerned with asset liquidity issues generally defined by [AMI 06] as the ease of trading the asset.

2.4.2. *Sources and characteristics of illiquidity*

Liquidity is an elusive notion, not only because it applies to different levels of the economy with complex linkages but also because it is a multi-dimensional concept that is difficult to capture in a single measure and thus to model. Liquidity is therefore subtle to define. Even if exogenous measures of liquidity can be computed, the notion itself is tightly linked to the notion of information and strongly depends on the timescale on which we try to study liquidity. Even on a single asset level, liquidity appears as a heterogeneous concept. [BRU 09] distinguished asset's market liquidity from trader's funding liquidity. While the former designates the ease of trading the asset in terms of transaction costs, the latter denotes the ease of finding funding in terms of costs such as capital requirement and margin calls. The two types of liquidity are positively related as the funding costs depend on the asset market liquidity. The term liquidity risk has a negative connotation as it implies costs and losses[19]. The cost of liquidity when trading an asset is typically captured by the bid-ask spread. This spread, at least from the market maker perspective, can be broken into two components:

– the *effective spread*, which compensates the market maker for insuring the liquidity of the market and corresponds to the technology and inventory costs incurred by the market maker;

– the *information spread*, which compensates the market makers for potential losses they may incur when taking an uninformed bet. As they cannot distinguish informed from uninformed bets, they might well be "the opposite side" of an informed order in their role of insuring market liquidity.

[AMI 06] split liquidity costs into three components:

– *direct trading costs*: deterministic transaction costs encompassing brokerage commissions, transaction taxes and exchange fees;

– *price impact costs*: correspond to the difference between the executed price and the mid-price. It is limited to (half) the bid-ask spread for small orders but can exceed this spread for higher positions. When trading a small position, a single counter party is sufficient to execute the order at the best price. As the size of the position increases, many counter parties are required to absorb the order, each with different beliefs about the fair value of the asset, which leads to a lower price;

– *search and delay costs*: incurred when traders delay the execution and search for a better execution price than the one "displayed" by the bid-ask spread. By doing so, traders undertake the risk of seeing the market move by the time they decide to execute their order. This trade-off between price impact costs and seeing the market move is particularly relevant for block orders.

By denoting a liquid market as one in which every agent can buy and sell a large quantity rapidly at low cost at any time, [HAR 90a] distinguished four interrelated dimensions for liquidity:

---

19 Negative basis strategy, e.g. when a CDS is lower than the underlying bond's spread, is a typical counterexample where liquidity offers very attractive risk reward opportunity for investors.

– *width,* which measures the cost incurred by a round trip transaction, for example, by instantaneously buying and selling a position. The incurred costs correspond thus to the price impact costs and direct trading costs;

– *depth,* which is the number of shares that can be traded at a given price without incurring additional costs above the bid-ask spread. According to [BAN 99], up to the quote spread, liquidity costs are exogenous as the market is able to absorb the position. The quote applies to all market participants irrespective of their characteristics. For higher positions, liquidity costs are assumed endogenous[20] as they are supposed to be specific to the individual trade position;

– *immediacy,* which captures how quickly positions can be traded and corresponds to the time between placing the order and its settlement;

– *resiliency,* which indicates the ability of the market to absorb random shocks, for example, uninformative orders.

In addition, [ALM 00] stresses the importance of distinguishing temporary price impact from permanent impact when determining the optimal execution of portfolio transactions in a dynamical liquidity framework. We will refine those notions to include costs in the optimization setting for portfolio allocation in section 3.7.1 p. 235. [STA 09] argues that liquidity is a continuous characteristic and distinguishes four degrees of liquidity according to the liquidity costs they incur, the cost of liquidity increasing with illiquidity in a nonlinear way:

– costless trading when any position can be traded without any cost;

– continuous trading when most of the orders are executed at a certain cost;

– interrupted trading when some orders are executed from time to time;

– no trading when the market is completely illiquid.

2.4.3. *Liquidity and asset classes*

Those degrees of liquidity depend on the asset type, the size of the position and the liquidation horizon. Exchanging cash is a costless trading as it does not require any value adjustment. Exotic securities are traded interruptedly while some structured credit products like CDO and ABS were typical illiquid asset during the 2008 financial crisis. Illiquidity increases with the size of the position. It occurs in the short term but vanishes over a longer horizon. Typically a security held to maturity has no liquidity cost. This differentiation is useful when selecting an appropriate method to incorporate liquidity adjustment and determine the fair value prices according to the degree of liquidity of the market (see [GAR 13a]).

20 The distinction between exogenous and endogenous liquidity is challenged by [STA 09] who argue that the whole price impact curve is exogenous because it is determined by the market.

Turning to equities, the need for a definition also arises through the study of the stylized facts of correlations between returns, squared returns and volumes (see in particular the discussion in [DAR 15]). The contributions on the subject are numerous and are roughly of three main natures. A first stream of literature is related to the risky nature of liquidity, both at a security level and the market level. Contributions in this field underline in particular its time-varying nature. Among others, [AMI 90], [HUB 01], [CHO 00] and [HAS 01] support this evidence. A second and wide-ranging subject in the literature deals with models that are able to link liquidity to price changes and returns. Contributions in this direction are numerous and include [AMI 86], [BRE 96], [PÁS 03], [ACH 05] and [KOR 08]. In particular [AMI 02], [CHO 01] and [BEK 07] identify how liquidity helps to explain future returns. A third and last subject when dealing with liquidity is the identification of the notion of information in the trading (see, e.g., [EAS 96]). The general idea is that volumes and activity should be related to either information-initiated trading or herding effects. In this respect, the notion of liquidity is sometimes treated as being exogenous or endogenous and academic works generally try to filter out the notion of information using models with latent variables. Two cornerstone contributions which help to understand the idea behind such an approach are [CLA 73] and [AND 96]. [CLA 73] studied the link between trading volume and volatility, by introducing a "*mixture of distribution*" hypothesis, i.e. a joint dependence of returns and volume on an unobserved, underlying variable modeling the information flow. In the same fashion, [AND 96] developed an empirical return volatility-volume model with a microstructure inspiration.

Still studying equities, empirically, there is a strong association between volatility and trading volume with a positive correlation between these two quantities ([CLA 73], [GAL 92], [AND 96], [ANE 00]). Compared to the volume itself, the number of trades seems to be even more correlated to volatility ([ANE 00]). This general picture is refined when the volatility definition is split as a sum between a continuous part and a jump component part. In this case, [GIO 10] found that the continuous component is positively correlated with volume, whereas the jump component is negatively correlated. The natural question that comes next is to know which kind of information lies behind each volatility component. It is believed that the negative correlation behind price jumps is related to public information ([WAN 12]) such as macroeconomic information ([AND 07]). The argument for this kind of link is that when public information is released, the consensus materializes quickly and the price change occurs without great trading activity. On the contrary, private information may need "*large trading to reveal itself*" ([WAN 12]). In short, diffusive volatility is associated with increased trading, but this is not the case for volatility linked to jumps. Jumps are believed in general to be driven by true, new information.

Except for contributions in the spirit of [AND 96], where the notion of liquidity is represented by an unobservable variable that has to be filtered out, exogenous and objective measures of liquidity on observable variables have to be defined. Because of the wide amount of literature on stock liquidity, there are many alternative measures. They generally use either market order data or daily data. For instance, to estimate liquidity, [AMI 86] used the bid-ask spread; [BRE 96] tried to interpret the link between order flow and changes in price and [PÁS 03] linked liquidity with the sensitivity of returns with respect to high volumes. [HOL 14] provided an empirical review of measures and challenges when studying stock liquidity. A short and complementary review is also available in [KOR 08] who also handle the general link between factors and liquidity.

2.4.4. *Measuring liquidity*

2.4.4.1. *Equities*

Following the previous discussions, we are interested here in examples of objective measures on observable data for individual stocks. Measures presented here are not our own, we rather compile the major ones that appear throughout the references we give throughout the paragraph. The work of [AMI 02] provided a measure of illiquidity (generally referred to as the acronym "*ILLIQ*") that diffused both among academics and practitioners. This measure is now quite famous and contributions of [BRE 13] or [ACH 05] review, and directly use this measure. For a given asset i, with observed returns $r_{i,t}$, the measure $ILLIQ_{i,t}$ is the average on a period T, of the absolute price change per dollar traded:

$$ILLIQ_{i,t} = \frac{1}{T} \sum_{t'=t-T+1}^{t} \frac{|r_i, t'|}{Dvol_{t'}},$$

where $Dvol_{t'}$ is the dollar value traded on a day t'. As $r_{i,t'}$ are dimensionless, the $ILLIQ$ measure has a $1/dollar$ dimension.

$ILLIQ$ is an illiquidity measure so one may find in the literature two related liquidity measures. The first one is to use $LIQ^{(1)}_{i,t} = 1/ILLIQ_{i,t}$. The other is to use the sum of the inverse terms, that is:

$$LIQ^{(2)}_{i,t} = \frac{1}{T} \sum_{t'=t-T+1}^{t} \frac{Dvol_{t'}}{|r_i, t'|}.$$

One possibility is to use the *turnover* that is the relative proportion of traded shares as a liquidity measure. Again, for an asset i, if we denote t', $v_{t'}$ and $s_{t'}$ for day, the volume of shares traded and the number of outstanding shares, respectively, it is possible to propose:

$$LIQ_{i,t}^{(3)} = \frac{1}{T} \sum_{t'=t-T+1}^{t} \frac{v_{t'}}{s_{t'}}.$$

Of course, it is possible to adapt $LIQ_{i,t}^{(3)}$ in various ways. For instance, it is possible to average the volume on the period but to consider only the number of outstanding shares at the end of the period:

$$LIQ_{i,t}^{(3)} = \frac{1}{T} \frac{\sum_{t'=t-T+1}^{t} v_{t'}}{s_t}.$$

These two measures appear empirically to have a bias that favors size. The solution may be to build a fourth measure by replacing in $LIQ_{i,t}^{(1,2)}$ the dollar-traded volume by the turnover (that is equivalent to $LIQ^{(3)}$). This idea is initially explored in [FLO 11] and handled also in [BRE 13], which even split this modified measure into signed measures: a positive and a negative one (see the original paper for more details).

The previous measures are based on daily data. We find in [KOR 08] two examples of measures based on trade data. The *quoted percentage spread* $Qspread$ is the mean of the spread scaled by the mid point. For an asset i, on the last observed T transactions $t' = 1, ..., T$, the $Qspread$ is:

$$Qspread_{i,t} = \frac{1}{T} \sum_{t=1}^{T} \frac{Ask_t - Bid_t}{Mid_t}$$

where $Mid_t = (Ask_t + Bid_t)/2$. Alternatively, [KOR 08] also defined the *effective quoted spread* $Espread$ which is the same except for the fact that the previous measure is modified in the following way:

$$Espread_{i,t} = \frac{1}{T} \sum_{t=1}^{T} \frac{p_t - Mid_t}{Mid_t}$$

where p_t is the effective transaction price for transaction t.

2.4.4.2. *Bonds*

As mentioned in [CHA 05], existing studies have focused on US equities due to data limitation and the sparse nature of the bond market. Extending equity liquidity measures to the bond market is not straightforward as they depend on bond intrinsic characteristics. Unlike stocks, bonds redeem. The liquidity of a 10-year bond is not the same as a 3-month one even for the same issuer. A traded volume-based liquidity measure can be quite misleading as a traded bond is not necessarily liquid, for example, forced selling and falling angels. And vice versa, bonds not traded are not necessary illiquid.

[DAS 09] introduced the liquidity cost score (LCS) to measure bond level liquidity. A bond's LCS represents the round-trip cost as a percentage of the bond's price of immediately executing a standard institutional transaction. Therefore, according to this definition, a lower LCS value denotes better liquidity. LCS is computed as follows:

$$LCS = \begin{cases} (\text{Bid spread} - \text{Ask spread}) \times \text{OASD} & \text{if the bond is spread quoted} \\ \dfrac{\text{Ask Price} - \text{Bid Price}}{\text{Bid Price}} & \text{if the bond is price quoted} \end{cases}$$

The liquidity on a security by security level improves with the issue size and the price. Higher LCS were concomitant to higher maturity issues, higher yield to maturity (YTM), Libor option adjusted spread (LOAS), duration and DTS. These findings suggest that liquidity risk is priced by the credit market, at least partially. Historical evolution of YTM and LCS for the Bloomberg-Barclays Euro Credit Corporates is depicted in Figure 2.33.

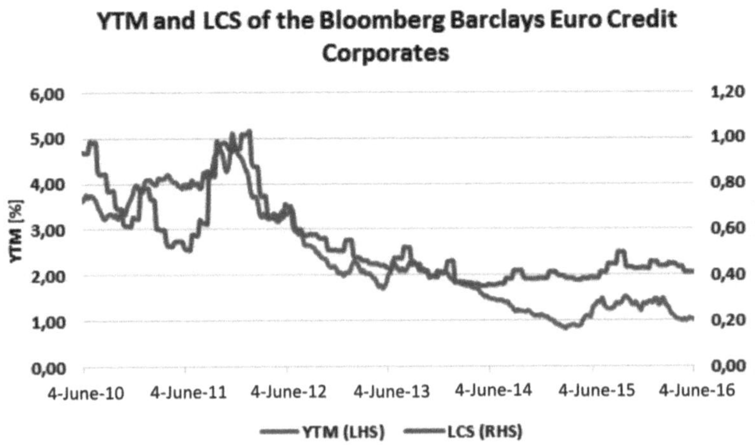

Figure 2.33. *YTM and LCS of the Bloomberg Barclays Euro Credit Corporates index.*

2.4.5. *The liquidity premium: empirical findings and theoretical elements*

The total liquidity premium can be divided into two parts, both being positively related: the liquidity level and the liquidity risk. [LOU 11] argued that the liquidity level corresponds to the average liquidity of the asset over time. As such, it can be regarded as a mean effect. The liquidity level is related to the ability to quickly trade large amounts with low price impacts. It depends on the asset's characteristics, such as maturity. The liquidity risk is based on the variation of the asset price due to unexpected change in the aggregate liquidity. It corresponds thus to a volatility effect. Investors ask to get compensated for holding an asset that would perform poorly in case of an adverse liquidity shock. This premium is closely related to the time variation of the liquidity risk factor and to the exposure of the asset to systematic shocks in aggregate liquidity. Time variation series in aggregate liquidity can be found in [SAD 14].

[AMI 86, AMI 88] showed that the relationship between asset returns and illiquidity is upward sloping and concave. Returns increase less for highly illiquid assets. This pattern holds for stocks and bonds as advocated in [AMI 91b]. [AMI 02] shows that expected market illiquidity positively affects *ex ante* stock excess return, suggesting that expected stock excess return partly represents an illiquidity premium. This complements the cross-sectional positive return - illiquidity relationship. This increasing relation between illiquidity and return still holds after controlling for risk and some other characteristics.

For corporate bonds, [CHE 07] found that illiquidity costs increase as rating deteriorates and that changes in bonds' illiquidity costs lead to changes in bonds' yield. [DAS 11] decomposed a bond's option-adjusted spread into three components: default cost measured by using credit default swap (CDS) quotes, liquidity cost as measured by LCS and the market risk premium captured by the intercept. The authors found that both the default risk and liquidity risk are significant contributors to the credit spread for both investment grade and high-yield bonds during the period January 2007 - April 2010. They also found that default risk premiums tend to vary by industry, whereas liquidity premiums are fairly constant across sectors, which raises the question of the effectiveness of a default risk hedging when most of a bond's spread is related to illiquidity concerns. [DE 12a] showed that corporate bond returns have significant exposure to liquidity fluctuations. Liquidity risk premium would be around 0.6% for investment grade bonds and 1.5% for speculative bonds. Furthermore, this liquidity risk is a priced factor for the expected returns. Because liquidity is a risk factor, investors ask for higher return to get compensated for bearing this risk.

[PÁS 03] explored the presence of a priced systematic liquidity factor in equity returns and showed that stocks with the largest exposure to the liquidity factor produced a higher return. [AMI 15b] found that both exposure to shocks in market liquidity and exposure to the market illiquidity return premium are priced. Evidence on the existence of a global liquidity risk factor can be also found in [AMI 15a] who highlight "commonality across 45 countries in the illiquidity return premium, controlling for common global return factors and variation in global illiquidity. This commonality is different from commonality in illiquidity itself and is greater in globally-integrated markets".

In the absence of an investable market benchmark for illiquid assets, [ANG 14a] identified four strategies to harvest the illiquidity premium: by passively allocating to an illiquid asset class, by selecting illiquid securities, by operating as a market maker and by dynamically rebalancing the portfolio. [ANG 11] detailed that the risk-adjusted return of illiquid asset classes may be exaggerated given that data issues are induced by infrequent trading, selection and survivorship biases. [ANG 14a] questioned the existence of an illiquidity premium across asset classes arguing that large illiquidity risk premiums exist mainly within asset classes. This mispricing of illiquidity across asset classes may be due to a limited integration across asset classes as investors do not consider the investment universe as a whole but rather segment it into silos managed by separate divisions. Moreover, the quest for higher returns pushed the prices of illiquid assets up[21], where within an asset class, the presence of illiquidity risk adverse investors willing to pay the price to be able to trade rapidly allows for the emergence of a liquidity premium. [MAR 16] questioned the existence and amplitude of liquidity premium due to the subjectivity of illiquidity measures and other data biases.

If some empirical studies suggest that liquidity risk is priced by the market, for example, higher illiquidity implies lower prices and higher expected returns, why should illiquidity concerns yield a liquidity premium? Are empirical findings in line with theoretical estimates? These questions are raised by [AMI 86] and [ANG 14b]. Their approaches point out the heterogeneity in investors' horizons and the uncertainty about the length of the period of illiquidity respectively as main reasons behind the emergence of a liquidity premium. [AMI 86] analyzed a model where investors with different holding horizons trade assets with different transaction costs. They found that expected returns are an increasing concave function of the bid-ask spreads. They also suggest that the expected net return of transaction costs is also increasing with the holding period, i.e. there exists a liquidity premium for long-term investors holding illiquid assets. [DE 15] illustrated these findings with a simple example. Consider two risk free assets with transaction costs of 1% and 5%, respectively. The risk-free rate is assumed to be equal to 2%. They consider two investors whose investment horizons are respectively 1 and 10 years. The short-term investor prefers the first, more liquid, asset, whose expected gross - of transaction

21 [ANG 14a] reports that the share of illiquid assets held by institutional investors rose from 5% in 1995 to 20% in 2012.

cost - return is given by the sum of the risk-free rate and the bid-ask spread, i.e. 2% + 1% = 3%. Hence, the short-term investor earns a net return of 2%. If the long-term investor holds the liquid asset, then he or she can achieve a 2.9% net return per annum, since he/she trades only once in 10 years, the annual transaction costs are now equal to 0.1%. In order for the illiquid asset to be attractive for the long-term investor, its net expected return should be at least equal to 2.9%. In fact, by holding the illiquid asset over a 10-year horizon, the long-term investor incurs an annual transaction cost of 0.5%. The illiquid asset should achieve a gross return of at least 2.9% + 0.5% = 3.4%. The liquidity premium is thus equal to 0.9%. It is positively related to the transaction cost of the liquid asset and the holding period of the long-term investor as highlighted in Figure 2.34.

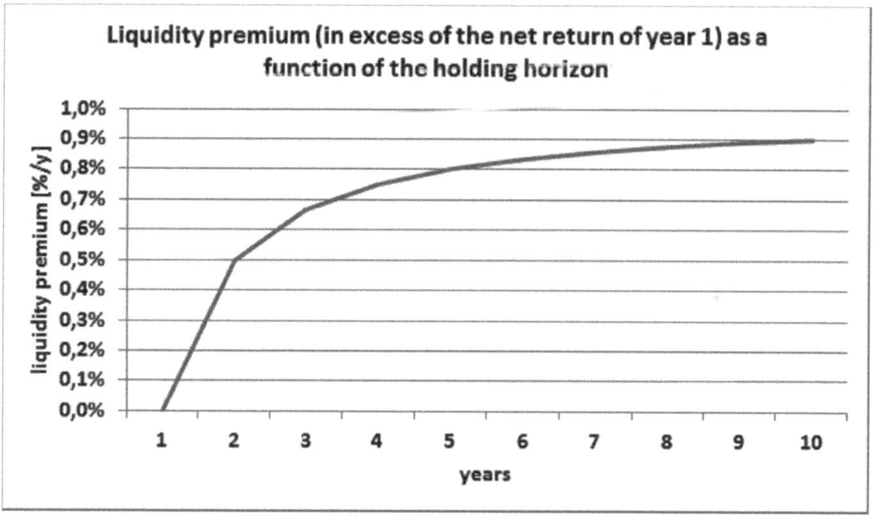

Figure 2.34. *Liquidity premium in excess of the net return of year one as a function of the investment horizon, obtained for a bid-ask spread of 1% for the liquid asset.*

[ANG 14b] extended the [MER 71] framework by allowing of infrequent trades of the risky asset for intervals of uncertain durations. They considered an economy composed of three assets: a risk-free asset, a liquid risky asset and a risky yet illiquid one. The latter can be traded only on random times selected according to a Poisson process of intensity λ. The expected illiquidity period is thus equal to $\frac{1}{\lambda}$. The investor chooses the amount of his/her wealth he/she would consume, the rest being invested in the liquid and the illiquid assets. Liquid assets can be converted into consumption at any time while illiquid holdings can be sold exclusively at random times. As the investor cannot trade his/her illiquid asset for an uncertain period of time, he/she is running a risk that cannot be hedged: the risk of not being able to exchange his/her illiquid wealth into consumption. The consumption might drop to zero for scenarios where liquid wealth is not enough. Therefore, the investor asks to get compensated for holding the illiquid asset. Uncertainty about the length of the illiquidity interval determines the cost of illiquidity. [ANG 14b] found that for an average interval of illiquidity as short as 1 week (λ = 50), the investor is willing to forgo 1.8% of his/her wealth to hedge out liquidity risk by making the second risky asset liquid. [ANG 14a] estimated the annual liquidity premium at 0.7% if the asset can be liquidated only twice a year on average (λ = 2). This premium grows up to 6% for once in a decade trading opportunities. Illiquidity risk has a very large effect on portfolio choice. When the average interval between trades is 6 months, the optimal allocation is 44%. For 10 years, this reduces to 5%. Relative to the Merton economy, illiquidity leads to a large reduction in the allocation to both illiquid and liquid assets, lower consumption rates and time-varying effective relative risk aversion.

2.4.6. *Managing liquidity risk: portfolio construction and the liquidity augmented VaR (L-VaR)*

The *ex ante* future distribution of P&L of the portfolio is the relevant objective function that a portfolio manager looks at and ensures that it has adequate properties especially from a risk perspective. Tracking Error Volatility (TEV) or Value at Risk (VaR) are synthetic risk statistics commonly used to measure the risk of yet to come P&L distribution. Even if the investor is absolutely certain about the out-performance of a specific strategy in the near future, would he/she go along with this strategy if liquidity concerns are prohibitive? The answer requires a general framework that explicitly takes into account liquidity risk for portfolio construction.

[ERN 12] distinguished three types of models, including market liquidity:

– models based on bid-ask spread data: liquidity costs are captured from observable bid-ask spreads and subtracted from prices. [BAN 99] and [ERN 12] developed a liquidity augmented VaR model. This class of model offers the advantage of simplicity. However, only exogenous liquidity costs are taken into account as the price impact is not explicitly modeled;

– models based on volume or transaction data: this class of model attempts to correct [BAN 99] drawbacks by estimating the price impact function. For instance, [BER 00] estimated it from past trades in the regression-wise approach;

– models based on limit order book or weighted spread data as in [FRA 01] or [STA 07].

Though liquidity risk cannot be hedged out, it can still be managed. Portfolio managers, for instance, may choose their liquidation policy with respect to the illiquidity cost profile of underlying securities keeping illiquid assets for a longer time and trading liquid securities more frequently. It is not without its disadvantages however, as liquidity management may cause some performance drawdown. These measures have been recently complemented by new practices such as swing pricing[22].

Illiquidity generally occurs over the short term but vanishes over the long term: a security held to maturity has no liquidity cost. Given that, the investor can adapt the risk-return profile of the portfolio by strategically allocating certain assets to the illiquid strategy bucket, for example, private debt. Such a bucket helps to boost the overall return of the portfolio by capturing an extra premium while offering potential diversification benefits.

From a risk perspective, ignoring liquidity risk tends to underestimate the overall risk of a position. [BAN 99] found that ignoring the liquidity effect leads to underestimating the market risk in emerging markets by more than 25%. More recently, [STA 07] proposed a weighted spread to improve on previous liquidity measures by taking into account the price impact costs in their VaR framework. They found that liquidity factor increases the 10-day VaR@99% by 25% for liquid DAX stocks. [BAN 99] included liquidity into a parametric VaR framework. On the basis of observed bid-ask spreads time series, they derived their liquidity augmented VaR model. Denoted by $r_{t+1} = \log(P_{mid,t+1}) - \log(P_{mid,t})$ the logarithmic return of the mid price at time t over one period of time, for example, from t to $t+1$. Assuming centered Gaussian returns, [BAN 99] exploited information embedded in the distribution of normalized spreads to incorporate the effect of liquidity risk into a parametric VaR framework. Price dynamics are given by the following equation:

$$P_{mid,t+1} = P_{mid,t}e^{r_{t+1}} - \frac{1}{2}P_{mid,t}S_{t+1},$$

22 Swing pricing aims to protect the overall performance of the portfolio for the benefit of existing investors. Trading activity incurs costs (brokerage fees, liquidity spread, taxes) that are traditionally charged to the fund and thus dilute the value of existing investors' investments. Swing pricing is a mechanism by which the NAV of a fund is adjusted upwards in the case of large net inflows and downwards in the case of large net outflows. Namely, if there are important subscriptions or net inflows (or redemptions or net outflows) exceeding a certain threshold, the NAV will be swung upwards (or downwards) by a predefined swing factor. Subscribers thus contribute to the cost that their transactions generate by entering the fund at a higher price, while redemptions are executed at a lower price. The swing factor and threshold level are reviewed on a regular basis by a committee dedicated to validating the parameters of the swing pricing. Swing pricing does not generate additional costs for holders; it modifies the allocation of costs among shareholders. Nonetheless, the mechanism may generate volatility in daily prices, thus increasing the tracking error or the volatility of the fund, irrespective of any fundamental change in the inherent risk of the portfolio.

where S_t denotes the normalized price' spread at time t, namely:

$$S_t = \frac{P_{ask,t} - P_{bid,t}}{P_{mid,t}}.$$

Given these assumptions, [BAN 99] derived a closed-form expression for the liquidity-adjusted VaR. Under perfect correlation between liquidity and return, they derived the following formula for the liquidity-adjusted VaR:

$$L - VaR_{99\%,t+1} = P_{mid,t}(1 - e^{-2.33\theta\sigma}) + \frac{1}{2}P_{mid,t}(\mu_S + \kappa\sigma_S),$$

where σ denotes the volatility of returns and θ is a scaling factor. $\theta = 1$ for Gaussian distribution and $\theta > 1$ to account for fat-tailed returns. μ_S and σ_S are the mean and standard deviation of the bid-ask spreads and κ is the 99% empirical percentile. They found that it ranges between 2 and 4.5 compared to 2.33 for the 99% percentile of the Gaussian distribution. Although their approach relies on restrictive assumptions, its main advantage relies on the low data set required to include liquidity into a risk framework. The historical spread series are sufficient. The drawdowns are the additive nature of liquidity risk irrespective of correlation issues, especially in the tail dependence. It also fails to take into account the price impact function, which leads to underestimation of higher positions.

Departing from the Gaussian assumption for prices of [BAN 99], [ERN 12] used a Cornish-Fisher approximation to develop a liquidity-adjusted total risk VaR. Although their specification yields a more precise risk forecast, it fails to capture the price impact as the liquidation occurs on the bid-ask spread cost and correlation among risk factors is assumed perfect. The advantage is still the same with the additive add-on scheme. [BAN 99] addressed the problem of computing liquidity VaR for a portfolio. They recommended computing the average portfolio spread and applying their above mentioned technique in order to avoid computing correlation among bid-ask spreads between securities. More recently, [BRI 10] accounted for liquidity by introducing randomness into the holding period. The operational time over which assets should be liquidated may differ from the one retained for computing risk measures, for instance, VaR. More generally, a portfolio manager who rebalances his/her portfolio on a regular basis, for example, monthly, may not be able to fully adjust his/her portfolio to his/her new set of views if liquidity conditions are degraded and a longer horizon is required. Their stochastic holding period shifts the P&L distribution downward and increases VaR.

[MEU 12] presented a framework for jointly modeling market risk and liquidity risk. Liquidity is not just a deterministic bid-ask but is modeled as a risk factor *per se* whose impact on the P&L of the portfolio is state-dependent. Thus, when volatility is high and market is down, the negative impact of liquidity is greater. The framework also takes into account endogenous liquidity risk stemming from forced selling in adverse market scenarios. The impact of liquidity risk on the portfolio P&L will also depend on the liquidation scheme or the turnover, in a take profit case or a stop loss one. To account for liquidity risk, conventional VaRs are computed over longer horizons in an *ad hoc* fashion. The Committee on Banking Supervision ([SUP 09]) extended the liquidity time horizon from 10 days to 3 months in the calculation of VaR@99%. The Committee acknowledged that the liquidity of traded assets varies substantially over time and that banks' exposures to market risk and credit risk vary with liquidity conditions in the market.

Following [GAR 13a], we present a liquidity augmented model based on LCS for the credit market. Although LCS does not account directly for price impact for large trades, [DAS 09] argued that it is highly correlated with price impact. It is found to be persistent on average: bonds with low LCS are likely to remain liquid according to the LCS measure for a while. The approach of [GAR 13a] differs from that of [BAN 99] in three ways as it departs from the normality assumption, models the liquidity for each security and aggregate positions holdings into the portfolio and takes into account dependency structure between traditional risk factors and liquidity ones. Moreover, their non-parametric approach allows for stress testing and scenario analysis.

For each security, we define the achieved return in h steps forward, as a function of the carry, market return and liquidity cost. Carry is proportional to the mid-YTM and the market return is proxied by the product of the modified duration by the sum of h variations of the mid-YTM. Liquidity at the liquidation horizon is assumed, as in [BAN 99], equal to half of LCS[23] prevailing at the end of the period, i.e. $t + h$:

$$LRet_{t\to t+h} = YTM_{mid,t} \times Coverage_{t\to t+h} - ModDur_{mid,t} \times \Delta YTM_{t\to t+h} - \frac{1}{2}\left(LCS_t + \Delta LCS_{t\to t+h}\right).$$

At the beginning of the period, i.e. at time t, the carry and coverage are known. We need to project YTM and LCS to the end of the period. We do that by modeling the variations of both YTM and those of LCS. For the sake of simplicity, we consider a portfolio of equally weighted generic securities corresponding to main credit sectors. The joint distribution of YTM and LCS weekly changes is calibrated over the period from June 2010 to June 2016. Omitting liquidity, VaR@99% underestimates by 22% over the short run. The underestimation decreases with the projection horizon as market risk takes over liquidity as depicted in Figure 2.35.

23 In [BAN 99], the bid-ask spread is normalized to the mid price, LCS is normalized to the bid price and hence is more conservative.

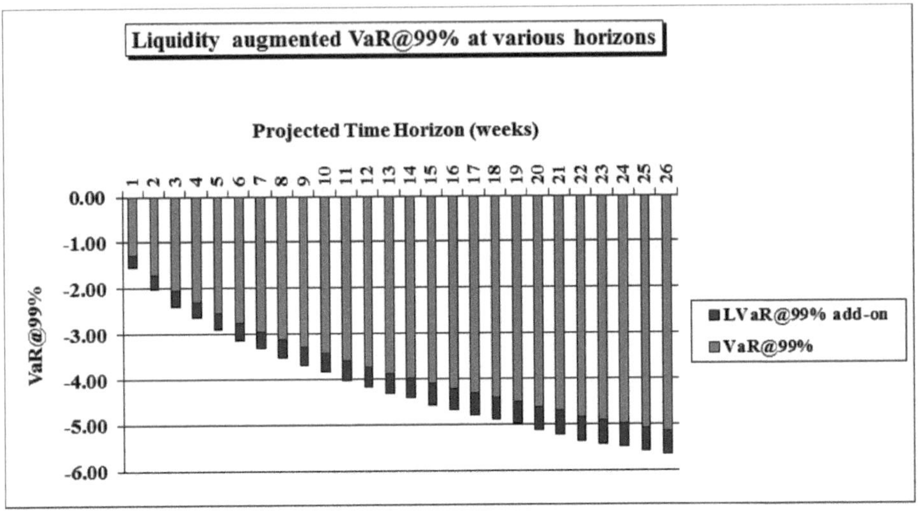

Figure 2.35. *Liquidity-augmented VaR. The red sticks correspond to the difference between the LVaR and the traditional VaR (in blue)*

In the long-term, the ratio of LVaR@99% to traditional VaR@99% would converge around 10%, as depicted in Figure 2.36, suggesting that usual market risk factors will take over liquidity risk factor over longer horizons.

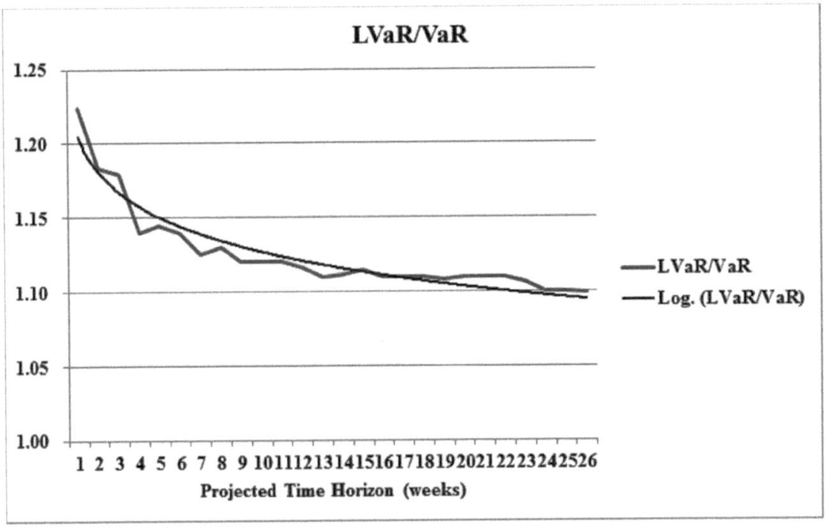

Figure 2.36. *Ratio of LVaR to VaR*

Portfolios can be ordered according to their liquidity profile. For instance, portfolios with lower LCS are preferred to less liquid ones. [MEU 12] proposed the liquidity efficiency score as a criterion for assessing portfolio's liquidity risk. Because the liquidity adjustment always hits the P&L downward, he defined the liquidity efficiency score as the percentage of deterioration of the left tail, for example, the ratio of traditional expected shortfall to the liquidity-augmented one. This ratio is larger than 0 and lesser than 1. The closer to 1, the lower the risk of liquidity. The 4 weeks' efficiency score of our sample portfolio is close to 90%.

2.5. Implications of low rates on risk modeling in fixed-income markets

If you borrow money, you have to pay for it. The price is given by the interest rate, which, similarly to the prices of other products, should be positive. This is known as the time value of money (see [MAR 03b]). As a result, traditional financial modeling precludes negative rates and relegates it to the status of anomaly. Rates dynamics such as [VAS 77] model were criticized for their inability to prevent negative rates in their diffusion. Rates were thought to be floored by zero. However, in recent years, the financial markets have witnessed the emergence and the amplification of negative rates. While the economic theory and the financial markets practitioners (see [BER 16] and [TEI 15]) argue that this floor moved from zero into negative territories, risk models have to be revisited to account for this new situation.

Rates and spreads volatilities are traditionally assumed to be Gaussian, i.e. constant irrespective of the underlying level, or log-normal. In a log-normal framework, volatility is proportional to the level of the underlying, either for rates or spreads. Should the underlying fall to zero, its volatility will also drop to null. Moreover, log-normal rates or spreads cannot be negative in which case volatility will be negative too! This paradigm has been challenged by the recent evolution of rates and spreads. The implications of these observations are particularly important in the case of risk models. In fact, a low-yield environment does not necessarily imply a low-risk world. In what follows, we examine the risk return trade-off when rates' levels reach their lower boundary and question the adequacy of volatility as a risk measure, after which we address adjustments to conduct in order to cope with the underestimation of risk. The first improvement affects the volatility of the risk factors, while the second concerns the sensitivity to these risk factors.

2.5.1. *The risk-return trade-off in a low-rate environment*

When rates are low, the risk-return trade-off is affected. The distribution of future rates movements becomes skewed because rate hikes are more likely to occur than rate tightenings. This pronounced asymmetry in rates distribution hampers the volatility of rate as a risk measure.

2.5.1.1. *The return*

The total return ($TR_{t \to t+1}$) over the period $t \to t+1$ of a bond bought at a yield z_t can be approximated by the following equation:

$$TR_{t \to t+1} \approx z_t.\delta - Dur_t \times dZ_{t \to t+1}. \qquad [2.20]$$

Dur denotes the duration of the bond, dZ represents the magnitude of variation of the yield and δ denotes the time coverage. The probability distribution of the yields' movements is asymmetric as the latter are floored by z_{floor}, which denotes the threshold under which yields cannot drop. This floor is traditionally null, although in current market conditions it moved into negative territories. Yield movements may thus vary inside a semi-bounded interval:

$$dZ_{t \to t+1} \in \left[-(z_t - z_{floor}); +\infty\right[$$

and the total return range becomes:

$$TR_{t \to t+1} \in \left]-\infty; z_t(1+\delta)Dur_t \times z_{floor}\right].$$

While the potential gain is bounded, potential loss is theoretically unlimited. It is the well-known asymmetry of returns of bonds inherited from the asymmetry of their yields. Still when yields level is fairly high, it is not uncommon to assume a symmetric distribution for the sake of simplicity. However, when yields approach their floor, little room is left for narrowing, and widening movements are more likely. Carry component becomes negligible, if not negative, and may not offset an adverse movement. Yields behave as if they were truncated: only upside movements are allowed. This also holds for each of the yield's traditional components, i.e. the reference rate Y_t and the spread S_t, with $Z_t = Y_t + S_t$.

Assuming that rates movements follow a Gaussian distribution over the long run, one can check in Figure 2.37 how the distribution of rates shifts to the right, increasing the likelihood of rate hikes and consequently the probability of occurrence of negative total return, when the truncation becomes greater. The asymmetry of the conditional distribution becomes more pronounced as the truncation threshold increases. We can note the impact of truncation threshold on the skewness of rates as depicted in Figure 2.38. The higher the truncation threshold, the more skewed the distribution is, thus boosting the likelihood of higher rates. In this simple framework, the lower the yields, the higher the probability of an adverse movement. Still the volatility does not capture this risk.

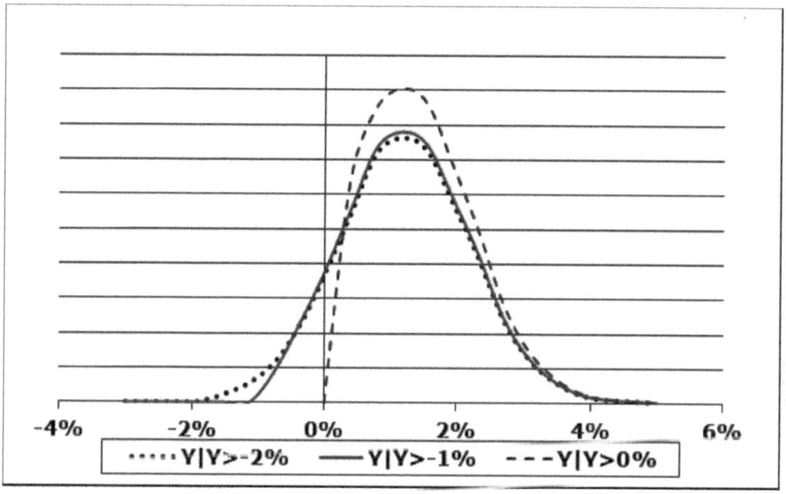

Figure 2.37. *Distribution of truncated rates with initial rate = 1%, volatility of the rates = 1%*

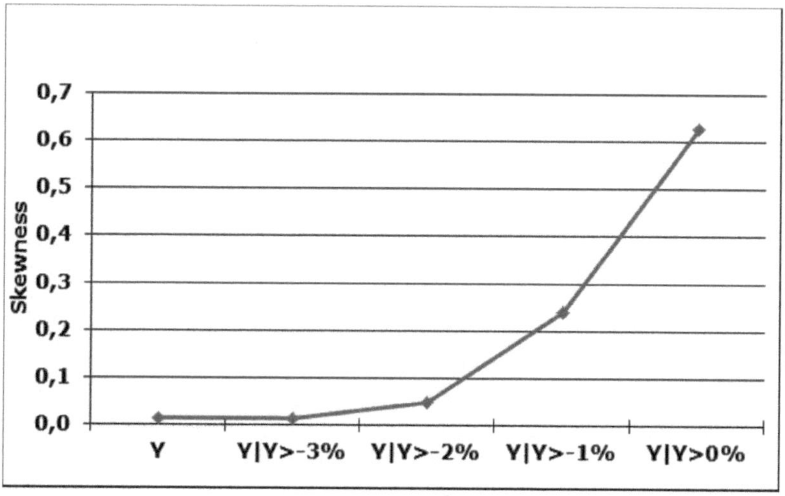

Figure 2.38. *Skewness of rates as a function of the truncation threshold with initial rate = 1%, volatility of the rates = 1%*

2.5.1.2. *The risk*

The impact of truncation on volatility can be analytically computed in the case of Gaussian distributions. The variance of a truncated Gaussian variable $u \rightsquigarrow \mathcal{N}(\mu, \sigma^2)$ is given by the following equation:

$$\sigma^2(u \mid u > c) = \sigma^2 \left(1 + \frac{c-\mu}{\sigma} M\left(-\frac{c-\mu}{\sigma}\right) - M^2\left(-\frac{c-\mu}{\sigma}\right)\right)$$

where $M(c) = \frac{\phi(c)}{\Phi(c)}$ denotes the ratio of Mill, i.e. the ratio of the density ϕ to the cumulative Gaussian distribution Φ evaluated at truncation threshold c. It is worth mentioning that the volatility of the truncated distribution is lower than that of the unconditional one, i.e. $\sigma(u \mid u > c) < \sigma(u)$, which bears out the assertion that volatility understates the risk of low-yield bonds[24].

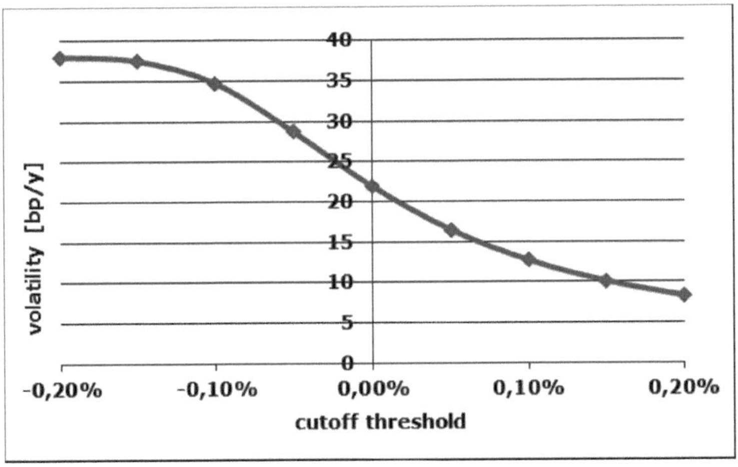

Figure 2.39. *Annualized volatility of weekly variations of the 3-year Euro swap rate as a function of the cut-off, below which the rate distribution is truncated. The sample taken from the period 11/10/2011 to 27/04/2015*

Consequently, we can compute the volatility of the truncated distribution of rates, i.e. the local conditional volatility, and compare it to the longer-term unconditional one. This is shown in Figure 2.39. The volatility of the 1-week variation of the 3-year Euro swap rate is about 39bp/y from 11/10/2011 to 26/01/2016. Over that period, we witnessed a drop of the 3-year swap rate from 1.69% to −0.08%. Should rates remain above −0.20% then only a movement above -12bp is authorized. The volatility of the

24 [TEI 15] argues that skewness can be deemed as a sensible risk measure.

conditional distribution is thus reduced by 4bp/y. In fact, the difference between the lower boundary of rates and their actual level defines the cut-off threshold for the conditional distribution. Should rates pursue their tightening and reach their lower boundary, assumed at –0.20%, then the annualized volatility should drop to 22bp. It is interesting to note that the volatility does not drop to null even if rates fall below –0.20%.

2.5.2. *Volatility in a low-yield environment*

Given equation [2.20], we can deduce that the volatility of TR can also be approximated by the following relation:

$$\sigma(TR_{t\to t+1}) \equiv Dur_t \times \sigma(dZ_{t\to t+1}).$$

As previously explained, in a low-yield environment, given the asymmetry of yield's distribution, volatility would underestimate the downside risk, which raises a number of questions: what is a good risk model? How to model $\sigma(dZ_{t\to t+1})$ in such a context? How does $\sigma(TR_{t\to t+1})$ behave as rates approach their floor level? Does the approximation $\sigma(TR_{t\to t+1}) \approx Dur_t \times \sigma(dZ_{t\to t+1})$ still hold?

2.5.2.1. *What is a good risk model?*

A good risk model should allow for accurate forecasting of the selected risk measure (Tracking Error, Value at Risk, Expected Shortfall, etc.) over the investment horizon. These measures are the historical estimation of the future risk level. An annual *ex ante* Tracking Error of 100bp means that if the portfolio composition remains unchanged, then the Tracking Error computed over a year horizon should be around 100bp. The validity of risk models and consequently of related allocation models relies on their ability of forecasting the future risk based on previous data with the implicit assumption that the future resembles the past. Thus, it is of primary importance to identify the law of motion of the market in order to achieve an accurate risk projection. We seek market invariants whose dynamics are mildly stable, i.e. risk factors that are stationary and useful for projecting the P&L of the portfolio. Failing that, practitioners settle for computing the product of sensitivity and the volatility of risk factors, mainly rates and spreads for fixed-income securities.

2.5.2.2. *Modeling the volatility of factors*

Traditionally, we distinguish two main approaches for modeling each of these factors, i.e. rates and spreads. We model either their absolute changes or their relative or log changes leading respectively to the normal model and log-normal model[25].

25 The terms "normal" and "log-normal" are not related to the Gaussian distribution which is by no means necessary since randomness can be modeled by a Student distribution or any other suitable probability law.

2.5.2.2.1. Normal volatility

In the normal volatility model, the volatility of changes in rates is considered to be locally stationary. The volatility of a bond would then be directly linked to that of rates. The volatility of rates is assumed to be independent of the rate level, for example, should rates widen from 2% to 4% their volatility remains the same. Rates dynamics are governed by the following equation:

$$dY = \kappa.\epsilon$$

with κ a positive scalar and ϵ a random variable of unit variance, which leads to the above mentioned constancy of rates volatility, i.e. $\sigma(dY) = \kappa$. In a benchmarked process, an active exposure of 1 year of duration would generate the same TE irrespective of rates level. Similarly, if OASD is retained as a credit risk yardstick, then spread volatility is assumed to be the same whether spreads are low or high.

2.5.2.2.2. Log-normal volatility

Alternatively, some argue (see, e.g., [DOU 13]) that a bond's risk is directly proportional to its interest rate level. The volatility of rates is thus proportional to rates level:

$$\frac{dY}{Y} = \vartheta.\eta \rightarrow \sigma(dY) = \vartheta.Y,$$

with ϑ denoting a positive scalar and η a random variable of unit variance.

The corollary of this assumption is that risk should drop to null as rates approach zero. Modeling the relative changes is particularly useful for spreads, since the volatility of spread variation is found to be proportional to spread level. We can conclude that the volatility of their relative variation is stable in time (see [BEN 05]) and the DTS would then be a superior measure of sensitivity to spread risk. However, log-normal processes do not allow for negative rates or spreads. Such conclusions are not compatible with current data where rates and spreads are low without observing a proportional drop in their volatilities. We show in Figure 2.40 a normal and a log-normal diffusion with similar parameters, i.e. same initial value and a 1-year volatility of 1% for both frameworks. We note that log-normal dynamics lead to higher volatilities (resp. lower) than those obtained under normal assumptions for forecasting horizons above (resp. under) 1 year.

2.5.3. *Volatility of returns and the adequacy of usual sensitivity measures, duration and DTS, in a low-yield environment*

For small figures of spreads, the volatility of spread is not null. Thus, the proportionality law is not observed for low spreads. Volatility seems to decrease as spreads tighten until reaching a floor below proportionality (see [DES 15]). Volatility seems to be normal below a threshold and "log-normal" above it. Bond credit risk is thus proportional to its spread as long as the latter is above the threshold. Should the spreads drop below the threshold, volatility flattens as it reaches an incompressible floor. An explanation for the existence of a floor stems from the assumption that spread volatility is not driven solely by changes in risk, but can also result from various noises caused by pricing errors and other frictions in the market. Similar results were found by [DOU 13] for rates. Addressing this issue can be achieved in two ways which are not mutually exclusive: by adjusting volatilities or by adjusting sensitivities.

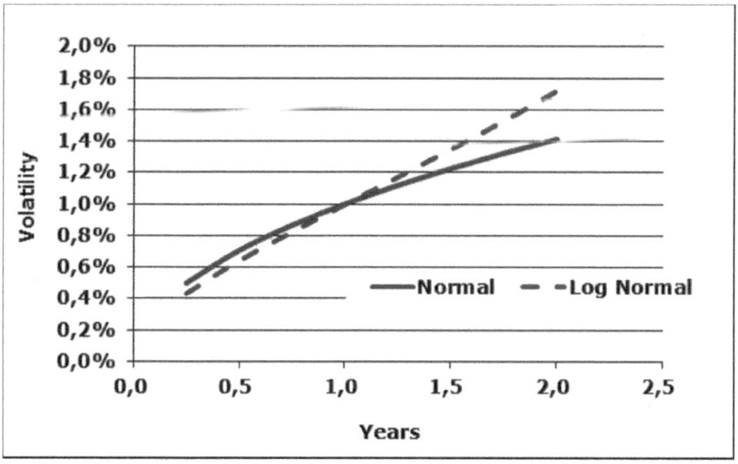

Figure 2.40. *Diffusion of normal versus log-normal volatility with the 1-year volatility of 1% for both specifications*

2.5.3.1. *Adjusting the volatilities of rates and spreads*

We present a non-exhaustive list of adjustments applied to volatilities in order to cope with negative rates or spreads:

– shifting the log-normal distribution into negative territory, i.e. by translating rates by a fixed number. Hence, rate variations are proportional to the rate level and a positive constant c and rate volatility is proportional to the rate level plus that constant:

$$\frac{dY}{(y+c)} = \vartheta.\eta \to \sigma(dY) = \vartheta(y+c).$$

Should rates drop to zero their volatility will not be null but equals $\vartheta.c$;

– adding a normal noise to the non-shifted log-normal volatility. Hence, the risk factor volatility is assumed to be the sum of two noises: a normal one that acts as a structural incompressible volatility level when rates approach zero and a log-normal one increasing when rates widen and dominating the first term:

$$dY = y.\vartheta.\eta + \chi.\epsilon \rightarrow \sigma(dY) = \sqrt{\vartheta^2.y^2 + \chi^2},$$

with $\chi > 0$. This modeling is found to better fit actual data for rates and spreads (see [BEN 05], [BEN 07] and [DOU 13]), although the structural volatility level is found to be different from one market to another;

– transforming rates by applying an inverse-call likewise function. The rationale behind this approach that finds its theoretical root in the work of [BLA 95] consists of considering rates as call options on some shadow rates. The approach has been recently generalized by [MEU 16]. It tolerates negative rates and allows for a smooth shift from normal to log-normal regimes;

– [BER 16] argued that adding jumps to the log-normal diffusion allows for a better fit of historical data for the 3-year Euro swap rate. The log-normal behavior is preserved. However, when the rate goes down to zero, the occurrence of jumps can produce a certain amount of variance, which is not compatible with the variance stemming from the diffusion part of the process. The low-rate environment seems to be compatible with a non-vanishing variance, when we accept to exit the settings of continuous processes.

2.5.3.2. *Adjusting the sensitivity to spreads*

The standard expression of DTS assumes proportionality of volatility of TR to spread level. This implies that volatility of TR should drop to null as spreads approach zero. As a consequence, DTS might understate risk when spreads are very low. In order to address this issue, one should floor DTS when spreads are below a certain threshold s_{floor}:

$$DTS = OASD \times max(s, s_{floor})$$

This correction implies that DTS remains the appropriate sensitivity measure for spreads above s_{floor}. Should spreads drop below s_{floor} then the sensitivity switches to spread duration and the volatility from log-normal to normal regime. s_{floor} can be estimated by maximum likelihood techniques as explained in [DES 15].

3

Active Portfolio Construction

3.1. Introduction

How do we transform investment ideas into a real portfolio? How do we turn views and predictions into effective positions? This essential part of an investment process is called the allocation procedure. A investment process needs a cautious, well-designed allocation scheme whose engineering is at least as important as any other part. A badly implemented idea is doomed to lose its potential profitability. We can summarize our view on allocation in simple terms: allocating is finding degrees of freedom in the markets, those degrees of freedom being materialized by portfolios of assets. Allocating is choosing between these portfolios while searching for potential expositions and correlations between them in a statistically uncertain environment. In fact, allocation may be purely an estimation challenge.

In this section, we will present *active* techniques in the sense that we will not discuss theoretical equilibrium models justifying the need for a market portfolio, and we will not confine ourselves to benchmarked investments. Within this context, allocation is active as soon as personal forecasts, bets or views are used, or when in-depth monitoring is used to actively manage the underlying risk of the strategy. Allocation covers a wide range of literature, from strong theoretical foundations and academic works, to empirical contributions of practitioners. Unfortunately, with this profusion of competing papers and techniques, there is more confusion and sometimes a lack of an unifying view. Hence, comparing allocation techniques is not always relevant in itself. It is surprising to see that competing allocation techniques are often (but hopefully not always) promoted as raw alternatives that are often compared through the lens of effective backtests. Backtesting or performance comparison is neither an explanation nor a proof of what an allocation technique achieves to do mathematically. Seemingly competing approaches are sometimes several paths to solve the same problem. Again, we would like to favor intuition rather than universality; we are more interested in putting allocation techniques in perspective rather than listing every feature of each technique. The interaction and differences between techniques is more interesting than backtests. In this respect, the discussion materializing the explicit links between portfolio allocation and inverse problems, developed and detailed in section 3.3.4, appears rather original[1] in the literature to the best of our knowledge.

3.1.1. *A statistical challenge and a need for regularization*

The aim of this chapter is to provide a wide framework in which allocation techniques with increasing levels of sophistication are described. Rather than comparing backtests (that are not always statistically significant in many papers), we prefer to explain the motivations and the theory they are rooted in. We want to adopt an unifying view, showing that many allocation techniques may appear different, but share in the end the same objective: reducing empirical disagreements by a statistical action. Those empirical disagreements are well illustrated by the example of mean-variance allocation. Again, mean-variance, this dusty concept? We want to elaborate on mean-variance, not for the setup in itself, but for the extraordinary powerful messages that it conveys. What appears to be one of the most famous and elegant setups for allocation is sometimes still badly understood in practice. What is usually observed is that using a mean-variance allocation with historical estimators leads to unstable and unrealistic weights: raw estimation leads to errors and misinterpretations. Within this context, assets' weights are proportional to the multiplication of the inverse covariance matrix with the expected returns. Any slight modification on the estimator of the expected returns makes the results to diverge in practice. This is a real limitation for a realistic use for a portfolio manager. Of course, alternatives to mean-variance usually seek to solve for this instability. As simple as it may seem, the mean-variance framework allows to thoroughly understand the statistical challenges of allocation and thus we are interested in studying it (again). The ill-posedness of the original problem using raw estimators lies in the spectral configuration of the estimated covariance matrix. The symptom occurs when estimated returns are updated, but the cause remains in the estimation of the risk component. Fighting this instability to get more stable weights, regardless of the technique, is called *regularization*.

And there is empirically still much pedagogical work to do. In a recent study led by EDHEC (see [GOT 09]), it has been estimated that up to 70% of the respondents (all financial practitioners) were still using the raw sample estimated covariance matrix. In the same study, only 15% of the respondents were using factor models and

1 It is of course not the first time that this topic is discussed: see, in particular, [CAR 11b] and [FAS 15] in addition to all the references that are given all along the chapter. Yet, precise discussions between portfolio allocation and inverse problems represent a small part of the portfolio allocation literature.

hardly 5% regularization techniques. This shows that this is still useful to spread theoretical cautionary messages and motivates one more time how important it is to stress the mathematical aspects of allocation. Section 3.2 is therefore dedicated to a theoretical diagnosis of the statistical challenges that are at play when allocating, and that mean-variance helps to uncover. The motivations and the properties of the techniques exposed afterward (even heuristic techniques) always elaborate on strong theoretical results. We strongly advise reading section 3.2 to understand the tools that will allow to handle the remaining of this chapter.

3.1.2. *Some alternative options*

How do we get a robust allocation process? You can still keep in mind the objectives of mean-variance allocation: maximizing expected profit while controlling for risk. The first option is to remain within this framework and to use for the expected return any signal that owns a strong predictive power. This defines the scope of section 3.5. A possibility is to *clean* the estimated covariance matrix in order to get more stable weights when inverting the covariance matrix. Cleaning the covariance matrix is a form of regularization (see in particular section 3.3.4). In some situations, specific manipulations of the signal may also be a solution. Replacing a sample mean of returns by a smoother version is a quite natural idea: the agnostic view that only considers historical returns leads to a sampling error that is too high. A cure is to introduce prior information that relies less on the data sample but more on the fund manager's experience, forecast or theory (see below developments on the Black-Litterman framework on section 3.5.3). The alternative consisting in mechanically confining weights within bounds by the application of constraints could be considered as an empirical recipe: paradoxically, this empirical "shortcut" is backed by a strong theory and is also a form of regularization (see section 3.5.2).

The second option is to drop the expected return estimation and to use a technique that focuses on risk: this will be at the heart of section 3.6. Such techniques do not require an explicit specification of the expected returns and seem to be strategy-free as they are agnostic on the return part. They, in fact, understate implicit bets, but the investor does not have to specifically build directional bets on assets or strategies. We will find among them techniques such as naive diversification, minimum variance, maximum diversification and risk-parity. Hopefully, all of them may be written as particular cases of a more general regularizing framework (see section 3.6.1.5). In any case, *all* the methods that employ a covariance matrix benefit from matrix cleaning; furthermore, this cleaning step is not still well incorporated in the daily life of many players of the financial industry, as underlined by the aforementioned study of [GOT 09].

3.1.3. *From strategies to expected returns*

The return of any security can be decomposed into a systematic and a residual part (see section 2.2 on *LFM*). The CAPM states that the residual part has zero expectation. It results that the expected (excess) return of the security is proportional to its beta relatively to the market. The risk, however, contains a residual part for which the investor is not getting any compensation. An investor following the CAPM should thus hold the market portfolio and achieve the consensus return. Under such conditions, it would not be possible to outperform the market bad news for active management. However, like all models, the CAPM is based on a set of assumptions, some of which are questionable. We already discussed this are point in introduction, but within the portfolio allocation context, the assumption that all market participants share the same expectations and differ only in their tolerance for risk lacks realism. The objective of active management is to beat the market; this can be made possible if the active portfolio is different from the market portfolio.

Market players have differential information that guides their distinct return expectations. Superior information is the key for accessing greater opportunities and potentially higher returns. Active management will be driven by expectations different from that of the consensus that can be recovered using the CAPM. In fact, starting with the market portfolio and assuming that it is optimal, we can infer the implied CAPM expected returns. They are also known as the consensus expected returns as the expected return of any portfolio would be thus proportional to its beta with respect to the optimal market portfolio. It follows that forecasting the return of any portfolio can be done easily by choosing the right beta. Still, is that sufficient for regularly beating the market?

As stressed by [GRI 00], "*Active management is forecasting*". Forecasting follows a thorough mechanism of information processing that transforms it from raw data into refined forecast according to the following rule of thumb:

$$\text{Alpha} = \text{Information Ratio} \times \text{Volatility}$$

where Alpha is the beta-adjusted excess return and Volatility is residual. The Information Ratio (IR) is defined as the ratio of excess return to the tracking error or the volatility of excess returns versus the benchmark. For a discussion of the nature of IR, see [GRI 00]. One implication of the aforementioned relationship between alpha and tracking error is that the efficient residual frontier would be linear as reported in Figure 3.1.

In active management, the added value is proportional to the square of the IR. IR role is twofold: it measures the quality of investment opportunities in an active management process, and its square defines the ability of a portfolio manager to add value. A natural question is thus to know where do these opportunities come from and how to increase IR. The answer is given by the Fundamental Law of Active Management (FLAM) that helps distinguishing two sources of value (see [GRI 89]):

– the forecasting capability of assets residual returns or *Skill* that can be measured by the *Information Coefficient* (IC) defined as the correlation of returns and forecasts.

– the number of times in a year we use this skill or the *breadth* (BR).

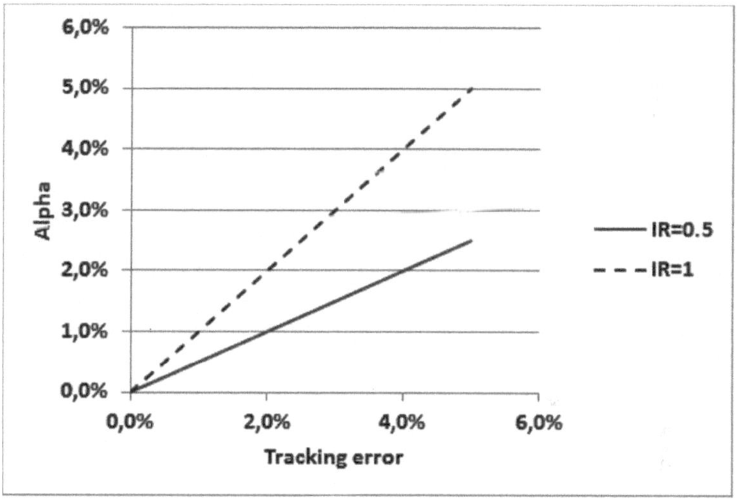

Figure 3.1. *Active efficient frontier as a function of Information Ratio*

Formally, the FLAM states that:

$$IR = IC \times \sqrt{BR}.$$

According to the FLAM, to achieve great performance, i.e. to achieve a high value of IR, the manager has to play well, i.e. she or he should possess a high IC, and has to play frequently , i.e. with a large BR. An implication of the FLAM is the trade-off between IC and BR. In fact, the same IR can be achieved by different combinations of IC and BR as highlighted in Figure 3.2. This gives an extra degree of freedom in defining the business model of the investment company, at least from a theoretical perspective: skill-oriented or breadth-oriented, the latter being costly in terms of transaction expenditure. Another direct implication of the FLAM is that:

$$\text{Alpha} = IC \times \sqrt{BR} \times \text{Volatility}.$$

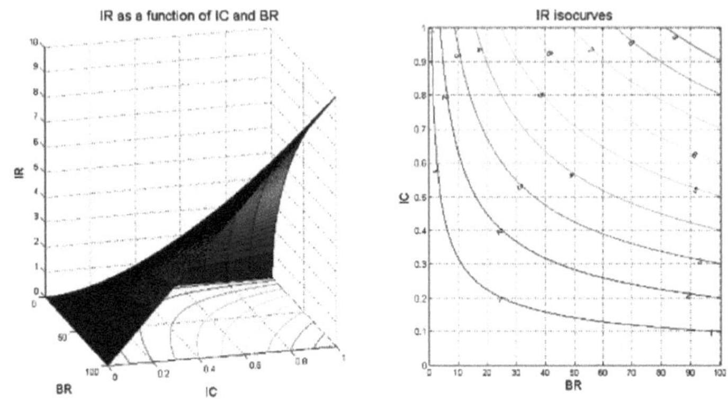

Figure 3.2. *Information Ratio as a function of Information Coefficient and breadth*

In its original formulation, the FLAM determines the (maximal) added value given forecasts without taking into account portfolio constraints such as no short sales. [CLA 02] provided an extended version of the FLAM in which IR is reduced because of restriction on active positions due to investment constraints. Denoting by TC the transfer coefficient defined as the correlation between positions and forecasts, [CLA 02] generalized the FLAM:

$$IR = IC \times \sqrt{BR} \times TC.$$

[QIA 04] highlighted the variability of the *IC* of a given strategy as an additional source of active risk that is ignored by the traditional tracking error measurement. Omitting this, "strategy risk" can lead to erroneous performance figures and an understatement of the active risk. Time variability of ICs led [DIN 10] to derive a generalization of the FLAM by distinguishing between standard cross-sectional *IC*s and temporal ICs. [DIN 10] found that the effect of the volatility of ICs on the portfolio IR is larger than the breadth. Another generalization that focuses on defining the breadth is given by [SEN 10].

[BUC 05] tackles the divergence between the returns anticipated by the FLAM and those really observed. Forecasting bias is due to violation in the underlying assumptions of the FLAM , mainly the existence of a trend. [MIC 16] questioned the applicability of the FLAM given the importance of estimation errors in reality. Estimation error was also addressed by [ZHO 08]. When breadth is large with respect to the amount of available data, benefits of the FLAM can be offset by estimation error. It follows a trade-off between breadth and estimation error. To cope with this additional drawdown, the author recommends scaling the estimated portfolios by an optimal factor that helps improve the portfolio performance.

There may be subtle differences between a signal and a strategy expressed in expected returns. In particular, [GRI 94] links *scores* (normalized signal on assets) or forecasts to expected returns through the product of volatility of the asset and the information coefficient (correlation of the score with the returns). Therefore, alphas must control for volatility, skill and expectations:

$$\text{Alpha} = \text{Volatility} \times IC \times \text{Score}.$$

Given a raw signal or score, alpha is estimated by scaling the score by the volatility of residual returns proportionally to the information coefficient or the correlation between returns and scores. When $IC = 0$, then informationless scores are transformed into null alphas!

"The rule of thumb converts "garbage in" to zeros."
— [GRI 00]

3.1.4. *Scope of this chapter*

We already underlined in the introduction of this book how the most played strategies gave birth to a whole industry through the use of systematic strategies to build smart beta products. For some years now, the difference between public and proprietary strategies has been blurred. [HAR 16] inventoried more than 300 factors that have been tried, and published in the academic literature. The need for innovation and in-house solutions is needed more than ever. We will consider views and strategies as an input in the following, and we explicitly do not address the problem of finding a performing trading signal. Our assumption is that this signal/strategy/expected return estimation is both exogenous and given. We consider in this chapter any strategy as being proprietary to the fund manager as the result of her/his knowledge, work and expertise. We will not discuss its construction, origin or motivation. Why? Mainly because the profitability of two strategies can only be conceived with the same allocation. One may be playing two strategies that may seem apparently different but ending up in the same portfolio with two different allocation procedures. Alternatively, one cannot compare two strategies if the allocation process is not the same. Having no reference allocation to promote, the quest for a winning strategy is out of the scope of this book. However, the underlying assets we will deal with are generic: they can equivalently be single assets, funds, stocks or asset classes. In any case, the path leading to the final, investable portfolio will strongly depend on the fund manager's mandate, objectives, abilities, possibilities, constraints and knowledge.

By lack of space, we cannot cover all the possible allocation techniques that have been published and proposed through years. We will, however, proceed to a wide overview of the most common alternatives, mainly driven by their potential regularizing effect. In particular, a wide stream of research is related to a *Bayesian modeling*. We will address Black-Litterman allocation that is often promoted as a Bayesian technique, but which is rather related, in our opinion, to the usual literature even if it presents a flavor of Bayesian statistics. Dealing with Bayesian allocation would be way too long to explain properly and would sophisticate our pitch. We nonetheless do not underestimate the importance and the interest of this framework: we deeply encourage any reader to explore this approach, as the core of its motivation is the use of prior information, which is a known remedy for the reduction of out-of-sample noise. References on the subject are wide, but a selected and chronological reading would include the works of [FRO 86], [CHO 93], [MAR 03a], [HAR 10], [JON 10], [AVR 10], [DEM 13], [KAY 14], [DEM 15]. In addition, we will not address *resampling techniques*. Resampling involves generally bootstrapping and Monte Carlo methods. The idea behind resampling is to increase the uncertainty in the allocation to give more importance to the out-of-sample properties of the estimator. Even if resampling methods are theoretically founded, they are mostly numeric and do not meet the regularizing effect we want to uncover in the presented techniques. References to learn more about resampling techniques for allocation include, in particular, the contributions of [JOR 92], [MIC 98] or [FLE 01b]. See also [SCH 02] and [HAR 08] for a critical view this approach.

3.2. A theoretical toolbox for allocation

3.2.1. *Motivations and notations*

Here, we review and unify the notations used throughout this chapter. We are interested in the allocation in discrete time between N assets at date t. Rebalancing at date t involves the determination for a future period $[t; t+1]$ of the relative weights between assets, denoted by w_t, which is a vector of $\mathbb{R}^N$, with possibly negative weights. We will also note $\Delta w_t = w_t - w_{t-1}$ the one-period difference of weights at each rebalancing. The set of N assets with weights w_t held between t and $t+1$ is understood as *the portfolio*. Random variables will generally be represented by uppercase letters, whereas their corresponding observations and realizations will be represented by lowercase letters, unless mentioned. In particular, for allocation at date t, we assume that the statistical sample of observations is made of T past observations. The random variable of the one-period $[t-1; t]$ return of asset i at date t writes $R_{i,t}$ and the corresponding random vector of size N is $R_t = (R_{1,t}, ..., R_{N,t})'$. The observed returns are therefore denoted by $r_{i,t}$ and $\mathbf{r}_t$. The random vector R_t is assumed to have finite unconditional first and second moments, respectively μ ($N \times 1$ dimensional vector) and Ω ($N \times N$ squared symmetric matrix), such that:

$$\mathbb{E}[R_t] = \mu \quad \text{and} \quad \mathbb{V}[R_t] = \Omega.$$

The random scalar that represents the returns of the portfolio is denoted by $R^P_{t+1} = w'_t R_{t+1}$ whose realizations r^P_{t+1} are observed in $t+1$. The volatility of the portfolio is denoted by σ_p by : $\sigma_P(w) = w'\Omega w$. Ω. Ω is the unobserved covariance matrix, and is related to the correlation matrix C through:

$$\Omega = diag(\sigma_1, ..., \sigma_N) \times C \times diag(\sigma_1, ..., \sigma_N),$$

where σ_i is the individual volatility of asset i, that is, the standard deviation of the returns of asset i (which coincides with the squared diagonal elements of Ω).

A signal or a strategy s_t will be potentially used and considered as an external proxy for μ, homogeneous to expected returns. s_t will be understood as a subjective view at date t of one-period expected returns at date $t+1$. Therefore, if the investor has an information set $\mathcal{I}_t$ made of private and public information, s_t has to be understood as the subjective expected gain on $[t; t+1]$ for each asset, conditionally on the observation of $\mathcal{I}_t$:

$$s_t = \mathbb{E}[R_{t+1}|\mathcal{I}_t].$$

Moreover, $w_t = (w_{1,t}, ..., w_{N,t})$ is a set of relative weights whose sum depends on the mandate of the fund manager. For instance:

– a long-only portfolio will be such that $\sum_{i=1}^N w_{i,t} = 1$ and $w_{i,t} \geq 0$, for all $i \in [1; N]$;

– a pure long-short portfolio will be such that $\sum_{i=1}^N w_{i,t} = 0$ and $w_{i,t} \in \mathbb{R}$, for all $i \in [1; N]$;

– a 130-30 portfolio will be such that $\sum_{i=1}^N w_{i,t} = 1$, $\sum_{i=1}^N w_{i,t}\mathbb{1}(w_{i,t} \geq 0) = 1.3$, $\sum_{i=1}^N w_{i,t}\mathbb{1}(w_{i,t} \leq 0) = 0.3$, and $w_{i,t} \geq 0$, for all $i \in [1; N]$.

We will denote the *net market value* by NMV and the *gross market value* invested by GMV. Relative weights are related to quantities $q_t = (q_{1,t}, ..., q_{N,t})$ (amount invested in currencies in each position) through $q_{i,t} = w_{i,t} \times GMV$. Regardless of the nature of the investment, we have:

$$\sum_{i=1}^N |q_{i,t}| = GMV \quad \text{and} \quad \sum_{i=1}^N q_{i,t} = NMV.$$

GMV is related to *assets under management* (henceforth AUM) through leverage. Let us assume that all AUM are invested in risky assets. Therefore, $GMV \geq AUM$ and if $GMV > AUM$, then the *leverage of the portfolio* is equal to GMV/AUM and the extra leverage $(GMV/AUM) - 1$ should be borrowed and financed.

3.2.2. *Modern Portfolio Theory*

3.2.2.1. *Gain versus risk*

We will start with some intuition to understand what is at stake behind Modern Portfolio Theory. The practical paradigm of any financial participant having to allocate in a portfolio made of N assets is usually (with very broad definition of profit and risk) to maximize her or his profit while minimizing the risk bared by his or her investment. Of course, the two potential realizations of the allocator's gain and risk are unknown in advance. However, they will be related to the positions in the N assets that will be taken and have before effective investment. Let us denote by $\mathcal{G}_{t,H}$ and $\mathcal{R}_{t,H}$, respectively, the (future) gain and the (future) risk of the investor on a forward period on a horizon of H periods of time as seen as date t of rebalancing. As the two quantities $\mathcal{G}$ and $\mathcal{R}$ are linked, it will not possible to proceed to an optimization in two separate steps. One should therefore find a function $f(\mathcal{G}, \mathcal{R})$ of gain and risk such as f is increasing with gain and decreasing with risk. The easiest way to describe f is to find two $\mathbb{R}$-valued functions f_1 and f_2, monotonically increasing such as:

$$f(\mathcal{G}_{t,H}, \mathcal{R}_{t,H}) = f_1(\mathcal{G}_{t,H}) - f_2(\mathcal{R}_{t,H}).$$

Yet an important aspect is missing, into: we are lacking for a degree of freedom that allows to optimize f since under this form we cannot allow for a trade-off between risk and gain. One should not hope this trade-off to come as a by-product of the optimization. The trade-off between risk and gain is driven by the risk-aversion of the investor that translates from her or his mandate, nature, experience or constraints. Then, f should be parametrized by a λ parameter such that:

$$f_\lambda(\mathcal{G}_{t,H}, \mathcal{R}_{t,H}) = f_1(\mathcal{G}_{t,H}) - \lambda f_2(\mathcal{R}_{t,H}).$$

Allocating between N assets, the only possibility for the investor to have an action on $\mathcal{G}_{t,H}$ and $\mathcal{R}_{t,H}$ is to act on the weights of the assets of the portfolio. Let us denote by w_t the vector of weights[2] held between t and $t{+}1$. Both $\mathcal{G}_{t,H}$ and $\mathcal{R}_{t,H}$ are functions $\mathcal{G}_{t,H}(w)$ and $\mathcal{R}_{t,H}(w)$ of the vector of weights. Of course, w_t has to be determined first through the optimization phase at date t so the optimal w_t^* to find is the one that maximizes the problem:

$$f_\lambda(w) = f_1(\mathcal{G}_{t,H}(w)) - \lambda f_2(\mathcal{R}_{t,H}(w)).$$

Some observations can be made at this stage.

---

2 We prefer for this chapter to state, most of the time, the allocation problem with weights. It is quite different from the usual approach developed in quantities as, for example, in [GOU 01]. We believe that working with weights allow to get more intuitive messages and a clearer picture of the mechanisms at play.

First, such an approach is adapted to any asset class or mix of asset classes as soon as $\mathcal{R}$ and $\mathcal{G}$ can be expressed under an analytical form. Second, this expression may be suited to an allocation when the weights are expressed in both relative weights and capital. The way we switch from one context to another involves the assets under management of the investment process, and the potential leverage available (because leverage is defined as $\sum_{i=1}^{N}|w_i|$ even with the relative weights). Third, the latter expression allows to integrate costs in the expression of $\mathcal{G}$. Moreover, the way $\mathcal{G}$ and $\mathcal{R}$ depend also on w will be explicitly left to the investor which has to build her or his own process. $\mathcal{G}$ may then involve a sophisticated modeling of costs, and $\mathcal{R}$ may be a sophisticated view of risk (asymmetric, nonlinear, tail-risk, etc.). In any case, $\mathcal{G}$ and $\mathcal{R}$ will be stochastic objects that will be defined and estimated. That is the reason why we previously said that allocating was making choices in an uncertain environment. Choices appear in the definition of f_1, f_2, $\mathcal{G}$ and $\mathcal{R}$. Choices are needed in the estimation procedure of the objects potentially involved. Choices again, as we have to pick a vector of weights. The environment is uncertain as $\mathcal{G}$ and $\mathcal{R}$ are not known in advance and have to be estimated and forecasted.

A last but capital remark remains. We may rebalance a portfolio at a shorter horizon than the horizon H of optimization. Let us assume that weights are rebalanced at every period t such as the positions w_t are held between t and $t+1$: H may be a multiple of the period of rebalancing, even infinite. As $\mathcal{G}$ and $\mathcal{R}$ will be estimated or forecasted (and replaced by their estimators $\hat{\mathcal{G}}$ and $\hat{\mathcal{R}}$), the final problem consists in finding an optimal w_t^* such that:

$$w_t^* = \text{argmax}_w \quad \underbrace{f_1(\hat{\mathcal{G}}_{t,H}(w))}_{\text{Gain forecast}} - \lambda \underbrace{f_2(\hat{\mathcal{R}}_{t,H}(w))}_{\text{Risk evaluation}}. \qquad [3.1]$$

3.2.2.2. *Some examples*

Equation [3.1] corresponds (up to the linear breakdown of f in $f_1 - f_2$) to a quite general representation of the allocation problem in the sense of Modern Portfolio Theory (see section 3.2.2.3). Such an explanation allows to understand the motivations and the writing of various allocation techniques. We illustrate how this equation appears in various applied financial contexts. In the following, Ω is again the $N \times N$ covariance matrix between assets and μ the $N \times 1$ vector of expected returns.

– $H = 1$: the horizon of optimization is the same than the one of rebalancing, then we are in a one-period, *myopic* allocation;

– $f_1 = f_2 = I_d$ and $\hat{\mathcal{R}}_t = w_t'\hat{\Omega}w_t$. If $\hat{\mathcal{G}}_t = 0$, we recover the minimum variance allocation optimization problem.

– $f_1 = f_2 = I_d$ and $\hat{\mathcal{R}}_t = w_t'\hat{\Omega}w_t$. If $\hat{\mathcal{G}}_t = w_t'\hat{\mu}$, we recover the mean-variance allocation optimization problem.

We will see that forecasting or estimating risk is usually, if not easier, at least more robust. Estimating $\mathcal{G}$, or finding a proxy for it, is the real challenge. Estimating future risk is an aspect of risk management and may be viewed as a hard science. Estimating future gain is forecasting–this is not a science at all and is instead the fruitful mix of experience, skills and beliefs. For instance, one may have at hand at date t some strategy s_t that will replace $\hat{\mu}$, or any approach to model $\mathcal{G}$ without using μ. Using a strategy and a signal is just having an expectation of future gain that is not only based on historical, past returns. If we want to introduce costs and that we note $\Delta w_t = w_t - w_{t-1}$, then:

– $\mathcal{G} = w_t' s_t - \xi \sum_{i=1}^{N} |\Delta w_t^i|$, where $\xi > 0$ is a fixed parameter, allows to introduce trading costs or broker fees in the optimization accounting for example.

– $\mathcal{G} = w_t' s_t - \gamma(\Delta w_t)^2$, where $\gamma > 0$ is a fixed parameter, allows to introduce quadratic costs in the optimization accounting for impact (see section 3.7.1).

Equation [3.1] is a particular case but remains quite general for many allocation schemes. It is easy to link this writing to mean-reversion, but the field of application is much wider. We can even be less specific, and this is detailed in the next section with the presentation of the general framework of Modern Portfolio Theory as defined by Markowitz.

3.2.2.3. *Modern Portfolio Theory: the general framework*

Harry Markowitz is recognized as the founder of the Modern Portfolio Theory. The original book of [MAR 59] tackled at the time the problem of rational choice under uncertainty, inspired from the work of [SAV 54]. Rationality has to be understood not in terms of information or future knowledge, or as in extra power in forecasting ability. Rationality behind the allocation problem is linked with the ability to make a perfect choice according to defined, assumed preferences of the investor. This does not account for perfect action or prevent the investor from making choices that appear to be detrimental to her or his wealth, as the information of the investor may be limited or incomplete.

Historically, the Markowitz framework is much wider than the famous mean-variance allocation. A very interesting reading is the contribution of [MAR 10] where Harry Markowitz reviews the use that has been made and the way other researchers have interpreted his original approach. Harry Markowitz particularly recalls that the original mean-variance problem is not restricted particularly to Gaussian returns and that the initial utility function (see below) was not doomed to be quadratic. He particularly underlines the differences between two cornerstone papers [MAR 52, MAR 59] and explains with humor, why the utility approach is not straightforward:

"The fundamental assumptions of [MAR 59] are presented late in the book because I feared that practitioners would not read a book that began with axioms of choice under uncertainty." — [MAR 10]

In the original setup, an investor has at hand her or his level of wealth $\mathcal{W}_t$ at date t and for a given horizon. $\mathcal{W}_t$ represents the accumulated wealth gained through the investment from 0 to t with $\mathcal{W}_0$ the initial amount invested. $\mathcal{W}_t$ is linked with assets returns through the budget constraint that drives the evolution equation for wealth:

$$\mathcal{W}_{t+1} = \mathcal{W}_t(w_t'\mathbf{r}_{t+1} + r_{f,t}), \qquad [3.2]$$

$r_{f,t}$ denoting the risk-free rate. Markowitz stressed the need for the investor to maximize the *expected utility* of wealth. A utility function $U(.)$ is a real-valued function of wealth that accounts for the preferences of the investor. It is usually positive, monotonically increasing. $U(.)$ is concave for risk-averse investors and convex for risk-seeking investors. At each period of rebalancing, the investor has to maximize the expectation of the utility of her or his future wealth. According to the evolution of wealth, for the one-period problem, maximizing U as a function of wealth is equivalent to maximize U as a function of returns, because in equation [3.2] at date t, $\mathcal{W}_t$, w_t and $r_{f,t}$ are known in advance. Therefore, up to a change in variables, the random variable $\mathcal{W}_{t+1}$ is tightly linked to the random variable $w_t'R_{t+1}$ (whose randomness is only linked with the one of the returns) and we will still note $U(w_t'R_{t+1})$ to represent utility. More generally, we could note $R_{t+1}^P = w_t'R_{t+1}$, where R_{t+1}^P is the return of the portfolio at date $t+1$. For the most common choice of utility functions, maximizing the expected value of wealth on the next period is equivalent to maximizing the expected return under a constraint of risk, using a dual formulation or minimizing risk for a conditional level of performance. Why? This is because, like any analytical function, the utility function may be approximated through a Taylor series expansion, up to an arbitrary power of the depending variable. If we stop at the second power, we implicitly use the two first moments of the return distribution. As a function of the random variable R_{t+1}, it is possible to approximate the utility function $U(w_t'R_{t+1})$ by:

$$U(w_t'R_{t+1}) \simeq U(0) + U'(0)w_t'R_{t+1} + \frac{1}{2}U''(0)(w_t'R_{t+1})^2.$$

If we assume a centered distribution (which is always easy to obtain if we center around the mean) by a simple Taylor expansion around 0, then:

$$\mathbb{E}[U] \simeq U(0) + U'(0)\mathbb{E}[w_t'R_{t+1}] + \frac{1}{2}U''(0)\Big[\mathbb{V}(w_t'R_{t+1}) + \mathbb{E}[w_t'R_{t+1}]^2\Big].$$

In this case, maximizing the expected utility $\mathbb{E}[U]$ leads to the mean-variance allocation problem. In [MAR 10], Harry Markowitz recalls that even in his original work, its "*defence of mean-variance is not unconditional*". In fact, the above problem is much more flexible:

> "*It is logically possible to accept the expected utility maxim and either accept or reject the use of mean and variance as criteria of portfolio selection. Conversely it is logically possible to accept the use of mean and variance and either accept or reject the expected utility maxim.*" — [MAR 59]

It holds exactly for a quadratic utility (as soon as the n-th derivative of U is zero for any $n \geq 3$) and for Gaussian returns. However, using distributions of returns that are strongly non-Gaussian, heavily skewed or with fat-tails, this approximation cannot hold on the whole support of the return distribution. The approximation holds for smooth or close to quadratic utility functions and distributions of returns that do not show a pathological asymmetry or frequent extreme events. Generalizing directly on the class of functions is a way to sophisticate the analysis by returning to the initial problem. There is in fact a clear link between the utility choice and the chosen measure of risk in a mean-risk allocation procedure. In theory, one could switch from one writing to another, by choosing either the utility function or the risk function $f(.)$ that will account for risk. As soon as we may estimate $\mathbb{E}[f(w_t' R_{t+1})]$ replacing the utility function by a new function $\tilde{U}$:

$$\tilde{U}(w_t' R_{t+1}) = \alpha + \beta w_t' R_{t+1} + \gamma f(w_t' R_{t+1})$$

is always possible. We will see, for instance, in section 4.3.4.1 on page 280 how the utility function appears if we replace variance by semi-variance. We could also include other moments of the distribution to deal with high-dimensional portfolios and with highly non-Gaussian return distribution, by including nonlinear effects or exponents of order greater than 2 in the expression of the utility function. For a detailed discussion on myopic portfolio choice with variations on the choice of utility functions, see [CAM 02]. To get more information on allocation methods involving higher-order moments, one may refer to the contributions of [LEV 79], [KRO 84], [HLA 94], [EDE 95], [JON 06], [MAR 09], or Chapter 9 of [JON 07a].

3.3. A focus on mean-variance

In this section, we will focus on the one-period mean-variance allocation with no friction. As simple as it may appear at first sight, mean-variance shows an exceptional versatility. It may be used as a stepping stone to more sophisticated approaches (as shown in section 3.7), while being mathematically simple and tractable. We want to emphasise here the intuitions of the model even if we do not expect our readers to reduce their own process to a simple, uncontrolled, one-stage mean-variance allocation. Why is it still important today to study mean-variance allocation in detail? First, mean-variance allocation is now quite a common tool for financial markets. It is therefore a necessary concept to study an ideal framework for understanding the issues of portfolio allocation. Even with some pitfalls, it remains a powerful tool, with several features that practitioners sometimes forget. In particular, it remains a smart way to control risk, and induces hedging relations within a portfolio. One of the main messages of the setup is that diversification is not relying on decorrelation but may be obtained even in the presence of correlation, and that the decrease of risk that we may obtain is linked to the strength of this correlation. Second, because even when using a sophisticated dynamical trading framework, we may also need a one-period allocation procedure and even in this respect, mean-variance allocation gives insight to set up those techniques. In this respect, a comprehensive understanding may then be a stepping stone that may be useful for handling dynamic trading issues. We will briefly review considerations relative to a fully dynamic trading framework in section 3.7.

3.3.1. *Mean-variance allocation*

The mean-variance optimization problem can be derived from the expectation utility writing developed in section 3.2.2.3. An expectation utility framework requires the choice of a utility function, and this choice will drive the specificities of the corresponding approach. With Gaussian returns and a quadratic utility function, it is a sufficient condition to recover the mean-variance allocation problem. The two contributions of [MAR 79] and [KRO 84] show that the minimum variance framework is suitable for common but various utility functions satisfying properties that are not too restrictive. Therefore, the precise choice of the utility function may appear as a second-order problem.

3.3.1.1. *Explicit specification*

Starting with a multitude of assets, an investor wants to select the optimal weights of each asset, while trying to control its expected performance and its expected level of risk. Mean-variance allocation aims at building such a portfolio by solving a one-period optimization program, through the maximization of the expected return of the portfolio for a given level of risk. This level of risk depends on the targeted or maximal budget of risk that the investor is ready, able or constrained to bear. Consequently, it requires in its simplest form two main objects: an estimation of the expected returns on the assets and an estimation of the risk between assets. Returns (R_t) are assumed to be i.i.d. in time and follow a Gaussian distribution with moments μ and Ω. The returns R_t^p of a portfolio made of those assets with generic weights w (we drop the indexation with time) are therefore also Gaussian with moments:

$$\mathbb{E}[R_t^p] = w'\mu \qquad \text{and} \qquad \mathbb{V}[R_t^p] = w'\Omega w.$$

The Gaussian assumption may be disappointing because this is a well-known fact that even for very large timescales (e.g. monthly returns), it is very difficult to support the fact that returns are Gaussian as widely discussed in Chapter 1. However, the allocation model may be decently robust to this assumption. In any case, the same optimization program holds if μ is replaced with any subjective view s_t of expected returns. The investor wants to maximize its one-period expected return while maintaining a low level of risk. The Lagrangian to optimize is the following:

$$\begin{aligned}\mathcal{L}(w) &= \mathbb{E}[R_t] - \frac{\lambda}{2}\mathbb{V}[R_t] \\ &= w'\mu - \frac{\lambda}{2}w'\Omega w. \end{aligned} \qquad [3.3]$$

The first-order condition of the Lagrangian gives:

$$\mu - \lambda\Omega w^* = 0,$$

where w^* is the solution of the problem and λ, the Lagrange multiplier, may be determined through the constraint on the variance (i.e. the level of risk). Hence, the optimal portfolio allocation (in the Markowitz sense) is an allocation w^* such that:

$$w^* = \frac{1}{\lambda}\Omega^{-1}\mu. \qquad [3.4]$$

REMARK 3.1.– It has been shown in theorem 1 of [BRI 99] that the same kind of expression for the weights of mean-variance, efficient portfolios may be obtained through the standard OLS regression of a fixed vector of ones on the matrix of returns, without any intercept:

$$e_N = \beta'\mathbf{R} + \epsilon \qquad [3.5]$$

where $\mathbf{R} = \{\mathbf{r}_k\}_{k=1}^N$ is the matrix of asset returns and ϵ is an i.i.d. perturbation. The weights are consequently the vector of parameters (normalized by their sum) as the OLS-estimate $\hat{\beta}$ is:

$$\begin{aligned}\hat{\beta} &= (\mathbf{R}'\mathbf{R})^{-1}(\mathbf{R}'e_N) \\ &= \hat{\Omega}^{-1}\hat{\mu},\end{aligned}$$

and $w^* = \hat{\beta}/(\hat{\beta}'.e_N)$. As underlined by the author, this kind of approach is quite unusual, because the dependent variable is a constant and therefore non-random; there is no intercept, the residuals may be correlated with the explanatory variable, violating the usual assumptions required by OLS estimation. Despite its simplicity and apparent redundancy, this framework is in fact quite practical as it allows to derive tests on the weights of the portfolio.

REMARK 3.2.– We provide in Appendix A.2 some simple and usual measures frequently used in the literature to analyze a set of portfolio weights through the lens of a single quantity to monitor diversification of the given portfolio.

3.3.1.2. *Working with quantities*

Working with weights is not standard but helps a lot to understand the issues of portfolio allocation in practice. The expression of the usual theoretical mean-variance problem uses in general quantities rather than weights. Indeed, working with weights, the parameter λ is in fact implicitly fixed, because with relative weights either $w_t' e_N$, $|w_t|' e_N$ or both are fixed (e.g. both equal to 1 for a long-only portfolio). Working with quantities, λ recovers in fact a risk aversion interpretation. Stating the problem in currency and in quantity should give a similar formula but in quantities:

$$q^* = \frac{1}{\lambda_q}\Omega^{-1}\mu,$$

where λ_q is still the Lagrange multiplier associated to the optimization problem stated in quantities, and is a proxy for the risk-aversion of the investor. Indeed, as λ_q tends to infinity, the norm of the vector of allocation in quantity vanishes. Reciprocally, λ_q close to zero implies high absolute levels of investment in risky assets. There is in implicit equation when working with weights, which is the relative constraint (say $w_t'.e_N = 1$). This constraint determines λ, but here, λ_q is rarely known from the investor. It is a "subjective risk-aversion", but it may be difficult for an investor to spontaneously give its subjective value of λ_q, which is determined by a problem that does not write:

$$q'\mu - \frac{\lambda_q}{2} q'\Omega q,$$

but rather:

$$q'\mu - \frac{\lambda_q}{2}(q'\Omega q - \sigma_H^2 AUM),$$

where AUM stands for the assets under management and σ_H is a target volatility measured on a H horizon. Then, the term $(q'\Omega q - \sigma_H^2 AUM)$ is a constraint in risk that has to be saturated and that helps to determine λ_q. In fact, λ_q is tightly linked to leverage.

For an illustration purpose (and illustration only), let us assume that at time t_0 a vector of positive quantities $q_{(t_0)} = w_{(t_0)} \times GMV$ is computed and held fixed with no rebalancing on a subsequent period $[t_0; t_0 + H]$. We consider no reinvested returns for sake of clarity and compute the out-of-sample risk through the computation of the *ex post* quadratic[3] risk $\mathcal{R}_H^{OS}([t_0; t_0 + H])$ of the strategy:

$$\begin{aligned}\mathcal{R}_H^{OS}([t_0; t_0 + H]) &= \frac{1}{H} \sum_{t=t_0}^{t_0+H-1} (q'_{(t_0)} \mathbf{r}_{t+1})^2 \\ &= \frac{1}{H} \sum_{t=t_0}^{t_0+H-1} \frac{1}{\lambda^2} (\hat{\mu}'_{t_0} \hat{\Omega}^{-1} \mathbf{r}_{t+1})^2 GMV^2 \\ &= \frac{1}{H} \sum_{t=t_0}^{t_0+H-1} (\hat{\mu}'_{t_0} \hat{\Omega}^{-1} \mathbf{r}_{t+1})^2 \left(\frac{L \times AUM}{\lambda} \right)^2,\end{aligned}$$

with weights such that $w_{(t_0)} = \hat{\Omega}^{-1} \hat{\mu}_{t_0}$ and $GMV = L \times AUM$, L being the leverage of the portfolio. Therefore, for achieving a target volatility σ_H we have to set L such that:

$$\underbrace{\sqrt{\frac{1}{H} \sum_{t=t_0}^{t_0+H-1} (\hat{\mu}'_{t_0} \hat{\Omega}^{-1} \mathbf{r}_{t+1})^2}}_{\hat{\psi}(t_0, H)} \frac{L}{\lambda} = \sigma_H,$$

since λ will be implicitly fixed by the mandate and nature of the fund, σ_H is exogenously given. However, the first term $\hat{\psi}(t_0, H)$ may vary with time as soon as financial returns are heteroskedastic. Indeed, the true volatility of underlying assets may vary ex post and an adaptive leverage allow us to control for the realized, effective volatility of the strategy. With a fixed leverage, the volatility of the strategy will never be constant. Acting on L helps to achieve σ_H: increase leverage in quiet markets and decrease it in case of volatility bursts. However, this comes at a cost, because the higher the leverage, the higher the cost as $(L - 1)AUM$ has at least to be borrowed and financed.

3.3.2. *Estimating moments*

Until now, we assumed that we had natural estimators for the return moments. We will in fact see throughout the chapter that allocation is in itself a global estimation challenge. The most natural estimators are sample counterparts, those previously defined in section 1.3.2. Sample counterparts are historical estimators, but it is not straightforward that this approach is optimal: with the words of [MAR 10], those estimators "*should be forward-looking rather than purely historical. Even a purely*

3 We neglect here the term $(\frac{1}{H} \sum_{t=t_0}^{t_0+H-1} q'_{(t_0)} \mathbf{r}_{t+1})^2$ that we assume to be negligible for H sufficiently large.

historical approach (...) involves judgement as to what estimation period to use". Their use without further treatment will in fact imply statistical problems whose study will be made afterward in section 3.3.3.

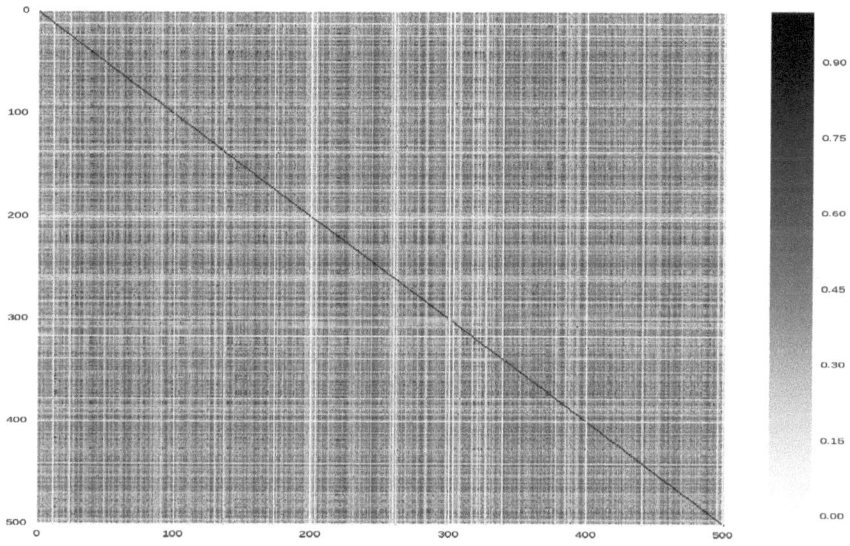

Figure 3.3. *Daily correlation matrix of S&P500 constituents at the date of 2015/01/01 for a period from 2002/01/01 to 2014/12/31. Data represents 502 assets on 3273 returns. Correlation is computed as the Pearson correlation. The mean correlation is equal to 0.346*

This general positive correlation accounts for the existence of a general "market mode" (all stocks generally co-moving with the market) reflecting the index nature of the S&P500, and the underlying motivations and message of the CAPM. However, the general correlation is expected to increase in the periods of market turmoils. In case of directional move of the market, stocks co-movements are higher in case of bear market than in case of bull markets. Stocks are relatively more correlated in bad times. This constitutes a well known stylized fact supported, for instance, by [ANG 02b], [ANG 02a] or [BAE 05] among others.

We illustrate this empirical evidence by plotting on Figure 3.4 the boxplot distribution of the correlation of S&P500 stocks with the relative index, per calendar year (the sample for the index as for each stock is therefore their returns within one calendar year). In this figure, this is not the correlation of stocks among others, but of stocks with the index, but this should convey roughly the same nature of information. We observe a neat spike in the correlations' distribution during the economic crisis lasting approximately from 2007 to 2009, assessing the observation that, in bear markets, stocks tend to correlate more with the market. We observe a neat spike in the correlations' distribution during the economic crisis lasting approximately from 2007 to 2009, assessing the observation that in bear markets, stocks tend to correlate more with the market.

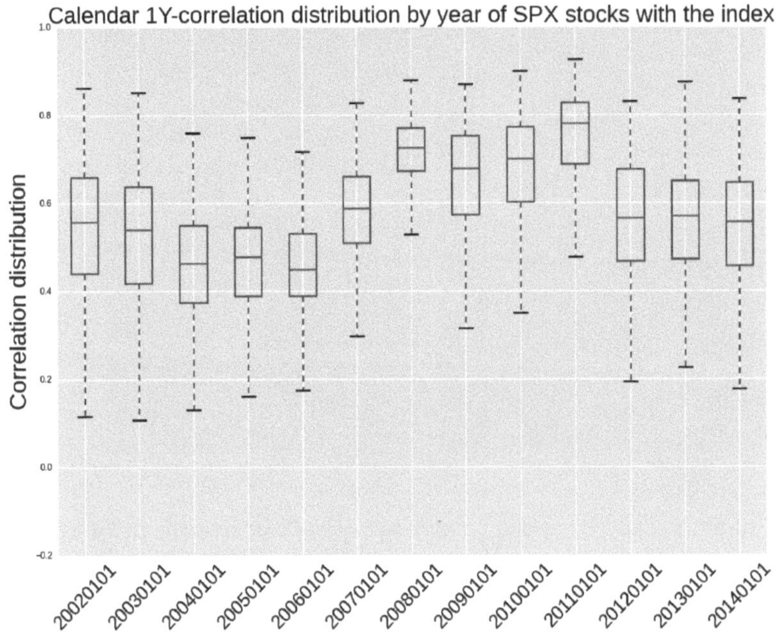

Figure 3.4. *Boxplot distribution of the correlation of S&P500 stocks constituents with the S&P500 index, per calendar year (one value per stock and per year). Total sample of returns still comprised between 2002/01/01 and 2014/12/31 for* 502 *fixed assets*

Figure 3.5 also illustrates this fact as we plot stock by stock the correlation with the index (x-axis) obtained on the overall period versus. the correlations with the index computed (y-axis) on the restrained crisis period (years 2007, 2008 and 2009). The plain line represents the identity line. We observe that the vast majority of correlations are shifted upward roughly 10–15%. This increase of the correlations seems to be a general pattern.

It is known for a long time (see, e.g. [BLA 76]) that the variance of returns is in general not constant, regardless of the asset class. Estimating Ω is quite straightforward in practice. The estimations do vary but quite slowly in time. It would be sufficient to refresh the estimator frequently. Usually, it may be improved by estimating separately correlations and volatilities, but it is comparatively a minor problem when compared to the problem of the estimation of μ. Estimating μ is a difficult task as underlined in a famous contribution of [MER 80]. The idea is that if we fix two points in time, t_0 and t_1, and observe a process S sampled at t_0 and t_1, the estimation of the drift we obtain would be dramatically impacted by the potential fluctuations of the stock between those two points. If the intrinsic volatility is huge, then the noise on the estimation of the drift is high and the estimator is of poor quality. Therefore, if we cannot subsample S between t_0 and t_1, we have no guess on the level of the volatility, no guess on the potential heteroskedasticity, etc. In other words, knowing where we start and where we end does not tell us much on the regularity of the path.

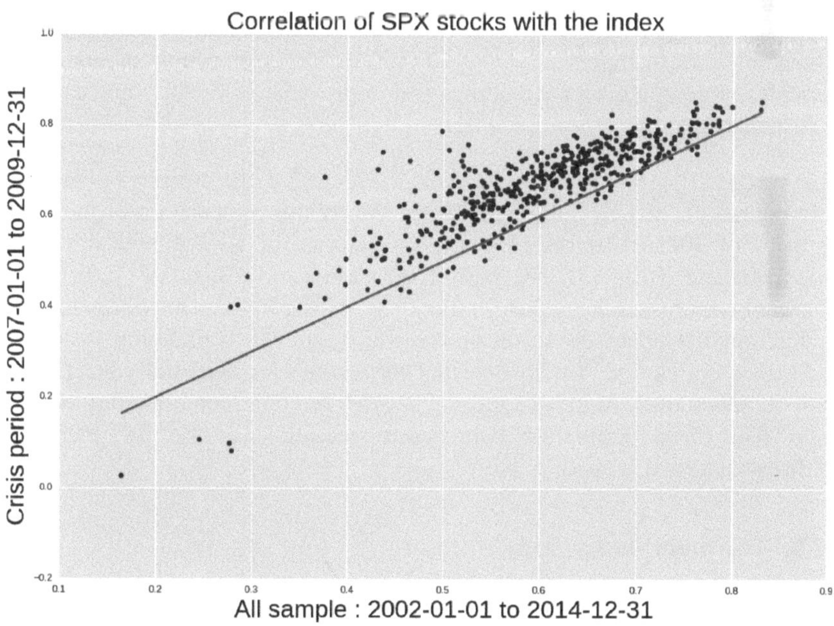

Figure 3.5. *Scatter-plot of stock-by-stock correlation with the S&P500 index obtained on the overall period 2002/01/01 and 2014/12/31 (x-axis) versus same correlations with the index computed on calendar years 2007, 2008 and 2009 (y-axis) representing crisis period. Plain line is the identity line. Total sample of returns still comprised between for* 502 *fixed assets*

It has been known since the work of [STE 56] that we may use in optimization estimators for the mean that are different from the sample mean that are more efficient out-of-sample. The work on Bayesian estimators for estimated moments is still the object of full academic research and the exhaustive list of contributions would be too long to present. We could, however, give the flavor of Bayesian estimation for estimating the expected returns. Following the original idea of [JAM 92], we may estimate $\hat{\mu}$ for the asset i through:

$$\hat{\mu}_i = \bar{\mu} + \alpha_i(\bar{\mu}_i - \bar{\mu}),$$

where $\bar{\mu}_i$ is the sample mean of asset i, $\bar{\mu}$ is the global sample mean averaged over assets and α_i is a mixing parameter belonging to $[0; 1]$ that is specific for the asset i and depends on its specificities, among all variance. The method of selection of α_i is at the heart of the method. The main focus and motivation of the method is to obtain better results in out-of-sample. We do not develop further the discussion of Stein estimators for sample means as it is not fully relevant in our analysis, because in the context of the use of proprietary strategies, the estimated mean will be dropped and replaced by bets or strategies. Yet, on the statistical part, the estimation problem remains of utmost importance, and this discussion is of course of utmost interest. Examples of complementary readings and improvements on the topic can be found, for instance, in [EFR 77] or [LED 01].

NUMERICAL EXAMPLE 3.1.– We plot in Figure 3.3 the correlation matrix of the daily returns of the S&P500 components. We fix the composition of the S&P500 at the date[4] of 2015/01/01 on 13 years, i.e. returns for all available prices between 2002/01/01 and 2015/01/01. We have in this case $T = 3273$ and $N = 502$ (502 stocks, 3,273 daily returns). This makes a ratio $T/N \sim 6.52$. Returns are normalized by their unconditional standard deviation on the whole sample. Correlation is computed as the Pearson correlation. We observe that correlations are essentially positive (only 14 negative terms over $N(N-1)/2 = 125,751$ possible combinations of couple of assets. The mean correlation over assets (measured as the flat average of the off-diagonal terms) is about 0.346[5].

3.3.3. *The inversion puzzle*

The use of raw sample estimators without correction, as just presented, is in practice detrimental to the out-of-sample performance and behavior of the mean-variance allocation. We will develop further throughout section 3.5 refinements

4 The example taken in this chapter is essentially useful for a statistical, descriptive study. We do not follow dynamically the S&P500 index on the period with stocks potentially leaving and entering the index, as we are mainly interested by the underlying statistical aspects of the study of a pool of stocks. A real backtest on such a pool of fixed stock would lead to survivorship bias but again, it is not our point here.

5 Note that this value is on daily returns. [POT 05] finds a value around 0.29 on S&P500 in a different period. However, the figures are lowered for intra-day data since it is more around 0.2 for 1 hour returns and around 0.05 for 5 minutes returns (see, again, [POT 05]).

to propose more robust estimators. However, it is crucial to explain why the blind application of expression 3.4 performs poorly empirically.

3.3.3.1. *Instability: a well-identified effect*

Practically, multiplying $\hat{\mu}$ by $\hat{\Omega}^{-1}$ in equation [3.4] leads to unstable solutions or extreme, overweighted vectors. [MER 80] already remarked the sensitivity of the resulting empirical portfolio to slight modifications of expected returns. [JOB 80, JOB 81b], [JOR 86], [FRO 86, FRO 88], [MIC 89], [BES 91], [CHO 93] among others, highlighted such problems when inverting the sample covariance matrix, because variations or errors in the return vector $\hat{\mu}$ are dramatically amplified. Coordinates with abnormal weights are unfortunately (or logically) those corresponding to the greatest estimation error. [MIC 89] even calls the mean-variance optimization the *"error maximization"* and recalls that we have to make a clear distinction between the *"financial optimality"* and the *"mathematical optimization"*.

This fact is a real limitation for practitioners. Proceeding to a rolling estimation of $\hat{\Omega}$ and $\hat{\mu}$ at two consecutive dates t and $t+1$, we end up with estimates $\hat{\mu}_t$ and $\hat{\mu}_{t+1}$ that are very close, then, even if $\hat{\Omega}_t$ and $\hat{\Omega}_{t+1}$ are also quite close (and $\hat{\Omega}$ may be also fixed), w_t^* and w_{t+1}^* may be far different due to the nearly singular nature of $\hat{\Omega}^{-1}$. The same feature remains with any estimator of μ varying (even slightly) in time, coming from an historical estimation or not. This is a drawback for the investor, as it implies a huge turnover of its portfolio, a deep rebalancing of its positions and a loss of interpretation in the views she or he tries to implement. This is an unwanted feature that generates practical limitations, turnover and high transaction costs. Most of all, this gives a bad understanding of what is going on and the potential profitability of the setup is wrecked by transaction costs. The instability problem does not come from the return estimator in itself but in the *spectral configuration* of $\hat{\Omega}$. When N is less than T, but still very large, the sample covariance matrix is invertible but numerically ill-conditioned. $\hat{\Omega}$ may be close to singular with eigenvalues close to zero. When N is larger than T, $\hat{\Omega}$ is not even invertible. This occurs especially when T is of the same order as N (T greater than N for identifiability but with T/N close to one). This fact has been well identified in the literature, seminal references may be found in the work of [MUI 87] or [PAF 04]. The asymptotic theory with $N, T \to \infty$ is developed in [LED 02].

The case of one single asset is statistically enlightening. As explored previously, using the results of section 1.3.2 and using the computations taken from [BRA 10], the variance of the weight writes:

$$\begin{aligned}\mathbb{V}[\hat{w}^*] &= \frac{1}{\lambda^2}\left(\frac{\mu}{\sigma^2}\right)^2\left(\frac{\mathbb{V}[\hat{\mu}]}{\mu^2} + \frac{\mathbb{V}[\hat{\sigma}^2]}{\sigma^4}\right) \\ &= (w^*)^2\left(\frac{\mathbb{V}[\hat{\mu}]}{\mu^2} + \frac{\mathbb{V}[\hat{\sigma}^2]}{\sigma^4}\right).\end{aligned}$$

Such an expression is useful since we see that the precision (inverse of the variance) of the estimator of the weights is increasing in the variance of the estimators (return and variance) itself scaled by the amplitude of the respective parameter. Let us clarify also that $\mathbb{V}[\hat{\sigma}^2]$ may largely drive and increase the variance of the estimator of the weights in case of departure from the i.i.d. Gaussian returns with large kurtosis. Each moment (and even higher order moments) has potentially an influence on the instability of weights estimators.

3.3.3.2. *Out-of-sample risk*

Even in the absence of costs, mean-variance portfolios with sample estimators may exhibit an *a posteriori* variance that is too high. The out-of-sample performance of the mean-variance process is consequently often rather poor. This is called *sampling error* in traditional statistics and reflects the fact that the estimator of moments is estimated on a subset, and not on the total population. Here, the subset of estimation is simply past data used afterward. The estimation error largely destroys the potential profitability of the signal and blurs the pertinence of the model. The mean-variance procedure is even qualified by [RON 14] as a "*quite aggressive model of active management*". [BOY 14] testing and investigating for the effects of each step of the process finds that estimation errors increases with the correlation among assets. When there is a high level of correlation among assets, this will have severe *a posteriori* effects due to estimation error.

We should at this stage, however, have a discussion[6] on the comparison of in-sample and out-of-sample risk when using the mean-variance framework. Let us assume that we are working on two periods: at time t_0 we have observed some past data on an unspecified period but we have at hand an estimated covariance matrix $\hat{\Omega}_{(0)}$ of the true but unknown matrix of returns covariance Ω, and a vector of weights $\hat{w}_{(0)} = (\hat{w}_{(0),1}, ..., \hat{w}_{(0),N})$ estimated thanks to $\hat{\Omega}_{(0)}$ and an arbitrary signal. $\hat{\Omega}_{(0)}$ is assumed to be an unbiased estimator of Ω. A direct consequence is that $\hat{\Omega}_{(0)}$ and $\hat{w}_{(0)}$ are not independent as $\hat{\Omega}_{(0)}$ is explicitly used in the computation of the weights. The in-sample risk, ISR, on the estimation period, may be computed *a posteriori* at t_0 and:

$$ISR = \hat{w}'_{(0)}\hat{\Omega}_{(0)}\hat{w}_{(0)}. \quad [3.6]$$

Weights $\hat{w}_{(0)}$ will be used on a subsequent period $[t_0; t_0 + T]$. Replace (see also on the beginning of next page as the equation is split by page break) – a footnote should appear...

6 This discussion is greatly inspired by the messages conveyed by [POT 05] and [BOU 11].

We are interested in measuring the out-of-sample risk, OSR, that will be observed and computed on the following period. If r_t^P is again the observed return of the portfolio P, we have[7]:

$$\begin{aligned} OSR &= \frac{1}{H}\sum_{t=t_0+1}^{t_0+H}(r_t^P)^2 \\ &= \sum_{t=t_0+1}^{t_0+H}\sum_{i,j=1}^{N}\hat{w}_{(0),i}\hat{w}_{(0),j}\frac{(r_{i,t}-\hat{\mu}_{(1)})(r_{j,t}-\hat{\mu}_{(1)})}{H} \\ &= \hat{w}'_{(0)}\hat{\Omega}_{(1)}\hat{w}_{(0)}, \end{aligned}$$

where $\hat{\mu}_{(1)}$ and $\hat{\Omega}_{(1)}$ are sample counterpart estimators of the moments of the return distributions estimated *a posteriori* on the $[t_0; t_0 + T]$ period. We have that:

$$\begin{aligned} \mathbb{E}[OSR] &= \mathbb{E}[\hat{w}'_{(0)}\hat{\Omega}_{(1)}\hat{w}_{(0)}] \\ &= \hat{w}'_{(0)}\mathbb{E}[\hat{\Omega}_{(1)}]\hat{w}_{(0)} \\ &= \hat{w}'_{(0)}\Omega\hat{w}_{(0)}? \end{aligned} \qquad [3.7]$$

as $\hat{\Omega}_{(1)}$ will be an unbiased estimator of Ω. However, $\hat{\Omega}_{(0)}$ is also an unbiased estimator of Ω! Therefore, we will have $\mathbb{E}[\hat{\Omega}_{(0)}] = \mathbb{E}[\hat{\Omega}_{(1)}] = \Omega$ and we naturally have by replacing in 3.7 that:

$$\mathbb{E}[OSR] = \hat{w}'_{(0)}\mathbb{E}[\hat{\Omega}_{(0)}]\hat{w}_{(0)}. \qquad [3.8]$$

As said before, $\hat{\Omega}_{(0)}$ and $\hat{w}_{(0)}$ are not independent and one consequence is therefore that in the most general case we have that:

$$\mathbb{E}[\hat{w}'_{(0)}\hat{\Omega}_{(0)}\hat{w}_{(0)}] \neq \hat{w}'_{(0)}\mathbb{E}[\hat{\Omega}_{(0)}]\hat{w}_{(0)}.$$

The most direct implication of this observation is that one *must not* measure *out-of-sample* risk with the same matrix that the one used formerly in the weight computation step. But how to rank those risks? The use of the Jensen inequality (stating that for a random variable X and a convex function f, we have that $\mathbb{E}[f(X)] \geq f(\mathbb{E}[X])$) on the appropriate variables should help us to show that when comparing equations [3.6] and [3.7] we have that:

$$ISR \leq OSR.$$

7 Here again we neglect the term $(\frac{1}{H}\sum_{t=t_0+1}^{t_0+H} r_t^P)^2$.

Is it possible to quantify the gap between in-sample and out-of-sample risk? [BOU 11] details this by interposing between the two terms a theoretical definition of risk TR involving Ω that allows to separate them, in such a way that[8]:

$$ISR = (1-q) \times TR = (1-q)^2 \times OSR,$$

where $q = N/T$ quantifies the amount of noise we have due to limited sample. Here again, the more data we have (high value of T), the highest distortion between in-sample and out-sample-risk we will get. This is an important message to have in mind, which we will recall in section 4.2.2. The best fit we get in-sample, the more trouble we will get out-of-sample and the more discrepancy we should expect out-of-sample.

3.3.4. *Operator writing and regularization*

The following section provides a suitable mathematical framework to introduce the concept of regularization as a global way of rediscovering allocation techniques explained later in the chapter. Again, allocation techniques are rarely developed under the prism of inverse problems in the traditional literature (however, with some exceptions like in, e.g., [LED 02], [LED 03]). We deliver a brief yet technical introduction to inverse problems in Appendix A.3 whose reading is preferable to understand the concepts elaborated here. As a complementary review on algebra and Hilbert spaces, one may also refer to [CAR 03].

Equation [3.4] elects for an inverse problem modeling under the framework described in Appendix A.3 since we try to recover the solution w^* such that $\Omega w^* = \mu$, where μ and Ω have to be estimated, and both lie in $\mathbb{R}^N$, endowed with its natural scalar product is an Hilbert space. The covariance matrix Ω is linked to such an operator $K = K_\Omega$:

$$K_\Omega : \begin{cases} \mathbb{R}^N \to \mathbb{R}^N \\ w \mapsto \Omega w. \end{cases}$$

K_Ω is unknown and estimated through $\hat{K} = K_{\hat{\Omega}}$. The problem is, in practice, $\hat{K}w = \hat{\mu}$. K_Ω is a linear operator with finite dimensional range, as obviously $\mathcal{R}(\Omega) \subset \mathbb{R}^N$. Thus, K_Ω is a compact and continuous operator. Moreover, K is self-adjoint (for the usual scalar product in $\mathbb{R}^N$) as Ω is a symmetric matrix.

Is this problem well-posed? Intuitively, well-posedness (whose true definition is, again, explored in Appendix A.3, more precisely in section A.3.1.2.6) is a measure of the sensibility of the solution of the problem to modifications of the input. Mild

8 The risks defined here are homogeneous to variances, not volatilities.

effects of slight changes of the input may be a sign of well-posedness. Strong or unbounded effects of slight changes of the input may be a sign of ill-posedness. Technically, it depends on the characteristics and the degree of knowledge of K (Ω in our case). If Ω is known, symmetric and has strictly positive eigenvalues, the answer is affirmative. The inverse exists and is continuous (because Ω can be diagonalized with strictly positive eigenvalues). When Ω is unknown, it has to be replaced by a consistent estimator $\hat{\Omega}$. When T/N is close to one, $\hat{\Omega}$ becomes close to singular. Then, $\hat{\Omega}^{-1}$ is in general unbounded and the ill-posedness of the Markowitz inverse problem arises.

Technically, any estimated matrix with strictly positive eigenvalues do not lead to an ill-posed problem. Indeed, in this case, operator $K_{\hat{\Omega}}$ will be continuous, and as we are in finite dimension, we are not, mathematically, in a pure case of ill-posedness, with the concepts defined in Appendix A.3. However, ill-posedness has to be understood through the effective numerical problems appearing in practice. Rather than pure unboundedness, we may face situations where numerical inversion is at least uncontrolled. Indeed, inversion problems arise also because periodically refreshing the estimation of the covariance matrix does not allow any control on the lowest and noisiest eigenvalues.

Finally, *regularization methods* (see again Appendix A.3.2) will consist of modifying the operator, often with a parametrized correction, with a parameter choice rule, such that if the regularization parameter is suitably chosen according to that rule, the regularized solution will converge to the true solution as the noise level vanishes. Regularization aims at solving the instability problem in problematic situations, in case of ill-posedness. Generally speaking, regularization will imply controlling the level of noise and in finite dimension, the dimension N of the spaces between whom K operates. The crucial point is always the same; there is the trade-off between precision and regularity of the solution. Leaving some precision should allow to increase stability.

3.4. Spectral insights for allocation

Section 3.3.3 helps to identify the source of the problems when using mean-variance allocation with sample moment estimators. The estimated sample covariance matrix is empirically badly conditioned and its inversion leads to unstable solutions. The most natural solution is to find better estimators. However, in order to build such estimators, we need to explore the fine spectral structure of the covariance matrix to understand what should be the suitable spectral pitfalls that estimators should dodge to behave decently out-of-sample.

3.4.1. *Should we work with covariance or correlation?*

This question seems trivial but is not so simple to address: should we estimate the correlation or the covariance matrix directly? Indeed the covariance matrix Ω of N asset returns should write:

$$\Omega = DCD,$$

$D = diag(\sigma_1, \ldots, \sigma_N)$ is the diagonal matrix of size N made of the individual volatilities of the assets on the diagonal (and 0 elsewhere), and C is the $N \times N$ correlation matrix between the assets. Either estimating Ω directly or not, we should end up with similar results but empirically, things seem to be different. The difficulty comes from the fact that the answer depends mainly on experience, preferences and habits of practitioners. Both academic and empirical references in finance are rather scarce because depending on the data, practitioners will rather trust their experience and their knowledge of the data set. The answer that comes more frequently is that it is preferable to separate the estimation of the volatility and the estimation of the correlation. A practical argument is that it allows first to build an expertise on each item to be estimated but also that the spectral analysis of the correlation matrix maybe more stable and less tricky.

Correlation estimation is not so difficult since the sample counterpart estimation is clear and easy to implement, and the matrix to obtain has properties that are identified (symmetry and diagonal terms equal to 1). The trace of the matrix is known and equal to N. The estimation of the volatility/variance (see, e.g., sections 1.3.2.3 and 1.5.2) may be more complicated but separating the problem allows any kind of sophistication: ARCH/GARCH models which are now quite common [ENG 82]; exponential moving averages, mixed frequencies, etc. For instance, [POT 05] adapts the usual covariance estimator using exponential moving averages of returns, and also deals with the mixed-frequency approach in the most general way. In addition, [ENG 16] mixes directly the estimation of a sophisticated time series model for volatility, while controlling for the correlation structure. Moreover, working on the correlation matrix is in a way a mean to "normalize" the data and proceeding to spectral analysis on variables that are set on a comparable scale. In the case where assets have volatilities of different scales, working on the spectral decomposition of the correlation matrix is far much safer and is therefore focused on the study of the real structure of linear dependence.

We will consequently mainly study in the following the spectral analysis of *correlation matrices* in the following. However, the eigenvalues of the correlation and the covariance matrix should only differ by the multiplication of the individual variances of the assets. On a universe assets, their returns are generally quite homogeneous: they show naturally different moments that are, however, of the same order of magnitude. Consequently, the level of variance involved are if not similar, at least comparable. Indeed, the potential differences in variances between them may be substantial but not sufficient to invalidate conclusions made on the spectrum of the correlation matrix, since the differences in numerical order of eigenvalues are way greater than differences in variances. Therefore, all the qualitative conclusions drawn from the spectrum of the correlation matrices should hold for the spectrum of the covariance matrix. We will study correlation matrices, but we will draw conclusions mechanically also for covariance matrices. In any case, it is important to note that working correlation does not prevent us to solve for the stationarity problem. Variance, asset by asset, can vary a lot, but so does correlation. Regardless of the object of interest, the non-stationarity of the estimated object is a main problem that will lead to estimation error, with consequences in out-of-sample.

3.4.2. *PCA and SVD*

When studying empirical correlation matrices, one may find alternating discussions on the use of "PCA" (Principal Component Analysis) or "SVD" (Singular Value Decomposition). What are they, is there a difference, is one more preferable than the other? This duality of notions may be confusing but fortunately they collapse in one and only in the present case as we deal with symmetric, semi-definite positive matrices. We provide in Appendix A.3 a full discussion of Singular Value Decomposition (henceforth SVD), operators and spaces, to which we will implicitly refer in the following.

In finite dimension, in the vectorial[9] spaces $\mathbb{R}^N$, which belongs to the vectors of weights w on the N assets, matrices are the natural incarnation of linear operators. If $\mathbf{R}$ is the $T \times N$ matrix of the return series of the N assets of length T and if $K\mathbb{R}^N \to \mathbb{R}^T$ is the operator that maps an N-dimensional real-valued vector w onto $\mathbf{R}w$, then the covariance matrix $\Omega = \frac{T}{N}\mathbf{R}'\mathbf{R}$ will represent (up to the normalizing factor) the $\mathbb{R}^N \to \mathbb{R}^N$ operator KK^* and the discussion of Appendix A.3 straightforwardly applies. This implies in particular that the eigenvalues of Ω coincide with the squared singular values of operator K. Said alternatively, in the linear, finite-dimensional case, diagonalizing Ω or proceeding to the SVD on the initial return observations is identical up to a square-root transformation of the eigenvalues. We will use either one term or the other in the following.

There is, however, one confusion to lift off when comparing SVD and PCA. PCA (see [HÄR 15] for an in-depth introduction) is a well-known learning technique aiming at finding linear combinations of the initial variables (vectors or axes) that allow to explain data at best in the sense of variance decomposition. The technique relies also on the diagonalization of the covariance matrix of the initial variables. The eigenvectors are homogeneous to axes of representation, and the eigenvalues are

9 We recall that $\mathbb{R}^N$ with its natural scalar product in an Hilbert space.

homogeneous to the proportion of variance represented by the vector. Should we keep only the most important combinations of data, we would retain only the axes where corresponding eigenvalues that are the highest. PCA is adapted to “any” kind of variable, that is to say not only to financial returns, and is widely used in data analysis. However, in finite dimension, SVD is also understood as the decomposition of the previous observation matrix $\mathbf{R}$ as:

$$\mathbf{R} = U\Delta V',$$

where U is a $T \times D$ matrix, Δ is $D \times D$ diagonal with descending diagonal elements, V is an orthonormal $D \times N$ matrix, and D is the rank of matrix $\mathbf{R}$. In particular as a particular consequence, an SVD is possible on non-squared matrix and this decomposition is unique. D will be equal to the number of non-zero eigenvalues of $\mathbf{R}'\mathbf{R} = V'\Delta^2 V$. In the case of covariance matrix estimated on financial returns, we would hope that r will be close to N even if this equality will be difficult to check due to estimation error.

Technically, using a PCA would be equivalent to diagonalize $\mathbf{R}'\mathbf{R}$ directly, but it is, in practice, numerically more efficient (or less problematic) to estimate the eigenvalues by estimating first the SVD decomposition through U, Δ and V and recover the eigenvalues as the squared values of the diagonal elements of Δ. The robustness of the estimation method for the empirical correlation matrix is indeed necessary numerically to compute directly the eigen decomposition of the correlation matrix but in this case, the sensitivity to problems in data (missing values, non-synchronized series, etc.) may be an additional source of instability (e.g. some negative empirical eigenvalues).

3.4.3. *Eigen decomposition and financial interpretation*

3.4.3.1. *Notations*

We decompose C the correlation matrix through its eigen decomposition. C is related to Ω through:

$$\Omega = diag(\sigma_1, ..., \sigma_N) C diag(\sigma_1, ..., \sigma_N),$$

and C is a $N \times N$ symmetric, positive, semi-definite matrix with 1 along its diagonal. We work with estimators: C, Ω, eigenvalues and vectors *should be understood as estimated values*. The estimator notations will then be skipped in this section for clarity unless precised. The eigen decomposition of C is made through:

$$C = \Phi' D \Phi. \quad [3.9]$$

Both Φ and D are $N \times N$ symmetric, squared matrices. D is the diagonal matrix:

$$\Omega = diag(\sigma_1, ..., \sigma_N)Cdiag(\sigma_1, ..., \sigma_N),$$

made of eigenvalues on the diagonal, 0 otherwise. We will assume throughout the chapter that the eigenvalues *are sorted in descending order*, that is,

$$\lambda_1 \geq \lambda_2 \geq ... \geq \lambda_N \geq 0,$$

and this sorting will also drive the indexation of associated eigenvectors. Φ is the matrix of eigenvectors $\Phi = (\phi_1, \ldots, \phi_N)$ with the additional assumption that this set of eigenvectors represent an orthonormal basis of $\mathbb{R}^N$, which means that for all $(i, j) \in [1; N]^2$, $\phi_i.\phi_j = \delta_{ij}$. In particular, we have $\Phi^{-1} = \Phi$ and:

$$\hat{\Omega}^{\ 1} = \Phi' diag(1/\lambda_1, \ldots, 1/\lambda_N)\Phi.$$

3.4.3.2. *Eigenvalues*

3.4.3.2.1. Interpretation

Eigenvalues are not so difficult to study as they form an ordered vector of size N, with positive elements. Eigenvalues represent the specific related variances and then the risk part that each eigenvector may explain. Eigenvalues of a covariance matrix are homogeneous to risk and also a proxy of *information*. The higher the eigenvalue, the higher the importance of the related eigenvector to explain the asset returns. The highest eigenvalues, with their associated eigenvectors, therefore represent the main directions for investment. As we will introduce it just below, if one uses an orthonormal basis to diagonalize the correlation matrix, eigenvectors will be orthogonal with each other. This means that any portfolio orthogonal to all of the F first eigenvectors (with F a fixed integer such that $N > F > 0$) will evolve in the subspace spanned by eigenvectors from order $F + 1$ to N and that the risk it will bare will be bounded from above by λ_{F+1}.

NUMERICAL EXAMPLE 3.2.– Figure 3.6 shows the eigenvalue distribution of correlation matrix previously displayed in Figure 3.3. The x-axis is in log10 scale for ease of visualization. The whole sum of the values of the spectrum is obviously equal to 502, the number of assets, because of trace preservation. Every eigenvalue is positive here. We can clearly see that apart from 10 or 20 values that are way greater than any others, the remaining (480 or so) values are very close and belonging to a main bulk of values. The amplitude of the values in the spectrum is wide because the smallest eigenvalue is equal to 0.06 and the highest one is equal to 183. The highest eigenvalue is related to the "first mode" of the matrix, which is commonly called the *market mode* (see below). The second highest eigenvalue is equal to only 15.2, which is far less than the highest one, this latter explaining alone nearly half of the total "normalized risk".

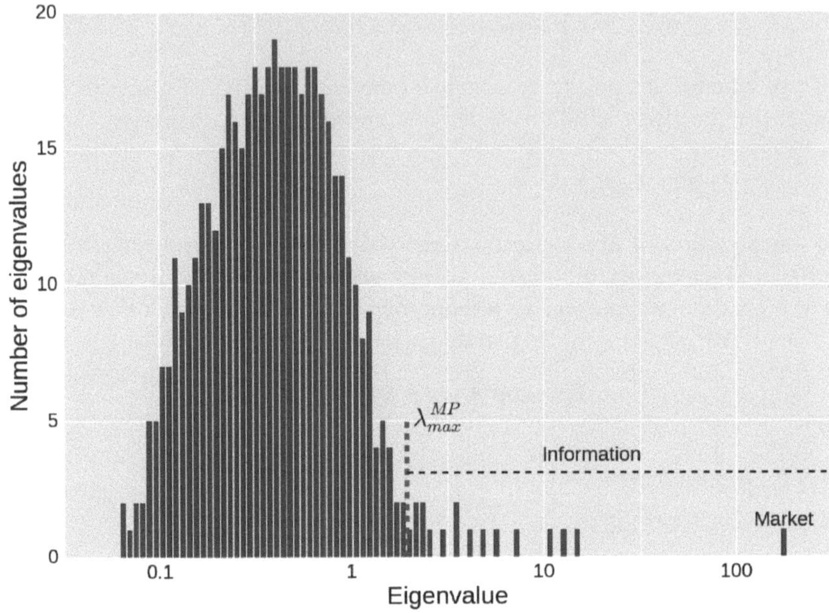

Figure 3.6. *Histogram of the eigenvalue distribution of the same correlation matrix shown in Figure 3.3. Eigenvalues are displayed as raw values but represented in a log10 scale. The eigenvector corresponding to the highest eigenvalue is to be understood as the "market" mode. The vertical dashed line indicates the value of the λ_{max} edge in the sense of the Marenko-Pastur analysis as detailed in example 3.3 for $\sigma^2 = 1$*

3.4.3.2.2. Random Matrix Theory

Eigenvalues of random matrices are the object of a flourishing literature and numerous contributions. The spectrum of sample correlation matrices is now well understood: we will see later that things are less clear for eigenvectors. However, the main implicit subtlety we deal with is that correlation matrices are estimated. Therefore, if the *true* matrix was constant in time (which is probably wrong) we will have to use finite time series in various periods of history in order to estimate them. The previous statements remain obviously correct, but the estimated eigenvalues will essentially be noisy estimators as the correlation matrix to be estimated remains a stochastic object.

Let us assume that the ratio $r = T/N$ is fixed, and greater than 1. When we assume that the coefficients of the matrix of assets price changes are independent and identically distributed, the distribution of the eigenvalues of the resulting correlation matrix is known when $N, T \to \infty$ and r stays fixed. This density makes sense only in an asymptotic framework and is known thanks to the work of [MAR 67]. This may become a guideline to evaluate the available information carried by a sample correlation matrix and a rather large number of studies have already been conducted on financial time series.

The study of random matrices, *Random Matrix Theory* (henceforth RMT), helps in this context to separate noise from real information. A detailed description would be unfortunately far beyond the scope of this book and we will be more interested here on the use of RMT in a financial context. However, for in-depth readings on RMT, we may refer, for instance, to the seminal work of [MAR 67], [MEH 04] for a complete review, [LAL 99], [MAL 04], [POT 05], [BOU 07], [BOU 11], the last sections of Chapter 1 of [BOU 09] and all the references therein. RMT provides insights on the spectrum[10] of the sample correlation matrix. Comparing eigenvalues of sample variance matrices of asset returns is generally quite similar to the spectrum of i.i.d. random variables, apart from the largest eigenvalues. The question becomes whether the information coming from this matrix, and conveyed through its eigenvalues, can be considered significantly different from pure noise. In case of pure randomness (even if this term should be handled with care!), the empirical density of the so-called Marenko-Pastur distribution $f(\lambda)$ of the eigenvalues of the empirical matrix should be equal to:

$$f(\lambda) = \frac{r}{2\pi\sigma^2} \frac{\sqrt{(\lambda_{max} - \lambda)(\lambda - \lambda_{min})}}{\lambda},$$

where σ^2 is the variance of the initial observations (returns, here) that led to the estimation of the matrix (for correlation or normalized returns, we should have $\sigma^2 = 1$). λ_{max} and λ_{min} depend explicitly on the noise ratio $r = T/N$. We have:

$$\lambda_{min} = \sigma^2\left(1 + \frac{1}{r} - 2\sqrt{\frac{1}{r}}\right) \quad \text{and} \quad \lambda_{max} = \sigma^2\left(1 + \frac{1}{r} + 2\sqrt{\frac{1}{r}}\right).$$

Some observations can be made. This density $f(.)$ has an inverted-V shape with finite support: the density is equal to zero outside the segment $[\lambda_{min}; \lambda_{max}]$. There is no eigenvalue to be expected in the $[0; \lambda_{min}]$ segment and the case where r is close to one is specific in the sense that λ_{min} becomes close to 0 and the mode of the distribution diverges. The width of the support is therefore driven by $\sqrt{1/r}$. Using this distribution in a financial context allows us to estimate which eigenvalues may be potential candidates for being representative of informative directions. Each eigenvalue below λ_{max}, i.e. inside the bulk of the MP distribution, may be considered as negligible and equivalent to noise.

---

10 It also provides insights into the expected distribution of eigenvectors coordinates in the case of true randomness: it is modeled by the *Porter-Thomas* distribution as highlighted in [LAL 99].

NUMERICAL EXAMPLE 3.3.– Following the previous analysis, we can estimate that as $N = 502$, $T = 3273$ and as we are working with a correlation matrix, $\sigma^2 = 1$, which gives a value of $\lambda_{max}^{MP} = 1.94$. This value is represented in Figure 3.6. With this value of λ_{max}^{MP}, we can estimate that only 17 eigenvalues are greater than this value, which means that only approximately 17 eigenvectors may support real information, with nearly 96.6% of eigenvalues in the bulk of the distribution. The sum of the corresponding eigenvalues is roughly equal to 267, which means that only 3% of the eigenvectors account for nearly 53% of the total volatility.

3.4.3.3. *Eigenvectors*

3.4.3.3.1. Interpretation

Eigenvectors are homogeneous to portfolios. The Matrix Φ, whose columns are the eigenvectors ϕ_i, is a basis of orthonormal portfolios best summarising the linear information available through the observation of asset returns. In financial terms, mixing those portfolios with expected returns is a way to find linear combinations of those orthonormal portfolios, which become the building blocks of the final arbitrage portfolios. Their returns are, in particular, uncorrelated by construction. The first eigenvectors (corresponding to the highest eigenvalues) explain best the information, in the sense that they have the greatest contribution to the overall variance. Hence, the last eigenvectors (i.e. ϕ_i with $i >> 1$) are the less informative. In the degenerate case, an eigenvector with a close-to-zero eigenvalue means that $C\phi_k \simeq 0$, which means in financial terms that portfolio k has a variance that is close to zero and may appear as risk-free. Then, if the expected return is positive, even slightly, the allocation process understands it as an arbitrage opportunity and overweighs the allocation in this portfolio, artificially considered by the algorithm as a "good opportunity": a positive profit with nearly no risk. In terms of information, this means that ϕ_k is co-linear to the other vectors and then it can be expressed as a linear combination of other eigenvectors. Thus, eigenvectors corresponding to the smallest eigenvalues are portfolios that are redundant in terms of information. Technically, an eigenvector is used to describe, represent and qualify one direction in an N-dimensional space. The sub-space that is spanned by a set of orthonormal vectors is identical to the one spanned by vectors where all signs of each coordinate are flipped.

Evaluating the noise of estimated eigenvectors on the whole spectrum is a much more sophisticated challenge. To the best of our knowledge, there is no complete overview or exhaustive framework able to model the entire set of eigenvectors of any given empirical matrix. Some enlightening results do exist; however, they are rather sparse in the sense that the amount of literature on the topic is far inferior to the equivalent amount of literature on empirical eigenvalues. Eigenvectors are consequently, represented or studied in the order implied by eigenvalues. They may convey some information, but a distinction has to be made depending on the eigenvalue they represent. Whereas the eigenvectors corresponding to the largest eigenvalues are rather stable (even if they may change through time), eigenvectors corresponding to the smallest eigenvectors are noisier, more unstable and near impossible to interpret.

For equities, the first top eigenvector coincides with the market mode and is a bit easier to study. Studying the variogram of the first eigenvector, [BOU 11] showed that the natural time of fluctuation of this mode is around 100 days, which is quite long but sufficient to understand that this mode is, however, changing and evolving. [ALL 12] identifies and study the dynamics of eigenvectors corresponding to the largest eigenvalues. Generally, eigenvectors electing for an interpretation are those associated to the highest eigenvalues and have an interpretation in terms of sectorial, geographical or macroeconomic bets. For instance, if we observe an eigenvector whose positive coordinates are associated to stocks from the financial sector whereas the negative coordinates are all the other stocks, this would indicate a sectorial bet buying financial stocks, shorting all other stocks. However, such patterns evolve in time, change, decrease, switch in order and are relatively hard to track down as it requires a qualitative reverse-engineering of the vectors. One main contribution that assesses precisely the economic and sector interpretation of the first eigenvectors is the work of [PLE 02], but see also [UEC 15]. References stating that sample eigenvectors corresponding to the eigenvectors of the smallest eigenvalues may be the support of a limited information have to be found, for example, in [BAI 10], [PAS 11] or [MON 15].

Another result that illustrates the specificity of eigenvectors is that contrary to the case of eigenvalues, making N growing to infinity does not allow to gain some stability. As N grows, the noise in eigenvectors in general do not decrease and fluctuations still appear. No limit is to be identified and in a large dimension N has no stabilizing effect on the estimated vectors.

NUMERICAL EXAMPLE 3.4.– We compare in Figure 3.7 the first and second eigenvectors of the correlation matrix shown in Figure 3.3. We have ranked the stocks according to the algebraic value of the coordinate on the second eigenvector for the sake of illustration. Consequently, each point on the x-axis represents a stock with its corresponding coordinates on the first and second eigenvectors. We observe in particular that:

– the first eigenvector (represented by points) associated to the highest eigenvalue (equal to 183) has coordinates that are all positive, with a mean equal to $1/502 \sim 0.002$ (thin dashed line);

– the second eigenvector (represented by a dashed line) associated to the second highest eigenvalue (equal to 15) has coordinates that are both positive and negative, with a zero mean.

The first eigenvector is often called the *market mode,* because up to minor variations, all the coordinates of the vector are nearly equal. This means that the return of this eigenvector seen as a portfolio is nearly the mean of the return of the set of stocks, then approximately the return of the market. This is even stronger in our present case, since dealing with components of the S&P500 index, we nearly obtain the returns of the index itself, potentially accounting for "the market". We recover a CAPM interpretation for this eigenvector, which represents major common market moves. Such an eigenvector will therefore generally always appear, regardless of the period and the set of estimation.

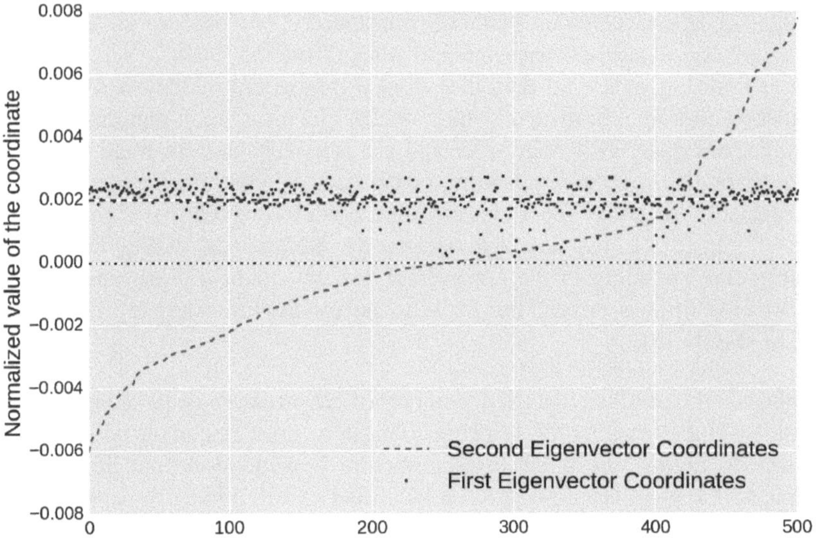

Figure 3.7. *Comparison of the first and second eigenvectors (both vectors' coordinates are normalized such that the sum of their absolute values sum to one) of the same correlation matrix shown in Figure 3.3. The x-axis is an arbitrary label of the stock after sorting the coordinates of the second eigenvector in ascending order. We plot on the y-axis the normalized value of the coordinate of the first and second eigenvectors*

The case of the second eigenvector has features that are easy to explain but is more difficult to interpret. The fact that we obtain positive and negative values is straightforward. As the basis of eigenvectors has to be orthogonal, if the first eigenvector is close to a unitary vector, all of the other $N - 1$ eigenvectors have to be orthogonal to it, that is, having a zero scalar product with the first eigenvectors, so (approximately) a zero sum of the coordinates. Therefore, regardless of the order of the eigenvector we could have represented along with the first eigenvector, we would observe such a pattern (positive and negative coordinates with zero sum). The fact that the median coordinate is around zero (as much positive as negative coordinates) may be commonly observed but is not compulsory.

3.4.3.3.2. Sample eigenvectors

What is the suitable tool[11] to study sample eigenvectors? The main quantity appears to be the *overlap* which is, for two N-dimensional vectors, the scalar product in $\mathbb{R}^N$ between them. In fact, as eigenvectors are identical up to their sign, the real quantity of interest is the squared overlap. The squared overlap lies between 0 and 1 and describes the similarity of the vectors between them. The overlap will be useful to answer two questions. The first question is the effective similarity between an eigenvector or order $i \in [1; N]$ coming from a sample matrix and the true vector of the same order i. The second question is the potential similarity between two eigenvectors of order i coming from two matrices estimated in two different contexts (e.g. two sample matrices estimating the same unknown matrix Ω but at two different times). A useful prism to answer for the first question, is that eigenvectors have to be studied correspondingly to the fact that the eigenvalue they are associated with, is, or is not, in the bulk of the eigenvalues distribution. If the corresponding eigenvalue is in the bulk of the distribution, few things may be said since the overlap between the sample vector and the corresponding true one is of order $1/N$. Intuitively, we could say that for the eigenvalues in the bulk of the distribution, there is so much noise that the notion of order in the spectrum is blurred and that there are few chances to get a precise mapping between sample vectors and the true ones. However, as soon as we study eigenvectors for eigenvalues standing out of the bulk (isolated eigenvalues that convey information), the overlap is of order 1 meaning that in this case, a clear link is maintained between the true vector and its estimation, stable and well identified. See for this [BEN 11] as a reference. References defining and using the overlap quantity include also, for instance, [ALL 14], [ALL 15] and [BUN 16] to which we refer for an extensive reading. In particular, recalling that the overlap between the first eigenvector and the other ones is always very weak, [MON 15] finds that it is still possible to exploit this accumulation of weak "cross-information" (materialized by the overlaps) between the first eigenvector[12] and the many other eigenvectors of the same matrix, to recover some additional information on the first one and improve prediction.

NUMERICAL EXAMPLE 3.5.– We plot in Figure 3.8 the shape of the overlap computed between eigenvectors coming from consecutive estimations of the matrix. We have estimated on several dates, 5-year correlation matrices, on each 1st of January of years from 2007 to 2016 included. We have then 10 matrices, and we compare two consecutive matrices that provide nine comparisons. Let us observe that

---

11 The authors would like to thank Joël Bun for his help on the topic of eigenvector interpretation.

12 Eigenvectors on a given matrix are built to be orthonormal, so scalar product between two different eigenvectors should be equal to zero. However, in the precise context of[MON 15], this scalar product has to be understood as the scalar product between eigenvectors of order > 2 on the estimated matrix and a first, "true" eigenvector where we have a prior (a theoretical one).

such matrices[13] have obviously a different N/T ratio than the matrix displayed in 3.3 as N is unchanged but for each matrix $T' = 5$ years, to be compared with $T = 14$ years for the matrix for the period 2002/01/01 – 2016/01/01. However, two consecutive matrices share the same ratio N/T'.

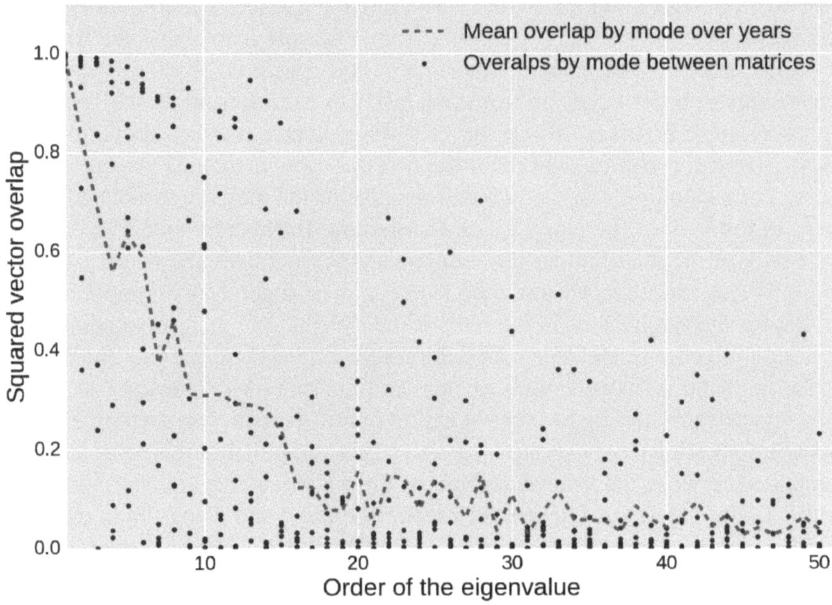

Figure 3.8. *Distribution of squared vector overlap between eigenvectors of the same index for two consecutive estimated matrices. The x-axis is the order of the eigenvector as sorted along the amplitude of its corresponding eigenvalue. Points represent the (squared) overlap for each eigenvector and for each couple of consecutive matrices. The dashed line is the mean, over years, by eigenvector, of those squared overlaps*

We compare them through the prism of each of their eigenvector, sorted along their associated eigenvalue, in descending order. Here again, the first vector (i.e. of order 1) will be the previously called *market mode*. On the x-axis is the index of the vector for which we plot the result of the nine eigenvector comparisons made in time in two consecutive years. Each dot represents a year and an eigenvector order, and is

13 We still use the Pearson correlation on daily returns that are kept normalized by their unconditional standard deviation on the initial sample of 14 years, but we hope that the implicit but weak notion of future information that is used is compensated by the fact that we compute correlation rather than covariance. Yet, we mainly insist on the illustration purpose of the present exercise.

equal to the squared scalar product. In other terms, for the order i, we represent the value $< \hat{\phi}_i^{(Y-1)}.\hat{\phi}_i^{(Y)} >^2$ for $i \in [1, 50]$ and Y in $[2008, 2016]$. We represent moreover with dashed line the mean of the quantity (averaged then over 9 comparisons) for each eigenvector order.

It is straightforward that as explained before, this quantity vanishes quite rapidly. Up to the order 5 the overlap remains high, whereas after order 15, the overlap is clearly weak and noisy. This means that the 10 first eigenvectors may convey some useful information with high probability, but for orders higher than 15 the underlying information may be rather considered as noise. The eigenvectors for an order greater than 10 or 15 are quite impossible to follow.

REMARK 3.3.– With a given covariance matrix, changing the expected return vector may lead to instability. As time passes by however, one may be concerned by the refresh of the covariance matrix. A possibility could be to refresh only the volatilities, to estimate a new correlation matrix and to test whether the correlation structure is similar or not to the previous one, to know whether they are different or not. For tests on the equality of two correlation matrices, see the test procedures described in [JEN 70] or [LAR 88].

3.4.3.4. *Spectral insights*

3.4.3.4.1. A link with predictability

There is a useful way to rewrite the allocation in the light of the former paragraph. For this, we will work alternatively with $C = \Phi' D \Phi$. All the objects (including expected returns and variances and covariances) are estimators, but we drop the notations for the sake of clarity. If the eigenvectors ϕ_k are of dimension $N \times 1$ and that we note $\tilde{\mu}$ the vector of individual asset expected returns normalized by their risk such that $\tilde{\mu}_i = \mu_i / \sigma_i$, then we may write:

$$\begin{aligned}
\Omega^{-1}\mu &= diag(1/\sigma_1, ..., 1/\sigma_N) \times \Phi' D \Phi \times diag(1/\sigma_1, ..., 1/\sigma_N) \times \mu \\
&= diag(1/\sigma_1, ..., 1/\sigma_N) \times \Big(\sum_{j=1}^{N} \frac{1}{\lambda_j} \phi_j . \phi_j' \Big) \times \tilde{\mu} \\
&= diag(1/\sigma_1, ..., 1/\sigma_N) \times \Big(\sum_{j=1}^{N} \frac{1}{\lambda_j} (\phi_j' . \tilde{\mu}) \phi_j \Big),
\end{aligned}$$

which means that for an asset $i \in [1; N]$:

$$(\Omega^{-1}\mu)_i = \frac{1}{\sigma_i} \times \Big(\sum_{j=1}^{N} \frac{1}{\lambda_j} (\phi_j' . \tilde{\mu}) \phi_{ji} \Big). \qquad [3.10]$$

Equation [3.10] is particularly enlightening as it presents what mean-variance allocation really do in the space of portfolios. If eigenvectors are orthonormal, normalized portfolios, mean-variance allocation will combine those portfolios depending both on the risk λ_k that is represented by each direction k (i.e. one-dimensional subspace of $\mathbb{R}^N$ spanned by ϕ_k) but also according to the expected, normalized gain in this direction, that is, $\phi'_k.\tilde{\mu}$. It is therefore crucial to understand that there is also an important re-scaling by λ_k. Therefore, any vector μ that will be close to co-linear to one of the eigenvectors of highest order will have a weight that will be relatively more decreased due to the magnitude of the corresponding eigenvalue. Conversely, investing in one specific eigenvector (e.g. market), we will have a direct re-weighting in risk. An alternative writing, partly inspired by a remark of [POT 05], for equation [3.10] is:

$$
\begin{aligned}
(\Omega^{-1}\mu)_i &= \frac{1}{\sigma_i} \times \Big(\sum_{j=1}^{N} \frac{1}{\lambda_j}(\phi'_j.\tilde{\mu})\phi_{ji} \Big) \\
&= \frac{1}{\sigma_i} \times \Big(\sum_{j=1}^{N} \big(\frac{1}{\lambda_j} - 1\big)(\phi'_j.\tilde{\mu})\phi_{ji} + \sum_{j=1}^{N} (\phi'_j.\tilde{\mu})\phi_{ji} \Big) \\
&= \frac{1}{\sigma_i} \times \Big(\sum_{j=1}^{N} \big(\frac{1}{\lambda_j} - 1\big)(\phi'_j.\tilde{\mu})\phi_{ji} + \sum_{j=1}^{N}\sum_{k=1}^{N} \phi_{jk}\tilde{\mu}_k\phi_{ji} \Big) \\
&= \frac{1}{\sigma_i} \times \Big(\sum_{j=1}^{N} \big(\frac{1}{\lambda_j} - 1\big)(\phi'_j.\tilde{\mu})\phi_{ji} + \sum_{k=1}^{N} \tilde{\mu}_k \sum_{j=1}^{N} \phi_{jk}\phi_{ji} \Big) \\
&= \frac{1}{\sigma_i} \times \Big(\sum_{j=1}^{N} \big(\frac{1}{\lambda_j} - 1\big)(\phi'_j.\tilde{\mu})\phi_{ji} + \sum_{k=1}^{N} \tilde{\mu}_k \underbrace{(\phi'_k.\phi_i)}_{\delta^i_k} \Big) \\
&= \frac{1}{\sigma_i} \times \Big(\tilde{\mu}_i + \sum_{j=1}^{N} \big(\frac{1}{\lambda_j} - 1\big)(\phi'_j.\tilde{\mu})\phi_{ji} \Big).
\end{aligned}
\qquad [3.11]
$$

We can remark now thanks to equation [3.11] that all the eigenvectors associated to eigenvalues λ_k such that $\lambda_k >> 1$ (i.e. the highest ones) are such that $(1/\lambda_k - 1)$ is close to -1 and the allocation in the direction supported by this eigenvector vanishes. This creates a link with section 3.4.4: the first eigenvectors (those associated to the highest eigenvalues) have then an influence that is decreased respectively to the other eigenvectors associated to the lowest eigenvalues, which is already a kind of *hedging* with respect to the first eigenvectors. As remarked by [POT 05], since those eigenvectors concentrate the majority of the overall risk, this will give a portfolio with a decent risk control (see again section 3.4.4 below).

REMARK 3.4.– In the perspective of the use of the risk-parity approach detailed in section 3.6.1.3, we can also remark that the risk associated to each stock

$\sigma_i w_i = \sigma_i(\Omega^{-1}\mu)_i$ is proportional to the "*Sharpe ratio*" of each asset as equation [3.11] allows to write that $\sigma_i w_i \propto \tilde{\mu}_i$.

3.4.3.4.2. Instability

We explain here the instability of the resulting portfolio from a spectral point of view. As expressed before, allocation is very sensitive to slight changes in estimated μ. We will show here that the problem does not lie in the estimation of μ but in the conditioning of the estimated covariance matrix and its spectral features. Suppose that μ is set at date t to a value that writes $\mu_t = (\mu_t^{(1)}, \ldots, \mu_t^{(N)})'$ and that there exists $k \in [1; N]$ such that only the kth component is modified when μ_{t+1} is estimated. What is the relative effect on allocation w^*? We denote with w_t^* the resulting vector of weights associated to the vector of estimated returns μ_t, and with w_{t+1}^* the new value associated to μ_{t+1}. Let E_l be the elementary $N \times 1$ vector with 1 on its lth coordinate, 0 elsewhere. Therefore:

$$\mu = \sum_{i=1}^{N} \mu^{(i)} E_i,$$

$$\mu_{t+1} - \mu_t = d\mu^{(k)} E_k.$$

What can then express the difference between the two allocations with μ_t replaced by μ_{t+1}:

$$w_{t+1}^* - w_t^* = \hat{\Omega}^{-1}(\mu_{t+1} - \mu_t) = \hat{\Omega}^{-1}(d\mu^{(k)} E_k).$$

Using equation [3.10], the ith component of w^* (with $i \in [1; N]$ not compulsorily equal to k) is modified such that:

$$\begin{aligned}(w_{t+1}^* - w_t^*)_i &= \frac{1}{\sigma_i} \times \Big(\sum_{j=1}^{N} \frac{1}{\lambda_j} \Big(\phi_j' . \frac{d\mu^{(k)} E_k}{\sigma_k} \Big) \phi_{ji} \Big) \\ &= \frac{1}{\sigma_i} \times \Big(\sum_{j=1}^{N} \frac{1}{\lambda_j} \Big(\delta_{jk} \phi_{jk} \frac{d\mu^{(k)}}{\sigma_k} \Big) \phi_{ji} \Big) \\ &= \frac{1}{\lambda_k} \frac{d\mu^{(k)}}{\sigma_i \sigma_k} \phi_{ki}^2 .\end{aligned}$$

It then becomes apparent that any modification on a given coordinate has a repercussion on each other coordinate depending on the eigenvectors coordinates, asset volatilities and eigenvalues. Conversely, we could also assume that μ is unchanged but that the estimation of the eigenvalue varies. As we do not have access to the true covariance matrix Ω, and we only have an estimator at hand: $(\lambda_l)_{l \in [1;N]}$ are the eigenvalues of the estimated matrix. Now assume that between t and $t + 1$, μ

is kept constant but that there exists $l \in [1; N]$ with $l \neq k$, such that our estimator of Ω has only its value of λ_l modified such that at $t+1$ λ_l is replaced by $\lambda_l - d\lambda_l$. This is not very realistic, but we will do the computation for illustration. Then, the effect on the ith component of a^* should write:

$$(w_{t+1}^* - w_t^*)_i = (\hat{\Omega}_{t+1}^{-1} - \hat{\Omega}_t)^{-1})\mu_t$$

$$= \frac{1}{\sigma_i} \times \Big(\sum_{j=1}^{N} \delta_{jl} \Big(\frac{1}{\lambda_l - d\lambda_l} - \frac{1}{\lambda_l} \Big) (\phi_j'.\tilde{\mu})\phi_{ji} \Big)$$

$$= \frac{1}{\sigma_i} \Big(\frac{1}{\lambda_l - d\lambda_l} - \frac{1}{\lambda_l} \Big) (\phi_l'.\tilde{\mu})\phi_{li}$$

$$= \Big(\frac{1}{\lambda_l - d\lambda_l} - \frac{1}{\lambda_l} \Big) \sum_{k=1}^{N} \frac{\phi_{lk}\mu_k\phi_{li}}{\sigma_i\sigma_k}.$$

A first-order development gives:

$$(w_{t+1}^* - w_t^*)_i \simeq \sum_{k=1}^{N} \frac{\phi_{lk}\mu_k\phi_{li}}{\sigma_i\sigma_k} \frac{d\lambda_l}{\lambda_l^2}.$$

Again, this is only for illustration, because, in practice, estimating Ω in t then in $t+1$ should probably lead to modifications in not only eigenvalues but also eigenvectors, and as eigenvalues are sorted in decreasing order, "true" eigenvalues may switch indices. But those (very) simple computations show an important empirical feature. A slight modification of the smallest eigenvalues is amplified of an order 2 with inversion. Then, a modification on $\mu^{(k)}$ does affect all the coordinates of the optimal weights, but its effect is amplified by the quantity $\frac{1}{\lambda_k}\frac{1}{\sigma_i\sigma_k}\phi_{ki}^2$. This quantity may be arbitrarily large if the smallest eigenvalues are close to zero.

3.4.4. *Benefits of mean-variance allocation*

Should we discard mean-variance allocation? We think that the answer is no. The drawbacks of the mean-variance framework, in practice, must not hide both the messages and advantages of the setup. In any case, mean-variance may be conceived as being either independent, decoupled or a particular case of the Markowitz setup. [RUB 02] recalls in particular the originality of the seminal papers of Harry Markowitz. The main messages is that diversification has positive effects on the overall portfolio construction, and that with an increased diversification, higher returns can be expected by an increase of target in risk.

"While diversification would reduce risk, it would not generally eliminate it. (...) Probably the most important aspect of Markowitz's work was to show that it is not a security's own risk that is important to an investor, but rather the contribution the security makes to the variance of his entire portfolio. (...) So the decision to hold a security should not be made simply by comparing its expected return and variance to others, but rather the decision to hold any security would depend on what other securities the investor wants to hold."

— [RUB 02]

Mean-variance is easy to explain, understand and apply. In addition, the underlying mathematical framework is quite simple since it involves mainly matrix inversion and simple statistics. Even in a simple case where we only end up with a covariance matrix and a potential proxy for expected returns, there is, hopefully, still some space to do something. In this paragraph we will gather some arguments (some of them are also given by [RON 14]) that account for the benefits of the setup as we still think that it remains a "*fabulous tool for combining risks and expected returns*" to quote the same reference. The fact is that there has been some confusion and also a lack of alternative methods to replace mean-variance, because historically no other method has gained, in practice, the same popularity. During the economic crisis of 2008, the practical use of diversification has not been able to prevent strategies to suffer. The problem is, as clearly stated again in [RON 14], that investors often mentally assimilate the principle of diversification with the inversion procedure, implicitly mixing the problems of the method with the problems of its parameter estimation, whereas the two topics may be clearly separated.

3.4.4.1. *Risk control*

Letting aside the specification of the correlation structure, mean-variance allocation weights implicitly expected returns with an inverse volatility scheme. Let us assume that Ω is simply equal to $diag(1/\sigma_1^2, \ldots, 1/\sigma_N^2)$ (no cross-correlation), then all our positions are weighted by $1/\sigma_i^2$. Benefits of volatility weighting have been explicitly highlighted in [HAL 12]. They are often used in practice (see, e.g. [BRA 09], [KIR 12], [ILM 12], [BAL 15] and [BAR 15] or [DAN 16] for momentum strategies). Resulting risk-adjusted performances are generally better, with an improved Sharpe ratio. This is a more general message: independently from the degree of sophistication the investor is ready to deal with, volatility weighting may often appear as the simplest risk management, and an helpful tool out-of sample.

Volatility weighting is also useful when put in perspective with the volatility-return link. The so-called *leverage effect* is a well-known stylized fact in finance (see [BOL 06]). Volatility and returns show generally a negative correlation: more precisely, clusters of high volatility are correlated with negative returns. Working with quantities with a constant risk-aversion, applying a volatility weighting implies that (if the volatility estimator is quite reactive) the absolute gross market value of the portfolio in times of huge volatility will be decreased, and increased it in times of low volatility. The benefits of volatility weighting appears naturally. If bursts of volatility are associated to bad returns, volatility weighting allows to diminish $\sum_i |q_i|$, then to potentially lower losses during hard times. Conversely, during market rallies with low-volatility levels, positions are increased and potentially beneficial bets may benefit from a higher leverage. Therefore, volatility weighting allows to time the exposition to market conditions, reducing potential losses during hard times, and increasing performance in good times. Evidently, this cannot be conceived without a decent risk-budgeting approach. Maximum positions, targets on risk and constraints on leverage may be envisaged to benefit from this weighting but with cautious empirical controls.

REMARK 3.5.– The notion of risk weighting is in fact implicitly present in the setting of [BRI 99] detailed in remark 3.1 stating that the mean-variance weights could be obtained as the coefficients of the regression of a constant vector on the return of assets. If we reflect on the assumptions underlying this setup, finding β coefficients for this OLS regression is equivalent to finding weights to apply to the returns to get a constant, unitary Sharpe by asset. Consequently, it is indeed already a way to normalize each bet in risk in order not to favor one with respect to the others.

3.4.4.2. *Implied hedging relations*

A particular and often forgotten feature of the mean-variance framework lies in the particular writing and explicit characterization of the inverse covariance matrix underlined in [STE 98]. It may be shown that multiplying by an inverse covariance matrix may be equivalent to specifying a specialized set of regression of one asset on all other assets. An explicit form for the inverse imply both the vector of regression coefficients and the resulting residual variance obtained by regressing assets' excess returns on the excess returns of all other risky assets. If $\Omega^{-1} = ((\Omega^{-1})_{i,j})_{(i,j)\in[1;N]^2}$ is the inverse covariance matrix, then we may write its coefficients as :

$$(\Omega^{-1})_{i,j} = \frac{-\beta_{i,j}}{\sigma_i^2(1-(R^2)_i)}, \qquad [3.12]$$

where σ_i^2 is the variance of the asset i and $(R^2)_i$ is not a return but the multiple regression coefficient of the returns of asset i on all other assets. $\beta_i = (\beta_{i,j})_{i\neq j}$ is the row vector of regression coefficients on the $N-1$ other assets. The term $\sigma_i^2(1-(R^2)_i)$ is then the portion of variance of asset i that cannot be hedged or diversified with a linear hedge in other assets. Consequently, working with a return estimator s, the weight of asset i resulting from the operation $\Omega^{-1}s$ will be proportional to $s_i - \sum_{k\neq i}\beta_{i,k}s_k$, which is the part of the strategy that cannot be explained by the other assets for the current strategy. The latter part of this term materializes the cost of the optimal hedge attainable as a linear combination of other assets for the particular asset i. Such an operation promotes assets that are weakly correlated with the others since all things equal, the weights will be increasing as β decreases, and a nearly perfect hedge (close to co-linearity) will lead to unstable and amplified weights.

3.5. Allocating using views

Having identified the source of the instability when using naive mean-variance allocation, we have several ways to solve this issue. We will explore in section 3.6 allocation methods that do not specify any explicit proxy for the expected returns. Prior to this we address in this section the use of allocation techniques that specify an estimator for the expected returns (in other words, that allows to use a strategy), regardless of its origin or motivations. Having understood the spectral features of Ω, we may try to correct the covariance estimator (see section 3.5.1) to make the estimator invertible. The action of making the covariance estimator more invertible is known under the term of *cleaning* in a financial context; in statistics or econometrics, it is associated to the term of *regularization*. Either by acting directly on the eigenvalues (spectral cut-off, section 3.5.1.1 and shrinkage, section 3.5.1.2), either by forcing the structure of the estimator to rely on a smallest number of parameters (parametric estimation, section 3.5.1.3). Other methods are rather empirical (practical use of constraints, section 3.5.2) but appear to have strong theoretical justification. Finally, we will address the Black-Litterman framework (see section 3.5.3) that will modify the expected return part, while compensating for the instability of the covariance matrix inversion in the meantime.

3.5.1. *Improving covariance estimation*

3.5.1.1. *Clipping / spectral cut-off*

According to the spectral analysis detailed in section 3.4, there is an intuitive procedure to ensure the stability of mean-variance portfolios: if the problem comes from the smallest eigenvalues, we have to just bound them! This technique is sometimes called *clipping* even if in the usual inverse problems literature, it is known under the term of *spectral cut-off*. The aim is then to stay in the initial framework of mean-variance allocation and to tackle the true source of instability. First, diagonalize the sample correlation $\hat{C}$ and get the eigenvalues $\hat{\lambda}_1, \ldots, \hat{\lambda}_N$ with corresponding eigenvectors $\hat{\phi}_1, \ldots, \hat{\phi}_N$. The next step is to choose an order k_0 (with an auxiliary criterion) such that all the eigenvalues of order $k' \in [k_0 + 1; N]$ are set to a constant value $\lambda_{k'} = \tilde{\lambda} \leq \hat{\lambda}_{k_0}$. However, the trace of the matrix may be modified since with such a modification the trace should shift from $Tr(\hat{C}) = \sum_{i=1}^{N} \lambda_i$ to $\sum_{i=1}^{k_0} \lambda_i + (N - k_0)\tilde{\lambda}$. It could be detrimental to modify this trace since it could lead to an overestimation of the total trace of the correlation then covariance matrix of the model and then to arbitrarily modify the total risk implied and estimated by the model. Unless this is wanted by the investor, we have to choose a suitable k_0 such that the trace is preserved. A simple computation gives us:

$$\tilde{\lambda} = \frac{1}{N - k_0} \sum_{i=k_0+1}^{N} \lambda_i.$$

In this case, the first eigenvalues are left unchanged and for all $i \in [1; N]$:

$$\tilde{\lambda}_i := \lambda_i \mathbb{1}(i \leq k_0) + \tilde{\lambda} \mathbb{1}(i > k_0).$$

This is less usual, but conversely, if both k_0 and $\tilde{\lambda}$ are fixed, we may also re-weight the first eigenvalues so that for all $i \in [1 : k_0]$:

$$\tilde{\lambda}_i := \lambda_i \frac{\sum_{i=1}^{N} \lambda_i - (N - k_0)\tilde{\lambda}}{\sum_{i=1}^{k_0} \lambda_i}.$$

The final estimator $\hat{\Omega}_{sc}$ for the covariance is:

$$\hat{\Omega}_{sc} = diag(\sigma_1, ..., \sigma_N) \times \hat{\Phi} \times \begin{pmatrix} \tilde{\lambda}_1 & 0 & ... & 0 \\ 0 & \tilde{\lambda}_2 & ... & 0 \\ ... & ... & ... & ... \\ 0 & ... & 0 & \tilde{\lambda}_N \end{pmatrix} \times \hat{\Phi} \times diag(\sigma_1, ..., \sigma_N).$$

It is in fact simple in practice to fix k_0, keep unchanged the k_0 first eigenvalues, and determine $\tilde{\lambda}$ in order to preserve the original trace. But how to choose k_0? In fact, the framework of RMT developed in section 3.4.3.2 is a powerful tool to determine the level beyond which all eigenvalues may be considered as being non-informative (see again [POT 05]).

NUMERICAL EXAMPLE 3.6.– With example 3.3 in mind and the previous analysis, we would have $k_0 = 17$ using RMT. We had that the 17 first eigenvalues were summing at 267. This means that the $502 - 17 = 485$ smallest eigenvalues should sum to $502 - 267 = 235$ in order to preserve the trace of the matrix. Consequently, $\tilde{\lambda} = 235/485 = 0.484$. The effect of spectral cut-off on eigenvalues is illustrated in Figure 3.9.

Such an approach naturally derives from a standard regularization[14] technique called, as said before, *spectral cut-off*: it is detailed in Appendix A.3.2.2.1. With the notations of Appendix A.3.2.2.1, we have:

$$q(\alpha, \lambda) = \mathbb{1}(\lambda \leq \lambda_{k_0}) + \frac{\lambda}{\bar{\lambda}}\mathbb{1}(\lambda > \lambda_{k_0}).$$

We have effectively that $\lim_{\alpha \to 0} q(\alpha, \lambda) = 1$ since in this context, $\alpha = \lambda_{k_0}$.

3.5.1.2. *Shrinkage*

3.5.1.2.1. Motivations

Shrinkage (also called *reduction*) aims at correcting the sample variance-covariance matrix when this latter ill-conditioned: the shrinkage estimator of the covariance matrix is built as a convex linear combination of the empirical estimator with some suitably chosen target matrix that has a better spectral structure. Initial work on shrinkage estimators for the mean of a multivariate normal distribution has been done by [STE 56] who showed that if we are willing to give up a little in terms of bias, we could do better in terms of mean squared errors. Shrinkage introduces biases in the resulting weights but compensates by reducing the estimation errors in the final weights. When the balance is satisfying, we gain much from the decrease in estimation error that hopefully compensates the biases [GOT 15]. Mathematically, the intensity of the reduction is a parameter[15] $\alpha \in [0; 1]$ that represents the relative weight of a target matrix in the new covariance matrix. If $\hat{\Omega}$ is the sample variance-covariance matrix and T_a denotes the target matrix, then the shrinkage estimator $\hat{\Omega}_s$ is computed as:

$$\hat{\Omega}_s = \alpha T_a + (1 - \alpha)\hat{\Omega}.$$

The mixing parameter α is chosen in order to provide an arbitrage between the estimation error coming from $\hat{\Omega}$ and the specification error of T_a. It quantifies the mix between bias and variance of the estimator. Shrinkage indeed reduces sampling error, but another goal is that despite of the potential singularity of $\hat{\Omega}$, the shrinkage estimator will hopefully inherit from a part of the spectral structure of the target matrix T_a. The greater the sample, the less estimation challenge we get, explaining that optimal α should decrease with the increasing size of the sample. However, all things equal, the more biased is the target T_a the lower is the parameter, with respect to the usual

14 We also see here the fact that we are not *strictly speaking* dealing with a true regularization scheme in finite dimension since the regularization that is at work here is not a finite range approximation with increasing dimension: the space spanned by the regularized operator is identical to the space of the true operator.

15 Despite its notation, this parameter α is not the same as the α parameter that will be introduced later in section 3.5.3 within the Black-Litterman framework.

"bias versus variance" dilemma. [LED 04] gives a review of shrinkage, including its application in practice. In their framework, α is chosen in a so-called "optimal way". One seeks to maximize the expected accuracy of the "shrunken" estimator, and to minimize the distance, computed using the Frobenius norm (see Appendix A.1.1), between the (true) covariance matrix and its shrinkage estimator, providing in the paper a detailed analysis and study for the optimal choice of α. When α is estimated, such procedures must not involve the inverse of the covariance matrix for obvious reasons. This is one of the main features of the method that allows to discard easily the unfavorable properties of the initial matrix and to work with a well-conditioned estimator at low implementation cost, even for large N.

REMARK 3.6.– We discuss in Appendix A.3.2.3 the link existing between shrinkage and regularization schemes. Few contributions exist on the subject (with the exception of [LED 03] e.g.). We develop, however, original arguments to explore under which conditions shrinkage could strictly speaking be considered as a regularization technique. The condition we obtain concerns the boundedness of the target matrix, with an uniformity in both the asset and time dimension.

3.5.1.2.2. Target matrices

The target matrix T_a has to be chosen and specified. Two common choices for T_a are a constant correlation matrix or a matrix derived from a market model.

1) In the constant correlation matrix model, the terms of the matrix T_a only depend on the variance of the assets. Its diagonal is made of the individual variances σ_i^2 of the assets. The non-diagonal terms T_{ij} are equal to $c\sigma_i\sigma_j$, where c is computed from an overall quantity estimated upon returns.

2) In the market model, we use the CAPM to write the following expression for an asset i of returns $R_{i,t}$:

$$R_{i,t} = \alpha_i + \beta_i R_{M,t} + \epsilon_t^i,$$

where $R_{M,t}$ is the return at time t of a market benchmark, whose volatility is σ_M and ϵ_t^i is assumed to be an i.i.d. noise with an idiosyncratic variance σ_i^2. Thus, if we note $\beta = (\beta_i)_{i=1:N}$, the target matrix T_a is set equal to:

$$T_a = diag(\sigma_1^2, ..., \sigma_N^2) + \sigma_M^2 \beta\beta'.$$

[LED 03] precises that when $T_a = \gamma I_N$, γ must be equal to the trace of the sample covariance matrix. This ensures that the initial allocation problem will be replaced by a problem with the same overall level of risk.

3.5.1.2.3. Effect on eigenvalues

The effect of shrinkage on the spectrum of the sample matrix is intuitive when $T_a = \gamma I_N, \gamma$ being the trace of the sample matrix:

$$\hat{\Omega}_s = \alpha\gamma I_N + (1 - \alpha)\hat{\Omega}.$$

Let λ_k be an eigenvalue of $\hat{\Omega}$ and ϕ_k the associated eigenvector. Then, ϕ_k is also an eigenvector of $\hat{\Omega}_s$ for the eigenvalue $\alpha\gamma + (1 - \alpha)\lambda_k$ since:

$$\begin{aligned}\hat{\Omega}_s\phi_k &= \alpha\gamma\phi_k + (1 - \alpha)\hat{\Omega}\phi_k \\ &= \alpha\gamma\phi_k + (1 - \alpha)\lambda_k\phi_k \\ &= (\alpha\gamma + (1 - \alpha)\lambda_k)\phi_k.\end{aligned}$$

As α lies between 0 and 1, when λ_k is greater than γ, $\alpha\gamma+(1-\alpha)\lambda_k$ is greater than γ but lower than λ_k. Conversely, when λ_k is lower than γ, this quantity is inferior to γ but greater than λ_k. The effect of shrinkage is then to *shrink* the range of the spectrum and to concentrate it around a mean value.

The major effect is on the lowest eigenvalues that are shifted upward. This is a simple intuition that confirms the argument of [LED 03] explaining that when the target matrix is γI_N, the shrinkage reduces the dispersion of the sample eigenvalues toward their mean. α is then interpreted as "*a normalized measure of the error of the sample covariance matrix*". The paper also shows why the eigenvalues of the sample covariance matrix are more dispersed than the eigenvalues of the true matrix, and why it is preferable to use estimators with eigenvalues that are less dispersed that the eigenvalues of the true covariance matrix. This dispersion is also a function of T/N.

In the general case, $\hat{\Omega}$ is replaced by $\hat{\Omega}_s = \alpha T_a+(1-\alpha)\hat{\Omega}$. Let $\hat{\lambda}_k$ be the eigenvalues of $\hat{\Omega}$ and $\hat{\phi}_k$ be the corresponding eigenvector. Without a target matrix, the solution w_* of $\hat{\Omega}w_* = \hat{\mu}$ is then obtained as since the eigenvectors have been assumed to be orthonormal:

$$w_* = \sum_{k=1}^{N} \frac{1}{\hat{\lambda}_k} < \hat{\mu}, \hat{\phi}_k > \hat{\phi}_k,$$

With $\hat{\Omega}_s = \alpha I + (1 - \alpha)\hat{\Omega}$, the weights w_*^s obtained with the shrinkage estimator are:

$$w_*^s = \sum_{k=1}^{N} \frac{1}{\alpha + (1 - \alpha)\hat{\lambda}_k} < \hat{\mu}, \hat{\phi}_k > \hat{\phi}_k, \qquad [3.13]$$

since $\hat{\Omega}_s$ has eigenvalues equal to $\hat{\lambda}_k(1 - \alpha) + \alpha$ with the same eigenvectors as $\hat{\Omega}$.

[LED 03] attributes the fact that the sample eigenvalues are more dispersed than the true ones to the presence of error also in the sample eigenvectors, and that shrinkage is a correction for this effect. Equation [3.13] provides a beginning of explanation to see how the eigenvectors are related to eigenvalues of the shrunken estimator. One important advantage of shrinkage techniques is that regardless of the proposed correction, it may easily allow to preserve the trace of the variance-covariance matrix if T_a is suitably chosen.

NUMERICAL EXAMPLE 3.7.– Figure 3.9 illustrates both the effect of shrinkage in addition to spectral cut-off for matrix displayed in Figure 3.3 for an *a-priori* value of α = 0.4, which is a strong value for illustration purpose. We focus on two regions: one region where eigenvalues of an order between 5 and 30 (top – the strong effect of spectral cut-off around k_0 = 17 is marked) ; and the other region between 20 and 502 (both the effects of shrinkage and spectral cut-off are materialized).

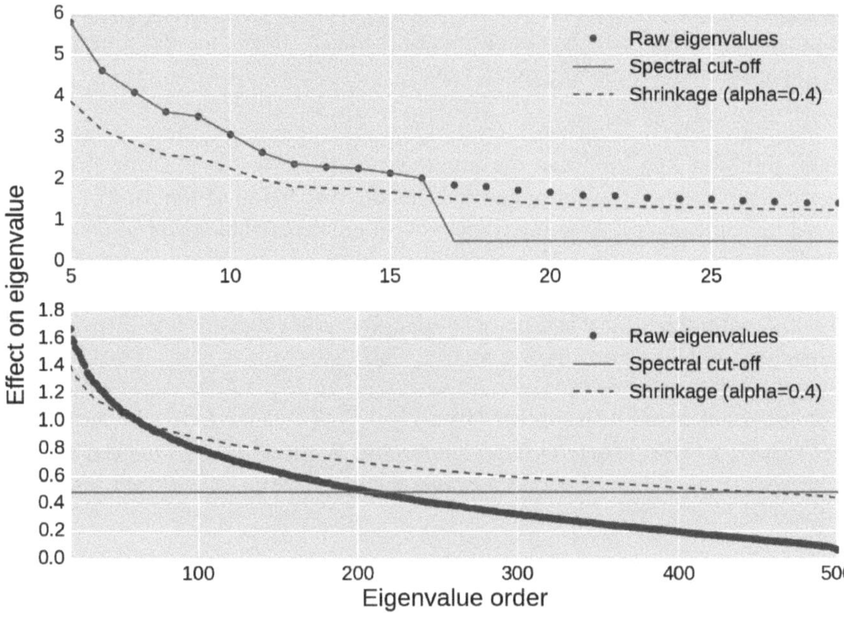

Figure 3.9. *Comparison of two regularization schemes on eigenvalues of the correlation matrix shown in Figure 3.3. Dots are the raw eigenvalues of the original sample matrix. The dashed line is the obtained eigenvalues of the shrinkage estimator for* α = 0.40. *The plain line is the effect of spectral cut-off as described in example 3.6*

3.5.1.2.4. Regularization scheme

We use the notions developed in Appendix A.3.2. We want to explore in which extent the shrinkage approach is a regularization method.

REMARK 3.7.– With notations of Appendix A.3.2.2 we get a regularization scheme $q_I(\alpha, \hat{\lambda})$:

$$q_I(\alpha, \hat{\lambda}) = \frac{\hat{\lambda}}{\alpha + (1-\alpha)\hat{\lambda}},$$

which is a first-order regularization scheme.

REMARK 3.8.– There is in fact a link between shrinkage and Tikhonov regularization (as noted in Appendix A.3.2.2.2). In numerical applications, where the problem to be regularized is of the form $Ka = \mu$, Tikhonov regularization is well known under the name of *ridge regression*. Ridge regression estimation was introduced by [HOE 70] in the multiple linear regression framework. When data on regressors are non-orthogonal, the OLS estimators are highly unreliable in the mean squared error sense and sensitive to small changes in data. The ridge regression technique has been extended to the general problem of matrix inversion by [VIN 76]. For portfolio allocation, the ridge technique computes:

$$a_* = (\Omega + \alpha I)^{-1}\mu,$$

where $\alpha > 0$ is a parameter unlinked to the sample size. This is quite similar to Tikhonov regularization and also very close to shrinkage techniques. [HOE 70] suggested to select the value for α through the so-called "ridge trace", which traces the values of the elements of the ridge estimator against α.

REMARK 3.9.– There is also a link between shrinkage and the Bayesian framework. Bayesian estimators and contributions are also mixing matrices coming from both *a priori* structures and confrontation to empirical estimators. However, the subtlety is that in the case of shrinkage the target matrix is known and assumed to have a predetermined structure that is different from the estimated matrix. Even if Bayesian estimators do shrink estimators with prior information, they do not assume that the target has to be different in general (see references given in [BAI 11] on this point).

Finally, we highlight also a recent paper by [ENG 16] that mixes elegantly the shrinkage approach with the *Dynamical Conditional Correlations (DCC)* of [ENG 02]. This work allows to conjugate a regularization technique (shrinkage) that acts to solve the problems appearing in the cross-section, with a parametric setting[16]

16 Consequently, it provides a transition for a procedure that appears at the interface with the techniques developed in section 3.5.1.3

that helps to improve the estimation on the time series aspect. The power of the method is to allow for heteroskedasticity, i.e. non-stationarity of moments, which was one of the problems discussed throughout section 3.4.

3.5.1.3. *Parametric estimation*

When identifying the problem of an ill-conditioned matrix inversion, it is natural to try to impose a structure on the matrix: controlling for the structure should help us to obtain a more stable inverse. This approach is quite natural and widely used in practice. In high-dimensional problems, reducing the complexity and the dimension of the problem is always a way to increase stability and obtain convergent solutions. In the case of infinite-dimensional inverse problems, being parametric allows to seek solutions in a finite-dimensional subspace, which is a closed subset of the space of solutions: this "brute force" dimensionality reduction allows us to find a convergent, stable and robust solution, potentially with a specification risk at the cost of losing in precision.

This is, for instance, the goal of factor model estimators that specify a given structure for $\hat{\Omega}$, in order to reduce the number of parameters to be estimated. A major contribution in this field was made by [FAN 08a] who showed that - surprisingly - this method works far better when using Ω^{-1} directly rather than Ω (which is of course of straightforward interest for the allocation problem). The obtained estimator is then always invertible and the asymptotic theory is derived, in the case where $N, T \to \infty$, with an increasing number of factors. Another approach is to define a more structured model for the covariance matrix, as for example in [SPE 03]. A PCA is made on the return series and the corresponding principal components are studied as univariate series through a given volatility model (e.g. GARCH). We review in the following subsections some of the widely used parametric methods to propose estimators for covariance matrices that are alternatives to the raw sample estimator.

3.5.1.3.1. Diagonal model

This is the most simple model where the correlation matrix is simply the $N \times N$ identity matrix. Consequently, the covariance matrix is the diagonal matrix where the matrix is made of the individual variance of the assets.

$$\Omega = \begin{pmatrix} \sigma_{11} & 0 & \dots & 0 \\ 0 & \sigma_{22} & \dots & 0 \\ \dots & \dots & \dots & \dots \\ 0 & \dots & 0 & \sigma_{NN} \end{pmatrix}.$$

In this case, we shift from $N(N+1)/2$ parameters (raw sample estimator) to N parameters (the N diagonal terms) to be estimated.

3.5.1.3.2. Constant correlation model

This is again a simple model where the correlation between stocks is supposed to be a constant equal to ρ. We may find in the literature the terms *market* or *single-index* correlation models. Empirically, even if this value fluctuates, depending on the market conditions, ρ is around 0.3 or 0.4 for stocks in usual conditions, as in example 3.1.

$$\Omega = diag(\sigma_1, ..., \sigma_N) \times \begin{pmatrix} 1 & \rho & ... & \rho \\ \rho & 1 & ... & \rho \\ ... & ... & ... & ... \\ \rho & ... & \rho & 1 \end{pmatrix} \times diag(\sigma_1, ..., \sigma_N).$$

Why is it sometimes called *market* model? In such a case, the spectrum of the correlation matrix is made of one large eigenvalue equal to $\lambda_1 = 1 + (N-1)\rho$, which is far greater than the remaining $N-1$ all equal to $1-\rho$. The eigenvector ϕ_1 corresponding to λ_1 is simply e_N, the unitary vector that spans all the universe of assets and may be thought in its simplest, unbiased form as representing "the market".

NUMERICAL EXAMPLE 3.8.– The equality $\lambda_1 = 1 + (N-1)\rho$ also directly provides an estimator of the mean correlation between assets, since:

$$\rho = \frac{\lambda_1 - 1}{N - 1}.$$

In our example with the S&P500, we obtained $\lambda_1 \sim 183$ (with $N = 502$), which provides an estimator of $\hat{\rho} = 182/501 \sim 0.363$, which is quite close to the flat average of the elements of the correlation matrix of 0.346 we estimated on Example 3.1.

To see it in another way, we could remark that this correlation structure is reproduced by a model where the returns of any asset $i \in [1; N]$ are written:

$$R_t^{(i)} = \sqrt{\rho} M_t + \sqrt{1-\rho}\epsilon_t^{(i)}, \qquad [3.14]$$

where $(M_t, \epsilon_t^{(1)}, ..., \epsilon_t^{(N)})$ are i.i.d. Gaussian variables $\mathcal{N}(0,1)$. Therefore, at date t, assets correlate only through the main market mode M_t, which is a common risk factor. This generic model helps to obtain the correlation matrix just above. Such a model is sometimes called the *One Factor Model* or *Single Index Model (SIM)* and have to be related to the work of [SHA 63]. Here again, the number of parameters decreases from $N(N+1)/2$ parameters $N+1$ (N diagonal terms plus ρ) to be estimated.

NUMERICAL EXAMPLE 3.9.– We may compute the instantaneous risk that an equal-weighted portfolio, i.e. for all $i \in [1; N]$, $w_i = 1/N$, bears to illustrate the effects of correlation. If we compute $w'\Omega w$ with the SIM model, with the additional assumption that all the volatilities are equal to σ, we obtain:

$$\begin{aligned} w'\Omega w &= \sum_{i=1}^{N} w_i^2\sigma_i^2 + \sum_{i,j=1|i\neq j}^{N} w_i w_j \sigma_i \sigma_j \rho \\ &= \left(\frac{1}{N}\right)^2 N\sigma^2 + N(N-1)\rho\left(\frac{1}{N}\right)^2 \\ &= \frac{\sigma^2}{N} + \left(1-\frac{1}{N}\right)\rho\sigma^2. \end{aligned} \qquad [3.15]$$

This shows the benefits and also the limits of diversification. When N is large, we see that correlation drives the risk of the portfolio. With $\rho = 0$, all the risk is effectively diversified. However, as soon as $\rho > 0$, risk evolves as $\sim \rho\sigma^2$. We have already underlined the few instances of negative correlations in the S&P500 (14 out of 125,751 in example 3.1), which shows that in an SIM model, diversification in our case leads to an overall variance that is divided by 3, since our estimation of correlation was around 0.36.

Dividing the overall risk by 3 is great, but all risk has not been diversified. And such an effect is strong since if we recompute equation [3.15] with $\rho = 0.36$ and a varying N we see that with $N = 5$, $w'\Omega w = 0.49$, with $N = 10$, $w'\Omega w = 0.42$ and with $N = 30$, $w'\Omega w = 0.38$. With approximately 5% of the assets, the same level of diversification is already achieved!

3.5.1.3.3. Market and factor models

The direct generalization of the constant correlation model occurs when Ω is assumed to be block-diagonal that is made of S blocks:

$$\Omega = diag(\sigma_1, ..., \sigma_N) \times \begin{pmatrix} C_1 & C_0 & ... & C_0 \\ C_0 & C_2 & ... & C_0 \\ ... & ... & ... & ... \\ C_0 & ... & C_0 & C_S \end{pmatrix} \times diag(\sigma_1, ..., \sigma_N),$$

where C_0 is a block matrix of constant ρ_0 such that $1 > \rho_0 > 0$ and each matrix C_i with $i \in [1; S]$ is a constant correlation matrix with 1 on the diagonal and ρ_i off the diagonal with $1 > \rho_i > \rho_0$. The S blocks may emulate the economic sectors within which each stock is more correlated than with any other stock outside the sector. Again, there is a statistical modeling behind this form and the model described in equation [3.14] easily extends in this situation to a finite number of specific factors in addition to the common market mode in order to obtain this block-diagonal structure for Ω (see [RON 14]). Moreover, let us assume that the S sectors are of homogeneous size N_S such as $S \times N_S = N$, and such that correlation is constant over blocks $1 > \rho_1 = ... =$

$\rho_S > \rho_0 > 0$. In this case, we have access to the full spectrum of the matrix with the largest eigenvalue equal to $\lambda_1 = 1 + (S-1)\rho_1 + (N-S)\rho$. The following $N_S - 1$ eigenvalues are all equal to $1 + (S-1)\rho_1 - S\rho$. The remaining $N - N_S$ eigenvalues are much lower, all equal to $1 - \rho_1$ (all of this is detailed in [PAF 04]). With such a model, we shift from $N(N+1)/2$ parameters to $N + S + 1$ (N variances of the assets and $S + 1$ correlations, one for each block).

The direct extension of this is a standard of the industry with the use of factor models. It is the multi-dimensional extension of the single factor and sector models such as macroeconomic factors, risk premia, Fama-French factors and industrial binary variables. It is, for example, at the heart of the famous BARRA risk model (see [BAR 07]). In this case, the factors are *observable* in the sense that the returns are modeled through:

$$R_t^{(i)} = \alpha^{(i)} + \beta_1^{(i)} F_{1,t} + \ldots + +\beta_K^{(i)} F_{K,t} + \epsilon_t^{(i)}, \qquad [3.16]$$

with observed, plug-in values of factors F (return of a strategy, belonging or not to an industry, etc.). Such an approach is sound because as soon as $K < N$, we gain in reducing the dimensionality of the problem. Moreover, being parametric in (α, β) allows to circumvent the ill-posedness nature of the inversion of the matrix. Such a method is one of the most widespread in the industry for the cleaning of the covariance matrices (when they are cleaned, see again [GOT 09]). Theoretical developments and estimation challenges are handled in [FAN 08a] and an in-depth review of such models is available in [CAM 97]. In particular, the sector model developed above may be viewed as a particular case of factor model with linear constraints. It is also possible to use non-observable factors (therefore called *latent factors*) to estimate the covariance matrix, but this is far beyond the scope of the present book (one may refer to [BAI 02], [BAI 03], [BAI 06], [BAI 12a], [BAI 16a]).

3.5.2. *Adding constraints*

3.5.2.1. *An empirical solution...*

"Constraints and judgment should play an essential role in portfolio choice. However, the implications for the portfolio-as-a-whole of such constraints and judgments should be thought trough, ideally with an expected-utility analysis with a properly chosen utility function. In the absence of the latter, I believe that some form of risk-return analysis is the best alternative."

—[MAR 10]

As expressed by [MAR 10] above, a natural heuristic approach often used in practice is simply to include constraints to prevent portfolio weights to take unrealistic values. This is a quick yet smart answer to a practical problem and has the advantage to control exactly the bounds for the weights of the portfolio and even to control for turnover if those bounds are quite strict. As we underlined previously, [GOT 09] found that hardly 30% of practitioners admitted to using a cleaning procedure. Yet in the same study, nearly 75% of the respondents did impose effective constraints on weights. The approximate symmetry of figures shows that everybody sees the problem, but the way to solve it is often either empirical, either theoretical.

With tight constraints, one may think that sharply following the target strategy becomes difficult, if not impossible. The constraints may be finally driving the allocation: monitoring the real performance becomes potentially pointless, the strategy losing its interpretability and its pertinence. However, in practice, constraints are not bad: on the contrary, they allow to control for *a posteriori* variance due to estimation error. A famous work by [JAG 03] shows that imposing a *no short-sell* constraint[17] allows in general to decrease the out-of-sample risk of a portfolio, even if the constraints are wrong or unjustified. Of course, this is adapted to long-only and not to long-short portfolios, where explicit short positions are needed. However, for portfolios with 100% net exposition (e.g. the so-called "1x0-x0" portfolios), this may be useful if the short positions introduce too much noise. They also document the fact that as soon as a no-short-sell constraint is involved, the introduction of upper bounds for the weights become useless. What is much more interesting is that this seemingly purely purpose-driven technique has in fact strong theoretical justification[18], as soon as it is applied in the right context. We keep on insisting on the fact that matrix inversion can lead to extreme weights in the resulting portfolio, but more precisely, this may be caused by stocks with a high average level of covariance with other assets. In this case, those stocks have a huge marginal contribution to the overall risk. When solving an optimization problem whose aim is to reduce risk, the weights of those assets have to be lowered to decrease their final contribution to the overall portfolio variance. However, when this level is really high, the algorithm tends to set artificially negative weights to those assets. The same mechanism is at play in the opposite situation where low covariance assets are unreasonably favored to solve the optimization problem. In both cases, this is mainly driven by the estimation of the covariance structure and the consequences of estimation error are disastrous out-of-sample (see [JAG 03] again for a full discussion).

REMARK 3.10.– Constraints may be clearly wrong, unjustified or seemingly inadequate, as they introduce specification error. However, the final gain comes through the existing trade-off between this misspecification error and the reduction of sampling error. However, it is documented that this approach may fail when assets are themselves already factors or large portfolios, and its success may also rely on the covariance estimation method.

17 See [JAC 05] for some insights on the practical inclusion of realistic short constraints for portfolio optimization with factors.

18 Even Maximum Sharpe Ratio portfolios may be interpreted as specific minimal-variance portfolios with modified constraints on the return: see [GOL 03b].

3.5.2.2. ...*but a theoretical justification*

Adding constraints within the optimization stage is equivalent to adding constraints in the estimation stage with constraints explicitly set in the optimization problem, with the corresponding Lagrange multipliers. This point is clearly identified by [LED 04] and thoroughly justified in Appendix A of [JAG 03]: adding constraints can be somewhat related to shrinkage. The explanation is the following. If $c_u = (c_u^1, \dots, c_u^N)$ and $c_l = (c_l^1, \dots, c_l^N)$ are the N-dimensional vectors of the Lagrange multipliers of the constraints for the upper and lower (non-negativity) constraints, respectively, the problem may be transformed into an unconstrained optimization problem where the covariance matrix Ω is replaced by:

$$\Omega_c = \Omega + C_u - C_l,$$

where C_u and C_l are $N \times N$ matrices such as $(C_u)_{i,j} = c_u^i + c_u^j$ and $(C_l)_{i,j} = c_l^i + c_l^j$. Let us recall that the mathematics behind Lagrange multipliers make that the product of the multiplier and its related constraint is equal to zero due to either the nullity of the multiplier or the fact the constraint is satisfied. When Ω is invertible, the existence of an upper bound and of a relative Lagrange multiplier allows us to shift the mean returns by a factor that is proportional to the Lagrange multiplier, and reciprocally when the lower bound is hit. In fact, constrained covariance matrices shrink large covariances in the direction of average covariances and imposing a constraint is equivalent to optimize an unconstrained problem with a modified matrix. This behaves exactly as shrinkage, and may be seen therefore as a regularization technique.

In the same spirit, [RON 11] exposes how the introduction of upper and lower bounds on portfolio weights may have an influence on the properties of the empirical covariance matrix in an unconstrained problem. Again, the constraints induce a correction on the original covariance matrix through their associated Lagrange multipliers. Why is this important? In fact, knowing that constraints are equivalent to modifications on the covariance matrix will also lead practitioners to see how their views will be *a priori* affected by their target constraints. [FAN 12a] explains why the constraints help to get a better out-of-sample risk. It is mathematically the same justification that is used in the proof of [JAG 03]. The fact is that with a given set of weights w, the risk obtained with an estimated covariance matrix $\hat{\Omega}$ is such that:

$$|w'\hat{\Omega}w - w'\Omega w| \leq ||\hat{\Omega} - \Omega||_\infty ||w||_1^2.$$

The right-hand term of the equation is the product of two terms. The first one, $||\hat{\Omega} - \Omega||_\infty$, will depend on the estimation method. $||w||_1 = \sum_{i=1}^N |w_i|$ is the expression of the gross market value of the portfolio and, in addition to the budget constraint $\sum_{i=1}^N w_i = 1$ is minimized in the case of the no-short-sell constraint where $w_i \geq 0$ for each asset. However, constraints help to easily control the $||w||_1$ term and hence the right-hand-side term in the previous equation, and as a consequence, the out-of-sample risk. This entailed the authors to express the fact that controlling the gross exposure of the portfolio is an easy empirical way to control weights and *a posteriori* risk, and builds a continuum between the no short-sale portfolio and the unconstrained mean-variance. It is an interesting alternative in case of long-short portfolios, or in the case of long-only portfolios as the no short-sell portfolio appears often not to be diversified enough.

REMARK 3.11.– Imposing constraints on the *a posteriori* weights is equivalent to modify the covariance matrix in a shrinkage-like approach. But we could also shrink the weights with a rule such that:

$$\tilde{w} = \alpha w^* + (1 - \alpha) w_0,$$

where w^* are the empirical weights of the initial unconstrained mean-variance problem and w_0 are some reference weights used to stabilize the resulting weights $\tilde{w}$. In practice, this solution seems to perform poorly empirically according to [DEM 13].

However, we already highlighted the result of [BRI 99] in remark 3.1 using the regression of a constant on assets' returns with an OLS framework. This writing could be particularly interesting in the perspective of using constraints setting because it allows to derive simple or more elaborated tests on weights. It is in particular possible to use this framework to make a nullity test on some particular weights or to test linear restrictions on subsets of weights using a joint test. This could be a helpful procedure to validate *ex ante* the pertinence of specific constraints.

Another approach could be to impose a structure not on the covariance matrix but directly on the inverse covariance matrix (called sometimes the *concentration*, *precision* or more often the *information matrix*). A way to reduce estimation error is to impose some sparsity to the inverse variance matrix. The fact is that even when an original covariance matrix is sparse, the inverse covariance matrix is not automatically sparse: inversion does not preserve sparsity. One of the first contributions on this topic may be found in the work of [DEM 72] whose aim is to find a method to impose some sparsity on the inverse covariance matrix. [GOT 15] elaborated on this to propose a method restricting some of the off-diagonal elements of the inverse covariance matrix. This is obtained by constraining the l_1-norm of those off-diagonal terms. As they present it, this is in a way "*equivalent to a strong form of shrinkage*". Such an approach is also developed, for instance, by [FAN 08a] and in [BRO 15]. Why does it work? As we have seen in section 3.4.4.2 the coefficients of the inverse covariance matrix may be viewed as regression coefficients from one asset on the others. Setting some of them to zero could be a way to take benefit only from the strongest hedging relations relatively to the others. Each line of the inverse matrix appears as a hedge portfolio:

trimming those portfolios may be a way to improve the overall estimator by selecting a subset of stocks, the strongest ones for the hedge.

[BRO 09] added a l_1 penalty term to the optimization program up to a parameter to be calibrated. This may be considered as a version of lasso regression. In addition to the regularizing effect, this allows us to take into account transaction costs, to control short-selling and finally to obtain preferentially sparse portfolios (i.e. with few non-zero positions). As expressed before, the constraint on short-selling ensures the stabilization of the portfolio. However, [BRO 09] also underlined that such a constraint naturally implies the construction of sparse portfolios. Empirically, this method works well as the obtained portfolio are more robust, less affected by estimation error and noisy information.

3.5.3. *Black-Litterman*

3.5.3.1. *Motivations*

The Black-Litterman approach (BL hereafter) is a technique proposed in [BLA 92] to integrate in the allocation process the forecasts of the investor, rather than trying to explicitly solve the instability of the inversion. Because of its appealing nature, this technique is now commonly used as it raised the attention of portfolio managers interested in incorporating personal views in the allocation. The technique suffers from the fact that a painstaking prior calibration is needed but is quite well adapted to situations where it is necessary to allocate between asset classes, providing a tactical asset allocation model which may thought of as being at the crossroads of several other techniques. The BL approach primarily focuses on the expected returns through active manipulation, but we will see that there is also an effective action on the covariance matrix. Even if the model is not usually presented as a regularization technique, we will see that regularization *may* be a by-product of the procedure. The idea is that the investor invests first in a reference or in an *equilibrium* portfolio that may be a market portfolio, her or his current portfolio, or any defined benchmark whose weights are explicitly known. Then, the investor deviates from the equilibrium portfolio in the direction of specific views or bets. If an asset is not concerned by any view, its corresponding allocation will be directly determined by the equilibrium portfolio. Under the original form of the setting, this portfolio is linked with the capitalization-weighted index but "philosophically" the portfolio could be any portfolio optimal in the idea of the manager. Afterward, the setting of the model remains the mean-variance framework and the covariance matrix that is used need not be cleaned.

3.5.3.2. *The framework*

The model starts with an equilibrium portfolio Π that is homogeneous to expected returns. The portfolio is implied from a vector of weights w_M that is at hand and Π is defined through:

$$\Pi = A\hat{\Omega}w_M,$$

where w_M is observed and $\hat{\Omega}$ is estimated (and need not to be inverted). A is a scalar parameter related to risk aversion. This portfolio may be the market portfolio (derived from the CAPM or from a capitalization-weighted index), the current portfolio of the manager or any desired portfolio. The portfolio has to be thought as a "fixed point" as only views that deviate from it will lead to weights that are different from w_M. Π is homogeneous to expected returns and is, in a way, a stability provider of the allocation procedure.

The method starts by assuming for the asset returns (R_t) a distribution $R \rightsquigarrow \mathcal{N}(\mu, \Omega)$, where μ cannot be observed and is itself random. The model specifies two distributions for μ: one suggested by the equilibrium portfolio and the other suggested by investors' forecasts. The model aims at specifying in the same time a distribution for Π, conditional on μ. Within a Bayesian framework the posterior distribution of μ conditional on Π may be derived. Rather than using the sample mean of μ as an estimator, this latter is replaced by the mean (denoted by $\overline{ER}$ in the following) of the posterior distribution of μ conditional on Π. The trick is that the expression of $\overline{ER}$ will incorporate $\hat{\Omega}$ and this will allow to tackle the ill-posedness.

The expression of the forecasts specifies the distribution of l linear combinations of the elements of μ, $P\mu \rightsquigarrow \mathcal{N}(V, F)$, where we adopt the following notations:

- P is a $l \times N$-dimensional matrix selecting the assets concerned with the views;
- F is a $l \times l$-dimensional diagonal covariance matrix of the errors on these views;
- V is a l-dimensional vector of the absolute expression of those views.

Π is assumed to be normally distributed as $\mathcal{N}(\mu, \alpha\hat{\Omega})$. The scalar parameter α has to be calibrated. Under those assumptions, μ is normal with mean $\overline{ER}$ and variance VR equal to:

$$\overline{ER} = [(\alpha\hat{\Omega})^{-1} + P'F^{-1}P]^{-1}[(\alpha\hat{\Omega})^{-1}\Pi + P'F^{-1}V]$$
$$VR = [(\alpha\hat{\Omega})^{-1} + P'F^{-1}P]^{-1}.$$

$\overline{ER}$ may be expressed in the following form, which is more intuitive from a financial point of view because it is expressed as the deviation from Π (the optimal portfolio being a deviation from the market portfolio):

$$\overline{ER} = \Pi + (\alpha\hat{\Omega})P'(F + \alpha P\hat{\Omega}P')^{-1}(V - P\Pi).$$

If no views are specified, we recover that:

$$\overline{ER} = [(\alpha\hat{\Omega})^{-1}]^{-1}[(\alpha\hat{\Omega})^{-1}\Pi] = \Pi.$$

Finally, the allocation uses $\overline{ER}$ instead of $\hat{\mu}$:

$$w^* = (A\hat{\Omega})^{-1}(\overline{ER}),$$

which rewrites:

$$w^* = w_M + \frac{\alpha}{A}P'(\alpha P\hat{\Omega}P' + F)^{-1}(V - P\Pi).$$

Several extensions of the BL model exist. All these are beyond the scope of this chapter as we initially wish to explore the regularization properties of the technique. We underline that the BL setting extends to various markets and asset classes of assets as returns in the following may represent risk factor returns. Many improvements may exist, where volatilities and correlations may also be stressed; even nonlinear and very general views can be included. See [MEU 08] for a general review.

3.5.3.3. *Limitations*

Practically, the manager can update at each date its equilibrium vector Π by replacing w_M by any w reflecting current or new information. Then, the allocation can be updated at each date through Π. We see easily that if both w_M and the views are unchanged at each allocation, the weights will not evolve. Yet, the calibration of the full model remains a hard task as it is sometimes difficult to give appropriate values for A, α and to specify F. Some empirical contributions are hopefully dedicated to the practical implementation of the model. Among them, we may identify the work of [HE 99], [LEE 00], [HER 03], [IDZ 07], [JON 07b] and [CHE 09]. In particular, the α parameter is puzzling by nature as it specified that the uncertainty of views is proportional to the assets' variance. It may be logical to think that for the more volatile assets induce predictions that have less precision. Yet it makes that all the uncertainty is driven by a single scalar, which may be a bit too hazardous as this scalar will have a huge influence on the overall variance. The works of [LEE 00] and [WAL 13] are both dedicated to the calibration of the α factor.

Some criticisms are often opposed to the model as it is originally presented. Apart from the difficulties met to calibrate the model, the model remains a mean-variance model with a raw covariance matrix. This is not really a problem because cleaning the matrix may be an independent step before applying the model. In addition, the deviation from the equilibrium portfolio is only driven by the manager and no tilt will be applied on any asset absent from the specification of the views. The views predetermine the vectorial space in which deviations from the reference portfolio will evolve. Moreover, the framework may not be suited to any kind of investment. Paradoxically, it may be not suited to benchmarked portfolios. It may seem odd since for benchmarked portfolios, an extra overlay is added on top of a reference benchmark. Yet, as developed by [SCH 09], the model remains intrinsically a mean-variance model[19] and the setting is the one of an unconstrained, global mean-variance model. The BL model helps to translate views into positions and controls the stability of the weights: yet the model does not seek to optimize any measure based on the overlay (the views). A last criticism comes from [MIC 13] and is linked to constraints and especially non-negativity ones. If one works with a non-zero position, long-only portfolio, the investor may add views that make the final BL portfolio to have negative weights. The only way to prevent from ending in such a situation if one is constrained to have positive weights is to decrease the α parameter up to a final value such that views do not twist the equilibrium so much. But decreasing α is equivalent to accepting an overall higher uncertainty in the views. The sign constraints then force artificially to recalibrate some parameters and to decrease the initial potential of the model, making it probably un-adapted to long-only portfolios.

3.5.3.4. *Is Black-Litterman really Bayesian?*

The fact that the BL model does not lead to unstable weights is widely recognized. For instance, [LEE 00] attributes the effect of the model through the "*spreading of the errors throughout the vector of expected returns*". The approach is self-coherent because modeling the distribution of Π conditional on μ means that conditional on the same μ, Π is on average equal to μ. If all the agents believe in the views μ, the equilibrium returns will tend to Π... itself centered on μ: this ensures the equilibrium nature of Π. Therefore, the BL approach looks similar to a Bayesian[20] setting since a prior distribution is specified on μ, which is supposed to be random, and this distribution is then updated to form new opinions. This is the commonly accepted view among practitioners. However, in order to have a Bayesian interpretation, we cannot use the conditional distribution of $R|\mu$ as sampling mechanism, even if it could seem the more natural candidate. Indeed, the reality of the strict Bayesian nature of BL can be discussed. This weakness for a Bayesian justification is expressed in [SAT 00], "*the interpretation of what is prior and what is sample information may differ from BL*". Another argument is the following:

19 In the original contribution however, it is underlined that the tracking error (defined under the name of *balance*) of a portfolio towards the equilibrium portfolio should be monitored.

20 This particular discussion, but more generally all the chapter owes a lot to a common work and thoughts shared with Anna Simoni that the authors want to sincerely thank here.

"since estimation of the mean is ancillary to estimation of variance, using a mean estimate that is a function of the covariance estimate is tantamount to believing that there is no information for the first moment of the data, while there is perfect information for the second moment, the expected squared deviations from the unknowable first moment. (...) Additionally, the α adjustment itself is an ad hoc modification of the prior distribution to steer the outcome towards some desirable result, which violates the principles of a rigorous Bayesian analysis."

— [MIC 13]

Anyway, a Bayesian interpretation is often given, which may seem natural at first glance. In practice, the prior-to-posterior transformation is not the same computation written down by Black and Litterman to obtain the modified expected excess returns $\overline{ER}$, but it gives the same result. Hence, it can be seen as a way to interpret the BL model from a Bayesian perspective.

3.5.3.5. *Regularizing effect*

Even if the main effort of the model is to focus on μ, we will show in this paragraph that the BL model provides in fact an indirect correction on the covariance matrix. To the best of our knowledge, such a reading of this correction is not provided in the literature, even if [MIC 13] identifies that "*BL does not solve but rather conceals the instability and estimation error problems of Markowitz mean-variance optimization.*" The expression of w^* is:

$$\frac{A}{\alpha}\underbrace{(\alpha\hat{\Omega})^{-1}}_{M_1:=}\underbrace{[(\alpha\hat{\Omega})^{-1}+P'F^{-1}P]^{-1}}_{(M_1+M_2)^{-1}:=}\underbrace{[(\alpha\hat{\Omega})^{-1}\Pi+P'F^{-1}V]}_{N\times 1\text{vector}}.$$

We will explicit the eigenvalues of matrix $M := M_1(M_1+M_2)^{-1}$ and for this we will study M^{-1}. M, M_1, M_2 are $N \times N$ matrices. We have:

$$[M_1(M_1+M_2)^{-1}]^{-1} = (M_1+M_2)M_1^{-1} = I_d + M_2M_1^{-1}.$$

Thus, the eigenvalues of M^{-1} have for lower bound:

$$\frac{A}{\alpha}(1+\inf sp(\alpha P'F^{-1}P\hat{\Omega})),$$

where $sp(.)$ stands for the set of eigenvalues of a matrix. Then, even if the eigenvalues of $P'F^{-1}P\hat{\Omega}$ tends to zero, the set of eigenvalues of M^{-1} is bounded from below (for fixed and calibrated A and α) and the eigenvalues of M cannot diverge, solving the instability of the initial problem.

3.6. Allocating without views

In this section, we explore techniques that do not use views or strategies, or at least not explicitly. As we have seen previously, it is difficult statistically to estimate an expected return vector. Consequently, if variance estimation is more robust (see [MER 80]), it makes sense to give more importance to the variance and to get rid of the return part. However, it would be wrong, technically, to speak about techniques that use "no views" at all. We use this term as all the techniques presented here do not make any explicit statement concerning any return estimation. This would be incorrect because *not using* views is in fact *having no active views,* which is slightly different, as it may cover an implicit bet on returns, hidden by the reformulation of the problem. Yet, no modeling of the future returns is explicitly needed. Historically, the advent of such techniques came with the introduction of the term *risk-parity* as [QIA 05] introduced it. This term is rather vague (and may sometimes be used for marketing purposes) as such methods have certainly been used before and recovers in fact several techniques that are not only applied to equities but to a variety of investment strategies. A cornerstone reference on the subject is [RON 14], which gives an in-depth exploration of risk-parity (along with properties and salient features and quantities), while recalling that such techniques remain investment models that rely on specific choices and parameters that are often to be estimated.

The success of such allocation techniques has natural justifications. Following the economic turmoil that started in 2008-2009, it is natural to look for defensive and low-risk assets. Second, independently from the economic context, if the fund manager has an explicit mandate constraining her or his overall level of risk, such allocation techniques are therefore a natural choice. Third, in the field of equities, low-volatility stocks have the particular behavior to deliver better returns. [ASN 12] puts forward a possible explanation for justifying the existence of this low-volatility anomaly. Their argument is that aversion or constraints toward leverage are at play. Playing safer assets with higher returns requires leverage, and all investors are not able to seize such opportunities. The advantage of risk-parity portfolios (see what follows) is that as they equalize the risks over asset classes, they mechanically overweight safer asset. Therefore, portfolios with an over-representation of defensive assets will lead to higher returns. In the same direction, [KAY 12] demonstrated in their appendix how minimum variance portfolios (again, in what follows) are biased toward low-idiosyncratic risk and low-beta assets. They moreover highlighted the fact that good performances of minimum variance portfolios may be due to the particular under-performance of high-beta bets in the recent decades. This is not a detail as the success of such techniques and the live debates on their relative interests, advantages and drawbacks one with respect to another, rely much on their good performance in a recent period. Another element is that regularization techniques are needed to correct the estimation of large covariance matrices implying a large number of assets, yet when allocating within a set of assets or a set of asset classes of lower dimension (typically 3 or 4 when allocating between asset classes). The instability aspect is less of a concern and risk-based allocation techniques are particularly adapted thanks to the intuitive action they have.

3.6.1. *Risk-based allocation*

We will present in this paragraph allocation methods that do not use views in the sense that they are risk-focused allocation methods, where explicit signal construction plays no active role. Thus, we may find them under the name of "*naive beta*" in the literature. Two streams of contributions may be identified in this field[21]. A first stream of papers is related to the study of returns and historical performance comparison. In our mind, this is not the most interesting way to begin with risk-based techniques as financial conditions are changing and evolving, and such studies may rely on particular historical biases or become obsolete within a finite range of time. Most of all, backtests are not the best way to understand analytics as they prove nothing. They may depend on the period, asset class, experimental protocol and subtleties that are not detailed in the papers, and differences are sometimes hardly noticeable. However, precise studies on the subject do exist and include, for instance, [CHO 11] or [LEO 12]. The second stream of papers deals with the mathematical analysis and empirical properties of the portfolios and see how they relate to the way portfolios are built. This is also the aim of the present section: reviewing and analyzing techniques along with their statistical and mathematical properties. We do not see those allocation techniques as being opposed and concurrent. We rather see them as alternatives where the focus is different from one to another. We do not aim to give an exhaustive list of properties or quantities as those are already given in the numerous references that we will refer to: we are rather mainly interested in the respective regularizing properties they present. In this paragraph, w will again be an N-dimensional vector of weights defining a portfolio P whose volatility will be written as $\sigma_P = \sqrt{w'\Omega w}$. The risk contribution of the asset i to portfolio P is $\partial\sigma_P/\partial w_i$.

3.6.1.1. *Equally weighted portfolios*

Equal weighting is the simplest allocation possible as it allocates equally between all the assets, regardless of their statistical properties. Allocation is made based on *capital* (i.e. in dollars) and not on risk, thus diversification in capital is maximized. No estimation is needed: neither the covariance matrix nor the expected return needs to be estimated. The only thing to do is to rebalance the mark-to-market. It is strange to begin a review of techniques dedicated to volatility-based allocation with a technique that requires nothing but the number of assets! However, we can conceive it as a zero-level benchmark. And we cannot discard the influence this approach had on the

21 This separation is in particular made by [JUR 15b], which constitutes an interesting contribution that will allow to build a common, transversal framework for risk-based allocation techniques as presented in section 3.6.1.5.

debates on allocation techniques recently. Empirically, the work of [DEM 09b] revived the debate and the interest in this "technique". Working on several data sets (mainly equity data), the authors found that naive equally weighted portfolios are even more interesting out-of-sample when compared to allocation strategies where parameters have to be estimated. The resulting portfolios are diversified in proportions and focus on performance, which is much better out-of-sample (compared to minimum variance portfolios, see below). What is sometimes forgotten is that in the original paper of [DEM 09b], the naive allocation is *explicitly* not promoted as a technique in itself, and the authors did not intend to "*advocate the use of the 1/N heuristic as an asset allocation strategy*". It is clearly presented as a benchmark to discuss empirical efforts to improve moment estimation. [DEM 09b] underlines that the 1/N benchmark must be dominated by classic techniques as soon as the estimation window is sufficiently long and if the number of assets is small. Obviously, naive diversification cannot be conceived as a technique in itself. From a statistical perspective, it comes not from a bad inspiration since it boils down to an extreme Bayesian approach that allows to prevent in-sample effects. If one has no trust at all in a return estimation, the safest way to allocate is to place the same level of confidence in each asset. In Bayesian terms, it could be observed that the $1/N$ weighting corresponds to an extreme choice of a totally uninformed prior.

This revived the debate around portfolio allocation and more precisely on volatility-related allocation, since this 1/N benchmark is often used in such studies. However, we should recall some facts on this study, mainly focused on the US equity market. The framework of the paper is monthly, which is a drawback for estimation, because more precision could be obtained with data at a higher frequency. Second, a very scarce number of assets is used (up to 20, but commonly 5 or 10). This is very small and is far from being pertinent as estimation error is even bigger in common situations with hundreds of assets. Last but not least, the data sets end in 2002 or 2004, which may be a favorable context for US equities (the technology bubble is included but not the 2008-2009 crisis). Quickly after the publication of the paper came some criticism to uphold the benefits of optimization versus naive diversification. [KRI 10] shows that the apparent superiority of the equal-weighted allocation procedure appears because of optimization problems coming from the use of rolling short-term means as proxies of expected returns. The use of longer-term samples or more plausible expected returns as signal still gives better results with optimized portfolios out-of-sample. Of course, the comparison with proprietary strategies is impossible. Finally, another critique came from [KIR 12] who underlines that the results of [DEM 09b] are largely driven by their research framework, focusing on a "*very theoretical*" mean-variance portfolio, known to be very sensitive to estimation noise and with an extreme turnover.

REMARK 3.12.– If all assets have identical excess returns and volatilities, with a constant and unique correlation between assets, the EW portfolio is optimal in the sense of the mean-variance criterion. However, this diversification argument fails in the case of heterogeneous statistical properties.

3.6.1.2. *Minimum Variance*

3.6.1.2.1. Motivations

The Minimum Variance portfolio (henceforth MV, see e.g. [HAU 91]) aims at minimizing the variance of the resulting portfolio, i.e. to minimize σ_P. This portfolio has a classical financial interpretation since it is known to be located on the left edge of the efficient frontier. It is simple to compute as it does not require to invert the covariance matrix. If we know that out-of-sample variance will be a problem, finding a portfolio with the minimum in-sample variance is a practical and logical attitude. The weights of the optimal portfolio obey to a risk-budgeting policy that equalizes the marginal contributions to risk, that is, for any $(i, k) \in [1; N]^2$:

$$\frac{\partial \sigma_P}{\partial w_i} = \frac{\partial \sigma_P}{\partial w_k},$$

with the condition that for all $i \in [1; N]$, $w_i \in [0; 1]$. Those portfolios are appealing: empirically they work well since they provide satisfying out-of-sample Sharpe ratios, even if the induced risk diversification is not sufficient (portfolios are too concentrated and potentially exposed to high drawdowns). Focusing on the UK equity market, [FLE 09] finds that minimum variance bring a reduction in risk with a significant decrease in volatility with respect to market-capitalization benchmarks for various covariance matrix alternatives. In addition, MV allocation (with constraints on weights) gives usually a greater Sharpe ratio than passive benchmarks [HAU 91].

REMARK 3.13.– When all assets have the same volatility, and when all the correlations are identical, the MV portfolio is equal to the equally weighted portfolio. If all the assets have the same expected return, the MV portfolio coincides with the portfolio of maximum Sharpe ratio. Indeed, if we think about the allocation formula $\Omega^{-1}\mu$, minimizing the variance of the portfolio is - schematically - quite equivalent to weighting only by variance and replacing the expected return vector by a constant vector.

3.6.1.2.2. Computing weights

It is interesting to compute the weights of the MV portfolio, especially in the market model. The motivations of the following computations are taken from [CLA 11]. Let us assume that the return model for an asset i writes: replace whole highlighted paragraph by (footnote also modified):

$$R_{i,t} = \alpha_i + \beta_i R_{M,t} + \epsilon_t^i,$$

where $R_{M,t}$ is the return of the market (or a benchmark) and (ϵ^i) are i.i.d. variables assumed to be independent from $R_{M,t}$, from β. We assume that ϵ_i has a zero mean and a variance equal to σ_i^2. Moreover we note σ_M^2 the variance of $R_{M,t}$ as a random variable. Consequently, the covariance matrix of the assets writes:

$$\Omega = diag(\sigma_1^2, ..., \sigma_N^2) + \sigma_M^2 \beta\beta',$$

with β the $N \times 1$ vector of $(\beta_1, ..., \beta_N)'$. Writing the minimization problem $\min_w w'\Omega w$ and stating the budget constraint $w'.e_N = 1$, we easily obtain $w_{MV} = \Omega^{-1}e_N/(e_N'\Omega^{-1}e_N)$. The use of the Woodbury matrix inversion formula[22] gives:

$$\Omega^{-1} = diag(1/\sigma_i^2) - \frac{(diag(1/\sigma_i^2)\beta)(diag(1/\sigma_i^2)\beta)'}{\sigma_M^{-2} + diag(1/\sigma_i^2)\beta'\beta}.$$

We have easily that:

$$(\Omega^{-1})_{i,j} = \frac{\delta_{ij}}{\sigma_i^2} - \frac{1}{\sigma_M^{-2} + \sum_k(\beta_k^2/\sigma_k^2)} \times \frac{\beta_i\beta_j}{\sigma_i^2\sigma_j^2}.$$

Therefore:

$$(\Omega^{-1}e_N)_i = \frac{1}{\sigma_i^2} - \frac{1}{\sigma_M^{-2} + \sum_k(\beta_k^2/\sigma_k^2)} \times \frac{\beta_i}{\sigma_i^2} \times \sum_k \frac{\beta_k}{\sigma_k^2}.$$

[CLA 11] defines the parameter β_{LS} as:

$$\beta_{LS} = \frac{\sigma_M^{-2} + \sum_k(\beta_k^2/\sigma_k^2)}{\sum_k(\beta_k/\sigma_k^2)}.$$

β_{LS} is a kind of harmonic mean of the β and is, in a way, a specific average of the β terms. β_{LS} may be computed *a priori* since after an estimation step of the β and volatilities, its value may be obtained independently and before the computation of the minimum variance portfolio. With those notations, we have:

$$(\Omega^{-1}e_N)_i = \frac{1}{\sigma_i^2} - \frac{1}{\beta_{LS}} \times \frac{\beta_i}{\sigma_i^2}.$$

As $\sigma_{MV}^2 = w_{MV}\Omega w_{MV}$ and $w_{MV} = \Omega^{-1}e_N/(e_N'\Omega^{-1}e_N)$ we get that:

$$w_{MV}^i = \frac{(\Omega^{-1}e_N)_i}{(e_N'\Omega^{-1}e_N)} = \frac{\sigma_{MV}^2}{\sigma_i^2}\left(1 - \frac{\beta_i}{\beta_{LS}}\right).$$

22 See Appendix, section A.1.2 with $M = diag(\sigma_1^2, ..., \sigma_N^2)$, $P = \beta$, $R = \beta'$, $D = diag(\sigma_M^2, ..., \sigma_M^2)$, and $Q = N$.

For long-short portfolios, the expression is enlightening. Indeed, by definition of the MV portfolio, its variance is inferior to the variance of the single portfolio made of one single asset i, then $\sigma^2_{MV} \le \sigma^2_i$ and the more volatile the asset, the lower its weight in the portfolio (which is coherent given the objective of variance minimization of the final portfolio). However, volatilities are only one element, since the weight of a stock becomes negative as soon as its β becomes greater than the average β_{LS}. The assets that become the more important absolute weights are those with the lowest volatility, and with the lowest beta. Things are more sophisticated if we add a long-only constraint as it allows to give insights to understand the low-volatility or low-beta anomaly as discussed previously. The addition of the long-only constraint in the market model leads (see again computations in [CLA 11]) to the following expression:

$$w^i_{MV} = \frac{(\Omega^{-1}e_N)_i}{(e'_N\Omega^{-1}e_N)} = \frac{\sigma^2_{MV}}{\sigma^2_i}\left(1 - \frac{\beta_i}{\beta_L}\right)\mathbb{1}(\beta_i < \beta_L)$$

where β_L is a modified version of β_{LS}:

$$\beta_L = \frac{\sigma_M^{-2} + \sum_{\beta_k<\beta_L}(\beta^2_k/\sigma^2_k)}{\sum_{\beta_k<\beta_L}(\beta_k/\sigma^2_k)}.$$

In contrast to the unconstrained case where β_{LS} is independently computable, the definition of β_L itself depends of the final value that is reached, so the problem is not analytically tractable in closed form. What is remarkable is the fact that the weights depend not only on the idiosyncratic risks but also on risk parameters computed at the portfolio level (which makes it difficult to obtain an analytical solution). The weights should decrease with their market beta and increase with lower specific risk, which is quite intuitive because the problem is to minimize the variance of the portfolio. A major finding of such an analysis is that a very large part of the risk is systematic and due to exposure to the market.

3.6.1.3. *Risk-Parity: Equally-weighted Risk Contributions*

Risk-Parity portfolios (henceforth RP) may be viewed as the equivalent of the $1/N$ strategy but in the world of risk. The first contribution introducing the term may be identified as the seminal work of [QIA 05]. The difference with the scheme known under the name of *Equally-weighted Risk Contributions* (henceforth ERC) is blurred[23]. ERC portfolios may be viewed as MV portfolios where a constraint is

23 The difference between RP and ERC is small even if the two frameworks share the same philosophy. One of the key difference between them is that the assumptions on correlations are stronger for RP than for ERC. In the following we will be mainly interested in the ERC framework but the difficulty is that the term *risk parity* sometimes encompasses broader notions and is used in a quite general meaning. In the following, we will also deal both with RP and ERC depending on the contributions and papers that explicitly refer to. In any case, [RON 14] is, again, a major reference on the subject for an in-depth understanding.

added on the risk diversification, as all assets are weighted to have an equal contribution in risk. Those allocation procedures are simple to build and appear to be a good empirical compromise between $1/N$ and MV allocation (see also [BAI 16b], [DEM 10] or [QIA 05]).

The philosophy of ERC allocation is to weigh the assets so that each of them has the same contribution to the overall variance. The volatility $\sigma_P(w)$ of the portfolio decomposes as follows:

$$\sigma_P(w) = \sum_{i=1}^{N} w_i \partial_{w_i} \sigma_P(w) = \sum_{i=1}^{N} w_i \frac{w_i \Omega_{ii} + \sum_{j \neq i} w_j \Omega_{ij}}{\sigma_P(w)}.$$

The resulting vectors of weights are such that for all $(i,j) \in [1;N]^2, i \neq j$:

$$w_i \partial_{w_i} \sigma_P(w) = w_j \partial_{w_j} \sigma_P(w)$$

under the constraint that $\sum_{i=1}^{N} w_i = 1$. Risk contribution of asset i is the term $w_i \partial_{w_i} \sigma_P(w)$. Analytically, it is not always possible to find a solution and the weighting is the solution of a nonlinear optimization program. We may think about ERC portfolios as a kind of MV portfolio that is implicitly constrained to have weights that are sufficiently diversified.

REMARK 3.14.– The ERC portfolio is equivalent:

– to the equally weighted portfolio when all assets have the same volatility and same correlations;

– to the MV portfolio when correlations are equal to $-(N-1)^{-1}$;

– to the MDP (see below) as soon as all correlations are the same;

– when all correlations are the same and that all assets have the same Sharpe ratio, RP is optimal in the sense of the mean-variance criterion.

REMARK 3.15.– The RP framework is the risk-based allocation technique that is probably the object of the highest number of contributions. In addition to the usual setting presented above, some alternative interpretations and extensions sometimes exist.

1) [KAY 14] delivers a Bayesian interpretation of RP. A Bayesian shrinkage argument is given to show that instead of the inputs, the shrinkage occurs directly at the weight level. This is also interesting as it may also be related to Bayesian regularization.

2) [RON 15] offers an extension that is a way to introduce assumptions on expected returns in RP portfolios. This approach remains infrequent in the RP

literature, but the idea is to wrap both the return part and the risk part of the traditional Markowitz problem into a single-risk measure, which is afterward used in an RP framework.

3.6.1.4. *Most Diversified Portfolio*

The Most Diversified Portfolio (henceforth MDP) developed by [CHO 08] tries to reach maximum diversification by maximizing the diversification ratio, which is the average of the volatilities of the assets divided by the portfolio volatility. The aim of the technique is to invest in stocks that have a low correlation with the others. This technique loads in fact a lot on the low-beta factor, which gives a coherent meaning to the purpose of maximizing diversification. The maximization of the *diversification ratio* writes:

$$max_w \frac{\sum_i w_i \sigma_i}{\sqrt{w'\Omega w}}.$$

The constraint implicitly imposed on weights w is (see, e.g., [DEM 10]) that for all $(i, j) \in [1; N]^2, i \neq j$:

$$\frac{1}{\sigma_i} \partial_{w_i} \sigma_P(w) = \frac{1}{\sigma_j} \partial_{w_j} \sigma_P(w).$$

It is difficult to understand the diversification ratio that is maximized as a proper measure of diversification. First, it may not be unique. Second, it is quite impossible to compare this ratio between two different portfolios, and to draw some conclusions on this measure, or to sort a set of portfolios sorting this criterion. Yet, this ratio confronts two versions of the volatility and scales the portfolio volatility where correlations are discarded, with the actual portfolio volatility (including correlations). Moreover, it is observed in [CHO 08] that in particular all assets have the same correlation to the MDP, and that all assets risk contributions are equal.

REMARK 3.16.– In the case where all volatilities are equal, the MDP coincides to the MV portfolio. When all the Sharpe ratios between assets are equal, the MDP is similar to the Maximum Sharpe Ratio portfolio and is optimal in the sense of the mean-variance criterion.

3.6.1.5. *A unifying framework for risk-based allocation*

A whole stream of literature tries to compare all the previous techniques, yet very few academic works are dedicated to the regularization mechanics behind those procedures. The contributions of [CLA 11], [SCH 10] or [KAY 12] study the analytical properties of risk-based portfolios and link parameters to their potential effects. A first step toward regularization was made by [DEM 09a] and [FAN 12a].

The work of [DEM 09a] encompasses well the cases of equally weighting and minimum variance. However, the work of [JUR 15b] is more general and highlighted the fact that all those techniques may be unified within a single framework.

Their unifying framework is that a risk-based allocation is a minimization of a convex function of weights, a dispersion metric, whose easiest "incarnation" is clearly variance. We will still minimize: $\text{argmin}_w w'\Omega w$, but the hint is that weights are constrained by both the usual budget constraint $\sum_{i=1}^N w_i = 1$ and an additional constraint that writes:

$$\sum_{i=1}^{N} \bar{w}_i \frac{(w_i^{1-\gamma} - 1)}{1-\gamma} \geq c \quad \text{with:} \quad \bar{w}_i = \frac{\sigma_i^\delta}{\sum_{j=1}^N \sigma_j^\delta},$$

and where c is an arbitrary constraint determined by the solution[24]; γ and δ are two additional, positive parameters that will play a specific role. The interest of such a constraint is that when deriving the first-order conditions of the problem, we obtain for all couple of assets $(i, j) \in [1; N]^2$:

$$\frac{w_i^\gamma}{\sigma_i^\delta} \times MRC_i = \frac{w_j^\gamma}{\sigma_j^\delta} \times MRC_j,$$

and we consequently observe that:

– $\gamma = 0$, $\delta = 0$ leads to allocate using an MV technique;

– $\gamma = 0$, $\delta = 1$ leads to allocate using an MDP technique;

– $\gamma = 1$, $\delta = 0$ leads to allocate using an ERC technique;

– $\gamma = \infty$, $\delta = 0$ leads to allocate using $1/N$ technique.

The whole framework is detailed in [JUR 15b], with additional Lagrange multipliers to control for positive weights: the paper points out the fact that the model is more general than the one developed in [DEM 09a] as the latter recovers MV and EW yet cannot extend easily to any risk-based model, because the set of constraints is too much binding and there is no parameter accounting for a risk tolerance. What interests us here in our context is that if δ may be interpreted (with the terms of [JUR 15b]) as an "*individual risk tolerance parameter*", γ may be thought as a "*regularization parameter*". Indeed, as δ grows, the preference for risky assets increases. However, as γ increases, we become more and more robust to estimation error, up to the extreme case of equally weighting in the case where γ goes to infinity.

24 Eventually with a rescaling by the sum of weights if necessary; let us recall that in the case of ERC, the objective is to equalize the risk contributions of each asset but the solution comes by solving an optimization program so the value of the risk contribution is not known in advance.

This shows that even if those allocations procedures do not provide an explicit, direct mathematical solution because they focus alternatively on sparseness, or nominal/risk diversification, they act as implicit regularization techniques. Meanwhile, as those methods do not get rid of the potential instability problem of the inverse matrix, a preliminary cleaning algorithm for the covariance matrix is still possible. The two approaches remain compatible and any risk-based allocation technique should take benefit from a spectral cleaning (regardless of its form) of the covariance matrix.

3.6.2. *Properties, pitfalls and differences*

It is useful to investigate briefly the out-of-sample properties of those allocation techniques, and to put their empirically observed features in perspective with their initial motivations. Such techniques are often discussed through the prism of their properties in terms of beta, volatilities, potentially under some simplifying assumptions (constant correlation, equal asset volatilities, equal asset returns, etc.) Again, those formulas have to be found in contributions such as [RON 14] or [JUR 15b]. Here, we will quickly review their out-of-sample behavior in terms of diversification, concentration, turnover and sensitivity to assumptions in correlations, in addition to the usual out-of-sample performance, as presented in many contributions.

3.6.2.1. *Empirical comparison*

Many publications are concerned by the comparison of the *out-of-sample performance* of risk-based allocation procedures. Performance should be a second-order objective given the fact that controlling risk is the first and main concern. Performance should come as a by-product, while robustness and diversification should be systematically monitored. Yet, gathering results on the empirical performance of RP allocation, [ASN 12] monitored a particular out-performance of RP portfolios over market-capitalization weighted portfolios. Conversely, [AND 12b] moderates those results that can be significantly affected by the periods of backtests, effective costs and frictions, and the fact that the results may be of limited significance. Moreover, [AND 12b] advocated that the resulting portfolios of [ASN 12] show very high values of unconditional leverage. The conclusions generally do not reach a consensus and this instability reinforces our intuition that ranking them as a function of their relative performance is not a suitable approach. This is being confirmed by [QIA 15] who found that for equities, risk-based or naive-beta strategies are generally outperformed by market-capitalization portfolios, especially in geographical zones outer from the United States and for emerging markets. However, ERC, MV and MD portfolios appear to have the advantage of being resilient in bear markets, but rather lagging in periods of bull markets, as identified by [LEO 12].

In particular, monitoring *concentration* in positions is important to ensure that diversification is effective. By definition of the ERC portfolios, those latter are generally less concentrated[25] than MV and MDP portfolios. Turning to long-only versions, MV and MDP can even show an important concentration in a small number of stocks as shown in [LEO 12]. It may be intuitive (yet unclear) that switching from a concentrated portfolio to a different concentrated portfolio should induce some *turnover* when positions change. [QIA 15] stated that MV and MDP portfolios have higher turnover and consequently higher transaction costs. Unfortunately, the link between turnover and returns is not straightforward, higher turnover does not compulsorily imply higher returns. Conversely, turnover of EW and ERC portfolios is in general weaker.

What is the sensitivity of those allocations toward *correlations*? Since those methods involve the use of correlation matrices, it is important to control how the different alternatives behave depending on correlations. [QIA 15] found that MDP is more sensitive to differences in correlations than other risk-based portfolios but that results may drastically depend on the risk model that is used, even if RP seems to be more robust relatively to this choice. This finding is also supported by [ALV 11], with a lower sensibility of RP toward heterogeneity in correlations. However, this sensibility increases with the average level of correlation. However, [LEO 12] found the opposite result, that is, ERC, MV and MD are relatively insensitive to the chosen risk model!

Studying risk-based allocation techniques, it is natural to explore their *sensitivity to risk inputs* and also the quantities related to out-of-sample risk. When used on stocks, EW allocation is, by construction, biased toward small stocks, since capitalization does not play a role. As no risk-measure is implied, no conclusion can be directly made on any other bias (beta, correlations, etc.) by the only observation of the weights alone! ERC generally favors first assets with low levels of volatility and low levels of correlations. MV and MDP also will overweight diversifying assets, seeking an exposition to low-beta ones. Of course, an MV portfolio will be loaded on low-volatility and low-beta assets, showing a strong dependence on the low-volatility anomaly. This point is handled in [CLA 06] who observed that in general MV portfolios are tilted toward value assets who tend to have low volatilities. In addition, [SCH 10] showed that MV portfolios have significant sensibilities[26] to the Fama-French factors and a particularly high sensitivity to low-beta assets.

25 It depends of course on the quantity used to quantify concentration. We tackle diversification measures in section A.2 of the Appendix. For instance, if concentration is monitored as a deviation of weights with respect to a $(1/N)$ benchmark, the EW portfolio is irrelevant for such an analysis by construction.

26 In addition, it is noticed that as soon as short positions are forbidden, high-volatility or highly correlated assets will tend to disappear from the portfolio with zero-weights.

Allocating specifically within the equity universe, MV and MDP allocations appear to be quite defensive techniques (since minimizing volatility and maximizing diversification is the goal) and may exhibit a significant intersection on the subset of stocks they are invested in. It is documented (see [MAI 10] for long-only portfolios) that ERC portfolios are more robust to estimation error. *Ex ante*, we should have that the volatility of the ERC portfolio is comprised between the volatility of the MV and the EW portfolio. Tracking error relatively to market-capitalization indices may be important, greater in practice than ERC portfolios. Those observations come again from [LEO 12], refining the analysis by the use of regressions of those strategies on some usual factors such as low-beta, small-cap, low residual volatility and value factors. It is shown that no extra-performance is added beyond the residual exposition to the aforementioned factors, and that all of these may be described as a five-factor benchmark, with explicit tilts in some idiosyncratic directions, in the direction of some stocks with characteristics and features that may be easily identified. This research effort largely contributed to decompose and dissect the particular behavior of those strategies. EW is mainly exposed to small capitalization stocks and has a greater volatility than the market-capitalization index (in contrast to the four other risk-based strategies).

3.6.2.2. *Which method for which context?*

Which method one should choose, and for which purpose? We recall here what is generally compiled by practitioners in the literature on the methods previously exposed. An empirical and extensive study made by [ALV 11] helps us for this and may be described in the following way. When the number of assets is low and correlations quite uniform[27], RP appears to be an appropriate choice. When the number of assets increase, RP keeps the nice feature to drive diversification on a larger number of assets (this can be an objective in itself). However, if the number of assets is large and that the investor is ready to accept a sparse portfolio (few number of non-zero positions) or that the volatilities are quite uniform, one has to choose MDP. With an arbitrary number of assets, MV is a suitable allocation procedure to choose, when the investor seeks or is constrained by an absolute constraint on the level of volatility to achieve... or alternatively when the absolute objective of the allocation is to minimize volatility!

A complementary reading is the work of [GAN 12]: in this contribution, the authors analyze the result of a hierarchical clustering on various indexing methods. This study is not exclusively focused on risk-based allocation techniques, but deals also with fundamental and return-based indexation, but the results are enlightening as it appears that intuitively, RP is more similar to MV than with EW. However, RP, MV and EW form a group that is closer to return-based indexing, and that this group

27 Or at least there is no possible forecast in the sense that the statistical significance of the estimated correlations is weak.

appears as a general alternative to the group formed by market-capitalization and fundamental indexation.

One may also want to use risk-based allocation in addition to other methods. Such techniques do exist in the literature and find a justification in [ODE 15]. In this paper, it is shown that under some general conditions, the optimal portfolio may be obtained as a linear mix between the market-capitalization weighted portfolio, and another one which may be decomposed as the sum of an MV portfolio and an ERC portfolio. Some other contributions try to use and combine risk-based portfolios with more sophisticated techniques. In particular, [KIR 12] proposed to build portfolios whose weights are obtained with the shrinkage of two portfolios, an MV and an EW portfolio, with a timing rule to allocate and balance in time between those two techniques. Some papers also using tilts and views do produce portfolios that lie between MV and ERC portfolios (see [HAE 14] and [JUR 15c]).

3.7. Dynamic trading

Until now, we insisted on features of allocation procedures that were more or less deriving from a mean-variance setting, which is frictionless and without costs. We want to relax in this section the no-costs assumption and to see how to solve equation [3.1]:

$$w_t^* = \text{argmax}_w \quad \underbrace{f_1(\hat{\mathcal{G}}_{t,H}(w))}_{\text{Gain forecast}} - \lambda \underbrace{f_2(\hat{\mathcal{R}}_{t,H}(w))}_{\text{Risk evaluation}}$$

in the most general case[28]. Indeed, each trade generates a cost. The allocation problem presented above assumes implicitly that when we decide to rebalance, the gain is simply the sum along the assets of the product of the weight of the asset times the return of the next period. The *real* gain, subsequent to trading, will be observable at $t + 1$ and will incorporate those costs; however, the *forecasted gain* as seen at date t should include those costs to come. Two aspects have not been taken into account in the previous analysis. First, the aforementioned costs have to be added at date t in the problem to be optimized. Second, the dynamics of the expected returns may be non-trivial and potentially useful to smooth the trading and reduce the costs: this will induce us to modify the problem in itself, not only its components. We will have to use a *dynamic approach*.

The mis-knowledge of transaction costs can dramatically affect the performance of the designed strategies and the final performance. To reduce the impact of costs in the effective P&L of the strategy, they have to be effectively included early in the

28 We want to thank here Mathieu Rosenbaum for clarifying discussions and sharp remarks that allowed to improve (greatly) the clarity of this section.

optimization design. The problem is in fact twofold. First, at least a fraction of the real costs has to be estimated. Their modeling and estimation may in itself be a challenge. The first attempt to incorporate transaction costs in the mean-variance allocation problem is sometimes linked to the early work of [POG 70]. [MER 73] identified the pertinence of the multi-horizon framework to define an intertemporal version of the CAPM, on which [MAG 76] worked later to incorporate costs. Other efforts in the financial literature to underline the importance to introduce costs in optimization problems are [DUM 91] or [LIU 02].

Meanwhile, [PER 88] popularized the concept of *implementation shortfall*. Modeling the return difference between a theoretical portfolio and the portfolio *implemented* for real, [PER 88] materializes the fact that the execution price is different from the *decision price* (that we understand as being the market price at the decision time i.e. the time of rebalancing decision and start of trading). Such a pattern is known for long by practitioners since with the words of [GRI 00] (re-quoted in [GAT 10]) the *trader's rule of thumb* states that "*it costs one day volatility to trade one day's volume*". Moreover, handling costs induce a "partitioning" of trades and orders: the bigger the trade, the higher the costs. Therefore, when using mean-variance framework, it is detrimental to execute trades that blindly follow the raw weights coming as output of the procedure. In this respect, a fine knowledge and estimation of costs is therefore needed: the aim of section 3.7.1 will be to define and model them precisely.

The difficulty comes from the fact that costs vary from one investor to another, and depends on their ability to execute or to deal with reactive market counterparties (with powerful infrastructure and low latency). One may conceive that for a same trade, two different investors may face different costs. This may be due either to the nature of the investor, her or his relation with brokers, her or his latency when executing, etc. Unfortunately, we cannot aim to be exhaustive on the subject, yet we will try to favor intuition and let the reader refer to the indicated references to build a complete view on the subject. In a second time, we will try to add those costs in the original problem stated in equation [3.1]. Equation [3.1] is indeed sufficiently generic to incorporate execution costs and a multi-period modeling for gain, risk and costs. The literature on transaction costs modeling is now flourishing and tightly linked to microstructure study. The modeling of costs is in fact necessary to understand how formulas arise and this will be the focus of section 3.7.1.2.5. We will then detail in section 3.7.2 how to incorporate costs in the optimization program to give a full picture of how, ideally, a realistic allocation procedure should be conceived in practice.

3.7.1. *Cost modeling*

Several typologies of costs have naturally appeared in the literature (see e.g. [KIS 03] for a description) and a clear mean to understand them is the way orders are executed. The first method for an investor is to deal with *over-the-counter* (OTC) orders. Price is directly negotiated with another market participant: there is no surprise in the price that is finally paid to execute this order. The second one is to delegate execution to a broker that can guarantee a defined execution price, for example, a price at close or a VWAP (volume-weighted average price). The investor then becomes the client of the broker. The execution risk is transferred by the client to the broker who bears the management and execution of the trades. The profit that the broker can generate is materialized by the difference between the price guaranteed by the broker to the client and the effective execution price the broker can achieve. The third possibility for the investor is to directly trade and execute on the markets (which is then equivalent to the role played by the broker in the second case). This needs more expertise and infrastructure, and a fine knowledge of order types. For this, we refer to [HAS 07], [LEH 13], [FOU 13] or [GUÉ 16], which will give a detailed insight into execution alternatives. However, in any case, trading remains costly, all that changes is the fact that we know or not in advance the cost of the trade, because delegating execution only transfers the responsibility of the execution, but does not offset the cost.

3.7.1.1. *Direct and indirect costs*

A natural separation remains between *direct* and *indirect* costs. Direct costs are sometimes called *explicit* costs. They represent a systematic compensation for every participant involved in a trade. They have to be included in the optimization program, but their estimation is not an issue since they are known in advance. Direct costs include commissions, brokerage fees, settlement and clearing fees, exchange fees (depending on the nature and proportion of orders used) and of course taxes, like the dividend tax, or even the stamp duty in the United Kingdom. They are known but may be changing and evolving with time. They may differ from one investor to another depending not only on their nature and geographical zone (taxes) but also on their size and relation to their prime brokers. Dividend tax reductions may depend on the total amount of time during which the asset has been held. In the case of long-short equity portfolios, there is also a shorting cost because for each stock each day, each broker issues a *locate* file that provides the maximal amount of shares that can be shorted this day with the associated cost of short-selling. In addition to the daily *easy-to-borrow* rate, which is generally negotiated, the *hard-to-borrow* rate potentially adds an incremental layer of cost when the resource in the related stock becomes scarce, and consequently more expensive to sell short. Such a cost can be dramatically increased suddenly (sometimes up to 500 times the usual cost) and proves that the usual, unconstrained allocation procedure is likely to be unrealistic.

Indirect costs (sometimes called *implicit* costs) are more subtle to evaluate and measure. They represent a variable part of execution costs, which is *not* known in advance[29] and represents usually the largest part of the execution cost for large trades. Implicit costs are already materialized in prices and are of course not paid separately. In the following, they will be understood as *impact costs*: the intuition is that the more we trade, the more impact we have on the market and the more costly it is. However, after the trade, it is not possible to exactly *observe* the execution cost. Only guesses, estimations and assumptions can be made, even in the post-trade analysis. This is the subtlety and the difficulty of indirect cost modeling: never observed, they have to be estimated through a functional form in order to be added in the optimization program for a rebalancing at date t, in prevision of the underlying costs affecting the gain that the trading will generate between t and $t+1$. Investors may face different indirect costs (depending on their execution choice, execution pattern, latency, procedures, speed and horizon), but allocation procedures for large funds must imperatively take those costs into account as one cannot scale trades arbitrarily in quantities as they become more and more costly. State of the art of modeling of such costs is handled in the next section.

3.7.1.2. *Insights into market impact modeling*

3.7.1.2.1. A link with liquidity

When a market participant is buying, she or he consumes a part of the liquidity of the order book, then pushes the price up. [FAB 08] defines market impact costs as "*the price an investor has to pay for obtaining liquidity*". The impact of a trade will depend of its size. [TÓT 11] links in addition the explicit modeling of impact with liquidity profiles through supply and demand configuration of the latent order book. Impact is not explicit and related to the (potential) activity of the investor on the market. The more precise way to estimate impact is for every investor to keep all proprietary executed orders, and fit his or her own impact model on his or her own trades. This implies a clear view and a historical archive of past trades, which is quite difficult as one's understanding on execution risk and costs builds up slowly. The other way is to use academic models that use functional approximations to model transaction costs and impact. Of course, such models are already generic and calibrated on real and proprietary data. In the literature, [ALM 05] estimates equity market impact on trades from Citigroup. [ENG 07] does the same on Morgan Stanley data and [MOR 09] uses metaorders from the Madrid and London Stock Exchange. The market impact costs are not confined to equities, since market impact formulas may be fitted for options ([TÓT 16]), futures ([MAS 14]), and even for bitcoin trading ([DON 16]). See [TÓT 11], [TÓT 16] and references therein for a review on the universality of the formula through time and asset classes.

29 Bid-ask spreads are a specific example of such costs. They are linked to the liquidity of the market, depend on the asset and the exchange, are indeed indirect costs, have to be estimated, but have a low variability across time. Therefore, their estimation may lead to considering them as a nearly systematic costs that are quite constant with time, even if technically unknown.

We do not, and could not, provide here a review of microstructure and impact models, their motivations and inspirations. We leave it to the reader and indicate that an in-depth review of models is available in [BOU 13] again or in [LEH 13]. We prefer to focus on their most consecrated form and will not enter the live debate of the precise estimation of the parameters of the laws as we are mainly interested in the interaction of the cost formulas with the initial allocation problem.

3.7.1.2.2. What is impact?

First, we have to define (or at least try!) more precisely the notion of impact. Our approach may appear quite non-standard to readers with a strong knowledge and experience on impact modeling. We only consider the price impact of a small *metaorder*[30] and do not explore any alternative definitions. We call here metaorder a master sequence of related, smaller subsequent trades made of elementary market orders. We thus assume that we are speaking here of one single non-trivial metaorder whose size is not negligible but whose trading will occur in a time scale that is inferior to the period of rebalancing. We also assume that the next decision to buy or sell will occur at a time where the former trade is complete. The sequence of trades however occurs in a time scale that is inferior to the day (typically minutes to few hours) and at a broader time scale (day or week) may appear as a single event.

Moreover, we only consider the impact of trades of an asset on its own price. If we study trades on an asset $A1$, we could assume the existence of cross-impact, i.e. the fact that trading on $A1$ could affect and influence the evolution of the prices of assets $A2$, $A3$, ... We voluntarily discard such effects[31] for the sake of clarity as it is far beyond our scope. We therefore only focus on the modeling of the definition of single impact, on a single asset for a single trade. This goal does not illustrate a lack of ambition, but is in itself already a major challenge.

3.7.1.2.3. Several notions of impact

An impact formula is a function $I(Q)$ that takes in argument a quantity Q and gives the price-impact in dollars of trading such a quantity: this means that the total price impact in dollars of a single trade of a quantity Q will be[32] $Q \times I(Q)$. As said before, the impact function will take the form of an explicit function plugged in the optimization program used for a rebalancing at date t. This impact function will emulate the indirect costs that the allocator (that does not delegate execution) will

30 Metaorders represent a more accurate and realistic way of trading, especially for large market participants, but data are mainly proprietary and consequently quite hard to be extracted for a study.

31 Moreover, we will not discuss the more subtle notion of *opportunity costs* , which is the loss that we may incur by the decision of not trading. For a discussion on this notion, see, for example, [FAB 08].

32 As it is a cost, $Q \times I(Q)$ will always be assumed to be *positive* and subtracted from the gains.

face by trading between t and $t + 1$. Here is the ambiguity and the challenge of impact modeling: $I(Q)$ is an explicit function that the allocator has to choose. With her or his own history of past trades, the allocator may estimate $I(Q)$ by a parametric fit on past trades. In the absence of such a data set, the choice for $I(Q)$ will mainly derive from previous empirical and academic studies. In any case, $I(Q)$ represents the functional form that represents best a *mean* impact. This function will induce a cost term that will affect the anticipated gain, which will be equal to the expected gain, purely coming from the strategy, minus an impact cost term driven by $I(Q)$. This distinction is crucial since empirically trade data are very noisy and the heuristics we describe (functional forms, impact profiles, etc.) describe average, stylized behaviors and do not account for mechanical effects.

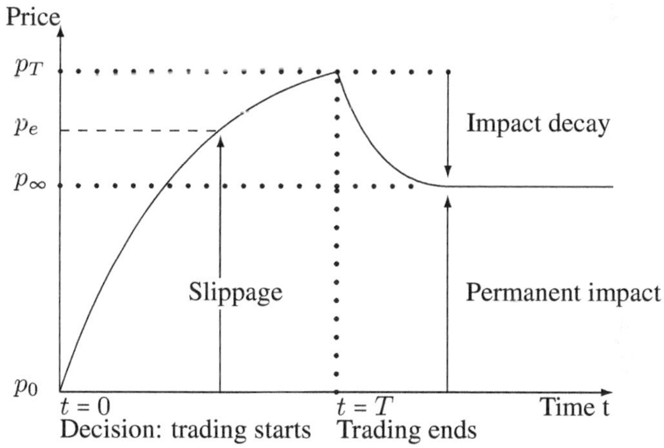

Figure 3.10. *A possible pattern for illustrating the mean impact of a small metaorder*

Until now, we have not yet explored the time aspect of impact. The conceptual scheme detailed in the current paragraph is schematically illustrated in Figure 3.10. Intuitively, we see that the time scale of observations may be important to understand impact. Suppose that the decision to trade is taken by the trader at time $t = 0$. At this time, the observed price (that we call the *decision* price) is denoted by p_0. Empirically, what we call the metaorder is not instantaneous and will last, say, a duration T: after that the trader does not trade any more. T is the total length of the time series of elementary orders that constitute the "metaorder". Our previous assumption was then that T was not interfering with the frequency of rebalancing: any decision of re-weighting should be taken only if the previous trade is complete. The final price p_T is the observed price when the trade is complete. Then, the price has been pushed from p_0 to p_T and the mean price paid overall on $[0;T]$ by the buyer will be denoted by p_e, which is the execution price and is equal to the convolution of prices and available fraction of volume between $t = 0$ and $t = T$. Conceptually, things do not end in $t = T$. One may think that numerous things can happen after the trade but in the absence of active, initiated trading after T, the price reverts to a limit value that we will denote p_∞. Again, the scheme described here is an *average* behavior which tries to illustrate the general consensus that impact studies tend to reach: prices rarely empirically exhibit such a clean and neat pattern.

With these notations, we can define the permanent price impact as the remaining part of the impact that can last after trade completion. Temporary impact should have an influence only through the execution price which is the price to pay "*for the liquidity cost*" [GAT 10]. The permanent component of impact models represents the influence of the action of trading on the "*fundamental value*" of the traded asset on the longer term; it is consequently logically argued that permanent impact[33] may not be considered as a true cost. [KYL 85] links in particular permanent impact to the "*information flow*". Permanent impact may be defined as:

$$\text{Permanent Price Impact:} \quad I_P = \left(\frac{p_\infty}{p_0} - 1\right). \qquad [3.17]$$

The realized impact, also called "*slippage*" is defined as:

$$\text{Slippage = Realized Impact:} \quad I_R = \left(\frac{p_e}{p_0} - 1\right). \qquad [3.18]$$

The temporary notion of impact is "temporary" in the sense that it appears as the difference of a full move of price and the permanent impact. It is more dependant on market conditions, the current liquidity conditions such as the number and nature of market participants, the asset, the order imbalances, etc. The slippage with respect to the decision price in equation [3.18] is what was presented before as *implementation shortfall.*

There is, however, a subtlety in definitions of quantities defined in equations [3.17] and [3.18]. Those definitions are not homogeneous in the literature. For instance, [HUB 04] collapsed the notion of slippage with the notion of temporary impact, whereas slippage has another definition in [GAT 10]. We implicitly assumed that p_0 was the suitable reference to which the execution price should be compared: this is not mandatory. We should be able to replace and/or to test alternative reference prices: this is what is sometimes called a *fair market benchmark price* [FAB 08]. We cannot observe the counterfactual price trajectory that would have occurred without the trade. Therefore, p_0 can be replaced in alternative measures of impact by the price at the close of the previous day, the price at the open or at the close of the same

33 Temporary and permanent impact are also discussed by [ALM 00] under slightly different definitions.

day, the price at the open of the next day, an averaged version of the price during the day, etc.

A subtle and critical question is the separation between alpha (performance) and pure impact. Indeed, only random trades in size and timing could theoretically help to model pure impact. Yet it is unrealistic to think that market participants will spontaneously initiate such a study and most of all, release its results freely. In practice, trades are motivated by information (or at least by what the trader thinks that information is). If an investor buys and the price rises, it may be the sum of two effects: real consensus of the market on the price evolving up (true alpha) and impact of the buyer. The function $I(Q)$ aims at modeling specifically the pure impact part after a trade that moved the price. Permanent impact may be related to *alpha* since when, say, buying, the initiator of the trade reveals her or his intentions as reflecting potentially some subjective (undervaluation, for instance) or private (news, for instance) information on the asset. The link between impact and alpha is a topic of utmost importance in our opinion, yet academic studies have not reached yet a clear view on the best way to include such information in impact estimation. In our framework, we will assume that the contribution of alpha is negligible as we are looking for a mean and general impact estimation: we do hope that estimating impact *on average*, the contribution of information is limited. The separation between impact and information is however not a trivial discussion and we refer to [GOM 15] and [BRO 15a] for further reading.

In any case, we are driven here by a need to build some intuition. We see that one may be tempted to trade few and slowly in order to minimize one's own impact on prices. Empirically this is of course unrealistic with large trades: unexecuted quantities can lead to an important risk. This is underlined in [ALM 00]: risk aversion will drive the trade-off between effective slippage and trading speed. The more the investor is risk-adverse, the fastest she or he will try to be. Of course, if an investor modulates her/his execution on a period covering a whole day, speed will be less of a concern and she or he will mainly try to minimize the average slippage.

3.7.1.2.4. Impact form and impact decay

Figure 3.10 illustrates an execution process that is continuous between $t = 0$ and $t = T$. The total impact of the trade completed between 0 and T is the integrated sum (i.e. the convolution) of all trades between 0 and T: this is compatible with a possible impact decay, which may be observed when trading ends in T. One possible approach is to use the formulation of [GAT 10] who provides a clear formulation for the price evolution of the price p of an asset with traded quantities q_t for $t > 0$ at time t, which is true for either $t > T$ or $t \leq T$:

$$p_t = p_0 + \int_0^t \tilde{I}_c(q_s)G_c(t-s)ds + \text{stochastic variation.} \quad [3.19]$$

In equation [3.19], $\tilde{I}_c$ is the *instantaneous market impact function* of one trade of an elementary quantity q_s (with $\int_0^t q_s = Q_t$ the total quantity traded between 0 and t) and G_c is a *decay factor*. We see that in this modeling, market impact affects the *drift* of the asset price process, not its volatility. The impact of other market participants has to be understood as being part of the stochastic variation, and it is not modeled but is sometimes called as the "*trading crowd*" (as defined, for instance, in [HUB 04] or [GAT 10]).

Another approach[34] could be to decompose impact in discrete time by writing:

$$p_t = p_0 + \sum_{t'=0}^{t} \tilde{I}_d(q_{t'})G_d(t' - s) + \text{perturbation term.}$$

Consequently,, the fact that impact has a temporary or permanent component is potentially compatible with the fact that impact is instantaneous: in this case, the impact function is a Dirac function and the decay is instantaneous. There is still a debate around the form and expression of functions $\tilde{I}$ and G. In [HUB 04], the permanent impact is supposed to be linear in quantity with a symmetric form for positive and negative quantities (buy or sell). The study of [BOU 04], based on trades autocorrelation, concludes that impact is temporary, with $\tilde{I}(q)$ proportional to $log(q)$, and that the decay function G is a power function. [ALM 05] accounts for an instantaneous decay $t' \mapsto G_c^{(t)}(t') = \delta_{tt'}$ and $\tilde{I}(q)$ is a power function of q, quite close to a square-root function of quantities. Finally, in [OBI 13], $\tilde{I}$ is linear and G is exponentially decaying. We can observe that with those notations and within this context, assuming that impact has a permanent component will be ensured by the fact that $\lim_{t' \to \infty} G_{c,d}(t') \neq 0$.

With our notations and the previous discussions, $I(Q_t)$ represents therefore the mean, overall impact cost generated by trading the total metaorder of quantity $Q_t = \int_0^t q_s$ between 0 and t, and results from the convolution of the instantaneous market impact function $\tilde{I}$ for elementary quantities q_s, with a corresponding decay kernel. Here again $I(Q)$ will *resume* the mean effect of impact induced by portfolio rebalancing.

3.7.1.2.5. Impact formulas

It is important to gain some intuition on the units of the quantities that are manipulated when modelling impact. [TOR 99] provides an enlightening risk-reward argument to understand the nature of impact. It is defined as the "*reward for the liquidity provider and must be proportional for the risk he takes*". Let us suppose that for a day and a given asset, the quantity traded by the allocator is equal to Q, for a

34 The subscript letters c and d are used here to distinguish that the impact function $\tilde{I}$ and the decay kernel G have no reason to be identical in continuous and discrete time.

total daily traded volume V on the market. Q/V is therefore the (daily here) traded fraction of volume for this asset. Q/V being dimensionless, a dual view is that this quantity may homogeneous to a time-horizon, the time-horizon beyond which the liquidity provider in front the trader will close its position. If we assume that the asset has a volatility σ: on this time-horizon $T = Q/V$ the extensive volatility of the asset will scale as $\sigma\sqrt{T}$. So the risk that the liquidity provider will face with open positions will be proportional to $\sigma\sqrt{Q/V}$. If impact is the "price to pay for liquidity", we have here an intuition, based on a risk view, of the functional form suitable for modelling impact. Alternative explanations to build an intuition to interpret the shape of the impact function are also available in [TÓT 11] and in [FAR 13].

Most of the time, impact is estimated through a power-law formula such that the impact function $I(Q)$ for a quantity Q writes (see [ALM 00], [ALM 03]):

$$I(Q) = \gamma\sigma\left(\frac{Q}{V}\right)^{\beta} \qquad [3.20]$$

where σ is the volatility of the traded asset; V is the usual (daily, for instance) traded volume of the asset; Q is the traded quantity; γ is a constant that is related to the time-horizon and $\beta > 0$ is the law exponent. Q/V is therefore dimensionless, and is the idiosyncratic fraction of the total liquidity that the trader executes. Q is known by the trader, but V has to be estimated as a typical value (by averaging past values, for instance).

Usually impact formulas tend to model slippage. Of course, this decision could be considered as being arbitrary. One could either model the permanent or the temporary impact. However, this requires after all strong beliefs and confidence in the way each investor understands her/his own impact, how she/he evaluates her/his impact persistence, her/his risk aversion, her/his need for size and speed, etc. What is certain however is that modeling slippage is both usual and realistic as execution price is a convenient and an objective, observables variable to look at and that whatever the notion of impact that is chosen, the fits and formulas are often noisy and remain approximations.

Yet we want to underline the nature of the functional form of the impact functions, since even distinguishing between permanent and temporary impact, [ALM 05] finds a power-law behavior toward Q/V, even if the exponents may vary. Such exponents are usually estimated thanks to nonlinear regression [ALM 05] or with the use of quantile-quantile plots [LIL 03]. Moreover, as we have seen before, the distinction between alpha (consensus on the increase of price) and pure impact is difficult to make. This induces a potential correlation between trades if those trades are the element of the same information-initiated metaorder. And speaking about costs, this also means that the measure of costs through slippage may be pessimistic and that real costs should be lower.

When focusing on temporary impact, it is commonly observed[35] that $\beta \in [0;1]$. As seen before, [TOR 99] suggests that $\beta = 1/2$ with a scaling of the impact as $\sqrt{Q/V}$. [ALM 05] finds rather β around $3/5$. The rationale for a sublinear impact is that when trading occurs, prices move and supplementary liquidity is discovered. For permanent impact, the exponent is rather around 1, which is a satisfying simplification for computation purposes to assume a linear impact (which implies quadratic trading costs). This is also found by [HUB 04]. In fact, [GAT 10] states that if impact has a permanent component, it has to be linear. This may seem quite paradoxical as we are giving two different formulas for two-related concepts. We recall first that we are trying to characterize mean effects, and that this apparent difference may be unified by the fact that it is all about scales: if we refer to Figure 3.10, permanent impact makes sense for times $t > T$, after trade completion and a potential decay. Therefore, the two notions of impact may co-exist, but are relevant depending on the timescale. See [JAI 15] for a discussion.

Two things must be added. First, it appears that impact function are quite symmetric, i.e. selling orders have the same price impact as buying orders. Some empirical studies tend to show that it is in general higher for buy orders, but as highlighted by [FAB 08], this may be due to a spurious bias of studies occurring in specific market conditions (bull or bear markets). Therefore, one may split one's own measures of impact on buy or sell orders, but may be fair to think about a symmetric function to model impact on buy and sell orders (see also [HUB 04] or [HU 09]). Second, a liquidity component is added by [ALM 05] for the estimation for permanent impact on equities. The formula in equation [3.20] is scaled by a coefficient $(1/T)^{\gamma}$, where T is turnover measured as the ratio N/V, where V is the previous share volume traded and N is the number of outstanding shares. γ is found as being around $1/4$. It is an important question to know the range within which those fits are coherent. [ALM 05] considered it as a good approximation when $|Q/V| < 10\%$, which is still a rather large range since trading 10% of the daily volume of a stock on a single trade is huge.

3.7.2. *A framework for optimal trading*

We now want to see how the very previous formulas derived for the mean-variance problem with no costs are modified if we keep the mean-variance objective, while introducing explicit and implicit costs in the optimization procedure. In this respect, equation [3.1] remains valid. Of course, the whole discussion on covariance cleaning, estimation error and in/out-of-sample risk will remain pertinent. It is generally accepted that the classical literature dealing with optimal trading includes major contributions of [MER 73], [CON 86b], [AMI 86], [VAY 98] or

35 In another context, [LIL 03] finds also a parameter β that lies in $[0;1]$ for single market orders.

[LIU 04]. If the first reference allows for a dynamic for the views on the expected returns, it does not take costs into account, on the contrary to the other references, which include costs but do not consider a dynamic on the expected returns. It is therefore important to include three elements in our analysis: transaction costs, multi-horizon optimization and consequently expected returns dynamics. This is an ambitious objective and we will mainly be interested in building a strong intuition rather than being able to master each detail of the computation of solutions. In a first approach, the one-period horizon optimization handled in section 3.7.2.1 will allow us to seize the intuition and concepts that will be fully developed later with more general assumptions in section 3.7.2.2. The fact is that there is a true gap between the one-period and multi-period horizon optimization is due to the mathematical tools involved. Yet the one-period modeling provides important heuristics to understand globally the underlying concepts of dynamic/optimal trading.

3.7.2.1. *One-period horizon*

Let us refer to equation [3.1]. We saw in section 3.7.1 that costs scale with the traded quantity. Our previous approach manipulating weights is therefore useless in this context and we will consider now throughout section 3.7.2 an investment in quantities.

We will fix specifically in section 3.7.2.1 horizon H to be equal to 1. Quantities will be denoted by q, an N-dimensional real-valued vector, with negative values indicating short positions. We are interested in the rebalancing of positions at date t, searching for an optimal allocation $q_t^{(0)}$ at the beginning of the period $[t; t+1[$ such that the budget constraint $e'_N.q_{t-1} = e'_N.q_t^{(0)}$ is satisfied. In other words, $q_t^{(0)}$ and q_t differ through the natural evolution of prices, $q_t^{(0)}$ being the decided quantity after rebalancing. δq is the absolute vector of quantities in the N assets traded by switching from q_{t-1} to q: δq is an N-dimensional real-valued vector such that $\delta q = q - q_{t-1}$. δq is the total quantity traded within our "metaorder" defined previously, whose scale and duration is inferior to the scale of rebalancing, and $|\delta q|$ will denote the vector $(|\delta q_1|, ..., |\delta q_N|)$. The optimal $\delta q^{(0)}$ to find satisfies: $\delta q_t^{(0)} = q_t^{(0)} - q_{t-1}$.

Equation [3.1] is modified in the following way:

$$q_t^{(0)} = \text{argmax}_q \quad \underbrace{f_1(\hat{\mathcal{G}}_{t,1}(q))}_{\text{Gain forecast}} - \lambda \underbrace{f_2(\hat{\mathcal{R}}_{t,1}(q))}_{\text{Risk evaluation}}. \qquad [3.21]$$

Costs will affect the *gain forecast* term $f_1(\hat{\mathcal{G}}_{t,1}(q))$. The gain forecast will be made of three terms:

– an *expected gain* term, which represents the underlying gain prediction due to the strategy (expected returns);

– a *linear cost* part accounting for direct costs: for a given traded quantity, this part of the costs is univocally determined. c will denote the N-dimensional vector, $\mathbb{R}^+$-valued, coefficients of linear costs.

– an *impact cost* part that accounts for indirect costs: the formula has to be specified and accounts at best of what the allocator thinks that the indirect costs will be. It is therefore a guess or an assumption of what a given trade should cost. $I(.)$ will denote the chosen, parametric impact function whose expression is also an $\mathbb{R}^{+N}$-valued function representing the impact component per asset. As discussed previously, $I(\delta q)$ will resume the mean impact of a metaorder of total traded quantity δq.

The modeling of the *risk* term $f_2(\hat{\mathcal{R}}_{t,1}(q))$ may be separated from the introduction of costs. We will see later that it is not always the case, but with this general writing in mind, one can revive the writing of equation [3.3] by stating a general form for the Lagrangian, which is:

$$\mathcal{L}(q,\delta q) = \underbrace{q'\mu}_{\text{Expected gain}} - \underbrace{c.|\delta q|}_{\text{Linear costs}} - \underbrace{\delta q.I(\delta q)}_{\text{Impact costs}} - \frac{\lambda}{2}\underbrace{q'\Omega q}_{\text{Risk evaluation}} . \qquad [3.22]$$

We have seen in section 3.7.1.2.5 that two possible forms for $I(\delta q)$ were $I(\delta q) = \gamma\delta q$ and $I(\delta q) = \gamma\sqrt{\delta q}$. We will therefore explore three situations:

– "*quadratic costs*": $I(\delta q) = \gamma\delta q$ and $\delta q I(\delta q) = \gamma(\delta q)^2$;

– "*3/2 costs*": $I(\delta q) = \gamma\sqrt{\delta q}$ and $\delta q I(\delta q) = \gamma(\delta q)^{3/2}$;

– "*linear costs*": $I(\delta q) = 0$ and only linear costs are assumed to be non-zero.

In a first step, we will first address the case where linear costs are dropped but impact costs are first quadratic, corresponding to the introduction of a $\gamma(\delta q)^2$ term in the optimization program. Then we will turn to the case where $\delta q I(\delta q) = \gamma(\delta q)^{3/2}$. The "3/2 formula" shares some similarities with the case of non-trivial linear costs that are finally presented. In the following, the term *ideal* will designate the ideal trade that we would have completed in the absence of costs and the term *optimal* will qualify the optimal trade for the problem where costs are taken into account, regardless of their nature.

3.7.2.1.1. Impact costs with a quadratic formula

It may seem odd to begin with the case where $I(\delta q) = \gamma\delta q$, whereas we stated clearly in section 3.7.1.2.5 that impact may be better represented by parametric fits such as $I(\delta q) = \gamma(\delta q)^\beta$ with β closer to $1/2$ rather than 1. Yet, choosing $I(\delta q) = \gamma\delta q$ provides a nice framework with a lot of technical convenience since all the optimization program will be easy to solve. Moreover, the final solution helps a lot to build a strong intuition on optimal trading in a dynamic framework. In this paragraph $c = 0$ and $\delta q I(\delta q) = \gamma \delta q^2$. If we define $q = q_{t-1} + u$, with u a generic variable representing δq the problem writes:

$$\mathcal{L}(u) = (q_{t-1} + u)'\mu - \gamma u^2 - \frac{\lambda}{2}(q_{t-1} + u)'\Omega(q_{t-1} + u).$$

Deriving the Lagrangian with respect to the mute variable u representing the shift in quantity traded, and equalizing to zero, we obtain:

$$\begin{aligned} 0 &= \frac{\partial \mathcal{L}}{\partial u} \\ &= \mu - 2\gamma u - \lambda\Omega(q_{t-1} + u). \end{aligned}$$

If we note q_t^* the solution of the no-cost mean-variance problem, q_t^* is such that $\mu - \lambda\Omega q_t^* = 0$ according to equation [3.4], which means that we can add this term in the previous equation, getting:

$$\begin{aligned} 0 &= \mu - 2\gamma u - \lambda\Omega(q_{t-1} + u) \\ &= \mu - 2\gamma u - \lambda\Omega(q_{t-1} + u) - \underbrace{(\mu - \lambda\Omega q_t^*)}_{=0} \\ &= -2\gamma u - \lambda\Omega(q_{t-1} + u - q_t^*) \\ &= -(2\gamma I_N + \lambda\Omega)u - \lambda\Omega(q_{t-1} - q_t^*), \end{aligned}$$

which gives finally an expression for the optimal $u^{(0)} = \delta q^{(0)}$ such as $q_t^{(0)} = q_{t-1} + \delta q^{(0)}$ that is:

$$\delta q = (2\gamma I_N + \lambda\Omega)^{-1}\lambda\Omega \underbrace{(q_t^* - q_{t-1})}_{\text{Trade if no costs}}. \qquad [3.23]$$

Equation [3.23] is very important: we already see that the optimal trade in the presence of quadratic costs is *proportional* to the trade that would have occurred in the absence of costs. Therefore, we see that the mean-variance solution of the problem with no friction still "*acts as a target*" (with the terms of [GAR 13b]). Two related observations are worth noting. First, q_t^* is a target even if q_{t-1} was not already optimal conditionally to the information available in $t - 1$. Second, we get a flavor of the usefulness of the multi-period framework, because if the target does not depend on

q_{t-1}, then being "more optimal" in $t-1$ is a way to diminish the trade to do between $t-1$ and t.

To gain more intuition on those computations, it may be fruitful to make the simplistic yet useful assumption that $\Omega = diag(\sigma_1^2, ..., \sigma_N^2)$. Recalling that $\gamma = (\gamma_1, ..., \gamma_N)$ is a vector, under this assumption, we have for each asset $i \in [1; N]$:

$$\begin{aligned}\delta q &= (2\gamma I_N + \lambda\Omega)^{-1}\lambda\Omega(q_{t-1} - q_t^*)\\ &= diag\Big(\frac{\lambda\sigma_1^2}{2\gamma_1 + \lambda\sigma_1^2}, ..., \frac{\lambda\sigma_N^2}{2\gamma_N + \lambda\sigma_N^2}\Big)(q_t^* - q_{t-1}).\end{aligned}$$

This expression is clear since the optimal trade in each asset, in the presence of quadratic costs, is in direction of the optimal trade in the absence of costs, but with an amplitude that is modulated by the friction introduced by the presence of impact costs. With γ_i close to zero, the trade will be quite identical to the one made in the absence of costs. On the contrary, the higher γ_i, the smaller the trade.

3.7.2.1.2. Impact costs with a "3/2 formula"

In this paragraph, we still suppose that $c = 0$, but now we assume that $\delta q I(\delta q) = \gamma|\delta q|^{3/2}$. This choice is coherent thanks to the discussion in section 3.7.1.2.5: a parametric fit for a mean impact formula with an exponent quite close to 0.5 is more plausible. We still denote $q = q_{t-1} + u$, with u representing the generic traded quantity, and the problem writes now:

$$\mathcal{L}(u) = (q_{t-1} + u)'\mu - \gamma|u|^{3/2} - \frac{\lambda}{2}(q_{t-1} + u)'\Omega(q_{t-1} + u).$$

Of course, the form of $\mathcal{L}$ is now a problem since the function $u \mapsto |u|^{3/2}$ may be derived in $u = 0$, but its derivative presents a singularity in 0. Thus, deriving the Lagrangian on a convenient zone of its support (either $\mathbb{R}^+$ or $\mathbb{R}^-$) with respect to u and equalizing to zero, we thus obtain:

$$\begin{aligned}0 &= \frac{\partial \mathcal{L}}{\partial u}\\ &= \mu - \frac{3}{2}\gamma\sqrt{|u|} - \lambda\Omega(q_{t-1} + u).\end{aligned}$$

If q_t^* is still the solution of the no-cost mean-variance problem, we have:

$$\begin{aligned}
0 &= \mu - \frac{3}{2}\gamma\sqrt{|u|} - \lambda\Omega(q_{t-1} + u) \\
&= \mu - \frac{3}{2}\gamma\sqrt{|u|} - \lambda\Omega(q_{t-1} + u) - \underbrace{(\mu - \lambda\Omega q_t^*)}_{=0} \\
&= -\frac{3}{2}\gamma\sqrt{|u|} - \lambda\Omega(q_{t-1} - q_t^*) - \lambda\Omega u,
\end{aligned}$$

which gives finally an expression for the optimal δq, which is more difficult to solve in closed form:

$$\frac{3}{2}\gamma\sqrt{|\delta q^{(0)}|} = \lambda\Omega(q_t^* - q_{t-1} - \delta q^{(0)}).$$

Here again, assuming that $\Omega = diag(\sigma_1^2, \ldots, \sigma_N^2,)$ is much beneficial, for each asset $i \in [1; N]$, we would have:

$$\frac{3\gamma_i}{2\lambda_i\sigma_i^2}\sqrt{|\delta q_i^{(0)}|} = (q_{i,t}^* - q_{i,t-1} - \delta q_i^{(0)}).$$

Taking the square expression of each side, some simple mathematics give us that if we define D_i to be equal to $D_i = 3\gamma_i/(4\lambda_i\sigma_i^2)$, then:

$$\delta q_i^{(0)} = sign(q_{i,t}^* - q_{i,t-1})\left(\sqrt{q_{i,t}^* - q_{i,t-1} + D_i^2} - D_i\right)^2.$$

This expression shows an hybrid behavior with two distinct regimes depending on the amplitude of $q_{i,t}^* - q_{i,t-1}$ compared to D_i. If D_i is negligible relatively to $q_{i,t}^* - q_{i,t-1}$, then δq_i is close to $q_{i,t}^* - q_{i,t-1}$, the total trade in the absence of costs to reach the ideal position, which is quite intuitive. Conversely, if D_i can no more be assumed to be negligible, a simple first-order development gives us that:

$$sign(q_{i,t}^* - q_{i,t-1})\delta q_i \simeq |q_{i,t}^* - q_{i,t-1}| - \underbrace{\left(2\sqrt{\frac{|q_{i,t}^* - q_{i,t-1}|}{D_i}} - \frac{3D_i}{2}\right)}_{\text{Affine "band"}}.$$

The optimal trade with costs is the ideal (i.e. no-costs) trade minus an affine *band*, increasing with the square-root of the ideal trade. We will see in the next paragraph that such an expression shares some similarities with the existence of a *no-trade zone* in the case of non-trivial linear costs. The term "*band trading*" comes from the fact that the corrective term makes that we follow the ideal position at a distance whose width is governed by the $2\sqrt{(|q_{i,t}^* - q_{i,t-1}|)/D_i} - 3D_i/2$ term.

3.7.2.1.3. Linear costs

We finally turn to the case where $c > 0$ and $I(\delta q) = 0$. The problem becomes:

$$\mathcal{L}(u) = (q_{t-1} + u)'\mu - c|u| - \frac{\lambda}{2}(q_{t-1} + u)'\Omega(q_{t-1} + u).$$

Similarly to the previous case, we see that the singularity in 0 of the derivative of the $u \mapsto |u|$ function sophisticates the analysis. On $\mathbb{R}^+$ or $\mathbb{R}^-$, we can, however, derive the Lagrangian, which gives again:

$$\begin{aligned} 0 &= \frac{\partial \mathcal{L}}{\partial u} \\ &= \mu - c.sign(u) - \lambda\Omega(q_{t-1} + u). \end{aligned}$$

Still by adding q_t^* in the equation, we obtain:

$$\begin{aligned} 0 &= \mu - c.sign(u) - \lambda\Omega(q_{t-1} + u) \\ &= \mu - c.sign(u) - \lambda\Omega(q_{t-1} + u) - (\mu - \lambda\Omega q_t^*) \\ &= -c.sign(u) - \lambda\Omega(q_{t-1} - q_t^*) - \lambda\Omega u. \end{aligned}$$

Such an equation is not always a closed-form solution, but the general conclusion is quite intuitive: as the cost of trading is linear and known in advance, if the expected return is not sufficient to beat this cost, there is no point in completing the trade. Conversely, if one believes that the expected trade is sufficient to exceed the linear cost, then it may be profitable. The optimal trade is then:

$$\delta q^{(0)} = q_t^* - q_{t-1} - \underbrace{\frac{1}{\lambda}\,\Omega^{-1}c.sign(\delta q^{(0)})}_{\text{“Band” or “No-trade zone”}}. \qquad [3.24]$$

However, this equation does not systematically have a solution. For an asset i, there are two situations. If $|q_{i,t}^* - q_{i,t-1}|$ is greater than the i-th component $\frac{1}{\lambda}(\Omega^{-1}c.sign(\delta q^{(0)}))_i$, then equation [3.24] defines $\delta q_i^{(0)}$ univocally: the optimal trade is the ideal trade minus a term of fixed width (whereas in the case of 3/2 costs, this term increases with the trade size). In the opposite situation, the ideal position is at close distance from the current position, which indicates that trading is useless, and the optimal action is to do nothing. This illustrates the term “no-trade zone”:

– if the positions are at close distance from the ideal, target positions, within the defined “band” around the target, no action is required: the marginal gain obtained from trading may be potentially wrecked by the future costs;

– if the current positions are outside of the band, a minimal action is required, that is the allocator trades just at the band width distance from the target.

3.7.2.2. *General case*

Until now, we have presented throughout the chapter a costless version of the mean-variance problem, and in the previous sections, the problem in the presence of costs. The last and more general case to explore deals with the introduction of costs when allocating at t. We try to use a horizon H such that $t + H > t + 1$, with H possibly infinite. We want to illustrate the dynamic trading problem under its more general form because it constitutes the last piece of our pedagogical puzzle. However, the step is quite high and if we still want to address this problem, this is with a completeness purpose: any reader with a strong knowledge in optimal control and dynamic programming will be quite disappointed by the content of this section. The reality is that explicitly addressing the general problem is mathematically intensive and begs for heavy developments. The content of the section is therefore mainly dedicated to readers looking for a soft introduction on the subject or for references in order to discover the topic.

We have seen previously that in the presence of costs with a one-period horizon, the mean-variance optimal solution is to trade a quantity in direction of a target, which is the ideal position in the absence of costs. As the presence of costs implies that the tracking of this ideal position will be imperfect, it is clear that the trade-off between our rebalancing frequency and the statistical properties of our return estimation have in particular a role to play. Intuitively, if our ideal position is based on a return estimation that is quite steady, with few rebalancing steps (i.e. in a finite and few number of periods) we would hope to follow closely this ideal position. Yet if the ideal target shows a high degree of variability at a finer scale, this goal is quite difficult to achieve.

Even with costs, the one-period solution of section 3.7.2.1 will not be optimal in the long-term because the statistical fluctuations of the ideal position will be difficult to follow with a one-period horizon (letting aside the discussion on the quality of the modeling of the impact). For instance, let us assume that the return estimation is well modeled by a mean-reverting process showing a given level of autocorrelation. If the level of autocorrelation is low, the ideal target may move quickly in various directions for consecutive periods. Therefore, in the presence of costs, it may be on average more profitable to do nothing than trying to follow sharply the target, due to transaction costs! Consequently, with a specific dynamics on the return estimation, the ideal position may not purely be the ideal position of the one-period mean-variance problem with no cost, but a transformation of it, depending on the statistical time-properties the return estimation. The role played by the dynamic nature of the process of expected returns in rebalancing has been well understood, for example, by [BAL 99], [BAL 00]. Obviously, we may sophisticate the problem if in addition to the time scale of evolution of the return estimation and the frequency of rebalancing, we allow for a slower pattern of execution and complex forms of impact, but we still make the assumption that between two rebalancing of the portfolio, the impact has already decayed to a stable value, allowing explicit formulas to be used for it.

The general literature is vast and quite technical. A seminal exploration of the problem is the work of [GRI 10], but unfortunately we cannot refer to all the contributions on the topic. We nonetheless stick to the contributions that we believe to be the closest to our pitch and a good way to discover what is at stake with optimal trading. In particular, two streams of literature are not explored: first, the literature linked to optimal trading for execution (with the exception of the contribution of [PAS 16]), which exploits often a continuous-time framework; and second, the literature related to portfolio optimization using the statistical nature of expected returns but without incorporating costs.

3.7.2.2.1. Reformulation of the problem

We try in this paragraph to describe progressively the approach that is needed to deal with optimal trading with a multi-period horizon. Let us start with a very naive and general description of what is at stake. We will denote by $\tilde{\mathcal{G}}_{t+1}(q_t)$ a modified version of gain minus risk such that $\tilde{\mathcal{G}}_{t+1}(q_t)$ is the gain materialized at $t+1$ with quantities decided at t and returns of assets R_{t+1} between t and $t+1$:

$$\tilde{\mathcal{G}}_{t+1}(q_t) = q_t' R_{t+1} - \text{ costs } - \frac{\lambda}{2}(q_t)'\Omega_t(q_t).$$

We would like to find $(q_t^{(0)}, q_{t+1}^{(0)}, \ldots)$ such that we maximize:

$$(q_t^{(0)}, q_{t+1}^{(0)}, \ldots) = \underset{(q_t, q_{t+1}, \ldots)}{\text{argmax}} \quad \sum_{i \geq t} \frac{\tilde{\mathcal{G}}_{i+1}(q_i)}{(1 + r_{f,i})^{i-t}}.$$

This problem is not realistic. Obviously, there are unknown objects: unknown not only because costs and expected returns (R_t) have to be estimated, but also because (R_t), Ω and $(r_{f,t})$ are stochastic and that future information is not known in t. The stochastic nature of the risk-free rate induces one more level of sophistication and is itself the object of numerous contributions in the literature for this specific problem. Taking into account the randomness of the aforementioned objects, we obtain the following problem:

$$(q_t^{(0)}, q_{t+1}^{(0)}, \ldots) = \underset{(q_t, q_{t+1}, \ldots)}{\text{argmax}} \quad \mathbb{E}_t[\tilde{\mathcal{G}}_{t+1}(q_t)] + \sum_{i > t} \mathbb{E}_t\Big[\frac{\tilde{\mathcal{G}}_{i+1}(q_i)}{(1 + r_{f,i})^{i-t}}\Big]. \qquad [3.25]$$

It is a bit better, but we have still a problem here, even with simplifying assumptions. Searching at t for the infinite sequence $(q_t, q_{t+1}, \ldots)$ is untractable and unrealistic. The allocator will have, in practice, only a control on q_t at date t, and determining q_{t+j} at t with $j > 0$ is pointless as we would need to incorporate also all possible new information between t and $t+j$.

What about the following problem?

$$(q_t^{(0)}) = \text{argmax}_\xi \quad \mathbb{E}_t[\tilde{\mathcal{G}}_{t+1}(\xi)] + \sum_{i>t} \mathbb{E}_t\Big[\frac{\tilde{\mathcal{G}}_{i+1}(q_i)}{(1+r_{f,i})^{i-t}}\Big].$$

The previous problem is also useless as it is equivalent to the original one-period horizon problem: for a fixed t, the second right-hand term is fixed and does not depend on ξ. What would be useful is a *different characterization* of the problem. For $t' > t$, allocating $q_{t'}$, the allocator will have the knowledge of q_t. What we would need is an information at t on the future $q_{t'}$! Of course, this information will translate through other elements: statistical properties of (R_t), $(r_{f,t})$, etc. A proper tool for solving this problem is the Bellman optimality principle detailed in the next paragraph.

3.7.2.2.2. Bellman optimality principle

The theoretical review of the Bellman optimality principle in every detail would be a painstaking effort: it would imply in particular heavy developments on partial differential equations, that we cannot make here by sake of concision and also because other works deal with this subject with much more talent and pertinence. The following section may appear very naive to readers with a high-level of knowledge in optimal control. But for others, interested in learning more on the subject, some major references to dive into the subject are of course the original work of [BEL 57] and also the book of [KAM 12]. For the particular case of contributions using the Bellman optimality principle in finance, in addition to the references compiled afterward through the section, one may also refer to the clear presentation of [BRA 10] or the Appendix of [RON 14]. [KOL 15] also provides a clear presentation of the usefulness of this principle in finance, for an optimal trading objective.

Here we briefly recall the intuition of the Bellman optimality principle (tightly linked to *dynamic programming*, from the title of the book of [BEL 57]). It has many nice features and applies to quite general contexts. Its use is of course not confined to finance or portfolio optimization. The Bellman optimality principle is in particular quite famous in advanced economics, in particular in fields such as macroeconomics, for instance, for the study of economic growth or monetary policy among other applications. In the particular case of asset pricing, [MER 73] used dynamic programming for his work on the Intertemporal CAPM. For the sake of clarity and to stay in line with our original problem, we will develop intuition in discrete time. When the problem is stated in continuous time, the characterization of the problem leads to differential equations called Hamilton-Jacobi-Bellman (HJB) equations. It shares in general very tight links with *variational calculus* but here again, see [KAM 12] for an exhaustive mathematical discussion.

What does the Bellman optimality principle state? Having a dynamic problem to optimize on a future horizon, the idea is to break the global problem into smaller ones, and to locally characterize maximums of the smaller local problems, rather than exploring all the potential trajectories of the future problem to find the right one. As previously highlighted, the smaller problems have to be solved by taking into account all the possible configurations, but not all the trajectories. The drawback of the exploration of all the potential trajectories to find the optimal one is not only computational: if for a reason or another we shift from this trajectory, we are doomed to be sub-optimal. Whereas if we seek at any moment an *optimal policy* conditionally to the initial or current state or action, it is therefore possible to accommodate for corrections from positions that are no more on what would have been the optimal, global trajectory. What matters is that it is always possible to seek future decisions/actions or states that will be optimal given this initial setup. Of course, to fulfill this objective, one may have a problem that has a decent structure and that is not purely stochastic in the sense that the allocator may have some action on the process. This is particularly well adapted to our case since even with costs, the mean-variance problem remains quite tractable and the allocator has a *control variable,* which is simply the trade to do (or alternatively the allocated position). The Bellman optimality principle therefore does not seek global optimal trajectories but characterizes maximums for an object called *value function* V that represents the remaining trajectory given the current state. This is the suitable definition of V that will allow us to split the global problem in smaller problems and to reduce the complexity of the computation. A main feature of the Bellman optimality principle is the fact that the problem will be solved by *backward recursion* as explained below.

3.7.2.2.3. Value function

Let us get back to the problem stated in equation [3.25] and let us decompose the problem. The general objective to maximize rewrites:

$$
\begin{aligned}
&\mathbb{E}_t[\tilde{\mathcal{G}}_{t+1}(q_t)] + \sum_{i>t} \mathbb{E}_t\Big[\frac{\tilde{\mathcal{G}}_{i+1}(q_i)}{(1+r_{f,i})^{i-t}}\Big] \\
&= \mathbb{E}_t\Big[q_t' R_{t+1} - \text{ costs } - \frac{\lambda}{2}(q_t)'\Omega_t(q_t)\Big] + \sum_{i>t} \mathbb{E}_t\Big[\frac{\tilde{\mathcal{G}}_{i+1}(q_i)}{(1+r_{f,i})^{i-t}}\Big] \\
&= q_t' \mu_t - \text{ estimated costs } - \frac{\lambda}{2}(q_t)'\Omega_t(q_t) + \sum_{i>t} \mathbb{E}_t\Big[\frac{\tilde{\mathcal{G}}_{i+1}(q_i)}{(1+r_{f,i})^{i-t}}\Big].
\end{aligned}
$$

Here again, the term μ_t is the expected return in the sense of the strategy along which we try to allocate, and Ω_t is in fact estimated, but for both terms, the estimator notations are implicitly skipped. This formulation is quite general and does not depend on the nature of the costs. For simplicity, we will assume that the risk-free rate is equal to zero: we could also assume that it is constant, in which case the $(1 + r_{f,i})^{i-t}$ terms are deterministic and become prefactors of the expectation terms. We do not define yet the chosen form of the estimated costs that are here again a product of the traded quantity times an impact function I of the traded quantity. The expression of the value function we look for appears quite naturally (with the notation $\delta q_t = q_t - q_{t-1}$):

$$\begin{aligned} V_t(q_{t-1}, q_t) &= \max_{(q_t, q_t+1, \ldots)} \Big(q_t' \mu_t - \delta q_t I(\delta q_t) - \frac{\lambda}{2}(q_t)' \Omega_t (q_t) \\ &+ \sum_{i>t} \mathbb{E}_t \Big[q_i' \mu_i - \delta q_i I(\delta q_t) - \frac{\lambda}{2}(q_i)' \Omega_t (q_i) \Big] \Big) \\ &= \max_{q_t} \Big(q_t' \mu_t - \delta q_t I(\delta q_t) - \frac{\lambda}{2}(q_t)' \Omega_t (q_t) \Big) + \mathbb{E}_t [V_{t+1}(q_t, q_{t+1})]. \end{aligned}$$

We could re-state the intuition by stating the maximum gain we could obtain from the current state q_{t-1} up to infinity, is the current gain plus the maximum gain afterward, having shifted from q_{t-1} to $q_{t-1} + \delta q_t$ at the next step. Moreover, the value function V is a maximum; therefore, our objects of interest (trades and positions) are the optimal values that have to be inputs of V, which is already a maximum. The characterization of the expression of V is the main mathematical challenge that will not be expressed here. V is not uniquely characterized but it is possible to find families of linear-quadratic functions that are natural candidates for V. A light review for those sophisticated concepts is available in the introduction of [CHA 15]. More detailed computations are available in all the papers we refer to throughout the section.

3.7.2.2.4. Solving for quadratic costs

In the case of quadratic costs, the problem has been the object of numerous contributions among which one may refer to [SKA 09], [GLA 13], [GAR 13b], [CUR 14], [CHA 15] or [GAR 16]. One contribution is generally recognized as being central for quadratic costs. Indeed, in spite of simplifying assumptions on the nature of the quadratic costs (the impact formula is explicitly proportional to the covariance matrix), we believe that [GAR 13b] is the most pedagogical approach to understand optimal trading (with quadratic costs but also in general). The simplifying assumptions made in the paper and the discrete-time framework make it possible to obtain closed formulas that are so simple to understand that it makes the article one of the best compromises, both to understand the Bellman optimality principle and the general ideas behind optimal trading. The analogies and the wording of the paper constitute an excellent trade-off between sophistication and intuition.

The message is very much in line with the previous conclusions provided in section 3.7.2.1 for the quadratic costs case. The optimal trade to make is of the form:

$$\delta q = r(\tilde{q}_t^* - q_{t-1}),$$

where: $r \in [0;1[$ is a scalar and $\tilde{q}_t^*$ is a slightly modified version of q_t^*, the ideal position in the case of the mean-variance problem with no cost. r is a trading rate given by the resolution of the optimal problem using the Bellman optimality principle. As in the one-period case however, r increases with costs and decreases with risk aversion. The difference between q_t^* and $\tilde{q}_t^*$ is the fact that the latter is scaled by a matrix term depending on r and on, roughly, the "autocorrelation" of the expected return as a statistical time series. The term is a matrix in the most general case, but in the case where the expected returns, as a vector, has no cross-autocorrelation (no statistical link of expected return of asset i and past expected return of asset j as soon as $i \neq j$), then the term is even more easy to identify since for each asset i, $\tilde{q}_{i,t}^* = \frac{q_{i,t}^*}{1+r\phi_i}$, where ϕ_i is the difference between the covariance of $(\mu_{i,t+1} - \mu_{i,t})$ and $(\mu_{i,t})$. The target positions are then close to the ideal ones (with no costs) but corrected from the influence of the risk-aversion, the transaction costs and the speed of the strategy. All things equal, with a same level of expected returns, the faster strategies will be given lower weights. An interesting property is also that if this optimal policy has been followed up to time t, the current positions are already the result of an exponential moving average of past target positions (see [GAR 13b]). Even if this discussion holds for a specific assumption on the costs formula (which is, however, quadratic), sophisticating the cost formula makes the expression of the solution more complex, but not its general form:

REMARK 3.17.– In general for strategies, there is a natural trade-off between performance, speed and capacity, i.e. for a given level of Sharpe ratio, the maximal amount of risk in dollars that can be obtained after costs. The quest for any manager remains a performing signal with a high capacity. Slower signals are said to be more capacitive than quicker ones. And strategies with a high Sharpe ratio can generally be played at a low level of assets under management, but their performance quickly deteriorates at higher levels. Very high Sharpe ratio strategies are generally obtained for quick signals, at a low level in assets. See [LAN 15] for a discussion.

3.7.2.2.5. Solving for linear costs

The problem with linear costs and a multi-period horizon leads to the same conclusion and the same heuristics to those developed in section 3.7.2.1 in a more simple context. Contributions of [SON 13] or [BIC 16], for instance, address the optimal trading problem with linear costs and [LIU 14] is a bit more general, allowing, in addition, for the inclusion of quadratic costs. Meanwhile, some contributions have enriched the expected return component with a dynamics for the expected return component, with, for instance, the work of [MAR 11], [MAR 12], or more recently, [DE 12b], [PAS 16] or [REJ 16]. The intuition remains, however, unchanged. As the problem is very sophisticated, and nearly impossible to solve in closed form, we have to recall that here again, in the presence of linear costs, the solution remains to follow the strategy within a no-trading zone around the current position. Therefore, regardless of the complexity of the problem, the rebalancing heuristics do not change. What varies is the computation of the width of the trading zone. Switching from an infinite to a finite horizon, and varying also the nature order (limit and market orders) [PAS 16] tries, for instance, to find coherent, tractable approximations for the computation of the width of the no-trading zone, which is tightly linked to the statistical properties of the asset, the dynamics of the return, the linear costs, risk aversion and the defined finite horizon.

4

Backtesting and Statistical Significance of Performance

"If past history is all there was to the game, the richest people would be librarians."
Warren Buffet[1]

4.1. Introduction

An investment process, as sharp and smart as it may be, requires proper ex-post analysis in order to assess its performance in a *backtest* exercise. A *backtest* is a simulated strategy on historical data applied to fictional money. Such an approach is quite universal and used from individual traders to the biggest funds. It may be used either by small funds without sufficient seeding or by larger ones testing for candidates strategies for production. In each case, an in-depth analysis of the strategy is carried out. The problem is of utmost importance for young funds. Inception and seeding process of funds is sometimes a closed loop: investors seek to invest in sufficiently large funds, postponing investment in some of them until they become sufficiently large! There is a real need for managers to adopt a critical approach towards their simulations.

We aim in Chapters 4 and 5 to provide a backtest framework articulated along two dimensions. In Chapter 4, we consider strategies as being analyzable as statistical objects: a strategy is a time series of returns. If the performance of a given strategy is statistically poor, then there is no need to trade it. This approach is rather strong since it does not require any insights on the nature of the strategy. The end of the chapter asks, however, the question of the nature of the strategy by trying, still based uniquely on the returns, to assess whether the strategy may be classified as a return premium or

1 See, e.g., [BUF 06].

a behavioral bias. But this approach is limited in real life, since it is not conceivable to trade a strategy and to sell it as a "black box" or to forget about the true nature of the bets or the peculiarities of the traded asset class. Unveiling the links of a given strategy with the real economy is natural, handling therefore strategies as a statistical *and* an economical object. This will be the aim of Chapter 5, which comes as the second stage of a wider analysis.

We have already underlined how important it is to produce clean backtests, but this task is difficult for at least three reasons. First, it may involve advanced statistical concepts. We should clearly identify the stochastic objects that are at play. Sharpe ratio, Sortino ratio and correlations are statistical variables, for which we observe one and only realization for a given strategy in a given set of data. An investor should therefore carefully identify what she or he wants to test, both the object and the assumption she or he wants to check. Second, it is sometimes necessary to store the number of trials that have been involved when setting up the strategy. Keeping a track of all parameters or all alternatives that are tested may be a good way to quantify the degree of statistical robustness of the strategy at test. The third reason is more pernicious: it is all about moderating the enthusiasm of the strategy designer! Unfortunately, this is perhaps the most difficult task to enforce since it may be exciting to go live with a strategy that works well in simulation. We need in practice to step back, and to look at all the potential drivers of performance. Is the backtest sufficiently long? Are there crisis periods incorporated in the backtest? Is the risk management correctly done? All these serve one fundamental goal that will make the performance repeatable: reduce the statistical part of the operational risk coming from the trading of fake signals.

The aim of this section is therefore to assess whether a given strategy is trustful enough to be traded *for real*. Of course, the mathematical aspects underlying the statistical study of a simulated strategy do also apply for past performance of a real strategy. But this chapter is also intended to allow us to understand all the subtleties and the potential traps of any simulation exercise. In the following, we will assume that a *manager* or a *fund manager* is a quantitative investor who designs a strategy in backtest with the aim of trading it for real afterwards if she or he sufficiently trusts the strategy. The *investor* will be a sophisticated agent potentially interested in becoming a client of a fund manager, who is able to design winning strategies. Whatever the point of view, at this point of the chapter, let us imagine that we are given a strategy. At the end of the chapter, we will progressively build a quantitative examination of the strategy in order to assess whether:

– the (potential) simulation framework of the strategy has no bias;

– the key features of the time series, made of the strategy returns, are statistically significant;

– the strategy is really performing in the sense that it is statistically significant;

– it is possible to precisely compute the main performance measures of interest, potentially annualized;

– the strategy represents behavioral bias or a risk premium.

In this chapter, we will generically note (R_t) as a series of random financial returns. The unconditional distribution of returns through time will be denoted by R and $(r_t)_{t\in[0;T]}$ as the observed time series of returns. If stationarity is not required for (R_t), it may be at least compatible with the analytics. The fact that the moments of (R_t) are identical to each date to the moments of R is, of course, related to effective stationarity. We will note (P_t) as a time series of observed quantities, where stationarity is hardly expected or has no sense: prices, cumulated or integrated returns, with or without reinvestment, etc. Moreover, in this chapter, (R_t) will quite never stand for the return of an underlying financial asset such as a stock, a bond or a future. (R_t) will have to be understood throughout the chapter as a time series of one-dimensional random return, representing the historical (after costs) return of a fund, strategy or portfolio return, either observed, reported or simulated. (P_t) may be understood as the integral or sum of R_t and emulates a current portfolio net asset value. The nature of the return (arithmetic or geometric) depends on the context and is in general precised. In this respect, r_f takes a more general sense. It may still be considered as a risk-free rate: if a fund or strategy cannot sustainably afford returns greater than r_f, then it is more profitable for the investor not to invest in the fund! However, r_f could be also a hurdle or reference rate to beat according to the prospectus of the fund, as a benchmark rate.

4.2. Backtesting

4.2.1. *Providing accurate backtests*

First, we have to define a *backtest*. A backtest consists of the use of historical market data to evaluate now, how a given strategy has, or would have performed, in the past. The most natural way to build a backtest is to regenerate the strategy on test, in the past, to assess its significance and pertinence. This exercise is, of course, subject to a rather large number of biases (see below) but it is the only way for a practitioner to test her or his strategy on "real" (but not live) data. This highlights a major difference between finance and experimental sciences: it is not possible in finance to make several attempts with a free parameter, and all others being fixed. The true difference between finance and other fields like physics is the repeatability of the experiment. It is impossible at two different dates to face identical market conditions, moreover in an environment that also changes technologically: repeatability in the conditions of the experiment will never be met. Backtests are then in essence imperfect approximations, but practitioners are forced to deal with fixed, past data and to evaluate their strategies on the past. Consequently, they will not be able to observe the effect of their virtual transactions on past realized trades. They just have to live with that.

Have you ever seen any professional presentation promoting losing strategies with dramatic drawdowns? No, of course. It is intuitive that any fund manager willing to attract new investors will rather try to sell strategies with a past, realized benefit. However, we often read in funds' prospectus forewords and warnings such as:

...past performance is not the guarantee of future results...
...past returns are not indicative of future performance...
...past performance may not be indicative of future benefits...

It is important to know that the Security and Exchange Commission (SEC) cautiously scrutinizes funds in order to check that they do not promote strategies or investments that are false, wrong or made with no caution. Effective abuses are heavily punished. The SEC is even concerned by performance promotion that is even just ambiguous enough, but do not necessarily step into prosecution in that case. They deliver in such situation *no-action letters* that are very insightful. [LO 16] quotes part of the no-action letter of 1986 responding to Clover Capital Management: we also believe that this example is particularly interesting for strategy designers, and as [LO 16], we also reproduce here a core part of the letter:

"We believe the use of model or actual results in an advertisement would be false or misleading (...) if it implies, or a reader would infer from it, something about the adviser's competence or about future investment results that would not be true had the advertisement included all material facts. Any adviser using such an advertisement must ensure that the advertisement discloses all material facts concerning the model or actual results so as to avoid these unwarranted implications or inferences. (...) In the staff's view, Rule 206(4)-1(a)(5) prohibits an advertisement that: - Fails to disclose the effect of material market or economic conditions on the results. (...) - Includes model or actual results that do not reflect the deduction of advisory fees, brokerage or other commissions, and any other expenses that a client would have paid or actually paid; - Fails to disclose whether and to what extent the results portrayed reflect the reinvestment of dividends and other earnings; - Suggests or makes claims about the potential for profit without also disclosing the possibility of loss; (...) - Fails to disclose prominently the limitations inherent in model results, particularly the fact that such results do not represent actual trading; (...) It is the responsibility of every adviser using model or actual results to ensure that the advertisement is not false or misleading."

SEC[2] Staff No-Action Letter, Clover Capital Management, Inc. - October 28, 1986.

2 Source: https://www.sec.gov/divisions/investment/noaction/clovercapital102886.htm. Quoted also in [LO 16].

We leave to the reader the consultation of the entire letter. Nonetheless we see how important it is, for statistical and legal reasons, to produce a serious and coherent backtest including costs, fees, dividends and taxes with a precise modeling of potential losses. The aforementioned forewords are, of course, needed for regulatory matters and help to remind the investors that nothing is ever certain. But statistically speaking, we should therefore be worried of seeing only positive past performing strategies! If past performance is not the guarantee of future benefit and is uncorrelated with future ones, we should be worried about not seeing more frequently losing strategies! This statement is, of course, a bit provocative, but this is not so innocent since evaluation biases may be more subtle than that. It is difficult (and in fact quite impossible) to assess the future profitability of a given strategy. At best, we can observe past performance of the strategy; we can understand why it seems to work and try to monitor both the performance statistics and the portfolio analytics. We can try to disentangle all the possible undergone biases. And cross fingers! It is interesting to note that if a fund manager is able to provide a successful past performance track, we hope that it will able to repeat it in the near future. On the contrary, when we see a deceiving performance track, we are quite sure that good future performance of the fund manager will be due to pure luck or general market moves. With those simple heuristics, we are already putting repeatability at the heart of the process and guessing that noise and randomness may also be at play.

4.2.2. *In/out-of-sample*

4.2.2.1. *General definitions*

One of the main risk practitioners face is *overfitting*. Using the whole set of data at hand, it is tempting to optimize over and over, with numerous tests and attempts, the parameters driving the strategy, in order to improve its backtested performance. This is doomed to give disappointing results when used live afterwards in production. The simplest sanity check is to split the historical dataset into two parts: a learning part and an evaluation part. The learning sample that allows us to tune the parameters of the strategy will deliver figures and performances that are called *in-sample*. The evaluation part of the dataset will bring *out-of-sample* performance figures. If one is in quest of generalization, universality or representativeness, there are alternative ways to split datasets. We may learn on one geographical zone and test the obtained strategy on the other zones: the out-of-sample will be made by the "rest of the world". We could also test a strategy on one asset class and backtest it out-of-sample on other asset classes. An alternative could be also to gather more data, but in the past, and to afterwards extend the size of the dataset. The most frequent problem is related to time series modeling and forecasting: in this case, the time series is split in time and the most common approach is to learn on past data and test on the more recent data. The out-of-sample is then the more recent part of the data on which the strategy has not been optimized.

Another approach is to fix the parameters of a strategy once and for all and to follow its live, subsequent behavior. Should this strategy become profitless, should its parameters have to change, this would be a sign of a potential overfitting. The out-of-sample backtest on past data is always a pseudo-out-of-sample test. Observed past data have been affected or generated by past trades of market participants. So, fictive trades in the past would have had an effect that is by definition, unobserved. This is the reason why there is often a degradation between backtested performance and effective performance. Therefore, a simple strategy with a small but decent performance may be preferable to a strategy with promising results that have not been tested cautiously. This explains why proceeding to due diligence, investors often trust funds that are live for sufficiently long rather than funds with short existence but impressive backtests.

To illustrate how hazardous the overconfidence in backtests comparison may be we would like to refer to an experiment of [QIA 15] in which the authors find that when comparing risk-based allocation techniques (presented in section 3.6.1) the ranks based on the out-of-sample returns of the portfolio that are built are completely reversed when compared with the order we would obtain after the training phase. In such an example, the generalization is poor and the bias induced by the trust that is devoted to the in-sample is amplified. Nevertheless, the in-sample/out-of-sample approach, even if imperfect, remains a necessary approach. From an informational point of view, it is known to be not optimal (since we do not use all the information for training) as discussed, for instance, in [SCH 12]. Despite this, as said before, we cannot vary the situations of a financial experiment: historical backtests remain the only mean to deal with the simulation of a new strategy since "*a genuinely meaningful out-of-sample experiment is difficult to carry out*" [SUL 99].

4.2.2.2. *Cross-validation*

We would like to mention *cross-validation.* Cross-validation is a way to assess the quality of estimation and is related to prediction purposes. Ideally, it would be great to have more datasets to evaluate the validity of estimated parameters in order to assess that the estimated model has nice properties when applied to unseen data. With a set of inputs X that helps to predict outputs Y, the strategy designer has estimated a function $f_{\hat{\theta}_1}$: $\hat{\theta}_1$ is a parameter that governs f and which has been estimated on an observation set S_1 of variables $X(S_1)$. With a new set S_2 of (X, Y) pairs, we hope that $f_{\hat{\theta}_1}(X(S2))$ is sufficiently close to $Y(S_2)$. In that case, we are ensured that the final modeling is quite able to generalize and that overfitting will be avoided. In its simplest form, cross-validation may be viewed as a sanity check: varying the training sets allows us to evaluate how the model behaves on new datasets.

In this respect, rolling regression may appear as a form of crude and basic cross-validation since we estimate a model on rolling data, mechanically varying the dataset. However, it is not strictly speaking a case of cross-validation since the estimation method does not change and the behavior on the new dataset provides no feedback to the estimation method: it is just that new parameters are observed each day! A true cross-validation procedure should in fact involve a partitioning of the initial dataset, where each partition is made of subsets with no overlap. One training set (in-sample) and one set for validation (out-of-sample), whose union may or may not represent all the data at hand. Partitioning again and again, validation sets (resp. training sets) may, of course, share data in common with previous partitions. The usual practice is, of course, to use the results obtained on each partition to give feedback on estimation, for instance by averaging with an appropriate weighting rule the parameters obtained with the various partitions. This approach allows reducing the out-of-sample error of the model and increases its forecast abilities in situations where the data are scarce or oddly distributed. There are, of course, many ways to perform cross-validation (exhaustive or not, repeated, n-fold, leave-n-out, etc.) and we refer to [HAS 09] for further reading.

4.2.2.3. *Examining particular events*

Most of the time, a backtest leaves us with a cumulative track of performance in function of time and potential additional statistics. We may compute correlations, Sharpe ratio, performance metrics, etc. This leaves us, however, with some patterns or events in the representation that either begs for an explanation or characterize the behavior of the strategy in particular circumstances. We advocate here that even after cautious quantification of the behavior of a strategy, it may be of utmost interest to focus on some precise time periods to assess how the strategy could react in some odd cases: bubbles, crises, squeeze periods, etc. It may tell a lot in terms of performance and also in terms of risk management. We may take the example of the momentum strategy: as presented in [DAN 16], this particular strategy may face turmoils and severe undesired losses under some market conditions. Those are particularly striking during the crises of 1929 and 2008–2009. [DAN 16] displays the graphs that illustrate how any quantitative backtest should include a visual inspection of the strategy and a reverse engineering of the striking events. Those striking events are dramatic drawdowns (or daw-ups!), increases or decreases of volatility, volatility clusters, etc. Other various examples of contributions that examine drivers and consequences of particular events in time for specific strategies may be found among many others in [JOR 00], [KHA 11], [BAR 12] or [CLA 09]. The study of the links of a strategy with the real economy (business cycles and economic conditions) will be tackled in Chapter 5.

4.2.3. *Biases*

"It amazes me how people are often more willing to act based on little or no data than to use data that is a challenge to assemble."

Robert J. Shiller[3]

3 Source: interview with Robert Shiller, available at http://www.advisorperspectives.com/newsletters10/pdfs/Unconventional_Wisdom-An_Interview_with_Robert_Shiller.pdf

Biases are usually the nightmare of quantitative financial practitioners. They are always implicit, hidden or unseen and their main hazard is that it is very difficult to disentangle biases from low/high forecasting abilities. However, some biases are more insidious and difficult to check for, the exhaustive list is, in general, impossible to address. We will try to list here some of the most common biases that we should check when dealing with strategy assessment. We are not always able to give a pre-formatted procedure to handle them, and propose sometimes only conservative behaviors rather than pre-determined solutions.

4.2.3.1. *A zoology of biases*

There is a wide scope of potential biases. The introduction of *future information* is a common yet spurious bias to systematically check, since the performance that is obtained is generally far greater than the usual performance that the common fund manager is able to generate (a Sharpe ratio of 10.0, for instance). In those situations, it is generally easy to check for the introduction of future information. Dealing with past data at date t, an example of the use of future information would be that the signal and its evaluation at date $t - 2$ include information of date $t - 1$ (that would not have been able at date $t - 1$). The term used in this case by data providers is that the data they provide is *point-in-time*. Point-in-time means that the historical data used now as past data was *really* available in the past at the date and time indicated.

We can give here two examples, for the sake of illustration. First, if we deal with a strategy executed once a day, using a daily refreshed data: the hour of refresh of the data in the past is compulsory, since if the data provider was not able, in the past, to deliver the file before the daily decision, the strategy may lose all its real forecasting power. The hour of the delivery of the data in the past then drives the significance of the backtest. Second, a similar example comes from the diffusion of the fundamental data of earnings announcement for stocks. Generally, fundamental data (income and cash-flow statements, with balance sheet) are provided some days (typically two weeks) after the end of the financial quarter. After the announcement by the CEO of the company, data providers process the financial statements and send them automatically. Those statements are never perfect and need a large amount of corrections within the next earning period. In fact, data providers do not release all the figures at the same time, they begin with the biggest companies, dealing with smaller ones afterwards. We may face a typical delay of roughly one month (and even longer) between the end of the financial period and the sending of a comprehensive, audited statement for smallest companies. In the meantime, one may find academic data, with clean figures for financial statements, for each financial period. Using this kind of data directly without a safety delay would inject inappropriate data that would not be point-in-time in the past, therefore introducing insidious information in the backtest.

Survivorship bias is yet another subtle example of potential and unwanted use of future information in simulations. Let us assume that we are testing a fund selection strategy on a pool of hedge funds, with a goal to select funds for a fund of funds. If we only consider living funds available today in a database, we will potentially have a very interesting strategy since we will be investing in the past on funds that are known to have performed sufficiently well in the past, since they have survived! The same example may be applied to stocks belonging today to a defined index. Stocks are members of this index because they have been performing well in the past, and have sufficiently increased their capitalization. The solution involves mainly infrastructure and work on data. It necessitates building dynamic investment pools, whatever the underlying assets, with living, dying or badly performing assets included. Assets have to be considered dynamically inside this pool in order to get a clear and exhaustive picture of the real potential of the strategy.

We may also face *operational biases* that all depend on the particular infrastructure of the practitioner. A straightforward example is the storing of orders and the modeling of execution costs. Young funds may forget to store their own historical information on execution (and so, whether or not they delegate their execution, see section 3.7.1). Some years later, they realize that they have lost or missed some crucial information on their own behavior. More generally, forgetting to include costs in the analysis of the strategies is a major problem that leads to a severe, systematic overestimation of the potential of a strategy. Another operational bias is linked to the way work is organized. It does not directly impact the estimated gain, but keeping track of all the strategies and attempts that do not work is rarely done, even if it should be. Keeping all the results of strategies that have worked or not will help to understand any intriguing behavior of a future strategy in test.

One final bias is the overconfidence in computers! Remember that not so long ago, even in the 80s, computers were not able to calculate so fast, and that processing information was slow and costly. A pure backtest on arbitrary past data is not always relevant, and recall that technological possibilities of today do not account for the lack of speed of the access to information some decades ago. [LO 16] makes the following remark:

> "*Any form of leverage including technology leveraged investing can create new and greater risks. In the financial industry, Moore's law must be weighted against the technology updated version of Murphy's law: anything that can go wrong will go wrong and will go wrong faster and bigger when computers are involved.*" —— [LO 16]

This is rather a cautionary message on the unmonitored use of technology than the description of a bias. Yet it may be useful if applied in the past! In the reverse way, we may produce backtests by applying an inverse Moore's law backwards, slowing down a strategy as we move back in the past. In any case, we have to think about an automated strategy only for periods of historical time where technology would have allowed it.

4.2.3.2. *The "in-sample trap"*

[LEI 07] presents an unusual exercise: can we explain the variations of the S&P500 index by trying a sufficiently high number of variables, potentially unrelated to financial information? The paper became famous since the author postulates a provoking message: we can explain the variations of the index (in a very satisfying statistical fashion) with Bangladesh butter production, US cheese production and US plus Bangladesh sheep population! The example is funny but highlights in fact a very deep concept. In a fixed universe and with an increasing number of tests, it will always be possible to find artificial strategies, parameters and variables that allow us to obtain positive performance on a given dataset. Such an approach is called *data snooping*. We find in [SUL 99] a possible definition of data snooping:

> "*Data-snooping occurs when a given set of data is used more than once for purposes of inference or model selection. When such data reuse occurs, there is always the possibility that any satisfactory results obtained may simply be due to chance rather than to any merit inherent in the method yielding the results. (...) Data-snooping need not be the consequence of a particular researcher's efforts. It can result from a subtle survivorship bias operating on the entire universe of technical trading rules that have been considered historically. (...) The effects of such data-snooping, operating over time and across many investors and researchers, can only be quantified provided that one considers the performance of the best trading rule in the context of the full universe of trading rules from which this rule is conceivably chosen.*" — [SUL 99]

The biases due to data snooping are very well known and often highlighted in financial statistical studies. The problem is clearly identified, yet it is rarely handled in financial textbooks whereas it should be systematically underlined. Historically, biases due to data snooping have been previously modeled and quantified by, for example, [LO 90] or [DIE 06a]. Using the procedure detailed in [WHI 00], [SUL 99] quantify the data-snooping biases of various usual technical trading rules on daily data in the DJIA Index. Along with the study of [BRO 92] some years ago, this was one of the first contributions to evaluate the probability that strategies in finance are subject to caution since they have been elaborated after too much data manipulation.

The general concept that encompasses data snooping is *statistical overfitting*. Statistical overfitting deals with the elaboration of a model or a strategy "*that owns a level of complexity which is higher than the reality has*" [BAI 15]). A model that is overfitted is typically not parsimonious, and has a very low reproducibility. An overfitted model is useless in the sense that is only able to describe the training data. If we try a lot of different versions of the same strategy, we will often find a strategy that works best. It is always tempting to retain the strategy and trade it for real. We may be very disappointed by its out-of-sample performance. Heuristically, a performing out-of-sample signal, already implemented for real, will be preferable to an in-sample model with a Sharpe ratio twice bigger.

A rule to assess the pertinence of the number of trials made has been given in [BAI 14a] who evaluates the sufficient number of attempts needed to reach a successful strategy. This well illustrates the problem underlying backtest overfitting since the higher the number of combinations tried, the greater the probability of finding a successful one. Unfortunately, with a given backtest, it is impossible to reverse engineer the number of trials that have been made. Managers generally come with a backtest, but rarely with the number of attempts needed to generate it. [BAI 12b] gives insights to measure the probability that a Sharpe ratio is too high and provides heuristics to assess the length of a minimal backtest for it to be statistically significant. The purpose of those heuristics is to criticize significance of real performance tracks for effective investments. The idea of [BAI 12b] is to introduce the concept of *Minimum Track Record Length* that is necessary to assess whether a measured Sharpe ratio is below a given critical level. The idea behind the paper is quite natural as it "simply" uses the asymptotic law of Sharpe ratio on a single track record.

The more trials are made, the longer the backtest an investor should ask for, even if those quantities are never disclosed. [BAI 14a] tackles the importance of the number of attempts made to simulate a winning strategy. For an expected level of annualized Sharpe ratio S_0 and N attempts, they derive a bound that defines the minimal number of years acceptable as being equal or greater than $\frac{2\log(N)}{S_0^2}$ years. For instance, if a manager seeks a strategy with a 1.0 yearly Sharpe ratio and that she or he proceeds to 20 tests to build the strategy, any backtest or proforma strategy of less than 6 years of history is difficult to trust. Some observations can be made. First, this is a sanity check since a very long backtest may very well be also overfitted! Second, the true formula is a bit more sophisticated (we give here only an order of magnitude) and leads in fact to real values slightly lower than this bound. Finally, the work developed in [BAI 16c] offers a more general framework. This latter work is less empirical, yet it delivers a whole framework to check and evaluate the probability of backtest overfitting (see this original reference for more details). Moreover, and more difficult to enforce, the N attempts are assumed to be independent. This is quite impossible to obtain, prove or even define: is changing one parameter an independent test? And if no, how to qualify the dependence between the two tests?

In order to figure out the difficulty of being discriminant with our own results, we could recall the heuristics given by [BAI 15] on random strategies. Building random signals, they give an interesting empirical rule: with 5 years of daily data, with roughly 45 trials, the best strategy we select in this experiment will have a Sharpe ratio of roughly 1.0 with a high probability. Another disturbing feature is that overfitted models have the unwanted behavior to generate out-of-sample negative performance and losses rather than zero performance!

4.3. Performance statistics

The previous section described the potential biases of backtesting and warned about the possible hazards of a simulation framework that is not well understood or mastered. Yet, after having defined a cautious and rigorous qualitative setting for backtesting strategies, there is a need for the definition of performance measures. The potential enthusiasm of a growing profit should not make the manager forget elementary caution concerning her or his own results. What is important is to consider the generic nature of what a strategy is: a time series of returns. We want to put the stress on the statistical nature of the performance measures, which are in any case, statistical estimators with their own specificities. We will make the choice to focus on some of them, and study them precisely rather than trying to list every way to measure and qualify performance. As an illustration, [ELI 07] observes that sorting hedge funds according to their relative Sharpe ratio is sufficient to rank and choose them. The performance measure may vary but the results generally do not change. This shows that in some circumstances, multiplying the metrics and their comparison is not always meaningful. What is, however, more interesting in the paper is that the authors document that this non-decidability holds even in case of a strong departure from the Gaussian assumption for the hedge fund returns. This underlines and illustrates that we have to study performance and risk ratios with their statistical and random nature in mind. Our aim is then not to compare the metrics between them or to promote one rather than another in itself.

4.3.1. *Numerical illustration*

We will illustrate the concepts presented in this chapter with the study of three fictive strategies, which are all anonymous and paper-trading exercises:

– the first one, called "Strategy 1", illustrated in Figure 4.1, runs from 2011/01/01 to 2014/12/31;

– the second one, called "Strategy 2", illustrated in Figure 4.2, runs from 1990/01/01 to 2014/12/31;

– the third one, "Strategy 3", illustrated in Figure 4.3, runs from 2013/01/01 to 2014/12/31.

The only things to know is that all three strategies represent the cumulated gain, with no reinvestment[4], of an after-costs daily investment decision. From Figures 4.1,

4 See section 1.2 for implications or assumptions concerning return computations. The no-reinvestment assumption may be viewed as an investment where profits and losses are taken out at each rebalancing. This is close to the modeling of geometric returns where returns are computed as "log-price" increments, except that here log prices are replaced by the logarithm of portfolio value.

4.2 and 4.3, it can be seen that the plain line is the total return (cumulated sum) and the dashed line on each figure represents the zero-volatility projection of profit, if we assume that the daily return is equal to the mean over the sample. We will keep those strategies on test unless one appears to fail one of our tests. In spite of their apparent positive profit and winning aspect, will those strategies be kept until the end of the chapter?

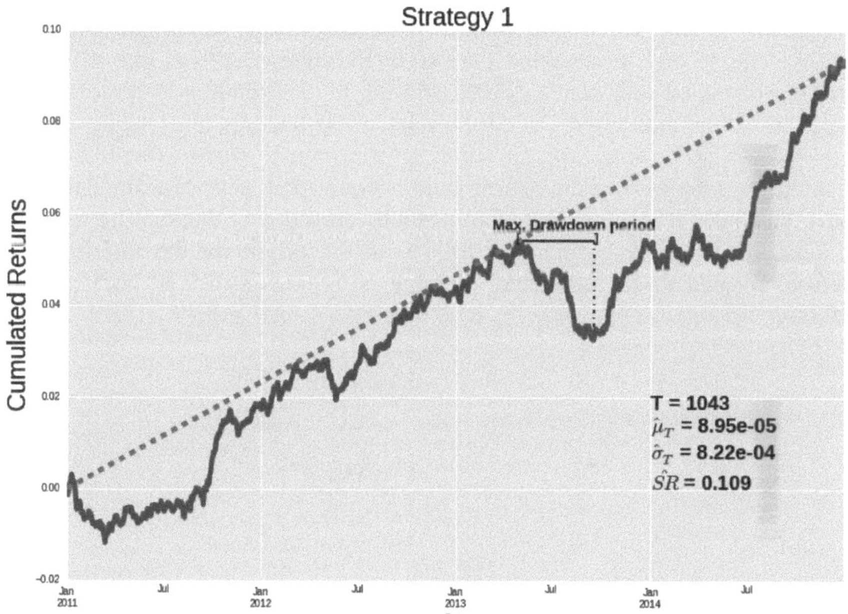

Figure 4.1. *Strategy 1 - 2011/01/01 to 2014/12/31. Plain line: cumulated return with no reinvestment. Dashed line: drift of the strategy. The maximum drawdown period is also indicated along with moments of the daily return distribution*

4.3.2. *Sharpe ratio*

To assess the profitability of a given strategy, one of the most widespread metrics is the Sharpe ratio. Its initial name, as it is originally presented in [SHA 66], is the *reward-to-variability ratio*. However, it rapidly gained in practice the name of its initial inventor. The Sharpe ratio is the ratio of the effective return of the strategy scaled by its volatility. The rationale of its use and success is twofold. First, let us observe that there is no *natural* total order in $\mathbb{R}^2$. This means that for any given couple of real numbers, it is not guaranteed to be able to compare it with another couple of real numbers, if no additional criterion is involved. In financial terms, if one is given a set of assets it is impossible to sort them along with their couple of first moments of their return distribution, all other things equal, without a defined rule. If (μ_1, σ_1) and (μ_2, σ_2) are the return and volatility of two assets 1 and 2, we are not certain to be able to order them. We would prefer asset 1 to asset 2 if it provides more gain with less risk ($\mu_1 > \mu_2$ and $\sigma_2 > \sigma_1$) but how to compare two assets such that $\mu_1 > \mu_2$ and $\sigma_1 > \sigma_2$? The Sharpe ratio does not solve this; however, it aggregates the two concepts in one scalar criterion, as it increases with return and decreases in volatility. The second idea behind the use of the Sharpe ratio is that it is directly rooted in Sharpe's theory of the CAPM. Indeed, in the (volatility $\times$ return) map, the Sharpe ratio of an underlying asset is the slope of the line that joins the asset with the origin (or with the intercept as soon as we include a risk-free asset in the computation). Maximizing the Sharpe ratio is equivalent to the maximization of the slope, which should be ultimately dominated by the slope of the security market line that joins the tangency optimal portfolio with the origin (or the intercept). It is, therefore, adapted to an "efficiency" reading in the perspective of finding efficient portfolios.

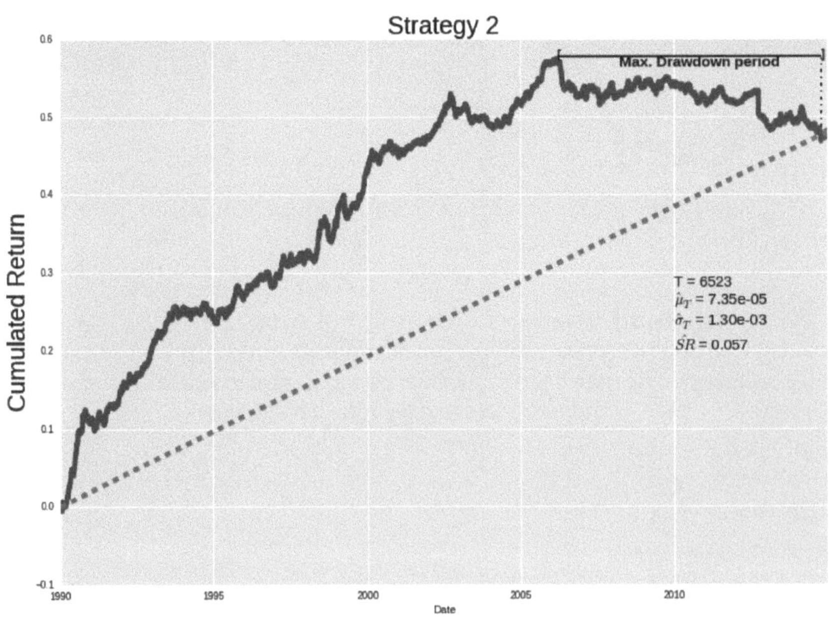

Figure 4.2. *Strategy 2 - 1990/01/01 to 2014/12/31. Plain line: cumulated return with no reinvestment. Dashed line: drift of the strategy. The maximum drawdown period is also indicated along with moments of the daily return distribution*

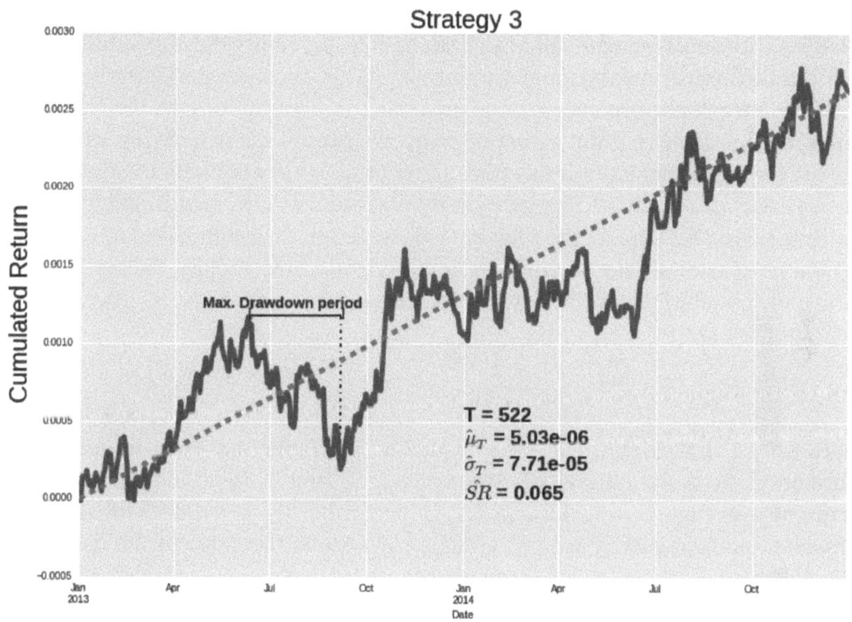

Figure 4.3. *Strategy 3 - 2013/01/01 to 2014/12/31. Plain line: cumulated return with no reinvestment. Dashed line: drift of the strategy. The maximum drawdown period is also indicated along with moments of the daily return distribution*

Even if the Sharpe ratio does not tell us everything, we dedicate a whole part of the chapter to its study since it is always monitored, published and compared. But as simple to compute it may appear, it relies on some assumptions that are most of the time forgotten or simply never explored. Let us assume that we deal with a strategy that provides a return series (R_t) on $[0;T]$, a T-length period where R_{t+1} is the return between t and $t+1$. If $\mu = \mathbb{E}[R_t]$ and $\sigma^2 = \mathbb{V}[R_t]$, then the theoretical expression of the Sharpe ratio SR as a random variable is defined as:

$$SR = \frac{\mu - r_f}{\sigma},$$

with r_f a fixed, constant rate. It may be a risk-free rate (as in the context of single assets - it still makes some sense when studying strategy returns) but it may also be a fixed, constant hurdle rate for a comparison purpose. In the following, we will assume that $r_f = 0$ for the sake of simplicity and notations; however, it does not change anything in the computations. If we take a Brownian model for the diffusion of the *returns* of the strategy, the Sharpe ratio is the ratio of the drift of the diffusion scaled by its diffusion coefficient (volatility). To get a precise estimation of the Sharpe ratio, we should plug into its definition the values of the diffusion parameters (drift and volatility). It would be equivalent to assume that the returns of the strategy are i.i.d. with the theoretical mean μ and variance σ^2. This becomes particularly sensitive if we study a track performance of a given strategy: assumptions on the independence of returns are sensitive if the nature or characteristics of the underlying strategy[5] have evolved through time. Even if this i.i.d. assumption is very unlikely to hold in practice, the heuristics of the use of Sharpe ratio by practitioners are often implicitly related to this framework. Of course, the moments of the return distribution are never available, and the most natural way to compute it empirically is to replace the estimators with the sample counterparts of the return moments, i.e.:

$$\hat{\mu}_T = \frac{1}{T}\sum_{t=1}^{T} r_t \quad \text{and} \quad \hat{\sigma}_T^2 = \frac{1}{T}\sum_{t=1}^{T}(r_t - \hat{\mu}_T)^2 \quad \text{and} \quad \widehat{SR} = \widehat{SR}_T = \frac{\hat{\mu}_T}{\hat{\sigma}_T}.$$

NUMERICAL EXAMPLE 4.1.– We compute in Table 4.1, the moments of the distribution of daily returns of Strategies 1, 2 and 3, whose cumulated gain is represented in Figures 4.1, 4.2 and 4.3. In particular, $\hat{\mu}_T$ is the drift of each curve of cumulated performance if seen as a random walk and the slope of the dashed line in each Figure 4.1, 4.2 and 4.3. Strategies 1 and 2 have a comparable level of gain (mean return) but the volatility of Strategy 2 is twice as much as that of Strategy 1, resulting in a final Sharpe ratio divided by 2. Strategy 3 has a mean return that is up to ten times less than Strategies 1 and 2 but with a reduced volatility, resulting in an equivalent daily Sharpe ratio compared with Strategy 2.

4.3.2.1. *Time scale and aggregation*

A crucial observation is that any measure of the Sharpe ratio remains an estimator, and therefore a statistical object computed as the ratio of the two estimators of the expected return and standard error of the same random return. But we have to observe that the main random variable under study is the *one-period return* of the strategy. Then, it is important to understand that any property, feature and test based on the Sharpe ratio depends for the assumptions made on the returns, and on the *time scale* of the observed realizations (i.e. the unit of time measure between t and $t + 1$).

When a fund manager designs a strategy, she or he generally wants to give figures that may be comparable with the figures of a concurrent for comparison purposes. Usually, both fund managers and clients are interested in *annualized* Sharpe ratios. But the annualization procedure depends both on the properties of the return time series and on the granularity or frequency of the series (daily, weekly, monthly, if the time between t and $t + 1$ is day, week or month). Under the former definition, we are in fact concerned by a normalized definition of the Sharpe ratio. Another possibility is to define the Sharpe ratio under a non-normalized version that is extensive with time.

5 Potentially unknown if we are looking, say, at a fund database.

In this case, the drift is replaced by the total return over $[0; T]$ and the volatility by the total volatility on the whole period. Under the i.i.d. assumption, the total return should be replaced by μT and the volatility by $\sigma\sqrt{T}$, then the Sharpe ratio becomes:

$$\widehat{SR}_{ext} = \frac{\hat{\mu}_T\sqrt{T}}{\hat{\sigma}_T} = \widehat{SR} \times \sqrt{T}. \qquad [4.1]$$

The $\sqrt{T}$-factor is related both to the length of the period but also to the data on which the Sharpe is measured. Indeed, one could measure a Sharpe ratio with daily data but express it at a different frequency. Let us assume that we deal with daily data on three years, with 750 points of data. The daily Sharpe ratio would be estimated on 750 points, giving a figure $\widehat{SR}^{(d)}$. The extensive Sharpe ratio for the total period would be approximately equal to $\widehat{SR}^{(d)}_{ext} \times \sqrt{750}$. However, if we deal with a Sharpe ratio $\widehat{SR}^{(a)}$, estimated on the 750 points of daily data, but already annualized, the multiplying factor is not $\sqrt{750}$ but $\sqrt{3}$, as 3 is the number of years of the period for a Sharpe ratio measured in years. Dealing with a monthly Sharpe ratio $\widehat{SR}^{(m)}$, the multiplying factor should be $\sqrt{36}$. This will be related to annualization (see section 4.4.1) since annualization is already an aggregation in time.

Strategy	No. of days T	Mean daily returns $\hat{\mu}_T$	Daily volatility $\hat{\sigma}_T$	Daily $\widehat{SR}^{(d)}$
Strategy 1	1043	$8.95e-05$	$8.22e-04$	0.109
Strategy 2	6523	$7.35e-05$	$1.30e-03$	0.057
Strategy 3	522	$5.03e-06$	$7.71e-05$	0.065

Table 4.1. *Daily moments of Strategies 1, 2 and 3*

NUMERICAL EXAMPLE 4.2.– We can compare the aggregation effect of the first moments of the return distribution of Strategies 1 to 3 to the daily figures given in Table 4.1. The drift (mean return) of each strategy is positive, and the mean and volatility of the returns are extensive with the scale (month, year) of the measure. With a monthly aggregation, we obtain Table 4.2. With an annual aggregation, we obtain Table 4.3. The obtained Sharpe ratio of Table 4.3 now has values whose order of magnitude is maybe more familiar to professional investors. Figures for Strategy 3 for yearly aggregation are (voluntarily) clearly flawed since computing a mean and a standard deviation on 2 points is meaningless: the yearly Sharpe ratio of Strategy 3 is very appealing but in fact totally pointless. Using yearly aggregated calendar data for Strategy 1 is hazardous, but for Strategy 3 it has no sense at all.

4.3.2.2. *Link with t-statistic*

Why is this important? In fact, the multiplying term in equation [4.1] gives a whole statistical sense to this measure. Indeed, $\widehat{SR}_{ext}$ is the expression of the Student t-statistic used for the test of (R_t) being issued (or not) of the draws of a random variable with zero mean. The interest is straightforward since computing the Sharpe ratio in its extensive version encompasses the test of the significance of the strategy under study! With i.i.d. Gaussian returns, the distribution at a finite distance T is a (biased[6]) Student's t-distribution with $T-1$ degrees of freedom. In the following, we still assume without loss of generality that r_f is equal to zero but we also drop the T indexation of the estimators of μ. $\widehat{SR}_{ext}$ follows a non-central t-distribution since the non-centrality parameter of the law is $\sqrt{T}(\mu/\sigma)$.

Strategy	No. of months M	Mean monthly returns $\hat{\mu}_M$	Monthly volatility $\hat{\sigma}_M$	Monthly $\widehat{SR}^{(m)}$
Strategy 1	48	$1.95e-03$	$4.14e-03$	0.469
Strategy 2	300	$1.59e-03$	$7.46e-03$	0.214
Strategy 3	24	$1.094e-4$	$2.65e-04$	0.412

Table 4.2. *Monthly moments of Strategies 1, 2 and 3*

Strategy	No. of years Y	Mean yearly returns $\hat{\mu}_Y$	Yearly volatility $\hat{\sigma}_Y$	Yearly $\widehat{SR}^{(y)}$
Strategy 1	4	$2.33e-02$	$1.33e-02$	1.74
Strategy 2	25	$1.92e-02$	$3.39e-02$	0.57
Strategy 3	2	$1.31e-03$	$3.67e-04$	3.57

Table 4.3. *Yearly moments of Strategies 1, 2 and 3*

The statistical subtlety here is that those parameters are not observed and define the theoretical, unobserved centrality parameters of the law that will help us to test the significance of the strategy. Should μ be equal to zero, the t-distribution would be central. In other fields (signal analysis, econophysics), the $\sqrt{T}(\mu/\sigma)$ is often called the *signal-to-noise ratio* which quantifies the proportion of real signal (strength of the drift) among noisy observations (random, volatile returns, quantified by the volatility here). We only draw this parallel between Sharpe ratio and t-statistic for the moment as we will fully expand on Sharpe ratio testing in section 4.4.2.

NUMERICAL EXAMPLE 4.3.– Using the previous context, the t-statistics related to the series of returns of Strategies 1, 2 and 3 are given in Table 4.4. If we want to compare our Strategies 1 and 2 with a random walk we should compare the t-value for each strategy with the related quantiles of test of the t-distribution. The null hypothesis is then:

$$H_0 : \mu = 0 \quad \text{against} \quad H_a : \mu \neq 0.$$

6 For a precise overview of the statistical nature of this link, and a discussion on the bias $\sqrt{T/(T+1)}$ that technically appears at finite distance, see [MIL 78].

Strategy	No. of days T	Daily $\widehat{SR}^{(d)}$	$t = \sqrt{T} \times \widehat{SR}^{(d)}$
Strategy 1	1043	0.109	3.52
Strategy 2	6523	0.057	4.60
Strategy 3	522	0.065	1.48

Table 4.4. *t-Statistics related to Strategies 1, 2 and 3*

We could conclude that with this kind of test, the two strategies appear to be significant and different from pure noise. Indeed, the value of the t-statistic at the 97.5% level is respectively equal to 1.962 and 1.960 with 1042 and 6522 degrees of freedom (number of observed returns minus 1), both less than 3.52 and 4.60 (with p-values respectively about $2e-4$ and nearly 0). The null hypothesis is then strongly rejected in the two cases and the two strategies seem to appear, with this simple test, as being not pure noise and statistically significant. However, we see that the effect of the magnitude of T is huge since even if the Sharpe ratio of Strategy 1 is higher than that of Strategy 2, the t-statistic is, however, lower.

For Strategy 3, however, even if its Sharpe ratio was apparently decent, the strategy is simulated on a period of time that is too short to assess its statistical meaning. The associated t-statistic is much too weak; this strategy is not statistically significant. In this respect, according to our previous goal to keep only meaningful strategies on test with our approach described on page 4.1, we will drop this strategy in the remainder of the chapter.

As a conclusion, from a statistical viewpoint, what matters is not the value of the Sharpe ratio itself but the product of Sharpe ratio with the square root of the number of observations, since this quantity is linked to the value of a t-statistic. We will see in the following that the study may be refined in various ways (including the study of higher moments to derive precise tests). Yet, using the extended Sharpe ratio for an initial guess on the significance of the strategy is a simple yet robust approach.

REMARK 4.1.– Working with a strategy that is benchmarked against another strategy B (often a representative index) whose returns are described by a series of observed returns (r_t^B), the previous quantities remain relevant if the analysis of observed returns (r_t) is replaced by $\tilde{r}_t = (r_t - r_t^B)$. In that case, the volatility of $(\tilde{r}_t)$ is called *tracking error* TE which is easily estimated by:

$$TE^2 = \frac{1}{T}\sum_{t=1}^{T}(\tilde{r}_t - \tilde{\mu})^2 \quad \text{where} \quad \tilde{\mu} = \frac{1}{T}\sum_{t=1}^{T}(r_t - r_t^B).$$

Moreover, the focus is no more on the absolute returns, but on the returns in excess relative to the benchmark. Therefore rather than the absolute Sharpe ratio, the *information ratio* is the quantity:

$$IR = \frac{\tilde{\mu}}{TE}.$$

4.3.3. *Skewness and kurtosis*

We already explored the basics of skewness and kurtosis for asset returns in section 1.3.3. The estimation of skewness and kurtosis in the context of strategies is of utmost importance but rather unstable, as illustrated in example 4.4. The intuitions developed previously in section 1.3.3 remain, but having a robust estimator for both quantities is important since they will appear in limit formulas for the Sharpe ratio asymptotics, significance tests, normality tests, and in tests for the potential overfitting of a given strategy.

However, we promote and highlight here a last measure for skewness, which can be seen in [LEM 15]. This measure is particularly adapted since it is specifically built for the study of strategies. The advantage of the measure is that it does not require the existence of the third moment of the distribution and may be computed as soon as the first moment exists, and is particularly adapted to the individual study of a given quantitative strategy. It first requires normalizing the returns to obtain a zero mean and unitary variance, and then to sort the absolute returns of the series in ascending order and to plot the returns as a function of their normalized rank from smallest to largest absolute returns. The final measure is detailed in the paper and may be related to standard measures of skewness, but it is interesting since it appears as the area between re-ranked curves in the aforementioned graph. This allows us to get a direct and visual diagnosis of skewness problems and singularities which makes the novelty of the measure. We will come back to this measure in section 4.4.5.

NUMERICAL EXAMPLE 4.4.– We compute and compare some estimators detailed in section 1.3.3 on Strategies 1 and 2. The results are stored in Table 4.5. We see that Strategy 1 is hardly skewed but Strategy 2 is relatively negatively skewed which suggests an asymmetry towards negative returns. The skewness estimators are, however, quite different since we observe a non-homogeneity in the estimators for Strategy 2. Moreover, the kurtosis of Strategy 1 is quite close to the value of a Gaussian distribution. Strategy 2 has a high kurtosis which means that extreme events are less infrequent. Those elements suggest that the unconditional distribution of returns of Strategy 1 (displayed on Figure 4.4) may be distributed according to the Gaussian distribution, but this is quite unlikely for Strategy 2 (see Figure 4.5) since Strategy 2 is characterized by more extreme and especially negative events.

Strategy	s	s_a	s_B	s_{P1}	s_{P2}	s_{GM}	k
Strategy 1	0.011	0.011	0.074	0.130	0.094	0.040	3.28
Strategy 2	−1.93	−1.93	0.054	0.101	0.070	0.047	45.7

Table 4.5. *Various measures of skewness and kurtosis of Strategies 1 and 2. Acronyms for estimators are homogeneous to the notations of section 1.3.3*

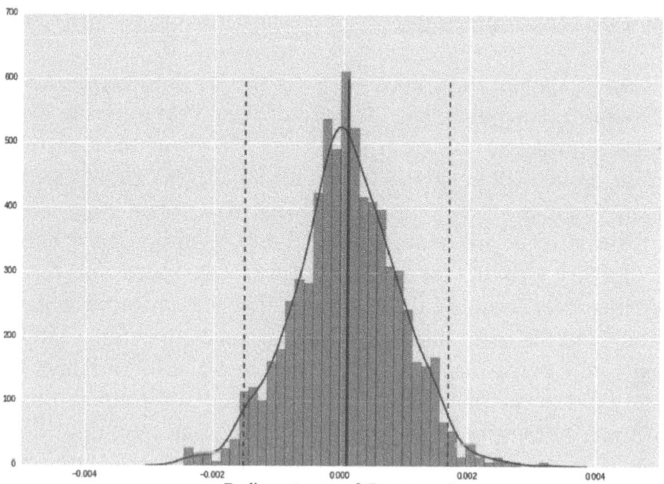

Figure 4.4. *Unconditional histogram of daily returns of Strategy 1 on the period from 2011/01/01 to 2014/12/31. The mean of the distribution is materialized by a plain vertical line. The vertical dashed lines represent two standard deviations around the mean*

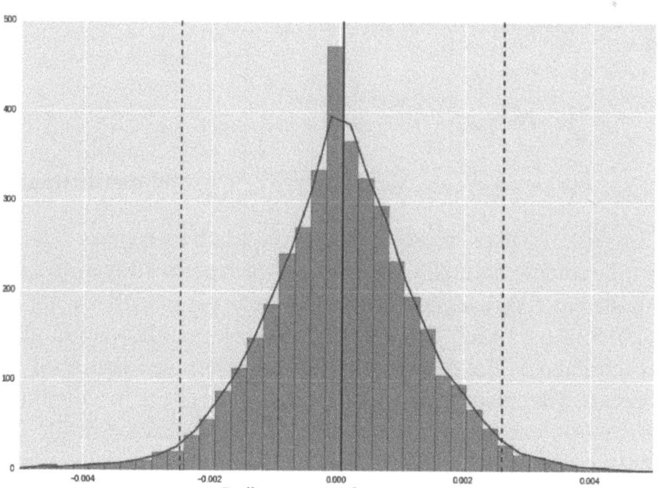

Figure 4.5. *Unconditional histogram of daily returns of Strategy 2 on the period from 1990/01/01 to 2014/12/31. The mean of the distribution is materialized by a plain vertical line. The vertical dashed lines represent two standard deviations around the mean*

4.3.4. *Downside risk measures*

We have mainly spoken until now, with the use of the Sharpe ratio, of variance which is a bilateral, i.e. a symmetric measure of risk. Two opposite events will have the same marginal effect in the measure of risk whatever their sign. However, an extreme negative return will generally have a negative consequence on the survival of a fund manager, whereas an extreme positive one will rather improve its reputation. And return distributions are empirically, rarely symmetrical. This natural yet important asymmetry drives, for some investors, the need for the definition of downside risk measures, namely the measures that weight more negative outcomes than positive ones. In the early times of mean-variance allocation, [ROY 52] defined similar concepts with semi-variance (see below) in place of variance. He named the approach "safety-first principle", which gave the name to the paper. Some years later, derivations of the CAPM with an asymmetric view of risk were developed, leading to the democratization of the use of new measures of risk accounting for this asymmetry.

4.3.4.1. *Semi-variance*

Semi-variance is a dispersion measure that takes only into account observations that lie below the mean of the sample. Of course, the mean may be replaced by any arbitrary value. For a discrete series of observations $(r_t)_{t\in[1;T]}$ of empirical mean $\bar{r}$, the semi-variance of the sample is given by:

$$\text{Semi-variance} = \frac{1}{N_<}\sum_{i=1}^{N} \mathbb{1}(r_t < \bar{r})(r_t - \bar{r})^2,$$

where $N_< = \sum_{i=1}^{N} \mathbb{1}(r_t < \bar{r})$. Semi-variance may be a useful metric to look at.

REMARK 4.2.– Yet, it takes more sense when used to replace variance in mean variance (that becomes naturally mean-semi-variance) allocation procedures for investors with strong risk aversion. Contributions using such an approach are, for instance, [ROY 52] or [ARZ 77]. This alternative is, however, also studied in [MAR 59] which handles the comparison between variance and semi-variance in an allocation context. The distribution of R is at stake since a cautious study of its empirical distribution can lead to the choice of semi-variance in the case, where R shows a strongly asymmetric or highly skewed distribution. Minimizing variance will weight less extreme returns regardless of their signs, whereas semi-variance will be more suited to investors for which reducing losses is a prime objective. In fact, [MAR 59] also recalls that there is a direct mapping between the chosen risk measure and the implicit utility function on use if we write the allocation procedure as an expected utility problem. Using variance is equivalent to the use of an utility function U_V such that:

$$U_V(R) = \alpha + \beta R + \gamma R^2.$$

The choice of the semi-variance risk measure corresponds in fact to an implicit utility function that can be written as:

$$U_{SV}(R) = \alpha + \beta R + \gamma[\mathbb{1}(R < \theta)(R - \theta)]^2,$$

where $\alpha, \beta, \gamma, \theta$ are real numbers. Elaborating on this, the Sortino ratio came as a simple redefinition of the Sharpe ratio where variance is replaced by semi-variance.

4.3.4.2. *Maximum drawdown*

Looking at *drawdowns* is also another way to monitor downside risk. A drawdown is the cumulated loss experienced after the reach of a local maximum, and before a recovery (we find sometimes the term of "peak-to-valley loss"). Of course, it makes sense only for *non-stationary* series since we are looking for a local negative drift that occurs as a rupture in an expected positive drift. The *Maximum Drawdown* (henceforth MaxDD) is the worst drawdown that is experienced on a period of interest. Consequently, drawdowns are not computed on returns but rather on a series of prices or cumulated/integrated returns.

What may also matter is the duration, the amplitude of the worst drawdown, and also the total number of drawdowns of a series or their cumulated size (as used in the Burke ratio). Let us take a series $(P_t)_{t\in[0;T]}$. MaxDD is computed by finding the quantity MaxDD(T):

$$MaxDD(T) = max_{t\in[0;T]}\Big(max_{t'\in[0;t]}P_t - P_{t'}\Big). \qquad [4.2]$$

With those notations, there are two observations to be made. First, this quantity is positive as it computes the highest peak-to-valley discrepancy on the whole series available. Of course, this quantity is obviously path-dependent and relies on the available data that have to be over as long a period as possible for the sake of statistical meaning. MaxDD(T) is usually normalized as the quantity computed in equation [4.2] is homogeneous to the unit of P_t which is commonly a price or a profit. We have to find a normalization that can be either an arbitrary level or a local price. In the first case, the reference is an arbitrary level of assets, for instance $P_{t=0}$ which is therefore constant in the case of non-reinvested returns, with P_t therefore being the integrated sum of returns. In the second case, we should normalize by a local value of price, in particular in presence of reinvested or cumulative returns: if there are two dates t_1 and t_2, such that $t_1 < t_2$ and $MaxDD(T) = P_{t_2} - P_{t_1}$, MaxDD$(T)$ is usually normalized by P_{t_1}, the level of price or profit experienced before the loss.

REMARK 4.3.– As with semi-variance, maximum drawdown is a downside risk-measure, and it is possible to use it as a risk component to replace variance in a mean-risk allocation framework. Portfolio allocation using maximum drawdown and related generalizations have been developed, for instance, in [CHE 03], [CHE 05].

REMARK 4.4.– A drawdown is different from the "peak-to-peak" distance, which is defined as the time needed for a series to reach a new maximum after experiencing a loss. Drawdowns have to be limited for young and fragile funds that have to minimize their losses especially in their early times. But peak-to-peak distances are also important for funds, in general, that are asking for fees only when they are at their maximum historic value of normalized profit (high water mark). Between two peaks, the funds in this situation cannot ask for performance fees as long as the performance is below the current high water mark. On the long run, remaining before the current historical maximum may threaten the survival of the fund.

NUMERICAL EXAMPLE 4.5.– We show in Figures 4.1, 4.2 and 4.3 the periods that allow us to represent the MaxDD for each strategy on the simulation period.

4.3.4.3. *Calmar, Sterling and Burke ratios*

As in the case of the Sortino ratio where variance is replaced by semi-variance, adaptations of the Sharpe ratio with drawdown measures do exist. They are detailed below. Still working with a profit/price series (P_t) on a T-length period we have:

$$Calmar(T) = \frac{(P_T - P_0)/P_0}{MaxDD(T)} \text{ and } Sterling(T) = \frac{(P_T - P_0)/P_0}{MaxDD(T) - c},$$

where c is a constant, typically set to 10%. The two measures are quite close and the Calmar ratio is often used in practice. Another measure that takes into account the whole distribution of drawdowns is the Burke ratio:

$$Burke(T) = \frac{(P_T - P_0)/P_0}{\sqrt{\sum_{i=1}^{N_d} D_i^2}},$$

where $(D_i)_{i=1,\ldots,N_d}$ is the series of N_d drawdowns experienced on the period.

4.3.4.4. *Statistical significance and tests*

We already mentioned that statistical significance of the Sharpe ratio is linked with the t-statistic, and consequently any un-normalized Sharpe ratio (total return over total variance) on a T-length period scales with $\sqrt{T}$. Alternatively, we could say that for two Strategies 1 and 2 with the same normalized Sharpe on periods T_1 and T_2 such that $T_1 < T_2$ the significance statistic of the second strategy will be greater by a factor $\sqrt{T_2/T_1}$.

Conversely, it will be useful to get the same statistics for MaxDD and Calmar ratio. Hopefully, this is possible thanks to the work of [MAG 04b] and [MAG 04a] whom we refer to for detailed calculation, formulas and extended discussion. In order to get such heuristics it is convenient to model the value of the strategy through a

Brownian motion[7], as soon as there is no reinvestment of the returns and where P_t is the cumulated sum of the returns. The framework to understand this section then requires modeling P_t thanks to a drift μ and a volatility σ with $SR = \mu/\sigma$. The procedure developed here helps to test for the nullity and the sign of μ with the help of the MaxDD. μ, σ and SR are, therefore, theoretical values on which we make some inference. In the case of a Brownian motion with no drift, the distribution of drawdowns at a given date is known (see [KAR 98]). When the drift is in addition equal to zero, still working with a Brownian motion, the distribution of the MaxDD may even be obtained (see [DOU 99]).

This assumption is, of course, irrelevant in the general context of strategies since investors are trying to find strategies with positive and significant drifts. We do not explicate the forms of the laws that describe the way the MaxDD scales with time since they are quite sophisticated and beyond our scope, we let the reader refer to the previous references. However, it is natural to observe that the way the (un-normalized) MaxDD scales with time is related to the sign of the drift. It scales with T for a negative drift, $\sqrt{T}$ for a null drift (pure random walk) and with $log(T)$ for a positive drift. This also opens the way for tests. If we plot for a growing period length T the quantity MaxDD(T) versus T, a shape departing for a $log(T)$ fit should raise an alert on the true positivity of the drift of the strategy under study. This, however, assumes that the moments of the underlying stochastic process are constant (i.e. the return process is at least weakly stationary). What is therefore interesting is the nature of the link[8] between Sharpe ratio SR and expected MaxDD.

For a null drift, $\mathbb{E}[MaxDD(T)] = 1.2533\sigma\sqrt{T}$ and for a strictly positive drift, formulas hold asymptotically as T goes to infinity and the formula is of the form:

$$\mathbb{E}[MaxDD(T)] \underset{T\to\infty}{\rightsquigarrow} \sigma SR\Big(0.64 + \frac{log(T)}{2} + log(SR)\Big), \qquad [4.3]$$

where SR is the raw value of the theoretical Sharpe ratio, and σ the volatility of the process. We see in Equation [4.3] that for a given period (fixed T), the $\mathbb{E}(MaxDD)/\sigma$ statistic will be a function $x \to xlog(x)$ of the Sharpe ratio for which sensitivity to T is much more pronounced for short periods of time and weak values of SR. To sum up, for a winning strategy with a positive drift, the expected MaxDD(T) should scale with time as $log(T)$ and for a fixed period should scale with Sharpe as volatility times $log(SR)/SR$.

NUMERICAL EXAMPLE 4.6.– Of course, such a test cannot be run with one single sample of observations since for one sample only one value for the MaxDD can be

7 As soon as profits are reinvested, a geometric Brownian motion is more relevant; the relative normalization of the MaxDD by the latest peak value is necessary.

8 [MAG 04b] gives equivalent scaling behaviors for exploring the Calmar ratio rather than the MaxDD.

computed! For a given sample, computing the MaxDD for an increasing time period will provide a chart with a stepwise profile. Obviously, such a study cannot be observed with a single series since we seek an expected value of $MaxDD(T)$.

What has to be done is to draw or bootstrap from the initial empirical distribution of returns new sample of various sizes parametrized by a varying length T'. If we make N_D draws for each value of T' and compute each value of $MaxDD_i([0;T'])$ for $i \in N_D$, we may compute the empirical estimation of $\mathbb{E}[MaxDD(T')]$ as the sample mean:

$$\hat{\mathbb{E}}[MaxDD(T')] = \frac{1}{N_D}\sum_{i=1}^{N_D} MaxDD_i([0;T']),$$

and then estimate how $\hat{\mathbb{E}}[MaxDD(T')]$ scales with T'. We proceed to such a test and represent the result in Figure 4.6 for Strategy 1 (only for sake of illustration). For each value of T' and each draw we block-bootstrap a sample within the original total sample to draw a sample of length T' on a grid of T' of size T and $N_D = 100$ draws, and compute $MaxDD$ as the un-normalized value of the drawdown (sum of returns). The plain line represents $\hat{\mathbb{E}}[MaxDD(.)]$ as a function of period length. The dashed line represents the scaling obtained with the formula in equation [4.3], in the case of a positive drift. The plain line represents the scaling obtained with $1.25\sigma\sqrt{T}$, in the case of a null drift.

There is on Figure 4.6 a bias between the empirical and the theoretical curve. This bias may be due to the fact that equation [4.3] holds asymptotically, and also because the original series of returns may be non-stationary or different from a Brownian motion, because of a time-varying drift or because of an autocorrelation in the returns. It would be natural to extend the theoretical formulas to distributions that are non-Gaussian, auto-correlated, skewed or with a high kurtosis. It is quite intuitive that a series with a positive drift but high negative kurtosis will show higher drawdowns than in an equivalent Gaussian case. If the significance of the nullity of the drift is not properly tested the formula fits well with our estimation, the assumption of null drift for Strategy 1 does not seem coherent with the data.

4.4. Statistical significance of performance

In the present section, we will, however, try to show how to accept or reject some strategies based on simple risk measures taken as whole statistical objects. We will mainly focus on the Sharpe ratio as even with this simple measure, widespread and used as it may be, some elementary statistical perspectives on its use are often missed by practitioners.

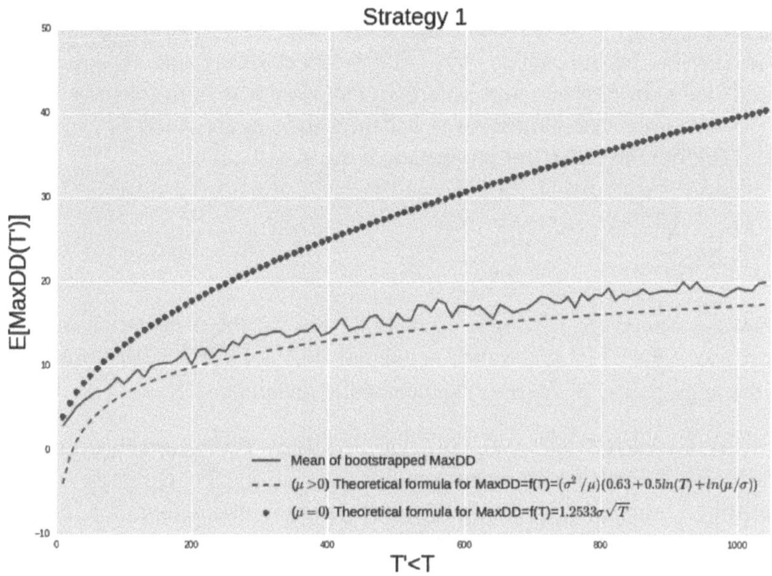

Figure 4.6. *Scaling for expected $MaxDD$ on $N_D = 100$ block-bootstrap draws compared with the theoretical formulas for Strategy* 1

4.4.1. *Sharpe ratio annualization*

We have already given some insights on the computation of the Sharpe ratio in section 4.3.2. We insisted on the fact that the quantity is computed on the same frequency of the returns of the strategy. This has two consequences. First, if we want to annualize the Sharpe for comparison purpose, it is preferable to take into account the statistical properties of the return series to give precise annualized figures. Second, if we want to make some statistical tests, we have to manipulate the correct statistical objects on the same time scale that the returns used to compute the Sharpe ratio.

4.4.1.1. *Intuition*

Annualization intrinsically has no statistical purpose. Computing the estimated Sharpe ratio is, in itself, stand alone. But how can we compare two strategies that are not on the same time scale? It is not possible to compare performance levels of two strategies with, on the one hand, say, intra-day strategies, and on the other macro bets with monthly liquidity. Therefore, the most reasonable time scale to convert performances is the yearly frequency that implicitly became a business standard to compare performances. The most common way to annualize the Sharpe ratio (i.e. to set the Sharpe ratio to an annual 'unit' whatever its time frame of computation) is to multiply the computed Sharpe by the square root of the frequency ratio N_y between the year and the frequency of the data. For instance, an estimated Sharpe ratio with monthly (respectively weekly, daily) data has a frequency ratio of $N_y = 12$ (resp. 52, 250) and has to be multiplied by $\sqrt{12}$ (respectively $\sqrt{52}$, $\sqrt{250}$) to get an annualized[9] value of Sharpe ratio. This is in fact only true in the case of independent returns through time. Annualization is in fact a time aggregation of N_y returns and consists of finding the statistical properties of the statistical object:

$$R_t^{(y)} = \sum_{t'=t}^{t+N_y-1} R_{t'}.$$

In the case where (R_t) is made up of i.i.d. returns, the distribution of $R_t^{(y)}$ has a mean equal to $N_y \times \mathbb{E}[R]$ and a variance equal to $N_y \times \mathbb{V}[R]$. Therefore, the Sharpe ratio of the aggregation of R_t over N_y periods is scaled by $\sqrt{N_y}$.

NUMERICAL EXAMPLE 4.7.– We compare in Table 4.6 the annualized values using either daily, monthly or yearly estimators of mean returns. For Strategy 1, we see that whatever the technique (aggregating then estimation or estimating then rescaling by a $\sqrt{N_y}$) the values are fairly equivalent. However, the figures are quite different in the case of Strategy 2. We will give the explanation for such a puzzle in the next section.

Strategy	$\sqrt{250} \times \widehat{SR}^{(d)}$	$\sqrt{12} \times \widehat{SR}^{(m)}$	$\widehat{SR}^{(y)}$
Strategy 1	1.72	1.62	1.74
Strategy 2	0.90	0.74	0.57

Table 4.6. *Comparing all moments of Strategies 1 and 2*

4.4.1.2. *Using statistical properties of the return series*

It is important to understand that any annualization process is an aggregation, not a mean, and scales with N_y. Note that the annualization step and the choice of the annualization coefficient are left to the practitioner who has to do things properly and must therefore understand the statistical challenges of the computation step. In fact, not only the frequency of data, but also the statistical properties of the series matter. We may face the following paradox: let us imagine that two fund managers are using the same strategy that display returns are positively autocorrelated. The first one is not aware of that, and the second one is. The first one will only take into account the N_y factor to annualize, and the first one will also take autocorrelation into account, in addition to the N_y factor. The annualization factor of the first manager will be more favorable than the second one, which is however aware of the particular structure of its return series. With promotion in mind, clients may be artificially entailed to invest in the first fund, the (correct) statistical approach of the second fund manager being seemingly detrimental in an advertisement perspective! However, the first one will be

9 For daily data, 250 is the number of business days in one year. Values such as 252, 256 and 260 may also be found and must be generally explicitly given.

artificially flawed by its estimation, overestimating the performance of her/his strategy, by underestimating her/his risk. That is what we explain below.

When returns are no longer assumed to be i.i.d. but still stationary, $\mathbb{E}[R^{(y)}]$ remains equal to $N_y \times \mathbb{E}[R]$ but the variance of $R^{(y)}$ does not scale linearly with N_y. The expression of $\mathbb{V}[R^{(y)}]$ is given, for example, in [LO 02] and becomes in this case:

$$\mathbb{V}[R^{(y)}] = N_y \times \sigma^2 \Big(1 + 2 \sum_{j=1}^{N_y - 1} (N_y - j)\rho_j\Big), \qquad [4.4]$$

where ρ_j is the j-th autocorrelation coefficient of R at its original frequency level. Therefore with an estimated Sharpe ratio $\widehat{SR}$, and autocorrelation coefficients $(\widehat{\rho}_j)_{j \in [1;N_y]}$ on a series (R_t), the more general expression of the annualized Sharpe ratio $(\widehat{SR}^{(y)})$ is:

$$\widehat{SR}^{(y)} = \frac{N_y}{\sqrt{N_y + 2\sum_{j=1}^{N_y - 1}(N_y - j)\widehat{\rho}_j}} \widehat{SR}. \qquad [4.5]$$

In practice, autocorrelation orders disappear quite slowly on common strategies, so if N_y is important, we may estimate autocorrelation coefficients on a finite number of orders, skipping estimation of greater order coefficients. If the strategy is not autocorrelated, we see simply that all the ρ terms disappear and that we are left with the former expression $\widehat{SR}^{(y)} = \sqrt{N_y}\widehat{SR}$.

NUMERICAL EXAMPLE 4.8.– We plot in Figure 4.7 the annualized Sharpe ratios for Strategies 1 and 2, which are obtained by taking into account the autocorrelation coefficients up to an increasing order (x-axis). The higher the order we consider, the more precise we are on the measure. Strategy 2 appears to be more autocorrelated than Strategy 1 (the first daily autocorrelation order of Strategy 2 is around 10%, whereas it is around 2% for Strategy 1). The effect is quite important for Strategy 2 whose "true" Sharpe ratio is equal to 0.57 rather than the measure of 0.90 given in Table 4.6. The measure integrating autocorrelation with daily returns of the series finally perfectly matches the value of $\widehat{SR}^{(y)}$ computed with re-sampled calendar returns by year. The precision of the match is due to the depth of the sample (25 years). However, the true Sharpe ratio of Strategy 1 may be instead around 1.35 which does not match the 1.74 value of $\widehat{SR}^{(y)}$ for Strategy 1. This may be explained by the low size of the sample (only 4 calendar years for estimation). The Sharpe ratio computed on re-sampled calendar data involves the computation of a standard deviation on 4 points (4 years) only, which is rather small. In this case, the formula integrating all of the correlation structure of the strategy is preferable since it provides a more precise and more conservative number (1.35 rather than 1.7).

In practice, a smoother and robust way to annualize Sharpe ratios with such a method would involve a parametric estimation of the autocorrelogram of the series, i.e. to estimate the $\widehat{\rho}_j$ terms in 4.5 with a parametric function.

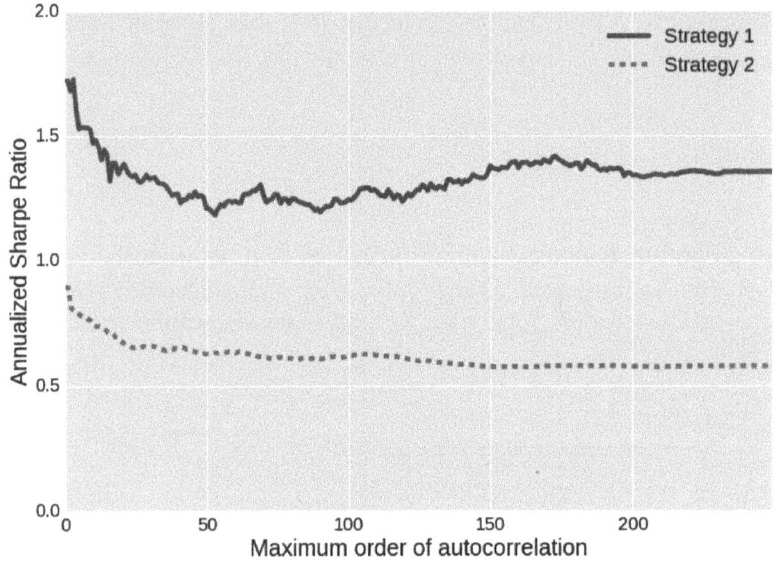

Figure 4.7. *Annualized Sharpe ratio taking into account autocorrelation for Strategy 1 (plain line) and Strategy 2 (dashed line) as a function of the maximal order of autocorrelation considered for variance correction*

4.4.2. *Testing significance with the Sharpe ratio*

Inference on a single Sharpe ratio from a given strategy is critical and should be a part of any quantitative manager's toolbox in order to assess the true performance and interest of a given strategy. We already specified that under the assumption of Gaussian i.i.d. returns, the extensive Sharpe ratio on T periods follows a t-statistic with $T - 1$ degrees of freedom. Therefore, this allows us to derive a simple significance test where we test:

$$H_0 : \mu = 0, \qquad [4.6]$$

or in other words, the nullity of the drift of the return process. In this case, for a test at the α significance level, the test statistic is the extensive Sharpe ratio directly and has to be compared with the following:

– a unilateral sided, $1 - \alpha$ quantile of the $T - 1$ central t-statistic, if the alternative hypothesis is $H_a : \mu < 0$ or $H_a : \mu > 0$;

– a two-sided bilateral quantile of the $T - 1$ central t-statistic, if the alternative hypothesis is $H_a : \mu \neq 0$.

Of course we could conduct this test with any other constant, and this test is related to the significance of the drift where the Sharpe ratio naturally appears as the test-statistic. The other possibility is to directly test the Sharpe ratio. A test of $SR \neq 0$ is quite useless since in that case, testing for the nullity of the drift is conceptually equivalent. In that case, it is better to test for a fixed value SR_1 of the *normalized* Sharpe ratio:

$$H_0 : SR = SR_1 \qquad \text{vs} \qquad H_a : SR > SR_1, \qquad [4.7]$$

and in that case the test statistic is still the extensive Sharpe ratio, which has to be compared with the sided, unilateral quantile of the $T - 1$ t-statistic with central parameter with a centrality parameter equal to no more than 0 this time, but equal to $\sqrt{T}SR_1$. Those tests use the finite distance distribution of the Sharpe ratio. A subtlety is that the estimator of the Sharpe ratio is biased at finite distance, even if this bias vanishes quickly (namely, for a fixed T, the expectation of the estimator is not strictly the estimated parameter).

However, this Sharpe ratio estimator is asymptotically Gaussian with asymptotic moments such that:

$$\sqrt{T}\left(\widehat{SR} - \frac{\mu}{\sigma}\right) \rightsquigarrow \mathcal{N}\left(0, 1 + \frac{\mu^2}{2\sigma^2}\right).$$

μ and σ are again the true values of the drift and the volatility of the underlying process. Such an expression is given in both [JOB 81a] and in [LO 02] (an equivalent obviously exists for the t-statistic and is available in [JOH 40]). This asymptotic law is useful since we could also test the significance of a given Sharpe ratio at the α confidence level and get confidence intervals for the Sharpe ratio. It will also allow (see below) providing tests when we will need to relax the assumption of Gaussian returns, and consequently to get an alternative to the use of the t-statistic, since in the case of strongly skewed returns for instance, the use of the Student t-test would be irrelevant. For an estimated Sharpe ratio $\widehat{SR}$, this value belongs at the α level in the segment:

$$\left[\widehat{SR} \pm q_N(\alpha) \times \frac{1}{T}\sqrt{1 + \frac{1}{2}\widehat{SR}^2}\right],$$

where $q_N(\alpha)$ is the bilateral α-quantile of a standardized, centered Gaussian distribution. At this stage, we deal with statistical objects, this implies that such tests are to be used on the most frequent data. So if this Sharpe is estimated on T daily points, the quantities to plug in to the test have to be the daily Sharpe, not any annualized version on another time scale. Of course, a test is simple to conduct since knowing the estimated Sharpe ratio is sufficient. A test as in Equation [4.7] means that we just have to check whether or not SR_0 belongs to the estimated confidence interval.

But what happens when we release the assumption of Gaussianity for the returns? The asymptotic framework helps retain the possibility of conducting such significance tests. If we still assume returns to be i.i.d., then the asymptotic variance is given by [OPD 07]. The expression is corrected in the following way:

$$\sqrt{T}\left(\widehat{SR} - \frac{\mu}{\sigma}\right) \rightsquigarrow \mathcal{N}\left(0, 1 + \frac{1}{2}SR^2 - \gamma_3 SR + \left(\frac{\gamma_4 - 3}{4}\right) SR^2\right), \quad [4.8]$$

where again $SR = \mu/\sigma$, γ_3 and γ_4 are[10] respectively skewness and (absolute) kurtosis of the distribution. Here again, the asymptotic variance should be estimated since SR will be replaced by its estimator. The test remains the same, only the bounds of the confidence interval changing:

$$\left[\widehat{SR} \pm q_N(\alpha) \times \frac{1}{T}\sqrt{1 + \frac{1}{2}\widehat{SR}^2 - \hat{\gamma}_3 \widehat{SR} + \left(\frac{\hat{\gamma}_4 - 3}{4}\right)\widehat{SR}^2}\right].$$

Conversely to the Gaussian case, however, the estimated Sharpe ratio is not sufficient and we need to estimate γ_3 and γ_4. In the Gaussian case, the two corrective terms should vanish and we end up with the former expression.

The more general and maybe more empirical case deals with the situation where returns are no longer i.i.d. at all. The main assumption that has to hold to compute asymptotic terms is that the returns have to be stationary. Consequently, even in the case where returns show some autocorrelation or heteroskedasticity, [LO 02] derives the asymptotic properties of the Sharpe ratio using a GMM method. The estimator remains asymptotically Gaussian and unbiased, yet the computation of the asymptotic variance is far more complex[11] and is left to the reader.

NUMERICAL EXAMPLE 4.9.– Using the previous estimation of skewness and kurtosis to estimate γ_3 and γ_4 provided in Table 4.5, we compute in Table 4.7 an estimation (up to the T factor) of the asymptotic variance for the estimator of the Sharpe ratio

10 See again section 1.3.3 for a discussion on skewness and kurtosis estimation. We voluntarily keep here γ_3 and γ_4 notation to recall that they have to be understood and estimated here as the third and fourth moment of the return distribution.

11 See appendix A of [LO 02] for the complete expression. [OPD 07] also extends this exercise to the non-i.i.d. case. However, in this precise setting, the results are subject to caution since they are dismissed by [LED 08].

provided in equation [4.8]. This factor is interesting since we see how far we are from Gaussianity and what we would miss by using only the t-statistic to test for the significance of the strategy.

At first order, using only the t-statistic is equivalent to using 1 as an approximation for $1 + \frac{1}{2}SR^2$ in 4.8. In the case of Strategy 2, this accounts only for a modification of $\frac{1}{2}(0.057)^2$ of the asymptotic variance. Consequently, the other $1.344 - (1 + 0.5 \times (0.57)^2) = 0.343$ correction comes from the departure from the Gaussian assumption. We see that in the case of Strategy 2, the effect is tremendous and any testing procedure should involve all our knowledge on the nature of the return distribution.

Strategy	$\widehat{SR}$	$\hat{\gamma}_3$	$\hat{\gamma}_4$	$1 + \frac{1}{2}\widehat{SR}^2 - \hat{\gamma}_3\widehat{SR} + \left(\frac{\hat{\gamma}_4-3}{4}\right)\widehat{SR}^2$
Strategy 1	0.109	0.011	3.28	1.005
Strategy 2	0.057	−1.93	45.7	1.344

Table 4.7. *Asymptotic variance estimator for Sharpe ratio for Strategies 1 and 2*

4.4.3. *A general test of significance*

We have just discussed the statistical analysis of a given sample backtest and its Sharpe ratio to evaluate whether the strategy is statistically significant. However, a Sharpe ratio is one and one figure only for a dataset but has to be understood as a selected strategy among a more extensive set of tests. In order to warn researcher and quants and prevent them from being too optimistic, [BAI 12b], [BAI 14b] propose a "*deflated measure*" of Sharpe ratio that is quite easy to implement in practice, as soon as an history of the tests that have been made are kept and analyzed. The measure has to be understood not as a replacement of the measure but as a corrected test that uses and crosses the notions aforementioned in this chapter (non-normality, overfitting, asymptotic law of the Sharpe ratio, etc.). The term "*deflated*" has to be understood as a correction on the Sharpe to redefine the test-statistic and obtain a more discriminant test. The initial statistical work has been developed in [BAI 12b], whereas [BAI 14b] tackles a more pragmatic approach. The deflating procedure accounts for two effects: the first one is the fact that multiple tests have been made and only the best have been kept to build the strategy; the second one is that the returns of the strategy may deviate from a Gaussian distribution. In order to repeat the procedure, we have to gather the series of T returns of the strategy and compute:

– the estimated Sharpe ratio $\widehat{SR}$ of the strategy;

– $\hat{\gamma}_3$ an estimator of the skewness of the return series;

– $\hat{\gamma}_4$ an estimator of the absolute kurtosis of the return series;

and also the following quantities:

– N the number of independent trials that finally led to the chosen strategy;

– $V(S)$ the variance among the N trials.

In practice, trials are rarely independent or this dependence is quite impossible to quantify. Suppose that we have in fact M trials and that those trials are not independent. [BAI 14b] give in the appendix some heuristics to replace N with an effective number of trials computed as:

$$\tilde{N} = \hat{\rho}_t + (1 - \hat{\rho}_t)M,$$

where $\hat{\rho}_t$ is in fact the average correlation between the M trials. With those notations, we can first define a reference Sharpe ratio SR_0 such that:

$$SR_{ref} = \sqrt{V(S)}(1-\gamma)\Phi^{-1}\left(1 - \frac{1}{\tilde{N}}\right) + \gamma_E \Phi^{-1}\left(1 - \frac{e^{-1}}{\tilde{N}}\right),$$

where Φ is the cumulative function for the normal distribution and γ_E is the Euler-Mascheroni constant which is approximately equal to 0.57. The "*Deflated Sharpe ratio statistic*" DSR in the sense of [BAI 14b] is therefore:

$$DSR(N, \hat{SR}, T) = \Phi\left(\frac{(\widehat{SR} - SR_{ref})\sqrt{T-1}}{\sqrt{1 - \hat{\gamma}_3 \widehat{SR} + \frac{\hat{\gamma}_4 - 1}{4}\widehat{SR}^2}}\right). \quad [4.9]$$

Some remarks can be made. First, it is better to compute the true Sharpe ratios on the raw returns without procceding to any annualization. DSR can be compared straightforwardly with a quantile statistic such as $1 - \alpha$ for a unilateral test of significance at the α level (testing $H_0 : SR = 0$ against $H_a : SR > 0$, for instance). The difficulty will come in practice from the collection or the estimation number of trials, i.e. giving coherent figures for N, $\hat{\rho}_t$ or M. Needless to say, the estimation of $V(S)$ could be a challenge, even more so as the values seem to depend critically on this value (that appears in the formula as a general pre-factor).

NUMERICAL EXAMPLE 4.10.– We may want to analyze Strategies 1 and 2 with such an approach. Unfortunately, we can not have access to the value $V(S)$. We will then make an assumption on $V(S)$ in order to estimate the acceptable number of tests, conditional on the statistical properties of the strategies, to consider them as being statistically significant. So, we assume that the dispersion of Sharpe ratios of tests that led to those strategies is equal to half the Sharpe ratio of each strategy, i.e. $V(S) = (\frac{1}{2}\hat{SR})^2$. This choice is completely discretionary but is a reasonable assumption for an illustration purpose.

Therefore, what is the maximal number of strategies N_0 such that for a given strategy the Deflated Sharpe ratio becomes less than the 5% test value that is N such that $DSR(N, SR, T) < 0.95$? We find in particular that with the quantities previously given, we find for Strategy 1 that $DSR(4, 0.109, 1043) = 0.951$ and for Strategy 2 that $DSR(5, 0.057, 6523) = 0.957$. This means that if the number of tests ran to choose Strategy 1 is greater than 4 and greater than 5 for Strategy 2, the strategies may appear as probably coming from overfitted experiments. It is surprising to see how low this figure is, especially for Strategy 1 which is, however, nearly Gaussian and significant. We underline here the importance of the time parameter. It is always preferable to have many observations to qualify a strategy, as this example illustrates it.

4.4.4. *Statistically equivalent strategies*

Having one strategy and concluding on its statistical pertinence is one thing. But we could also have two strategies (or more) and want to know whether one strategy is clearly different from the other, or if roughly speaking, using or one the other boils down to the same thing. Are those two precise strategies statistically different? Therefore, inference should be made on two time series of same length. It may be seen as the extension of [LO 02] that explores statistical inference on a single Sharpe ratio both with i.i.d. normal and also for non-normal returns. The main academic contribution on this topic started with [JOB 81a], but has been followed by the work of [MEM 03]. Practical case studies are, for instance, used in [LEU 08] or [DEM 09b]. Here we only give a general picture, and let the reader refer to the given references for the general and detailed framework. The test made on two strategies with observed returns $(r_t^1)_{t=1,\ldots,T}$, $(r_t^2)_{t=1,\ldots,T}$ generally starts with the assumption that the two first moments of their respective distribution are $\mu = (\mu_1, \mu_2)$ and Σ:

$$\Sigma = \begin{pmatrix} \sigma_1^2 & \sigma_{12}^2 \\ \sigma_{12}^2 & \sigma_2^2 \end{pmatrix}.$$

The estimator of the difference of the two Sharpe ratios is simply:

$$\frac{\hat{\mu_1}}{\hat{\sigma_1}} - \frac{\hat{\mu_2}}{\hat{\sigma_2}}.$$

When the returns are assumed to be i.i.d. and normal, [MEM 03] shows that:

$$\sqrt{T}((\hat{\mu_1}, \hat{\mu_2}, \hat{\sigma}_1^2, \hat{\sigma}_2^2) - (\mu_1, \mu_2, \sigma_1^2, \sigma_2^2))$$

follows asymptotically a $\mathcal{N}(0, \Omega)$, where Ω is given by:

$$\Omega = \begin{pmatrix} \sigma_1^2 & \sigma_{12}^2 & 0 & 0 \\ \sigma_{12}^2 & \sigma_2^2 & 0 & 0 \\ 0 & 0 & 2\sigma_1^4 & 2\sigma_{12}^4 \\ 0 & 0 & 2\sigma_{12}^4 & 2\sigma_2^4 \end{pmatrix}$$

Any deviation from the i.i.d. and normality assumption modified the asymptotic variance and the expression of Ω. But in the present context, the test to be performed is a classical one. To decide between the two strategies, the fund manager has to test the statistical nullity of the four-dimensional vector $((\hat{\mu_1}, \hat{\mu_2}, \hat{\sigma}_1^2, \hat{\sigma}_2^2) - (\mu_1, \mu_2, \sigma_1^2, \sigma_2^2))$ under a Gaussian assumption, using Ω which is estimated, e.g. with sample counterparts. In the more general case, returns are, of course, not Gaussian and such a statistic is not pertinent. The general case is much more sophisticated and is fully developed in [LED 08].

4.4.5. *How to differentiate anomalies from risk premia?*

Trading a profitable strategy is sometimes puzzling: why does the strategy work? Generally speaking, it is difficult to answer but it may be interesting to check whether the profit comes from the exposition to risk (performance being a reward for bearing this risk) or whether the strategy is playing a true anomaly that has not yet been arbitraged away by the market. This is an endless debate among academics and professionals, even on strategies played for decades. For instance, [COC 99] already discusses the difference between risk premia and (potentially arbitrage-based) anomalies. The intuition is that in the case of a risk premium, investors may not trade it, thus contributing to the persistence of the high reward associated with it. Alternatively, any easy arbitrage should be traded as soon as it is detected, causing the anomaly to disappear. [LO 04], [LO 16] propose basing the semantic difference on a sustainability criterion. If a "*sustainable risk premium may be available to investors for a period of time, given the financial environment*" a "*behavioral bias premium may be sustainable*" in a more permanent way.

We already highlighted the striking departure of the CAPM represented by the low-volatility anomaly: high-volatility stocks deliver on average poor returns when compared with low-volatility stocks. The low-volatility anomaly remains a general stylized fact of stock markets, and is above all a robust puzzle. The academic literature provides several paths for an explanation, including behavioral biases ([BAR 08] or [IWA 13]), overoptimism of analysts or institutional incentives [HAU 12]. [BOU 16] shows that the anomaly is tightly linked with dividends but that the anomaly remains strong for ex-dividend returns, and reaches the final conclusion that it is difficult to support the fact that the strategy may qualify as a risk premium. Anyway, a clear and final word is still missing, showing that the separation between risk premia and market anomalies may be difficult to define, even on premia/anomalies that have stood for several decades.

But is it possible to build some simple intuition with a given strategy to assess whether it is a risk premium or a behavioral anomaly? We certainly do not aim to bring a conclusion or to individually qualify here a variety of strategies. Instead, we want to highlight the existence of a simple procedure to get an intuition on the potential risk premium nature of a strategy only with the series of returns. We recall here the framework of [LEM 15] that we already described in section 4.3.3. where insights are proposed and developed in order to differentiate risk premia from market anomalies. The main message is that a risk premium is probably more related to skewness[12] than to volatility, as a reward for tail risk. Why? Because as detailed in [LEM 15], positive expected returns attract potential investors, increase prices but may also lead to crowdedness, then to a greater risk of crash, consequently materialized by a greater downside tail risk. Crowdedness may also reduce capacity and future returns. The anomaly generally finishes to "*stabilize (...) around an acceptable skewness/excess return tradeoff.*" The authors provide a general definition of what a risk premium is in terms of skewness, and compensate for negative extreme events rather than for the "simple" volatility, the relation between effective Sharpe ratio and skewness is quite linear.

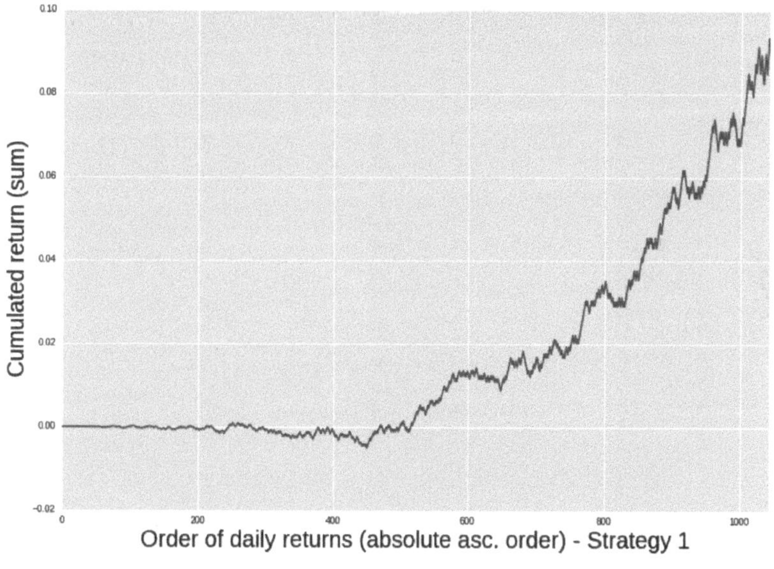

Figure 4.8. *Skew of Strategy 1 studied through the returns cumulated after having being ordered by their absolute value*

NUMERICAL EXAMPLE 4.11.– In practice, the idea is simple: with a series of observed returns $(r_t)_{t=0,...,T}$, order them by their absolute value in increasing order, and plot the cumulated sum of signed returns (the final cumulated return of the series should therefore be equal to $\sum_{t=0}^{T} r_t$. Any strategy qualifying as a risk premium

12 The introduction of a term related to skewness in the Markowitz problem is discussed in particular in [LEM 15] through the introduction of a condition on the third derivative of the utility function.

should be associated with negative tail risk: this implies, in the previous graph, a very specific behavior for the highest absolute returns that appear to mostly negative in the area of the graph relative to the most extreme absolute returns.

We plot such a cumulated gain sorted by absolute returns for Strategy 1 in Figure 4.8 and for Strategy 2 in Figure 4.9. We clearly see that for Strategy 1 the biggest returns are not particularly negative ones. However for Strategy 2, the biggest returns are quite exclusively negative ones. This is what we already observed *supra* as the returns of the second strategy are negatively skewed with fat tails. Figure 4.9 accounts for such a feature by materializing the fact that the biggest returns are the negative ones. With such a statistical behavior, we should be tempted to propose Strategy 1 as a behavioral bias and Strategy 2 as a risk premium.

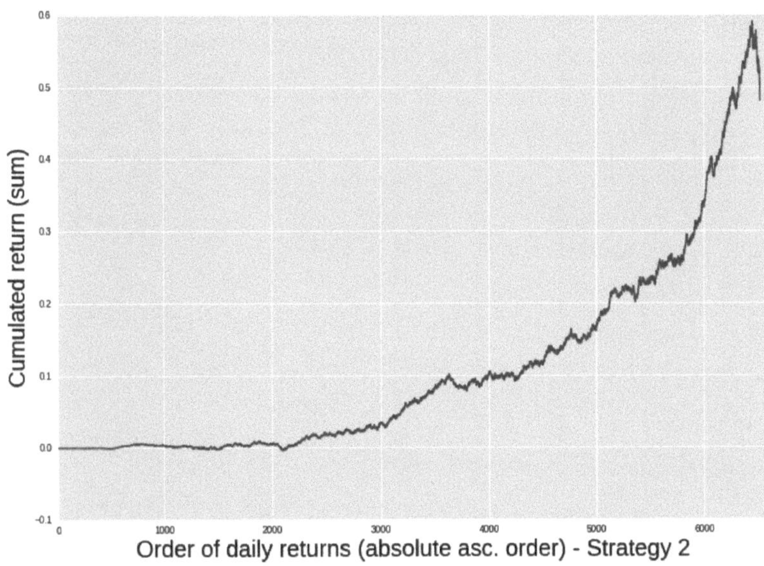

Figure 4.9. *Skew of Strategy 2 studied through the returns cumulated after having being ordered by their absolute value*

5

Gauging Economic Influences on Quantitative Strategies

One important step of any active strategy – quantitative or not – is to understand how different types of environments can have an impact on the strategy's profits and losses. Chapter 4 voluntarily dismissed the study of the nature of the strategy to consider strategy performance as a statistical object. Yet, if a strategy is statistically a performing one, what are its links towards the real economy? What is its sensitivity to economic conditions? One of the least explored topics in the academic research literature is the connection between financial assets' cycles and macroeconomic ones. One of the main explanations for that is probably to be found in the disappointing empirical results obtained across various research articles, in spite of the very intuitive idea that both cycles should be connected. When only focusing on equities, the intuition is that, during periods of growth, earnings should be getting more and more positive, and equity prices should consequently trend upward. On the contrary, during periods of recession, the very same earnings should deteriorate, leading equity prices into a slump. What is more, depending on how deep the recession is, the scale of the impact of the economic downturn should be different. From this perspective, the 2001 versus 2008 US recession episodes reinforce the impression that economic and market cycles should be connected.

Another case can be made with bonds: interest rates have been collapsing since the 1980s. Many macroeconomic observers are seeing in this collapse the reflection of two broad-based phenomena: on the one hand, inflation slowed down considerably – from more than 10% per year, to levels far below the 2% level, across OECD country members. On the other hand, potential growth across developed countries has also been through a negative trend. Gross domestic product (GDP hereafter) growth in the US dropped from 4% in the 1980s to roughly 2% between 2010 and 2015. Many see in both phenomena the explanation for the lower levels of yields (they should compensate investors for the erosion of the value of money, i.e. inflation). However, across empirical experiments, the correlation between changes in yields and changes in economic conditions is rather disappointing.

Simple correlation estimates are presented in Table 5.1. This table shows correlation results between the quarterly returns on the S&P 500, the quarterly changes in the US 10-year yields and two macroeconomic variables: the US GDP quarterly growth and the year-over-year change in the US Consumer Price Index (CPI). The signs of the relationships are in line with expectations: with a higher growth and a lower inflation, higher returns on equities can be expected and higher bond yields as well. The problem is the scale of these correlations: if aggregate growth and inflation phenomenon have an impact on aggregate indices like the S&P 500, then this relation should be overwhelmingly high. The maximum correlation in the table is obtained in rate to growth connection, and it only reaches 23% – nothing overwhelming.

	GDP growth	Yearly change in the Consumer Price Index
Quarterly returns on S&P 500	11%	–9%
Quarterly variations in the US 10-year rate	23%	16%

Table 5.1. *Historical correlation between financial assets and macroeconomic aggregates (1962–2016)*

The crude results obtained from Table 5.1 are very consistent with a large part of the empirical results obtained by various academic research articles. The academic debate is probably best summarized by the contribution of [WEL 08]: using a large set of economic variables – that are actually bottom-up variables – the authors assess systematically the in-sample and out-of-sample ability of these fundamental metrics to predict equity returns. Their results are unanimous: the explanatory power of the wide spectrum of selected variables is more than limited. Since the publication of this article, many other scholars have tried to understand why the intuition that fundamentals should be on average priced in stock prices appears to be so statistically wrong. [RAP 10] finds that combining forecasts helped to increase the forecast accuracy: individual fundamentals have a lesser explanatory power than aggregated fundamentals. They conclude with the fact that aggregated fundamental signals were tightly related to aggregated economic variables. From the perspective of their results, fundamentals are connected to business conditions and returns on stocks are showing signs of pricing in these factors. [PAY 12] also shows that stock markets' volatility forecast could be improved by conditioning regressions upon business conditions. [COO 09] finds that the output gap – a measure of the saturation of production capacities – showed a statistically significant predictive ability over stock returns. [RAP 13] provides an in-depth overview of the research situation, and Table 6.3 in their book sheds light on another phenomenon: business conditions seem to matter all the more for data analysis that is conducted using lower frequency data. By essence, financial returns are more volatile than economic fundamentals: for example, over the 1962–2016 period, quarterly returns on the S&P 500 have had a 16% volatility. The corresponding GDP growth volatility is only 7%, which is less than half of the stock index's volatility. Several other research articles diagnosed a statistically significant explanatory power for various business cycle-related data series: [NEL 76] and [CAM 04] highlight the relationship between stock returns and inflation; [RAN 06] connects returns on equities to aggregate output measures and, finally, [CAM 09] finds that expected business conditions are also reliable forecasters of returns on stocks.

A similar debate is also to be found in the credit bond-related literature. [COL 01] shows that a large number of fundamental data have a limited explanatory power over credit spreads variations. These conclusions are reviewed and extended in [DUF 11]. Here again, more recent contributions actually highlight that when accounting for regime shifts - and more broadly for model and parameter uncertainty - a connection between aggregated indices' spreads variations and aggregated macroeconomic conditions could actually be found. Examples of such empirical findings are [GIL 12] and [GIL 09].

The case of government bonds is very different: the classical interest rate theory of Irvin Fisher states that rates should equate the sum of a compensation for growth and for inflation. Naturally, an environment of lower inflation and growth should coincide with a period of lower rates. The empirical investigations of such a research trail actually proved to be quite fruitful: [ANG 03] draws a direct connection between interest rates on government bonds and macro-economic fundamentals. Most short-rate models are based on an economic understanding of the connection between economic fundamentals and the dynamics of interest rates, using monetary policy as a transmission channel. Equally interesting results are to be found in [DIE 05], [ANG 06b] and [ANG 07b].

Two other cases are probably worth mentioning. The case of currencies followed the same path as the equity literature, starting by empirically rejecting the influence of economic forces on currencies, to finally assess that the relationship between markets and fundamentals is complex and requires a potentially more sophisticated modeling approach. The seminal and very famous article by [MEE 83] tests various empirical models of the dynamics of exchange rates, only to find that none of them were actually showing any forecasting power. Their empirical findings led them to conclude that currencies evolve in a very similar way to a random walk. Since then, and very similarly to the equity-related literature, the introduction of modeling sophistication helped solve the puzzle raised by [MEE 83]. For example, [MAR 95] relates money stocks and relative revenues to currencies evolution in the case of the German, the Canadian, the Swiss and the Japanese currencies over 1973 to 1991. [ENG 05] shows that when asset prices' valuation actually depend on fundamentals that are integrated variables, the transitory part of the fundamentals' process matters much less to asset prices' dynamics. Relative inflation, for instance, stands a good chance to be a fundamental to exchange rates, as it is an integrated time series process: its cycles should not be statistically relevant explanatory variables, but its trend should be. [HSI 82], [DE 94] or [FRO 95] present empirical evidence that the labor productivity gap between two currency zones can explain the empirical departure of the currencies' value with the purchasing power parity rule. [FRO 91], [BLO 97] and [GOL 95] investigate the relationship between foreign direct investments and currencies, finding evidence of a connection between trends in currency markets and the net international investment positions of currency zones. Again, economic fundamentals are everywhere.

Finally, the case of commodities is our last analogy here. Since [GOR 06] and [ERB 06], an increasing number of investors have been driven towards commodity markets for two reasons. First, it seemed that they generated an empirical risk premium despite the fact that commodity futures distributed no revenue. Second, they showed a low correlation with the rest of the asset classes over the period of time covered in those two contributions. After the 2008 economic and financial crisis, a renewed interest focused on the behavior of commodities over the 2007 and 2008 period: the low correlation with the rest of asset classes was no more, and one way to connect the recent behavior of commodities to the rest of the asset classes was through their connection to the economic cycle. An early paper by [BJO 97] showed that when interest rates expected inflation and economic growth was high, the returns on commodities were usually at their lowest. More recently, [NGU 11] underscored the relation between commodity markets and major macroeconomic variables (e.g. business cycle indicators and monetary policy regimes) by evaluating commodity performance during the early, middle and late phases of expansionary and recessionary periods. The authors conclude that it is profitable to invest in commodities when monetary policy is restrictive during the middle and late stages of the expansion phase, during recession, and when monetary policy is expansive, that is, during recovery periods. [CHE 13] and [CHE 14a] highlight that during overstressed economic periods, commodity markets tend to react more to economic news than over quiet periods. There again, economic conditions seem to have an influence on markets.

Building a connection between returns and economic conditions is a complex task, but it remains necessary. Growth prospects are now weaker than over the 1940–2008 period, as the US, the EMU and even the Chinese growth are showing signs of deceleration. Inflation around the world is now at its lowest levels since the Great Depression, as highlighted by every International Monetary Fund report. Finally, monetary conditions are also of importance, as showed by the role played by central banks around the globe, particularly since 2008: it remains an early research subject, but already contributions such as [JOY 11] and [KRI 11] are connecting the dots between returns and monetary conditions. This chapter provides an overview of several methods that can be used to connect the returns obtained with a quantitative strategy with economic conditions. We rely on three examples: a risk-parity equity strategy, a commodity trend-following strategy and a currency carry strategy. We do not use those strategies *per se*, but we need here precise and realistic examples to illustrate our framework of analysis. In section 5.1, we explain how each strategy has been built. In section 5.2, we connect the returns on these strategies to measures of economic conditions. In section 5.3, we show how the release of economic information can impact the returns on those three strategies.

5.1. A tale of three strategies

The main objective of this chapter is to walk the reader through the possibilities that he or she can use to better understand the impact of economic influences on strategies. In essence, this chapter will naturally bend towards empirical applications. In order to help a wider spectrum of readers understand the arguments developed in this chapter, coming from various parts of the investment world, we will focus on three broad systematic strategies. Each of these strategies will focus on a specific part of financial markets: equities, currencies and commodities. The three strategies are: an equity equal risk contribution strategy, a currency carry strategy and commodity trend-following strategy. They have two things in common: first, in their crudest form, they are simple strategies that could be maintained in an Excel spreadsheet, making the reproduction of the results presented here simpler. Second, they all seek to exploit what seems to be a market inefficiency, something on which the quant part of the industry heavily relies. The equity strategy exploits the low-volatility anomaly, the currency strategy exploits the carry anomaly and, finally, the commodity strategy exploits the time series momentum anomaly.

5.1.1. *An equity equal risk contribution strategy*

The first systematic strategy on which our experiments will rely on is an equity strategy: the equivalent risk contribution equity portfolio, applied to the S&P 500 investment universe. This strategy amounts to investing capital across the stocks in an index with weights that are inversely proportional to the volatility of the underlying stock. It may seem simplistic, but its performance proved to be consistently high, outperforming the corresponding market index by a significant information ratio. We use here a simplified version in which ω_i the weights attached to stock i are derived from the following formula:

$$\omega_i \propto \frac{1}{\sigma_i}, \qquad [5.1]$$

where $\sigma_i = \sqrt{\mathbb{V}(R_{i,t})}$, with $R_{i,t}$ the return on stock i at time t. Weights are proportional to the inverse of each stock's volatility, and the proportionality will depend on the targeted volatility of the final portfolio. In what follows, each strategy's volatility has been made comparable, reaching roughly 9%. The data set starts in January 1999 and ends in March 2016. It is made of the daily returns on the S&P 500 sub-components. We use such an investment universe in order to rely on a well-known equity index and avoid having to rationalize the impact of the currency exposures found in broader indices such as the MSCI Index. See discussions on low-volatility strategy on pages xxix and 222, and, more generally, the developments on risk-based allocation techniques can be seen in section 3.6, previously in this book. Figure 5.1 shows the historical evolution of the strategy, along with the NBER recession periods. As for many equity strategies, the strategy delivered positive returns for most of the samples, but during the 2008 recession period as well as in 2015. Key statistics for the strategy are presented in Table 5.2.

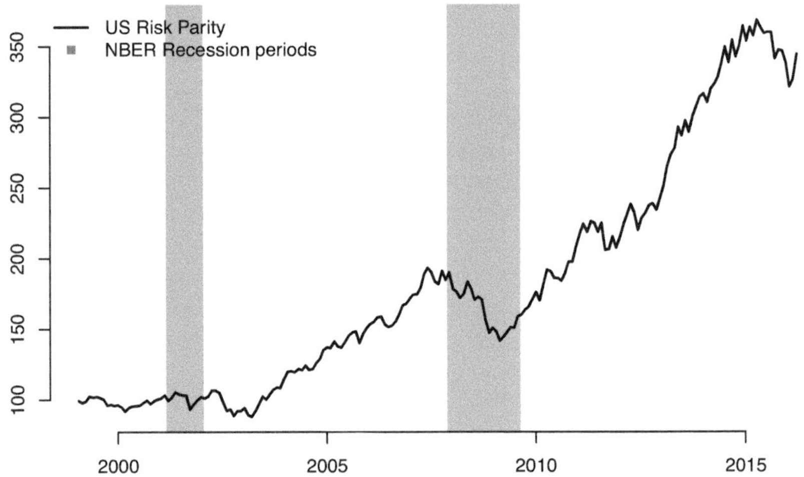

Figure 5.1. *Historical performance of the US risk-parity strategy described in section 5.1.1 (1999–2015)*

5.1.2. *A carry strategy*

Right after the collapse of the 2001 dot-com bubble, various quantitative analysts around the globe started promoting what came to be known as "carry strategies". These strategies in their simplest version borrow money in a currency with low rates to lend money in a currency with higher rates. In our experiments, we will narrow the investment universe to the G10 currency markets: US dollar, Canadian dollar, the Euro, the Japanese Yen, the Swiss Franc, the British Pound, the Swedish Krona, the Norwegian Krona, the Australian dollar and the New Zealand dollar. The strategy would go short the currencies with the lowest interest rates (as measured by the 2-year government bond rates[1]) and long the currencies to which higher rates are attached.

More formally, we rely here on a simple carry strategy. Say $y_{i,t}$ is the yield to maturity of a government bond issued in currency i at time t. Let $r_{i,t}$ be the return on currency i between periods $t-1$ and t. Every currency is here considered against dollar, that will act as a muted currency. This gives a set of $N_C = 9$ potential sources of returns. The strategies goes long the four currencies with the highest rates and short the four currencies with the lowest rates. The return r_t^S on the strategy S at date t can therefore be formulated the following way:

$$r_t^S = \sum_{i=1}^{N_C} \text{sign}(y_{i,t-1} - \text{med}(y_{t-1,.}))r_{i,t}, \qquad [5.2]$$

with the convention that $\text{sign}(0) = 0$. $\text{med}(y_{t-1,.})$ is the median value of the set of the N_C interest rates time series at time $t-1$.

Carry strategies have already been placed under the focus of academic research. [HEA 07] and [BUR 11] highlight the importance of this factor in currency movements. [CHR 11] connects the performance of carry strategies with systematic risk, which is very consistent with the point of view that is the backbone of the present chapter, as systemic risk can be viewed as being the reflection of economic cycles. Figure 5.2 shows the historical evolution of the strategy, along with the NBER recession periods. The strategy delivered a next-to-zero return over the whole period, despite a positive momentum between 2003 and 2007. Key statistics for the carry strategy are presented in Table 5.2.

5.1.3. *A commodity trend-following strategy*

The third and final strategy that is going to be analyzed here is a trend-following strategy, applied to a universe of commodity futures. The strategy is based on a set of 22 commodity futures belonging to the four key commodity sectors: agriculture, energy, industrial metals and precious metals. We rely on daily prices. As for the previous two strategies, the trend-following strategy has been designed to be simple and replicable by an interested reader who has access to the relevant data set.

The strategy boils down to going long for the assets that showed a positive trend in the past and short for those with a negative one. The trend indicator selected is the three-month return on each of the commodity futures, consistent with the [MOS 12]'s article on time series momentum. The paper argues that momentum in markets is a

1 Other rates could be used, such as Libor rates, but when willing to have a consistent rates measure for each currency zone, government bond rates are probably an easier way.

statistically persistent anomaly, and that the trend followers who are very present in the hedge fund industry seek to exploit this anomaly. In order to let every commodity future contribute to the overall trend-following portfolio, the final long and short weights are proportional to the underlying asset's volatility. Therefore, the weight $\omega_{i,t}$ associated with asset i at time t will be written as

$$\omega_{i,t} \propto \text{sign}(r_{i,t-60:t-1})\frac{1}{\sigma_{i,t}}, \qquad [5.3]$$

where $r_{i,t-60:t-1}$ is the observed return on asset i over the past 60 trading days and $\sigma_{i,t}$ is the asset's volatility at time t. Here, the asset's volatility is proxied using a rolling 20 days standard deviation. The final scaling factor will control the final targeted volatility, here about 9%.

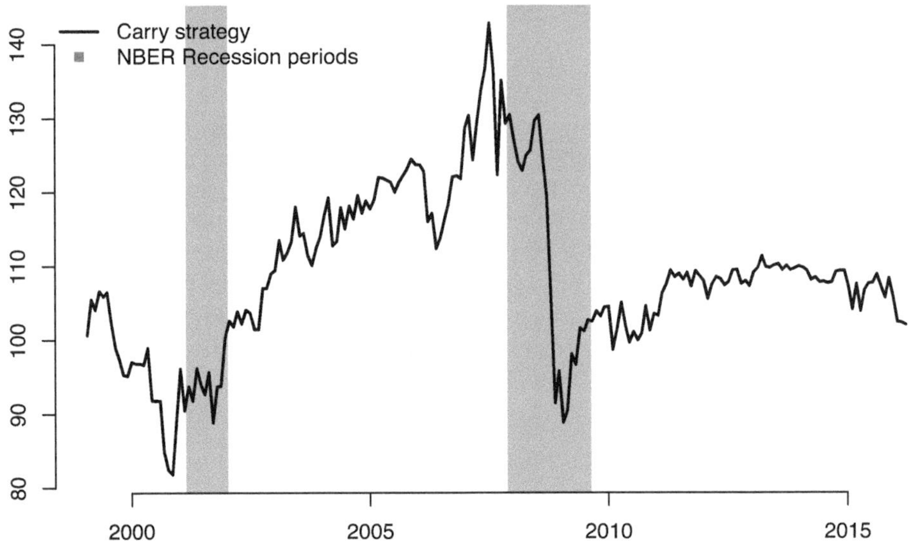

Figure 5.2. *Historical performance of the carry strategy described in section 5.1.2 (1999–2015)*

As mentioned earlier, there is evidence that there exists a time series momentum factor – very different from what equity managers refer to when thinking of a momentum factor – in many financial markets. The equity momentum factor seeks at under-weighting stocks that performed less well and overweighting stocks that showed the best performance. Even if all stocks generated a positive return, there would be under-weighted assets. [MOS 12]'s time series momentum factor seeks to go long assets with a past positive performance and short those with a negative one. A lot of the existing research on trends in markets were primarily focused on commodities: they seemed to display the strongest trends of all, and the now famous "turtle trading" premises explicitly sought to exploit this anomaly[2]. Currency markets are also a natural investment universe to trend followers, due to the lower correlation of this market compartment. [CHE 14c] explicitly focus on an inventory of the existing type of trends in commodity markets, showing that standard assets exhibit more complex trends on average than commodities.

Figure 5.3 shows the historical evolution of the strategy, along with the NBER recession periods. The strategy delivered a very positive performance, showing a very strong momentum over periods of commodity markets collapses as in 2008 or in 2015. Key statistics for the strategy are presented in Table 5.2.

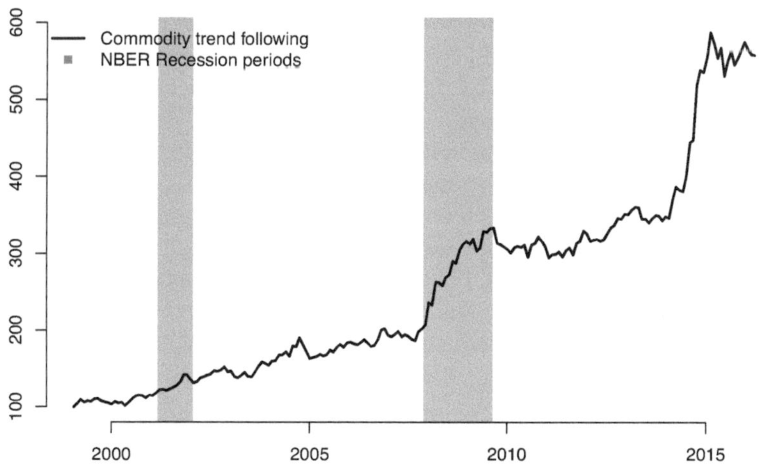

Figure 5.3. *Historical performance of the commodity trend-following strategy described in section 5.1.3 (1999–2015)*

	US Equity Risk Parity Index	Carry Index	Commodity Trend Following Index	S&P 500	US bonds	Dollar Index
Annualized return (%)	7.5	0.1	10.5	2.1	10.7	0.0
Volatility (%)	9.55	9.11	9.11	9.32	9.29	9.28
Risk-adjusted performance	0.83	0.01	1.16	0.22	1.15	0.00
Max. drawdown	–0.29	–0.73	–0.18	–0.78	–0.18	–0.85
Calmar ratio	0.25	0.00	0.58	0.03	0.58	0.00

Table 5.2. *Performance analysis for the three strategies (1999–2015)*

2 To learn more on the "turtle trading" phenomenon, see [COV 07].

5.2. Building economic condition indices

The aim of this chapter is to provide the reader with various ways to gauge the potential impact of economic conditions on a strategy's returns. The stage of the strategies having been set in the previous section, this section will focus on relating returns and macroeconomic conditions.

The very definition of "economic conditions" needs to be discussed first. What we mean in this section by this is that we want to assess in which phase of the economic cycle the world is. This remains for the moment a vague statement, but it remains one of the most heavily debated questions across markets. Questions such as "Is activity strong?" or "Is there a recession at work in the world?" or "Is inflation set to rise?" are all related to this question, but we first need to be much more precise regarding what we mean by economic conditions. First, economic conditions are actually a proxy to business cycle conditions. Most of the attention around business cycle has been set on GDP growth: evolution of growth is essential to markets such as equities. In the end, what makes the valuation of equities is partially the overall evolution of sales, which is from an aggregate perspective nothing more than the goods and services exchanged in an economy – which is precisely what GDP growth is measuring. The earliest observers of business cycle fluctuations focused both on GDP growth and the proxies of it. [KON 35] analyzed the evolution of GDP growth in the UK during the first industrial revolution, finding that, beyond the apparent trend in rising production, long lasting cyclical evolution was also at work. An earlier attempt to isolate economic cycles had been made by [JUG 62], highlighting that fixed capital formation was at the origin of 7-year cycles. [KIT 23] highlighted a shorter cycle, which involves variations in the quantity of goods produced as well as in their selling price. From the perspective of these three earlier pioneers of business cycle research, different types of cycles can affect the economy, and signs of them can be found in both the output and the overall prices.

Later contributions focused on exploiting the emerging datasets that various statistical offices came up with after the end of the Second World War. [BUR 46] were among the first gathering statistical measures of the US economy, showing how swings in the business cycle exhibit statistical regularities. A whole tradition of business cycle analysis then followed, even if this topic retained only a limited attention from academic research until the 1980s. [LON 83] among others then renewed the foundations of a scientific method to analyze and understand the cyclical variations any capitalist economy can go through. Later summarized in [KIN 99], this stream of research focuses on understanding the potential sources to variations in real activity, as opposed to the variations in goods and services' prices. To the real phenomenon studied in this literature, articles such as [BER 95] and later [BER 99] then extended business cycle studies to monetary phenomenon: the "financial accelerator" explains how financial conditions can impact the investment cycle, which is an essential dimension of economic activity. The recent very high impact of central banks on liquidity conditions is very consistent with this type of research articles: by manipulating both interest rates and credit spreads, monetary conditions progressively became a factor of the utmost importance.

Now, the question is to create measures of such a phenomenon, in order to assess economic conditions and in the end to answer the question: where are we in terms of the different phases of the business cycle, across output, prices and monetary conditions? This question has been a research topic over the past 15 years, strongly fostered by Central Banks' research department. Now, a larger set of methodologies are available to do so, with clear differences. These economic condition indices can be split into three categories:

1) The first type of indicators, which has been proposed, is based on a large number of data-series that are combined into a single metric. Individual indicators having been found to be volatile and partial indicators of economic conditions, the cross-section of a large number of them makes up for both these flaws. It probably started with [STO 02]: using a large number of data, the authors construct a smaller set of factors using PCA (see also section 3.4.2) to reduce the dimensionality of the problem. They show how using these factors makes it possible to forecast various economic time series in a better way than when using individual data. Their conclusions hold when forecasting both output related data as well as inflation-related data. Another example of such indices is the index proposed in [ARU 09]: here again, they extract one single factor out of a large sample of time series. The refinement is that they rely on a model with unobservable factors, estimated using a Kalman filtering approach. In essence, the business cycle is an unobservable phenomenon: each data carries its load of noisy information regarding its evolution. The Kalman filtering approach (see section 2.3.1) makes it possible to assume a particular dynamic to it and therefore to make forecasts about it. The PCA does a similar job, but the structure of the business cycle factor is only emerging from the dataset and is not controlled by the way the index is built or defined. The precision of the measure is a question tackled in [BER 05b]: what they call the "single step" approach provides its users with a precision that is as satisfactory as the more complex Kalman filtering approach[3]. The [ARU 09] index is available from the Fed of Philadelphia's website[4] with a long history. Other examples of such indicators can be found in [BEB 15]: here again, they gather economic time series by type – output- and inflation-related factors – before aggregating along these lines a large set of time series. The Chicago Fed National Activity Index (CFNAI) proposes a similar approach and is based on [STO 89]: it aggregates 85 macroeconomic time series into a single business cycle indicator[5]. It has been used in empirical applications in articles such as [BEB 11].

3 On this point, see as well the discussion in [IEL 15] and the references in it.

4 See https://www.philadelphiafed.org/research-and-data/real-time-center/business-conditions-index.

5 Here again, the time series of the index is available at: https://www.chicagofed.org/publications/cfnai/index.

What is common to all these contributions is that they let the factors truly latent and unspecified: economic conditions remain what they are, a concept that is broad and sometimes quite vague.

2) The second stream of research papers that emerged more recently describes itself as "nowcasting". Nowcasting is the contraction of two words, "forecasting" and "now", and means making forecasts about the current economic conditions: not only are business conditions unobservable but also they are difficult to assess in a coincident way. For example, the most genuine indicator assessing current growth conditions is probably GDP growth, but this quarterly data series is usually available between 30 and 50 days after the end of a quarter – the quarter for which it measures economic activity. In such a situation, "nowcasting" therefore makes a lot of sense, and many central banks have invested heavily in such a technology. The Fed of Atlanta proposes an online nowcasting indicator for the US economy[6] that follows the methodology presented in [HIG 14]. [BAN 12] provides an overview of the existing literature on nowcasting indicators. One of the first attempts to create a methodology to "nowcast" GDP growth in the USA using the timely economic newsflow can be found in [EVA 05]: the very key difference between the index technology presented earlier and the nowcasting one is that, in the case of nowcasting indicators, economic news are turned into a GDP estimate. By essence, nowcasting methodologies are relying on the fact that both hard data such as industrial nowcasting production and soft data such as surveys can be used to nowcast GDP growth. The bulk of the existing contributions are based on the US economy: see, for example, [GIA 08], [KUZ 11] and [GIA 09] in the case of the Eurozone, [MIT 09] for the UK, [D'AG 12] for Ireland and [ROS 10] and [FER 14] for the global economy.

3) Finally, other attempts to gauge economic activity or business cycle fluctuations have been carried out using a single data series, used as a proxy instead of the cross-section of a large number of economic time series. Even though there is a lower number of attempts in that direction, they remain interesting studies around specific indicators. [BAK 11b] is a good example of such research articles: the authors use the Baltic dry index as a proxy for global activity. It is an indicator of transportation costs for raw materials shipped by sea. The authors find that it is a reliable predictor of assets' returns, highlighting its interest as a business cycle measure. Another interesting article in this stream of research approach is the work of [KIL 09]. The article seeks to disentangle the contribution from demand shocks on real oil prices from that of the supply ones. In order to answer such an essential question to any commodity markets, [KIL 09] relies on a business cycle-related measure that naturally excludes the influence of the service sector: cargo freight data[7]. The dataset is monthly and can be downloaded from the author's website. The conclusion of the article shows the significance of demand shocks on real oil prices. Finally, the last type of articles

6 See https://www.frbatlanta.org/research/publications/wp/2014/07.aspx.

7 See http://www-personal.umich.edu/ lkilian/reaupdate.txt.

that could be mentioned in this section are articles relying on univariate time series to gauge economic conditions. The most renowned article in this line of research is probably the contribution of [HAM 89]: introducing a time series model (known as "Markov-switching" model, MS hereafter – see also discussion in section 2.3.2), the author estimates the regime in which the economy is at every observation point. The model relies on the assumption that the conditional probability from one regime to another is time invariant, which is enough to obtain time-varying probabilities for each date in the estimation sample. It uses the model to estimate recession periods in the USA using real GDP growth and obtains dates that are close to those of the National Bureau of Economic Research – which are the US official recession dates. The methodology has been widely used since then and remains one of the key time series models used in dating turning points in the business cycle. The Federal Reserve of Saint Louis extensively uses this technology, providing turning point dates for a broad spectrum of countries[8]. On this line of research, see the literature review available in [IEL 12].

Here, we intend to rely on these different approaches, building economic condition indices encompassing three dimensions: GDP growth or economic activity, inflation dynamics and, finally, monetary conditions – a synonym for a measure on how active central banks around the world are. We have created three time series where each is a mix of a larger number of time series, following a methodology that every Bloomberg© user will be able to reproduce. Here are the steps that we have followed:

1) First of all, in order to obtain a list of macroeconomic data series that are used by markets watchers, we have restrained ourselves to the data belonging to the Bloomberg© calendar for the G8 countries[9]. These time series have been split between growth, inflation and monetary conditions. Any Consumer or Producer Price Index data have been labeled inflation, any Central Bank-related information has been labeled monetary conditions and the rest of it has been grouped under the growth label.

2) The list of the time series extracted is reported in Tables A.1 and A.2 for the growth index, A.3 for inflation and A.4 for the Monetary Condition Index. The longest list is for growth, given its significance for market participants. Then comes inflation and, finally, monetary conditions. For growth, the earliest data available date back to November 1986[10] and ends in December 2015. Inflation follows exactly the same *modus operandi*. In the case of monetary conditions, the situation is slightly different: with the creation of the euro-zone, the sample has to start in 1999. It also ends in 2015.

8 See https://fred.stlouisfed.org/.

9 Under Bloomberg©, type WECO <GO> and then select the G8 option.

10 Some US data date back to an earlier date, but for the sake of what we intend to do with it, we have limited the sample to 30 years.

3) Among all the data, we have screened for data that have a frequency that is quarterly and decided to discard them. We want to rely on a typical "high-frequency" macroeconomic data set that is with a monthly frequency.

4) Then, we ran unit-root test: this type of test intends to verify whether a time series is stationary or not[11]. The series that are found not to be stationary are differentiated, that is, the series are replaced by their one-month change. Stationarity is a key hypothesis for what we intend to do with the data set later.

5) Finally, the data are gathered by type (i.e. growth, inflation or monetary policy) and each of them are z-scored: each time series is scaled, by subtracting its average and then dividing it by its standard deviation. This is done for two reasons: it makes the time series comparable, when a comparison between them is necessary and it will make it possible to run a PCA using a decomposition of their correlation matrix – that is, our analysis will be driven by covariation – instead of the covariance of these initial data – which would have been driven by the time series' respective volatilities. We intend on creating economic condition indices: the correlation between them is an essential information, much more important than their respective volatilities.

6) Once all of these steps are done, a PCA is performed in order to extract the first factor attached to each data set: given what has been done in the previous steps, it should provide us with a gauge for each of the three dimensions to the economic cycle.

The three macroeconomic condition factors are presented in Figure 5.4, highlighting their respective behavior alongside the NBER recession periods in the USA. The growth condition index follows recession periods closely, dropping for each of them with various intensities. Around the 1992–1993 period, the indicator dropped during a period without US recessions: it actually matched European recessions as dated by the Center for Economic Policy Research[12] (CEPR). Another drop was observed around 2011, which matched a European recession of that time. The inflation index is slightly more volatile on the graphic, following the growth condition index closely but only for a couple of periods. Most of these occurrences actually take place during recessions such as the US 1991, 2001 and 2008 recessions. It highlights how price dynamics have a tendency to lag behind growth. Another peak is visible in 2011 right before the European recession. Finally, the Monetary Condition Index shows how monetary policy loosened or tightened from 1999 to 2015: the more positive it became the tighter the monetary conditions were. Such periods took place right before the 2001 and the 2008 recessions. Since the end of 2008, monetary conditions remained loose to show signs of recovery in the indicator

11 To gain insights into those tests, see any time series book like, for example, [HAM 94]. Computation using, for example, R or Matlab is in general quite easy.

12 See http://cepr.org/content/euro-area-business-cycle-dating-committee.

after the 2013 "taper tantrum", when the Fed announced its willingness to exit from its quantitative easing (henceforth QE) policy.

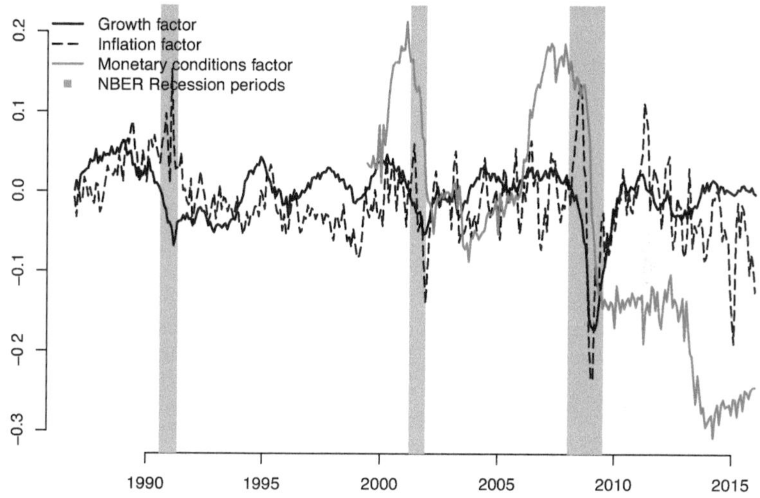

Figure 5.4. *Economic condition indices time series (1986–2015)*

5.3. Relating business conditions to market performances

Now, with these economic condition indices having been created, this section will focus on exploiting this information in order to relate economic conditions and market performances. There are several ways to do this, and these can be divided into two types of approaches. A first possibility is to slice and dice history according to the regime each economic condition index is in. For example, suppose that the growth index can be described by two regimes – say expansion and recession – then it becomes possible to compute a given strategy's returns during each type of regime. This type of approach has been used in [ANG 04], [BLI 11] or [GUI 07]. Another type of approach tries to relate the level of each indicator to the scale of returns. If economic conditions reach very high levels, should returns not be all the more positive or negative? Such an approach has been undertaken in a limited number of contributions. In a way, the regression of returns on economic variables listed in the introduction of this chapter can be seen as following this type of methodology: regressions' beta are a measure of how economic indicators translate into a certain level of returns. [BOO 16] use a block-bootstrap approach to deal with the difference in the persistence between economic indicators and assets' returns. In this section, we will briefly use both approaches, applied to the three quantitative strategies mentioned previously.

5.3.1. *Economic condition regimes and returns on quantitative strategies*

In this section, we aim to turn the economic condition indices into regimes using a Markov-switching (MS) model. Let x_t be a realization of a given time series. A MS model is based on a regime representation such that the variable X_t follows at t the distribution:

$$X_t \rightsquigarrow \mathcal{N}(\mu_i, \sigma_i), \qquad [5.4]$$

$$S_t = i, \qquad [5.5]$$

where S_t is an unobservable variable that states in which regime the time series is at time t. During regime i, X_t is distributed as a Gaussian random variable with an expectation equal to μ_i and volatility equal to σ_i. In the case of two regimes, when i in equation [5.5] can either be equal to 0 or 1, the probability at time t to be in regime i is written as:

$$\begin{aligned} P(S_t = i) = {} & P(S_t = i|S_{t-1} = 0) \times P(S_{t-1} = 0) \\ & + P(S_t = i|S_{t-1} = 1) \times P(S_{t-1} = 1), \end{aligned} \qquad [5.6]$$

where $P(S_t = i|S_{t-1} = j)$ is the conditional probability that the time series is in regime i at time t, being in regime j at time $t - 1$. The conditional probabilities are time invariant, while the unconditional probabilities are time varying. The model can be estimated by MLE following the methodology provided in [HAM 86] (see, in addition, [HAM 89] and also the discussion in section 2.3.2 for a more elaborated presentation of these models).

We estimated such a model with two regimes: a high regime and a low regime. The difference between both regimes is that μ_i is higher in the case of the high regime than in the case of the low regime. The estimation has been done using one of the MS estimation routines in R. Table 5.3 shows the estimated μ_i for each regime, as a sanity check that the previously mentioned difference between a high and a low regime is consistent with the intuition of it. The probability associated with the regimes is charted in Figure 5.5. Table 5.4 displays the annualized performance of each strategy for each of the regimes of each of the economic indicators.

	High regime	Low regime
Growth	0.02	–0.04
Inflation	0.00	–0.02
Monetary conditions	0.06	–0.19

Table 5.3. *Estimated expectations from the Markov-switching model*

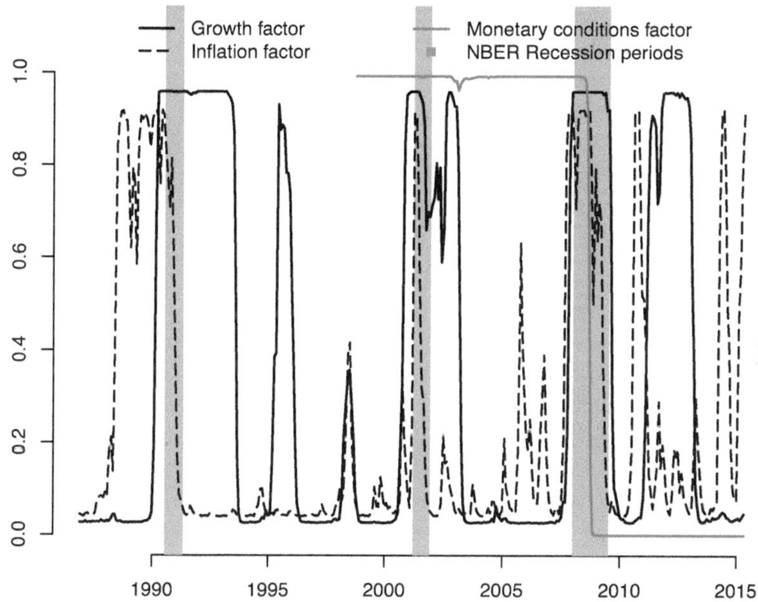

Figure 5.5. *Estimated probability that (1) the growth factor is in its recession regime, (2) the inflation factor is in its high regime and (3) monetary conditions are in the tighter regime (1986–2015)*

		Equity risk parity	Carry	Trend following	S&P 500	US bonds	US Dollar
Global average		7.2%	0.1%	10.0%	2.1%	10.1%	0.0%
Growth	Expansion	13.7%	0.0%	7.5%	7.7%	5.9%	1.8%
	Recession	–2.2%	0.3%	13.7%	–6.1%	16.3%	–2.7%
Inflation	Higher inflation	1.2%	–7.2%	14.7%	–4.6%	9.5%	4.4%
	Lower inflation	8.5%	1.7%	9.0%	3.6%	10.2%	–1.0%
Monetary conditions	Tight conditions	5.7%	1.9%	11.0%	0.6%	11.8%	–2.7%
	Loose conditions	9.1%	–2.2%	8.8%	4.0%	8.0%	3.5%

Table 5.4. *Performance analysis across the economic regimes*

Figure 5.5 shows the merit of performing this regime analysis: first of all, the G8 recession periods that are estimated are close to that of the US NBER recession periods, while still showing selected differences. As detailed earlier, European recessions are also highlighted by the regime probabilities on the graph. The regime estimates also show that recessions across the G8 world have a tendency to last longer than the pure US ones: it is particularly true in the case of 1991 and 2001. For both these recessions, the US recessions appear shorter than across the full spectrum of G8 countries. In the case of inflation, there is no existing official dating scheme: the regime probabilities are the only element on which we can rely. The regime probability emphasizes the 1988–1989 inflation shock, as well as the surges in inflation in 2001, 2008 and 2011. Finally, the monetary condition regimes appear to be quite binary, as the pre- and post-QE periods are clearly visible in the estimated probability.

Now, let us focus on the performances of each strategy per regime to try to understand how these strategies react during each of them. Such an analysis is at the heart of the motivations of this chapter. Results are displayed in Table 5.3. Before turning to the three strategies, the first table offers a point of comparison using standard assets: the S&P 500, a Government Bonds Index (Barclays US Treasuries) and the US Dollar Index. The performance of these assets has been rescaled, so that each of them has the same volatility as the three strategies over the full period. The analysis is performed over the 1999–2015 period. Analyzing the performance of these assets per regime will help the reader understand how equities, bonds and the US dollar react across each of these types of periods. Here are the key points to take away from reading this table:

1) First, in the case of the growth factor, the performance of the S&P 500 is in line with the intuition. During periods of recession, the index shows an average negative performance (–6% per annum) when this performance is positive during expansion periods (+8%). Given its overall 2% performance per year, the difference between both performances seems to be large enough to see the potential explanatory power of economic conditions. A similar pattern is observable in the case of bonds: the bond index delivers a 16% performance during periods of recession, and a 6% one during periods of expansion. Bonds have been delivering positive returns almost every quarter in the sample, explaining why the performance per regime does not show any difference in sign as in the S&P 500 case. Still, the 10% difference in performance between both types of periods says a lot about the explanatory power of the growth regimes with respect to bonds. Finally, in the case of the US dollar, the situation is quite different: the spread between the return per regime is much smaller. Periods of expansion have been accompanied on average by a positive return on the dollar, while periods of recession have been accompanied on average by negative returns. First, this difference is insignificant as both figures are very small, especially when compared with the 9% volatility of the returns. Second, the 2001 crisis is playing a significant role in this finding: during the 2001 US recession, the US dollar lost a lot of value after the DotCom bubble burst. From the perspective of this analysis, growth regimes matter to stocks and bonds and a lot less to currencies. What about the three strategies? The equity risk parity strategy looks a lot like the S&P 500: recession periods lead to negative returns, when positive ones bring about positive returns. The key difference about this strategy is that it suffers less from recession periods than the S&P 500 while profiting more from expansion periods. As in the

US dollar case, the carry strategy shows a limited sensitivity to growth regimes. In the case of the trend-following strategy, recession periods – creating large negative trends in commodity markets – are particularly positive periods for trend followers. When risk parity strategy shows signs of being defensive during periods of recession, the trend-following strategy is actually profiting from it. These are key features that should be taken into account when designing a quant strategy.

2) Turning now to inflation regimes, periods of low inflation seem to profit stocks: they usually appear at the end of a recession, therefore matching periods of recovery. Inflation regimes show little impact on bonds: low inflation means a 10.2% return on bonds versus 9.5% for higher inflation. The order relation between both figures seems to be intuitive (higher inflation periods are periods of increasing rates and therefore lower returns on bonds), but the spread between both returns is insignificant. One reason for this situation is the fact that high-inflation regimes are often coincident with recessions, as shown in Figure 5.5: from the growth regime analysis bonds seem to deliver higher returns during periods of recession. Finally, periods of higher inflation seem to correlate well with that of a rising dollar: here again, the carry argument should explain a lot of this phenomenon. Higher inflation means higher rates, especially in the USA – explaining the rise in the US dollar, as higher rates turn US bonds into more attractive assets to non-US investors. Now, when it comes to the three strategies, several conclusions can be drawn from Table 5.3. First, inflation regimes seem to show a reasonable explanatory power over the strategies: not only are growth conditions important to quantitative strategies, but inflation should also be taken into consideration. Second, periods of higher inflation seem to profit the trend-following strategy but not the carry strategy: historically, over periods of higher inflation, the carry strategy has on average delivered a strongly negative return (–7.2% for a volatility of 9%, quite something). Finally, the equity risk parity case is also interesting: periods of low inflation have been historically very positive for this type of strategy. Not only does the strategy generate a 8.5% return (i.e. risk-adjusted performance in the neighborhood of 1), but it also sharply outperforms the S&P 500 Index. Periods of higher inflation are still periods of positive returns for the strategy, but at a much smaller scale.

3) Finally, monetary condition regimes are actually splitting the sample into a before/after 2008 situation, creating a distinction between the pre- and post-QE period. In a nutshell, the QE period profited to the S&P 500 and to the US dollar, while weighing a little on the returns on bonds (with much lower yields). On the contrary, the non-QE period has been a detrimental period to stocks and to the US dollar, with bonds generating a higher level of return. Turning to the strategies, they offer a lower sensitivity to the monetary condition regimes than to the two other types of regimes. The QE period has offered a positive support to the risk parity strategy, the strategy having delivered a return per annum that is 3% higher than that in the non-QE case. The loose monetary condition regime has been globally detrimental to the carry and the trend-following strategy, without a marked difference between both periods' returns.

In the end, the interest of this analysis is to understand under which type of economic conditions would a quantitative strategy deliver a more positive or negative return. From the analysis above, the risk parity strategy delivers returns that should be all the more positive as the world economy is in an expansion period, with lower inflation and loose monetary conditions. Carry strategies deliver all the more negative returns during periods of higher inflation and loose monetary conditions, probably explaining why currency carry strategies have been attracting less attention over the past 5 years. Finally, the commodity trend-following strategy seems to profit a lot from recession periods, when inflation is higher and monetary conditions are loose.

A similar analysis can be easily done without even relying on the methodology mentioned previously, but by using the regime indicators provided by the FRED database[13]. The website provides a lot of pre-estimated regimes using a wide spectrum of indicators that are not purely US focused.

5.3.2. *Economic condition indices' level and returns on quantitative strategies*

As discussed earlier, assessing the performance of a strategy during certain types of periods – such as recession or inflationary periods – is essential, but there are other interesting ways to connect the returns on a strategy to the prevailing macroeconomic conditions. Not only regime analysis matters to building a strategy, but understanding how more structural economic evolutions can impact a strategy also matters. The developed world has been through a period of very accommodative monetary policy: how does this structural element impact a trend-following strategy? GDP growth is said to be set on a declining path: how does it impact any strategy? These questions are essential when thinking of backtesting a strategy, beyond assessing the average impact any type of regime can have on a given strategy.

In order to give some consistency to this chapter, we will keep on working using the economic condition indices built in the previous sections. As mentioned in this chapter's introduction, when computing correlations between economic data and financial returns, the results are usually disappointing and this low correlation is an interesting empirical puzzle. When using data at a lower frequency, the correlation between the returns on standard assets and economic data is found to be increasing, leading to the conclusion that the holding period is likely to be a key when connecting returns to any economic data. Say $X_{t,t+H}$ is a variable containing information regarding economic fundamentals, over the period t to $t + H$ on a H-periods horizons. With fundamental data coming from p sources, then $X_{t,t+H}$ is a vector of size p. Then, let us assume that $R_{i,t,t+H}$ is the observed return on asset i

13 See https://fred.stlouisfed.org/.

(that can also be a strategy) over the period going from t to $t + H$. A linear connection between the two variables can be built using the following regression:

$$R_{i,t,t+H} = \alpha + \beta X_{t,t+H} + \epsilon_t, \qquad [5.7]$$

where α and β are, respectively, the intercept and the slope coefficients that relate both variables and ϵ_t is the usual scaled random variable, likely to be chosen to be distributed following a Gaussian distribution for estimation consistency reasons. Now, given that H can be large, there can be a significant overlap from $X_{t,t+H}$ and $X_{t+1,t+H+1}$, for example. A cleaner way to run such a regression is use a block-bootstrap approach: generating random starting investment dates t and then computing the associated returns and macroeconomic condition level over the H periods following this starting date. Replicating this experiment a large number of times will provide its users with a better representation of the law of motion embedded in the data. Such estimation results are presented in Tables 5.5 and 5.6.

	Risk parity	Carry	Trend following	S&P 500	US bonds	Dollar
1 day	0.10%	0.03%	0.07%	0.07%	0.06%	0.07%
1 month	0.15%	0.15%	0.07%	0.84%	1.08%	0.15%
3 months	2.20%	0.42%	0.07%	4.37%	3.48%	0.25%
6 months	4.61%	0.92%	0.08%	8.79%	7.15%	0.88%
1 year	9.99%	3.06%	0.30%	17.27%	17.79%	2.40%
2 years	25.02%	9.97%	8.61%	31.65%	25.06%	5.60%

Table 5.5. *R^2 per strategy obtained from a regression on economic condition indices as given in equation [5.7]*

Coefficient	Risk parity	Carry	Trend following	S&P 500	US bonds	Dollar
α	0.00017*	–0.00001*	0.00029*	0	0.00036*	–0.00004*
β_{Growth}	0.0028*	0.00216*	0.00001	0.00291*	–0.00116*	0.0006*
$\beta_{\text{Inflation}}$	–0.00134*	–0.00158*	–0.00011	–0.00202*	0.00283*	–0.00089*
$\beta_{\text{Monetary conditions}}$	–0.00082*	–0.00009*	0.0002*	–0.00081*	0.00061*	–0.00042*

Table 5.6. *Beta coefficient obtained from the regression presented in equation [5.7] in the case of a one-year holding period*

For the sake of comparison, results have been computed both in the case of the previous quantitative strategies and in the case of three more traditional assets: the returns on US stocks obtained from the S&P 500 Index, the returns on a Treasury Bond Index and, finally, the returns on the US dollar, using a Trade-Weighted Index. Table 5.5 shows the term structure of R^2 obtained from the regression of returns on the three previous economic condition indices using equation [5.7]. In the case of traditional assets such as equities or bonds, the regressions show a R^2 that is an increasing function of the holding period: starting from a very low R^2 for a holding period of a month, it then increases until it reaches a level of about 25 to 30%. When using growth in the industrial production as a fundamental data, [BOO 16] finds even higher readings. The US dollar on the contrary does seem to exhibit a strong connection to the three economic condition indices. Turning to the three strategies, there are significant differences between the three of them: on the one hand, the risk parity strategy shows R^2 that are only slightly weaker than those obtained with the S&P 500. For 2 years, on the one hand, the risk parity strategy shows R^2 that are only slightly weaker than those obtained with the S&P 500. For a 2-year holding period, the regression's R^2 reaches 25%, that compares well with the S&P 500's 32%. On the other hand, the trend-following and the carry strategies show a rather low connection to the economic indices: for a one-year holding period, the trend-following strategy shows a R^2 of only 0.3%, when that of the carry strategy is about 3%. This does not mean that both those strategies are not connected to any economic evolution: it only shows that there are only limited evidence that the three economic condition indices are linearly connected to them. When building a systematic strategy, this type of behavior is usually welcome, when the designer of the strategy has no certainty regarding the future of economic conditions. An "all-weather" characteristic in a strategy, that is, a weak sensitivity to economic conditions over the long run is a feature to look for.

Now, turning to Table 5.6, the reader can also analyze the sign of the connection between returns and economic condition indices. The table denotes with an "*" the parameter estimates for which a Student t-test would diagnose a statistical significance at a 5% risk level. Focusing first on the equity case with one year as a holding period, the signs and statistical significance in the case of the S&P 500 and in the case of the risk-parity strategy are very similar: both of them are positively related to growth, while being negatively connected to monetary conditions and inflation. From the perspective of these results, it seems that stronger inflation and tighter monetary conditions are both detrimental to the performance of equities – should they be considered from the perspective of a market capitalization index or from a risk-based perspective. But there is more to it. Here again, this type of analysis can provide investment solutions with information that can be used to better understand and control the behavior of a strategy: here, in the case of equities, most estimates are very comparable except in the case of inflation. The risk parity strategy shows a slope coefficient that is lower than that of the S&P 500: the difference between both series of returns from this perspective is that inflation is less detrimental to risk parity strategies than to the S&P 500 Index, probably explaining part of the outperformance of the risk-based strategy. The carry strategy's estimates are equity like: their estimates have the same signs and the same significances. The commodity trend-following strategy shows a different pattern: with a one-year holding period, none of the estimates are statistically significant, but in the case of the Monetary Condition Index: when monetary conditions are getting tighter, it seems to profit to the returns on this strategy. Again, those sensitivities should be taken into consideration when conceiving a quantitative strategy as they can be the source of unexplained performance, which is only rarely positive.

5.3.3. *Nonlinearities between economic information and financial returns*

Another source of information is to be found in assessing the potential nonlinearities between returns and economic conditions. The previous regression analysis already shed some light on the relation between returns and fundamentals, but the assumed linear relationship in equation [5.7] can actually hide some tail dependence between economic conditions and returns. What is more, linearity can also hide an asymmetric relationship: extreme positive and negative environment could actually have a similar impact on market returns. Nonlinear econometrics can bring an answer to those questions. Despite the fact that this type of econometric model can be mathematically quite complex, some of its estimators are actually simple to program and to use.

Let X_t be a variable used to explain Y_t, with a relation such that:

$$Y_t = f(X_t) + \epsilon_t, \quad [5.8]$$

where ϵ_t is a uniform $(0,1)$ i.i.d. random variable. Again, we assume that we have at hand T of observations $((x_t, y_t))_{t \in [1;T]}$ of (X_t, Y_t). The function $f(.)$ is unknown and needs to be approximated. One of the most commonly used non-parametric estimates to $f(.)$ is the Nadaraya–Watson estimator, named after the work of [NAD 64] and [WAT 64], and also known as kernel regression. Let $K(.)$ be the kernel function, which is going to play the role of a weighting function. Then, $f(.)$ can be expressed in the neighborhood of x_0 as follows:

$$f(x_0) = \frac{\sum_{t=1}^{T} K(x_t - x_0) y_t}{\sum_{t=1}^{N} K(x_t - x_0)}, \quad [5.9]$$

where T is the total number of observations. Now, it should be clear to the reader that $K(.)$ is a weight function, and that it should be selected such that it is also a distance function: when x_t is very close to x_0, $K(x_t - x_0)$ should be higher than that when it is very different from it. One of the most used specifications for $K(.)$ is the distribution function of a Gaussian random variable:

$$K(z, h) = \frac{1}{\sqrt{2\pi}h} \exp\left(-\frac{1}{2}\frac{z^2}{h^2}\right), \quad [5.10]$$

where h is a smoothing parameter to the non-parametric regression[14]. [JAC 00] recommends to select h according to:

$$h = \frac{1.8\sigma}{\sqrt[5]{T}}, \quad [5.11]$$

14 h is actually the standard deviation parameter in the Gaussian distribution function.

where σ is the standard deviation of x_t, replaced in empirical experiments by its empirical estimate. Using the block-bootstrap methodology detailed previously, (X_t) is set to be the economic condition indices built previously and (Y_t) the returns on the three quantitative strategies detailed above. Figures 5.6, 5.7 and 5.8 present non-parametric estimates, respectively, relating for various holding periods:

– the relation between the growth economic index and the returns on the carry strategy;

– the relation between the inflation economic index and the returns on the equity risk parity strategy;

– the relation between the monetary condition economic index and the returns on the trend-following strategy.

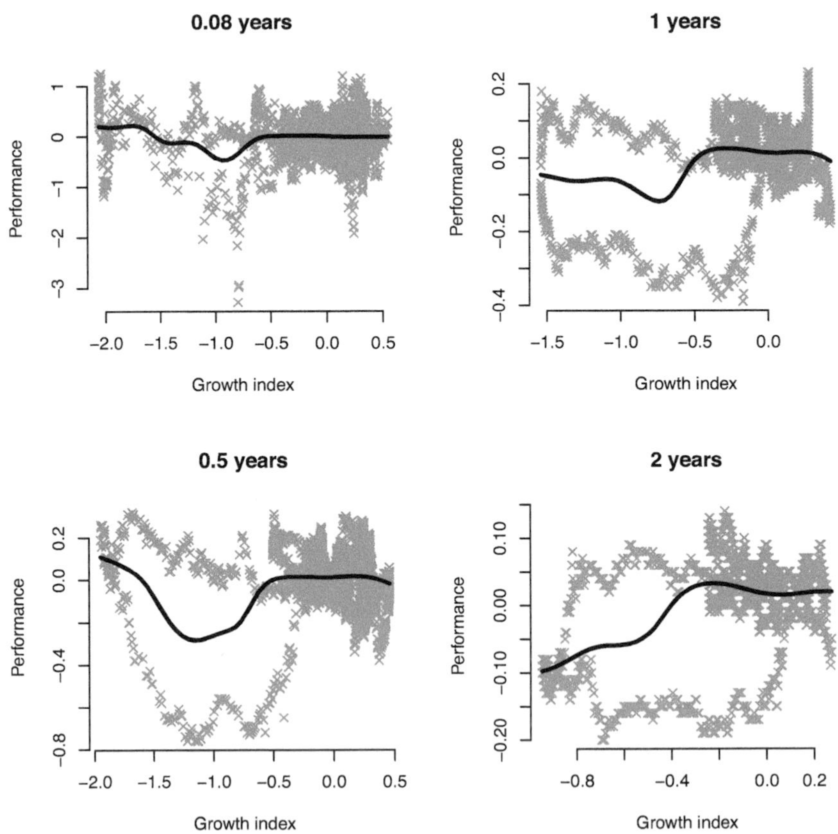

Figure 5.6. *Nonlinear estimation of the relation between returns on the carry strategy and the growth economic condition index*

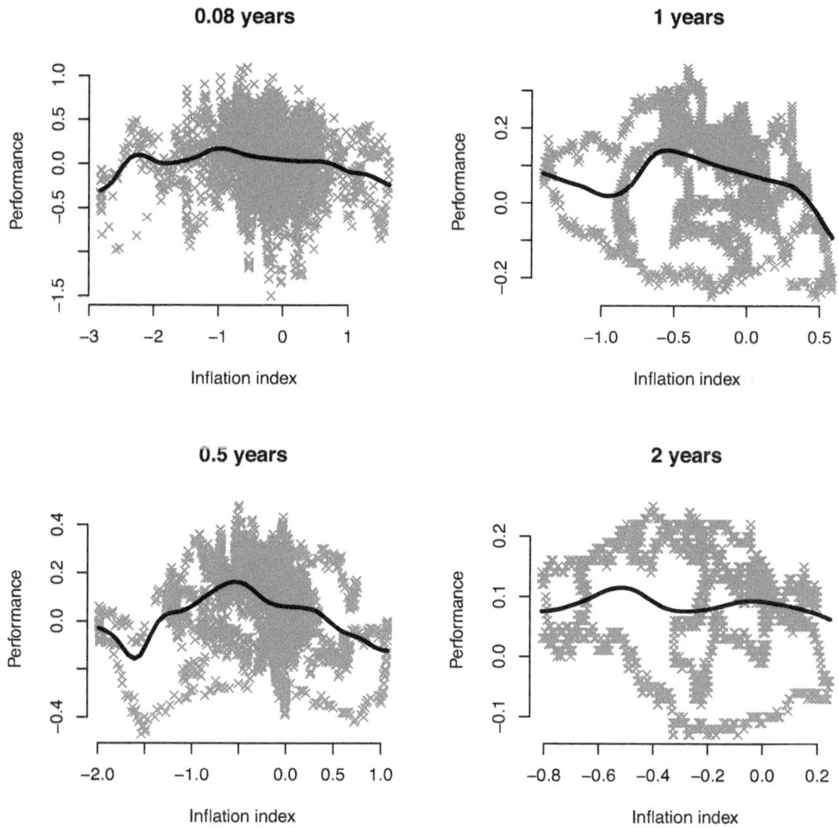

Figure 5.7. *Nonlinear estimation of the relation between returns on the equity risk parity strategy and the inflation economic condition index*

Beyond the pieces of evidence already collected using the previous linear regressions, more information can be obtained from each of these graphs. First, in the case of growth and the carry strategy for a 2-year holding period, an asymmetric relation appears: returns on a carry strategy seem to be weekly related to growth when the indicator is positive. When it is negative, a negative relationship appears on the graph: the more negative the growth index, the more negative the returns on the carry strategy. The positive relationship diagnosed in the previous section actually seems to be an asymmetric one. Figure 5.7 shows different kinds of empirical evidence about the connection between inflation and equity risk parity strategies: for a 6-month holding period, the estimates seem to draw a tent-shaped relationship. When the inflation index is around –0.5, the strategy seems to deliver positive returns. As it goes to more extreme readings, the returns on the strategy become more and more negative. Overall, the relationship remains negative (the tent-shaped estimates remain overall downward sloping), but it exhibits an empirical asymmetry that must also be taken into consideration. Finally, Figure 5.8 provides some insight into the nature of the connection between the trend-following strategy and monetary conditions. For a 2-year holding period, the non-parametric estimate also shows an asymmetric V shape: extremely loose monetary conditions seem to be profitable to trend-following strategies such as extremely tight ones. Again, the overall relationship remains a positive one, but the linear approximation looks rather poor from this angle: very tight and very loose monetary policies seem to almost equally profit to commodity trend-following strategies[15].

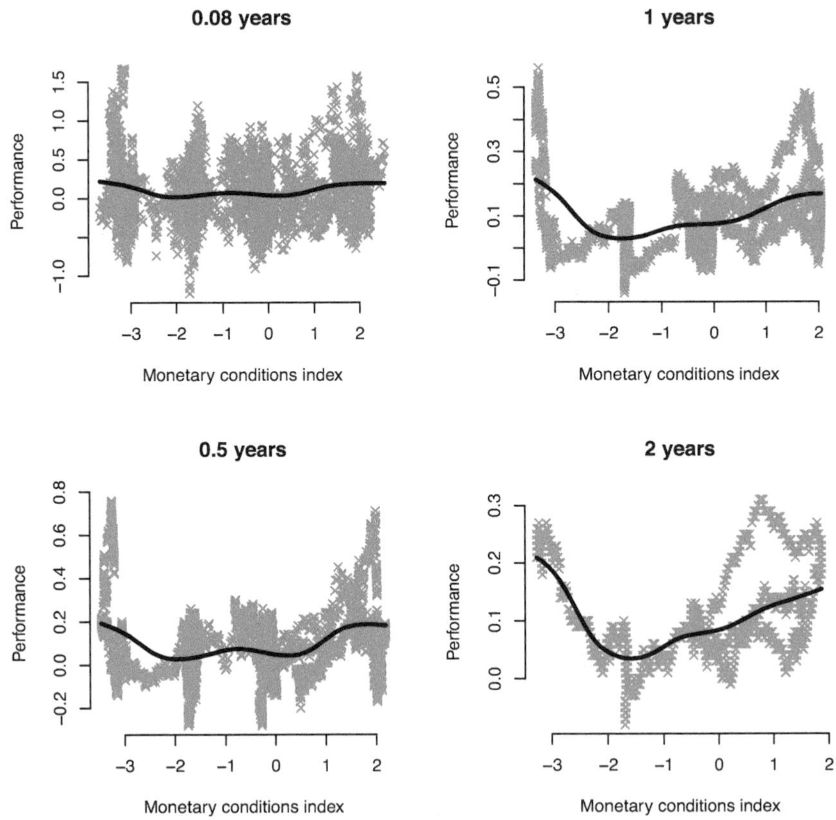

Figure 5.8. *Nonlinear estimation of the relation between returns on the trend-following strategy and the Monetary Condition Index*

15 They are typically periods corresponding to either an extreme commodity rally, as in the oil bull market of 2007–2008, or an extreme collapse, as in the aftermath of the 2008 crisis.

The returns on these three very common strategies therefore exhibit selected macroeconomic sensitivities to which a portfolio manager should be sensitive. These sensitivities can then be controlled by monitoring each of the macroeconomic risk factors, using indices similar to those presented in this chapter, as least from a hedging perspective. Now, there is a last potential approach to understanding how these strategies are influenced by economic information by looking at how this information is incorporated into the strategies' returns. There is a large amount of literature assessing how economic news impacts returns on a large set of returns. The next section will review this literature before presenting evidence on how the disclosure of economic information influences the three quantitative strategies.

5.4. The impact of economic information on a strategy's performance

The disclosure of information and its impact on markets has been a very early focus of the financial academic literature. Pieces of information regarding the future of a company or about the overall evolution of growth or inflation around the world make the daily news of most market participants. Here, we will focus on the later: our quantitative strategies include a large number of assets and the diversification effects across them significantly weaken the impact of company-specific news. Early literature focused on the impact of news on interest rates and bond prices, as seen in [URI 81], [HAR 84], [EDE 93], [EDI 96], [FLE 97], [FLE 99], [FLE 01a], [BAL 01] or, more recently, [GUÉ 09]. Most of these articles find that a significant departure between actual and expected economic figures can lead to rather violent changes in interest rates. While most of this literature is US focused, there are other contributions focusing on European assets, such as [EHR 02], [GOL 03a] and [BRI 08]. Other types of assets have also been analyzed, with similar findings: economic information can have a tremendous influence on financial assets. In the case of volatility, see, for example, how monetary policy announcements impact implied volatilities in [BRI 06]. [CHE 14a] provides a lengthy literature review in the case of commodities and presents evidence showing that commodities are also reacting to economic news, especially during periods of recession. This literature is now abundant, and we do not intend to provide the reader with an extended literature review. However, little has been done so far to try to assess how these announcements impact quantitative strategies: this section will provide an initial overview in that direction.

5.4.1. *The integration of surprises in economic information in asset prices*

In this section, we intend to measure how positive or negative surprises observed when selected economic figures are disclosed impact the three previous quantitative strategies. Let r_t be the return at date t of a given strategy. Let F_T^i be the forecast at time t for the ith economic figure: financial information providers such as Bloomberg© typically provide their users with the result of a survey conducted among economists about upcoming economic figures. For example, a couple of days before the publication of the US GDP figure, a survey is conducted and then the median of this survey is used as a "market consensus", that is, the forecast F_t^i. Then, on the day of the publication of the GDP numbers, the actual number A_t^i is disclosed. Empirical investigations define the "surprise" in this publication as the difference between A_t^i and F_t^i. The time series of these differences are usually scaled, that is , they are divided by their standard deviation in order to make surprises comparable across economic figures. Let us define the surprises S_t^i the following way:

$$S_t^i = \frac{A_t^i - F_t^i}{\sigma(i)}, \qquad [5.12]$$

where $\sigma(i)$ is the standard deviation associated with the ith surprise. In what follows, we will run OLS regressions, to draw a linear relationship between returns and the economic surprises. The surprises that we intend on using are mainly US focused, as US data have been consistently found to have an impact on assets' returns in the literature. The list of the news is as follows: the US Unemployment Rate, the US Consumer Sentiment, the German Industrial Production, the US Initial Jobless Claims, the US Conference Board Consumer Confidence Index, the US Construction Spendings, the European Unemployment Rate, the US Capacity Utilization Rate, the US Industrial Production, the European Economic Sentiment Index, the US Building Permits, the Eurozone Retail Sales, the US Chicago Business Barometer, the US Fed Consumer Credit Index, the US Leading Index, the US Job creation Payroll Survey, the German IFO, the European Industrial Construction Figures, the US Retail Sales, the US Phili Fed Survey and, finally, the US ISM. This is a total of 21 economic news, over a period that started roughly in 1999 and ends in 2016.

Using this list of news indexed by the index i, we will run the following regression:

$$r_{t^{(i)}} = \alpha + \beta s_{t^{(i)}}^i + \epsilon_{t^{(i)}}^i, \qquad [5.13]$$

where $t^{(i)}$ are the dates for which there has been an announcement regarding the ith series of economic data, $s_{t^{(i)}}^i$ is the observed value of S_t^i at the time of release $t = t^{(i)}$, r_t is the observed return of a strategy or of an index, which we want to explain with economic series, and ϵ_t is again a i.i.d. centered, reduced Gaussian variable.

5.4.2. *An analysis of the impact of economic news on each strategy*

The estimation of equation [5.13] will be done in two ways. First, a global estimation will be performed, using the full sample available and making it possible then to assess which economic figure should be watched when having to manage one of the three quantitative strategies investigated here. Then, a shorter term analysis will be performed, using rolling estimates to assess whether the news can impact the strategies only during certain periods of time: in the case of commodities, for example, [CHE 14a] shows how economic news typically impacts more commodity markets during US recession periods than during US expansion periods.

	Risk parity	Carry	Trend following	S&P 500	Bonds	Dollar
Retail Sales	0.1076**	0.0965**	–0.0763	0.132**	–0.2559**	0.0902*
Construction Spendings	–0.0092	–0.0012	–0.0122	–0.0271	0.0996	9e–04
Conference Board Consumer Confidence	–0.0208	–0.1511**	0.0668	–0.0433	–0.102**	0.0819*
Leading Index	0.0494	0.1179**	–0.0703	0.0273	–0.0647	0.0581
EC Economic Sentiment	0.011	–0.0235	0.0319	–0.0468	–0.0882	0.0457
European Industrial Construction	0.0796	0.102**	0.0686	0.0672	–0.0378	–0.161**
Eurozone Retail Sales	0.0405	0.0027	0.0041	0.0203	–0.0215	–0.0264
European Unemployment Rate	0.0012	–0.0292	–0.0603	0.0206	–0.0341	0.138**
Fed Consumer Credit	0.0426	0.0343	0.0355	0.0444	0.065	–0.0138
German Industrial Production	–0.0229	–0.0695	–0.0188	–0.0672	–0.0732	–0.047
IFO	0.0644	0.0391	0.0288	0.0212	–0.0647	–0.0748
US ISM	0.1483**	0.0237	–0.0039	0.1019*	–0.3078**	0.1708**
Chicago Business Barometer	0.0415	–0.0072	0.0506	0.0264	–0.2136**	0.0859*
Phili Fed Survey	0.1479**	0.0755	–0.0949**	0.0895*	–0.1806**	–0.0104
Building Permits	0.0114	0.0384	0.1199**	0.0554	–0.133**	0.109**
US unemployment rate	–0.0516	–0.0254	0.0301	0.0064	–0.023	–0.1132*
US Consumer Sentiment	–0.0267	0.1038**	–0.0242	–0.0379	–0.025	–0.0181
Capacity Utilization	0.0056	–0.0701	–0.0349	0.012	–0.1281**	0.0414
Job Creation Payroll Survey	0.0516	4e–04	0.035	–0.01	–0.4275**	0.2914**
Industrial Production	0.0062	–0.0927**	0.0025	–0.0354	–0.0791	0.0285
Initial Jobless Claims	–0.0212	–0.0229	0.023	–0.0374	0.1399**	–0.01

Table 5.7. *Estimated slopes when running the regression of equation [5.13]. "*" indicates a statistical significance at a 10% risk level and "**" indicates a statistical significance at a 5% risk level*

5.4.2.1. *Overall sample analysis*

Table 5.7 provides the results obtained for the three key strategies, alongside results for the returns on the V, a US Treasury Bond Index and returns on the US dollar. In Table 5.7, the explained returns are in columns, while each line represents an explicative variable. First of all, there is an obviously low number of surprises that show a statistical significance over the period covered here. The risk parity strategy shows a reaction to only two of them, five of them in the case of the carry strategy and two of them in the case of the trend-following strategy. The S&P 500 shows a reaction to two of them, the bond index to 9 of them and the Dollar to 8 of them. These quantitative strategies show here one of their advantages when compared with standard assets: a lower sensitivity to economic news. Now, when comparing the risk parity strategy to the S&P 500 Index, both of them react to the same news, but not with the same intensity: the risk parity strategy has a lower positive sensitivity to US retail sales, but has a stronger sensitivity to the US industrial surveys that are the ISM and Phili Fed surveys. The composition of the strategy versus the S&P 500 must be the reason for that. The carry strategy has a positive sensitivity to retail sales, the leading index and US consumer confidence but a negative one to US industrial production and Conference Board Consumer Confidence. Finally, the trend-following strategy exhibits a positive reaction to US building permits and a negative one to the Phili Fed survey. Now, this appeal of lower than standard assets' sensitivity to economic news might be mitigated when running a rolling regression: the sample used here covers two very different periods in terms of monetary policy. The QE period must have had an impact on these sensitivities.

5.4.2.2. *Rolling analysis*

Having highlighted that the three strategies exhibit lower sensitivities to economic news than bonds and exchange rates, this part of this section will now provide information regarding how stable this finding can be. Using the very same data set as for the previous section, we now run the regression using a rolling window of four years. Given that most of the economic news are monthly news, this gives a rolling sample of 48 observations and follows the methodology used in [CHE 14a]. In this article, the authors show how returns on commodities display a low sensitivity to economic news over the long run, but over shorter periods of time how this sensitivity can rise sharply, weakening the celebrated decorrelation obtained from commodities precisely over periods, over which investors need it the most – market downturns. Figure 5.9 shows one of the outcomes of this methodology: it charts the percentage of all the news (within the spectrum of the 21 selected news), for which a 5% significance is found for the slope parameter in equation [5.13]. It also compares this rolling percentage with its value using the long-term results discussed previously.

The cases of the risk parity and the trend-following strategies are of the utmost importance for investment managers willing to use such quantitative strategies: despite the low long-term percentage of news to which the strategies have reacted, this percentage can substantially increase during particular periods. In the case of the risk parity strategy, this percentage actually varies between 0 and 25% over the 2007–2016 period – quite a change in sensitivities. In the case of the trend-following strategy, it also ranges within similar bounds. Figure 5.10 illustrates the difference between the percentages of news with a statistically significant impact on the long run versus using the rolling estimation scheme: for these two strategies, the average number of news increases when running the rolling regression. This implies that connecting economic news and the returns on those strategies can prove to be complex: they show a tendency to react to certain news over shorter periods of time that a long run analysis fails at highlighting. Finally, in the case of the carry strategy, its connection to economic news is somewhat more stable, and stronger in the meantime as discussed previously. Carry strategies exhibit a sensitivity to economic news that is in line with a previous diagnosis regarding the connection between this strategy and the economic cycle.

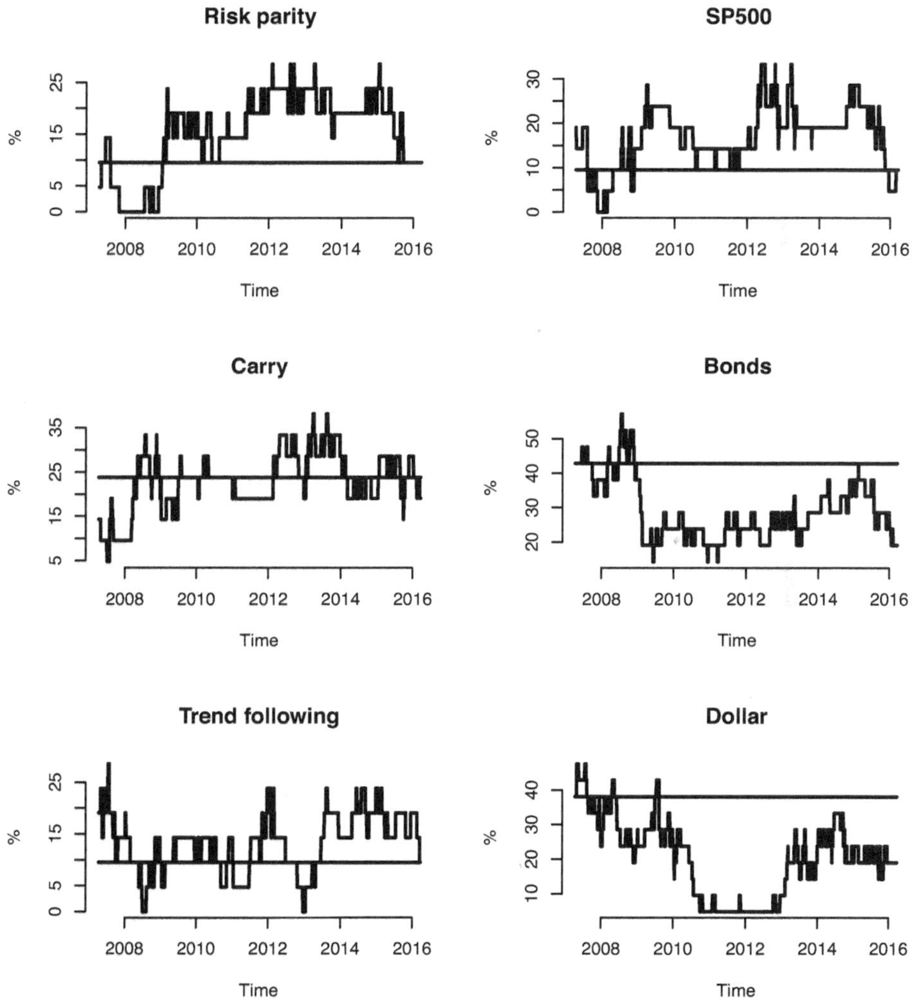

Figure 5.9. *Percentage of news that is statistically significant for rolling regressions over 4-year periods following equation [5.7]*

5.4.2.3. *Some final words*

Quantitative strategies are often backtested and assessed using historical performance metrics: their realized performance, their Sharpe ratio or their maximum drawdown. This chapter tried to gather evidence that it should not be the only assessment to be run prior to the launch of a new strategy or to its inclusion in a broader investment process. The three simple but yet very common strategies investigated here – the risk parity strategy, the currency carry strategy and the commodity trend-following strategy – exhibit selected economic sensitivities. In the case of the risk parity strategy, its connection to recessions and expansion was quite clear – not to mention the connection between the level of the economic indices and the shape of the returns on this strategy. This is only one example among the three and a deeper discussion for each of them could be detailed here – at the cost of making this chapter heavier than it already is. This chapter has been more shaped in a way that any reader with quantitative skills could be using the methodology presented here to run tests on his or her own: the economic dimension of quantitative strategies is not to be ignored.

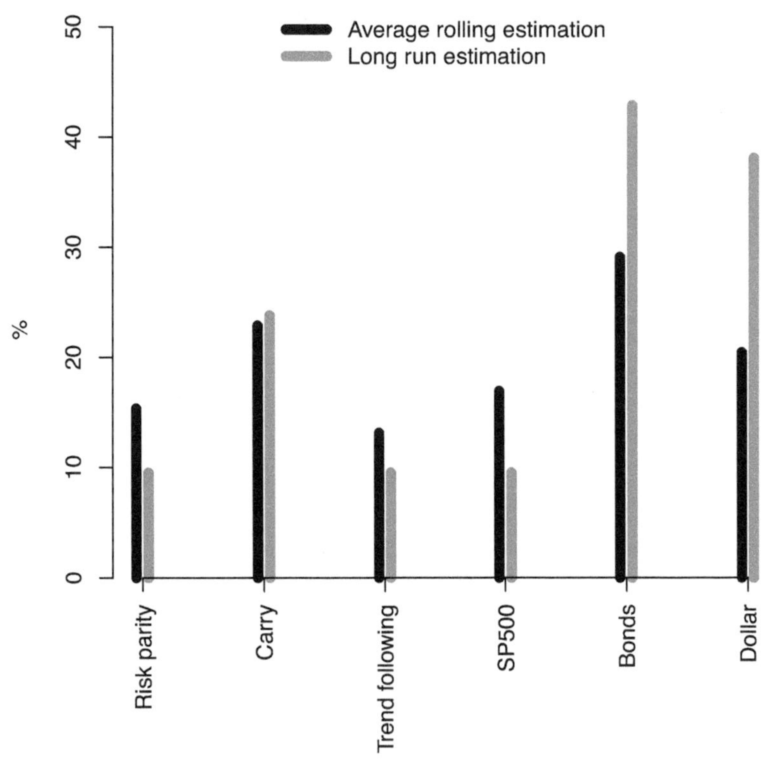

Figure 5.10. *Comparison between the average percentage of news that is statistically significant for rolling regressions versus over the long run*

Appendix

A.1. Useful formulas

A.1.1. *Frobenius norm*

Let M be an $N \times K$ real-valued matrix. The *Frobenius norm* $||M||_F$ of M is computed as the square root of the sum of squared values of the elements of M, which is:

$$||M||_F = \sqrt{\sum_{i=1}^{N} \sum_{j=1}^{K} M_{i,j}^2}.$$

If M' is the transpose matrix of M, then we also have:

$$||M||_F = \sqrt{Tr(MM')}.$$

A.1.2. *Sherman-Morrison-Woodbury formula*

The Woodbury formula (see [WOO 49]) helps to obtain the inverse of a matrix M_0 that decomposes:

$$M_0 = M + PDR,$$

where Ω and M are the $N \times N$ matrices, P is $N \times Q$, R is $Q \times N$ and D is $N \times N$. In this case, we have:

$$(M + PDR)^{-1} = M^{-1} - M^{-1}P(D^{-1} + RM^{-1}P)^{-1}RM^{-1}.$$

The easiest way to prove it is to compute directly:

$$\begin{aligned}
&(M+PDR)(M^{-1}-M^{-1}P(D^{-1}+RM^{-1}P)^{-1}RM^{-1}) \\
&= I_N + PDRM^{-1} - P(D^{-1}+RM^{-1}P)^{-1}RM^{-1} \\
&\quad -PDRM^{-1}P(D^{-1}+RM^{-1}P)^{-1}RM^{-1} \\
&= I_N + PDRM^{-1} - (P+PDRM^{-1}P)(D^{-1}+RM^{-1}P)^{-1}RM^{-1} \\
&= I_N + PDRM^{-1} - PD(D^{-1}+RM^{-1}P)(D^{-1}+RM^{-1}P)^{-1}RM^{-1} \\
&= I_N + PDRM^{-1} - PDRM^{-1} \\
&= I_N. \qquad [A.1]
\end{aligned}$$

A.2. Diversification measures

Following the individual weights of assets in a portfolio is difficult. It has been quite usual in practice to develop heuristics to monitor and study the weights of a portfolio within one scalar criterion. We briefly explore here various diversification measures. This is useful since it allows us to aggregate in one single figure the information of dispersion or of concentration of a N-dimensional vector of weights w. The *Herfindahl index* is one of the most commonly computed. If we note it as D_H we compute it in the following way:

$$D_H = 1 - w'w = 1 - \sum_{i=1}^{N} w_i^2.$$

To measure a dispersion towards a $1/N$ prior, we may also define the *modified Herfindahl index*:

$$D_{MH} = 1 - \frac{\sum_i w_i^2 - \frac{1}{N}}{1 - \frac{1}{N}}.$$

Rather than a quantity between 0 and 1, we may seek an extensive quantity homogeneous to the number of assets. The *effective number* of assets $N_{eff} \leq N$ may be of help. The lower the quantity, the lower the degrees of freedom of the portfolio. The number of effective assets may be computed as the *inverse Herfindahl index*. This measure is interesting since it may account for positive and negative weights, lies is $[0; N]$, and in fact allows monitoring of how we are effectively invested in the N assets:

$$N_{eff} = \left[\frac{\sum_i w_i^2}{(\sum_i |w_i|)^2}\right]^{-1}.$$

There are of course other measures of diversification, and successful ones use entropy. Entropy measures are tailored for situations where $w_i \geq 0$ for each asset i. The use of entropy for long-only portfolios has been proposed and used, for instance, in [BER 08]:

$$D_E = -\sum_i w_i log(w_i).$$

D_E vanishes for fully concentrated portfolios concentrated in one single asset and is bounded by a maximum value of $log(N)$ for an equal-weighted portfolio and is directly inspired from the expression of the Shannon entropy. [HAN 77] generalized this kind of measure by introducing a power diversification measure D_γ parametrized by a real number $\gamma > 0$ that writes:

$$D_\gamma = -(\sum_{i=1}^{n} w_i^\gamma)^{\frac{1}{\gamma-1}},$$

with $\gamma > 0$. We may remark that $D^2 = D_H - 1$.

Finally, all those measures do not account for correlations and volatilities. They only account for a static dispersion in weights. To take into account those correlation effects, the *differential diversification measure* D_D has been proposed in the academic work of [STE 10]:

$$D_D = \sum_i w_i \sqrt{\Sigma_{ii}} - \sqrt{w'\Sigma w}.$$

The use of such a measure is surprisingly rare, as it should quite naturally be of interest in any portfolio monitoring.

REMARK A.1.– As popularized by [CRE 09], the measure of *Active Shares* allows us to derive a quantity to monitor how far a portfolio is from a benchmark B of weights $(w_i^B)_{i=1,\ldots,N}$. The Active Shares are simply computed as:

$$AS = \frac{1}{2}\sum_{i=1}^{N} |w_i - w_i^B|.$$

A.3. A brief introduction to inverse problems

Inverse problems are at the heart of many scientific fields ranging from astronomy to quantum physics. We present here the minimal yet necessary mathematical background to understand and use them in a financial context, since a complete mathematical presentation would be impossible. We strongly recommend referring to major references as [ENG 96], [KRE 99] and [KAL 08] for an in-depth understanding of those subtle concepts.

A.3.1. *Mathematical background*

A.3.1.1. *Statistical motivation*

Suppose that we dispose of indirect observations y of a random object Y that arise as the transformations of an object of interest f that we wish to identify as our final object of interest. This object f is usually a vector or a function. The transformations on f are represented by the application of an operator $T : \mathcal{E} \to \mathcal{F}$ to f, where $\mathcal{E}$ and $\mathcal{F}$ are two Hilbert spaces[1]:

$$Tf = y. \qquad [A.2]$$

We wish to estimate f after having observed y, possibly through noisy observations. The difficulty may come from what we really know, observe or have to estimate: either T, y or both, may be unknown. A classical dichotomy between well-posed and ill-posed inverse problem has been stated by Hadamard. A problem is well-posed if three conditions are fulfilled:

1) there is at least one solution to the problem (*existence*);

2) this solution is unique (*unicity*);

3) the solution f depends continuously of the data y (*stability*).

If one of those conditions is not met, the problem is said to be *ill-posed*. The two first conditions are not usually difficult to obtain but the last condition may be the hardest to verify in practice. Historically, solutions were believed to always depend continuously on the data. In cases of instability, the blame was put on the mathematical model, assumed to be inappropriate. As soon as y is observed, the existence of a solution is not the main obstacle. The unicity of the solution is less easy to deal with. If $\text{Ker}(T) \neq \{0\}$ and f_0 is a solution, each $f_\epsilon \in \text{Ker}(T)\backslash\{0\}$ is such that $f_0 + f_\epsilon$ is the solution of equation A.2 different from f_0. To assess unicity, we first check the statistical conditions under which T is effectively injective. Alternatively, we can add some conditions or information on the desired solution. The last and major challenge remains the stability of the solution. Instability is materialized by the fact that as soon as T^{-1} is unbounded any small perturbation in $y \to y + \delta$ is dramatically amplified. As the solution is estimated through $T^{-1}(y + \delta)$, if we do not have any control of δ the estimated solution may be far different from the true one. The definition of the statistical properties of the noise is then a topic of utmost importance. Depending on the problem, this perturbation may appear not only in y but also in T.

1 See, for example, [ENG 96]. Hilbert spaces are Banach spaces endowed with a norm issued from a scalar product. $\mathbb{R}^N$ is a simple example of Hilbert space.

A.3.1.2. *Concepts and operators*

A.3.1.2.1. Linear problems

Inverse problems may be either linear or non-linear, depending on T. Linear problems are the most simple way to understand ill-posed inverse problems, but may also be at the heart of the resolution of non-linear problems. Let us suppose that T is a linear operator between two Hilbert spaces $T : \mathcal{E} \to \mathcal{F}$. T is assumed to be known and bounded. The problem is estimating f from a noisy version of equation [A.2]: $Tf = y + \delta$, where δ is a perturbative error but only $y + \delta$ is observed. The case of δ being deterministic has been handled in [TIK 63] and [TIK 77]. The case where δ is considered as stochastic is called a *statistical inverse problem*. The inversion of T is then at the heart of the control of the stability of the solution. Examining the spectrum of the operator (when it exists and may be obtained) will allow in particular a precise diagnosis of the potential stability of the problem.

A.3.1.2.2. Adjoint operator

We will mainly focus on linear operators, and a useful notion to define in our context is the concept of *adjoint operators*. Let $T : \mathcal{E} \to \mathcal{F}$ be an operator between two Hilbert spaces endowed with respective scalar products $< .,. >_{\mathcal{E}}$ and $< .,. >_{\mathcal{F}}$. If T is bounded, then[2] there exists a linear operator $T^* : \mathcal{F} \to \mathcal{E}$ such that for each $(\phi, \psi) \in \mathcal{E} \times \mathcal{F}$ we have:

$$< T\phi, \psi >_{\mathcal{F}} = < \phi, T^*\psi >_{\mathcal{E}} .$$

Operator T^* is called the *adjoint operator* of T and is always uniquely determined and bounded, such that $||T||_{\mathcal{E}} = ||T^*||_{\mathcal{F}}$. Moreover, the Riesz theorem (see [ENG 96]) ensures that the adjoint operator always exists in Hilbert spaces. A *self-adjoint operator* is an operator such that $T = T^*$ (in this case $\mathcal{E} = \mathcal{F}$). In addition, all the eigenvalues of a self-adjoint operator are real and the relative eigenfunctions are mutually orthogonal. The stream of eigenvalues is called the *spectrum* $Sp(T)$ of the operator. In the most general case, it may be of infinite size and potentially uncountable. In finite dimension, where linear operators are represented by the matrices, if M represents the operator T, then the transpose matrix M' represents the action of the adjoint operator T^*.

A.3.1.2.3. Compact operators

An operator $K : \mathcal{E} \to \mathcal{F}$ is said to be *compact* between two Hilbert spaces $\mathcal{E}$ and $\mathcal{F}$ as soon as $T(\mathcal{B}_{\mathcal{E}})$ is relatively compact in $\mathcal{F}$ (with $\mathcal{B}_{\mathcal{E}}$ being $\{x \in \mathcal{E} | ||x|| \leq 1\}$), i.e. $\overline{T(\mathcal{B}_{\mathcal{E}})}$ is compact in $\mathcal{F}$. Another definition is that for any bounded sequence $\{x_n\}$ of $\mathcal{E}^{\mathbb{N}}$, $\{Tx_n\}$ has converging subsequences in $\mathcal{F}$. This is a topological definition and we will see that such operators may be characterized by spectral properties that are very

2 See [CAR 03].

interesting with real interest in practice. Without further notice, the generic operator T will be noted K in the following when $T = K$ is assumed to be compact.

In particular, K compact is equivalent to K^*, KK^* or also to K^*K compact. It implies also that K is continuous and bounded (which becomes an equivalence in the case where K is linear).

A.3.1.2.4. Singular value decomposition

In finite dimensions an operator is one-to-one as soon as it is surjective. So, the injectivity is the only notion to check in order to assess the invertibility of the operator. In infinite dimensions however, a bounded operator may be surjective without being injective and reciprocally. The study of compact operators is consequently more thrilling in infinite dimension. When $dim(\mathcal{E}) = \infty$, then for $T = K$ compact, $0 \in Sp(K)$, where $Sp(K)$ is the spectrum of K, and we have either one of the three situations (see [ENG 96]):

1) $Sp(K) = \{0\}$;

2) $Sp(K)$ is finite;

3) $Sp(K)$ is a sequence that tends to 0.

When $dim(\mathcal{E}) = +\infty$ and K is self-adjoint (still compact, linear), its eigensystem exists and is characterized by the sequence (λ_n, ϕ_n) of eigenvalues λ_n and eigenvectors such that $K\phi_n = \lambda_n\phi_n \quad \forall n \in \mathbb{N}$. K may be rewritten:

$$K\phi = \sum_{n=1}^{\infty} \lambda_n < \phi.\phi_n > \phi_n.$$

Unfortunately, such an eigensystem do not exist for an operator K which is not self-adjoint. The singular system generalizes this definition in the most general case. Let us consider again $K : \mathcal{E} \rightarrow \mathcal{F}$ a compact operator, linear, between two Hilbert spaces. K is not compulsory self-adjoint, but KK^* and K^*K are self-adjoint and positive in any case. This means in particular that their eigenvalues are all non-negative. The square roots of the eigenvalues of K^*K are the *singular values*. A compact operator is injective if and only if all its singular values are different from 0. If it is the case, 0 is not an eigenvalue of K^*K but may be one of KK^*. $(\lambda_j, \phi_j, \psi_j)$ is called a *singular system*.

A.3.1.2.5. Why compact operators?

Why are compact operators so important? For several reasons, both empirical and theoretical. First, numerous problems in econometrics appear to be inverse ones with underlying operators that appear to be compact. A precise mathematical description of linear econometric inverse problems is provided in [CAR 03], including the generalized method of moments, deconvolution, instrumental variables or general additive regression models.

In addition to their frequent representativeness in econometrics and statistics, the second reason is more theoretical and is linked to the many useful spectral properties they have. First, compact operators have a *discrete spectrum*, even in the case of infinite dimension spaces. If K is both compact and self-adjoint, the set of its eigenvalues (λ_j) is countable, and in infinite dimensions, if K has infinitely many eigenvalues such that if they are ranked in descending absolute order:

$$|\lambda_1| > |\lambda_2| > ... \quad \text{and} \quad lim_{j \to \infty} \lambda_j = 0.$$

If $\mathcal{K}(\mathcal{E}, \mathcal{F})$ is the vector space of compact operators, $\mathcal{K}(\mathcal{E}, \mathcal{F})$ is closed in the space of linear operators $\mathcal{L}(\mathcal{E}, \mathcal{F})$ and *contains all the finite rank operators*. A useful property if $\mathcal{F}$ is a Hilbert space, any compact operator $K : \mathcal{E} \longrightarrow \mathcal{F}$ is limit in $\mathcal{L}(\mathcal{E}, \mathcal{F})$ of a sequence of operators of finite rank. This property is the source of major regularization techniques that will be exposed later. This means that any compact operator, even in infinite dimension, is the limit of a sequence of operators of finite dimensional range. A sequence of finite dimensional operators could approach K using an increasing sequence of the spectrum of K.

A.3.1.2.6. Ill-posedness and compacity

Let us suppose that we work with a linear, compact operator $K : \mathcal{E} \to \mathcal{F}$ between two Hilbert spaces. In finite dimension ($dim(\mathcal{F}) < \infty$), the injectivity of K is linked to its surjectivity: invertibility and stability of the inverse are consequently well mastered. When $dim(\mathcal{F}) = \infty$ and K is a finite range operator with $dim(\mathcal{R}(K)) = N_K < \infty$. In many examples, the singular value decomposition is known. $(\lambda_k, \phi_k, \psi_k)_{k \in \mathbb{N}}$ is finite (finite number of non-zero singular values). The inverse is then bounded and:

$$K^{-1}\phi = \sum_{k=1}^{N_K} \frac{1}{\lambda_k} < \phi, \psi_k > \phi_k.$$

In this case the problem is not ill-posed. $\mathcal{R}(K)$ is closed as a subspace of finite dimension of an infinite dimension space. When $dim(\mathcal{R}(K)) = \infty$, $\mathcal{R}(K)$ is non-closed and:

$$K^{-1}\phi = \sum_{k=1}^{\infty} \frac{1}{\lambda_k} < \phi, \psi_k > \phi_k.$$

As $\lambda_n \to_{>} 0$, we have that K is unbounded and the problem is ill-posed. Moreover, if K is compact and $dim(\mathcal{F}) = \infty$, then the problem is ill-posed if and only if $\mathcal{R}(K)$ is non-closed.

The properties of the operator are related to the well/ill-posed nature of the problem. The asymptotic behavior of the sequence $\{\lambda_k\}$ allows us to quantify the degree of ill-posedness of the problem. The faster the convergence of λ_k towards 0, the more instable the problem, and greater the ill-posedness. The terminology is usually the following: if $\lambda_j = \mathcal{O}(j^{-\beta})$, $\beta > 0$, the problem is said to be *mildly* ill-posed; if $\lambda_j = \mathcal{O}(exp(-\beta j^r))$, $\beta > 0$, $r > 0$, the problem is said to be *severely* ill-posed. The parameter β is the degree of ill-posedness of the problem.

A.3.1.3. *Least-squares solutions*

It is also important to view inverse problems through the study of best approximate solutions. If $T : \mathcal{E} \to \mathcal{F}$ is a bounded linear operator, then $f \in \mathcal{E}$ is the *best approximate solution* of A.2 if f is a least-square solution of A.2 and if:

$$||f|| = inf\{ \ ||\phi|| \mid \phi \text{ is a least square solution of A.2}\}.$$

When dealing with linear compact operators with non-closed range, A.2 is ill-posed and the best approximate solution does not depend continuously on y. The Moore-Penrose inverse[3] $T^\dagger$ of T generalizes the notion of inverse operator and is defined as the operator mapping y with the corresponding best approximate solution. An important property is that $T^\dagger$ is bounded (or continuous as linear) if and only if the range of T is closed. The Moore-Penrose inverse is closely related to inverse problems and stability topics. An important property is that for $y \in \mathcal{D}(T^\dagger)$, f is a least-squares solution of A.2 if and only if we have:

$$T^*Tf = T^*y. \qquad [A.3]$$

Equation [A.3] is called the *normal equation* and a consequence of this is that:

$$T^\dagger = (T^*T)^\dagger T^*.$$

If $(\lambda_n, \phi_n, \psi_n)$ is the singular system of K (linear and compact) we have:

$$K^\dagger y = \sum_{i=1}^{\infty} \frac{< y, \phi_n > \psi_n}{\lambda_n},$$

for $y \in \mathcal{D}(K^\dagger)$ if and only if:

$$\sum_{n=1}^{\infty} \frac{| < y, \phi_n > |^2}{\lambda_n^2} < +\infty. \qquad [A.4]$$

3 More precisely, $T^\dagger$ is the linear extension of $\overline{T}^{-1}$ to the space $\mathcal{R}(T) \dot{+} \mathcal{R}(T)^\perp = \mathcal{D}(T^\dagger)$ with: $\overline{T} := T|_{\text{Ker}(T)^\perp} \to \mathcal{R}(T)$. Thus, $\text{Ker}(T^\dagger) = \mathcal{R}(T)^\perp$.

Equation [A.4] is called the *Picard criterion* ensures that $y \in \mathcal{D}(K^\dagger)$. This criterion ensures that the Fourier coefficients $< y, \phi_n >$ decay sufficiently fast with respect to the sequence of λ_n. This is the first time that we can observe that the relative properties of the operator (through the λ_n) are intrinsically linked to y (through $< y, \phi_n >$) to control stability. The error in y that affects $< y, \phi_n >$ for small eigenvalues is greatly amplified by the $1/\lambda_n$ factor.

A.3.2. *Regularization*

A.3.2.1. *Definition*

> "*A regularization method consists of a regularization operator and a parameter choice rule which is convergent in the sense that, if the regularization parameter is chosen according to that rule, the regularized solutions converge (in norm) as the noise level tends to zero.*" — [ENG 96]

Regularization aims at solving the instability problem in ill-posed situations. The general idea is to build a sequence (in the sense of $n \to +\infty$, where n is the size of the data sample) of well-posed problems that approximate the initial ill-posed one. Regularization requires the introduction of additional parameters that quantify the distance between the regularized and the raw solution, but also requires the rules that allow choosing those parameters. The focal point in the study of the convergence of the solution is the trade-off between the precision and the regularity of the solution. In fact, any compact operator is the limit of a sequence of finite-rank operators (see [ENG 96]): this again increases the interest for compact operators. y will denote the exact data and y^δ is its observed, noisy version, where δ will quantify the noise level (in practice $\delta = \delta_n$).

Looking for the best approximate solution (see section A.3.1.3) $f^\dagger = T^\dagger y$, we will have access to $f^\delta = T^\dagger y^\delta$. The approximations will be controlled by a regularization parameter α, which will provide stable solutions f_α^δ depending continuously on y^δ. When $n \to +\infty$, we expect $\alpha = \alpha_n \to 0$ and the regularization technique to make that $f_{\alpha_n}^\delta$ converges towards the true solution. Generally speaking, the estimation of f_α^δ must take into account the nature of the operator T. In this respect, the problem $f^\delta = T^\dagger y^\delta$ is replaced by $f_\alpha^\delta = R_\alpha y^\delta$, where $\{R_\alpha\}$ is a family of continuous (but not necessarily linear) operators that depend on α. Intuitively, as the amount of noise δ diminishes, the regularizing operators chosen in $\{R_\alpha\}$ are closer to T (in a sense that has to be precised), and the estimated solution is closer to the true one.

In fact, the choice of a regularization technique and of its parameters must also be linked to the total noise δ, the observed data y^δ and the operator T. What should also be considered is *a priori* information available on the true data y and most of all on the nature/type of solution that we seek to obtain. Solutions with minimal norm may be viewed as a selection criterion among the set of solutions, thus being additional information added in the estimation procedure.

If α is chosen only according to the level of noise δ, and regardless of the observed data, $\alpha = \alpha(\delta)$ is called an *a priori parameter choice rule.* If $\alpha = \alpha(\delta, y^\delta)$ then it is an *a posteriori* parameter choice rule[4]. A family $\{R_\alpha\}$ (with R_α continuous $\forall \alpha > 0$) is a regularization for $T^\dagger$ if the convergence of R_α towards $T^\dagger$ on $\mathcal{D}(T^\dagger)$ with $\alpha \to 0$ is pointwise. It is difficult to conclude on the speed of convergence of solutions of ill-posed problems without restricting oneself to specific subsets of solutions, defined via the smoothness of the true solution. Doing this, we get a precise and accurate control on the speed of convergence of the solution. Using the dual of the operator helps to recover the problem:

$$T^*Tf = T^*y^\delta.$$

Then solution f could be computed if we could get the inverse of T^*T which cannot be obtained in ill-posed situations. Regularization procedures use functions F_α to provide an estimator $\hat{f}_\alpha$ of f defined as:

$$\hat{f}_\alpha^\delta = F_\alpha(T^*T)T^*y^\delta,$$

where F_α depends on the so-called regularization parameter.

A.3.2.2. *Some regularization methods*

We present here some regularization methods. We do not aim at being exhaustive and refer to [ENG 96] and [KAL 08] for a complete review. An ill-posed inverse problem may be solved by regularization schemes. For a compact, one-to-one operator $K : \mathcal{E} \to \mathcal{F}$ in the equation $Ka = \mu$, a regularization scheme involves a sequence of operators R^α indexed by a positive real parameter α known as regularization parameter. As approximation of the solution, we then take $a_\alpha = R^\alpha \mu$ which can be computed in a stable way since R^α is assumed to be continuous. The regularization parameter α must be chosen such that, as the noise in the data $\hat{\mu}$ goes to zero, the regularized solution a_α converges to $a^\dagger$. Regularization schemes can be of first or of second order. A regularization scheme of first order is of the form:

$$R^\alpha \mu = \sum_{j=1}^{\infty} \frac{q(\alpha, \lambda_j)}{\lambda_j} < \mu, \psi_j > \phi_j, \qquad [A.5]$$

4 Methods that depend only on y^δ but not on δ cannot be involved in convergent regularization methods. This does not imply, however, that such methods may be satisfying at a given finite δ: this must be understood in an asymptotic perspective.

with:

$$q : \mathbb{R}_+^* \times]0, ||K||] \to \mathbb{R}, \quad \forall \lambda : |q(\alpha, \lambda)| \leq c(\alpha)\lambda, \quad \lim_{\alpha \to 0} q(\alpha, \lambda) = 1, \quad c(\alpha) > 0.$$

The regularization scheme of the second order allows us to write R^α as the product $R^\alpha = A^\alpha K^*$ with A^α self-adjoint and bounded for a given α and:

$$\forall \lambda : |q(\alpha, \lambda^2)| \leq d(\alpha)\lambda^2, \quad d(\alpha) > 0, \quad ||A^\alpha|| \leq d(\alpha),$$

$$A^\alpha \phi = \sum_{j=1}^{\infty} \frac{q(\alpha, \lambda_j^2)}{\lambda_j^2} < \phi, \phi_j > \phi_j. \qquad [A.6]$$

We will explore here several methods: spectral cut-off, Tikhonov regularization and shrinkage. Other methods are unfortunately far beyond our scope and will not be addressed here.

A.3.2.2.1. Spectral cut-off

The idea behind spectral cut-off is to replace the original problem with a projected one, where the projection is on a space with dimension smaller than $dim(\mathcal{F})$. Let P_k be the finite-dimensional orthogonal projector on $span\{\psi_1, \ldots, \psi_k\}$, the spectral cut-off approximation of the problem $Kf = y$ is $Kf = P_k y$, with $f \perp Ker(K)$. This problem has a unique solution that we denote with f_α. We introduce a regularization parameter α defined as a function of k: $\alpha = \alpha(k) := sup\{\tilde{\alpha} \in \mathbb{R}; \lambda_k \geq \sqrt{\tilde{\alpha}}\}$. Hence, the spectral cut-off approximated solution writes:

$$f_\alpha = \sum_{j;\lambda_j \geq \sqrt{\alpha}} \frac{1}{\lambda_j} < y, \psi_j > \phi_j.$$

Spectral cut-off is a first-order regularization scheme and corresponds to setting $q(\alpha, \lambda) = 1(\lambda \geq \sqrt{\alpha})$ in vRegSchemeFirstOrder.

A.3.2.2.2. Tikhonov regularization

Tikhonov regularization is a method introduced by [TIK 77] in order to remedy the instability of the solution (even the best approximate solution) of an inverse problem. A penalty is added to the norm of the solution to compensate the non-invertibility of T^*T. The solution f_0 is then the solution of:

$$f_0 = argmin_f ||Tf - y^\delta||^2 + \alpha||f||^2 \qquad [A.7]$$

where α is the regularization parameter. The right term ensures the regularity and the smoothness of the solution. The spectral expression for the estimated function is thus:

$$\hat{f}_\alpha = \sum_{n=1}^{\infty} \frac{\lambda_n}{\alpha + \lambda_n^2} < y^\delta, \psi_n > \phi_n.$$

Using the singular value decomposition of K, the Tikhonov regularized solution can be rewritten as:

$$f_\alpha = \sum_{j=1}^{\infty} \frac{\lambda_j}{\lambda_j^2 + \alpha} < \hat{\mu}, \psi_j > \phi_j, \qquad \text{[A.8]}$$

that makes it clear that this regularization scheme simply consists of moving the spectrum of K^*K away from 0 by a translation of α. With notations of equation [A.6], we get $q(\alpha, \lambda^2) = \frac{\lambda^2}{\alpha+\lambda^2}$, $d(\alpha) = 1/\alpha$ and $A^\alpha = (\alpha I + K^*K)^{-1}$ that show that Tikhonov regularization is a second order regularization scheme. However, when K is self-adjoint the Tikhonov regularized solution takes the form $f_\alpha = (K + \alpha I)^{-1}\hat{\mu}$ since we do not have to project $\hat{\mu}$, but only to correct for the lack of stability of K^{-1}. In this latter case, the Tikhonov scheme becomes a regularization scheme of first order.

A.3.2.3. *Shrinkage as a regularization method*

We refer here to the framework tackled in section 3.5.1.2. We consider a general target matrix T_a with eigenvalues l_k and corresponding eigenvectors φ_k. We want to explore here in particular under which terms shrinkage can be defined as a regularization scheme of first or second order. This complements the work of [LED 03].

PROPOSITION A.1.– Let T_a be a non-singular square matrix and $\Omega_s = \alpha T_a + (1-\alpha)\hat{\Omega}$ be the shrinkage estimator of Ω. The approximate solution $w_*^s = \Omega_s^{-1}\hat{\mu}$ corresponds to a regularized solution obtained through a first order regularization scheme. Moreover, if $(\hat{\lambda}_j, \hat{\phi}_j)_j$ denote the eigensystem associated with $\hat{\Omega}$, then Ω_s has eigenvectors $(\hat{\phi}_j)_j$ and eigenvalues $((1-\alpha)\hat{\lambda}_j + \sum_{u=1}^N \alpha l_u < \varphi_u, \hat{\phi}_j >^2)_j$ and w_*^s can be rewritten as:

$$w_*^s = \sum_{j=1}^{N} \frac{1}{(1-\alpha)\hat{\lambda}_j + \sum_{u=1}^N \alpha l_u < \varphi_u, \hat{\phi}_j >^2} < \hat{\mu}, \hat{\phi}_j > \hat{\phi}_j,$$

In particular, since $\sum_{u=1}^N l_u < \varphi_u, \hat{\phi}_j >^2 = ||T_a^{\frac{1}{2}} \hat{\phi}_j||^2$ when $Ker(\hat{\Omega}) = \{0\}$, we see that w_*^s takes a similar form to equation [A.8] so that the shrinkage technique corresponds to a generalized Tikhonov regularization scheme. The asymptotic theory is here quite particular but interesting. This aspect has been treated in [LED 02]. It is implicit that when $N \to \infty$, we must have also $T \to \infty$ in order to keep the relation $T \geq N$. Intuitively, the degree of ill-posedness is decreasing in T (with N fixed) and increasing in N (with T fixed, $T \geq N$). This point has been underlined by [LED 03]: they found that the shrinkage intensity α has to increase with the estimation error made on the sample covariance matrix, and to decrease with the misspecification error due to the target matrix T_a. The estimation error disappears as T increases while the latter does not. Hence, the misspecification error is negligible when T is small, but its influence matters as T becomes large. This is coherent if we interpret α as a true regularization parameter. [LED 03] derive the behavior of the optimal α (optimal as defined in paragraph 3.5.1.2.1 on page 206) that must be of order $O(1/T)$, with a specified constant of proportionality that can be estimated.

From a regularization perspective, the point of interest is to know whether $\lim_{\alpha \to 0} q(\alpha, \lambda) = 1$. In usual regularization schemes, α is increasing in the measurement error, given in our case by the estimation error made on $\hat{\Omega}$. In portfolio allocation, the sample has two dimensions: N and T, one linked to the misspecification error and the other one to the measurement error. Therefore, α must be decreasing in T. This is satisfied if α depends on T, but we have also to control that T remains greater than N as $N \to \infty$ (we can still consider α as a $O(1/T)$). This asymptotic framework is known as *general asymptotics* ([LED 03]). Moreover, we must keep in mind that for a given $j \in [1; N]$, $q(\alpha, \lambda_j)$ depends on the term $\sum_{u=1}^{N} l_u < \varphi_u, \phi_j >^2$, but all the terms change with N.

A very simple assumption can help to solve this situation. Up to our knowledge, we never met such an analysis before in the literature.

PROPOSITION A.2.– If we assume that the spectrum of the target matrices is uniformly bounded from above (uniformly in N and T) by a constant M_0 (i.e. for every N, and sample of size T, $\forall u \in [1; N]$, $|l_u| \leq M_0$), then $\lim_{\alpha \to 0} q(\alpha, \lambda) = 1$ and shrinkage is a regularization technique.

The assumption that the spectrum of the covariance matrix is bounded from *below* may often be found in the literature. For obvious reasons, and as compact operators appear commonly in ill-posed inverse problems, this is typically a class of assumption that we *cannot* make as we aim at studying the opposite.

With assumptions of propositions A.3.2.3 and A.3.2.3 we have:

$$0 \leq \sum_{u=1}^{N} l_u < \varphi_u, \hat{\phi}_j >^2 \leq M_0 \sum_{u=1}^{N} < \varphi_u, \hat{\phi}_j >^2 = M_0,$$

since $\sum_{u=1}^{N} < \varphi_u, \phi_j >^2 = ||\phi_j||^2 = 1$ as (ϕ_j) is an orthonormal family for each N. Then, we can control for the convergence of $q(.,.)$ independently of the order of the eigenvalue, as a general function of λ (and no more λ_j), as $\lambda \to q(\alpha, \lambda) = \lambda/((1 - \alpha)\lambda + \alpha M)$ so that $\lim_{\alpha \to 0} q(\alpha, \lambda) = 1$.

A.4. Tables from Chapter 5

Time series	Economic region
Canada Mortgage and Housing Corp Total Starts SAAR	Canada
STCA Canada Industrial Product Price MoM NSA	Canada
STCA Canada Labor Force Participation Rate SA	Canada
STCA Canada Labor Force Unemployment Rate SA	Canada
STCA Canada Net Change in Full Time Labor Force Employment SA	Canada
STCA Canada Net Change in Labor Force Employment SA	Canada
STCA Canada Net Change in Part Time Labor Force Employment SA	Canada
STCA Canada New Housing Price MoM	Canada
STCA Canada New Housing Price YoY	Canada
STCA Canada Raw Materials Price MoM	Canada
STCA Canada Value of Building Permits Month-over-Month % change SA	Canada
European Commission Consumer Confidence Indicator Eurozone	Europe
European Commission Economic SentiMent Indicator Eurozone	Europe
European Commission Euro Area Business Climate Indicator	Europe
European Commission Manufacturing Confidence Eurozone Industrial Confidence	Europe
Bank of France Business Sentiment Indicator	France
France Business Confidence Composite Overall Indicator	France
France Business Confidence General Production Expectations	France
France Business Confidence Manufacturing Industry Sentiment Index	France
France Business Confidence Personal Production Expectations	France
France Consumer Confidence Overall Indicator SWDA	France
France Households Consumption Goods Expenditure Total MoM	France
France Households Consumption Goods Expenditure Total YoY	France
France Industrial Production YoY SA	France
France Manufacturing Production MoM SA 2005 = 100	France
France Manufacturing Production YoY SA 2005 = 100	France
Germany Current Account EUR NSA	Germany
Germany Import Prices MoM	Germany
Germany Import Prices YoY	Germany
Germany Producer Prices MoM	Germany
Germany Producer Prices YoY	Germany
Germany Retail Sales Constant Prices NSA YoY	Germany
Germany Retail Sales Constant Prices SWDA MoM	Germany
Germany Trade Balance EUR NSA	Germany
Germany Wholesale Prices MoM 2010 = 100	Germany
Germany Wholesale Prices YoY 2010 = 100	Germany

Italy General Govt Debt	Italy
Italy New Car Registrations YoY NSA	Japan
Japan Big 50 Constructors Orders by Contract Value YoY	Japan
Japan Capacity Utilization Operating Ratio Manufacturing MoM SA	Japan
Japan Housing Starts Ann	Japan
Japan Housing Starts YoY NSA	Japan
Japan Indices of Industrial Production MoM SA 2010 = 100	Japan
Japan Indices of Industrial Production: Production YoY NSA 2010 = 100	Japan
Japan Jobs to Applicants Ratio SA	Japan
Japan Merchandise Trade Exports YoY NSA	Japan
Japan Merchandise Trade Imports YoY NSA	Japan
Japan New Composite Index of Business Cycle Indicators Coincident Index	Japan
Japan New Composite Index of Business Cycle Indicators Leading Index	Japan
Japan Official Reserve Assets	Japan
Japan Producer Price Index MoM	Japan
Japan Producer Price Index YoY	Japan
Japan Services Producer Price YoY	Japan
Japan Small Business Confidence All Industries	Japan
Japan Trade Statistics Balance NSA	Japan
Japan Unemployment Rate SA	Japan
Japan Vehicle Sales YOY	Japan
CBI MTE Full Average Selling Prices Next 3 Months Balance	UK
CBI MTE Full Volume of Total Order Book Balance	UK
CBI Retailing Q1 Monthly Volume Sales Compared Year Earlier Reported Balance	UK
CBI Total Distribution Monthly Q1 Vol. Sales Compared Year Earlier Reported Bal.	UK
GFK UK Consumer Confidence Indicator	UK
RICS England & Wales Housing Market Survey Price Balance SA	UK
UK Cent Govt Net Cash Requirement ex.Northern Rock Asset Mgmt & Bradford&Bingley	UK
UK Claimant Count Rate SA	UK
UK HBOS House Prices 3 Mth YoY	UK
UK HBOS House Prices All UK MoM SA	UK
UK Industrial Production MoM SA	UK
UK Industrial Production YoY SA	UK
UK Manufacturing Production MoM SA	UK
UK Manufacturing Production YoY SA	UK
UK PSNCR Public Sector Net Cash RequireMent	UK
UK Trade Balance in Goods SA	UK
UK Trade Balance Value of Trade Balance SA	UK
UK Unemployment Claimant Count Monthly Change SA	UK
UK Unemployment ILO Unemployment Rate SA	UK

Table A.1. *List of time series used to create the growth index*

Time series	Economic region
Average Monthly Change in Fed Labor Market Conditions Index - LMCI 19	US
Bloomberg US Weekly Consumer Comfort Index	US
Capital Goods New Orders Nondefense Ex Aircraft & Parts MoM	US
Capital Goods Shipments Ex Air %	US
Chicago Fed National Activity Index	US
Conference Board Consumer Confidence SA 1985 = 100	US
Conference Board US Leading Index MoM	US
Federal Reserve Consumer Credit Total Net Change SA	US
ISM Manufacturing PMI SA	US
ISM Manufacturing Report on Business New Orders SA	US
ISM Manufacturing Report on Business Prices Index NSA	US
MNI Chicago Business Barometer (sa)	US
National Association of Home Builders Market Index SA	US
NFIB Small Business Optimism Index	US
Philadelphia Fed Business Outlook Survey Diffusion Index General Conditions	US
Private Housing Authorized by Bldg Permits by Type Total SAAR	US
Private Housing Units Started by Structure Total Monthly % Change SA	US
Private Total Housing Authorized by Building Permits MoM SA	US
U-3 US Unemployment Rate Total in Labor Force Seasonally Adjusted	US
UMich Expected Change in Prices During the Next 5-10 Years: Median	US
UMich Expected Change in Prices During the Next Year: Median	US
University of Michigan Consumer Expectations Index	US
University of Michigan Consumer Sentiment Index	US
University of Michigan Current Economic Conditions Index	US
US Auto Sales Domestic Vehicles Annualized SAAR	US
US Auto Sales Total Annualized SAAR	US
US Capacity Utilization % of Total Capacity SA	US
US Continuing Jobless Claims SA	US
US Durable Goods New Orders Total ex Transportation MoM SA	US
US Employees on Nonfarm Payrolls Manufacturing Industry Monthly Net Change SA	US
US Employees on Nonfarm Payrolls Total MoM Net Change SA	US
US Employees on Nonfarm Payrolls Total Private MoM Net Change SA	US
US Employment Total in Labor Force Net Change SA	US
US Foreign Net Transactions	US
US Industrial Production Industry Groups Manufacturing MoM SA	US
US Industrial Production MOM SA	US
US Initial Jobless Claims SA	US
US Labor Force Participation Rate SA	US
US Manufacturers New Orders Total MoM SA	US
US Manufacturing & Trade Inventories Total MoM SA	US
US New One Family Houses Sold Annual Total MoM SA	US

US New One Family Houses Sold Annual Total SAAR	US
US New Privately Owned Housing Units Started by Structure Total SAAR	US
US Personal Consumption Expenditure Core Price Index MoM SA	US
US Personal Consumption Expenditure Core Price Index YoY SA	US
US Personal Consumption Expenditures Chain Type Price Index MoM SA	US
US Personal Consumption Expenditures Chain Type Price Index YoY SA	US
US Personal Consumption Expenditures Nominal Dollars MoM SA	US
US Personal Income MoM SA	US
US Treasury Federal Budget Debt Summary Deficit Or Surplus NSA	US
US Treasury International Capital Net Monthly Inflows Total	US

Table A.2. *List of time series used to create the growth index – continued*

Time series	Economic region
STCA Canada CPI Ex the 8 Most Volatile Components And Indirect Taxes MoM NSA	Canada
STCA Canada CPI Ex the 8 Most Volatile Components And Indirect Taxes YoY	Canada
STCA Canada CPI MoM NSA 2002 = 100	Canada
STCA Canada CPI NSA 2002 = 100	Canada
STCA Canada CPI YoY NSA 2002 = 100	Canada
Eurostat PPI Eurozone Industry Ex Construction MoM	Europe
Eurostat PPI Eurozone Industry Ex Construction YoY	Europe
France CPI YoY 2015 = 100	France
Germany CPI Baden Wuerttemberg MoM	Germany
Germany CPI Baden Wuerttemberg YoY	Germany
Italy CPI FOI Ex Tobacco NSA	Italy
Japan CPI Nationwide Ex Food & Energy YoY%	Japan
Japan CPI Nationwide Ex Fresh Food YoY	Japan
Japan CPI Nationwide YoY	Japan
Japan CPI Tokyo Ex Food & Energy YoY%	Japan
Japan CPI Tokyo Ex Fresh Food YoY	Japan
Japan CPI Tokyo YoY	Japan
UK Money Supply M4 MoM SA	UK
UK Money Supply M4 YoY SA	UK
UK RPI All Items NSA	UK
UK RPI Less Mortgage Interest PayMents YoY NSA	UK
UK RPI MoM NSA	UK
UK RPI YoY NSA	UK
US CPI Urban Consumers Less Food & Energy MoM SA	US
US CPI Urban Consumers Less Food & Energy SA	US
US CPI Urban Consumers Less Food & Energy YoY NSA	US
US CPI Urban Consumers MoM SA	US
US CPI Urban Consumers NSA	US
US CPI Urban Consumers YoY NSA	US

Table A.3. *List of time series used to create the inflation index*

Time series	Economic region
Bank of Canada Overnight Lending Rate	Canada
ECB Deposit Facility Announcement Rate	Europe
ECB M3 Annual Growth Rate SA	Europe
ECB Main Refinancing Operations Announcement Rate	Europe
ECB Marginal Lending Facility Announcement Rate	Europe
BOJ Monetary Base Avg Outstanding YoY NSA	Japan
BOJ Monetary Base End of period Outstanding	Japan
Japan Money Stock M2 avg amt outstanding YoY%	Japan
Japan Money Stock M3 avg amt outstanding YoY%	Japan
Bank of England UK Mortgage Approvals	UK
UK Bank of England Official Bank Rate	UK
UK Consumer Credit Supplied (Ex SLC) SA	UK
UK Lending to Individuals Net Lending Secured On Dwellings in Billions	UK
UK Official Reserves Changes in Net Reserves	UK
Federal Funds Target Rate - Lower Bound	US
Federal Funds Target Rate - Upper Bound	US

Table A.4. *List of time series used to create the monetary condition index*

Conclusion

With deep upcoming changes in the financial world resulting from the increased use of learning algorithms, we may be tempted to use more and more black-box techniques to make our way into the wonderful world of performance generation. These techniques include for instance machine learning, deep learning, convolutional neural networks, support vector machines, random forests and boosting. In recent years, the surge of interest in such trendy techniques is, in our view, more a symptom of the evolution of investors than a true revolution in asset management. Learning techniques does not constitute a paradigm shift in the approach *per se*: investors have now realized how important it is to find new sources of performance, and they are trying to use tools that have perhaps just been used more confidentially by few participants until now.

Likewise, dealing with data remains a challenge. Diversifying the data sources is a potential source of new alpha , and trying to build strategies based on the data extracted from social networks, Internet requests, tick-by-tick data, or even geo-localization and satellite pictures is a natural goal. But are trivial sanity checks on those data done correctly? Do investors check their quality and depth, and do they discuss their biases, sustainability or their "point-in-timeness"? A funny yet insightful example is given by the negative correlation between the size of a person and the length of the person's hair. Based on an evaluation over a global population, irrespective of cultural bias, it has been found that, on average, men have shorter hair than women. She or he should not expect to become taller by simply cutting their hairs! A similar reasoning applied to finance should underline how some quick and spurious conclusions, even drawn from sophisticated algorithms, may be hazardous. New sources of data may also be understood as new markets or new asset classes: are they well understood; do they have any specific hidden feature, tax or behavior? Financial investment is now a whole industrial process whose raw material is data. This process therefore requires perfect understanding of the quality of the inputs that are used.

This quest for alpha and this appetite for new data and new black-box algorithms should paradoxically be an inducement to set up a more ambitious investment process. First of all, it is not only because we view this growing interest in sophisticated mathematics purely as a good thing. It is also because we hope that students, quants, investors and managers will be more and more involved in the scientific understanding of the whole process, being more and more demanding on the scientific quality of each step of their investment process. It is all about marginal gains: no step should be ignored and no decision should be taken lightly. From the nature of the data to risk management, from allocation to backtesting, from statistical to economic significance, leaving the complexity to an unmastered algorithm to build a strategy would be useless if no effort is made to understand the main drivers of performance generation. Even with the use of simple OLS regressions, we can often observe that for years, some practitioners (not all, hopefully) have been tempted to regress $Y = Something$ on $X = Whatever$, regardless of the nature of the explicative variables, regardless of the modeling of the error term and regardless of the pertinence of the model.

In conclusion, the increase in sophistication should not ideally start from the desire to use unknown techniques; it should begin from a greater strictness in mastering each aspect of the investment process. However, we are quite sure that with the pressure of performance and an increased competition, this ambition will naturally percolate gradually among financial habits. A robust investment process should be viewed as a holistic approach for efficiently delivering repeatable alpha. Each of its part has to be coherent with the whole: the investment horizon, the universe and its underlying risk factors, the data and its transformation into informed bets and strategies, allocation and portfolio construction within a risk budget, performance and risk attributions. Contrary to mathematics where the law of large numbers ensures that perturbations offset each other, the greatest hazard for a fund manager is that financial errors tend to sum up along the alpha production chain.

Bibliography

[AAS 09] AAS K., CZADO C., FRIGESSI A. *et al.*, "Pair-copula constructions of multiple dependence", *Insurance: Mathematics and Economics*, vol. 44, no. 2, pp. 182–198, 2009.

[ACH 05] ACHARYA V., PEDERSEN L., "Asset pricing with liquidity risk", *Journal of Financial Economics*, vol. 77, no. 2, pp. 375–410, 2005.

[AÏT 15] AÏT-SAHALIA Y., CACHO-DIAZ J., LAEVEN R., "Modeling financial contagion using mutually exciting jump processes", *Journal of Financial Economics*, vol. 117, no. 3, pp. 585–606, 2015.

[ALE 08] ALEXANDER C., *Moving Average Models for Volatility and Correlation, and Covariance Matrices*, John Wiley & Sons, 2008.

[ALE 10] ALESSI L., CAPASSO M.B.M., "Improved penalization for determining the number of factors in approximate factor models", *Statistics and Probability Letters*, vol. 80, nos. 23–24, pp. 1806–1813, 2010.

[ALL 12] ALLEZ R., BOUCHAUD J.-P., "Eigenvector dynamics: general theory and some applications", *Physical Review E*, vol. 86, p. 046202, 2012.

[ALL 14] ALLEZ R., BOUCHAUD J.-P., "Eigenvector dynamics under free addition", *Random Matrices: Theory and Applications*, vol. 3, no. 3, 2014.

[ALL 15] ALLEZ R., BUN J., BOUCHAUD J.-P., "The eigenvectors of Gaussian matrices with an external source", available at: https://arxiv.org/abs/1412.7108, 2015.

[ALM 00] ALMGREN R., CHRISS N., "Optimal execution of portfolio transactions", *Journal of Risk*, vol. 3, no. 2, pp. 5–39, 2000.

[ALM 03] ALMGREN R., "Optimal nonlinear impact functions and trading-enhanced risk", *Applied Mathematical Finance*, vol. 10, no. 1, pp. 1–18, 2003.

[ALM 05] ALMGREN R., THUM C., HAUPTMANN E. *et al.*, "Direct estimation of equity market impact", *Risk*, vol. 18, no. 7, pp. 58–62, 2005.

[ALV 11] ALVAREZ M., LUO Y., CAHAN R. *et al.*, Risk parity and risk-based allocation, Report, Deutsche Bank Quantitative Strategy, Markets Research, New York, October 2011.

[AMI 86] AMIHUD Y., MENDELSON H., "Asset pricing and the bid-ask spread", *Journal of Financial Economics*, vol. 17, no. 2, pp. 223–249, 1986.

[AMI 88] AMIHUD Y., MENDELSON H., "Liquidity and asset prices: financial management implications", *Financial Management*, vol. 17, no. 1, pp. 5–15, 1988.

[AMI 90] AMIHUD Y., MENDELSON H., WOOD R., "Liquidity and the 1987 stock market crash", *Journal of Portfolio Management*, vol. 13, pp. 65–69, 1990.

[AMI 91a] AMIHUD Y., MENDELSON H., "Liquidity, asset prices and financial policy", *Financial Analysts Journal*, vol. 47, pp. 1411–1425, 1991.

[AMI 91b] AMIHUD Y., MENDELSON H., "Liquidity, maturity, and the yields on US treasury securities", *Journal of Finance*, vol. 46, no. 4, pp. 1411–1425, 1991.

[AMI 02] AMIHUD Y., "Illiquidity and stock returns: cross-section and time-series effects", *Journal of Financial Markets*, vol. 5, no. 1, pp. 31–56, 2002.

[AMI 03] AMIN G., KAT H., "Welcome to the dark side: hedge fund attrition and survivorship bias over the period 1994–2001", *Journal of Alternative Investments*, vol. 6, no. 1, pp. 57–73, 2003.

[AMI 06] AMIHUD Y., MENDELSON H., "Stock and bond liquidity and its effect on prices and financial policies", *Financial Markets & Portfolio Management*, vol. 20, no. 1, pp. 19–32, 2006.

[AMI 07] AMISANO G., GIACOMINI R., "Comparing density forecasts via weighted likelihood ratio tests", *Journal of Business & Economic Statistics*, vol. 25, no. 2, pp. 177–190, 2007.

[AMI 15a] AMIHUD Y., HAMEED A., KANG W. *et al.*, "The illiquidity premium: international evidence", *Journal of Financial Economics*, vol. 117, no. 2, pp. 350–368, 2015.

[AMI 15b] AMIHUD Y., MENDELSON H., "The pricing of illiquidity as a characteristic and as a factor", *Multinational Finance Journal*, vol. 19, no. 3, pp. 149–168, 2015.

[AND 96] ANDERSEN T., "Return volatility and trading volume: an information flow interpretation of stochastic volatility", *Journal of Finance*, vol. 51, no. 1, pp. 169–204, 1996.

[AND 03a] ANDERSEN T., BOLLERSLEV T., DIEBOLD F. *et al.*, "Modeling and forecasting realized volatility", *Econometrica*, vol. 71, no. 2, pp. 579–625, 2003.

[AND 03b] ANDERSEN T., *An Introduction to Multivariate Statistical Analysis*, Probability and Statistics, 3rd ed., Wiley, 2003.

[AND 07] ANDERSEN T., BOLLERSLEV T., DIEBOLD F. *et al.*, "Real-time price discovery in global stock, bond and foreign exchange markets", *Journal of International Economics*, vol. 73, no. 2, pp. 251–277, 2007.

[AND 12a] ANDERSEN T., DOBREV D., SCHAUMBURG E., "Jump-robust volatility estimation using nearest neighbor truncation", *Journal of Econometrics*, vol. 169, no. 1, pp. 75–93, 2012.

[AND 12b] ANDERSON R., BIANCHI S., GOLDBERG L., "Will my risk-parity strategy outperform?", *Financial Analysts Journal*, vol. 68, no. 6, pp. 75–93, 2012.

[ANE 00] ANE T., GEMAN H., "Order flow, transaction clock, and normality of asset returns", *Journal of Finance*, vol. 55, no. 5, pp. 2259–2284, 2000.

[ANG 02a] ANG A., BEKAERT G., "International asset allocation with regime shifts", *Review of Financial Studies*, vol. 15, no. 4, pp. 1137–1187, 2002.

[ANG 02b] ANG A., CHEN J., "Asymmetric correlations of equity portfolios", *Journal of Financial Economics*, vol. 63, no. 3, pp. 443–494, 2002.

[ANG 03] ANG A., PIAZZESI M., "A no-arbitrage vector autoregression of term structure dynamics with macroeconomic and latent variables", *Journal of Monetary Economics*, vol. 50, no. 4, pp. 745–787, 2003.

[ANG 04] ANG A., BEKAERT G., "How do regimes affect asset allocation", *Financial Analysts Journal*, vol. 60, no. 2, pp. 86–99, 2004.

[ANG 06a] ANG A., HODRICK R., XING Y. *et al.*, "The cross-section of volatility and expected returns", *Journal of Finance*, vol. 61, no. 1, pp. 259–299, 2006.

[ANG 06b] ANG A., PIAZZESI M., WEI M., "What does the yield curve tell us about GDP growth?", *Journal of Econometrics*, vol. 131, no. 1, pp. 359–403, 2006.

[ANG 07a] ANG A., CHEN J., "CAPM over the long run: 1926–2001", *Journal of Empirical Finance*, vol. 14, no. 1, pp. 1–40, 2007.

[ANG 07b] ANG A., DONG S., PIAZZESI M., No-arbitrage Taylor rules, Working Paper no. 13448, National Bureau of Economic Research, September 2007.

[ANG 09a] ANG A., GOETZMANN W., SCHAEFER S., "Evaluation of active management of the Norwegian Government Pension Fund – Global", Report, Report to the Norwegian Ministry of Finance, 2009.

[ANG 09b] ANG A., HODRICK R., XING Y. *et al.*, "High idiosyncratic volatility and low returns: international and further US evidence", *Journal of Financial Economics*, vol. 91, pp. 1–23, 2009.

[ANG 11] ANG A., GOETZMANN W., SCHAEFER S., "The efficient market theory and evidence: implications for active investment management", *Foundations and Trends in Finance*, vol. 5, no. 3, pp. 157–242, 2011.

[ANG 14a] ANG A., *Asset Management: A Systematic Approach to Factor Investing, Financial Management Association Survey and Synthesis*, Oxford University Press, 2014.

[ANG 14b] ANG A., PAPANIKOLAOU D., WESTERFIELD M., "Portfolio choice with illiquid assets", *Management Science*, vol. 60, no. 11, pp. 2737–2761, 2014.

[ARN 95] ARNOLD B., GROENEVELD R.A., "Measuring skewness with respect to the mode", *American Statistician*, vol. 49, no. 1, pp. 34–38, 1995.

[ARN 05] ARNOTT R., HSU J., MOORE P., "Fundamental indexation", *Financial Analysts Journal*, vol. 61, no. 2, pp. 83–99, 2005.

[ARU 09] ARUOBA S., DIEBOLD F., SCOTTI C., "Real-time measurement of business conditions", *Journal of Business & Economic Statistics*, vol. 27, no. 4, pp. 417–427, 2009.

[ARZ 77] ARZAC E., BAWA V., "Portfolio choice and equilibrium in capital markets with safety-first investors", *Journal of Financial Economics*, vol. 4, no. 3, pp. 277–288, 1977.

[ASN 12] ASNESS C., FRAZZINI A., PEDERSEN L., "Leverage aversion and risk parity", *Financial Analysts Journal*, vol. 68, no. 1, pp. 47–59, 2012.

[ASN 13] ASNESS C., MOSKOWITZ T., PEDERSEN L., "Value and momentum everywhere", *Journal of Finance*, vol. 68, no. 13, pp. 929–985, 2013.

[AVR 10] AVRAMOV D., ZHOU G., "Bayesian portfolio analysis", *Annual Review of Financial Economics*, vol. 2, pp. 25–47, 2010.

[BAE 05] BAELE L., "Volatility spillover effects in European equity markets", *Journal of Financial and Quantitative Analysis*, vol. 40, no. 2, pp. 373–401, 2005.

[BAI 02] BAI J., NG S., "Determining the number of factors in approximate factor models", *Econometrica*, vol. 70, no. 1, pp. 191–221, 2002.

[BAI 03] BAI J., "Inferential theory for factor models of large dimensions", *Econometrica*, vol. 71, no. 1, pp. 135–171, 2003.

[BAI 06] BAI J., NG S., "Evaluating latent and observed factors in macroeconomics and finance", *Journal of Econometrics*, vol. 131, nos. 1–2, pp. 507–537, 2006.

[BAI 10] BAI Z., SILVERSTEIN J., *Spectral Analysis of Large Dimensional Random Matrices*, 2nd ed., Springer-Verlag, New York, 2010.

[BAI 11] BAI J., SHI S., "Estimating high dimensional covariance matrices and its applications", *Annals of Economics and Finance*, vol. 12, no. 2, pp. 199–215, 2011.

[BAI 12a] BAI J., LI K., "Statistical analysis of factor models of high dimension", *Annals of Statistics*, vol. 40, no. 1, pp. 436–465, 2012.

[BAI 12b] BAILEY D., LOPEZ DE PRADO M., "The Sharpe ratio efficient frontier", *Journal of Risk*, vol. 15, no. 2, pp. 191–221, 2012.

[BAI 14a] BAILEY D., BORWEIN J., LOPEZ DE PRADO M. *et al.*, "Pseudo-mathematics and financial charlatanism: the effects of backtest overfitting on out-of-sample performance", *Notices of the American Mathematical Society*, vol. 61, no. 5, pp. 458–471, 2014.

[BAI 14b] BAILEY D., LOPEZ DE PRADO M., "The deflated Sharpe ratio: correcting for selection bias, backtest overfitting and non-normality", *Journal of Portfolio Management*, vol. 40, no. 5, pp. 94–107, 2014.

[BAI 15] BAILEY D., GER S., LOPEZ DE PRADO M. *et al.*, *Statistical Overfitting and Backtest Performance*, in JURCZENKO E. (ed.), *Risk-based and Factor Investing*, ISTE Press, London and Elsevier, Oxford, 2015.

[BAI 16a] BAI J., LI K., "Maximum likelihood estimation and inference for approximate factor models of high dimension", *Review of Economics and Statistics*, vol. 98, no. 2, pp. 298–309, 2016.

[BAI 16b] BAI X., SCHEINBERG K., TUTUNCU R., "Least-squares approach to risk parity in portfolio selection", *Quantitative Finance*, vol. 16, no. 3, pp. 357–376, 2016.

[BAI 16c] BAILEY D., BORWEIN J., LOPEZ DE PRADO M. *et al.*, "The probability of backtest overfitting", *Journal of Computational Finance*, forthcoming, 2016.

[BAK 11a] BAKER M., BRADLEY B., WURGLER J., "Benchmarks as limits to arbitrage: understanding the low-volatility anomaly", *Financial Analysts Journal*, vol. 67, no. 1, pp. 40–54, 2011.

[BAK 11b] BAKSHI G., PANAYOTOV G., SKOULAKIS G., "The Baltic Dry Index as a predictor of global stock returns, commodity returns, and global economic activity", available at: www.ssrn.com/abstract=1787757, 2011.

[BAL 84] BALL C., TOROUS W., "The maximum likelihood estimation of security price volatility: theory, evidence, and application to option pricing", *Journal of Business*, vol. 57, no. 1, pp. 97–112, 1984.

[BAL 99] BALDUZZI P., LYNCH A., "Transaction costs and predictability: some utility cost calculations", *Journal of Financial Economics*, vol. 52, no. 1, pp. 47–78, 1999.

[BAL 00] BALDUZZI P., LYNCH A., "Predictability and transaction costs: the impact on rebalancing rules and behavior", *Journal of Finance*, vol. 55, no. 5, pp. 2285–2309, 2000.

[BAL 01] BALDUZZI P., ELTON E., GREEN T., "Economic news and bond prices: evidence from the US treasury market", *Journal of financial and Quantitative analysis*, vol. 36, no. 4, pp. 523–543, 2001.

[BAL 15] BALTAS N., KOSOWSKI R., "Demystifying time-series momentum strategies: volatility estimators, trading rules and pairwise correlations", available at: www.ssrn.com/abstract=2140091, 2015.

[BAL 16] BALCHUNAS E., "How the US government inadvertently launched a $3 trillion industry", available at: http://www.bloomberg.com/features/2016-etf-files/, 2016.

[BAN 99] BANGIA A., DIEBOLD F., SCHUERMANN T. *et al.*, "Liquidity on the outside", *Risk*, vol. 12, pp. 68–73, 1999.

[BAN 12] BANBURA M., GIANNONE D., MODUGNO M. *et al.*, Now-casting and the real-time data flow, Working Paper, no. ECARES 2012-026, ULB Brussels, 2012.

[BAR 77] BARNDORFF-NIELSEN O., "Exponentially decreasing distributions for the logarithm of particle size", *Proceedings of the Royal Society of London A, Mathematical, Physical and Engineering Sciences*, vol. 353, no. 1674, pp. 401–419, 1977.

[BAR 97] BARNDORFF-NIELSEN O., "Normal inverse Gaussian distributions and stochastic volatility modelling", *Scandinavian Journal of Statistics*, vol. 24, no. 1, pp. 1–13, 1997.

[BAR 02] BARNDORFF-NIELSEN O., SHEPHARD N., "Econometric analysis of realized volatility and its use in estimating stochastic volatility models", *Econometrica*, vol. 72, no. 3, pp. 885–925, 2002.

[BAR 07] BARRA M., MSCI BARRA Risk Model Handbook, Report, MSCI BARRA, 2007.

[BAR 08] BARBERIS N., HUANG M., "Stocks as lotteries: the implications of probability weighting for security prices", *American Economic Review*, vol. 98, no. 5, pp. 2066–2100, 2008.

[BAR 12] BARBERIS N., "Psychology and the financial crisis of 2007–2008", in HALIASSOS M., (ed.), *Financial Innovation: Too Much or Too Little?*, MIT Press, Cambridge, 2012.

[BAR 15] BARROSO P., SANTA-CLARA P., "Momentum has its moments", *Journal of Financial Economics*, vol. 116, pp. 111–120, 2015.

[BAT 96] BATES D., "Jumps and stochastic volatility: exchange rate processes implicit in deutsche mark options", *Review of Financial Studies*, vol. 9, no. 1, pp. 69–107, 1996.

[BEB 11] BEBER A., BRANDT M., KAVAJECZ K., "What does equity sector orderflow tell us about the economy?", *Review of Financial Studies*, vol. 24, no. 11, pp. 3688–3730, 2011.

[BEB 15] BEBER A., BRANDT M., LUISI M., "Distilling the macroeconomic news flow", *Journal of Financial Economics*, vol. 117, no. 3, pp. 489–507, 2015.

[BED 01] BEDFORD T., COOKE R., "Probability density decomposition for conditionally dependent random variables modeled by Vines", *Annals of Mathematics and Artificial Intelligence*, vol. 32, no. 1, pp. 245–268, 2001.

[BED 02] BEDFORD T., COOKE R., "A new graphical model for dependent random variables", *Annals of Statistics*, vol. 30, no. 4, pp. 1031–1068, 2002.

[BEK 07] BEKAERT G., HARVEY C., LUNDBLAD C., "Liquidity and expected returns: lessons from emerging markets", *Review of Financial Studies*, vol. 20, pp. 1783–1831, 2007.

[BEL 57] BELLMAN R., *Dynamic Programming*, Princeton University Press, Princeton, 1957.

[BEN 05] BEN DOR A., DYNKIN L., HYMAN J., DTS – Further insights and applicability, Report, Lehman Brothers, 2005.

[BEN 07] BEN DOR A., DYNKIN L., HOUWELING P. *et al.*, "Duration Times Spread (DTS): a new measure of spread exposure in credit portfolios", *Journal of Portfolio Management*, vol. 33, no. 2, pp. 77–100, 2007.

[BEN 11] BENAYCH-GEORGES F., NADAKUDITI R., "The eigenvalues and eigenvectors of finite, low rank perturbations of large random matrices", *Advances in Mathematics*, vol. 227, no. 1, pp. 494–521, 2011.

[BEN 14] BENDER J., BRETT HAMMOND P., MOK W., "Can alpha be captured by risk premia?", *Journal of Portfolio Management*, vol. 40, no. 2, pp. 18–29, 2014.

[BER 95] BERNANKE B., GERTLER M., "Inside the black box: the credit channel of monetary policy transmission", *Journal of Economic Perspectives*, vol. 9, no. 4, pp. 27–48, 1995.

[BER 99] BERNANKE B., GERTLER M., GILCHRIST S., "The financial accelerator in a quantitative business cycle framework", in TAYLOR J.B., WOODFORD M., (eds), *Handbook of Macroeconomics*, vol. 1, Elsevier, Oxford, 1999.

[BER 00] BERKOWITZ J., "Breaking the silence", *Risk*, vol. 13, no. 10, pp. 105–108, 2000.

[BER 05a] BERNADELL C., COCHE J., NYHOLM K., Yield curve prediction for the strategic investor, ECB Working Paper, April 2005.

[BER 05b] BERNANKE B., BOIVIN J., ELIASZ P., "Measuring the effects of monetary policy: a factor-augmented vector autoregressive (FAVAR) approach", *The Quarterly Journal of Economics*, vol. 120, no. 1, pp. 387–422, 2005.

[BER 07] BERTHOLON H., MONFORT A., PEGORARO F., "Pricing and inference with mixtures of conditionally normal processes", available at: www.ssrn.com/abstract=1688953, 2007.

[BER 08] BERA A., PARK S., "Optimal portfolio diversification using the maximum entropy principle", *Econometric Reviews*, vol. 27, nos. 4–6, pp. 484–512, 2008.

[BER 16] BERNIS G., BOTTE A., MERHY C. *et al.*, Fixed Income portfolio management in a low rate environment, Research Paper NATIXIX Asset Management, June 2016.

[BES 91] BEST M., GRAUER R., "On the sensitivity of mean-variance-efficient portfolios to changes in asset means: some analytical and computational results", *The Review of Financial Studies*, vol. 4, no. 2, pp. 315–342, 1991.

[BIC 16] BICHUCH M., SIRCAR R., "Optimal investment with transaction costs and stochastic volatility", available at: https://arxiv.org/abs/1401.0562, 2016.

[BJO 97] BJORNSON B., CARTER C., "New evidence on agricultural commodity return performance under time-varying risk", *American Journal of Agricultural Economics*, vol. 79, no. 3, pp. 918–930, 1997.

[BLA 73] BLACK F., SCHOLES M., "The pricing of options and corporate liabilities", *Journal of Political Economy*, vol. 81, no. 3, pp. 637–654, 1973.

[BLA 76] BLACK F., "Studies of stock price volatility changes", *Proceedings of the 1976 Meetings of the Business and Economics Statistics Section, American Statistical Association*, pp. 177–181, 1976.

[BLA 92] BLACK F., LITTERMAN R., "Global portfolio optimization", *Financial Analysts Journal*, vol. 48, pp. 28–43, 1992.

[BLA 95] BLACK F., "Interest rates as options", *Journal of Finance*, vol. 50, no. 5, pp. 1371–76, 1995.

[BLI 07] BLITZ D., VAN VLIET P., "The volatility effect: lower risk without lower return", *Journal of Portfolio Management*, vol. 34, no. 1, pp. 102–113, 2007.

[BLI 11] BLITZ D., VAN VLIET P., "Dynamic strategic asset allocation: risk and return across economic regimes", *Journal of Asset Management*, vol. 12, no. 5, pp. 360–375, 2011.

[BLO 50] BLOMQVIST N., "On a measure of dependence between two random variables", *The Annals of Mathematical Statistics*, vol. 21, no. 4, pp. 593–600, 1950.

[BLO 97] BLONIGEN B., "Firm-specific assets and the link between exchange rates and foreign direct investment", *American Economic Review*, vol. 87, no. 3, pp. 447–465, 1997.

[BOL 06] BOLLERSLEV T., LITVINOVA J., TAUCHEN G., "Leverage and volatility feedback effects in high-frequency data", *Journal of Financial Econometrics*, vol. 4, no. 3, pp. 353–384, 2006.

[BON 11] BONATO M., "Robust estimation of skewness and kurtosis in distributions with infinite higher moments", *Finance Research Letters*, vol. 8, no. 2, pp. 77–87, 2011.

[BOO 14] BOON L.-N., IELPO F., "Determining the maximum number of uncorrelated strategies in a global portfolio", *Journal of Alternative Investment*, vol. 16, no. 4, pp. 8–27, 2014.

[BOO 16] BOON L.-N., IELPO F., "An anatomy of global risk premiums", *Journal of Asset Management*, vol. 17, no. 4, pp. 229–243, 2016.

[BOU 04] BOUCHAUD J.-P., GEFEN Y., POTTERS M., WYART M., "Fluctuations and response in financial markets: the subtle nature of random price changes", *Quantitative Finance*, vol. 4, pp. 176–190, 2004.

[BOU 07] BOUCHAUD J.-P., LALOUX L., MICELI A. *et al.*, "Large dimension forecasting models and random singular value spectra", *The European Physical Journal B*, vol. 55, no. 2, pp. 201–207, 2007.

[BOU 09] BOUCHAUD J.-P., POTTERS M., *Theory of Financial Risk and Derivative Pricing: From Statistical Physics to Risk Management*, 2nd ed., Cambridge University Press, 2009.

[BOU 11] BOUCHAUD J.-P., POTTERS M., *Financial Applications of Random Matrix Theory: A Short Review*, Oxford University Press, 2011.

[BOU 13] BOUCHAUD J.-P., *The Endogenous Dynamics of Markets: Price Impact, Feedback Loops and Instabilities*, 2nd ed., Risk Books, 2013.

[BOU 16] BOUCHAUD J.-P., POTTERS M., LALOUX L. *et al.*, "Deconstructing the Low-Vol anomaly", *Journal of Portfolio Management*, forthcoming, 2016.

[BOW 20] BOWLEY A., *Elements of Statistics*, Scribner, New York, 1920.

[BOX 15] BOX G., JENKINS G., REINSEL G. *et al.*, *Time Series Analysis: Forecasting and Control*, 4th ed., John Wiley & Sons, New York, 2015.

[BOY 14] BOYNTON W., "Allocations for optimal portfolios when there is estimation error", available at: http://publix.newhaven.edu/hanko/BoyntonArticle.pdf, 2014.

[BRA 95] BRAUN P., NELSON D., SUNIER A., "Good news, bad news, volatility and betas", *Journal of Finance*, vol. 50, no. 5, pp. 1575–1603, 1995.

[BRA 09] BRANDT W., SANTA-CLARA P., VALKANOV R., "Parametric portfolio policies: exploiting characteristics in the cross section of equity returns", *Review of Financial Studies*, vol. 22, pp. 3411–3447, 2009.

[BRA 10] BRANDT M., *Portfolio Choice Problems*, vol. 1, Elsevier, Cambridge, 2010.

[BRE 96] BRENNAN M., SUBRAHMANYAM A., "Market microstructure and asset pricing: on the compensation for illiquidity in stock returns", *Journal of Financial Economics*, vol. 41, no. 3, pp. 441–464, 1996.

[BRE 13] BRENNAN M., HUH S., SUBRAHMANYAM A., "An analysis of the Amihud illiquidity premium", *Review of Asset Pricing Studies*, vol. 3, no. 1, pp. 133–176, 2013.

[BRI 99] BRITTEN-JONES M., "The sampling error in estimates of mean-variance efficient portfolio weights", *Journal of Finance*, vol. 54, no. 2, pp. 655–671, 1999.

[BRI 06] BRIÈRE M., "Market reactions to central bank communication policies: reading interest rate options smiles", Solvay Business School WP-CEB, pp. 006–009, 2006.

[BRI 08] BRIÈRE M., IELPO F., "Yield curve reaction to macroeconomic news in Europe: disentangling the US in influence", in DANIEL S., STANISLAV P. (eds), *Consequences of the European Monetary Integration on Financial Markets*, Cambridge Scholars Publishing, Newcastle, 2008.

[BRI 10] BRIGO D., NORDIO C., "Liquidity-adjusted market risk measures with stochastic holding period", available at: www.ssrn.com/abstract=1679698, 2010.

[BRI 15] BRIÈRE M., SZAFARZ A., "Factor-based v. Industry-based asset allocation: the contest", available at: www.ssrn.com/abstract_id=2615703, 2015.

[BRO 92] BROCK W., LAKONISHOK J., LEBARON B., "Simple technical trading rules and the stochastic properties of stock returns", *Journal of Finance*, vol. 47, no. 5, pp. 1731–1764, 1992.

[BRO 99] BROWN S., GOETZMANN W., IBBOSTSON R., "Offshore hedge funds: survival and performance", *Journal of Business*, vol. 72, pp. 91–117, 1999.

[BRO 01] BROWN S., GOETZMANN W., PARK J., "Careers and survival: competition and risk in the hedge fund and CTA industry", *Journal of Finance*, vol. 56, no. 5, pp. 1869–1886, 2001.

[BRO 09] BRODIE J., DAUBECHIES I., DE MOL C., GIANNONE D., LORIS I., "Sparse and stable Markowitz portfolios", *Proceedings of the National Academy of Science*, vol. 106, no. 30, pp. 12267–12272, 2009.

[BRO 15a] BROKMANN X., SÉRIÉ E., KOCKELKOREN J. *et al.*, "Slow decay of impact in equity markets", *Market Microstructure and Liquidity*, vol. 1, no. 2, p. 1550007, 2015.

[BRO 15] BROWNLEES C., NUALART E., SUN Y., "Realized networks", available at: www.ssrn.com/abstract_id=2506703, 2015.

[BRU 09] BRUNNERMEIER M., PEDERSEN L., "Market liquidity and funding liquidity", *Review of Financial Studies*, vol. 22, no. 6, pp. 2201–2238, 2009.

[BUC 05] BUCKLE D., "Ex post reality versus ex ante theory of the fundamental law of active management", *Journal of Asset Management*, vol. 6, no. 1, pp. 21–32, 2005.

[BUF 06] BUFFET M., CLARK D., *The Tao of Warren Buffett: Warren Buffett's Words of Wisdom*, Scribner, New York, 2006.

[BUN 16] BUN J., BOUCHAUD J.-P., POTTERS M., "On the overlaps between eigenvectors of correlated random matrices", available at: https://arxiv.org/abs/1603.04364, 2016.

[BUR 46] BURNS A., MITCHELL W., *Measuring Business Cycles*, NBER Books, 1946.

[BUR 11] BURNSIDE C., EICHENBAUM M., REBELO S., "Carry trade and momentum in currency markets", *Annual Review of Financial Economics*, vol. 3, no. 1, pp. 511–535, 2011.

[CAI 05] CAILLAULT C., GUÉGAN D., "Empirical estimation of tail dependence using copulas. Application to Asian Markets", *Quantitative Finance*, vol. 5, no. 5, pp. 489–501, 2005.

[CAL 16] CALLUZZO P., MONETA F., TOPALOGLU S., "Information travels quickly, institutional investors react quickly, and anomalies decay quickly", 2016.

[CAM 81] CAMBANIS S., HUANG S., SIMONS G., "On the theory of elliptically contoured distributions", *Journal of Multivariate Analysis*, vol. 11, no. 3, pp. 368–385, 1981.

[CAM 97] CAMPBELL J., LO A., MACKINLAY A., *The Econometrics of Financial Markets*, Princeton University Press, 1997.

[CAM 02] CAMPBELL J., VICEIRA L., *Strategic Asset Allocation*, Oxford University Press, 2002.

[CAM 04] CAMPBELL J., VUOLTEENAHO T., "Inflation illusion and stock prices", *American Economic Review*, vol. 94, no. 2, pp. 19–23, 2004.

[CAM 09] CAMPBELL S., DIEBOLD F., "Stock returns and expected business conditions: half a century of direct evidence", *Journal of Business and Economic Statistics*, vol. 27, no. 2, pp. 266–278, 2009.

[CAR 97] CARHART M., "On persistence in mutual fund performance", *Journal of Finance*, vol. 52, no. 1, pp. 57–82, 1997.

[CAR 03] CARRASCO M., FLORENS J.-P., RENAULT E., "Linear inverse problems in structural econometrics: estimation based on spectral decomposition and regularization", in HECKMAN J., LEAMER E., (eds), *Handbook of Econometrics*, vol. 6B, Elsevier, Cambridge, 2003.

[CAR 11a] CARR P., WU L., "Leverage effect, volatility feedback, and self-exciting market disruptions", available at: http://faculty.baruch.cuny.edu/lwu/papers/CarrWuJFQA2016.pdf, 2011.

[CAR 11b] CARRASCO M., NOUMON N., "Optimal portfolio selection using regularization", available at: http://www.admissions.american.edu/cas/economics/info-metrics/pdf/upload/Carrasco-Nov-2011-submission.pdf, 2011.

[CHA 83] CHAMBERLAIN G., ROTHSCHILD M., "Arbitrage, factor structure and mean-variance analysis in large asset markets", *Econometrica*, vol. 51, pp. 1305–1324, 1983.

[CHA 05] CHACKO G., "Liquidity risks in the corporate bond markets", available at: www.ssrn.com/abstract=687619, 2005.

[CHA 15] CHAN P., SIRCAR R., "Optimal trading with predictable return and stochastic volatility", available at: www.ssrn.com/abstract=2478751, 2015.

[CHE 02] CHERUBINI U., LUCIANO E., "Bivariate option pricing with copulas", *Frontiers in Finance and Economics*, vol. 9, no. 2, pp. 69–85, 2002.

[CHE 03] CHEKHLOV A., URYASEV S., ZABARANKIN M., *Portfolio Optimization with Drawdown Constraints*, Risk Books, 2003.

[CHE 04] CHERUBINI U., LUCIANO E., VECCHIATO W., *Copula Methods in Finance*, Wiley Finance, 2004.

[CHE 05] CHEKHLOV A., URYASEV S., ZABARANKIN M., "Drawdown measure in portfolio optimization", *International Journal of Theoretical and Applied Finance*, vol. 8, no. 1, , pp. 13–58, 2005.

[CHE 07] CHEN L., LESMOND D., WEI J., "Corporate yield spreads and bond liquidity", *Journal of Finance*, vol. 62, no. 1, pp. 119–149, 2007.

[CHE 09] CHEUNG W., "The Black–Litterman model explained", *Journal of Asset Management*, vol. 11, no. 4, pp. 229–243, 2009.

[CHE 12] CHEVALLIER J., DING W., IELPO F., "Implementing a simple rule for dynamic stop-loss strategies", *Journal of Investing*, vol. 21, no. 4, pp. 111–114, 2012.

[CHE 13] CHEVALLIER J., IELPO F., *The Economics of Commodity Markets*, John Wiley & Sons, New York, 2013.

[CHE 14a] CHEVALLIER J., GATUMEL M., IELPO F., "Commodity markets through the business cycle", *Quantitative Finance*, vol. 14, no. 9, pp. 1597–1618, Taylor & Francis, 2014.

[CHE 14b] CHEVALLIER J., IELPO F., "Investigating the leverage effect in commodity markets with a recursive estimation approach", *Research in International Business and Finance*, 2014.

[CHE 14c] CHEVALLIER J., IELPO F., ""Time series momentum" in commodity markets", *Managerial Finance*, vol. 40, no. 7, pp. 662–680, 2014.

[CHI 12] CHICHEPORTICHE R., BOUCHAUD J.-P., "The joint distribution of stock returns is not elliptical", *International Journal of Theoretical and Applied Finance*, vol. 15, no. 3, p. 1250019, 2012.

[CHI 15] CHICHEPORTICHE R., BOUCHAUD J.-P., "A nested factor model for non-linear dependencies in stock returns", *Quantitative Finance*, vol. 15, no. 11, pp. 1789-1804, Taylor & Francis, 2015.

[CHO 93] CHOPRA V., ZIEMBA W.T., "The effect of errors in means, variances, and covariances on optimal portfolio choice", *Journal of Portfolio Management*, vol. 19, no. 2, pp. 6–11, Winter 1993.

[CHO 00] CHORDIA T., ROLL R., SUBRAHMANYAM A., "Commonality in liquidity", *Journal of Financial Economics*, vol. 56, no. 1, pp. 3–28, 2000.

[CHO 01] CHORDIA T., SUBRAHMANYAM A., ANSHUMAN V., "Trading activity and expected stock returns", *Journal of Financial Economics*, vol. 59, no. 1, pp. 3–32, 2001.

[CHO 08] CHOUEIFATY Y., COIGNARD Y., "Toward maximum diversification", *Journal of Portfolio Management*, vol. 35, no. 1, pp. 40–51, 2008.

[CHO 11] CHOW T.-M., HSU J., KALESNIK V., LITTLE B., "A survey of alternative equity index strategies", *Financial Analysts Journal*, vol. 67, no. 5, pp. 37–57, 2011.

[CHO 12] CHORRO C., GUÉGAN D., IELPO F., "Option pricing for GARCH-type models with generalized hyperbolic innovations", *Quantitative Finance*, vol. 12, no. 7, pp. 1079–1094, 2012.

[CHO 15] CHORRO C., GUÉGAN D., IELPO F., *A Time Series Approach to Option Pricing*, Springer, Berlin Heidelberg, 2015.

[CHO 16] CHOY J., DAVIS C., PRINEAS A., JOHNSON B., LAMONT K., Morningstar, a global guide to strategic-beta exchange-traded products, Report, Morningstar, 2016.

[CHR 06] CHRISTOFFERSEN P., HESTON S., JACOBS K., "Option valuation with conditional skewness", *Journal of Econometrics*, vol. 131, no. 1, pp. 253–284, 2006.

[CHR 11] CHRISTIANSEN C., RANALDO A., SÖDERLIND P., "The time-varying systematic risk of carry trade strategies", *Journal of Financial and Quantitative Analysis*, vol. 46, no. 4, pp. 1107–1125, 2011.

[CLA 73] CLARK P., "A Subordinated stochastic process model with finite variance for speculative prices", *Econometrica*, vol. 41, no. 1, pp. 135–155, 1973.

[CLA 02] CLARKE R., DE SILVA H., THORLEY S., "Portfolio constraints and the fundamental law of active management", *Financial Analysts Journal*, vol. 58, no. 5, pp. 48–66, 2002.

[CLA 06] CLARKE R., DE SILVA H., THORLEY S., "Minimum variance portfolios in the U.S. equity market", *Journal of Portfolio Management*, vol. 33, no. 1, pp. 10–24, 2006.

[CLA 09] CLAUSS P., RONCALLI T., WEISANG G., "Risk management lessons from Madoff fraud", *International Finance Review*, vol. 10, pp. 505–543, 2009.

[CLA 11] CLARKE R., DE SILVA H., THORLEY S., "Minimum variance portfolio composition", *Journal of Portfolio Management*, vol. 31, no. 2, pp. 31–45, 2011.

[CLA 13a] CLARE A., MOTSON N., THOMAS S., An evaluation of alternative equity indices – Part 1: Heuristic and optimised weighting schemes, Report, Cass Business School, 2013.

[CLA 13b] CLARE A., MOTSON N., THOMAS S., An evaluation of alternative equity indices – Part 2: Fundamental weighting schemes, Report, Cass Business School, March 2013.

[COC 99] COCHRANE J., "Portfolio advice for a multifactor world", *Economic Perspectives*, vol. 23, no. 3, pp. 59–78, 1999.

[COC 01] COCHRANE J., *Asset Pricing*, Princeton University Press, 2001.

[COC 11] COCHRANE J., "Presidential address: discount rates", *Journal of Finance*, vol. 66, no. 4, pp. 1047–1108, 2011.

[COL 01] COLLIN-DUFRESNE P., GOLDSTEIN R., MARTIN J., "The determinants of credit spread changes", *Journal of Finance*, vol. 56, no. 6, pp. 2177–2207, 2001.

[COM 94] COMON P., "Independent component analysis, a new concept?", *Signal Process*, vol. 36, no. 3, pp. 287–314, 1994.

[COM 07] COMMANDEUR J., KOOPMAN S., *An Introduction to State Space Time Series Analysis*, Oxford University Press, 2007.

[CON 86a] CONNOR G., KORAJCZYK R., "Performance measurement with the arbitrage pricing theory: a new framework for analysis", *Journal of Financial Economics*, vol. 15, no. 3, pp. 373–394, 1986.

[CON 86b] CONSTANTINIDES G.M., "Capital market equilibrium with transaction costs", *Journal of Political Economy*, vol. 94, no. 4, pp. 842–62, 1986.

[CON 88] CONNOR G., KORAJCZYK R., "Risk and return in an equilibrium APT: application of a new test methodology", *Journal of Financial Economics*, vol. 21, no. 2, pp. 255–289, 1988.

[CON 93] CONNOR G., KORAJCZYK R., "A test for the number of factors in an approximate factor model", *Journal of Finance*, vol. 48, no. 4, pp. 1263–1291, 1993.

[CON 95] CONNOR G., "The three types of factor models: a comparison of their explanatory power", *Financial Analysts Journal*, vol. 51, no. 3, pp. 42–46, 1995.

[CON 97] CONT R., POTTERS M., BOUCHAUD J.-P., *Scaling in Stock Market Data: Stable Laws and Beyond*, Springer, Berlin, Heidelberg, 1997.

[CON 01] CONT R., "Empirical properties of asset returns: stylized facts and statistical issues", *Quantitative Finance*, vol. 1, pp. 223–236, 2001.

[CON 07] CONT R., *Volatility Clustering in Financial Markets: Empirical Facts and Agent-Based Models*, Springer, Berlin, Heidelberg, 2007.

[CON 10a] CONNOR G., KORAJCZYK R., "Factor models in portfolio and asset pricing theory", in GUERARD JOHN B.J. (ed.), *Handbook of Portfolio Construction*, Springer, New York, 2010.

[CON 10b] CONNOR G., KORAJCZYK R., "Factor models of asset returns", in CONT R. (ed.), *Encyclopedia of Quantitative Finance*, Wiley, 2010.

[COO 09] COOPER I., PRIESTLEY R., "Time-varying risk premiums and the output gap", *Review of Financial Studies*, vol. 22, no. 7, pp. 2801–2833, 2009.

[COR 09] CORSI F., "A simple approximate long-memory model of realized volatility", *Journal of Financial Econometrics*, vol. 7, no. 2, pp. 174–196, 2009.

[COU 01] COUTANT S., DURRLEMAN V., RAPUCH G. *et al.*, "Copulas, Multivariate Risk – Neutral Distributions and Implied Dependence Functions", available at: www.ssrn.com/abstract=1032562, 2001.

[COV 07] COVEL M., *The Complete Turtle Trader: The Legend, the Lessons, the Results*, Harper Business, 2007.

[COX 85] COX J., INGERSOLL J., ROSS S., "A Theory of the term structure of interest rates", *Econometrica*, vol. 53, pp. 385–408, 1985.

[CRÉ 10] CRÉPON B., JACQUEMET N., *Économétrie: Méthode et Applications*, Ouvertures Économiques, De Boeck, 2010.

[CRE 09] CREMERS M., PETAJISTO A., "How active is your fund manager? A new measure that predicts performance", *Review of Financial Studies*, vol. 22, pp. 3329–3365, 2009.

[CRO 67] CROWN E., SIDDIQUI M., "Robust estimation of location", *Journal of the American Statistical Association*, vol. 62, pp. 353–389, 1967.

[CUR 14] CURATO G., GATHERAL J., LILLO F., "Optimal execution with nonlinear transient market impact", available at: https://arxiv.org/abs/1412.4839, 2014.

[D'AG 73] D'AGOSTINO R., PEARSON E., "Tests for departure from normality", *Biometrika*, vol. 60, no. 3, pp. 613–622, 1973.

[D'AG 12] D'AGOSTINO A., MCQUINN K., O'BRIEN D., "Nowcasting Irish GDP", *OECD Journal. Journal of Business Cycle Measurement and Analysis*, vol. 2, no. 7, pp. 21–31, 2012.

[DAN 97] DANIEL K., GRINBLATT M., TITMAN S. *et al.*, "Measuring mutual fund performance with characteristic-based benchmarks", *Journal of Finance*, vol. 52, no. 3, pp. 1035–1058, 1997.

[DAN 16] DANIEL K., MOSKOWITZ T., "Momentum crashes", *Journal of Financial Economics*, 2016.

[DAR 09] DAROLLES S., GOURIÉROUX C., JASIAK J., "L-performance with an application to hedge funds", *Journal of Empirical Finance*, vol. 16, no. 4, pp. 671–685, 2009.

[DAR 12] DARVAS Z., VARGA B., Uncovering Time-varying parameters with the Kalman-Filter and the flexible least squares: a Monte Carlo study, Working Paper no. 1204, Corvinus University of Budapest, 2012.

[DAR 13] DAROLLES S., DUVAUT P., JAY E., *Multi-factor Models and Signal Processing Techniques: Application to Quantitative Finance*, ISTE Ltd, London and John Wiley & Sons, New York, 2013.

[DAR 15] DAROLLES S., LE FOL G., MERO G., "Who is acting strategically", available at: http://www.u-cergy.fr/thema/repec/2015-14.pdf, 2015.

[DAS 09] DASTIDAR S., PHELPS B., Introducing LCS liquidity cost scores for US credit bonds, Qps Working Paper, Barclays Capital, 2009.

[DAS 11] DASTIDAR S., PHELPS B., "Credit spread decomposition: decomposing bond-level credit OAS into default and liquidity components", *Journal of Portfolio Management*, vol. 37, no. 3, pp. 70–84, 2011.

[DE 94] DE GREGORIO J., WOLF H., Terms of trade, productivity, and the real exchange rate, Report no. 4807, National Bureau of Economic Research, 1994.

[DE 12a] DE JONG F., DRIESSEN J., "Liquidity risk premia in corporate bond markets", *Quarterly Journal of Finance*, vol. 2, no. 2, p. 1250006, 2012.

[DE 12b] DE LATAILLADE J., DEREMBLE C., POTTERS M., BOUCHAUD J.-P., "Optimal trading with linear costs", *Journal of Investment Strategy*, vol. 1, no. 3, 2012.

[DE 15] DE JONG F., DRIESSEN J., "Can large long-term investors capture illiquidity premiums?", *Bankers, Markets & Investors*, vol. 134, pp. 34–60, 2015.

[DEH 79] DEHEUVELS P., "La fonction de dépendance empirique et ses propriétés – Un test non paramétrique d'indépendance", *Académie Royale de Belgique*, Bulletin de la Classe des Sciences, 5e Série, vol. 65, pp. 274–292, 1979.

[DEL 71] DELLACHERIE C., MEYER P.-A., *Probabilités et Potentiels*, Hermann, 1971.

[DEM 72] DEMPSTER A., "Covariance selection", *Biometrics*, vol. 28, no. 1, pp. 157–175, 1972.

[DEM 05] DEMARTA S., MCNEIL A., "The t copula and related copulas", *International Statistical Review*, vol. 73, no. 1, pp. 111–129, 2005.

[DEM 09a] DEMIGUEL V., GARLAPPI L., NOGALES F., *et al.*, "A generalized approach to portfolio optimization: improving performance by constraining portfolio norms", *Management Science*, vol. 55, no. 5, pp. 798–812, 2009.

[DEM 09b] DEMIGUEL V., GARLAPPI L., UPPAL R., "How inefficient are simple asset-allocation strategies?", *Review of Financial Studies*, vol. 22, no. 5, pp. 1915–1953, 2009.

[DEM 10] DEMEY P., MAILLARD S., RONCALLI T., "Risk-based indexation", available at: www.lyxor.com, 2010.

[DEM 13] DEMIGUEL V., MARTIN-UTRERA A., NOGALES F., "Size matters: optimal calibration of shrinkage estimators for portfolio selection", *Journal of Banking and Finance*, vol. 37, no. 8, pp. 3018–3034, 2013.

[DEM 15] DEMIGUEL V., MARTIN-UTRERA A., NOGALES F., "Parameter uncertainty in multiperiod portfolio optimization with transaction costs", *Journal of Financial and Quantitative Analysis*, vol. 50, no. 6, pp. 1443–1471, 2015.

[DES 15] DESCLÉE A., MAITRA A., POLBENNIKOV S., Adjusting DTS of Euro sovereign bonds to a low spread environment, Qps Working Paper, Barclays Capital, 2015.

[DID 09] DIDERICH C., *Positive Alpha Generation, Designing Sound Investment Processes*, John Wiley & Sons, New York, 2009.

[DIE 05] DIEBOLD F., PIAZZESI M., RUDEBUSCH G., Modeling bond yields in finance and macroeconomics, Working Paper no. 2005/03, Center for Financial Studies (CFS), 2005.

[DIE 06a] DIEBOLD F., *Elements of Forecasting*, 4th ed., Cengage Learning, 2006.

[DIE 06b] DIEBOLD F., LI C., "Forecasting the term structure of government bond yields", *Journal of Econometrics*, vol. 130, no. 2, pp. 337–364, 2006.

[DIN 93] DING Z., GRANGER C., ENGLE R., "A long memory property of stock market returns and a new model", *Journal of Empirical Finance*, vol. 1, no. 1, pp. 83–106, 1993.

[DIN 96] DING Z., GRANGER C., "Modeling volatility persistence of speculative returns: a new approach", *Journal of Econometrics*, vol. 73, no. 1, pp. 185–215, 1996.

[DIN 10] DING Z., "The fundamental law of active management: time series dynamics and cross-sectional properties", available at: https://www.math.nyu.edu/faculty/avellane/FundamentalLawFT.pdf, 2010.

[DON 16] DONIER J., BONART J., "A million metaorder analysis of market impact on the Bitcoin", available at: https://arxiv.org/abs/1412.4503, 2016.

[DOO 08] DOORNIK J., HANSEN H., "An Omnibus test for univariate and multivariate normality", *Oxford Bulletin of Economics and Statistics*, vol. 70, no. 1, pp. 927–939, 2008.

[DOU 99] DOUADY R., SHIRYAEV A., YOR M., "On probability characteristics of "downfalls" in a standard Brownian motion", *Theory of Probability and is Applications*, vol. 44, no. 1, pp. 29–38, 1999.

[DOU 13] DOUADY R., The volatility of low rates, Report, Riskdate, 2013.

[DRO 14] DROESBEKE J.-J., SAPORTA G., THOMAS-AGNAN C., *Les approches statistiques du risque*, Éditions Technip, 2014.

[DUA 06] DUAN J.-C., RITCHKEN P., SUN Z., Jump starting GARCH: pricing and hedging options with jumps in returns and volatilities, Working Paper, nos. 06–19, 2006.

[DUF 11] DUFFIE D., *Measuring Corporate Default Risk*, Oxford University Press, 2011.

[DUM 91] DUMAS B., LUCIANO E., "An exact solution to a dynamic portfolio choice problem under transactions costs", *Journal of Finance*, vol. 46, no. 2, pp. 577–95, 1991.

[DUR 12] DURBIN J., KOOPMAN S., *Time Series Analysis by State Space Methods*, 2nd ed., Oxford University Press, 2012.

[EAS 96] EASLEY D., KIEFER N., O'HARA M., PAPERMAN J., "Liquidity, information and infrequently traded stocks", *Journal of Finance*, vol. 51, pp. 1405–1436, 1996.

[EBE 02] EBERLEIN E., PRAUSE K., "The generalized hyperbolic model: financial derivatives and risk measures", *Mathematical Finance–Bachelier Congress 2000*, Springer, pp. 245–267, 2002.

[EDE 93] EDERINGTON L., LEE J., "How markets process information: news releases and volatility", *Journal of Finance*, vol. 48, no. 4, pp. 1161–1191, Wiley Online Library, 1993.

[EDE 95] EDERINGTON L., *Mean-variance as an Approximation to Expected Utility Maximization: Semi Ex-ante Results*, vol. 1, Mark Hirschey and Wayne Marr Editors, Emerald, London, 1995.

[EDI 96] EDISON H., "The reaction of exchange rates and interest rates to news releases", *FRB International Finance Discussion Paper*, vol. 570, 1996.

[EFR 77] EFRON B., MORRIS C., "Stein's paradox in statistics", *Scientific American*, vol. 236, no. 5, pp. 119–127, 1977.

[EHR 02] EHRMANN M., FRATZSCHER M., Interdependence between the euro area and the US: What role for EMU?, Working Paper, European Central Bank, 2002.

[ELI 07] ELING M., SCHUHMACHER F., "Does the choice of performance measure influence the evaluation of hedge funds", *Journal of Banking and Finance*, vol. 31, pp. 2632–2647, 2007.

[EMB 99] EMBRECHTS P., MCNEIL A., STRAUMANN D., "Correlation and dependence in risk management: properties and pitfalls", in DEMPSTER M., (ed.), *Risk Management: Value at Risk and Beyond*, Cambridge University Press, 1999.

[EMB 01] EMBRECHTS P., LINDSKOG F., MCNEIL A., "Modelling dependence with copulas and applications to risk management", available at: https://people.math.ethz.ch/embrecht/ftp/copchapter.pdf, 2001.

[ENG 82] ENGLE R., "Autoregressive conditional heteroscedasticity with estimates of the variance of United Kindom inflation rate", *Econometrica*, vol. 50, pp. 987–1007, 1982.

[ENG 86] ENGLE R., BOLLERSLEV T., "Modelling the persistence of conditional variances", *Econometric Reviews*, vol. 5, no. 1, pp. 1–50, 1986.

[ENG 96] ENGL H., HANKE M., NEUBAUER A., *Regularization of Inverse Problems, Mathematics and its Applications*, Springer, Netherlands, 1996.

[ENG 02] ENGLE R., "Dynamic conditional correlation", *Journal of Business & Economic Statistics*, vol. 20, no. 3, pp. 339–350, 2002.

[ENG 05] ENGEL C., WEST K., "Exchange rates and fundamentals", *Journal of Political Economy*, vol. 113, pp. 485–517, 2005.

[ENG 07] ENGLE R., FERSTENBERG R., "Execution risk", *Journal of Portfolio Management*, vol. 33, no. 2, pp. 34–45, 2007.

[ENG 16] ENGLE R., LEDOIT O., WOLF M., "Large dynamic covariance matrices", available at: http://www.econ.uzh.ch/static/wp/econwp231.pdf, 2016.

[ERB 06] ERB C., HARVEY C., "The strategic and tactical value of commodity futures", *Financial Analysts Journal*, vol. 62, no. 2, pp. 69–97, 2006.

[ERN 12] ERNST C., STANGE S., KASERER C., "Accounting for non normality in liquidity risk", *Journal of Risk*, vol. 14, no. 3, pp. 3–21, 2012.

[EVA 05] EVANS M., "Where are we now? Real-time estimates of the macro economy", *International Journal of Central Banking*, vol. 1, no. 6, pp. 127–175, 2005.

[EVA 15] EVANS J., "Smart Beta is no guarantee you will beat the market", available at: http://www.ft.com/intl/cms/s/0/2d00969c-a32f-11e4-9c06-0144feab7de.html, 2015.

[FAB 08] FABOZZI F., FOCCARDI S., KOLM P., *Financial Modeling of the Equity Market: From CAPM to Cointegration*, Wiley, 2008.

[FAM 65] FAMA E., "The behavior of stock-market prices", *Journal of Business*, vol. 38, no. 1, pp. 34–105, 1965.

[FAM 92] FAMA E., FRENCH K., "The cross-section of expected stock returns", *Journal of Finance*, vol. 47, no. 2, pp. 427–465, 1992.

[FAM 93] FAMA E., FRENCH K., "Common risk factors in the returns on stocks and bonds", *Journal of Financial Economics*, vol. 33, no. 1, pp. 3–56, 1993.

[FAM 96] FAMA E., FRENCH K., "Multifactor explanations of asset pricing anomalies", *Journal of Finance*, vol. 51, no. 1, pp. 55–84, 1996.

[FAM 10] FAMA E., FRENCH K., "Luck versus skill in the cross-section of mutual fund returns", *Journal of Finance*, vol. 65, no. 5, pp. 1915–1947, 2010.

[FAM 15] FAMA E., FRENCH K., "A five-factor asset pricing model", *Journal of Financial Economics*, vol. 116, no. 1, pp. 1–22, 2015.

[FAN 90] FANG K., KOTZ S., NG K.-W., *Symmetric Multivariate and Related Distributions*, Chapman & Hall, 1990.

[FAN 08a] FAN J., FAN Y., LV J., "High dimensional covariance matrix estimation using a factor model", *Journal of Econometrics*, vol. 147, no. 1, pp. 186–197, 2008.

[FAN 08b] FANTAZZINI D., "Dynamic copula modelling for value at risk", *Frontiers in Finance and Economics*, vol. 5, no. 2, pp. 72–108, 2008.

[FAN 12a] FAN J., ZHANG J., YU K., "Vast portfolio selection with gross-exposure constraints", *Journal of the American Statistical Association*, vol. 107, no. 498, pp. 592–606, 2012.

[FAN 12b] FANG Y., IELPO F., SÉVI B., "Empirical bias in intraday volatility measures", *Finance Research Letters*, vol. 9, no. 4, pp. 231–237, 2012.

[FAR 13] FARMER D., GERIG A., LILLO F. *et al.*, "How efficiency shapes market impact", *Quantitative Finance*, vol. 13, no. 11, pp. 1743–1758, 2013.

[FAS 15] FASTRICH B., PATERLINI S., WINKER P., "Constructing optimal sparse portfolios using regularization methods", *Computational Management Science*, vol. 12, no. 3, pp. 417–434, 2015.

[FEL 68] FELLER W., *An Introduction to Probability Theory and its Applications*, 3rd ed., Wiley, 1968.

[FER 14] FERRARA L., MARSILLI C., "Nowcasting global economic growth: a factor-augmented mixed-frequency approach", 2014.

[FLE 97] FLEMING M., REMOLONA E., "What moves the bond market?", *Economic Policy Review*, vol. 3, no. 4, pp. 31–50, 1997.

[FLE 99] FLEMING M., REMOLONA E., "Price formation and liquidity in the US Treasury market: the response to public information", *Journal of Finance*, vol. 54, no. 5, pp. 1901–1915, 1999.

[FLE 01a] FLEMING M., REMOLONA E., The term structure of announcement effects, Working Paper no 71, 2001.

[FLE 01b] FLETCHER J., HILLIER J., "An examination of resampled portfolio efficiency", *Financial Analysts Journal*, vol. 57, no. 5, pp. 66–74, 2001.

[FLE 09] FLETCHER J., "Risk reduction and mean–variance analysis: an empirical investigation", *Journal of Business Finance & Accounting*, vol. 36, pp. 951–971, 2009.

[FLO 07] FLORENS J.-P., MARIMOUTOU V., PEGUIN-FEISSOLLE A., *Econometric Modeling and Inference*, Cambridge University Press, 2007.

[FLO 11] FLORACKIS C., GREGORIOU A., KOSTAKIS A., "Trading frequency and asset pricing on the London Stock Exchange: evidence from a new price impact ratio", *Journal of Banking and Finance*, vol. 35, no. 12, pp. 3335–3350, 2011.

[FOU 13] FOUCAULT T., PAGANO M., ROELL A., *Market Liquidity: Theory, Evidence, and Policy*, Oxford University Press, 2013.

[FRA 01] FRANCOIS-HEUDE A., VAN WYNENDAELE P., Integrating liquidity risk in a parametric intraday VaR framework, Research Paper, 2001.

[FRO 86] FROST P., SAVARINO J., "An empirical Bayes approach to efficient portfolio selection", *Journal of Financial and Quantitative Analysis*, vol. 21, pp. 293–305, 1986.

[FRO 88] FROST P., SAVARINO J., "For better performance: constrain portfolio weights", *Journal of Portfolio Management*, vol. 15, no. 1, pp. 29–34, 1988.

[FRO 91] FROOT K., STEIN J., "Exchange rates and foreign direct investment: an imperfect capital markets approach", *Quarterly Journal of Economics*, vol. 106, no. 4, pp. 1191–1217, 1991.

[FRO 95] FROOT K., ROGOFF K., "Perspectives on PPP and long-run real exchange rates", in *Handbook of International Economics*, vol. 3, Elsevier, 1995.

[FUL 11] FULOP A., LI J., YU J., Bayesian learning of self-exciting return dynamics, Working Paper, Singapore Management University, 2011.

[FUN 97] FUNG W., HSIEH D., "Survivorship bias and investment style in the return of CTAs", *Journal of Portfolio Management*, vol. 24, no. 1, pp. 30–41, 1997.

[FUS 08] FUSAI G., RONCORONI A., *Implementing Models in Quantitative Finance: Methods and Cases*, Springer-Verlag, Berlin-Heidelberg, 2008.

[GAL 92] GALLANT R., ROSSI P., TAUCHEN G., "Stock prices and volume", *Review of Financial Studies*, vol. 5, no. 2, pp. 199–242, 1992.

[GAN 12] GANDER P., LEVEAU D., PFIFFNER T., "Categorization of indices: do all roads lead to Rome?", *Journal of Index Investing*, vol. 3, no. 3, 2012.

[GAR 80] GARMAN M., KLASS M., "On the estimation of security price volatilities from historical data", *Journal of Business*, vol. 53, no. 1, pp. 67–78, 1980.

[GAR 13a] GARCIN M., MERHY C., PISTRE N., Liquidity risk in fixed income markets: valuation adjustement, risk assessement, stress testing and portfolio construction, Report, Natixis Asset Management, 2013.

[GAR 13b] GARLEANU N., PEDERSEN L., "Dynamic trading with predictable returns and transaction costs", *Journal of Finance*, vol. 68, no. 6, pp. 2309–2340, 2013.

[GAR 16] GARLEANU N., PEDERSEN L., "Dynamic portfolio choice with frictions", *Journal of Economic Theory*, vol. 165, no. 6, pp. 487–516, 2016.

[GAT 10] GATHERAL J., "No-dynamic-arbitrage and market impact", *Quantitative Finance*, vol. 10, no. 7, pp. 749–759, 2010.

[GEN 86] GENEST C., MACKAY J., "The joy of copulas: bivariate distributions with uniform marginals", *American Statistician*, vol. 40, pp. 280–283, 1986.

[GEN 95] GENEST C., QUESADA MOLINA J., RODRIGUEZ LALLENA J., "De l'impossibilité de construire des lois à marges multidimensionnelles données à partir de copules", *Comptes Rendus de l'Académie des Sciences de Paris*, vol. 320, pp. 723–726, 1995.

[GIA 03] GIARDINA I., BOUCHAUD J., "Bubbles, crashes and intermittency in agent based market models", *The European Physical Journal B-Condensed Matter and Complex Systems*, vol. 31, no. 3, pp. 421–437, 2003.

[GIA 08] GIANNONE D., REICHLIN L., SMALL D., "Nowcasting: the real-time informational content of macroeconomic data", *Journal of Monetary Economics*, vol. 55, no. 4, pp. 665–676, 2008.

[GIA 09] GIANNONE D., REICHLIN L., SIMONELLI S., "Nowcasting euro area economic activity in real time: the role of confidence indicators", *National Institute Economic Review*, vol. 210, no. 1, pp. 90–97, 2009.

[GIL 09] GILCHRIST S., YANKOV V., ZAKRAJSEK E., "Credit market shocks and economic fluctuations: evidence from corporate bond and stock markets", *Journal of Monetary Economics*, vol. 56, no. 4, pp. 471–493, 2009.

[GIL 12] GILCHRIST S., ZAKRAJSEK E., "Credit spreads and business cycle fluctuations", *American Economic Review*, vol. 102, no. 4, pp. 1692–1720, 2012.

[GIO 10] GIOT P., LAURENT S., PETITJEAN M., "Trading activity, realized volatility and jumps", *Journal of Empirical Finance*, vol. 17, no. 1, pp. 168–175, 2010.

[GIV 13] GIVORD P., D'HAULTFŒUILLE X., La régression quantile en pratique, Working Paper, Institut National de la Statistique et des Études Économiques, 2013.

[GLA 13] GLASSERMAN P., XU X., "Robust portfolio control with stochastic factor dynamics", *Operations Research*, vol. 61, no. 4, pp. 874–893, 2013.

[GLO 92] GLOSTEN L., JAGANNATHAN R., RUNKLE D., "On the relation between the expected value and the volatility of the nominal excess return on stocks", *Journal of Finance*, vol. 48, no. 5, pp. 1779–1801, 1992.

[GOL 73] GOLDFELD S., QUANDT R., "A Markov model for switching regressions", *Journal of Econometrics*, vol. 1, no. 1, pp. 3–15, 1973.

[GOL 95] GOLDBERG L., KOLSTAD C., "Foreign direct investment, exchange rate variability and demand uncertainty", *International Economic Review*, vol. 36, no. 4, pp. 855–73, 1995.

[GOL 03a] GOLDBERG L., LEONARD D., "What moves sovereign bond markets? The effects of economic news on US and German yields", *Current Issues in Economics and Finance*, vol. 9, no. 9, 2003.

[GOL 03b] GOLDFARB D., IYENGAR G., "Robust portfolio selection problems", *Mathematics of Operations Research*, vol. 28, no. 1, pp. 1–38, 2003.

[GOM 15] GOMES C., WAELBROECK H., "Is market impact a measure of the information value of trades? Market response to liquidity vs. informed metaorders", *Quantitative Finance*, vol. 15, no. 5, pp. 773–793, 2015.

[GOR 06] GORTON G., ROUWENHORST K., "Facts and fantasies about commodity futures", *Financial Analysts Journal*, vol. 62, no. 2, pp. 47–68, 2006.

[GOT 09] GOTZ F., "A long road ahead for portfolio construction: practitioners' views of an EDHEC survey", available at: http://faculty-research.edhec.com/servlet/com.univ.collaboratif.utils.LectureFichiergw?ID_FICHIER=1328885973150, 2009.

[GOT 15] GOTO S., XU Y., "Improving mean variance optimization through sparse hedging restrictions", *Journal of Financial and Quantitative Analysis*, vol. 50, no. 6, pp. 1415–1441, 2015.

[GOU 97] GOURIÉROUX C., SCAILLET O., SZAFARZ A., *Econométrie de la finance, analyses historiques*, Economica, 1997.

[GOU 01] GOURIÉROUX C., JASIAK J., *Financial Econometrics: Problems, Models, and Methods*, Princeton University Press, 2001.

[GRE 02] GREGORIOU G., "Hedge fund survival lifetimes", *Journal of Asset Management*, vol. 3, no. 3, pp. 237–252, 2002.

[GRE 07] GRECU A., MALKIEL B., SAHA A., "Why do hedge funds stop reporting their performance?", *Journal of Portfolio Management*, vol. 34, no. 1, pp. 119–126, 2007.

[GRI 89] GRINOLD R., "The fundamental law of active management", *Journal of Portfolio Management*, vol. 15, no. 3, pp. 30–37, 1989.

[GRI 94] GRINOLD R., "Alpha is volatility times IC times score", *Journal of Portfolio Management*, vol. 20, no. 4, pp. 9–16, 1994.

[GRI 00] GRINOLD R., KAHN R., *Active Portfolio Management: a Quantitative Approach for Producing Superior Returns and Controlling Risk*, 2nd ed., McGraw-Hill, 2000.

[GRI 10] GRINOLD R., "Signal weighting", *Journal of Portfolio Management*, vol. 36, no. 4, pp. 24–34, 2010.

[GRO 84] GROENEVELD R., MEEDEN G., "Measuring skewness and kurtosis", *Journal of the Royal Statistical Society. Series D (The Statistician)*, vol. 33, no. 4, pp. 391–399, 1984.

[GUÉ 09] GUÉGAN D., IELPO F., "Further evidence on the impact of economic news on interest rates", *Frontiers in Finance and Economics*, vol. 6, no. 2, pp. 1–45, 2009.

[GUÉ 10] GUÉGAN D., MERHY C., A note on fair value and illiquid markets, CES Working Paper, University Pantheon-Sorbone (Paris 1), 2010.

[GUÉ 13] GUÉGAN D., IELPO F., LALAHARISON H., "Option pricing with discrete time jump processes", *Journal of Economic Dynamics and Control*, vol. 37, no. 12, pp. 2417–2445, 2013.

[GUÉ 16] GUÉANT O., *Optimal Execution and Liquidation in Finance*, Financial Mathematics, Chapman and Hall/CRC, 2016.

[GUI 07] GUIDOLIN M., TIMMERMANN A., "Asset allocation under multi variate regime switching", *Journal of Economic Dynamics and Control*, vol. 31, no. 11, pp. 3503–3544, 2007.

[HAE 14] HAESEN D., HALLERBACH W., MARKWAT T. *et al.*, "Enhancing risk parity by including views", available at: www.ssrn.com/abstract=2478751, 2014.

[HAL 12] HALLERBACH W.G., "A proof of the optimality of volatility weighting over time", *Journal of Investment Strategies*, vol. 1, no. 4, pp. 87–99, 2012.

[HAM 86] HAMILTON J., "State-space models", in ENGLE R., MCFADDEN D., (eds), *Handbook of Econometrics*, vol. 4, Elsevier, 1986.

[HAM 89] HAMILTON J., "A new approach to the economic analysis of nonstationary time series and the business cycle", *Econometrica*, vol. 57, no. 2, pp. 357–384, 1989.

[HAM 94] HAMILTON J.D., *Time Series Analysis*, Princeton University Press, 1994.

[HAN 77] HANNAH L., KAY J., *Concentration in Modern Industry: Theory, Measurement and the U.K. Experience*, Macmillan, 1977.

[HAN 91] HANSEN L., JAGANNATHAN R., "Restrictions on intertemporal marginal rates of substitution implied by asset returns", *Journal of Political Economy*, vol. 99, pp. 225–262, 1991.

[HAR 84] HARDOUVELIS G., "Market perceptions of federal reserve policy and the weekly monetary announcements", *Journal of Monetary Economics*, vol. 14, no. 2, pp. 225–240, 1984.

[HAR 90a] HARRIS L., "Statistical properties of the roll serial covariance bid/ask spread estimator", *Journal of Finance*, vol. 45, pp. 579–590, 1990.

[HAR 90b] HARVEY A., *The Econometric Analysis of Time Series*, 2nd ed., MIT Press, 1990.

[HAR 99] HARVEY C., SIDDIQUI A., "Autoregressive conditional skewness", *Journal of Financial and Quantitative Analysis*, vol. 34, no. 4, pp. 465–487, 1999.

[HAR 00] HARVEY C., SIDDIQUI A., "Conditional skewness in asset pricing tests", *Journal of Finance*, vol. 55, no. 3, pp. 1263–1295, 2000.

[HAR 08] HARVEY C., LIECHTY J., LIECHTY M., "Bayes vs. resampling: a rematch", *Journal of Investment Managements*, vol. 6, no. 1, pp. 1–17, 2008.

[HAR 10] HARVEY C., LIECHTY J., LIECHTY M. *et al.*, "Portfolio selection with higher moments", *Quantitative Finance*, vol. 10, no. 5, pp. 469–485, 2010.

[HAR 12] HARVEY A., KOOPMAN S., SHEPHARD N., *State Space and Unobserved Component Models*, Cambridge University Press, 2012.

[HÄR 15] HÄRDLE W., SIMAR L., *Applied Multivariate Statistical Analysis*, 4th ed., Springer-Verlag, 2015.

[HAR 16] HARVEY C., LIU Y., ZHU H., "... and the cross-section of expected returns", *Review of Financial Studies*, vol. 29, no. 1, pp. 5–68, 2016.

[HAS 01] HASBROUCK J., SEPPI D., "Common factors in prices, order flows and liquidity", *Journal of Financial Economics*, vol. 59, no. 3, pp. 383–411, 2001.

[HAS 07] HASBROUCK J., *Empirical Market Microstructure: The Institutions, Economics, and Econometrics of Securities Trading*, 1st ed., Oxford University Press, 2007.

[HAS 09] HASTIE T., TIBSHIRANI R., FRIEDMAN J., *The Elements of Statistical Learning*, 2nd ed., Springer, 2009.

[HAU 91] HAUGEN R., BAKER N., "The efficient market inefficiency of capitalization-weighted stock portfolios", *Journal of Portfolio Management*, vol. 17, no. 3, pp. 35–40, 1991.

[HAU 12] HAUGEN R., BAKER N., "Low risk stocks outperform within all observable markets of the world", available at: http://ssrn.com/abstract=2055431, 2012.

[HE 99] HE G., LITTERMAN R., The intuition behind Black–Litterman model portfolios, Report, Goldman Sachs Asset Management, 1999.

[HEA 07] HEATH A., GALATI G., MCGUIRE P., "Evidence of carry trade activity", *BIS Quarterly Review*, pp. 27–41, September 2007.

[HEN 93] HENDRICKS D., PATEL J., ZECKHAUSER R., "Hot Hands in Mutual Funds: Short-Run Persistence of Relative Performance, 1974–1988", *Journal of Finance*, vol. 48, no. 1, pp. 93–130, 1993.

[HÉR 87] HÉRAULT J., JUTTEN C., "Space or time adaptive signal processing by neural network models", *AIP Conference Proceedings 151 on Neural Networks for Computing*, American Institute of Physics Inc., pp. 206–211, 1987.

[HER 03] HEROLD U., "Portfolio construction with qualitative forecasts", *Journal of Portfolio Management*, vol. 30, no. 1, pp. 61–72, 2003.

[HES 93] HESTON S., "A closed-form solution for options with stochastic volatility with applications to bond and currency options", *Review of Financial Studies*, vol. 6, no. 2, pp. 327–343, 1993.

[HEV 14] HEVIA C., GONZÁLEZ-ROZADA M., SOLA M. *et al.*, "Estimating and forecasting the yield curve using a Markov switching dynamic Nelson and Siegel model", *Journal of Applied Econometrics*, vol. 30, no. 6, pp. 987–1009, 2014.

[HIG 14] HIGGINS P., GDPNow: a model for GDP "nowcasting", Working paper, Fedral Reserve Bank of Atlanta, 2014.

[HIN 75] HINKLEY D., "On power transformation to symmetry", *Biometrika*, vol. 62, no. 1, pp. 101–111, 1975.

[HLA 94] HLAWITSCHKA W., "The empirical nature of Taylor-series approximations to expected utility", *American Economic Review*, vol. 84, no. 3, pp. 713–719, 1994.

[HOE 70] HOERL A., KENNARD R., "Ridge regression: biased estimation for nonorthogonal problems", *Technometrics*, vol. 12, no. 1, pp. 55–67, 1970.

[HOG 72] HOGG R., "More light on the kurtosis and related statistics", *Journal of the American Statistical Association*, vol. 67, pp. 422–424, 1972.

[HOL 14] HOLDEN C., JACOBSEN S., SUBRAHMANYAM A., "Empirical analysis of liquidity", *Foundations and Trends in Finance*, vol. 8, no. 4, pp. 263–365, 2014.

[HOT 32] HOTTELING H., SOLOMONS L.M., "The limits of a measure of skewness", *Annals of Mathematicals Statistics*, vol. 3, no. 2, pp. 141–142, 1932.

[HSI 82] HSIEH D., "The determination of the real exchange rate: the productivity approach", *Journal of International Economics*, vol. 12, nos. 3–4, pp. 355–362, 1982.

[HU 09] HU G., "Measures of implicit trading costs and buy–sell asymmetry", *Journal of Financial Markets*, vol. 12, no. 3, pp. 418–437, 2009.

[HUB 01] HUBERMAN G., HALKA D., "Systematic liquidity", *Journal of Financial Research*, vol. 24, no. 2, pp. 161–178, 2001.

[HUB 04] HUBERMAN G., STANZL W., "Price manipulation and quasi-arbitrage", *Econometrica*, vol. 72, no. 4, pp. 1247–1275, 2004.

[HWA 99] HWANG S., SATCHELL S., "Modelling emerging market risk Premia using higher moments", *International Journal of Finance and Economics*, vol. 4, no. 4, pp. 271–296, 1999.

[IDZ 07] IDZOREK T., "A step-by-step guide to the Black–Litterman model", in SATCHELL S. (ed.), *Forecasting Expected Returns in The Financial Markets*, Academic Press, 2007.

[IDZ 13] IDZOREK T., KOWARA M., "Factor-based asset allocation vs. asset-class-based asset allocation", *Financial Analysts Journal*, vol. 69, no. 3, pp. 19–29, 2013.

[IEL 12] IELPO F., "Equity, credit and the business cycle", *Applied Financial Economics*, vol. 22, no. 12, pp. 939–954, 2012.

[IEL 15] IELPO F., "Forward rates, monetary policy and the economic cycle", *Journal of Forecasting*, vol. 34, no. 4, pp. 241–260, 2015.

[ILM 12] ILMANEN A., KIZER J., "The death of diversification has been greatly exaggerated", *Journal of Portfolio Management*, vol. 38, no. 3, pp. 15–27, 2012.

[IWA 13] IWASAWA S., USHIWAMA T., "A behavioral economics exploration into the volatility anomaly", *Public Policy Review*, vol. 9, no. 3, pp. 457–490, 2013.

[JAC 00] JACKWERTH J., "Recovering risk aversion from option prices and realized returns", *Review of Financial Studies*, vol. 13, no. 2, pp. 433–451, 2000.

[JAC 05] JACOBS B., LEVY K., MARKOWITZ H., "Portfolio optimization with factors, scenarios, and realistic short positions", *Operations Research*, vol. 53, no. 4, pp. 586–599, 2005.

[JAG 03] JAGANNATHAN R., MA T., "Risk reduction in large portfolios, why imposing the wrong constraints help", *Journal of Finance*, vol. 58, no. 4, pp. 1651–1684, 2003.

[JAI 15] JAISSON T., "Market impact as anticipation of the order flow imbalance", *Quantitative Finance*, vol. 15, no. 7, pp. 1123–1135, 2015.

[JAM 92] JAMES W., STEIN C., "Estimation with quadratic loss", vol. 1, of *Statistics*, pp. 443–460, Springer-Verlag, 1992.

[JAR 80] JARQUE C., BERA A.K., "Efficient tests for normality, homoscedasticity and serial independence of regression residuals", *Economics Letters*, vol. 6, no. 3, pp. 255–259, 1980.

[JEG 93] JEGADEESH N., TITMAN S., "Returns to buying winners and selling losers: implications for stock market efficiency", *Journal of Finance*, vol. 48, no. 1, pp. 65–91, 1993.

[JEN 68] JENSEN M., "The Performance of Mutual Funds in the Period 1945–1964", *Journal of Finance*, vol. 23, no. 2, pp. 389–416, 1968.

[JEN 70] JENNRICH R., "An asymptotic $\chi;^2$-test for the equality of two correlation matrices", *Journal of the American Statistical Association*, vol. 65, no. 330, pp. 904–912, 1970.

[JIA 05] JIANG G., TIAN Y., "The model-free implied volatility and its information content", *Review of Financial Studies*, vol. 18, no. 4, pp. 1305–1342, 2005.

[JIA 07] JIANG G., YAO T., YU T., "Do mutual funds time the market? Evidence from portfolio holdings", *Journal of Financial Economics*, vol. 86, pp. 724–758, 2007.

[JOB 80] JOBSON J., KORKIE R., "Estimation for Markowitz efficient portfolios", *Journal of the American Statistical Association*, vol. 75, pp. 544–554, 1980.

[JOB 81a] JOBSON J., KORKIE R., "Performance hypothesis testing with the Sharpe and Treynor measures", *Journal of Finance*, vol. 36, no. 4, pp. 889–908, 1981.

[JOB 81b] JOBSON J., KORKIE R., "Putting Markowitz theory to work", *Journal of Portfolio Management*, vol. 7, no. 4, pp. 70–74, 1981.

[JOE 90] JOE H., "Families of min-stable multivariate exponential and multivariate extreme value distributions", *Statistical and Probability Letters*, vol. 9, pp. 75–81, 1990.

[JOE 96] JOE H., "Families of m-variate distributions with given margins and $m(m-1)/2$ bivariate dependence parameters", in RUSCHENDORF L. (ed.), in *Distributions with Fixed Marginals and Related Topics*, Institute of Mathematical Statistics, 1996.

[JOE 97] JOE H., *Multivariate Models and Dependence Concepts*, Chapman & Hall, 1997.

[JOE 14] JOE H., *Dependence Modeling with Copulas*, Chapman & Hall, 2014.

[JOH 40] JOHNSON N., WELCH B., "Applications of the non-central t-distribution", *Biometrika*, vol. 3–4, no. 31, pp. 362–389, 1940.

[JOH 15] JOHNSON B., BOCCELLARI T., BRYAN A. *et al.*, Morningstar's Active/Passive Barometer, A New Yardstick for an Old Debate, Report, Morningstar, June 2015.

[JON 03] JONDEAU E., ROCKINGER M., "Conditional volatility, skewness, and kurtosis: existence, persistence, and comovements", *Journal of Economic Dynamics and Control*, vol. 27, no. 10, pp. 1699–1737, 2003.

[JON 06] JONDEAU E., ROCKINGER M., "Optimal portfolio allocation under higher moments", *European Financial Management*, vol. 12, no. 1, pp. 29–55, 2006.

[JON 07a] JONDEAU E., POON S., ROCKINGER M., *Financial Modeling Under Non-Gaussian Distributions*, Springer-Verlag, 2007.

[JON 10] JONDEAU E., ROCKINGER M., "Portfolio allocation for European markets with predictability and parameter uncertainty", *Swiss Finance Institute Research Paper Series*, vol. 10, no. 41, 2010.

[JON 07b] JONES R., LIM T., ZANGARI P., "The Black-Litterman model for structured equity portfolios", *Journal of Portfolio Management*, vol. 33, no. 2, pp. 24–33, 2007.

[JOR 86] JORION P., "Bayes-stein estimation for portfolio analysis", *Journal of Financial and Quantitative Analysis*, vol. 21, pp. 279–292, 1986.

[JOR 88] JORION P., "On jump processes in the foreign exchange and stock markets", *Review of Financial Studies*, vol. 1, no. 4, pp. 427–445, 1988.

[JOR 92] JORION P., "Portfolio optimization in practice", *Financial Analysts Journal*, vol. 48, no. 1, pp. 68–74, 1992.

[JOR 00] JORION P., "Risk management lessons from of long-term capital management", *European Financial Management*, vol. 6, no. 3, pp. 277–300, 2000.

[JOY 11] JOYCE M., LASAOSA A., STEVENS I. *et al.*, "The financial market impact of quantitative easing in the United Kingdom", *International Journal of Central Banking*, vol. 7, no. 3, pp. 113–161, 2011.

[JUG 62] JUGLAR J., *Des Crises commerciales et leur retour périodique en France, en Angleterre, et aux Etats-Unis*, Guillaumin, 1862.

[JUL 97] JULIER S., UHLMANN J., "A new extension of the Kalman filter to nonlinear systems", *Proceedings of AeroSense: The 11th International Symposium on Aerospace/Defense Sensing, Simulations and Controls*, vol. 3068, pp. 182–193, 1997.

[JUR 15a] JURCZENKO E. (ed.), *Risk-Based and Factor Investing*, ISTE Press, London and Elsevier, Oxford, 2015.

[JUR 15b] JURCZENKO E., MICHEL T., TEILETCHE J., "A unified framework for risk-based investing", *Journal of Investment Strategies*, vol. 4, no. 4, pp. 1–29, 2015.

[JUR 15c] JURCZENKO E., TEILETCHE J., "Active risk-based investing", available at: www.ssrn.com/abstract_id=2592904, 2015.

[JUT 91] JUTTEN C., HÉRAULT J., "Blind separation of sources, Part 1: an adaptive algorithm based on neuromimetic architecture", *Signal Processing*, vol. 24, no. 1, pp. 1–10, 1991.

[KAC 05] KACPERCZYK M., SIALM C., ZHENG L., "On the industry concentration of actively managed equity mutual funds", *Journal of Finance*, vol. 60, no. 4, pp. 1983–2011, 2005.

[KAL 60] KALMAN R.E., "A new approach to linear filtering and prediction problems", *Journal of Basic Engineering*, vol. 82, pp. 35–45, 1960.

[KAL 88] KALABA R., TESFATSION L., "The flexible least squares approach to time-varying linear regression", *Journal of Economic Dynamics and Control*, vol. 12, no. 1, pp. 43–48, 1988.

[KAL 89] KALABA R., TESFATSION L., "Time-varying linear regression via flexible least squares", *Computers & Mathematics with Applications*, vol. 17, nos. 7–8, pp. 1215–1245, 1989.

[KAL 08] KALTENBACHER B., NEUBAUER A., SCHERZER O., "Iterative regularization methods for nonlinear ill-posed problems", *Radon Series on Computational and Applied Mathematics*, vol. 6, Walter de Gruyter, 2008.

[KAM 12] KAMIEN M., SCHWARTZ N., *Dynamic Optimization: The Calculus of Variations and Optimal Control in Economics and Management*, 2nd ed., Dover Publications, 2012.

[KAR 98] KARATZAS I., SHREVE S., *Brownian Motion and Stochastic Calculus*, 2nd ed., Springer-Verlag, 1998.

[KAY 12] KAYA H., LEE W., Demystifying Risk Parity, Report, Neuberger Bergman, 2012.

[KAY 14] KAYA H., "The Bayesian roots of risk balancing", *Journal of Investment Strategies*, vol. 3, no. 3, pp. 19–39, 2014.

[KEL 70] KELKER D., "Distribution theory of spherical distributions and a location-scale parameter generalization", *Sankhya: The Indian Journal of Statistics, Series A*, vol. 32, no. 4, pp. 419–430, 1970.

[KEN 77] KENDALL M., STUART A., *The Advanced Theory of Statistics*, vol. 1, Griffin, 1977.

[KEN 90] KENDALL M., *Rank Correlation Methods*, 5th ed., Charles Griffin Book Series, Oxford University Press, 1990.

[KHA 11] KHANDANI A., LO A., "What happened to the quants in August 2007? Evidence from factors and transactions data", *Journal of Financial Markets*, vol. 14, no. 1, pp. 1–46, 2011.

[KIL 09] KILLIAN L., "Not all oil price shocks are alike: disentangling demand and supply shocks in the crude oil market", *American Economic Review*, vol. 99, no. 3, pp. 1053–1069, 2009.

[KIM 94] KIM C.-J., "Dynamic linear models with Markov-switching", *Journal of Econometrics*, vol. 60, nos. 1–2, pp. 1–22, 1994.

[KIM 99] KIM C.-J., NELSON C., *State Space Model with Regime Switching: Classical and Gibbs-Sampling Approaches with Applications*, MIT Press, 1999.

[KIM 08] KIM C.-J., PIGER J., STARTZ R., "Estimation of Markov regime-switching regression models with endogenous switching", *Journal of Econometrics*, vol. 143, no. 2, pp. 263–273, 2008.

[KIM 04] KIM T., WHITE H., "On more robust estimation of skewness and kurtosis", *Finance Research Letters*, vol. 1, pp. 56–73, 2004.

[KIN 99] KING R., REBELO S., "Resuscitating real business cycles", in TAYLOR J., WOODFORD M. (eds), *Handbook of Macroeconomics*, vol. 1, Elsevier, 1999.

[KIR 12] KIRBY C., OSTDIEK B., "It's all in the timing: simple active portfolio strategies that outperform naive diversification", *Journal of Financial and Quantitative Analysis*, vol. 47, no. 2, pp. 437–467, 2012.

[KIS 03] KISSELL R., GLANTZ M., *Optimal Trading Strategies: Quantitative Approaches for Managing Market Impact and Trading Risk*, Amacom, 2003.

[KIT 23] KITCHIN J., "Cycles and trends in economic factors", *Review of Economics and Statistics*, vol. 5, no. 1, pp. 10–16, 1923.

[KLA 05] KLADROBA A., "Flexible least squares estimation of state space models: an alternative to Kalman-filtering", University of Duisburg-Essen, Institute of Business and Economic Studie (IBES), 2005.

[KNI 05] KNIGHT J., SATCHELL S., *Linear Factor Models in Finance*, Elsevier Finance, 2005.

[KOE 05] KOENKER R., *Quantile Regression*, Cambridge University Press, 2005.

[KOL 15] KOLM P., RITTER G., "Multiperiod portfolio selection and bayesian dynamic models", available at: www.ssrn.com/abstract=2472768, 2015.

[KON 35] KONDRATIEFF N., "The long waves in economic life", *Review of Economics and Statistics*, vol. 17, no. 6, pp. 105–115, 1935.

[KOO 15] KOOPMAN S., SHEPHARD N., *Unobserved Components and Time Series Econometrics*, Oxford University Press, 2015.

[KOR 99] KORAJCZYK R., *Asset Pricing and Portfolio Performance: Models, Strategy and Performance Metrics*, Risk Books, 1999.

[KOR 08] KORAJCZYK R., SADKA R., "Pricing the commonality across alternative measures of liquidity", *Journal of Financial Economics*, vol. 87, no. 1, pp. 45–72, 2008.

[KOS 06] KOSOWSKI R., TIMMERMANN A., WERMERS R. *et al.*, "Can hedge funds "stars" really pick stocks? New evidence from a bootstrap analysis", *Journal of Finance*, vol. 61, no. 6, pp. 2551–2595, 2006.

[KRE 99] KRESS R., *Linear Integral Equations*, 2nd ed., Springer, 1999.

[KRI 10] KRITZMAN M., PAGE S., TURKINGTON D., "In defense of optimization: the fallacy of 1/N", *Financial Analysts Journal*, vol. 66, no. 2, pp. 31–39, 2010.

[KRI 11] KRISHNAMURTHY A., VISSING-JORGENSEN A., "The effects of quantitative easing on interest rates: channels and implications for policy", *Brookings Papers on Economic Activity*, vol. 43, no. 2, pp. 215–287, 2011.

[KRO 84] KROLL Y., LEVY H., MARKOWITZ H., "Mean-variance versus direct utility maximization", *Journal of Finance*, vol. 39, no. 1, pp. 47–61, 1984.

[KUZ 11] KUZIN V., MARCELLINO M., SCHUMACHER C., "MIDAS vs. mixed-frequency VAR: nowcasting GDP in the euro area", *International Journal of Forecasting*, vol. 27, no. 2, pp. 529–542, 2011.

[KYL 85] KYLE A., "Continuous auctions and insider trading", *Econometrica*, vol. 53, no. 6, pp. 1315–1336, 1985.

[LAH 11] LAHAYE J., LAURENT S., NEELY C., "Jumps, cojumps and macro announcements", *Journal of Applied Econometrics*, vol. 26, no. 6, pp. 893—921, 2011.

[LAL 99] LALOUX L., CIZEAU P., BOUCHAUD J.-P. *et al.*, "Noise dressing of financial correlation matrices", *Physical Review Letters*, vol. 83, no. 7, pp. 1467–1470, 1999.

[LAN 15] LANDIER A., SIMON G., THESMAR D., "The capacity of trading strategies", available at: www.ssrn.com/abstract=2585399, 2015.

[LAR 88] LARNTZ K., PERLMAN M., "A simple test for the equality of correlation matrices", vol. 2, pp. 289–298, Springer-Verlag, 1988.

[LED 01] LEDOIT O., WOLF M., "Improved estimation of the covariance matrix of stock returns with an application to portfolio selection", *Journal of Empirical Finance*, vol. 10, pp. 603–621, 2001.

[LED 02] LEDOIT O., WOLF M., "Some hypothesis tests for the covariance matrix when the dimension is large compared to the sample size", *Annals of Statistics*, vol. 30, no. 4, pp. 1081–1102, 2002.

[LED 03] LEDOIT O., WOLF M., "A well-conditioned estimator for large dimensional covariance matrices", *Journal of Multivariate Analysis*, vol. 88, no. 2, pp. 365–411, 2003.

[LED 04] LEDOIT O., WOLF M., "Honey, I shrunk the sample covariance matrix ", *Journal of Portfolio Management*, vol. 30, no. 4, pp. 110–119, 2004.

[LED 08] LEDOIT O., WOLF M., "Robust performance hypothesis testing with the Sharpe ratio", *Journal of Empirical Finance*, vol. 15, no. 5, pp. 850–859, 2008.

[LEE 00] LEE W., *Theory and Methodology of Tactical Asset Allocation*, Wiley, 2000.

[LEH 13] LEHALLE C.-A., LARUELLE S., *Market Microstructure in Practice*, World Scientific Publishing, 2013.

[LEI 07] LEINWEBER D.J., "Stupid data miner tricks, overfitting the S&P 500", *Journal of Investing*, vol. 16, no. 1, pp. 15–22, 2007.

[LEM 15] LEMPÉRIÈRE Y., DEREMBLE C., NGUYEN T.-T. *et al.*, "Risk Premia: Asymmetric Tail Risks and Excess Return", available at: https://arxiv.org/abs/1409.7720, 2015.

[LEO 12] LEOTE DE CARVALHO R., LU X., MOULIN P., "Demystifying equity risk-based strategies", *Journal of Portfolio Management*, vol. 38, no. 3, pp. 56–70, 2012.

[LEU 08] LEUNG P.-L., WONG W.-K., "On testing the equality of the multiple Sharpe ratios, with the application on the evaluation of iShares", *Journal of Risk*, vol. 10, no. 3, pp. 1–16, 2008.

[LEV 79] LEVY H., MARKOWITZ H., "Approximating expected utility by a function of mean and variance", *American Economic Review*, vol. 69, no. 3, pp. 308–317, 1979.

[LHA 12] LHABITANT F.-S., "Correlation vs. trends in portfolio management: a common misinterpretation", *Journal of Wealth Management*, vol. 15, no. 3, pp. 63–66, 2012.

[LI 14] LI X., SULLIVAN R., GARCIA-FEIJÓO L., "The limits to arbitrage and the low-volatility anomaly", *Financial Analysts Journal*, vol. 70, no. 1, pp. 52–63, 2014.

[LIL 03] LILLO F., FARMER D., MANTEGNA R., "Master curve for price-impact function", *Nature*, vol. 421, pp. 129–130, 2003.

[LIN 65] LINTNER J., "The valuation of risk assets and the selection of risky investments in stock portfolios and capital budgets", *The Review of Economics and Statistics*, vol. 47, no. 1, pp. 13–37, 1965.

[LIT 91] LITTERMAN R., SCHEINKMAN J., "Common factors affecting bond returns", *Journal of Fixed Income*, vol. 1, no. 1, pp. 54–61, 1991.

[LIU 02] LIU H., LOWENSTEIN M., "Optimal portfolio selection with transaction costs and finite horizons", *Review of Financial Studies*, vol. 15, no. 3, pp. 805–835, 2002.

[LIU 04] LIU H., "Optimal consumption and investment with transaction costs and multiple risky assets", *Journal of Finance*, vol. 59, no. 1, pp. 289–338, 2004.

[LIU 14] LIU R., MUHLE-KARBE J., WEBER M., "Rebalancing with Linear and Quadratic Costs", available at: https://arxiv.org/abs/1402.5306, 2014.

[LO 90] LO A., MACKINLAY A., "Data-snooping biases in tests of financial asset pricing models", *Review of Financial Studies*, vol. 3, pp. 431–467, 1990.

[LO 91] LO A., "Long-term memory in stock market prices", *Econometrica*, vol. 59, no. 5, pp. 1279–1313, 1991.

[LO 02] LO A., "The statistics of Sharpe ratios", *Financial Analysts Journal*, vol. 58, no. 4, pp. 36–52, 2002.

[LO 04] LO A., "The adaptative market hypothesis: market efficiency from an evolutionary perspective", *Journal of Portfolio Management*, vol. 30, no. 5, pp. 15–29, 2004.

[LO 16] LO A., "What is an index?", *Journal of Portfolio Management*, vol. 42, no. 2, pp. 21–36, 2016.

[LON 83] LONG J., PLOSSER C., "Real business cycles", *Journal of Political Economy*, vol. 91, no. 1, pp. 39–69, 1983.

[LOP 16] LOPEZ DE PRADO M., "Mathematics and economics: a reality check", *Journal of Portfolio Management*, vol. 43, no. 1, pp. 5–8, 2016.

[LOU 11] LOU X., SADKA R., "Liquidity level or liquidity risk? Evidence from the financial crisis", *Financial Analyst Journal*, vol. 67, no. 2, pp. 36–44, 2011.

[MAC 00] MACKINLAY A., PÁSTOR L., "Asset pricing models: implications for expected returns and portfolio selection", *Review of Financial Studies*, vol. 13, no. 4, pp. 883–916, 2000.

[MAG 76] MAGILL M., CONSTANTINIDES G., "Portfolio selection with transaction costs", *Journal of Economic Theory*, vol. 13, no. 2, pp. 245–263, 1976.

[MAG 04a] MAGDON-ISMAIL M., ATIYA A., "Maximum drawdown", available at: http://alumnus.caltech.edu/amir/mdd-risk.pdf, October 2004.

[MAG 04b] MAGDON-ISMAIL M., ATIYA A., PRATAP A. *et al.*, "On the maximum drawdown of a brownian motion", *Journal of Applied Probability*, vol. 41, no. 1, pp. 147–161, 2004.

[MAI 10] MAILLARD S., RONCALLI T., TEILETCHE J., "The properties of equally-weighted risk contribution portfolios", *Journal of Portfolio Management*, vol. 36, no. 4, pp. 60–70, 2010.

[MAL 04] MALEVERGNE Y., SORNETTE D., "Collective origin of the coexistence of apparent RMT noise and factors in large sample correlation matrices", *Physica A: Statistical Mechanics and its Applications*, vol. 331, nos. 3–4, pp. 660–668, 2004.

[MAN 63] MANDELBROT B., "The variation of certain speculative prices", *Journal of Business*, vol. 36, p. 394, 1963.

[MAR 67] MARČENKO V., PASTUR L., "Distribution of Eigenvalues of Some Sets of Random Matrices", *Mathematics of the USSR-Sbornik*, vol. 1, no. 4, pp. 457–483, 1967.

[MAR 95] MARK N., "Exchange rates and fundamentals: evidence on long-horizon predictability", *American Economic Review*, vol. 85, no. 1, pp. 201–218, 1995.

[MAR 04] MARKOV M., MOTTL V., MUCHNIK I., Principles of nonstationary regression estimation a new approach to dynamic multi factor models in finance, Dimacs technical report, Rutgers University, October 2004.

[MAR 52] MARKOWITZ H., "Portfolio selection", *Journal of Finance*, vol. 7, no. 1, pp. 77–91, 1952.

[MAR 59] MARKOWITZ H., *Portfolio Selection: Efficient Diversification of Investments*, Basil Blackwell, 1959.

[MAR 79] MARKOWITZ H., LEVY H., "Approximating expected utility by a function of mean and variance", *American Economic Review*, vol. 69, no. 3, pp. 308–317, 1979.

[MAR 03a] MARKOWITZ H., USMEN N., "Resampled frontiers vs diffuse Bayes: an experiment", *Journal of Investment Management*, vol. 1, no. 4, pp. 9–25, 2003.

[MAR 10] MARKOWITZ H., "Portfolio theory: as i still see it", *Annual Review of Financial Economics*, vol. 2, pp. 1–23, December 2010.

[MAR 03b] MARTELLINI L., PRIAULET P., PRIAULET S., *Fixed-income securities: valuation, risk management, and portfolio strategies*, Wiley, 2003.

[MAR 09] MARTELLINI L., "Toward the design of better equity benchmarks", *Journal of Portfolio Management*, vol. 34, no. 4, pp. 1–8, 2009.

[MAR 11] MARTIN R., SCHÖNEBORN T., "Mean reversion pays, but costs", *Risk*, vol. 24, no. 2, pp. 96–101, 2011.

[MAR 12] MARTIN R., "Optimal multifactor trading under proportional transaction costs", available at: https://arxiv.org/abs/1204.6488, 2012.

[MAR 16] MARKWAT T., MOLENAAR R., "The ins and outs of investing in illiquid assets", *Alternative Investment Analyst Review*, vol. 5, no. 1, pp. 23–33, 2016.

[MAS 14] MASTROMATTEO I., TÓTH B., BOUCHAUD J.-P., "Agent-based models for latent liquidity and concave price impact", *Physical Review E*, vol. 89, p. 042805, 2014.

[MCL 16] MCLEAN D., PONTIFF J., "Does academic research destroy stock return predictability?", *Journal of Finance*, vol. 71, no. 1, pp. 5–32, 2016.

[MEE 83] MEESE R., ROGOFF K., "Empirical exchange rate models of the seventies: do they fit out of sample?", *Journal of international economics*, vol. 14, no. 1, pp. 3–24, 1983.

[MEH 04] MEHTA M., *Random Matrices*, Pure and Applied Mathematics, 3rd ed., Elsevier, 2004.

[MEM 03] MEMMEL C., "Performance hypothesis testing with the Sharpe ratio", *Finance Letters*, vol. 1, pp. 21–23, 2003.

[MER 71] MERTON R., "Optimal consumption and portfolio rules in a continuous-time model", *Journal of Economic Theory*, vol. 3, pp. 373–413, 1971.

[MER 73] MERTON R., "An intertemporal capital asset pricing model", *Econometrica*, vol. 41, no. 5, pp. 867–87, 1973.

[MER 80] MERTON R., "On estimating the expected return on the market: an exploratory investigation", *Journal of Financial Economics*, vol. 8, no. 4, pp. 323–361, 1980.

[MEU 05] MEUCCI A., *Risk and Asset Allocation*, Springer, 2005.

[MEU 08] MEUCCI A., "Fully flexible views, theory and practice", *Risk*, vol. 21, no. 10, pp. 97–102, 2008.

[MEU 11] MEUCCI A., "A new breed of copulas for risk and portfolio management", *Risk*, vol. 24, no. 9, pp. 122–126, 2011.

[MEU 12] MEUCCI A., "A fully integrated liquidity and market risk model", *Financial Analyst Journal*, vol. 68, no. 8, pp. 55–67, 2012.

[MEU 14] MEUCCI A., "Linear factor models: theory, applications and pitfalls", available at: www.ssrn.com/abstract=1635495, 2014.

[MEU 16] MEUCCI A., LOREGIAN A., "Neither "Normal" nor "Lognormal": modeling interest rates across all regimes", *Financial Analysts Journal*, vol. 72, no. 3, pp. 68–82, 2016.

[MIC 89] MICHAUD R., "The Markowitz optimization enigma: is "Optimized" optimal", *Financial Analysts Journal*, vol. 45, pp. 31–42, 1989.

[MIC 98] MICHAUD R., *Efficient Asset Management: A Practical Guide to Stock Portfolio Management and Asset Allocation*, HBS Press, 1998.

[MIC 13] MICHAUD R., ESCH D., MICHAUD R., "Deconstructing Black-Litterman: how to get the portfolio you already knew you wanted", *Journal of Investment Management*, vol. 11, no. 1, pp. 6–20, 2013.

[MIC 16] MICHAUD R., ESCH D., MICHAUD R., "The 'Fundamental Law of Active Management' is no law of anything", available at: www.ssrn.com/abstract=2834020, 2016.

[MIL 78] MILLER R., GEHR A., "Sample size bias and Sharpe's performance measure: a note", *Journal of Financial and Quantitative Analysis*, vol. 13, no. 5, pp. 943–946, 1978.

[MIT 09] MITCHELL J., "Where are we now? The UK recession and nowcasting GDP growth using statistical models", *National Institute Economic Review*, vol. 209, no. 1, pp. 60–69, 2009.

[MON 15] MONASSON R., VILLAMAINA D., "Estimating the principal components of correlation matrices from all their empirical eigenvectors", *Europhysics Letters*, vol. 112, no. 5, p. 50001, 2015.

[MON 07a] MONFORT A., PEGORARO F., "Switching VARMA term structure models", *Journal of Financial Econometrics*, vol. 5, no. 1, pp. 105–153, 2007.

[MON 07b] MONTIER J., *CAPM Is CRAP (or, The Dead Parrot Lives!)*, in MONTIER J., *Behavioural Investing: A Practitioner's Guide to Applying Behavioural Finance*, Wiley, 2007.

[MON 09] MONTANA G., TRIANTAFYLLOPOULOS K., TSAGARIS T., "Flexible least squares for temporal data mining and statistical arbitrage", *Expert Systems with Applications*, vol. 36, no. 2, pp. 2819–2830, 2009.

[MOO 88] MOORS J., "A quantile alternative for kurtosis", *The Statistician*, vol. 37, no. 1, pp. 25–32, 1988.

[MOR 15] MORGAN S., WINSHIP C., *Counterfactuals and Causal Inference: Methods and Principles for Social Research*, 2nd ed., Cambridge University Press, 2015.

[MOR 09] MORO E., VICENTE J., MOYANO L. *et al.*, "Market impact and trading profile of hidden orders in stock markets", *Physical Review E*, vol. 80, p. 066102, American Physical Society, 2009.

[MOS 12] MOSKOWITZ T., OOI Y., PEDERSEN L., "Time series momentum", *Journal of Financial Economics*, vol. 104, no. 2, pp. 228–250, 2012.

[MOS 66] MOSSIN J., "Equilibrium in a capital asset market", *Econometrica*, vol. 34, no. 4, pp. 768–783, 1966.

[MUI 87] MUIRHEAD R., "Developments in eigenvalue estimation", in GUPTA A., (ed.), *Advances in Multivariate Statistical Analysis*, Springer, 1987.

[NAD 64] NADARAYA E., "On estimating regression", *Theory of Probability and Its Applications*, vol. 9, no. 1, pp. 141–142, 1964.

[NEL 76] NELSON C., "Inflation and rates of return on common stocks", *Journal of Finance*, vol. 31, no. 2, pp. 471–483, 1976.

[NEL 87] NELSON C., SIEGEL A., "Parsimonious modeling of yield curves", *Journal of Business*, vol. 60, no. 4, pp. 473–89, 1987.

[NEL 91] NELSON D., "Conditional heteroskedasticity in asset returns: a new approach", *Econometrica*, vol. 59, no. 2, pp. 347–370, 1991.

[NEL 06] NELSEN R., *An Introduction to Copulas*, Statistics, Springer-Verlag, 2006.

[NG 15] NG K., PHELPS B., "The hunt for a low-risk anomaly in the USD corporate bond market", *Journal of Portfolio Management*, vol. 42, no. 1, pp. 63–84, 2015.

[NGU 11] NGUYEN V., SERCU P., "Tactical asset allocation with commodity futures: implications of business cycle and monetary policy", available at: www.ssrn.com/abstract=1695889, 2011.

[NIK 09] NIKOLAOU K., "Liquidity (risk) concepts definitions and interactions", ECB Working Paper No. 1008, available at: https://ssrn.com/abstract=1333568, 2009.

[NYH 07] NYHOLM K., "A new approach to predicting recessions", *Economic Notes*, vol. 36, no. 1, pp. 27–42, 2007.

[OBI 13] OBIZHAEVA A., WANG J., "Optimal trading strategy and supply/demand dynamics", *Journal of Financial Markets*, vol. 16, no. 1, pp. 1–32, 2013.

[ODE 15] ODERDA G., "Stochastic portfolio theory optimization and the origin of rule-based investing", *Quantitative Finance*, vol. 15, no. 8, pp. 1259–1266, 2015.

[ONA 09] ONATSKI A., "Testing hypotheses about the number of factors in large factor models", *Journal of Financial Economics*, vol. 77, no. 5, pp. 1447–1479, 2009.

[OPD 07] OPDYKE J., "Comparing Sharpe ratios: so where are the p-values?", *Journal of Asset Management*, vol. 8, no. 5, pp. 308–336, 2007.

[PÁS 03] PÁSTOR L., STAMBAUGH R., "Liquidity risk and expected stock returns", *Journal of Political Economy*, vol. 111, no. 3, pp. 642–685, 2003.

[PAF 04] PAFKA S., KONDOR I., "Estimated correlation matrices and portfolio optimization", *Physica A: Statistical Mechanics and Its Applications*, vol. 343, pp. 623–634, 2004.

[PAR 80] PARKINSON M., "The extreme value method for estimating the variance of the rate of return", *Journal of Business*, vol. 53, no. 1, pp. 61–65, 1980.

[PAS 11] PASTUR L., SHCHERBINA M., *Eigenvalue Distribution of Large Random Matrices*, Mathematical Surveys and Monographs, American Mathematical Society, 2011.

[PAS 16] PASSERINI F., VÁZQUEZ S., "Optimal trading with alpha predictors", *Journal of Investment Strategies*, vol. 5, no. 3, 2016.

[PAT 06] PATTON A., "Modelling asymmetric exchange rate dependence", *International Economic Review*, vol. 47, no. 2, pp. 527–556, 2006.

[PAY 12] PAYE B., "'Déjà vol': predictive regressions for aggregate stock market volatility using macroeconomic variables", *Journal of Financial Economics*, vol. 106, no. 3, pp. 527–546, 2012.

[PEL 15] PELAGATTI M., *Time Series Modelling with Unobserved Components*, CRC Press, 2015.

[PER 88] PEROLD A., "The implementation shortfall: paper versus reality", *Journal of Portfolio Management*, vol. 14, no. 3, pp. 4–9, 1988.

[PER 04] PEROLD A., "The capital asset pricing model", *Journal of Economic Perspectives*, vol. 18, no. 3, pp. 3–24, 2004.

[PER 07] PEROLD A., "Fundamentally flawed indexing", *Financial Analysts Journal*, vol. 63, no. 6, pp. 31–37, 2007.

[PLE 02] PLEROU V., GOPIKRISHNAN P., ROSENOW B. *et al.*, "A random matrix approach to cross-correlations in financial data", *Physical Review Letter E*, vol. 65, no. 6, p. 066126, 2002.

[POG 70] POGUE G., "An extension of the Markowitz portfolio selection model to include variable transactions' costs, short sales, leverage policies and taxes", *Journal of Finance*, vol. 25, no. 5, pp. 1005–1027, 1970.

[POO 05] POON S.-H., *A Practical Guide to Forecasting Financial Market Volatility*, John Wiley & Sons, 2005.

[POT 05] POTTERS M., BOUCHAUD J.-P., LALOUX L., "Financial applications of random matrix theory: old laces and new pieces", *Acta Physica Polonica B*, vol. 36, no. 9, pp. 623–634, 2005.

[PUK 15] PUKTHUANTHONG K., ROLL R., "A protocol for factor identification", available at: www.ssrn.com/abstract=2342624, 2015.

[QIA 04] QIAN E., HUA R., "Active risk and information ratio", *Journal of Investment Management*, vol. 2, no. 3, pp. 20–34, 2004.

[QIA 05] QIAN E., "Risk parity portfolios", Report , PanAgora Asset Management, 2005.

[QIA 15] QIAN E., ALONSO N., BARNES M., "The triumph of mediocrity: a case study of Naïve Beta", *Journal of Portfolio Management*, vol. 41, no. 4, pp. 19–34, 2015.

[RAN 06] RANGVID J., "Output and expected returns", *Journal of Financial Economics*, vol. 81, no. 3, pp. 595–624, 2006.

[RAP 10] RAPACH D., STRAUSS J., ZHOU G., "Out-of-sample equity premium prediction: combination forecasts and links to the real economy", *Review of Financial Studies*, vol. 23, no. 2, pp. 821–862, 2010.

[RAP 13] RAPACH D., ZHOU G., "Forecasting stock returns", *Handbook of Economic Forecasting, 2(Part A)*, pp. 328–383, 2013.

[REJ 16] REJ A., BENICHOU R., DE LATAILLADE J. *et al.*, "Optimal trading with linear and (small) non-linear costs", 2016.

[RIC 93] RICHARDSON M., SMITH T., "A test for multivariate normality in stock returns", *Journal of Business*, vol. 66, no. 2, pp. 295–321, 1993.

[ROG 91] ROGERS L., SATCHELL S., "Estimating variance from high, low and closing prices", *Annals of Applied Probability*, vol. 1, no. 4, pp. 504–512, 1991.

[RON 11] RONCALLI T., "Understanding the impact of weights constraints in portfolio theory", available at: www.ssrn.com/abstract_id=1761625, 2011.

[RON 14] RONCALLI T., *Introduction to Risk Parity and Budgeting*, Chapman & Hall/CRC, 2013.

[RON 15] RONCALLI T., "Introducing expected returns into risk parity portfolios: a new framework for asset allocation", *Bankers, Markets & Investors*, vol. 138, September 2015.

[ROS 76] ROSS S., "The arbitrage theory of capital asset pricing", *Journal of Economic Theory*, vol. 13, no. 3, pp. 341–360, 1976.

[ROS 10] ROSSITER J., "Nowcasting the global economy", *Bank of Canada Discussion Paper*, vol. 2010–12, 2010.

[ROY 52] ROY A., "Safety first and the holding of assets", *Econometrica*, vol. 20, no. 3, pp. 431–449, 1952.

[RUB 02] RUBINSTEIN M., "Markowitz's "Portfolio Selection": a fifty-year retrospective", *Journal of Finance*, vol. 62, no. 3, pp. 1041–1045, 2002.

[SAD 14] SADKA R., "Asset class liquidity risk", *Bankers, Markets & Investors*, vol. 128, pp. 20–30, 2014.

[SAL 07] SALVADORI G., DE MICHELE C., KOTTEGODA N. *et al.*, *Extremes in Nature: An Approach Using Copulas*, Springer, 2007.

[SAT 00] SATCHELL S., SCOWCROFT A., "A demystification of the Black-Litterman model: managing quantitative and traditional portfolio construction", *Journal of Asset Management*, vol. 1, no. 2, pp. 138–150, 2000.

[SAV 54] SAVAGE L., *The Foundations of Statistics*, Wiley, 1954.

[SCH 76] SCHWEIZER B., WOLFF E., "Sur une mesure de dépendance pour les variables aléatoires", *Comptes Rendus de l'Académie des Sciences de Paris*, vol. 283, pp. 659–661, 1976.

[SCH 81] SCHWEIZER B., WOLFF E., "On nonparametric measures of dependence for random variables", *Annals of Statistics*, vol. 9, no. 4, pp. 879–885, 1981.

[SCH 89] SCHWERT W., "Why does stock market volatility change over time?", *Journal of Finance*, vol. 44, no. 5, pp. 1115–1153, 1989.

[SCH 02] SCHERER B., "Portfolio resampling: review and critique", *Financial Analysts Journal*, vol. 58, no. 6, pp. 98–109, 2002.

[SCH 09] SCHUTEL DASILVA A., LEE W., PORNROJNANGKOOL B., "The Black-Litterman model for active portfolio management", *Journal of Portfolio Management*, vol. 35, no. 2, pp. 61–70, 2009.

[SCH 10] SCHERER B., "A new look on minimum variance investing", available at: www.ssrn.com/abstract=1681306, 2010.

[SCH 12] SCHORFEIDE F., WOLPIN K., "On the use of holdout samples for model selection", *American Economic Review*, vol. 102, no. 3, pp. 477–481, 2012.

[SEN 10] SENECHAL E., "The empirical law of active management perspectives on the declining skill of U.S. fund managers", *Journal of Portfolio Management*, vol. 37, no. 1, pp. 121–132, 2010.

[SHA 63] SHARPE W., "A simplified model for portfolio analysis", *Management Science*, vol. 9, no. 2, pp. 277–293, 1963.

[SHA 64] SHARPE W., "Capital asset prices: a theory of market equilibrium under conditions of risk", *Journal of Finance*, vol. 19, no. 3, pp. 425–442, 1964.

[SHA 66] SHARPE W., "Mutual fund performance", *Journal of Business*, vol. 39, no. 1, pp. 119–138, 1966.

[SHI 82] SHILLER R., "Consumption, asset markets and macroeconomic fluctuations", *Carnegie-Rochester Conference Series on Public Policy*, vol. 17, no. 1, pp. 203–238, 1982.

[SIE 88] SIEGEL S., CASTELLAN J., *Nonparametric Statistics for the Behavioral Sciences*, 2nd ed., McGraw-Hill, 1988.

[SIE 14] SIEGEL L.B., SCANLAN M., "No fear of commitment: the role of high-conviction active management", *Journal of Investing*, vol. 23, no. 3, pp. 7–22, 2014.

[SKA 09] SKAF J., BOYD S., "Multi-period portfolio optimization with constraints and transaction costs", available at: https://web.stanford.edu/boyd/papers/pdf/dyn_port_opt.pdf, 2009.

[SKL 59] SKLAR A., "Fonctions de répartitions à n dimensions et leurs marges", *Publications de l'Institut Statistique de l'Université de Paris*, vol. 8, no. 1, pp. 24–35, 1959.

[SON 13] SONER H., TOUZI N., "Homogenization and asymptotics for small transaction costs", *SIAM Journal on Control and Optimization*, vol. 51, no. 4, pp. 2893–2921, 2013.

[SOR 68] SORENSON H., STUBBERUD A., "Non-linear filtering by approximation of the a posteriori density", *International Journal of Control*, vol. 8, no. 1, pp. 33–51, 1968.

[SPE 03] SPECHT K., GOHOUT W., "Portfolio selection using the principal components GARCH model", *Financial Markets and Portfolio Management*, vol. 17, no. 4, pp. 450–458, 2003.

[STA 07] STANGE S., KASERER C., "Why and how to integrate liquidity risk into a VaR-framework", available at: www.ssrn.com/abstract=1292289, 2007.

[STA 09] STANGE S., KASERER C., "Market liquidity risk – an overview", available at: www.ssrn.com/abstract=1362537, 2009.

[STE 56] STEIN C., "Inadmissibility of the usual estimator for the mean of a multivariate normal distribution", *Proceedings of the 3rd Berkeley Symposium on Mathematical and Statistical Probability, Berkeley*, University of California Press, vol. 1, pp. 197–206, 1956.

[STE 98] STEVENS G., "On the inverse of the covariance matrix in portfolio analysis", *Journal of Finance*, vol. 53, no. 5, pp. 1821–1827, 1998.

[STE 10] STEFANOVITS D., Equal Contributions to Risk and Portfolio Construction, PhD Thesis, ETH Zürich, 2010.

[STO 89] STOCK J., WATSON M., "New indexes of coincident and leading economic indicators", *NBER Macroeconomics Annual*, vol. 4, pp. 351–409, MIT Press, 1989.

[STO 02] STOCK J., WATSON M., "Macroeconomic forecasting using diffusion indexes", *Journal of Business and Economic Statistics*, vol. 20, no. 2, pp. 147–162, 2002.

[SUL 99] SULLIVAN R., TIMMERMANN A., WHITE H., "Data-snooping, technical trading rule perofrmance, and the bootstrap", *Journal of Finance*, vol. 54, no. 5, pp. 1647–1691, 1999.

[SUP 09] SUPERVISION C.O.B., "Guidelines for computing capital for incremental risk in the trading book", available at: http://www.bis.org/publ/bcbs149.pdf, 2009.

[TÓT 11] TÓTH B., LEMPÉRIÈRE Y., DEREMBLE C. *et al.*, "Anomalous price impact and the critical nature of liquidity in financial markets", *Physical Review X*, vol. 1, no. 2, p. 021006, American Physical Society, 2011.

[TAN 10] TANIZAKI H., *Nonlinear Filters: Estimation and Applications*, 2nd ed., Springer, 2010.

[TAY 07] TAYLOR S., *Modelling Financial Time Series*, 2nd ed., World Scientific Publishing Company, 2007.

[TEI 15] TEILETCHE J., "The risky asymmetry of low bond yields", http://www.agefi.fr/sites/agefi.fr/files/migrate/etudereference/PTTIFYCZBZ_3_Unigestion_Research%2520Paper_The%2520risky%2520asymmetry%2520of%2520low%2520bond%2520yields_Febr%2520%25202015.pdf, 2015.

[TER 11] TERÄSVIRTA T., ZHAO Z., "Stylized facts of return series, robust estimates and three popular models of volatility", *Applied Financial Economics*, vol. 21, nos. 1–2, pp. 67–94, 2011.

[THO 02] THODE H., *Testing for Normality*, CRC Press, 2002.

[THO 06] THOMPSON J., BAGGETT L., WOJCIECHOWSKI W. *et al.*, "Nobels for nonsense", *Journal of Post Keynesian Economics*, vol. 29, no. 1, pp. 3–18, 2006.

[TIK 63] TIKHONOV A., "Regularization of incorrectly posed problems", *Soviet Mathematics Doklady*, vol. 4, pp. 1035–1038, 1963.

[TIK 77] TIKHONOV A., ARSENIN V., *Solutions of Ill-Posed Problems*, Winston & Sons, 1977.

[TOR 99] TORRE N., FERRARI M., "The market impact model(TM)", Report, MSCI BARRA, BARRA Research Insights, 1999.

[TÓT 16] TÓTH B., EISLER Z., BOUCHAUD J.-P., "The square-root impact law also holds for option markets", *Wilmott*, vol. 85, pp. 70–73, 2016.

[TRE 61] TREYNOR J., *Market Value, Time, and Risk*, Unpublished Manuscript, 1961.

[TRE 07] TREYNOR J., *Toward a Theory of Market Value of Risky Assets*, Wiley, 2007.

[UEC 15] UECHI L., AKTSU T., STANLEY E. *et al.*, "Sector dominance ratio analysis of financial markets", *Physica A: Statistical Mechanics and Its Applications*, vol. 421, pp. 488–509, 2015.

[UNG 15] UNG D., FERNANDES R., HAHN B., "SPIVA Europe Scorecard, Year-End 2015", Report , S&P Dow Jones Indices, 2015.

[URI 81] URICH T., WACHTEL P., "Market response to the weekly money supply announcements in the 1970s", *Journal of Finance*, vol. 36, no. 5, pp. 1063–1072, Wiley Online Library, 1981.

[VAN 00] VAN DER VAART A., *Asymptotic Statistics*, Cambridge University Press, 2000.

[VAN 10] VAN DER VAART A., "Time series", available at: https://staff.fnwi.uva.nl/p.j.c.spreij/onderwijs/master/aadtimeseries2010.pdf, 2010.

[VAS 77] VASICEK O., "An equilibrium characterization of the term structure", *Journal of Financial Economics*, vol. 5, no. 2, pp. 177–188, 1977.

[VAY 98] VAYANOS D., "Transaction costs and asset prices: a dynamic equilibrium model", *Review of Financial Studies*, vol. 11, no. 1, pp. 1–58, 1998.

[VES 00] VESSEREAU T., Factor analysis and independent component analysis in presence of high idiosyncratic risks, Working paper, CIRANO, 2000.

[VIN 76] VINOD H., "Canonical ridge and econometrics of joint production", *Journal of Econometrics*, vol. 4, no. 2, pp. 147–166, 1976.

[WAL 13] WALTERS J., "The factor tau in the Black-Litterman model", available at: www.ssrn.com/abstract=1701467, 2013.

[WAN 12] WANG T., HUANG Z., "The relationship between volatility and trading volume in the Chinese stock market: a volatility decomposition perspective", *Annals of Economics and Finance*, vol. 13, no. 1, pp. 211–236, 2012.

[WAT 64] WATSON G., "Smooth regression analysis", *Sankhya: The Indian Journal of Statistics, Series A*, vol. 26, no. 4, pp. 359–372, 1964.

[WEL 08] WELCH I., GOYAL A., "A comprehensive look at the empirical performance of equity premium prediction", *Review of Financial Studies*, vol. 21, no. 4, pp. 1455–1508, 2008.

[WER 12] WERMERS R., YAO T., ZHAO J., "Forecasting stock returns through an efficient aggregation of mutual fund holdings", *Review of Financial Studies*, vol. 25, no. 12, pp. 3490–3529, 2012.

[WES 11] WESTLING T., "Male organ and economic growth: does size matter?", available at: https://helda.helsinki.fi/bitstream/handle/10138/27239/maleorga.pdf, July 2011.

[WHI 00] WHITE H., "A reality check for data snooping", *Econometrica*, vol. 68, no. 5, pp. 1097–1126, 2000.

[WIL 08] WILLIAMSON S., "Liquidity constraints", DURLAUF S., BLUME L., (eds), *The New Palgrave Dictionary of Economics*, 2nd ed., Palgrave Macmillan, Basingstoke, 2008.

[WIM 13] WIMMER B., CHHABRA S., WALLICK D., "The bumpy road to outperformance", Report , Vanguard Research, 2013.

[WOO 49] WOODBURY M., *The Stability of Out-Input Matrices*, University of Chicago Press, Chicago, 1949.

[XIA 13] XIANG J., ZHU X., "A regime-switching Nelson-Siegel term structure model and interest rate forecasts", *Journal of Financial Econometrics*, vol. 11, no. 3, pp. 522–555, 2013.

[YAN 00] YANG D., ZHANG Q., "Drift-independent volatility estimation based on high, low, open, and close prices", *Journal of Business*, vol. 73, no. 3, pp. 477–91, 2000.

[ZEN 13] ZENG Y., WU S., *State-Space Models: Applications in Economics and Finance*, Statistics and Econometrics for Finance, Springer, 2013.

[ZHA 05] ZHANG L., MYKLAND P., AIT-SAHALIA Y., "A tale of two time scales: determining integrated volatility with noisy high-frequency data", *Journal of the American Statistical Association*, vol. 100, no. 472, pp. 1394–1411, 2005.

[ZHO 08] ZHOU G., "On the fundamental law of active portfolio management what happens if our estimates are wrong?", *Journal of Portfolio Management*, vol. 34, no. 4, pp. 26–33, 2008.

[ZHU 15] ZHU X., SHAHIDUR R., "A regime-switching Nelson–Siegel term structure model of the macroeconomy", *Journal of Macroeconomics*, vol. 44, pp. 1–17, 2015.

Index

E, F

G, H, I, J, K

L, M, N

O, P, Q, R

S, T, U, V, W